Lecture Notes in Computer Scienc

T0238353

Commenced Publication in 1973
Founding and Former Series Editors:
Gerhard Goos, Juris Hartmanis, and Jan van Leeuwen

Editorial Board

Pierpaolo Degano   Joshua Guttman
Fabio Martinelli (Eds.)

Formal Aspects in Security and Trust

5th International Workshop, FAST 2008
Malaga, Spain, October 9-10, 2008
Revised Selected Papers

 Springer

Volume Editors

Pierpaolo Degano
Università di Pisa
Dipartimento di Informatica
Largo Bruno Pontecorvo 3, 56127 Pisa, Italy
E-mail: degano@di.unipi.it
www.di.unipi.it/~degano

Joshua Guttman
The MITRE Corporation
202 Burlington Road, Bedford, MA 01730-1420, USA
E-mail: guttman@mitre.org

Fabio Martinelli
Istituto di Informatica e Telematica (IIT)
Consiglio Nazionale delle Ricerche (CNR)
Pisa Research Area, Via G. Moruzzi 1, 56125 Pisa, Italy
E-mail: fabio.martinelli@iit.cnr.it

Library of Congress Control Number: Applied for

CR Subject Classification (1998): C.2.0, D.4.6, E.3, K.4.4, K.6.5

LNCS Sublibrary: SL 4 – Security and Cryptology

ISSN	0302-9743
ISBN-10	3-642-01464-X Springer Berlin Heidelberg New York
ISBN-13	978-3-642-01464-2 Springer Berlin Heidelberg New York

springer.com

© Springer-Verlag Berlin Heidelberg 2009
Printed in Germany

Typesetting: Camera-ready by author, data conversion by Scientific Publishing Services, Chennai, India
Printed on acid-free paper   SPIN: 12654567   06/3180   5 4 3 2 1 0

Preface

The present volume contains the proceedings of the 5th International Workshop on Formal Aspects in Security and Trust (FAST 2008), held in Malaga, Spain, October 9-10, 2008. FAST is an event affiliated with the 13th European Symposium on Research in Computer Security (ESORICS 2008). FAST 2008 was held under the auspices of the IFIP WG 1.7 on Foundations of Security Analysis and Design.

The 5th International Workshop on Formal Aspects in Security and Trust (FAST 2008) aimed at continuing the successful effort of the previous three FAST workshop editions for fostering the cooperation among researchers in the areas of security and trust. As computing and network infrastructures become increasingly pervasive, and as they carry increasing economic activity, society needs well-matched security and trust mechanisms. These interactions increasingly span several enterprises and involve loosely structured communities of individuals. Participants in these activities must control interactions with their partners based on trust policies and business logic. Trust-based decisions effectively determine the security goals for shared information and for access to sensitive or valuable resources.

FAST sought for original papers focusing on formal aspects in: security and trust policy models; security protocol design and analysis; formal models of trust and reputation; logics for security and trust; distributed trust management systems; trust-based reasoning; digital assets protection; data protection; privacy and ID issues; information flow analysis; language-based security; security and trust aspects in ubiquitous computing; validation/analysis tools; Web service security/trust/privacy; GRID security; security risk assessment; case studies.

The proceedings consist of an invited paper by Gilles Barthe and 20 revised papers selected out of 59 submissions. Each paper was reviewed by at least three members of the Program Committee (PC).

We wish to thank the the PC members for their valuable efforts in properly evaluating the submissions, and the ESORICS 2008 organizers for accepting FAST as an affiliated event and for providing a perfect environment for running the workshop.

October 2008

Pierpaolo Degano
Joshua Guttman
Fabio Martinelli

Organization

Program Chairs

Pierpaolo Degano
Joshua Guttman
Fabio Martinelli

Program Committee

Gilles Barthe
Frederic Cuppens
Theo Dimitrakos
Roberto Gorrieri
Masami Hagiya
Chris Hankin
Christian Jensen
Audun Josang
Yuecel Karabulut
Igor Kotenko
Ninghui Li
Javier Lopez
Steve Marsh
Catherine Meadows
Mogens Nielsen
Flemming Nielson
Indrajit Ray
Peter Ryan
Steve Schneider
Jean-Marc Seigneur
Vitaly Shmatikov
Ketil Stoelen
William Winsborough
Ron van der Meyden

External Reviewers

Aldini, Alessandro
Autrel, Fabien
Ben Ghorbel, Meriam
Bodei, Chiara
Bouzida, Yacine
Bravetti, Mario
Bucur, Doina
Cederquist, Jan
Costa, Gabriele
Crafa, Silvia
Cuppens, Nora
Durante, Luca
Garcia-Alfaro, Joaquin
Guidi, Claudio
Hoa, Feng
Kawamoto, Yusuke
Koutny, Maciej
Liu, Alex
Lund, Mass Soldal
Luo, Zhengqin
Maillé, Patrick
Matos, Ana
Matteucci, Ilaria
Mazzara, Manuel
Nadales, Damian
Pacalet, Anne
Petri, Gustavo
Piazza, Carla
Refsdal, Atle
Riis Nielson, Hanne
Rossi, Sabina
Sakurada, Hideki
Seehusen, Fredrik
Takahashi, Koichi
Tishkov, Artem
Toahchoodee, Manachai
Xia, Zhe
Zanella Beguelin, Santiago

Table of Contents

Formal Certification of ElGamal Encryption[*]
A Gentle Introduction to CertiCrypt

Gilles Barthe[1], Benjamin Grégoire[2,3], Sylvain Heraud[3],
and Santiago Zanella Béguelin[2,3]

[1] IMDEA Software, Madrid, Spain
Gilles.Barthe@imdea.org
[2] Microsoft Research - INRIA Joint Centre, France
[3] INRIA Sophia Antipolis - Méditerranée, France
{Benjamin.Gregoire,Sylvain.Heraud,Santiago.Zanella}@inria.fr

Abstract. CertiCrypt [1] is a framework that assists the construction of machine-checked cryptographic proofs that can be automatically verified by third parties. To date, CertiCrypt has been used to prove formally the exact security of widely studied cryptographic systems, such as the OAEP padding scheme and the Full Domain Hash digital signature scheme. The purpose of this article is to provide a gentle introduction to CertiCrypt. For concreteness, we focus on a simple but illustrative example, namely the semantic security of the Hashed ElGamal encryption scheme in both, the standard and the random oracle model.

1 Introduction

CertiCrypt [1] is a framework that assists the construction of machine-checked cryptographic proofs in the style advocated by *provable security* [2,3]. According to this style, the interplay between the cryptographic system and the adversary must be specified precisely and the proof of security must be established rigorously, making explicit all the assumptions used in the process. CertiCrypt concentrates on the game-playing approach to cryptographic proofs [4,5,6]. This approach uses techniques that help reduce the complexity of cryptographic proofs by structuring them in steps of manageable size. To date, CertiCrypt has been used to prove formally the exact security of widely studied cryptographic systems, such as the OAEP padding scheme and the Full Domain Hash digital signature scheme, and to establish results of wide applicability to cryptographic proofs, such as the PRP/PRF Switching Lemma and the Fundamental Lemma of game-playing.

CertiCrypt is built on top of the general purpose proof assistant Coq [7], from which it inherits a high level of trustworthiness and the ability to provide independently verifiable evidence that proofs are correct. One long-term ambition of CertiCrypt is to contribute to increase confidence in cryptographic proofs. Indeed, constructing a correct security proof can be such a delicate task that some

---

[*] This work has been partially supported by the ANR project SCALP.

P. Degano, J. Guttman, and F. Martinelli (Eds.): FAST 2008, LNCS 5491, pp. 1–19, 2009.
© Springer-Verlag Berlin Heidelberg 2009

cryptographic systems are notorious for having flawed proofs that stood unchallenged for years. The situation is even worse, as there are concerns about the trustworthiness of cryptographic proofs in general [4,5]. As a possible solution, Halevi [5] suggested the construction and use of dedicated tools, and singled out some desirable features and functionalities of these tools. In a sense, CertiCrypt provides a first step towards the completion of Halevi's programme, although it focuses more in delivering automation, expressiveness and high assurance, than in providing a user interface to sketch proofs.

The main difficulty in building a tool to certify cryptographic proofs is that they usually involve a broad set of concepts and reasoning methods, drawing on probability, group and complexity theory. In the case of the game-playing approach, proofs additionally rely on programming language semantics and program transformation and verification. While all these aspects are covered in CertiCrypt, this is the first time we address some essential details that arise when using the tool to build a concrete proof.

The purpose of this article is to provide a gentle introduction to CertiCrypt. We give a step-by-step presentation of security proofs for (Hashed) ElGamal encryption, in the hope of helping readers understand some fine-grained details of the framework. Following Shoup's introductory paper on game-based proofs [6], we provide proofs both in the standard model, assuming that the hash function is entropy smoothing, and in the random oracle model, assuming the hash function is indistinguishable from a truly random function. These proofs generalize our earlier proof of ElGamal encryption, which was presented briefly in [1].

2   Provable Security and the Game-Playing Technique

The aim of cryptography is to achieve a particular security goal, independently of the behavior of adversaries. However, one cannot just enumerate every way an adversary may behave to break the security goal and design a cryptographic system to counter them all. That methodology is bound to fail because adversaries will behave in unpredicted ways to overcome any anticipated countermeasures. Therefore, valid proofs must establish security against all feasible adversaries. As explained below, not all adversaries are feasible, and some restrictions on their abilities are necessary to construct a security proof. In particular, it must be assumed that the adversary is not omniscient (i.e. it does not know some secrets) nor omnipotent (i.e. it cannot perform arbitrarily expensive computations). Both assumptions will be formalized using access control and resource usage policies on the one hand, and complexity classes on the other hand.

In the flavour of the game-playing technique that is adopted by CertiCrypt, the security goal is expressed through a probabilistic program that captures the interaction between the cryptographic system and an adversary. In the context of this paper, we shall focus on public-key encryption schemes and on their semantic security (equivalently, IND-CPA security), which guarantees ciphertext indistinguishability against chosen plaintext attacks. Informally, a public-key encryption scheme is semantically secure if any feasible adversary that only knows the public key and that chooses a pair of messages (m_0, m_1), cannot distinguish a scenario where it is given an encryption of m_0 from a scenario where it is given an encryption of m_1. Clearly, a necessary condition for an encryption scheme to be semantically secure is to be probabilistic, because otherwise an adversary can just compare the encryption of m_0 with the ciphertext it is given to tell apart both scenarios. In a game-based setting, semantic security is specified by means of the following probabilistic program:

> **Game** IND-CPA :
> $(sk, pk) \leftarrow$ KG( );
> $(m_0, m_1) \leftarrow \mathcal{A}(pk);$
> $b \xleftarrow{\$} \{0, 1\};$
> $\zeta \leftarrow$ Enc$(pk, m_b);$
> $b' \leftarrow \mathcal{A}'(pk, \zeta);$
> $d \leftarrow b = b'$

Here, KG is the key generation algorithm of the scheme and Enc the encryption algorithm, whereas $\mathcal{A}$ and $\mathcal{A}'$ are procedures representing an adversary. In addition to the procedures that appear in the above program, the game may involve oracles that can be called by the adversary; e.g. in Hashed ElGamal the adversary is given access to a public hash oracle. The specification of the IND-CPA game is completed by stating that the adversary belongs to the class of probabilistic polynomial time (PPT) programs, and that has access to a global variable to maintain state, read-only access to pk, but does not have access to sk or b. There are two ways to control access to variables: one can declare a variable as local, in which case it shall only be accessible in the scope of the procedure, or global, in which case its access is restricted by an explicit policy.

The IND-CPA property states that the probability of an adversary guessing which message has been encrypted is not significantly higher than $1/2$. The precise definition involves a security parameter η (which determines the scheme parameters) and requires that the probability of $d = 1$ holding at the end of the game, written $\Pr_{\text{IND-CPA}^\eta}[d = 1]$, is negligibly close to $1/2$ as a function of η. Formally, a function $\nu : \mathbb{N} \to \mathbb{R}$ is negligible iff

$$\text{negligible}(\nu) \stackrel{\text{def}}{=} \forall c.\ \exists n_c.\ \forall n.\ n \geq n_c \Rightarrow |\nu(n)| \leq n^{-c}$$

We say that a function ν is negligibly close to a constant k when the function $\lambda \eta. |\nu(\eta) - k|$ is negligible.

The essence of the game-playing technique is to prove a security property, such as the IND-CPA security of an encryption scheme, through successive transformations of the original attack game. More precisely, proofs that follow the game-playing technique are organized as a sequence of transitions of the form $G, A \to G', A'$ where G and G' are games, and A and A' are events. The goal is to establish for each transition $\Pr_G[A] \leq f(\Pr_{G'}[A'])$, for some monotonic function f. By combining the consecutive inequalities drawn from each transition, one can extract from a game-based proof an inequality $\Pr_{G_0}[A_0] \leq f(\Pr_{G_n}[A_n])$. Thus, if G_0, A_0 denotes the original attack game and event, one can obtain a bound of $\Pr_{G_0}[A_0]$ from a bound of $\Pr_{G_n}[A_n]$.

In many cases, transitions $G, A \rightarrow G', A'$ are such that $\Pr_G[A] = \Pr_{G'}[A']$. Such transitions, which are called bridging steps, include semantics-preserving program transformations. Formally, semantics preservation is defined by means of probabilistic non-interference [8], since we are only interested in preserving the observable behavior of games. However, there are many cases in which semantics preservation is context-dependent; to account for such cases, it is necessary to resort to a relational logic that generalizes probabilistic non-interference and that allows to reason modulo pre- and postconditions.

Game-based proofs also rely frequently on failure events, which help bound the probability loss in transitions by the probability of a flag being raised. One essential tool to reason about failure events is the so-called Fundamental Lemma: given two games G_1 and G_2 whose code only differ after a certain bad flag is raised (i.e. after an assignment bad ← true, where bad is initially set to false and always remains raised once set), one can conclude that for any event A, $\Pr_{G_1}[A \wedge \neg\mathsf{bad}] = \Pr_{G_2}[A \wedge \neg\mathsf{bad}]$. This implies in turn

$$|\Pr_{G_1}[A] - \Pr_{G_2}[A]| \leq \Pr_{G_1}[\mathsf{bad}] = \Pr_{G_2}[\mathsf{bad}]$$

provided both games terminate with the same probability.

Finally, some transitions are justified by security assumptions. For instance, the proof in Section 4.2 relies on the Decisional Diffie-Hellman assumption or DDH assumption for short. For a family of finite cyclic groups, this assumption states that no efficient algorithm can distinguish between triples of the form (g^x, g^y, g^{xy}) and triples of the form (g^x, g^y, g^z), where x, y, z are uniformly sampled from $\mathbb{Z}_q$, q is the (prime) order of the group, and g a generator. One characteristic of game-based proofs is to formulate these assumptions using games; the DDH assumption is formulated as follows

Definition 1 (DDH assumption). *Consider the games*

Game DDH_0 :
$x, y \xleftarrow{\$} \mathbb{Z}_q;$
$d \leftarrow \mathcal{B}(g^x, g^y, g^{xy})$

Game DDH_1 :
$x, y, z \xleftarrow{\$} \mathbb{Z}_q;$
$d \leftarrow \mathcal{B}(g^x, g^y, g^z)$

and define
$$\epsilon_{\mathsf{DDH}}(\eta) \overset{def}{=} |\Pr_{\mathsf{DDH}_0^\eta}[d = 1] - \Pr_{\mathsf{DDH}_1^\eta}[d = 1]|$$

Then, for every PPT *adversary* $\mathcal{B}$, ϵ_{DDH} *is a negligible function. Note that the semantics of the above games (and in particular the order q of the group) depends on the security parameter η.*

3   An Introduction to **CertiCrypt**

The goal of this section is to provide a brief overview of the framework. We first present the syntax and semantics of the language used to describe games, and then the tools the framework provides to reason about them.

3.1 Syntax and Semantics of Games

The lowest layer of CertiCrypt is the formalization of a probabilistic programming language with procedure calls. Given a set $\mathcal{V}$ of variables and a set $\mathcal{P}$ of procedure names, commands can be defined inductively by the clauses:

$$
\begin{aligned}
\mathcal{I} ::= & \ \mathcal{V} \leftarrow \mathcal{E} && \text{deterministic assignment} \\
| & \ \mathcal{V} \xleftarrow{\$} \mathcal{D} && \text{random assignment} \\
| & \ \text{if } \mathcal{E} \text{ then } \mathcal{C} \text{ else } \mathcal{C} && \text{conditional} \\
| & \ \text{while } \mathcal{E} \text{ do } \mathcal{C} && \text{while loop} \\
| & \ \mathcal{V} \leftarrow \mathcal{P}(\mathcal{E}, \dots, \mathcal{E}) && \text{procedure call} \\
\mathcal{C} ::= & \ \text{nil} && \text{nop} \\
| & \ \mathcal{I}; \ \mathcal{C} && \text{sequence}
\end{aligned}
$$

where $\mathcal{E}$ is the set of expressions and $\mathcal{D}$ is the set of distributions from which values can be sampled in random assignments. Common data types and operators are provided, but in order to adapt to different settings, the syntax is user-extensible: users can define new data types and operations by providing an adequate interpretation in terms of Coq constructions. In addition, the syntax is typed, so that operators and expressions have a total semantics.

Games consist of a main command and an environment that maps a procedure identifier to its declaration, consisting of a list of formal parameters, a body, and a return expression (we use an explicit return when writing games, though),

$$
\text{declaration} \overset{\text{def}}{=} \{\text{params} : V^\star; \ \text{body} : \mathcal{C}; \ \text{re} : \mathcal{E}\}
$$

Formally, the type of games is $\mathcal{C} \times (\mathcal{P} \to \text{declaration})$. The semantics of games is defined using the measure monad $M(X)$ of Audebaud and Paulin [9]; its type constructor, unit and binding are defined as:

$$
\begin{aligned}
M(X) & \overset{\text{def}}{=} (X \to [0,1]) \to [0,1] \\
\text{unit} \quad & : \ X \to M(X) \overset{\text{def}}{=} \lambda x. \ \lambda f. \ f \ x \\
\text{bind} \quad & : \ M(X) \to (X \to M(Y)) \to M(Y) \\
& \overset{\text{def}}{=} \lambda \mu. \ \lambda M. \ \lambda f. \ \mu(\lambda \ x. \ M \ x \ f)
\end{aligned}
$$

This monad can be viewed as a specialization of the continuation monad, and allows to provide a continuation-passing style semantics of games. Intuitively, an element in $M(X)$ may be interpreted as the expectation operator of a (sub) probability distribution on X. Thus, the denotation of a game relates an initial memory to the expectation operator of the (sub) probability distribution of final memories that results from its execution. The denotational semantics of games is defined internally by means of a small-step semantics that uses frames to deal with procedure calls. From a user point of view, however, these details can be ignored without hindering understanding; the formal definition of small-step semantics can be found in [1]. The denotation of games is presented in Fig. 1; in the figure we represent a memory m as a pair $(m.\text{loc}, m.\text{glob})$, making explicit its local and global components. Expressions are deterministic and their semantics is given by a function $[\![\cdot]\!]_{\mathcal{E}}$ that evaluates an expression in a given memory and returns a value. The semantics of distributions in $\mathcal{D}$ is given by another function $[\![\cdot]\!]_{\mathcal{D}}$; we give as examples the semantics of the uniform distribution on $\mathbb{B}$ and on integer intervals of the form $[0..n]$. In the figure, we have omitted the procedure environment E for the sake of readability. In the remainder we will frequently make no distinction between a game $G = (c, E)$ and its main command c when the environment where it is evaluated either has no relevance, or is clear from the context.

$$
\begin{aligned}
[\![\mathsf{nil}]\!]\; m &= \mathsf{unit}\; m \\
[\![i;\; c]\!]\; m &= \mathsf{bind}\; ([\![i]\!]\; m)\; [\![c]\!] \\
[\![x \leftarrow e]\!]\; m &= \mathsf{unit}\; m\{[\![e]\!]_{\mathcal{E}}\; m/x\} \\
[\![x \,\xLeftarrow{\$}\, d]\!]\; m &= \mathsf{bind}\; ([\![d]\!]_{\mathcal{D}}\; m)\; (\lambda v.\; \mathsf{unit}\; m\{v/x\}) \\
[\![x \leftarrow f(e)]\!]\; m &= \begin{aligned} &\mathsf{bind}\; ([\![E(f).\mathsf{body}]\!]\; (\emptyset\{[\![e]\!]_{\mathcal{D}}\; m/E(f).\mathsf{params}\}, m.\mathsf{glob})) \\ &(\lambda m'.\; (m.\mathsf{loc}, m'.\mathsf{glob})\{[\![E(f).\mathsf{re}]\!]_{\mathcal{E}}\; m'/x\}) \end{aligned} \\
[\![\mathsf{if}\; e\; \mathsf{then}\; c_1\; \mathsf{else}\; c_2]\!]\; m &= \begin{cases} [\![c_1]\!] \text{ if } [\![e]\!]_{\mathcal{E}}\; m = \mathsf{true} \\ [\![c_2]\!] \text{ if } [\![e]\!]_{\mathcal{E}}\; m = \mathsf{false} \end{cases} \\
[\![\mathsf{while}\; e\; \mathsf{do}\; c]\!]\; m &= [\![\mathsf{if}\; e\; \mathsf{then}\; c;\; \mathsf{while}\; e\; \mathsf{do}\; c]\!]\; m \\[1em]
[\![\{0,1\}]\!]_{\mathcal{D}}\; m &= \lambda f.\; \frac{1}{2}\; f(\mathsf{true}) + \frac{1}{2}\; f(\mathsf{false}) \\
[\![[0..e]]\!]_{\mathcal{D}}\; m &= \lambda f.\; \sum_{i=0}^{n} \frac{1}{n+1}\; f(i) \quad \text{where } n = [\![e]\!]_{\mathcal{E}}\; m
\end{aligned}
$$

Fig. 1. Denotational semantics of games

CertiCrypt provides an alternative, more convenient rule for *while* loops:

$$[\![\mathsf{while}\; e\; \mathsf{do}\; c]\!]\; m\; f = \sup\{[\![[\mathsf{while}\; e\; \mathsf{do}\; c]_n]\!]\; m\; f : n \in \mathbb{N}\}$$

where $[\mathsf{while}\; e\; \mathsf{do}\; c]_n$ is the n-step unrolling of the loop, i.e.

$$
\begin{aligned}
[\mathsf{while}\; e\; \mathsf{do}\; c]_0 &= \mathsf{nil} \\
[\mathsf{while}\; e\; \mathsf{do}\; c]_{n+1} &= \mathsf{if}\; e\; \mathsf{then}\; c;\; [\mathsf{while}\; e\; \mathsf{do}\; c]_n
\end{aligned}
$$

Note that the function $[\![\cdot]\!]$ maps $\mathcal{M}$ to $M(\mathcal{M})$, but it is trivial to define a semantic function $[\![\cdot]\!]'$ from $M(\mathcal{M})$ to $M(\mathcal{M})$ using the bind operator of the monad: $[\![G]\!]'\; \mu \stackrel{\text{def}}{=} \mathsf{bind}\; \mu\; [\![G]\!]$. One of the major advantages of using the monad $M(\mathcal{M})$ is that the probability of an event A, represented as a Boolean predicate over memories, can be readily defined using the characteristic function $\mathbb{I}_A$ of A:

$$\Pr_{G,m}[A] \stackrel{\text{def}}{=} [\![G]\!]\; m\; \mathbb{I}_A \tag{1}$$

In what follows, we sometimes omit the initial memory m; in that case one may safely assume that the memory initially maps variables to default values of the right type.

3.2   Reasoning about Games

In game-based proofs, bridging steps correspond in a sense to semantics preserving transformations; they are used to restate the way certain quantities are computed to prepare the ground for a subsequent transformation. Hence, in a bridging step from G, A to G', A' the goal is to establish $\Pr_{G,m}[A] = \Pr_{G',m}[A']$. If we take a look at definition (1), this amounts to proving that $[\![G]\!] \, m \, \mathbb{I}_A = [\![G']\!] \, m \, \mathbb{I}_{A'}$, or generalizing this to a pair of initial memories m_1, m_2 and arbitrary functions $f, g : \mathcal{M} \to [0,1]$, that $[\![G]\!] \, m_1 \, f = [\![G']\!] \, m_2 \, g$.

The main tool CertiCrypt provides to establish such equalities is the relational logic pRHL, which generalizes Relational Hoare Logic [10] to a probabilistic setting. Judgments in pRHL are of the form $\models G_1 \sim G_2 : \Psi \Rightarrow \Phi$, where G_1 and G_2 are games, and Ψ and Φ are relations over deterministic states. A judgment $\models G_1 \sim G_2 : \Psi \Rightarrow \Phi$ is valid iff for every pair of initial memories m_1, m_2 such that $m_1 \, \Psi \, m_2$, $[\![G_1]\!] \, m_1 \sim_\Phi [\![G_2]\!] \, m_2$ holds. The relation $\sim_\Phi$ is a lifting of Φ to measures. If Φ is a PER, the definition of $\sim_\Phi$ is rather intuitive:

$$\mu_1 \sim_\Phi \mu_2 \overset{\text{def}}{=} \forall a. \ \mu_1 \, \mathbb{I}_{[a]} = \mu_2 \, \mathbb{I}_{[a]}$$

where $\mathbb{I}_{[a]}$ is the characteristic function of the equivalence class of a. The definition of $\sim_\Phi$ for arbitrary relations is less immediate, and involves an existential quantification:

$$\text{range } P \ \mu \overset{\text{def}}{=} \forall f. \ (\forall a. \ P \ a \Rightarrow f \ a = 0) \Rightarrow \mu \ f = 0$$
$$\mu_1 \sim_\Phi \mu_2 \overset{\text{def}}{=} \exists \mu. \ \pi_1(\mu) = \mu_1 \wedge \pi_2(\mu) = \mu_2 \wedge \text{range } \Phi \ \mu$$

where the projections of μ are defined as

$$\pi_1(\mu) \overset{\text{def}}{=} \text{bind } \mu \ (\lambda p.\text{unit } (\text{fst } p)) \qquad \pi_2(\mu) \overset{\text{def}}{=} \text{bind } \mu \ (\lambda p.\text{unit } (\text{snd } p))$$

This definition stems from work on probabilistic bisimulations, and generalizes lifting to arbitrary relations. Both definitions coincide for PERs [11].

In order to reason about pRHL judgments, CertiCrypt provides a set of derived rules and a (partial) weakest precondition calculus. The rules can be found in [1]. An important implication of a pRHL judgment $\models G_1 \sim G_2 : \Psi \Rightarrow \Phi$, is that if two functions f and g are unable to distinguish memories in the Φ relation, i.e.

$$\forall m_1 \, m_2. \ m_1 \, \Phi \, m_2 \Rightarrow f \ m_1 = g \ m_2$$

then

$$\forall m_1 \, m_2. \ m_1 \, \Psi \, m_2 \Rightarrow [\![G_1]\!] \, m_1 \, f = [\![G_2]\!] \, m_2 \, g \qquad (=_{[\![]\!]})$$

In particular, if Φ is the equality on the free variables of a Boolean predicate A, we obtain $\Pr_{G_1,m_1}[A] = \Pr_{G_2,m_2}[A]$. This property extends to the $\leq$ relation.

By specializing pRHL judgments to equality predicates on sets of variables, one recovers probabilistic non-interference: given a set X of variables, define

$$m_1 =_X m_2 \overset{\text{def}}{=} \forall x \in X, m_1 \ x = m_2 \ x$$

Probabilistic non-interference w.r.t. a set I of input variables and a set O of output variables is defined as $\models \cdot \sim \cdot : =_I \Rightarrow =_O$, we use $\models \cdot \simeq_O^I \cdot$ as a shorthand.

CertiCrypt provides several tools to reason about non-interference. In particular, CertiCrypt implements several tactics that help establish non-interference or reduce it to a simpler goal. For example, the tactic eqobs_in implements a semi-decision procedure for judgments of the form $\models c, E \simeq_O^I c, E'$. Other tactics, such as eqobs_hd, eqobs_tl, eqobs_ctxt, deadcode, and swap simplify the goal by using functions that take games c_1, E_1 and c_2, E_2 and sets of variables I, O and return c_1', c_2' and I', O' such that

$$\models c_1', E_1 \simeq_{O'}^{I'} c_2', E_2 \quad \Rightarrow \quad \models c_1, E_1 \simeq_O^I c_2, E_2$$

The tactics differ in their strategy to compute c_1', c_2' and I', O'. Tactic eqobs_tl searches for a maximal common prefix c such that $c_1 = c; c_1'$ and $c_2 = c; c_2'$, eqobs_hd searches similarly for a maximal suffix, and eqobs_ctxt combines both. The tactic swap rearranges instructions in programs to generate a largest common suffix while preserving observational equivalence, i.e. $c_1' = \hat{c}_1; c$ and $c_2' = \hat{c}_2; c$ are permutations of c_1 and c_2 (and $I' = I$ and $O' = O$). The tactic deadcode produces slices of the original commands using the variables in O as slicing criteria.

In addition, CertiCrypt automates other common program transformations: expression propagation (ep), variable allocation (alloc), and inlining (inline). These tactics are shown to preserve non-interference. The tactic sinline combines inline, alloc, ep, and deadcode in one powerful tactic.

To be able to deal with procedure calls the tactics need information about procedures in the environment of games. This information cannot be computed recursively due to the presence of adversaries whose code is unknown. Given two environments E_1 and E_2, and a procedure f, tactics assume the following information is given:

– For each environment: a set W_i of global variables that f might modify, sets I_i and O_i of global variables, and a subset P_i of its formal parameters such that for every execution of the body of the procedure, the final values of variables in $O_i \cup \mathsf{fv}(E_i(f).\mathsf{re})$ depend only on the initial values of variables in $I_i \cup P_i$. Formally,

$$\begin{aligned} W_i &= \mathsf{globals}(\mathsf{modifies}(E_i(f).\mathsf{body}, E_i)) \wedge \\ P_i &\subseteq E_i(f).\mathsf{params} \wedge \\ &\models E_i(f).\mathsf{body}, E_i \simeq_{O_i \cup \mathsf{fv}(E_i(f).\mathsf{re})}^{I_i \cup P_i} E_i(f).\mathsf{body}, E_i \end{aligned}$$

(modifies computes an over approximation of the variables modified by a piece of code.) This information is used by the tactics swap, deadcode, ep, and inline;

– Relational information: sets I and O of global variables, and a subset P of the formal parameters of f such that the execution of the body of f in each environment, starting from memories equal on variables in $I \cup P$, results in measures equivalent on $O \cup \mathsf{fv}(E_i(f).\mathsf{re})$. We further require that $E_1(f).\mathsf{re} = E_2(f).\mathsf{re}$. Formally,

$$P \subseteq E_1.(f).\mathsf{params} \;\wedge\; P \subseteq E_2.(f).\mathsf{params} \;\wedge\;$$
$$\models E_1(f).\mathsf{body}, E_1 \sim^{I \cup P}_{O \cup \mathsf{fv}(E_i(f).\mathsf{re})} E_2(f).\mathsf{body}, E_2$$

This information is used by tactics eqobs_in, eqobs_hd, and eqobs_tl.

CertiCrypt provides several mechanisms to build the above information incrementally and automatically when the bodies of procedures in E_1 and E_2 are observationally equivalent modulo expression propagation and dead code elimination. It is also possible to derive the information for an adversary from the information about the oracles it may call. This is possible provided the adversary is well-formed, since in this case we know that the adversary and any subprocedures it may call respect an access control policy $(\mathcal{O}, \mathcal{RO}, \mathcal{RW})$: they may only call oracles in $\mathcal{O}$, read global variables in $\mathcal{RO}$, and read or modify global variables in $\mathcal{RW}$.

As said before, some transformations performed during proofs are context-dependent. CertiCrypt allows for a rich specification of the context in which a transformation is valid using program invariants. Tactics are thus extended to deal with invariants on global variables; the information they use is specified instead by judgments of the form

$$\models c_1, E_1 \sim c_2, E_2 : =_I \wedge \phi \Rightarrow =_O \wedge \phi$$

4 Semantic Security of Hashed ElGamal Encryption

Let G be a cyclic group of prime order q and g a generator, and let $(H_k)_{k \in K}$ be a family of keyed hash functions mapping elements in G to bitstrings of a certain length ℓ. Hashed ElGamal is a public-key encryption scheme whose security is believed to be related to the discrete logarithm problem in G. Its key generation, encryption and decryption algorithms are defined as follows:

$$\mathsf{KG}(\,) \quad \stackrel{\mathrm{def}}{=} \quad k \stackrel{\$}{\leftarrow} K;\; x \stackrel{\$}{\leftarrow} \mathbb{Z}_q;\; \mathsf{return}\; ((k, x), (k, g^x))$$
$$\mathsf{Enc}(k, \alpha, m) \quad \stackrel{\mathrm{def}}{=} \quad y \stackrel{\$}{\leftarrow} \mathbb{Z}_q;\; h \leftarrow H_k(\alpha^y);\; \mathsf{return}\; (g^y, h \oplus m)$$
$$\mathsf{Dec}(k, x, \beta, \zeta) \quad \stackrel{\mathrm{def}}{=} \quad h \leftarrow H_k(\beta^x);\; \mathsf{return}\; h \oplus \zeta$$

The plaintext space of Hashed ElGamal is $\{0, 1\}^\ell$, in contrast to the original ElGamal encryption scheme whose plaintext space is simply G.

In the remainder of this section we present game-based proofs of the semantic security of Hashed ElGamal encryption in two different settings. The first proof is done in the standard model of cryptography; it assumes that the family $(H_k)_{k \in K}$ of hash functions is entropy smoothing and reduces semantic security to the hardness of the DDH problem. The second proof is done in the Random Oracle Model (ROM); it assumes hash functions behave as perfectly random functions and reduces semantic security to the hardness of the (list) CDH problem.

To formalize the proofs in CertiCrypt we first need to extend the syntax and semantics of games to include the types and operators used in the description of the scheme that are not already defined. As explained in Sec. 3, this is done in a modular way. We declare a family of cyclic groups $(G_\eta)_{\eta \in \mathbb{N}}$ indexed by the security parameter and extend the types of the language with user-defined types for elements in G_η and bitstrings of length ℓ. We extend $\mathcal{D}$ with the uniform distribution on bitstrings of length ℓ. We finally extend the language operators with nullary operators q and g to retrieve the order and a generator of G_η respectively, binary operators for the product and power in the group, and $\oplus$ for exclusive or on bitstrings of length ℓ. For the security proof in the standard model, we represent the hash function of the scheme as a binary operator taking a key in K and a value in G_η and returning a bitstring of length ℓ, whereas in the proof in the random oracle model we directly encode the hash function as a procedure and no further extensions are needed.

4.1   Security in the Standard Model

The proof we present next relies on two assumptions: the assumption that the family of hash functions $(H_k)_{k \in K}$ is entropy smoothing, and the hardness of the DDH problem in G_η. The latter assumption was already formalized in Sec. 2 as Definition 1. The former is formally stated below.

Definition 2 (Entropy Smoothing (ES) assumption). *Consider the games*

Game ES_0 :	Game ES_1 :
$k \stackrel{\$}{\leftarrow} K;\ h \stackrel{\$}{\leftarrow} \{0,1\}^\ell;$	$k \stackrel{\$}{\leftarrow} K;\ z \stackrel{\$}{\leftarrow} \mathbb{Z}_q;$
$d \leftarrow \mathcal{D}(h)$	$d \leftarrow \mathcal{D}(H(k, g^z))$

and define

$$\epsilon_{\mathsf{ES}}(\eta) \stackrel{def}{=} |\Pr_{\mathsf{ES}_0}[d = 1] - \Pr_{\mathsf{ES}_1}[d = 1]|$$

Then, for every PPT *adversary* $\mathcal{D}$, ϵ_{ES} *is a negligible function.*

To avoid cluttering the description of games, we slightly modify the presentation of the key generation algorithm: instead of returning the hash key as a component of the secret and public key, we model it as a global variable k. This will allow us at the same time to nicely illustrate the use of global variables in CertiCrypt.

Theorem 1 (Security of Hashed ElGamal in the standard model). *For every* PPT *and well-formed adversary* $(\mathcal{A}, \mathcal{A}')$,

$$\left| \Pr_{\mathsf{IND\text{-}CPA}}[d] - \frac{1}{2} \right| \leq \epsilon_{\mathsf{DDH}}(\eta) + \epsilon_{\mathsf{ES}}(\eta)$$

Furthermore, under the DDH *and* ES *assumptions,* $\Pr_{\mathsf{IND\text{-}CPA}}[d]$ *is negligibly close to* $\frac{1}{2}$.

Figure 2 gives an overview of the proof; proof scripts appear inside grey boxes. We model the adversary as two procedures sharing state via global variables in

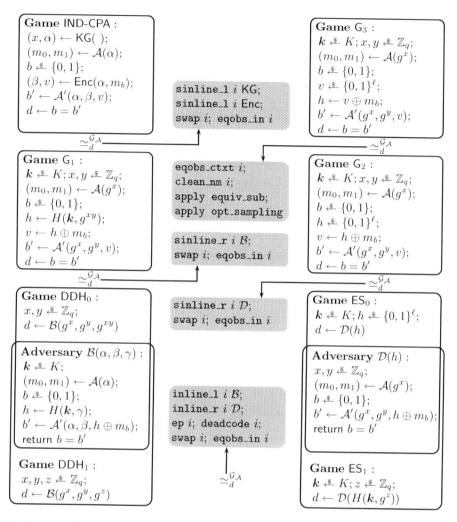

Fig. 2. Game-based proof of semantic security of Hashed ElGamal encryption in the standard model

$\mathcal{G_A}$. The well-formedness condition simply states that the adversary has read-only access to $\boldsymbol{k}$ and that it cannot call procedures named $\mathcal{B}$ or $\mathcal{D}$ as these are the names reserved for adversaries in the reduction. Note that this is without loss of generality, and the adversary is free to define and call any other private procedures of its own as long as they are also well-formed. The information i used by the tactics is thus inferred automatically.

We begin by proving

$$\Pr_{\mathsf{IND\text{-}CPA}}[d] = \Pr_{\mathsf{DDH}_0}[d] \tag{2}$$

For clarity, we introduce an intermediate game G_1 and show that

$$\models \mathsf{IND\text{-}CPA} \sim_d^{\mathcal{G_A}} \mathsf{G}_1 \quad \text{and} \quad \models \mathsf{G}_1 \sim_d^{\mathcal{G_A}} \mathsf{DDH}_0$$

Since the $\simeq$ relation is transitive,

$$\frac{\models c \simeq_O^I c' \quad \models c' \simeq_O^I c''}{\models c \simeq_O^I c''} \; \text{[R-Trans]}$$

we obtain $\models \mathsf{IND\text{-}CPA} \simeq_d^{\mathcal{G}_A} \mathsf{DDH}_0$. Equation (2) follows then from $(=_{\llbracket\rrbracket})$. Next we show that

$$\mathrm{Pr}_{\mathsf{DDH}_1}[d] = \mathrm{Pr}_{\mathsf{ES}_1}[d] \tag{3}$$

To this end, we prove first $\models \mathsf{DDH}_1 \simeq_d^{\mathcal{G}_A} \mathsf{ES}_1$. We illustrate this transition in detail, showing the intermediate goals obtained after applying each tactic in the proof script:

| $x,y,z \xleftarrow{\$} \mathbb{Z}_q; \; d \leftarrow \mathcal{B}(g^x, g^y, g^z)$ | $\simeq_d^{\mathcal{G}_A}$ | $k \xleftarrow{\$} K; \; z \xleftarrow{\$} \mathbb{Z}_q; \; d \leftarrow \mathcal{D}(H(k, g^z))$ |

$$\text{inline\_l } i \; \mathcal{B}; \; \text{inline\_r } i \; \mathcal{D}$$

| $x,y,z \xleftarrow{\$} \mathbb{Z}_q; \; \alpha \leftarrow g^x; \beta \leftarrow g^y; \gamma \leftarrow g^z;$ $k \xleftarrow{\$} K; \; (m_0, m_1) \leftarrow \mathcal{A}(\alpha);$ $b \xleftarrow{\$} \{0,1\}; \; h \leftarrow H(k, \gamma);$ $b' \leftarrow \mathcal{A}'(\alpha, \beta, h \oplus m_b); \; d \leftarrow b = b'$ | $\simeq_d^{\mathcal{G}_A}$ | $k \xleftarrow{\$} K; \; z \xleftarrow{\$} \mathbb{Z}_q; \; h \leftarrow H(k, g^z);$ $x,y \xleftarrow{\$} \mathbb{Z}_q; \; (m_0, m_1) \leftarrow \mathcal{A}(g^x);$ $b \xleftarrow{\$} \{0,1\};$ $b' \leftarrow \mathcal{A}'(g^x, g^y, h \oplus m_b); \; d \leftarrow b = b'$ |

$$\text{ep } i$$

| $x,y,z \xleftarrow{\$} \mathbb{Z}_q; \; \alpha \leftarrow g^x; \beta \leftarrow g^y; \gamma \leftarrow g^z;$ $k \xleftarrow{\$} K; \; (m_0, m_1) \leftarrow \mathcal{A}(g^x);$ $b \xleftarrow{\$} \{0,1\}; \; h \leftarrow H(k, g^z);$ $b' \leftarrow \mathcal{A}'(g^x, g^y, H(k, g^z) \oplus m_b);$ $d \leftarrow b = b'$ | $\simeq_d^{\mathcal{G}_A}$ | $k \xleftarrow{\$} K; \; z \xleftarrow{\$} \mathbb{Z}_q; \; h \leftarrow H(k, g^z);$ $x,y \xleftarrow{\$} \mathbb{Z}_q; \; (m_0, m_1) \leftarrow \mathcal{A}(g^x);$ $b \xleftarrow{\$} \{0,1\};$ $b' \leftarrow \mathcal{A}'(g^x, g^y, H(k, g^z) \oplus m_b);$ $d \leftarrow b = b'$ |

$$\text{deadcode } i$$

| $x,y,z \xleftarrow{\$} \mathbb{Z}_q;$ $k \xleftarrow{\$} K; \; (m_0, m_1) \leftarrow \mathcal{A}(g^x);$ $b \xleftarrow{\$} \{0,1\};$ $b' \leftarrow \mathcal{A}'(g^x, g^y, H(k, g^z) \oplus m_b);$ $d \leftarrow b = b'$ | $\simeq_d^{\mathcal{G}_A}$ | $k \xleftarrow{\$} K; \; z \xleftarrow{\$} \mathbb{Z}_q;$ $x,y \xleftarrow{\$} \mathbb{Z}_q; \; (m_0, m_1) \leftarrow \mathcal{A}(g^x);$ $b \xleftarrow{\$} \{0,1\};$ $b' \leftarrow \mathcal{A}'(g^x, g^y, H(k, g^z) \oplus m_b);$ $d \leftarrow b = b'$ |

$$\text{swap } i$$

| $x,y,z \xleftarrow{\$} \mathbb{Z}_q;$ $k \xleftarrow{\$} K; \; (m_0, m_1) \leftarrow \mathcal{A}(g^x);$ $b \xleftarrow{\$} \{0,1\};$ $b' \leftarrow \mathcal{A}'(g^x, g^y, H(k, g^z) \oplus m_b);$ $d \leftarrow b = b'$ | $\simeq_d^{\mathcal{G}_A}$ | $x,y,z \xleftarrow{\$} \mathbb{Z}_q;$ $k \xleftarrow{\$} K; \; (m_0, m_1) \leftarrow \mathcal{A}(g^x);$ $b \xleftarrow{\$} \{0,1\};$ $b' \leftarrow \mathcal{A}'(g^x, g^y, H(k, g^z) \oplus m_b);$ $d \leftarrow b = b'$ |

$$\text{eqobs\_in } i$$

We first inline the calls to $\mathcal{B}$ and $\mathcal{D}$ in each game. When inlining a procedure call, the expressions appearing in the list of actual parameters are assigned to the corresponding formal parameters appearing in its declaration and the return expression is assigned to the return variable. We use ep to propagate assignments along the game, and deadcode to eliminate instructions that do not affect — either directly or indirectly— the value of d. (The tactic sinline would achieve the same result as this combination of tactics.) At this point the resulting programs are the same modulo reordering of instructions; we use swap to rearrange the instructions of the program in the right hand side in the same order as in the program in the left hand side. The tactic `eqobs_in` concludes by performing a dependency analysis to show that in the resulting program the value of d depends only on the initial value of variables in $\mathcal{G}_\mathcal{A}$.

Finally, we show that

$$\Pr_{\mathsf{ES}_0}[d] = \Pr_{\mathsf{G}_3}[d] \tag{4}$$

As before, we introduce an intermediate game G_2 and prove $\models \mathsf{ES}_0 \simeq_d^{\mathcal{G}_\mathcal{A}} \mathsf{G}_2$, and $\models \mathsf{G}_2 \simeq_d^{\mathcal{G}_\mathcal{A}} \mathsf{G}_3$. By [R-Trans] we get $\models \mathsf{ES}_0 \simeq_d^{\mathcal{G}_\mathcal{A}} \mathsf{G}_3$ which together with $(=_{[\![]\!]})$ gives (4). The transition from ES_0 to G_2 is similar to the one detailed above. However, the transition from G_2 to G_3 is more interesting since we use an algebraic property of $\oplus$ which we call *optimistic sampling*:

$$\models x \xleftarrow{\$} \{0,1\}^\ell; y \leftarrow x \oplus z \simeq_{\{x,y,z\}}^{\{z\}} y \xleftarrow{\$} \{0,1\}^\ell; x \leftarrow y \oplus z \tag{5}$$

Let us give a step-by-step trace of the interaction with CertiCrypt:

$k \xleftarrow{\$} K;\ x,y \xleftarrow{\$} \mathbb{Z}_q;$ $(m_0,m_1) \leftarrow \mathcal{A}(g^x);\ b \xleftarrow{\$} \{0,1\};$ $h \xleftarrow{\$} \{0,1\}^\ell;\ v \leftarrow h \oplus m_b;$ $b' \leftarrow \mathcal{A}'(g^x, g^y, v);$ $d \leftarrow b = b'$	$\simeq_d^{\mathcal{G}_\mathcal{A}}$	$k \xleftarrow{\$} K;\ x,y \xleftarrow{\$} \mathbb{Z}_q;$ $(m_0,m_1) \leftarrow \mathcal{A}(g^x);\ b \xleftarrow{\$} \{0,1\};$ $v \xleftarrow{\$} \{0,1\}^\ell;\ h \leftarrow v \oplus m_b;$ $b' \leftarrow \mathcal{A}'(g^x, g^y, v);$ $d \leftarrow b = b'$

eqobs_ctxt i

$h \xleftarrow{\$} \{0,1\}^\ell;\ v \leftarrow h \oplus m_b$	$\simeq_{\{k,x,y,b,v\}\cup\mathcal{G}_\mathcal{A}}^{\{k,x,y,m_0,m_1,b\}\cup\mathcal{G}_\mathcal{A}}$	$v \xleftarrow{\$} \{0,1\}^\ell;\ h \leftarrow v \oplus m_b$

clean_nm

$h \xleftarrow{\$} \{0,1\}^\ell;\ v \leftarrow h \oplus m_b$	$\simeq_{\{v\}}^{\{k,x,y,m_0,m_1,b\}\cup\mathcal{G}_\mathcal{A}}$	$v \xleftarrow{\$} \{0,1\}^\ell;\ h \leftarrow v \oplus m_b$

apply equiv_sub

$h \xleftarrow{\$} \{0,1\}^\ell;\ v \leftarrow h \oplus m_b$	$\simeq_{\{h,v,m_b\}}^{\{m_b\}}$	$v \xleftarrow{\$} \{0,1\}^\ell;\ h \leftarrow v \oplus m_b$

apply opt_sampling

First, `eqobs_ctxt` is used to remove the common prefix and suffix in the programs. Then, `clean_nm` removes from the output set the variables appearing in the input set that are not modified throughout the programs. This is justified by the rule:

$$\frac{X \cap \mathsf{modifies}(c_1) = \emptyset \quad X \cap \mathsf{modifies}(c_2) = \emptyset \quad X \subseteq I \quad \models c_1 \simeq_O^I c_2}{\models c_1 \simeq_{O\cup X}^I c_2}$$

Finally, we apply the subsumption rule

$$\frac{I' \subseteq I \quad \models c_1 \simeq_O^I c_2 \quad O \subseteq O'}{\models c_1 \simeq_{O'}^{I'} c_2} \quad [\text{R-Sub}]$$

to strengthen the postcondition and weaken the precondition so as to obtain a goal that suits the statement of optimistic sampling (5), which allows us to conclude the proof.

The last transition effectively removed the dependency of v on b, and thus the dependency of b' on b. It is then easy to prove that

$$\Pr_{\mathsf{G}_3}[d] = \frac{1}{2} \tag{6}$$

Indeed, in G_3 the variable b is only used to compute h, which is not used anymore. We can use tactics `swap` and `deadcode` to prove that the game is equivalent to a game where b is sampled after calling $\mathcal{A}'$. Since $\forall G\ e\ d$, $\mathrm{Pr}_{G;d\leftarrow e}[d] = \mathrm{Pr}_G[e]$, we have $\mathrm{Pr}_{G_3}[d] = \mathrm{Pr}_{G_3}[b = b']$. To conclude, we use the fact that for any game G and Boolean variables b, b', $\mathrm{Pr}_{G;b\xleftarrow{\$}\{0,1\}}[b = b'] = \frac{1}{2}$, provided G is absolutely terminating. CertiCrypt provides a semi-decision procedure for absolute termination which can automatically discharge this condition for G_3 based on the assumption that $\mathcal{A}$ and $\mathcal{A}'$ are PPT procedures and thus absolutely terminating.

To summarize, from Equations (2), (3), (4), and (6) we obtain

$$
\begin{aligned}
|\mathrm{Pr}_{\mathsf{IND\text{-}CPA}}[d] - \tfrac{1}{2}| &= |\mathrm{Pr}_{\mathsf{DDH}_0}[d] - \tfrac{1}{2}| \\
&= |\mathrm{Pr}_{\mathsf{DDH}_0}[d] - \mathrm{Pr}_{\mathsf{DDH}_1}[d] + \mathrm{Pr}_{\mathsf{DDH}_1}[d] - \tfrac{1}{2}| \\
&\leq |\mathrm{Pr}_{\mathsf{DDH}_0}[d] - \mathrm{Pr}_{\mathsf{DDH}_1}[d]| + |\mathrm{Pr}_{\mathsf{DDH}_1}[d] - \tfrac{1}{2}| \\
&= |\mathrm{Pr}_{\mathsf{DDH}_0}[d] - \mathrm{Pr}_{\mathsf{DDH}_1}[d]| + |\mathrm{Pr}_{\mathsf{ES}_1}[d] - \tfrac{1}{2}| \\
&= |\mathrm{Pr}_{\mathsf{DDH}_0}[d] - \mathrm{Pr}_{\mathsf{DDH}_1}[d]| + |\mathrm{Pr}_{\mathsf{ES}_1}[d] - \mathrm{Pr}_{G_3}[d]| \\
&= |\mathrm{Pr}_{\mathsf{DDH}_0}[d] - \mathrm{Pr}_{\mathsf{DDH}_1}[d]| + |\mathrm{Pr}_{\mathsf{ES}_1}[d] - \mathrm{Pr}_{\mathsf{ES}_0}[d]| \\
&= \epsilon_{\mathsf{DDH}}(\eta) + \epsilon_{\mathsf{ES}}(\eta)
\end{aligned}
$$

From the above equation, $\mathrm{Pr}_{\mathsf{IND\text{-}CPA}}[d]$ is negligibly close to $\frac{1}{2}$ under the DDH and ES assumptions. It suffices to check that the adversaries $\mathcal{B}$ and $\mathcal{D}$ used in the reduction are PPT procedures. This is indeed the case because we assumed that both $\mathcal{A}$ and $\mathcal{A}'$ are PPT procedures. In CertiCrypt, the tactic `PPT_proc` proves this automatically.

4.2   Security in the Random Oracle Model

Hashed ElGamal encryption is semantically secure in the random oracle model under the Computational Diffie-Hellman (CDH) assumption on the underlying group family $(G_n)_{n\in\mathbb{N}}$. This is the assumption that it is hard to compute g^{xy} given g^x and g^y where x and y are uniformly random elements in $\mathbb{Z}_q$. If the DDH assumption holds for the group family, then it is computationally unfeasible to test the success of an adversary against CDH (knowing only g^x and g^y). For this reason, we consider the following slightly different formulation that is equivalent in an asymptotic setting.

Definition 3 (List CDH assumption). *Consider the game*

$$
\boxed{
\begin{array}{l}
\textbf{Game LCDH :} \\
x, y \xleftarrow{\$} \mathbb{Z}_q; \\
L \leftarrow \mathcal{C}(g^x, g^y)
\end{array}
}
$$

and define

$$
\epsilon_{\mathsf{LCDH}}(\eta) \stackrel{def}{=} \mathrm{Pr}_{\mathsf{LCDH}}[g^{xy} \in L]
$$

Then, for every PPT *adversary* $\mathcal{C}$, ϵ_{LCDH} *is a negligible function.*

The DDH assumption implies the CDH assumption which in turns is equivalent to the list CDH assumption. To see this, note that an adversary against list

CDH whit a non-negligible advantage can be converted into an adversary against CDH by returning a random element in the result list L; since L is necessarily of polynomial size, the list CDH advantage of the resulting adversary is still non-negligible.

Theorem 2 (Security of Hashed ElGamal in the ROM). *For every* PPT *and well-formed adversary* $(\mathcal{A}, \mathcal{A}')$,

$$\left| \Pr_{\text{IND-CPA}}[d] - \frac{1}{2} \right| \leq \epsilon_{\text{LCDH}}(\eta)$$

Furthermore, under the CDH *assumption,* $\Pr_{\text{IND-CPA}}[d]$ *is negligibly close to* $\frac{1}{2}$.

What allows us to achieve semantic security under a (possibly) weaker assumption on the group family is a stronger assumption about the underlying family of hash functions. In the random oracle model, we model hash functions as truly random functions represented as stateful procedures. Queries are answered consistently: if some value is queried twice, the same response is given. In this model, there is no reason to continue viewing hash functions as keyed, so in the following we drop hash keys in the formalization.

The proof is sketched in Figure 3. The figure shows the sequence of games used to relate the success of the IND-CPA adversary in the original attack game to the success of the list CDH adversary $\mathcal{C}$ in game LCDH; the definition of the hash oracle is shown alongside each game. As in the proof in the standard model, we begin by inlining the calls to KG and Enc in the IND-CPA game to obtain an observationally equivalent game G_1 such that

$$\Pr_{\text{IND-CPA}}[b = b'] = \Pr_{G_1}[b = b'] \tag{7}$$

Then, we perform a nonlocal program transformation: at the beginning of the game we sample the value h^+ that the hash oracle gives in response to g^{xy}. This is an instance of *lazy sampling*, a technique automated in CertiCrypt that is described in greater detail in [1]. We get

$$\Pr_{G_1}[b = b'] = \Pr_{G_2}[b = b'] \tag{8}$$

We can then modify the hash oracle so to not store in L the response given to a g^{xy} query; this will later let us remove h^+ altogether from the hash oracle. To do this, define the following relational invariant

$$\phi_{23} \stackrel{\text{def}}{=} (\Lambda \in \text{dom}(L) \implies L[\Lambda] = h^+)\langle 1 \rangle \wedge$$
$$\forall \lambda, \lambda \neq \Lambda \langle 1 \rangle \implies L[\lambda]\langle 1 \rangle = L[\lambda]\langle 2 \rangle$$

where by $e\langle 1 \rangle$ (resp., $e\langle 2 \rangle$) we mean the value that expression e takes in the left hand side (resp., right hand side) program. It is easy to prove that oracles H_2 and H_3 are semantically equivalent under this invariant and preserve it. Since ϕ_{23} is established just before calling $\mathcal{A}$ and is preserved throughout the games, we can prove $\models G_2 \sim G_3 : \mathcal{G}_{\mathcal{A}} \Rightarrow \{b, b'\} \wedge \phi_{23}$ by inlining the call to H in game G_2, hence

$$\Pr_{G_2}[b = b'] = \Pr_{G_3}[b = b'] \tag{9}$$

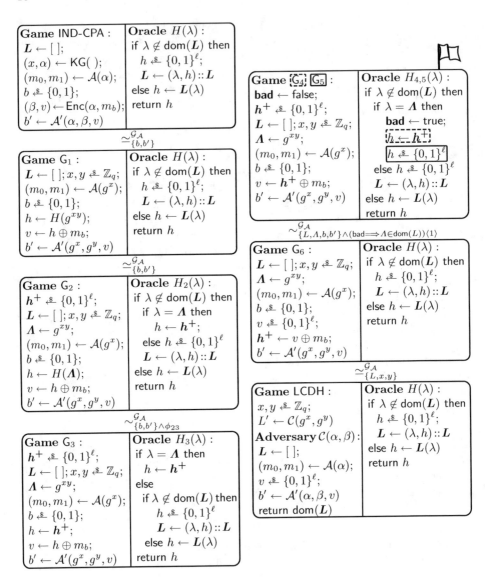

Fig. 3. Game-based proof of semantic security of Hashed ElGamal encryption in the Random Oracle Model

Then, we *undo* the modification to the hash oracle to prove that games G_3 and G_4 are observationally equivalent, i.e. $\models G_3 \sim^{\mathcal{G}_\mathcal{A}}_{\{b,b'\}} G_4$, from which we obtain

$$\mathrm{Pr}_{G_3}[b = b'] = \mathrm{Pr}_{G_4}[b = b'] \tag{10}$$

Games G_4 and G_5 are syntactically equal to up to the point where the flag **bad** is raised. From the Fundamental Lemma described in Sec. 2, it follows that

$$|\mathrm{Pr}_{\mathsf{G}_4}[b = b'] - \mathrm{Pr}_{\mathsf{G}_5}[b = b']| \leq \mathrm{Pr}_{\mathsf{G}_5}[\mathbf{bad}] \tag{11}$$

We then prove

$$\vDash \mathsf{G}_5 \sim \mathsf{G}_6 : =_{\mathcal{G}_{\mathcal{A}}} \Rightarrow =_{\{L,\Lambda,b,b'\}} \wedge (\mathbf{bad} \Longrightarrow \Lambda \in \mathrm{dom}(\boldsymbol{L}))\langle 1 \rangle$$

Using ep we coalesce the branches in the innermost conditional statement of H_5 to recover the original hash oracle. We defer the sampling of $\boldsymbol{h}^+$ in G_5 to the point just before computing v using swap, and we substitute

$$v \xleftarrow{\$} \{0,1\}^\ell;\ \boldsymbol{h}^+ \leftarrow v \oplus m_b \qquad \text{for} \qquad \boldsymbol{h}^+ \xleftarrow{\$} \{0,1\}^\ell;\ v \leftarrow \boldsymbol{h}^+ \oplus m_b$$

using the equivalence (5) presented in Sec. 4.1. Thus,

$$\mathrm{Pr}_{\mathsf{G}_5}[b = b'] = \mathrm{Pr}_{\mathsf{G}_6}[b = b'] \tag{12}$$

and by $(\leq_{[\![}])$,

$$\mathrm{Pr}_{\mathsf{G}_5}[\mathbf{bad}] \leq \mathrm{Pr}_{\mathsf{G}_6}[\Lambda \in \mathrm{dom}(\boldsymbol{L})] \tag{13}$$

Observe that in G_6, b' does not depend anymore on b, so we may as well sample b at the end of the game, thus obtaining

$$\mathrm{Pr}_{\mathsf{G}_6}[b = b'] = \frac{1}{2} \tag{14}$$

We construct an adversary $\mathcal{C}$ against list CDH that interacts with the adversary $(\mathcal{A}, \mathcal{A}')$ playing the role of an IND-CPA challenger. It returns the list of queries that the adversary $(\mathcal{A}, \mathcal{A}')$ makes to the hash oracle. Observe that $\mathcal{C}$ does not need to know x or y because it gets g^x and g^y as parameters. The success probability of $\mathcal{C}$ is the same as the probability of $\Lambda = g^{xy}$ being in the domain of $\boldsymbol{L}$ in G_6. Therefore, we finally have that

$$\mathrm{Pr}_{\mathsf{G}_6}[\Lambda \in \mathrm{dom}(\boldsymbol{L})] = \mathrm{Pr}_{\mathsf{G}_6}[g^{xy} \in \mathrm{dom}(\boldsymbol{L})] = \mathrm{Pr}_{\mathsf{LCDH}}[g^{xy} \in L'] \tag{15}$$

To summarize, from Equations (7)—(15) we obtain

$$\begin{aligned}
|\mathrm{Pr}_{\mathsf{IND\text{-}CPA}}[b = b'] - \tfrac{1}{2}| &= |\mathrm{Pr}_{\mathsf{G}_4}[b = b'] - \tfrac{1}{2}| \\
&= |\mathrm{Pr}_{\mathsf{G}_4}[b = b'] - \mathrm{Pr}_{\mathsf{G}_6}[b = b']| \\
&= |\mathrm{Pr}_{\mathsf{G}_4}[b = b'] - \mathrm{Pr}_{\mathsf{G}_5}[b = b']| \\
&\leq \mathrm{Pr}_{\mathsf{G}_5}[\mathbf{bad}] \\
&\leq \mathrm{Pr}_{\mathsf{G}_6}[\Lambda \in \mathrm{dom}(\boldsymbol{L})] \\
&= \mathrm{Pr}_{\mathsf{LCDH}}[g^{xy} \in L'] \\
&= \epsilon_{\mathsf{LCDH}}(\eta)
\end{aligned}$$

From the above equation and under the list CDH assumption (or equivalently, under the plain CDH assumption), the IND-CPA advantage of adversary $(\mathcal{A}, \mathcal{A}')$ results negligibly close to $\frac{1}{2}$. To see this, it suffices to verify that adversary $\mathcal{C}$ runs in probabilistic polynomial time. This is the case because adversary $(\mathcal{A}, \mathcal{A}')$ does, and $\mathcal{C}$ does not perform any costly computations.

5   Related Work

ElGamal is a standard example of a game-based cryptographic proof that provides a benchmark against which other works can be compared. We briefly comment on three proofs that are closely related to ours. For a more general account of related work, we refer to [1].

The most recent, and closely related is a formalization in Coq of a game-based proof of ElGamal semantic security by Nowak [12]. While we opt for a deep embedding, Nowak uses a shallow embedding and models adversaries directly as Coq functions. As a consequence, the resulting framework only provides limited support for proof automation. For the same reason, Nowak's formalization cannot deal with random oracles, so that he only presents the proof of Hashed ElGamal in the standard model of cryptography. Finally, it is not clear how to formalize complexity in the context of a shallow embedding, and Nowak's formalization ignores complexity altogether; as a result, security assumptions such as DDH cannot be modelled faithfully.

An earlier work by Barthe, Cederquist and Tarento [13] provides the foundations of a formal proof of security of Signed ElGamal encryption in Coq. In contrast to our work, they consider an idealized model of cryptography that abstracts away many details of the system and the security definition. Thus, the connection between the formalization and the security statement is not as strong as desired.

Corin and den Hartog [14] developed a (non-relational) Hoare logic for reasoning about probabilistic algorithms. They used it to construct a proof of semantic security of ElGamal encryption, but we are not aware of any other system verified using this logic. Being based on a mere probabilistic extension of Hoare logic, their formalism is not sufficiently expressive to model the notion of PPT complexity, and so security goals and hypotheses cannot be expressed precisely. More generally, the logic by itself provides no means to reason about context-dependent program transformations or transformations made in oracles.

6   Conclusion

CertiCrypt is a fully formalized framework that assists the construction of cryptographic game-based proofs. Proofs in CertiCrypt rely on a minimal trusted base and their correctness can be verified automatically by third parties. In this paper, we have illustrated some key aspects of CertiCrypt through the formalization of semantic security proofs of the Hashed ElGamal public-key encryption scheme in the standard and random oracle model, and we have highlighted some essential differences between our proofs and those that appear in the literature.

Acknowledgments. We would like to thank Daniel Hedin for his helpful comments on an earlier draft of this work.

References

1. Barthe, G., Grégoire, B., Zanella Béguelin, S.: Formal certification of code-based cryptographic proofs. In: Proceedings of the 36th ACM Symposium on Principles of Programming Languages. ACM Press, New York (2009)
2. Goldwasser, S., Micali, S.: Probabilistic encryption. J. Comput. Syst. Sci. 28(2), 270–299 (1984)
3. Stern, J.: Why provable security matters? In: Biham, E. (ed.) EUROCRYPT 2003. LNCS, vol. 2656. Springer, Heidelberg (2003)
4. Bellare, M., Rogaway, P.: The security of triple encryption and a framework for code-based game-playing proofs. In: Vaudenay, S. (ed.) EUROCRYPT 2006. LNCS, vol. 4004, pp. 409–426. Springer, Heidelberg (2006)
5. Halevi, S.: A plausible approach to computer-aided cryptographic proofs. Cryptology ePrint Archive, Report 2005/181 (2005)
6. Shoup, V.: Sequences of games: a tool for taming complexity in security proofs. Cryptology ePrint Archive, Report 2004/332 (2004)
7. The Coq development team: The Coq Proof Assistant Reference Manual v8.2 (2008), http://coq.inria.fr
8. Sabelfeld, A., Sands, D.: A per model of secure information flow in sequential programs. Higher-Order and Symbolic Computation 14(1), 59–91 (2001)
9. Audebaud, P., Paulin-Mohring, C.: Proofs of randomized algorithms in Coq. Science of Computer Programming (2008)
10. Benton, N.: Simple relational correctness proofs for static analyses and program transformations. In: Proceedings of the 31th ACM Symposium on Principles of Programming Languages, pp. 14–25. ACM Press, New York (2004)
11. Jonsson, B., Larsen, K.G., Yi, W.: Probabilistic extensions of process algebras. In: Handbook of Process Algebra, pp. 685–711. Elsevier, Amsterdam (2001)
12. Nowak, D.: A framework for game-based security proofs. In: Qing, S., Imai, H., Wang, G. (eds.) ICICS 2007. LNCS, vol. 4861, pp. 319–333. Springer, Heidelberg (2007)
13. Barthe, G., Cederquist, J., Tarento, S.: A machine-checked formalization of the generic model and the random oracle model. In: Basin, D., Rusinowitch, M. (eds.) IJCAR 2004. LNCS, vol. 3097, pp. 385–399. Springer, Heidelberg (2004)
14. Corin, R., den Hartog, J.: A probabilistic Hoare-style logic for game-based cryptographic proofs. In: Bugliesi, M., Preneel, B., Sassone, V., Wegener, I. (eds.) ICALP 2006. LNCS, vol. 4052, pp. 252–263. Springer, Heidelberg (2006)

Secure Information Flow as a Safety Property*

Gérard Boudol

INRIA, 06902 Sophia Antipolis, France

Abstract. In this paper we argue that, in the perspective of developing "security-minded" programming languages, the secure information flow property should be defined (as well as disciplined access) as a standard *safety* property, based on a notion of a security error, namely that one should not put in a public location a value elaborated using confidential information. We show that this is the property guaranteed by a standard security type system, and that, for a simple language, it is strictly stronger than non-interference. Moreover, we show that this notion of secure information flow allows us to give natural semantics to various security-minded programming constructs, including declassification.

1 Introduction

In this work we are concerned with the issue of software security, that is, more precisely, how to ensure that the software that we execute does not run into security violations. There are two possible attitudes with respect to software security:

- a *defensive attitude*, with the aim of protecting confidential information or precious resources against untrusted, potentially malicious code;
- a *constructive attitude*, with the aim of providing tools to design, develop and maintain secure software.

In the first case, one has to analyze compiled code before executing it, which can be very difficult (see [5], and subsequent work by the authors), or perform run-time security checks to block suspicious behaviour. Clearly, it is sometimes necessary to adopt the defensive attitude, setting severe limitations to what can be done using foreign code. But obviously, it would be preferable to get some a priori confidence in the software we run, thus opening more possibilities for trusted code to perform interesting interactions. Developing "security-minded" programming languages, such as JIF [15] or Flow CAML [21], is surely a way to enhance the trust we may have in the software we use. This is the topic we study, from a semantical perspective, in this paper, focusing on the confidentiality dimension of security. (As it is well-known, integrity may be dealt with by duality.) More precisely, we address the following question: what should we adopt as an appropriate semantics for a programming language that includes constructs designed to dynamically handle security issues?

* Work partially supported by the CRE FT-R&D no 46136511, and by the ANR-SETI-06-010 grant.

P. Degano, J. Guttman, and F. Martinelli (Eds.): FAST 2008, LNCS 5491, pp. 20–34, 2009.

Is the Non-interference Property Appropriate?

Access control is a well-established technique to ensure a clear safety property, namely that the code cannot read (and possibly execute) information unless it is granted the appropriate access right. Programming constructs have been proposed and studied to deal with access control at the application level, to dynamically enhance, restrict or check the current access right granted to the code (see [3,13,15,17,22]). However, it has been often argued that this is not enough to ensure end-to-end confidentiality, and that the code should also be checked for not disclosing confidential information it has the right to read. That is, one should also control the *flow of information* implemented by a program [10]. A static analysis for secure information flow was first proposed in [11], with a certification mechanism which was later on identified as a type system [25].

Regarding the security property to ensure, a semantical formulation was proposed by Cohen [8], under the name of *strong dependency*, nowadays referred to as *non-interference*, following the terminology of Goguen and Meseguer. This property states that *"variety in a secret input should not be conveyed to public output."* Then the work on static analysis of secure information flow has largely focused on developing security type systems for various languages, with the aim of showing a soundness result, namely that typable programs are non-interfering. We refer to the survey [19] for a review on the work done (till 2002) in this area.

The non-interference property has been, however, a matter of debate, from various points of view (see [18]). From the programming point of view, a fundamental observation is that non-interference rules out, by its very definition, programs that deliberately *declassify* information from a confidential level to a more public one. These programs are quite common and very useful, and therefore we should have ways to program with declassification. The JIF language [15] for instance includes such a downgrading facility. In [1] we argued that using declassification requires two different kinds of guarantees (see [20] for a discussion of the various aspects of declassification). First, the programmer has to have good reasons to think that it is safe to declassify a value. This, however, generally requires a semantical analysis of the program, and is therefore beyond the scope of standard static means. Second, though perhaps more modestly, the programmer would still like to have some guarantee, hopefully ensured by static analysis, that, even when using declassification constructs, his code does conform to some information flow policy – a guarantee similar to what we have with standard security type systems. Clearly however, the standard non-interference criterion is of no help here.

In [1] we have proposed a way to deal with declassification, first by introducing a programming construct to dynamically relax the flow policy, and then by defining an extended notion of (termination sensitive) non-interference, based on the notion of a bisimulation. However, although the programming construct is, to our view, quite simple to understand, this is admittedly not the case for our "non-disclosure" property. In particular, it is certainly not easy to find counter-examples to this property in case type checking fails for instance. This actually holds even without considering declassification, see [24]. As a matter of fact, it is generally impossible to find a counter-example to non-interference for programs that fail to type-check, simply because there is quite a deep mismatch between the security type system and the non-interference property. For instance, the two programs below, where we use the ML notation ! for reading the value from a memory location (that is, dereferencing in ML jargon):

$$P \; ; (v_{public} := \; ! \, u_{secret}) \; ; Q \tag{1}$$

$$v_{public} := (\text{if } ! \, u_{secret} \text{ then } E \text{ else } E') \tag{2}$$

are both rejected by a standard security type system, even though these programs are in some cases non-interfering. Indeed, the first one is non-interfering when either P updates the contents of location u or Q updates the contents of location v, in both cases with a value that does not depend on initial confidential information, and the second one is non-interfering in the case where E and E' always return the same value. However, from the intuitive point of view of secure information flow, both contain a *programming error*, since both exhibit a (direct or indirect) flow from *secret* to *public* information, and the type system is right in rejecting these programs: one should not hope to write secure software in this way. (Of course, in an expressive programming language, this kind of error may arise in much more subtle ways, see [1].)

Summarizing, we found two reasons why non-interference does not provide us with an appropriate semantical setting to use, with the purpose of developing security-minded programming languages: one is that it does not easily account for dynamic manipulations of the security policy, and the second is that it does not rely on an intuitive notion of a security error that could be used to explain why a program is faulty. It is therefore interesting to look for another security setting, which would allow us in particular to reduce the gap with type systems.

Safe Information Flow
Some work has recently been done to find methods to make the analysis of a program closer to the non-interference property, see [2,4,23]. Here we aim at reducing the gap in the other way: as we said non-interference, or its refinements, is not an appropriate security criterion in the programming of secure software. As a matter of fact, non-interference does not formalize the intuitive notion of secure information flow, which is, according to [11], that *"no execution results in a flow unless this is allowed by the information flow policy"*. Obviously, to make this definition precise, we have to give a formal meaning to *"execution results in a flow."* That is, we have to give an *information-flow-aware semantics* to programs, such that, typically, it is an error to attempt executing a statement $v_{public} := E$ if computing the value of expression E uses confidential information, as in the examples above. This has been done long ago by Fenton with his Data Mark Machine [12], which is a Minsky's machine where one tracks the confidentiality level of knowledge that is acquired, by reading at some level into the memory, while computing a piece of code. A similar idea has been used to give the semantics of some high-level languages [14,26,27]. This is the way we shall follow here, as it allows one to define in a natural and simple way the notion of a *security error* we are looking for, both from the access control (as in [3,17]) and information flow control point of view. Then the security property – no

run-time security error – is a standard *safety* property, which, from a programmer's point of view, is easy to understand. This notion of security was explicitly stated by Fenton in [12], but, even though one finds in [14,26] a similar idea of a security error, it seems that since Fenton's work, this was never officially adopted as a formal security criterion.

We show that, with respect to the formulation we have of secure information flow as a safety property, a security type (and effect) system that extends the one of [1,6] indeed ensures security. This *type safety* property (which is also suggested in [14,26], for a different language, security semantics, and type system) is not very difficult, at least when compared to the proofs of non-interference in [1,16,27] for instance. Moreover, we prove that our safety property is indeed, for a simple language (without declassification), strictly stronger than non-interference, and this shows that the gap with the type system is therefore reduced. As far as we can see, this has never been proved before. As in [1] we have in the language the construct (flow F in M) for locally relaxing, by extending it, the current flow policy, and in our semantics this policy is used to dynamically check that no illegal information flow is performed[1]. (Obviously, for typable programs, the type safety result ensures that these run-time checks are not needed). To further illustrate the flexibility of the approach, we add a new, dual construct for dynamically managing the flow policy, namely (revoke F in M), the semantics of which is that the flow policy F is explicitly disallowed when executing M. These constructs do not cause any particular difficulty when establishing type safety, but they are obviously beyond the scope of standard non-interference. We already explained this as regards declassification. For what concerns revocation of a flow policy, the standard non-interference property is not appropriate either, for a dual reason, because it would deem a program such as

$$(\text{revoke } public \prec secret \text{ in } u_{secret} := \, ! \, v_{public})$$

secure, whereas the assignment clearly violates the current flow policy. We could also easily add for instance to the language a construct that checks whether or not a particular flow policy holds at the current state of computation, and branches accordingly.

Note. For lack of space, the proofs are omitted. They can be found in the full version of the paper

2   Secure Programs

2.1   Security (Pre-)Lattices

Since the pioneering work of Denning [10], the classical way of abstractly specifying secure information flow is to use a *lattice of security levels*. The "objects" – information containers – of a system are then labelled by security levels, and information is allowed to *flow* from one object to another if the source object has a lower confidentiality level than the target one. In this paper we shall base our study on Core ML, a call-by-value λ-calculus extended with imperative constructs, where the "information containers," to which security levels are assigned,

---

[1] In [1] the operational semantics of (flow F in M) was the one of M.

are memory locations – "references", in ML's jargon (in an extended setting, that could also be files, entries in a database, or library modules).

We shall use here a slightly more flexible structure for confidentiality levels, namely the one of a *pre-lattice*, that is a structure defined as a pair $(\mathcal{L}, \preceq)$, where $\preceq$ is a preorder relation over the set $\mathcal{L}$, that is a reflexive and transitive, but not necessarily anti-symmetric relation, such that for any $x, y \in \mathcal{L}$ there exist a meet $x \curlywedge y$ and a join $x \curlyvee y$. The pre-lattices we use are defined as follows. We assume given a set $\mathcal{P}$ of *principals*, ranged over by $p, q \ldots$ (From an access control perspective, these are also called *permissions* [3,13], or *privileges* [17,22], while a "principal" is a set of permissions.) A *confidentiality level* is any set of principals, that is any subset ℓ of $\mathcal{P}$. The intuition is that whenever ℓ is the confidentiality label of an object, i.e. a reference, it represents a set of programs that are allowed to get the value of the object, i.e. to read the reference. Then a confidentiality level is similar to an access-control list (i.e. a set of permissions). From this point of view, a reference labelled $\mathcal{P}$ (also denoted $\bot$) is a most public one – every program is allowed to read it –, whereas the label $\emptyset$ (also denoted $\top$) indicates a secret reference, and reverse inclusion of security levels may be interpreted as indicating allowed flows of information: if a reference u is labelled ℓ, and $\ell \supseteq \ell'$ then the value of u may be transferred to a reference v labelled ℓ', since the programs allowed to read this value from v were already allowed to read it from u.

We follow the approach of [1], where the information flow policy can be dynamically updated, thereby modifying the security lattice that is currently in force during execution. A *flow policy* is a binary relation over $\mathcal{P}$. We let $F, G \ldots$ range over such relations. A pair $(p, q) \in F$ is to be understood as "*information may flow from principal p to principal q.*" We denote, as usual, by F^* the preorder generated by F (that is, the reflexive and transitive closure of F). Any flow policy F determines a preorder on confidentiality levels that extends reverse inclusion, as follows:

$$\ell \preceq_F \ell' \iff_{\text{def}} \forall q \in \ell' \, (\exists p \in \ell. \, p \, F^* \, q \text{ or } \forall p \in \mathcal{P}. \, p \, F^* \, q)$$

which is denoted $\preceq$ (instead of $\supseteq$) when $F = \emptyset$. Clearly $\{p\} \preceq_F \{q\}$ iff $p \, F^* \, q$, and $\preceq_F = \preceq_{F^*}$. For any F there is a least security level $\bot = \mathcal{P}$, and a greatest level with respect to $\preceq_F$, namely

$$\top_F = \{ q \mid \forall p \in \mathcal{P}. \, p \, F^* \, q \}$$

In particular $\top_\emptyset = \emptyset$, which we denote by $\top$. It is not difficult to see that the preorder $\preceq_F$ induces a pre-lattice structure on the set of confidentiality levels, where a meet is simply the union, and a join of ℓ and ℓ' is

$$\{ q \mid \forall p \in \mathcal{P}. \, p \, F^* \, q \text{ or } \exists p \in \ell. \, \exists p' \in \ell'. \, p \, F^* \, q \, \& \, p' \, F^* \, q \}$$

This observation justifies the following definition.

Definition (Security Pre-Lattices) 2.1. A confidentiality level is any subset ℓ of the set $\mathcal{P}$ of principals. Given a flow policy $F \subseteq \mathcal{P} \times \mathcal{P}$, the confidentiality levels are pre-ordered by the relation

$$\ell \preceq_F \ell' \iff_{\text{def}} \forall q \in \ell' \, (\exists p \in \ell. \, p \, F^* \, q \text{ or } \forall p \in \mathcal{P}. \, p \, F^* \, q)$$

$$M, N \ldots \in \mathcal{E}xpr ::= V \mid (\text{if } M \text{ then } N \text{ else } N') \mid (MN) \qquad \text{expressions}$$
$$\mid \ M \,; N \ \mid \ (\text{ref}_\ell \, N) \ \mid \ (!\,N) \ \mid \ (M := N)$$
$$\mid \ (\text{restrict } M \text{ to } \ell) \ \mid \ (\text{enable } \ell \text{ in } M) \ \mid \ (\text{test } \ell \text{ then } M \text{ else } N)$$
$$\mid \ (\text{flow } F \text{ in } M) \ \mid \ (\text{revoke } F \text{ in } M)$$
$$V \in \mathcal{V}al ::= x \ \mid \ u_\ell \ \mid \ \lambda x M \ \mid \ tt \ \mid \ ff \ \mid \ () \qquad\qquad values$$

Fig. 1. Syntax

The meet and join, w.r.t. F, of two security levels ℓ and ℓ' are respectively given by $\ell \cup \ell'$ and

$$\ell \curlyvee_F \ell' = \{\, q \mid \forall p \in \mathcal{P}.\ p\,F^*\,q \text{ or } \exists p \in \ell.\ \exists p' \in \ell'.\ p\,F^*\,q \ \& \ p'\,F^*\,q \,\}$$

One can see that each security level has a minimal representative with respect to a given flow policy. More precisely, let

$$\ell\!\downarrow_F\ =_{\text{def}} \{\, q \mid \forall p \in \mathcal{P}.\ p\,F^*\,q \text{ or } \exists p \in \ell.\ p\,F^*\,q \,\}$$

Then we have:

Lemma 2.2
(i) $\ell \preceq_F \ell' \ \Leftrightarrow \ \ell' \subseteq \ell\!\downarrow_F$
(ii) $\ell \curlyvee_F \ell' = \ell\!\downarrow_F \cap \ell'\!\downarrow_F$

2.2   Language

The language we consider is a higher-order imperative language à la ML, extended with constructs for dynamically granting and testing access rights, as in [3,13,17,22], and constructs for dynamically manipulating local flow policies, as in [1,7]. The construct (restrict M to ℓ) is used to restrict the access right of M by ℓ (this is similar to the "framed" expressions of [13], and to the "signed" expressions of [17]). This is a scoping construct: the current reading clearance is restored after termination of M. Dually, the (enable ℓ in M) construct is used to locally extend the read access right of M by ℓ. The test expression checks whether a given level is granted by the current evaluation context. The local flow declaration (flow F in M) enables the policy F to be used, in addition to the flow policy provided by the evaluation context, while reducing M, usually for declassification purposes. The (revoke F in M) construct is new. Its effect is dual to the one of flow, namely, it is to disallow the flow policy F when evaluating M, thus enforcing a policy that is more strict than the one granted by the evaluation context. One could also consider (check F then M else N), that behaves like M if F is entailed by the current flow policy G (that is, $F \subseteq G^*$), and like N otherwise. For more comments on the syntax, we refer to [1,3,13,17].

The syntax is given in Figure 1, where x is any variable, ℓ is any confidentiality level, and F is any flow policy. A *reference* is a memory location u to which is assigned a confidentiality level ℓ. For reasons explained below (and in [1,6]), we do not regard sequential composition as a derived construct. We let fv(M) be the set of variables occurring free in M, and we denote by $\{x \mapsto V\}M$ the capture-avoiding substitution of V for the free occurrences of x in M, where $V \in \mathit{Val}$.

2.3 Operational Semantics

For the purpose of proving our main results, and more specifically Theorem 1. below, it is convenient to formalize the operational semantics of the language following the "big-step" style. In this format, one describes how a pair made of an expression and an input memory reduces to a value and an output memory. As usual, a *memory* μ is a mapping from a finite set $\mathsf{dom}(\mu)$ of references to values, and we denote by $\mu[u_\ell := V]$ the memory obtained by updating in μ the value stored at reference u_ℓ into value V. We shall assume we start with a *well-formed* configuration, that is a configuration where every reference which occurs either in the expression or in a value stored in the memory is bound to a value in the memory (that is, it belongs to the domain of the memory). This property will be preserved by reduction.

In order to give the semantics of access control constructs, we maintain a current reading clearance for the evaluated expression, that is a security level that we denote by rc. Similarly, to control information flow, we maintain a current flow policy G. (In an implementation, both these components would be computed by means of a stack inspection mechanism, see [1,7].) As we said in the Introduction, the semantics has to formalize the fact that one should not store in a location labelled ℓ a value which has been elaborated using, directly or indirectly, information labelled ℓ' if $\ell' \not\preceq_G \ell$, according to the flow policy G that is in force when the storing operation is attempted. In our setting, "elaborated using information labelled ℓ" means that a reference labelled ℓ has been read. Then, to control the flow of information, the semantics will compute, for each expression, the level of knowledge that is acquired while evaluating the expression. Since this level may also be used, in the semantics of compound expressions, as an input for the next computing steps (as explained below), evaluation is starting with a given security level, traditionally denoted pc, initially $\bot$, that represents the level of knowledge that has been acquired prior to reducing the expression. Then the operational semantics of our language consists in a relation

$$\mathsf{rc}; G \vdash (\mathsf{pc}, M, \mu) \Downarrow^{\mathsf{m}} (\ell, V, \nu)$$

meaning that, starting with a knowledge level pc and a memory μ in the context of a reading clearance rc and a flow policy G, the expression M reduces to the value V, having acquired knowledge level ℓ, and updates the memory into ν. In Figure 2, we give the main rules of the semantics (the complete specification is to be found in the full version of the paper).

The superscript m in this relation is meant to indicate that the semantics is *monitored*. Indeed, we see that the side effects of an expression – creating, reading, or updating a reference – are subject to security constraints (put into boxes in Figure 2), to check that, in the case of $!\,u_\ell$, the code is granted the appropriate reading clearance, and that, in the cases of $\mathsf{ref}_\ell V$ and $u_\ell := V$, the code does not implement illegal flows. The current reading clearance rc is modified when evaluating the constructs restrict and enable, and checked when

$$\frac{\begin{array}{c} \mathsf{rc}; G \vdash (\mathsf{pc}, M, \mu) \Downarrow^m (\ell', \lambda x M', \mu') \\ \mathsf{rc}; G \vdash (\mathsf{pc}, N, \mu') \Downarrow^m (\ell'', V', \nu') \quad \mathsf{rc}; G \vdash (\ell' \curlyvee_G \ell'', \{x \mapsto V'\} M', \nu') \Downarrow^m (\ell, V, \nu) \end{array}}{\mathsf{rc}; G \vdash (\mathsf{pc}, (MN), \mu) \Downarrow^m (\ell, V, \nu)}$$

$$\frac{\mathsf{rc}; G \vdash (\mathsf{pc}, M, \mu) \Downarrow^m (\ell', b_i, \mu') \quad \mathsf{rc}; G \vdash (\ell', N_i, \mu') \Downarrow^m (\ell, V, \nu)}{\mathsf{rc}; G \vdash (\mathsf{pc}, (\text{if } M \text{ then } N_0 \text{ else } N_1), \mu) \Downarrow^m (\ell, V, \nu)} \quad b_0 = \mathit{tt}, \ b_1 = \mathit{ff}$$

$$\frac{\mathsf{rc}; G \vdash (\mathsf{pc}, M, \mu) \Downarrow^m (\ell', V', \mu') \quad \mathsf{rc}; G \vdash (\mathsf{pc}, N, \mu') \Downarrow^m (\ell, V, \nu)}{\mathsf{rc}; G \vdash (\mathsf{pc}, M \ ; \ N, \mu) \Downarrow^m (\ell, V, \nu)}$$

$$\frac{\mathsf{rc}; G \vdash (\mathsf{pc}, N, \mu) \Downarrow^m (\ell', V, \nu) \quad u_\ell \notin \mathsf{dom}(\nu)}{\mathsf{rc}; G \vdash (\mathsf{pc}, (\mathsf{ref}_\ell N), \mu) \Downarrow^m (\mathsf{pc}, u_\ell, \nu \cup \{u_\ell \mapsto V\})} \quad \boxed{\ell' \preceq_G \ell}$$

$$\frac{\mathsf{rc}; G \vdash (\mathsf{pc}, N, \mu) \Downarrow^m (\ell', u_\ell, \nu) \quad \nu(u_\ell) = V}{\mathsf{rc}; G \vdash (\mathsf{pc}, (! \, N), \mu) \Downarrow^m (\ell \curlyvee_G \ell', V, \nu)} \quad \boxed{\ell \preceq \mathsf{rc}}$$

$$\frac{\mathsf{rc}; G \vdash (\mathsf{pc}, M, \mu) \Downarrow^m (\ell_0, u_\ell, \mu') \quad \mathsf{rc}; G \vdash (\mathsf{pc}, N, \mu') \Downarrow^m (\ell_1, V, \nu)}{\mathsf{rc}; G \vdash (\mathsf{pc}, (M := N), \mu) \Downarrow^m (\mathsf{pc}, (), \nu[u_\ell := V])} \quad \boxed{\ell_0 \curlyvee_G \ell_1 \preceq_G \ell}$$

$$\frac{\mathsf{rc}; G \cup F \vdash (\mathsf{pc}, M, \mu) \Downarrow^m (\ell, V, \nu)}{\mathsf{rc}; G \vdash (\mathsf{pc}, (\mathsf{flow} \ F \ \mathsf{in} \ M), \mu) \Downarrow^m (\mathsf{pc} \curlyvee_G (\ell \!\downarrow_{G \cup F}), V, \nu)}$$

$$\frac{\mathsf{rc}; G^* - F \vdash (\mathsf{pc} \!\downarrow_G, M, \mu) \Downarrow^m (\ell, V, \nu)}{\mathsf{rc}; G \vdash (\mathsf{pc}, (\mathsf{revoke} \ F \ \mathsf{in} \ M), \mu) \Downarrow^m (\ell, V, \nu)}$$

Fig. 2. Big Step Monitored Evaluation (Main Rules)

a test expression is to be evaluated. Similarly, the current flow policy is updated when evaluating the body of flow and revoke expressions.

Let us now explain how the information flow is controlled. The security level ℓ that is returned when evaluating an expression is built upon the level of reads that are performed, as one can see from the semantics of $(! \, N)$. Indeed, this level remains identical to the initial pc (up to the current flow policy) when no read is performed. However, the acquired level ℓ that is returned only records the level of the "significant" reads, those which may influence the value returned by the expression. To see this, we have to look at the way in which the intermediate acquired knowledge levels are transmitted – or not – when evaluating compound expressions. The rule is that, *if the fact that an expression M gains control depends upon the particular value of a previously computed expression N, then the level of knowledge acquired in computing N is recorded prior to evaluating M*. In particular, evaluating one of the two branches in a conditional branching depends upon the level acquired when evaluating the boolean predicate. In this way, the evaluation controls indirect information flow.

In an application (MN), the level acquired in computing the function M is not transmitted to the evaluation of the argument N^2, because the fact that we turn to evaluate N does not depend on the particular value returned by M. When we arrive at reducing a redex $(\lambda x M' V')$, both levels acquired in computing the function and the argument are taken into account, since this particular redex generally depends on the information used in computing M and N (we refer to [1] for examples of indirect information flows in this case). On the contrary, in a sequential composition $M\,;\,N$, we can safely discard the level acquired after computing M, since we know that the returned value is not relevant for computing N. Similarly, when an assignment $(M := N)$ terminates, we restore the initial pc, since the value that is returned – namely $()$ – does not depend on any intermediate value. Then for instance any sequence of assignments does not gain any knowledge, that is, it returns the pc it started with.

Finally, let us comment on the semantics of (flow F in M) and (revoke F in M). In the case of (flow F in M), since the pc is an upper bound (of prior, relevant read operations) with respect to the current flow policy, we can keep it to evaluate M, since

$$\forall \ell.\ \text{pc} \preceq_G \ell \ \Rightarrow\ \text{pc} \preceq_{G \cup F} \ell$$

Regarding the level of knowledge that is returned, we have to keep at least the initial pc (otherwise declassification could affect some read operations outside of its scope), but we can take the level returned by ℓ as what it meant w.r.t. the more liberal policy $G \cup F$, and the way to do this is to take the minimal representative w.r.t. this policy (see Lemma 2.2). In the case of (revoke F in M), we have to minimize the initial pc with respect to the restricted policy, and we know by Lemma 1 (i) that this can be done replacing it by $\text{pc}\downarrow_G$ since

$$\forall \ell.\ \text{pc} \preceq_G \ell \ \Rightarrow\ \text{pc}\downarrow_G \preceq_{G^* - F} \ell$$

One should notice that the notion of secure information flow that is defined in this semantics is actually insensitive to the particular values that are involved in a computation, as it only tracks the places (or regions) – that is, the confidentiality levels in the memory – from which and where information flows.

As indicated in the Introduction, our semantics takes inspiration in Fenton's Data Mark Machine. Similar semantics have been given in [14,26,27] for higher-order imperative languages, without security-minded constructs. An important difference however is that we follow a *state-oriented* approach to information flow, as in [9,10,12,25], where the security labels are attached to memory locations, and not to values, as in the above mentioned work (and [16,21]).

The following lemma shows that one can only increase the level of acquired knowledge by evaluating an expression:

Lemma 2.3. $\text{rc}; G \vdash (\text{pc}, M, \mu) \Downarrow^m (\ell, V, \nu) \ \Rightarrow\ \text{pc} \preceq_G \ell$

To conclude this section, we observe that, since the level of knowledge acquired while computing an expression is directly accessible in the semantics, one could have programming constructs that use or modify it. For instance, we

---

[2] With a termination sensitive notion of secure information flow in mind, one would have to record part of this level, see [1,6].

considered in [1] a "reclassification" construct, namely $[\ell_0 \diagdown \ell_1]M$, that evaluates M, checks that the level of M is less than ℓ_0 (according to the current flow policy), and turns it into ℓ_1. This coercion, or cast construct, which could be called declassification whenever $\ell_1 \preceq_G \ell_0$, is more general than the declassification construct that is usually considered (see [15] for instance), since $\mathsf{declassify}(M, \ell) = [\top \diagdown \ell]M$. We can derive this construct here:

$$[\ell_0 \diagdown \ell_1]M =_{\mathrm{def}} (\mathsf{let}\ x = \mathsf{ref}_{\ell_0} M\ \mathsf{in}\ !\mathsf{ref}_{\ell_1}(\mathsf{flow}\ U\ \mathsf{in}\ !\, x))$$

where $U = \mathcal{P} \times \mathcal{P}$ (although a direct semantics would obviously be more efficient).

2.4   Secure Programs

In this section we define secure programs (from the confidentiality point of view), which do not run into security errors, or, more accurately, do not violate access restrictions, nor the current flow policy. A *security error* is a configuration where a security check has to fail, and where the monitored evaluation is stuck (since here we wish to avoid such errors, we are not considering ways of pulling through them, such as raising an exception). There are three kinds of security violations. The first one is an access right violation, namely a configuration $(\mathsf{pc}, (!\, u_\ell), \mu)$ in the context of an insufficient reading clearance, that is rc such that $\ell \not\preceq \mathsf{rc}$. The two other ones are attempts at implementing an illegal flow, either by creating or by updating a reference at confidentiality level ℓ with a value elaborated using information that, according to the current flow policy G, should not flow into level ℓ. Typical examples of these are $(\mathsf{ref}_\ell\,(!\, u_{\ell'}))$ and $(u_\ell := (!\, v_{\ell'}))$ with $\ell' \not\preceq_G \ell$, and more generally $(\mathsf{ref}_\ell\, N)$ and $(u_\ell := N)$ where the evaluation of N acquires a level ℓ' of information that should not flow at level ℓ.

To define our notion of a secure program, we introduce an uncontrolled variant of the operational semantics, denoted $\Downarrow$, which is defined exactly as $\Downarrow^{\mathsf{m}}$ except that we remove the side security conditions (inside the boxes) involved in the definition of the latter. It is clear that in the definition of $\Downarrow$, the security components G, pc and ℓ do not play any rôle, that is, if $\mathsf{rc}; G \vdash (\mathsf{pc}, M, \mu) \Downarrow (\ell, V, \nu)$ then for any G' and pc' there exists ℓ' such that $\mathsf{rc}; G' \vdash (\mathsf{pc}', M, \mu) \Downarrow (\ell', V, \nu)$. Therefore, we shall regard the unmonitored semantics as defined on configurations of the form (M, μ). We could give a direct definition of $\mathsf{rc} \vdash (M, \mu) \Downarrow (V, \nu)$ (which is the obvious one) but, for lack of space, we omit it. Notice that, in particular, the expressions $(\mathsf{restrict}\ M\ \mathsf{to}\ r)$, $(\mathsf{enable}\ \ell\ \mathsf{in}\ M)$, $(\mathsf{flow}\ F\ \mathsf{in}\ M)$ and $(\mathsf{revoke}\ F\ \mathsf{in}\ M)$ all behave like M in the unrestricted semantics. It should be clear that the uncontrolled semantics is more permissive than the monitored ones, that is

$$\mathsf{rc}; G \vdash (\mathsf{pc}, M, \mu) \Downarrow^{\mathsf{m}} (\ell, V, \nu) \;\Rightarrow\; \mathsf{rc} \vdash (M, \mu) \Downarrow (V, \nu)$$

Our definition of the security property is, roughly, that a program M is secure if the converse implication holds, that is, if all the security checks made during the evaluation of M succeed, or, in other words, that these checks are useless for such a program. However, we have to make this definition relative to a class of memories, because obviously a program such as $((!\, u_\ell)())$ is only secure if the memory binds u_ℓ to a secure value, that is, in this case, a function V such that $(V())$ is secure.

Definition (Secure Programs) 2.4. An expression M is secure (from the confidentiality point of view) w.r.t. a reading clearance rc, a flow policy G and a class $\mathcal{M}$ of memories if and only if

$$\text{rc} \vdash (M, \mu) \Downarrow (V, \nu) \;\Rightarrow\; \exists \ell. \; \text{rc}; G \vdash (\bot, M, \mu) \Downarrow^m (\ell, V, \nu)$$

for any $\mu \in \mathcal{M}$. This definition is inspired by the one of Fenton in [12]. This is a definition of a *safety* property, stating that nothing bad can possibly happen during execution. (This would be made more obvious by introducing a "small-step" variant of the semantics, which we omit here.) With this definition, we can easily explain the meaning of the "security-minded" programming constructs:

Lemma 2.5. For any expression M, the following holds:

(i) (restrict M to r) is rc-secure $\Leftrightarrow$ M is rc $\curlywedge$ r-secure;

(ii) (enable ℓ in M) is rc-secure $\Leftrightarrow$ M is rc $\curlyvee$ ℓ-secure;

(iii) (flow F in M) is G-secure $\Leftrightarrow$ M is $G \cup F$-secure;

(iv) (revoke F in M) is G-secure $\Leftrightarrow$ M is $(G^* - F)$-secure.

(The proof is immediate.) We shall see in Section 4 that our secure programs, when they do not involve dynamic manipulations of the flow policy, also satisfy the non-interference property. Our security property is *strictly* stronger than non-interference, however. Indeed, the program of Example (2) in the Introduction, with $E = tt = E'$ for instance, is not secure with respect to a flow policy G such that $secret \not\preceq_G public$. Similarly, the program of Example (1) is insecure whenever P terminates.

3   Type Safety

Our type system elaborates on the ones of [1,6,7,25], and, as such, is actually a *type and effect system*. This is consistent with our *"state-oriented"* approach – as opposed to the "value-oriented" approach of [14,16,17,21,22,26,27] for instance –, where only the access to the "information containers", that is, to the references in the memory, is protected by access rights. In particular, a value is by itself neither "secret" nor "public" (in a richer setting, there would be no such thing as a secret list of public integers for instance), and the types do not need to be multiplied by the set of confidentiality levels. Then the types are

$$\tau, \sigma, \theta \ldots \; ::= \; t \;|\; \text{bool} \;|\; \text{unit} \;|\; \theta\,\text{ref}_\ell \;|\; (\tau \xrightarrow[\ell, F]{e} \sigma)$$

where t is any type variable and e is any "security effect" – see below. Notice that a reference type $\theta\,\text{ref}_\ell$ records the type θ of values the reference contains, as well as the "region" ℓ where it is created, which is the confidentiality level at which the reference is classified. Since a functional value wraps a possibly effectful computation, its type records this *latent effect* e, which is the effect the function may have when applied to an argument. It also records the reading clearance ℓ and the flow policy F that are assumed to hold when the function is called in order to evaluate its body. The judgements of the type and effect system have the form

$$\text{rc}; G; \Gamma \vdash M : e, \tau$$

where Γ is a typing context, assigning types to variables and to references, and e is a *security effect*, that is a pair $(e.\mathsf{r}, e.\mathsf{w})$ of confidentiality levels. The intuition is:

- rc is the current read access right that is in force when reducing M;
- G is the current flow policy;
- e.r is the *reading level* of M. This is an upper bound (up to the current flow relation) of the confidentiality levels of the references the expression M reads that may influence its resulting value;
- e.w is the *writing level*, that is a lower bound (w.r.t. the relation $\preceq$) of the level of references that the expression M may update.

According to this, the security effects are ordered componentwise, in a covariant manner as regards the reading level, and in a contravariant way as regards the writing level. Then we abusively denote by $\perp$ the pair $(\perp, \top)$. In the typing rules for compound expressions, we will use the join operation on security effects:

$$e \curlyvee_G e' =_{\mathrm{def}} (e.r \curlyvee_G e'.r, e.w \cup e'.w)$$

The main rules of the typing system are given in Figure 3. This is essentially the system of [1,6,7], without the "termination level," and with a typing rule for the new (revoke F in M) construct. In order to get simple proofs, we adopt a syntax-directed style, with no subtyping rule, or more accurately no "subeffecting" rule (see [25]). We only use "subeffecting" in the (FLOW) and (REVOKE) rules, where we allow the reading effect to be weakened, with respect to the flow policy that has been used to derive this effect. For instance if $G = L \preceq H$ and $F = H \preceq L$ we have $\{H\} \preceq_{F \cup G} \{L\}$, and therefore if M reads at level H, the expression (flow F in M) appears to read at level L w.r.t. policy G. Similarly, if $G = A \preceq B$ we have $\{A, B\} \preceq \{A\}{\downarrow}_G$, and therefore if M reads at both levels A and B, with no flow policy relating these principals, the expression (revoke G in M) appears to read at level A w.r.t. policy G. For further explanations, comments and examples about the type system, we refer to [1,6,7].

In order to show the Type Safety result, asserting that typable expressions are secure, that is, that one may dispense of run-time checks when evaluating typable expressions, we have to extend typability to memories, that is, we define $\Gamma \vdash \mu$ as follows:

$$\Gamma \vdash \mu \Leftrightarrow_{\mathrm{def}} \forall u_\ell. \, u_\ell \in \mathrm{dom}(\mu) \Rightarrow u_\ell \in \mathrm{dom}(\Gamma) \ \& \ \Gamma \vdash \mu(u_\ell) : \Gamma(u_\ell)$$

Theorem (Type Safety) 3.1. Let M be an expression that is typable at confidentiality level rc, with a flow policy G, in the Γ context, that is, rc; G; $\Gamma \vdash M : e, \tau$ for some e and τ. Then M is secure w.r.t. rc, G and the class of memories $\{\mu \mid \Gamma \vdash \mu\}$.

Proof Hint. Assuming that rc; G; $\Gamma \vdash M : e, \tau$ and $(M, \mu) \Downarrow (V, \nu)$ where $\Gamma \vdash \mu$, we show, by induction on the inference of $(M, \mu) \Downarrow (V, \nu)$ and by case on M, that the following holds:

(i) for all pc if pc $\preceq_G$ e.w then rc; $G \vdash (\mathrm{pc}, M, \mu) \Downarrow^{\mathrm{m}} (\ell, V, \nu)$ for some ℓ.
(ii) for all pc if rc; $G \vdash (\mathrm{pc}, M, \mu) \Downarrow^{\mathrm{m}} (\ell, V, \nu)$ then $\ell \preceq_G \mathrm{pc} \curlyvee_G e.r$ and $\Gamma' \vdash V : \tau$ with $\Gamma' \vdash \nu$ for some Γ' such that $\Gamma \subseteq \Gamma'$.   ❑

As usual, there are secure programs, like (if tt then () else $v_\perp := \, ! u_\top$), that are not typable, since typability does not involve semantical considerations.

$$\frac{\mathsf{rc};G;\Gamma \vdash M : e, \mathsf{bool} \quad \mathsf{rc};G;\Gamma \vdash N_i : e_i, \tau \quad e.\mathsf{r} \preceq_G e_0.\mathsf{w} \curlywedge e_1.\mathsf{w}}{\mathsf{rc};G;\Gamma \vdash (\mathsf{if}\ M\ \mathsf{then}\ N_0\ \mathsf{else}\ N_1) : e \curlyvee_G e_0 \curlyvee_G e_1, \tau} \quad (\text{Cond})$$

$$\frac{\begin{array}{cc}\mathsf{rc};G;\Gamma \vdash M : e, \tau \xrightarrow[r,F]{e'} \sigma & r \preceq \mathsf{rc} \quad F \subseteq G^* \\ \mathsf{rc};G;\Gamma \vdash N : e'', \tau & e.\mathsf{r} \curlyvee_G e''.\mathsf{r} \preceq_G e'.\mathsf{w}\end{array}}{\mathsf{rc};G;\Gamma \vdash (MN) : e \curlyvee_G e' \curlyvee_G e'', \sigma} \quad (\text{App})$$

$$\frac{\mathsf{rc};G;\Gamma \vdash M : e, \tau \quad \mathsf{rc};G;\Gamma \vdash N : e', \sigma}{\mathsf{rc};G;\Gamma \vdash M\ ;\ N : (\bot, e.\mathsf{w}) \curlyvee e', \sigma} \quad (\text{Seq})$$

$$\frac{\mathsf{rc};G;\Gamma \vdash N : e, \theta \quad e.\mathsf{r} \preceq_G \ell}{\mathsf{rc};G;\Gamma \vdash (\mathsf{ref}_\ell\ N) : (\bot, e.\mathsf{w} \curlywedge \ell), \theta\ \mathsf{ref}_\ell} \quad (\text{Ref}) \qquad \frac{\mathsf{rc};G;\Gamma \vdash N : e, \theta\ \mathsf{ref}_\ell \quad \ell \preceq \mathsf{rc}}{\mathsf{rc};G;\Gamma \vdash (!\,N) : e \curlyvee_G (\ell, \top), \theta} \quad (\text{Deref})$$

$$\frac{\mathsf{rc};G;\Gamma \vdash M : e, \theta\ \mathsf{ref}_\ell \quad \mathsf{rc};G;\Gamma \vdash N : e', \theta \quad e.\mathsf{r} \curlyvee_G e'.\mathsf{r} \preceq_G \ell}{\mathsf{rc};G;\Gamma \vdash (M := N) : (\bot, e.\mathsf{w} \curlywedge e'.\mathsf{w} \curlywedge \ell), \mathsf{unit}} \quad (\text{Assign})$$

$$\frac{\mathsf{rc};F \cup G;\Gamma \vdash M : e, \tau \quad e.\mathsf{r} \preceq_{F \cup G} r}{\mathsf{rc};G;\Gamma \vdash (\mathsf{flow}\ F\ \mathsf{in}\ M) : (r, e.\mathsf{w}), \tau} \quad (\text{Flow})$$

$$\frac{\mathsf{rc};G^* - F;\Gamma \vdash M : e, \tau \quad e.\mathsf{r} \preceq_{G^* - F} r{\downarrow}_G}{\mathsf{rc};G;\Gamma \vdash (\mathsf{revoke}\ F\ \mathsf{in}\ M) : (r, e.\mathsf{w}), \tau} \quad (\text{Revoke})$$

Fig. 3. The Type and Effect System (Main Rules)

4   Non-interference

In this section, our aim is to show that our security property is stronger than non-interference. Obviously, this cannot hold for programs involving declassification, and therefore we show this result for programs in a sublanguage, namely the one given by the following grammar:

$$M,\ N \ldots ::= V \ |\ (\mathsf{if}\ M\ \mathsf{then}\ N\ \mathsf{else}\ N') \ |\ (MN)$$
$$|\ M\ ;\ N \ |\ (!\,N) \ |\ (M := N)$$

Even though they do not cause any particular difficulty – as they are orthogonal to the issue –, we have discarded also the constructs related to access control, for simplicity. For the same reason, we do not consider here the reference creation construct. This construct entails some complications in defining the non-interference property. It should be possible to include it, using the notion of "in view/out of view" parts of a configuration of [9]. In the rest of this section we only consider expressions that belong to the simple sublanguage.

Definition (Low Equality of Memories) 4.1. Let ℓ be a confidentiality level and G a global flow policy. Then two memories μ and ν are low equal below ℓ with respect to G, in notation $\mu \simeq_G^\ell \nu$, if and only if they satisfy:

$$\mathsf{dom}(\mu) = \mathsf{dom}(\nu) \ \& \ \forall u_{\ell'} \in \mathsf{dom}(\mu). \ \ell' \preceq_G \ell \ \Rightarrow \ \mu(u_{\ell'}) = \nu(u_{\ell'})$$

The relation $\simeq_G^{\ell}$ is clearly an equivalence.

Definition (Non-Interference) 4.2. An expression M (of the simple language) satisfies the non-interference property with respect to a flow policy G if an only if

$$\mu \simeq_G^{\ell} \nu \ \& \ (M, \mu) \Downarrow (V, \mu') \ \& \ (M, \nu) \Downarrow (V', \nu') \ \Rightarrow \ \mu' \simeq_G^{\ell} \nu'$$

for any ℓ, μ and ν. Notice that this definition is extremely simple, and does not in particular mention typing, nor any particular syntax, as opposed to definitions of non-interference in the "value-oriented" approach of [14,16,26,27] (and also [9]). As noticed in [20], this definition is still a little too intensional, since it deems the program of Example (2) insecure in the case where $E = \lambda x()$ and $E' = \lambda x(\lambda y y())$ for instance. However, the definition is fine for our purpose, which is to prove that, for expressions of the simple language, our (intensional) security property is stronger than non-interference. This is our second main result:

Theorem 4.3. For any expression M of the simple language, if M is secure with respect to G then M satisfies the non-interference property with respect to G.

5   Conclusion

We have argued that, for the purpose of developing secure software, the non-interference property is not a good criterion. We proposed to replace it with a more intensional notion of security, based on a notion of a security error, or security violation, that should be easy to understand and use from a programming point of view. We have shown that this intensional notion of a secure program is indeed closer than non-interference to the programming practice, where type systems, in particular, provide a very useful tool for developing safe software. Moreover, we have shown that this approach is well-suited for describing the semantics of various programming constructs that allow the programmer to deal with security issues.

References

1. Almeida Matos, A., Boudol, G.: On declassification and the non-disclosure policy. In: CSFW 2005, pp. 226–240 (2005); revised version accepted for publication in the J. of Computer Security, available from the authors web page
2. Amtoft, T., Banerjee, A.: Information flow analysis in logical form. In: Giacobazzi, R. (ed.) SAS 2004. LNCS, vol. 3148, pp. 100–115. Springer, Heidelberg (2004)
3. Banerjee, A., Naumann, D.A.: Stack-based access control for secure information flow. J. of Functional Programming 15, 131–177 (2005); special issue on Language-Based Security
4. Barthe, G., D'Argenio, P., Rezk, T.: Secure information flow by self- composition. In: CSFW 2004 (2004)

5. Barthe, G., Rezk, T.: Non-interference for a JVM-like language. In: ACM SIG-PLAN Workshop on Types in Language Design and Implementation, pp. 103–112 (2005)
6. Boudol, G.: On typing information flow. In: Van Hung, D., Wirsing, M. (eds.) ICTAC 2005. LNCS, vol. 3722, pp. 366–380. Springer, Heidelberg (2005)
7. Boudol, G., Kolundžija, M.: Access control and declassification. In: MMM- ACNS 2007. Communications in Computers and Information Science, vol. 1 (2007)
8. Cohen, E.: Information transmission in computational systems. In: 6th ACM Symp. on Operating Systems Principles, pp. 133–139 (1977)
9. Crary, K., Kliger, A., Pfenning, F.: A monadic analysis of information flow security with mutable state. J. of Functional Programming 15(2), 249–291 (2005)
10. Denning, D.E.: A lattice model of secure information flow. CACM 19(5), 236–243 (1976)
11. Denning, D.E., Denning, P.J.: Certification of programs for secure information flow. CACM 20(7), 504–513 (1977)
12. Fenton, J.S.: Memoryless subsystems. Computer Journal 17(2), 143–147 (1974)
13. Fournet, C., Gordon, A.: Stack inspection: theory and variants. In: POPL 2002, pp. 307–318 (2002)
14. Heintze, N., Riecke, J.: The SLam calculus: programming with secrecy and integrity. In: POPL 1998, pp. 365–377 (1998)
15. Myers, A.: JFlow: practical mostly-static information flow control. In: POPL 1999 (1999)
16. Pottier, F., Simonet, V.: Information flow inference for ML. ACM TOPLAS 25(1), 117–158 (2003)
17. Pottier, F., Skalka, C., Smith, S.: A systematic approach to static access control. ACM TOPLAS 27(2), 344–382 (2005)
18. Ryan, P., McLean, J., Millen, J., Gligor, V.: Non-interference, who needs it? In: CSFW 2001 (2001)
19. Sabelfeld, A., Myers, A.C.: Language-based information-flow security. IEEE J. on Selected Areas in Communications 21(1), 5–19 (2003)
20. Sabelfeld, A., Sands, D.: Dimensions and principles of declassification. In: CSFW 2005, pp. 255–269 (2005); revised version accepted for publication in the J. of Computer Security, available from the authors web page
21. Simonet, V.: The Flow Caml system: documentation and user's manual, INRIA Tech. Rep. 0282 (2003)
22. Skalka, C., Smith, S.: Static enforcement of security with types. In: ICFP 2000, pp. 34–45 (2000)
23. Terauchi, T., Aiken, A.: Secure information flow as a safety problem. In: Hankin, C., Siveroni, I. (eds.) SAS 2005. LNCS, vol. 3672, pp. 352–367. Springer, Heidelberg (2005)
24. Unno, H., Kobayashi, N., Yonezawa, A.: Combining type-based analysis and model checking for finding counterexamples against non-interference. In: PLAS 2006 (2006)
25. Volpano, D., Smith, G., Irvine, C.: A sound type system for secure flow analysis. J. of Computer Security 4(3), 167–187 (1996)
26. Zdancewic, S.: Programming Languages for Information Security, PhD Thesis, Cornell University (2002)
27. Zdancewic, S., Myers, A.C.: Secure information flow via linear continuations. HOSC 15(2-3), 209–234 (2002)

Who Can Declassify?

Alexander Lux and Heiko Mantel

Department of Computer Science, TU Darmstadt
Hochschulstraße 10, 64289 Darmstadt, Germany
{lux,mantel}@cs.tu-darmstadt.de

Abstract. Noninterference provides reliable guarantees for the confidentiality of sensitive information, but it is too restrictive if exceptions shall be permitted. Although many approaches to permitting and controlling exceptional information release have been proposed, the problem of declassification is not yet satisfactorily solved. The aim of our project is to provide adequate control for declassification in language-based security. The main contribution of this article is a novel approach for controlling who can initiate a declassification. Our contributions include a formal security condition and a sound approach to statically enforcing this condition. This article complements our earlier work on controlling where declassification can occur and what can be declassified.

1 Introduction

Before private data is given as input to an application, one would like a guarantee that the program is sufficiently trustworthy. The desired guarantee can be formalized by the noninterference property, which ensures that there is no danger of undesired information leakage. This is expressed by requiring that the program's output to untrusted sinks must be completely independent from any confidential input. While noninterference constitutes a reliable guarantee about the flow of information, it is a too restrictive requirement for some domains. For instance, the output of a password-based authentication mechanism differs for a given input depending on the stored password, i.e. on a secret. Therefore, such a mechanism necessarily cannot satisfy the noninterference property.

It is clear that the noninterference property can be relaxed in order to permit such exceptional information leakage. However, the problem of controlling such exceptions is not yet satisfactorily solved. To clarify the aims and virtues of previous approaches, three dimensions of controlling declassification were identified in [1], namely, *what* can be declassified, *where* declassification can occur, and *who* can initiate declassification. A recent classification of existing approaches to controlling declassification [2] shows that we do not yet have an integrated approach that provides adequate control in all of these dimensions.

In this article, we propose a novel approach to controlling the third dimension of declassification, i.e. who can initiate declassification. This work complements our earlier work on controlling the first two dimensions [3]. In addition, we present prudent principles of declassification that can be used as a sanity check for new security conditions. Our principles extend and refine the ones proposed in [2]. The second novel contribution is the security condition WHO that we

P. Degano, J. Guttman, and F. Martinelli (Eds.): FAST 2008, LNCS 5491, pp. 35–49, 2009.

integrate with our earlier condition WHERE to WHERE&WHO, in order to control who can initiate which declassifications. We prove that WHERE&WHO satisfies all prudent principles of declassification, the novel as well as the established ones. Interestingly, we could show that, in some cases, it is possible to refine the security policy such that WHERE&WHO can be enforced by the simpler condition WHERE, which we developed for controlling where declassification can occur. We also present an approach to statically enforcing WHERE&WHO by refining the policy and applying a type system for WHERE.

2   A Motivating Example

We consider a program that is used by a video store to control the delivery of movies to customers. After a customer decides to buy a movie, his payment data is fetched, and it is forwarded to a bank. The movie is delivered only after the payment has been confirmed by the bank. Movies can be ordered either via a web interface or at a vending machine in the store. Regular customers may become preferred customers, who may obtain a movie also without confirmation of their payment by the bank. However, this preferred treatment is limited to orders at the vending machine because the vendor does not have sufficient trust in the authentication mechanism of the web interface.

The example program is written in a simple imperative language with explicit I/O-instructions. Execution of an instruction $x <- in$ sets the value of the variable x to a value read from the input channel in. Execution of $x -> out$ writes the current value of x to the output channel out. As a convention, names of input and output channels end with I or O, respectively. Instructions in brackets (like, e.g., $[public:=movie]_1$) mark assignments that are intended as declassifications. For now such declassification statements should be read as usual assignments.

```
if byMachine then                              % branch on whether purchase at machine
    paydatvd <- machineI;                      % get payment data from vending machine
    paydatvd -> bankO;                         % pass payment data to bank
    payOK <- bankI;                            % get confirmation of payment from bank
    if (payOK or isPreferred(paydatvd)) then
        [public:=movie]₁;                      % copy movie to public variable
        public -> machineO fi                  % pass movie to machine
else
    paydatweb <- webI;                         % get payment data from web interface
    paydatweb -> bankO;                        % pass payment data to bank
    payOK <- bankI;                            % get confirmation of payment from bank
    if payOK then
        [public:=movie]₂;                      % copy movie to public variable
        public -> webO fi                      % pass movie to web interface
fi
```

For the store, it is essential that a movie is not leaked accidently. That is, a movie is a secret that must be protected from the customer until his credentials have been confirmed. As a movie is a secret, it must be explicitly declassified before it can be delivered to a customer. A preferred customer can initiate this declassification also without the bank's confirmation by declaring his special status. However, exceptions should be limited to purchases at the vending machine. It is the vendor's policy that a customer's input at the web interface cannot initiate a declassification. While our first example program satisfies this security requirement, the following program is vulnerable to attacks via the web interface. The problem with this program is that the check isPreferred(paydat) can depend on the input from the web interface, which violates the vendor's policy.

```
if byMachine
   then paydat <- machineI
   else paydat <- webI fi;
paydat -> bankO;                       % pass payment data to bank
payOK <- bankI;                        % get confirmation of payment from bank
if (payOK or isPreferred(paydat)) then
   [public:=movie]₁;                   % copy movie to public variable
   if byMachine
      then public -> machineO
      else public -> webO fi
fi
```

The objective of this article is to develop a security condition that adequately controls who can initiate a declassification. In particular, it should reject vulnerable programs like our second example, and it should accept secure programs like the first example. The subscripts at declassification statements (e.g., 1 and 2 in the first example and 1 in the second example) will be used to specify in a policy which declassification statements may be initiated by whom.

3   Adequate Control of Declassification

We aim for security conditions that formalize the intuitive notion of secure information flow on a semantic level and that are suitable points of reference for a soundness argument of a given syntactic security analysis. However, defining a security condition that adequately captures the security of information flow becomes non-trivial if exceptional information release shall be permitted. There is an inherent trade-off between relaxing information flow control in order to permit declassification and reliably ensuring security by rigorous information flow control. In the following, we present prudent principles of declassification that can be used as a sanity check for security conditions. The principles extend and refine the ones proposed by Sabelfeld and Sands [2]. The principles are presented in Section 3.1. In Section 3.2, we introduce the model of computation and the programming language used in the rest of the article. The prudent principles are formalized and specialized to this setting in Section 3.3.

3.1   Prudent Principles of Controlling Declassification

In the following, we use the term *noninterference* as a place-holder for a security condition that adequately characterizes information flow security in a setting without declassification. In order to apply the principles as a sanity check, this place-holder must be instantiated with a suitable security condition.

Semantic consistency [2]. The (in)security of a program is invariant under semantic-preserving transformations of declassification-free subprograms.

Whether a program is secure depends on its behavior. Semantic consistency ensures that the classification of a program is not effected by syntactic modifications that do not change the program's behavior. This principle is desirable for security definitions, in general, including ones that permit declassification.

Relaxation. Every program that satisfies noninterference also satisfies the given security condition.

Monotonicity of release [2]. Adding further declassifications to a secure program cannot render it insecure.

These principle are reasonable, because the whole purpose of introducing declassification is to accept more programs as secure. The principles *relaxation* and *monotonicity* impose a lower bound on the set of programs that are accepted by security conditions. This distinguishes them from the principles below, which impose upper bounds on the set of acceptable programs.

Non-occlusion [2]. The presence of a declassification operation cannot mask other covert information leaks.

Non-occlusion is crucial, because it summarizes the goal of controlling declassification. However, a bootstrapping problem occurs when formalizing this principle because such a formalization itself would constitute a characterization of secure information flow, which would need to be checked for non-occlusion. We introduce further prudent principles that can be formalized in the following.

Noninterference up-to. Every program that satisfies the given security condition also satisfies noninterference if it were executed in an environment that terminates the program when it is about to perform a declassification.

Persistence. For every program that satisfies the given security condition, all programs that are reachable also satisfy the security condition. If this only holds for programs that are reached by an execution where the last step is a declassification, then the given security condition is called *weakly persistent*.

The principle *noninterference up-to* ensures that the security condition is not more permissible than noninterference as long as no declassification occurs. Persistence and weak persistence, both ensure, after a declassification occurred, that one again obtains the original security guarantee for the resulting configuration.

The fourth principle introduced in [2], *conservativity*, is subsumed by *noninterference up-to* and *relaxation*. *Conservativity* requires that a security condition must be equivalent to noninterference for programs without declassification. One direction of the equivalence is implied by *relaxation* and the other by *noninterference up-to*. Note, however, that *noninterference up-to* also establishes guarantees for programs with declassification while conservativity does not.

While the previous principles provide a check of adequacy for security conditions with declassification, in general, the following principle is especially intended to check the adequacy of the control of *who* can initiate declassification.

Protection. A security property complies with *protection*, if for all programs satisfying this property, an attacker from whom declassification should be protected, cannot effect declassification by his behavior.

3.2   Policies, Programs, and a Definition of Noninterference

We capture the intended security guarantees by flow policies:

Definition 1. *An* MLS *policy with exceptions is a triple* $(\mathcal{D}, \leq, \leadsto)$, *where* $\mathcal{D}$ *is a finite set of security domains,* $\leq \subseteq \mathcal{D} \times \mathcal{D}$ *is a partial order and* $\leadsto \subseteq \mathcal{D} \times \mathcal{D}$.

The relation $\leq$ determines, between which domains information may flow normally. The relation $\leadsto$ determines, between which domains information may flow exceptionally, i.e. by declassification. An example is the two-level flow policy ($\{low, high\}, \{(low, high), (low, low), (high, high)\}, \leadsto$), which permits information flow from *low* to *high* but not from *high* to *low*. Declassification from *high* to *low* is permitted or not depending on whether *high* $\leadsto$ *low* or *high* $\not\leadsto$ *low*.

We assume a set of programs *Com*, a set of variables *Var* and a set of values *Val*. A *memory* assigns values to variables $s : Var \rightarrow Val$. A *domain assignment* is a function $dom : Var \rightarrow \mathcal{D}$. It establishes a connection between memories and a flow policy by assigning a domain to each variable. We say that *an observer has a security domain D* if he can see the values of all variables x with $dom(x) \leq D$, but not of other variables. Hence, a D-observer can distinguish memories, if and only if they differ in the value of at least one variable x with $dom(x) \leq D$.

Definition 2. *For a given domain* $D \in \mathcal{D}$, *two memories* s *and* s' *are* D-equal, *denoted by* $s =_D s'$, *if* $\forall x \in Var. (dom(x) \leq D \Rightarrow s(x) = s'(x))$.

We define the set of *configurations Conf* as the set of all pairs of a program C (or of the special symbol ϵ) and a memory s, denoted by $\langle C, s \rangle$ or $\langle \epsilon, s \rangle$, respectively. The operational semantics are given by a deterministic step relation $\rightarrow$ between configurations. We partition $\rightarrow$ into disjoint sub-relations $\rightarrow_k^{D_1 \rightarrow D_2}$ and $\rightarrow_O$ where $k \in \mathbb{N}$ and $D_1, D_2 \in \mathcal{D}$. A $\rightarrow_k^{D_1 \rightarrow D_2}$-step models the execution of a declassification instruction with label k, source domain D_1, and destination domain D_2. We call such steps *declassification steps* and $\rightarrow_O$-steps *ordinary steps*.

In the following, we assume a flow policy $(\mathcal{D}, \leq, \leadsto)$ and domain assignment *dom*. As notational convention we denote elements of $\mathcal{D}$ by D, of *Com* by C, of *Var* by x and y, of *Val* by v, of memories by s and t, of *Conf* by *cnf*, and of instruction labels in $\mathbb{N}$ by k, all possibly with indices or primes.

In Sect. 3.1, we used the term *noninterference* as a place-holder for a security condition that characterizes the absence of unintended information flow in a setting without declassification. We instantiate this place-holder with the *strong security condition*, which was originally introduced in [4] for multi-threaded programs. This is an established definition of security for which there already exist variants that permit and control declassification [1,3]. Strong security is based on the PER-approach [5], i.e. information flow security is characterized based on non-reflexive indistinguishability relations on programs. Two programs are indistinguishable for a D-observer, if they do not reveal information to D, when started in D-equal memories. As strong security does not permit declassification, the relation $\rightsquigarrow$ does not occur in the following definition.

Definition 3 (Strong Security for Sequential Programs). *A strong D-bisimulation is a symmetric relation R on programs that satisfies*

$$\forall C_1, C_1'. \ \forall s, s', t. \ \forall C_2. \left[\begin{array}{c} (C_1 \ R \ C_1' \land \langle C_1, s \rangle \rightarrow \langle C_2, t \rangle \land s =_D s') \\ \Rightarrow \exists C_2', t' : (C_2 \ R \ C_2' \land \langle C_1', s' \rangle \rightarrow \langle C_2', t' \rangle \land t =_D t') \end{array} \right]$$

The relation $\cong_D$ is defined as the union of all strong D-bisimulations. A program C is strongly secure if $C \cong_D C$ holds for all $D \in \mathcal{D}$.

For two programs being strongly D-bisimilar means that individual computation steps from D-equal memories can be simulated, such that the resulting memories also are D-equal and the resulting programs also are strongly D-bisimilar.

We instantiate programs and the operational semantics with a simple while language (WL), augmented with a declassifying assignment. The set Com is defined by the following grammar.

$$C ::= \mathsf{skip} \mid x{:=}Exp \mid C_1; C_2 \mid \mathsf{if}\ B\ \mathsf{then}\ C_1\ \mathsf{else}\ C_2\ \mathsf{fi} \mid \mathsf{while}\ B\ \mathsf{do}\ C\ \mathsf{od} \mid [x{:=}y]_k$$

As further condition we require that no two declassification assignments with the same instruction label may appear in a given program. That is, an instruction label uniquely determines the occurrence of a declassification in the program code. To denote expressions from a language $\mathcal{E}$ we use B or Exp. That expression Exp evaluates to value v in memory s is denoted by $\langle Exp, s \rangle \downarrow v$. Here, we do not fully define the language $\mathcal{E}$, but only assume that the evaluation of expressions is total, atomic, and unambiguous. Moreover, we assume a function $vars : \mathcal{E} \rightarrow \mathfrak{P}(Var)$ such that

$$\forall Exp, s, s'. \ [(\forall x \in vars(Exp).\ s(x) = s'(x)) \Rightarrow \forall v. \ (\langle Exp, s \rangle \downarrow v \Rightarrow \langle Exp, s' \rangle \downarrow v)]$$

For instance, $vars(Exp)$ could be the set of variables appearing in Exp.

$$\frac{}{\langle \mathsf{skip}, s \rangle \rightarrow_O \langle \epsilon, s \rangle} \qquad \frac{\langle Exp, s \rangle \downarrow v}{\langle x{:=}Exp, s \rangle \rightarrow_O \langle \epsilon, [x = v]s \rangle}$$

$$\frac{\langle B, s \rangle \downarrow v \quad v \neq 0}{\langle \mathsf{if}\ B\ \mathsf{then}\ C_1\ \mathsf{else}\ C_2\ \mathsf{fi}, s \rangle \rightarrow_O \langle C_1, s \rangle} \qquad \frac{\langle B, s \rangle \downarrow 0}{\langle \mathsf{if}\ B\ \mathsf{then}\ C_1\ \mathsf{else}\ C_2\ \mathsf{fi}, s \rangle \rightarrow_O \langle C_2, s \rangle}$$

$$\frac{\langle B, s \rangle \downarrow v \quad v \neq 0}{\begin{array}{c} \langle \mathsf{while}\ B\ \mathsf{do}\ C\ \mathsf{od}, s \rangle \\ \rightarrow_O \langle C; \mathsf{while}\ B\ \mathsf{do}\ C\ \mathsf{od}, s \rangle \end{array}} \qquad \frac{\langle B, s \rangle \downarrow 0}{\langle \mathsf{while}\ B\ \mathsf{do}\ C\ \mathsf{od}, s \rangle \rightarrow_O \langle \epsilon, s \rangle}$$

$$\frac{D_1 = dom(y) \quad D_2 = dom(x) \quad D_1 \not\leq D_2}{\langle [x{:=}y]_k, s \rangle \rightarrow_k^{D_1 \rightarrow D_2} \langle \epsilon, [x = s(y)]s \rangle} \qquad \frac{dom(y) \leq dom(x)}{\langle [x{:=}y]_k, s \rangle \rightarrow_O \langle \epsilon, [x = s(y)]s \rangle}$$

$$\frac{\langle C_1, s \rangle \rightarrow_O \langle \epsilon, s' \rangle}{\langle C_1; C_2, s \rangle \rightarrow_O \langle C_2, s' \rangle} \qquad \frac{\langle C_1, s \rangle \rightarrow_O \langle C_1', s' \rangle}{\langle C_1; C_2, s \rangle \rightarrow_O \langle C_1'; C_2, s' \rangle}$$

$$\frac{\langle C_1, s \rangle \rightarrow_k^{D_1 \rightarrow D_2} \langle \epsilon, s' \rangle}{\langle C_1; C_2, s \rangle \rightarrow_k^{D_1 \rightarrow D_2} \langle C_2, s' \rangle} \qquad \frac{\langle C_1, s \rangle \rightarrow_k^{D_1 \rightarrow D_2} \langle C_1', s' \rangle}{\langle C_1; C_2, s \rangle \rightarrow_k^{D_1 \rightarrow D_2} \langle C_1'; C_2, s' \rangle}$$

Fig. 1. Operational semantics of WL

The instantiation of the step relations is given by the rules in Fig. 1. Most rules are standard. Exceptions are the rules for declassifying assignments $[x:=y]_k$, which result in $\rightarrow_k^{D_1 \rightarrow D_2}$ steps, if the domains are not $\leq$-related. Declassifying assignments with $\leq$-related domains result in ordinary steps, because the direct information flow conducted by such instructions intuitively complies with $\leq$.

For simplicity, we require the right-hand side of declassifying assignments to be a variable. In Sect. 4.1, we extend WL with statements for input and output.

3.3   Formalization of the Principles

The purpose of a security condition is to formally characterize which programs obey a given flow policy. Hence, we can view a security condition as a function from an MLS-policy and a domain assignment to a set of WL-programs. As a notational convention, we write $PROP$ instead of $PROP((\mathcal{D}, \leq, \rightsquigarrow), dom)$ if $(\mathcal{D}, \leq, \rightsquigarrow)$ and dom are determined by the context.

We are now ready to formalize all prudent principles from Sect. 3.1 (with the exception of *non-occlusion* as explained before, and of the *who*-specific principle *protection* whose formalization is deferred to Sect. 4.1) by meta-properties of security conditions. To formalize *monotonicity* and *semantic consistency*, we define a *context* as a program $\mathcal{C}$, where the hole $\bullet$ may occur as an atomic sub-program. We use $\mathcal{C}\langle C \rangle$ to denote the program that one obtains by replacing each occurrence of $\bullet$ with C. As suggested in [2], we define semantic equivalence between programs by $\cong = \approx_{high}$, where $\approx_{high}$ is the strong *high*-bisimulation for the single-domain policy $(\{high\}, \{(high, high)\}, \emptyset)$.

Definition 4 (Semantic consistency). *A security property PROP is* semantically consistent, *if $C' \cong C$ and $\mathcal{C}\langle C \rangle \in PROP$ imply $\mathcal{C}\langle C' \rangle \in PROP$ for all commands C, C' without declassification instructions and for all contexts $\mathcal{C}$.*

Definition 5 (Relaxation). *A security property PROP is* relaxing, *if C is strongly secure implies $C \in PROP$.*

Definition 6 (Monotonicity). *A security property PROP complies with* monotonicity of release, *if*

1. $\mathcal{C}\langle x:=y \rangle \in PROP$ *implies* $\mathcal{C}\langle [x:=y]_k \rangle \in PROP$ *for all $\mathcal{C}$, x, y, and k and*
2. $\rightsquigarrow \subseteq \rightsquigarrow'$ *and* $C \in PROP((\mathcal{D}, \leq, \rightsquigarrow), dom)$
   imply $C \in PROP((\mathcal{D}, \leq, \rightsquigarrow'), dom)$.

The intuition of Definition 6 with respect to declassifying assignments is the following. If a program C_2 is obtained from a given program C_1 by replacing a declassifying assignment with an ordinary assignment and C_2 is accepted already, then C_1, (i.e. the same program with additional brackets indicating that declassification is permissible) should certainly also be accepted.

To formalize *noninterference up-to* we have to consider executions of programs under a monitor. Whenever a program is about to execute a declassification step $\rightarrow_k^{D_1 \rightarrow D_2}$, the monitor terminates the execution. This is similar to changing the operational semantics by removing the rule for declassification steps with the condition $D_1 \not\leq D_2$, because in the operational semantics an execution is stopped, if no further transition from the current configuration is possible.

Definition 7 (Noninterference up-to). *A security property PROP is non-interferent up-to, if $C \in PROP$ implies that the program C is is strongly secure if it were executed with a declassification-prohibiting monitor.*

Definition 8 (Persistence). *A security property PROP is persistent, if $C' \in PROP$ holds for all C' that are reachable from some $C \in PROP$, i.e. if $C \in PROP$ and $\langle C, s \rangle \twoheadrightarrow^* \langle C', s' \rangle$ for some C, s , and s' implies $C' \in PROP$.*

A property PROP is weakly persistent, if $C \in PROP$, $\langle C, s \rangle \twoheadrightarrow^* cnf$, and $cnf \twoheadrightarrow_k^{D_1 \to D_2} \langle C', s' \rangle$ for some C, s, s', cnf, D_1, D_2, and k implies $C' \in PROP$.

The formalizations of the prudent principles in this section will serve as a sanity check for our new security condition in the next section.

4   Characterization of Security

In this section we define a novel security property to adequately control *who* may influence declassification, by his input on a given channel.

4.1   Input and Output

We extend the notions of programs and security with input and output. We assume two disjunctive sets, a set of *input channels* $\mathcal{I}$, and a set of *output channels* $\mathcal{O}$. Now, the *domain assignments* assign security domains to channels, too: $dom : (Var \cup \mathcal{I} \cup \mathcal{O}) \to \mathcal{D}$. A D-observer knows the input of channels *in* with $dom(in) \leq D$ and observes the output of channels *out* with $dom(out) \leq D$. The step relation $\twoheadrightarrow$ additionally has the disjoint sub-relations $\twoheadrightarrow_{chan,v}$, where $chan \in \mathcal{I} \cup \mathcal{O}$ and $v \in Val$. A $\twoheadrightarrow_{in,v}$-step models the input of the value v on the channel $in \in \mathcal{I}$. A $\twoheadrightarrow_{out,v}$-step models the output of the value v on the channel $out \in \mathcal{O}$. As convention we denote elements of $\mathcal{I}$ by *in*, of $\mathcal{O}$ by *out*, and of $\mathcal{I} \cup \mathcal{O}$ by *chan*. We extend WL by atomic programs for input $x\ \text{<-}\ in$ and for output $Exp \text{ -> } out$. The operational semantics contains the following new rules in addition to the ones in Fig. 1.

$$\frac{}{\langle x\ \text{<-}\ in, s \rangle \twoheadrightarrow_{in,v} \langle \epsilon, [x = v]s \rangle} \qquad \frac{\langle Exp, s \rangle \downarrow v}{\langle Exp \text{ -> } out, s \rangle \twoheadrightarrow_{out,v} \langle \epsilon, s \rangle}$$

$$\frac{\langle C_1, s \rangle \twoheadrightarrow_{chan,v} \langle \epsilon, s' \rangle}{\langle C_1; C_2, s \rangle \twoheadrightarrow_{chan,v} \langle C_2, s' \rangle} \qquad \frac{\langle C_1, s \rangle \twoheadrightarrow_{chan,v} \langle C_1', s' \rangle}{\langle C_1; C_2, s \rangle \twoheadrightarrow_{chan,v} \langle C_1'; C_2, s' \rangle}$$

Unlike the rest of the operational semantics of WL, the input value v in the annotation of input steps is not deterministic. To account for that, we need to adapt the definition of a strong D-bisimulation accordingly. We define strong security as before (see Definition 3), however, now we define strong D-bisimulations as symmetric relations satisfying the sub-formula in Figure 2 without the box in

$$\forall C_1, C_1'. \; \forall s, s', t. \; \forall C_2.$$
$$(C_1 \; R \; C_1' \wedge s =_D s')$$

$$\Rightarrow \left[\begin{array}{l} \forall chan, v. \left[\begin{array}{c} (\langle C_1, s \rangle \rightharpoonup_{chan,v} \langle C_2, t \rangle \wedge dom(chan) \le D) \\ \Rightarrow \exists C_2', t'. \; (\langle C_1', s' \rangle \rightharpoonup_{chan,v} \langle C_2', t' \rangle \wedge C_2 \; R \; C_2' \wedge t =_D t') \end{array} \right] \\ \\ \wedge \left[\begin{array}{l} \langle C_1, s \rangle (\rightharpoonup \backslash (\bigcup_{dom(chan) \le D, v} \rightharpoonup_{chan,v})) \langle C_2, t \rangle \\ (\exists C_2', t'. \; \langle C_1', s' \rangle (\rightharpoonup \backslash (\bigcup_{dom(chan) \le D, v} \rightharpoonup_{chan,v})) \langle C_2', t' \rangle) \\ \Rightarrow \wedge \; \forall C_2', t'. \left[\begin{array}{l} \langle C_1', s' \rangle (\rightharpoonup \backslash (\bigcup_{dom(chan) \le D, v} \rightharpoonup_{chan,v})) \langle C_2', t' \rangle \\ C_2 \; R \; C_2' \\ \Rightarrow \wedge \left[t =_D t' \vee \left[\begin{array}{l} \exists D_1, D_2 \in \mathcal{D}. \; \exists k \in \mathbb{N}. \\ \langle C_1, s \rangle \rightharpoonup_k^{D_1 \to D_2} \langle C_2, t \rangle \\ \wedge \; D_1 \rightsquigarrow D_2 \\ \wedge \; D_2 \le D \wedge s \neq_{D_1} s' \end{array} \right] \right] \end{array} \right] \end{array} \right] \end{array} \right]$$

Fig. 2. Strong Bisimulation Relations with I/O

dark-gray background. The boxes with light-gray background mark the new elements of the formula compared to Definition 3. Now, strong D-bisimulations give different guarantees depending on whether a step is an I/O-step with a D-visible channel or not. If it is an I/O-step with a D-visible channel (first box with light-gray background), then the simulating step needs to be an I/O-step on the same channel and with the same value. However, it is important, that for D-visible input steps only the step with the same value needs to satisfy the requirements $C_2 \; R \; C_2'$ and $t =_D t'$. This captures the assumption, that a D-observer knows the input values of D-visible channels. For steps that are not I/O-steps with D-visible channels, the guarantees are required for all possible step results (last two boxes with light-gray background). This is necessary, because for input steps with non-D-visible channels the step result depends on the input value, which is not known to the observer and which should not be revealed to him.

To specify the input channels that must not effect a declassification step with a given instruction label, we assign sets of input channels to instruction labels.

Definition 9. *A protection labeling is a function* $prot : \mathbb{N} \to \mathfrak{P}(\mathcal{I})$.

Now we formalize the principle *protection*. An attacker cannot effect declassification k in a program by his behavior if the occurrence of a declassification k is invariant under change of the attacker's behavior. Hence, for the definition we fix the behavior of everybody else. Here behavior of everybody else means, the input provided by channels that are not in $prot(k)$. In the following for each $P \subseteq \mathcal{I}$ we define $\overline{P} = \mathcal{I} \backslash P$. We define the sets $\mathcal{B}_k$ of behaviors of channels that are not in $prot(k)$ as lists of input events (in, v) and no-input events $\perp$: $\mathcal{B}_k = ((\overline{prot(k)} \times Val) \cup \{\perp\})^*$. For $b \in \mathcal{B}_k$ we define $\to_{b,k} \subseteq \rightharpoonup^*$ inductively by $cnf \to_{b,k} cnf$, if b has length 0, and $cnf_1 \to_{b,k} cnf_2$, if b consists of the prefix b' and the last element a, and there is a cnf' such that $cnf_1 \to_{b',k} cnf'$ and either $a = (in, v) \wedge cnf' \rightharpoonup_{in,v} cnf_2$, or $a = \perp \wedge cnf'(\rightharpoonup \backslash (\bigcup_{in \in \overline{prot(k)}, v} \rightharpoonup_{in,v})) cnf_2$. The relation $(\rightharpoonup \backslash (\bigcup_{in \in \overline{prot(k)}, v} \rightharpoonup_{in,v}))$ contains any step, that is not an input step of a channel, that may effect declassification k. I.e. a behavior b determines when an input step of a channel in $\overline{prot(k)}$ occurs and what value is read. The inputs of channels in $prot(k)$ are not determined by a $b \in \mathcal{B}_k$. As abbreviation we define $\rightarrow_k := \bigcup_{D_1, D_2} \rightarrow_k^{D_1 \rightarrow D_2}$ and $\rightarrow_{\bar{k}} := \rightarrow \setminus \rightarrow_k$ for all k.

Definition 10 (Protection). *A security property PROP is protecting, if, given $C \in PROP$, it holds that*

$$\forall k, b \in \mathcal{B}_k, s, cnf_1, cnf_2, cnf'_1.$$
$$\left[\left(\begin{array}{c} \langle C, s \rangle \rightarrow_{b,k} cnf_1 \wedge cnf_1 \rightarrow_{\bar{k}} cnf_2 \\ \wedge \langle C, s \rangle \rightarrow_{b,k} cnf'_1 \end{array} \right) \Rightarrow \neg \exists cnf'_2. (cnf'_1 \rightarrow_k cnf'_2) \right]$$

The intuition is, that whether a given k-labeled execution step occurs or not is independent from the inputs of all channels from which k should be protected.

4.2   The Security Property for *Who*

First, to ensure that exceptional information flow only can occur by declassification steps, we define a supporting security property characterizing control of *where*. The property is defined similar to strong security, however, it permits declassification by declassification steps, if the exceptional flow complies with $\rightsquigarrow$. The property is an adaption of WHERE in [3] to the language with I/O.

Definition 11 (WHERE with I/O). *A strong $(D, \rightsquigarrow)$-bisimulation is a symmetric relation R on programs that satisfies the whole formula in Figure 2. The relation $\approx_D^{\rightsquigarrow}$ is the union of all strong $(D, \rightsquigarrow)$-bisimulations. A program C has secure information flow while complying with the restrictions where declassification can occur if $C \approx_D^{\rightsquigarrow} C$ holds for all $D \in \mathcal{D}$ (brief: C is where-secure or $C \in WHERE((\mathcal{D}, \leq, \rightsquigarrow), dom))$.*

Declassification is possible, since strong $(D, \rightsquigarrow)$-bisimulations do not always require the memory states after bisimulation steps to be D-indistinguishable. However, such exceptions are restricted: they may only occur after declassification steps $\rightarrow_k^{D_1 \rightarrow D_2}$, where the declassification target is visible to D ($D_2 \leq D$), the flow complies with the exceptional flow relation ($D_1 \rightsquigarrow D_2$), and the declassified information is D_1-visible ($s =_{D_1} s'$). The restrictions of WHERE on exceptional information flow offer the possibility to control *who* may effect declassification by only restricting further the occurrence of declassification steps.

Definition 12. *Let $P \subseteq \mathcal{I}$ and $k \in \mathbb{N}$. A (P, k)-protecting bisimulation is a symmetric relation $R \subseteq \text{Conf} \times \text{Conf}$ such that for all $cnf_1 R cnf'_1$ it holds that*

- $\forall cnf_2. (cnf_1 \rightarrow^* cnf_2 \Rightarrow \neg \exists cnf_3 cnf_2 \rightarrow_k cnf_3)$ *or*
- *for all cnf_2 with $cnf_1 \rightarrow cnf_2$ it is*
  $$\exists cnf'_2. cnf'_1 \rightarrow cnf'_2$$
  $$\wedge \forall cnf'_2.$$
  $$\left[\begin{array}{l} [(cnf_1 \rightarrow_k cnf_2 \wedge cnf'_1 \rightarrow cnf'_2) \Rightarrow cnf'_1 \rightarrow_k cnf'_2] \\ \wedge [(cnf_1(\rightarrow \setminus (\bigcup_{in \in \overline{P}, v} \rightarrow_{in,v})) cnf_2 \wedge cnf'_1 \rightarrow cnf'_2) \Rightarrow cnf_2 R cnf'_2] \\ \wedge \forall in \in \overline{P}, v. \left[\begin{array}{c} \left(\begin{array}{c} cnf_1 \rightarrow_{in,v} cnf_2 \\ \wedge cnf'_1(\rightarrow \setminus (\bigcup_{v' \neq v} \rightarrow_{in,v'})) cnf'_2 \end{array} \right) \\ \Rightarrow cnf_2 R cnf'_2 \end{array} \right] \end{array} \right]$$

Given C, a protection labeling prot : $\mathbb{N} \to \mathfrak{P}(\mathcal{I})$, and k, $WHO_{C,prot}(k)$ holds, iff for all from C reachable programs C' there is a $(prot(k), k)$-protecting bisimulation R such that $\forall s.\ \langle C', s \rangle\ R\ \langle C', s \rangle$. A program C is who-protected if $WHO_{C,prot}(k)$ holds for all k (brief: $C \in WHO$).

Configurations are related by a $(prot(k), k)$-protecting bisimulation, if there is no reachable declassification step k, because in this case such a step cannot be effected by any channel input. Else, if such a step occurs, it has to be simulated by a step with the same annotation. The results of bisimulation steps also need to be in the bisimulation relation, except, when the steps are input steps of channels in $\overline{prot(k)}$ and have differing values. This exception captures that these channels may effect declassification. The predicate $WHO_{C,prot}(k)$ initially only requires configurations with equal memories to be related by a bisimulation. This captures that there are no restrictions on the influence of initial values of variables on declassification. Hence, any difference in occurrence of a declassification step k is not caused by input channels that must not effect declassification.

We define the security property for control of *who* may effect declassification.

Definition 13 (WHERE&WHO). *A program C has secure information flow while complying with the restrictions where declassification can occur and who may effect declassification if C is* where-secure *and* who-protected. *(brief: C is* where&who-secure *or* $C \in WHERE\&WHO((\mathcal{D}, \leq, \leadsto), dom))$.

Example 1. We consider the example from Sect. 2 with the two-level flow policy where *high* $\leadsto$ *low*, a domain assignment *dom* assigning *high* to movie and *low* to every other variable or channel, and $prot(1) = prot(2) = \{webl\}$. We first consider the first program. The variable movie is only read by the declassifying assignments. The channel webl either is not read at all, or, if the input of bankl is fixed, the execution of declassification does not depend on the input from webl. Hence, the program is *where&who*-secure. Now we consider the second program. Consider two configurations, both consisting of the branching instruction with the branch condition (payOK or isPreferred(paydat)), and of memories, where in both payOK is 0 and in one isPreferred(paydat) is 1 and in the other 0. These configurations, are not $(\{webl, 1\})$-protecting bisimilar. However, their bisimilarity is required by WHO-protection of 1, when we consider an initial memory that assigns to byMachine the value 0. Hence, this program is not *where&who*-secure. This classification of the two programs is according to our intuition.

The property WHERE&WHO complies with all the principles from Sect. 3.

Theorem 1 (Compliance to Principles). WHERE&WHO *is*

1. semantically consistent.
2. relaxing,
3. monotonic,
4. noninterferent up-to,
5. persistent, *and*
6. protecting.

5   Enforcing Who Control by a Type System for WHERE

There are some cases, where WHERE is equivalent to WHERE&WHO. These are not only the trivial cases, but also cases where restrictions on *who* are imposed. We capture these cases by the following theorem.

Theorem 2. *Let C be given. Let $range(\rightsquigarrow) := \{D \in \mathcal{D} | \exists D' \in \mathcal{D}.\ D' \rightsquigarrow D\}$. If*
1. *C is where-secure and*
2. *$\forall in \in \bigcup_{k \in \mathbb{N}} prot(k).\ \forall D \in range(\rightsquigarrow).\ \neg\big(dom(in)(\leq \cup \rightsquigarrow)^* D\big)$,*

then C satisfies WHERE&WHO.

Since WHERE is parameterized with multi-level flow policies, which can be used to express integrity aspects, and since WHERE already restricts declassification within this policy, satisfaction of WHERE with a suitable flow policy can ensure WHERE&WHO. Inspired by this result, given a protection labeling *prot*, an MLS-policy $(\mathcal{D}, \leq, \rightsquigarrow)$, and a domain assign *dom*, we call *prot flow-enforced by* $(\mathcal{D}, \leq, \rightsquigarrow)$ *and dom*, whenever the second hypothesis of Theorem 2 is satisfied. By this theorem, if we have given a policy such that *prot* is flow-enforced, it just remains to check that a program is *where*-secure to check *where&who*-security.

5.1   Refining Flow Policies

To apply Theorem 2 to a given program and security policy, it might be necessary to refine the MLS-policy and the domain assignment, in order to capture the desired integrity aspect.

Definition 14. *Given MLS-policies $(\mathcal{D}_1, \leq_1, \rightsquigarrow_1)$, $(\mathcal{D}_2, \leq_2, \rightsquigarrow_2)$ and domain assignments $dom_1 : (Var \cup \mathcal{I} \cup \mathcal{O}) \rightarrow \mathcal{D}_1$, $dom_2 : (Var \cup \mathcal{I} \cup \mathcal{O}) \rightarrow \mathcal{D}_2$, we call a function $abs : \mathcal{D}_1 \rightarrow \mathcal{D}_2$ abstracting, iff*

1. *abs is surjective,*
2. *$\forall D_1, D_1' \in \mathcal{D}_1.\ (D_1 \leq_1 D_1' \Rightarrow abs(D_1) \leq_2 abs(D_1'))$,*
3. *$\forall D_1, D_1' \in \mathcal{D}_1.\ (D_1 \rightsquigarrow_1 D_1' \Rightarrow abs(D_1)(\rightsquigarrow_2 \cup \leq_2)abs(D_1'))$,*
4. *$\forall a \in (Var \cup \mathcal{I} \cup \mathcal{O}).\ dom_2(a) = abs(dom_1(a))$.*

We call $(\mathcal{D}_1, \leq_1, \rightsquigarrow_1)$ and dom_1 a policy refinement of $(\mathcal{D}_2, \leq_2, \rightsquigarrow_2)$ and dom_2, iff there is an abstracting function $abs : \mathcal{D}_1 \rightarrow \mathcal{D}_2$.

In a refinement of a given policy, security domains may be split up and the flow relations may impose additional restrictions. However, a refinement must not relax the restrictions on the flow of information between variables and channels. For our purpose, only flow-enforcing refinements are relevant.

Example 2. For instance, we consider the first program in Sect. 2 with the policy and domain assignment we present for the program in Sect. 4. The security domain of the channel webl is *low* and *low* is in the range of $\rightsquigarrow$, i.e. *prot* is not flow-enforced. However, there is a more restrictive policy, such that *prot* is flow-enforced and the program is *where*-secure: we add a security domain *web*, extend the flow relation to $\leq' = \leq \cup \{(low, web), (web, web)\}$, and we assign *web* to webl, paydatweb and bankO. The function *abs* defined by $abs(low) = low$, $abs(web) = low$, and $abs(high) = high$ is abstracting, i.e. the new MLS-policy and domain assignment are a policy refinement.

Lemma 1. *Let* $(\mathcal{D}_1, \leq_1, \leadsto_1)$, $dom_1 : (Var \cup \mathcal{I} \cup \mathcal{O}) \to \mathcal{D}_1$, $(\mathcal{D}_2, \leq_2, \leadsto_2)$, $dom_2 :$ $(Var \cup \mathcal{I} \cup \mathcal{O}) \to \mathcal{D}_2$, *and* $prot : \mathbb{N} \to \mathfrak{P}(\mathcal{I})$ *be given. If* $abs : \mathcal{D}_1 \to \mathcal{D}_2$ *is abstracting then*

1. $\forall D_2. \ \forall s, s'. \ [(\forall D_1 \in \mathcal{D}_1. \ (abs(D_1) \leq_2 D_2 \Rightarrow s =_{D_1,1} s')) \Leftrightarrow s =_{D_2,2} s']$, *and*
2. $\forall D_2. \ \forall C, C'. \ [(\forall D_1 \in \mathcal{D}_1. \ (abs(D_1) \leq_2 D_2 \Rightarrow C \approx_{D_1}^{\leadsto_1} C')) \Rightarrow C \approx_{D_2}^{\leadsto_2} C']$,

where $=_{D_1,1}$ *is the* D_1-*equality with respect to* $\leq_1$ *and* dom_1 *for all* $D_1 \in \mathcal{D}_1$, *and* $=_{D_2,2}$ *is the* D_2-*equality with respect to* $\leq_2$ *and* dom_2 *for all* $D_2 \in \mathcal{D}_2$.

Theorem 3. *Let* C, $(\mathcal{D}_2, \leq_2, \leadsto_2)$, dom_2 *and* $prot$ *be given. If there is a refinement* $(\mathcal{D}_1, \leq_1, \leadsto_1)$ *and* dom_1 *of* $(\mathcal{D}_2, \leq_2, \leadsto_2)$ *and* dom_2 *such that*

- $C \in WHERE((\mathcal{D}_1, \leq_1, \leadsto_1), dom_1)$ *and*
- $prot$ *is flow-enforced by* $(\mathcal{D}_1, \leq_1, \leadsto_1)$ *and* dom_1,

then $C \in WHERE\&WHO((\mathcal{D}_2, \leq_2, \leadsto_2), dom_2)$.

Theorem 3 shows, that even if policies are not beforehand designed to flow-enforce, flow-enforced protection labelings can be exploited.

5.2   Static Enforcement of WHERE&WHO

We propose an enforcement mechanism for WHERE&WHO in two steps. The first step is to find a refinement of the given flow policy and domain assignment such that *prot* is flow-enforced. The second step is to apply a type system enforcing WHERE with respect to the policy refinement, and to apply Theorem 3.

To find a suitable refinement for a given policy, we split up security domains from that information may flow to security domains in the range of $\leadsto$ into two security domains, with the intuition, that one has high integrity and one has low integrity with respect to the input channels. We construct the normal flow relation such that it relates domains of high integrity with the respective domains of low integrity, however, not the other way round. We construct the exceptional flow relation such that it has only security domains of high integrity as source. To input channels, from that declassification should be protected, we assign security domains of low integrity. To determine for each variable and output channel, whether it needs to be assigned to the respective domain of low or high integrity, a type inference based on the type system has to be pursued, which is out of the scope of this paper. The type system to enforce WHERE is identical to the one of [3]. A program C is *typable*, which we denote by $\vdash C$, if $\vdash C$ can be derived by the rules in Fig. 3.

Theorem 4 (Soundness of Security Type System). *Let* $\vdash C$.

1. C *is* where-*secure*.
2. *If* $prot$ *is flow-enforced by* $(\mathcal{D}, \leq, \leadsto)$ *and* dom *then* C *is* where&who-*secure*.

Note that *flow-enforced* is a property of just the MLS policy, the domain assignment, and the protection labeling, that can be checked by checking whether security domains are related by the transitive closure of $\leq$ and $\leadsto$.

$$\frac{\forall x \in vars(Exp).\ dom(x) \leq D}{\vdash Exp : D} \qquad \overline{\vdash \text{skip}} \qquad \frac{\vdash Exp : D \quad D \leq dom(x)}{\vdash x{:=}Exp} \qquad \frac{dom(y) \rightsquigarrow dom(x)}{\vdash [x{:=}y]_k}$$

$$\frac{\vdash C_1 \quad \vdash C_2}{\vdash C_1 ; C_2} \qquad \frac{\vdash B : low \quad \vdash C}{\vdash \text{while } B \text{ do } C \text{ od}} \qquad \frac{\vdash C_1 \quad \vdash C_2 \quad \vdash B : D \quad \forall D' \not\geq D : C_1 \approx_{D'}^{\rightsquigarrow} C_2}{\vdash \text{if } B \text{ then } C_1 \text{ else } C_2 \text{ fi}}$$

$$\frac{dom(in) \leq dom(x)}{\vdash x \text{ <- } in} \qquad \frac{\vdash Exp : D \quad D \leq dom(out)}{\vdash Exp \text{ -> } out}$$

Fig. 3. Rules of the Security Type System enforcing WHERE

The rule for conditional branches contains a semantic side condition ($\forall D' \not\geq$ $D : C_1 \approx_{D'}^{\rightsquigarrow} C_2$). To be able to fully automatize the analysis, we additionally need a syntactic approximation of this side condition. A simple solution is to require $\vdash B : low$. Examples for less restrictive approaches to syntactic approximations for similar side conditions can be found in [1,6,3].

6   Related Work

The development of adequate control for noninterference-like conditions is an active research area. In the following discussion, we focus on related work that targets the control of *who* can initiate declassification. For other dimensions of declassification, we refer to the overview on declassification in [2].

Approaches, based on *robustness* [7,8,9,8] permit any information to leak, as long as the leak appears for all possible behaviors of attackers. Hence, *robust declassification* does not comply to *noninterference up-to*. Possible behaviors of an attacker are explicitly defined as programs with limited capability to write [8]. Different to WHERE&WHO, *robust declassification* does not differentiate which channels may influence which declassifications.

A different kind of control of *who* can be conducted on the basis of authorization. The decentralized label model [10] explicitly defines the flow policy using ownership labels, that state which principal permits reading to which other principals for each information. Here, declassification is restricted in that each principal may only relax the requirements imposed by his label. Abstract noninterference [11] is also claimed to control the dimension *who*. However, here *who* is not used in the sense of who may influence, but in the sense of attackers with different observational capabilities.

Our prudent principles of declassification extend and, in some cases, refine the ones in [2]. Interestingly, the conjunction of *noninterference up-to* and *weak persistence* has similarities to *noninterference unless* in [12].

7   Conclusion

We presented a novel approach to controlling who can initiate declassification. Our security condition WHO permits to control who can effect a given declassification in a program. We integrated WHO with the previously defined condition WHERE, which controls where in the program and where in the flow policy declassification may occur. We argued for the adequacy of the combined condition WHERE&WHO with the help of prudent principles of controlling declassification. We showed that WHERE&WHO can be reduced to WHERE for some flow policies. Based on this result, we developed a technique for enforcing WHERE&WHO by, firstly, refining a given flow policy and, secondly, applying an existing type system for WHERE.

Acknowledgments. We thank the anonymous reviewers for their suggestions. This work was funded by the DFG in the Computer Science Action Program and by the Information Society Technologies program of the European Commission, Future and Emerging Technologies under the IST-2005-015905 MOBIUS project. This article reflects only the authors' views, and the Commission, the DFG, and the authors are not liable for any use that may be made of the information contained therein.

References

1. Mantel, H., Sands, D.: Controlled Declassification based on Intransitive Noninterference. In: Chin, W.-N. (ed.) APLAS 2004. LNCS, vol. 3302, pp. 129–145. Springer, Heidelberg (2004)
2. Sabelfeld, A., Sands, D.: Dimensions and Principles of Declassification. In: Proc. of the 18th IEEE Computer Security Foundations Workshop, pp. 255–269. IEEE, Los Alamitos (2005)
3. Mantel, H., Reinhard, A.: Controlling the What and Where of Declassification in Language-Based Security. In: De Nicola, R. (ed.) ESOP 2007. LNCS, vol. 4421, pp. 141–156. Springer, Heidelberg (2007)
4. Sabelfeld, A., Sands, D.: Probabilistic Noninterference for Multi-threaded Programs. In: Proc. of the 13th IEEE Computer Security Foundations Workshop, pp. 200–215. IEEE, Los Alamitos (2000)
5. Sabelfeld, A., Sands, D.: A per model of secure information flow in sequential programs. In: Swierstra, S.D. (ed.) ESOP 1999. LNCS, vol. 1576, pp. 50–59. Springer, Heidelberg (1999)
6. Köpf, B., Mantel, H.: Transformational typing and unification for automatically correcting insecure programs. International Journal of Information Security (IJIS) 6(2–3), 107–131 (2007)
7. Zdancewic, S., Myers, A.: Robust declassification. In: Proc. of IEEE Computer Security Foundations Workshop, pp. 15–26. IEEE, Los Alamitos (2001)
8. Myers, A.C., Sabelfeld, A., Zdancewic, S.: Enforcing Robust Declassification and Qualified Robustness. Journal of Computer Security 14, 157–196 (2006)
9. Chong, S., Myers, A.C.: Decentralized robustness. In: Proc. of the 19th IEEE workshop on Computer Security Foundations, pp. 242–256. IEEE, Los Alamitos (2006)
10. Myers, A.C., Liskov, B.: Protecting Privacy using the Decentralized Label Model. ACM Trans. Softw. Eng. Methodol. 9(4), 410–442 (2000)
11. Mastroeni, I.: On the role of abstract non-interference in language-based security. In: Yi, K. (ed.) APLAS 2005. LNCS, vol. 3780, pp. 418–433. Springer, Heidelberg (2005)
12. Goguen, J.A., Meseguer, J.: Unwinding and Inference Control. In: Proceedings of the IEEE Symposium on Security and Privacy, pp. 75–86. IEEE, Los Alamitos (1984)

Non-Interference for Deterministic Interactive Programs

David Clark[1] and Sebastian Hunt[2]

[1] King's College London
david.j.clark@kcl.ac.uk
[2] City University, London
seb@soi.city.ac.uk

Abstract. We consider the problem of defining an appropriate notion of non-interference (NI) for deterministic interactive programs. Previous work on the security of interactive programs by O'Neill, Clarkson and Chong (CSFW 2006) builds on earlier ideas due to Wittbold and Johnson (Symposium on Security and Privacy 1990), and argues for a notion of NI defined in terms of strategies modelling the behaviour of users. We show that, for deterministic interactive programs, it is not necessary to consider strategies and that a simple stream model of the users' behaviour is sufficient. The key technical result is that, for deterministic programs, stream-based NI implies the apparently more general strategy-based NI (in fact we consider a wider class of strategies than those of O'Neill et al). We give our results in terms of a simple notion of Input-Output Labelled Transition System, thus allowing application of the results to a large class of deterministic interactive programming languages.

1 Introduction

We consider the problem of defining an appropriate notion of non-interference (NI) [8] for deterministic interactive programs. By interactive programs we mean programs which perform channel-based IO, reading and writing primitive values on named channels over time, as the system executes, in contrast to the simple "batch-processing" style of computation assumed by much of the work in language-based security. Moving away from the simple batch-processing model introduces a number of complications and subtleties. Even so, in this paper we show that a relatively simple stream-based model of interaction may be adequate for the special (but common) case of deterministic programs.

Previous work on the security of interactive programs by O'Neill, Clarkson and Chong [14] builds on earlier ideas due to Wittbold and Johnson [16], and argues for a notion of NI defined in terms of strategies modelling the behaviour of users. We show that, for deterministic interactive programs, it is not necessary to consider strategies and that a simple stream model of the users' behaviour is sufficient. The key technical result is that, for deterministic programs, stream-based NI implies the apparently more general strategy-based NI (in fact we consider a wider class of strategies than those of O'Neill et al). We give our results in terms of a simple notion of Input-Output Labelled Transition System, thus allowing application of the results to a large class of deterministic interactive programming languages.

P. Degano, J. Guttman, and F. Martinelli (Eds.): FAST 2008, LNCS 5491, pp. 50–66, 2009.

2   Overview

We start by considering some motivating examples. These examples show that interactive programs may enable quite subtle covert channels, in which attackers can exploit information gained from previous outputs in order to leak information via later outputs. Moreover the examples show that a simple stream-based model of user behaviour may not suffice to reveal the presence of such channels. We also argue that such channels are significant even outside the typical "military" scenario in which an insider collaborates to send secrets to an outsider, by showing how a trusted user may be duped into sending information on such channels without knowing it.

Following [16] and [14] we then show how such channels can be guarded against by requiring a more sophisticated notion of NI, one defined in terms of user *strategies* rather than input streams.

It is striking that the example covert channels mentioned above all involve the *combination* of interaction and internal nondeterminism. The main result of this paper is to show that this is not accidental: for purely deterministic systems, such covert channels do not arise. We formalise this by showing how input streams can be represented as a special class of strategy and then showing that defining NI over this restricted class of strategies is equivalent to the more general notion when the system (though not necessarily the environment) behaves deterministically. Rather than tie our results to a specific programming language, we define a simple notion of Input-Output Labelled Transition System (IOLTS) and sate our definitions and results for any IOLTS. To illustrate how programming languages can be modelled in such a setting, we give an IOLTS semantics for a simple deterministic interactive language.

We conclude with a discussion of the scope and limitations of the chosen definition of NI and, more generally, of the use of strategies to model a program's environment.

3   Information Flow in Interactive Programs

We start with two simple examples of interactive programs illustrating ways in which such programs may be insecure.

The first program is insecure because there is a direct flow from High input to Low output:

```
x := 0;
input y from H;
output (x XOR y) to L;
```

The second program is an example of indirect flow from High to Low. If we consider that Low and High are feeding a stream of inputs to the program, information about the High stream can be deduced from the way in which the program is consuming Low's inputs:

```
input x from H;
if (x = 0) then input y from L;
input z from L;
output z to L;
```

For example, suppose the Low input stream starts 01. Then the Low output will be 1 if High inputs 0, otherwise the Low output will be 0.

3.1 Two Approaches to Defining Security

Users interact with the programs via input and output on named channels each of which is associated with a security level in a Denning-style multi-level security classification system, whereby security levels form a lattice, $\langle L, \sqsubseteq \rangle$, $L = \{a, b, c, \ldots\}$ [6]. For simplicity's sake we identify a channel's name with its security level. We write $\downarrow a$ for the set of channels visible to users at level a, ie $\downarrow a = \{a' \in L | a' \sqsubseteq a\}$.

Consider two users with access to channels a and b respectively where $a \not\sqsubseteq b$, i.e. the security policy specifies that no information should flow from channel a to channel b. We might reasonably try to capture this requirement in two alternative ways:

$$\text{All outputs on channel } b \text{ are consistent with all possible inputs on channel } a. \quad (1)$$

$$\text{Users of channel } a \text{ cannot send messages to the users of channel } b. \quad (2)$$

These both seem reasonable, but are they equivalent? First, observe that $2 \Rightarrow 1$: if some outputs seen by Bob are inconsistent with some possible inputs from Alice, then Bob can deduce something about the values input by Alice so Alice clearly *can* send messages to Bob, hence (by contraposition) 2 implies 1. At first sight it seems as though 1 $\Rightarrow$ 2 should also hold. After all, if what Bob sees tells him nothing about what Alice has input, surely she cannot send him a message.

In fact, as Wittbold and Johnson show in [16], this reasoning is unsound: some systems which satisfy property 1 allow Alice to send Bob messages. Let $L \sqsubseteq H$ and suppose that the only values which may be sent on these channels are 0 and 1. Consider **Program 1a:**

```
while (true) do
    x := 0 | 1;
    input y from H;
    output x to H;
    output (x XOR y) to L;
```

Here $|$ is a non-deterministic choice operator, so 0 $|$ 1 evaluates to either 0 or 1, with the choice being made in a way which is unpredictable to any observer of the running program. Writing output of value v on channel a as $a!v$ and input as $a?v$, the possible traces for the first iteration of the loop are:

```
H?0 H!0 L!0
H?0 H!1 L!1
H?1 H!0 L!1
H?1 H!1 L!0
```

Observation of the first L-output thus reveals nothing to L-users about the value of the first H-input: L-users cannot observe the H-outputs and hence, whether L-users see 0 or 1, both 0 and 1 are possible values for the input on H. This clearly holds for longer traces as well: no matter how much of the stream of L-outputs is observed, nothing is learned about which values have been input on H. Program 1a thus satisfies property 1 and, indeed, would seem to be a secure program.

Now consider the variant **Program 1b:**

```
while (true) do
    x := 0 | 1;
    output x to H;
    input y from H;
    output (x XOR y) to L;
```

In this example, the value of x is output *before* the H-input is demanded. The possible traces for the first iteration of this variant are:

```
H!0 H?0 L!0
H!0 H?1 L!1
H!1 H?0 L!1
H!1 H?1 L!0
```

It clearly remains the case that, in ignorance of the value of x, any observation of an output on channel L is consistent with both possible inputs on H, and thus property 1 holds also for Program 1b. Crucially, though, with Program 1b, H-users can exploit their knowledge of x to *control* what is output on L. This allows H-users to send messages to L-users, thus violating property 2. For example, if an H-user wants to send a particular message to L, say $x_1 \ldots x_n$, behaving as follows will suffice:

```
for (i = 1 to n) do
    input  k from H;
    output (k XOR xi) to H;
```

When composed with Program 1b, this behaviour results in the message $x_1 \ldots x_n$ being delivered on L without error.

Program 1b first appears in this form in O'Neill, Clarkson and Chong's paper [14]. This was an adaptation of a synchronous nondeterministic state machine used by Wittbold and Johnson [16] to illustrate the same phenomenon. (It is interesting to note that, in state machine form, the example actually appears much earlier in a paper by Shannon [15]. In this paper Shannon showed how, in certain cases, making "side information" available at the transmitting point may increase the capacity of a communication channel.)

Using Program 1b, an H-user is able deliberately to communicate secrets to L-users. But, even when a user does not *intend* to leak a secret, such covert channels can still pose a security risk, since one user's "cooperation" with another may be unwitting. Suppose we have two users, Alice and Bob, at incomparable security levels A and B, respectively. The following example is originally due to David Sands [11].

Alice is interacting with a web site. Alice is assured by the site that her credit card details are never sent to Bob, and this assurance is backed up by a proof of property 1. The web site requests Alice to input her credit card and then offers her a "special offer" code, inviting her to input this code at a later time to obtain a discount or free gift. Unbeknownst to Alice, this code is actually her own credit card number in encrypted form. If Alice does enter the code when requested, the system simply decrypts it and sends it to Bob. In simplified form (a boolean credit card number!), this may be coded as **Program 2**:

```
input   x from A;
k := 0 | 1;
output (k XOR x) on A;
.

.

.
input y from A;
output (k XOR y) on B;
```

The possible traces for this system are:

```
A?0 A!0 A?0 B!0      (*)
A?0 A!0 A?1 B!1
A?0 A!1 A?0 B!1
A?0 A!1 A?1 B!0      (*)
A?1 A!0 A?0 B!1      (*)
A?1 A!0 A?1 B!0
A?1 A!1 A?0 B!0
A?1 A!1 A?1 B!1      (*)
```

Now, since Bob cannot see channel A, both outputs 0 and 1 are consistent with all four possible input sequences by Alice, hence property 1 is satisfied. Clearly, though, if Alice behaves as expected - the traces marked (*) - her credit card number is leaked to Bob.

These examples illustrate that a simple security property based on consistency of one user's observed outputs with another user's possible inputs may not be adequate to provide desirable security guarantees. In particular, it seems that the problem with property 1 is that it fails to take account of the *interactive* nature of such systems, whereby a user's inputs may depend on previously seen outputs. Wittbold and Johnson [16] proposed instead a property stated in terms of consistency of observed outputs with user's *behaviours*, modelling behaviours as the *strategies* by which users provide inputs based on their observations of the system so far.

This use of a strategy-based security property is very elegant and is successful in accepting Program 1a while rejecting Program 1b and Program 2. On the other hand, it is also technically less straightforward than a security property based simply on the input and output streams of a program. It is striking that the examples above involve the *combination* of interactivity and non-determinism. In this paper we consider the (very common) sub-class of *deterministic* interactive systems and show that for this sub-class, stream-based and strategy-based security properties are actually equivalent. The intuition is that, for a deterministic program, a sufficiently high security user can, in principle, choose inputs and predict all outputs statically. Thus there should be no need to model dynamic behaviours of users in order to verify the security property.

3.2   Input-Output Labelled Transition Systems (IOLTS)

As illustrated by the examples above, we are interested in security properties of programs written in languages with input and output primitives. However, our treatment is not specific to a given language. Instead we express security properties at the level of input/output traces.

Definition 1. *An Input-Output Labelled Transition System (IOLTS) is an* input-neutral *labelled transition system with a set of labels given by*

$$A ::= \tau \mid a?v \mid a!v$$

where $a \in L$ and $v \in \mathbb{V}$ (where $\mathbb{V}$ is some unspecified non-empty set of possible values). By input-neutral *we mean that branching on inputs is never restricted for a state in which input is possible, i.e. for a state s of the LTS: if $\exists v.s \xrightarrow{a?v}$ then $\forall v.s \xrightarrow{a?v}$.*

Let s range over the states of IOLTSs. Let Tr denote the set of all possible IOLTS traces: $\mathrm{Tr} = A^*$. Let t, u range over Tr. For $t = \ell_1 \cdots \ell_n \in \mathrm{Tr}$ we write $s \xrightarrow{t} s'$ to mean that there exist states $s_1, \ldots, s_n$ such that $s \xrightarrow{\ell_1} s_1 \cdots \xrightarrow{\ell_n} s_n = s'$. We write $s \xrightarrow{t}$ to mean that there exists s' such that $s \xrightarrow{t} s'$.

Definition 2. *An IOLTS is* deterministic *iff:*

1. *If $s \xrightarrow{\ell_1} s_1$ and $s \xrightarrow{\ell_2} s_2$ and $\ell_1 \neq \ell_2$ then $\ell_1 = a?v_1$ and $\ell_2 = a?v_2$, for some channel a and values v_1, v_2.*
2. *If $s \xrightarrow{\ell} s_1$ and $s \xrightarrow{\ell} s_2$ then $s_1 = s_2$.*

3.3   IOLTS Example: A Simple Interactive Imperative Language

The simple interactive imperative language used for the examples above is essentially the same language defined in [14]. To demonstrate one possible instantiation of an IOLTS at the language level, we present a semantics for this language and observe that it does indeed define an IOLTS (see Figure 1). Note that the IOLTS for this particular language will be deterministic iff the expression evaluation relation is single valued (which will not be the case if the $\mid$ operator is admitted).

4   Strategies and Non-Interference

We assume that a user at level a can only observe input/output events on channels $b \sqsubseteq a$ and that no user can see τ actions (modelling internal state transitions), making this a timing insensitive model. Different traces may thus appear the same to a given user. We write $t =_a t'$ to mean that two traces look the same to a user at level a. More generally, for a subset of security levels $A \subseteq L$, we write $t =_A t'$ to mean that $t{\restriction}A = t'{\restriction}A$, where $t{\restriction}A$ is t with all τ events removed and with all IO events $b?v$ and $b!v$ removed except those for which $b \in A$. Each such $=_A$ is clearly an equivalence relation on traces. Note that, since users at level a can see events at level a and below, $=_a$ is shorthand for $=_{\downarrow a}$ rather than $=_{\{a\}}$ (wherever we actually intend $=_{\{a\}}$ we will write this explicitly).

4.1   Strategies

Each user provides inputs on the channel corresponding to his or her security level and is aware of the history of usage (both inputs and outputs) on all channels at or below

$$[\text{Skip}] \; \langle \text{skip}, \sigma \rangle \; \xrightarrow{\tau} \; \langle \text{skip}, \sigma \rangle$$

$$[\text{Seq1}] \; \langle \text{skip}; c_2, \sigma \rangle \; \xrightarrow{\tau} \; \langle c_2, \sigma \rangle$$

$$[\text{Seq2}] \; \frac{\langle c_1; c_2, \sigma \rangle \; \xrightarrow{l} \; \langle c_1'; c_2, \sigma' \rangle}{\langle c_1; c_2, \sigma \rangle \; \xrightarrow{l} \; \langle c_1'; c_2, \sigma' \rangle} \; l \in A$$

$$[\text{Assign}] \; \frac{\sigma \vdash e \to v}{\langle x := e, \sigma \rangle \; \xrightarrow{\tau} \; \langle \text{skip}, \sigma[x := v] \rangle}$$

$$[\text{If1}] \; \frac{\sigma \vdash e \to v \neq 0}{\langle \text{if } e \text{ then } c_1 \text{ else } c_2, \sigma \rangle \; \xrightarrow{\tau} \; \langle c_1, \sigma \rangle}$$

$$[\text{If2}] \; \frac{\sigma \vdash e \to 0}{\langle \text{if } e \text{ then } c_1 \text{ else } c_2, \sigma \rangle \; \xrightarrow{\tau} \; \langle c_2, \sigma \rangle}$$

$$[\text{While}] \; \langle \text{while } e \text{ do } c, \sigma \rangle \; \xrightarrow{\tau} \; \langle \text{if } e \text{ then } (c; \text{while } e \text{ do } c) \text{ else skip}, \sigma \rangle$$

$$[\text{In}] \; \langle \text{input } x \text{ from } a, \sigma \rangle \; \xrightarrow{a?v} \; \langle \text{skip}, \sigma[x := v] \rangle$$

$$[\text{Out}] \; \frac{\sigma \vdash e \to v}{\langle \text{output } e \text{ to } a, \sigma \rangle \; \xrightarrow{a!v} \; \langle \text{skip}, \sigma \rangle}$$

Fig. 1. IOLTS semantics for a simple language

that level. The behaviour of a user in choosing inputs on a channel may be influenced by this knowledge of the history (as when High uses Program 1 as a covert channel) and is modeled as a channel strategy: a function from what the user knows to the user's choice of the next input on the channel. We allow strategies to be nondeterministic, thus we define them to be functions from traces to non-empty sets of values:

Definition 3. *An a-strategy is a function* $\omega_a : \text{Tr} \to (\wp(\mathbb{V}) - \emptyset)$ *such that* $t_1 =_a t_2 \Rightarrow \omega_a(t_1) = \omega_a(t_2)$.

In the special case that ω_a is deterministic, we will write $\omega_a(t) = v$ as shorthand for $\omega_a(t) = \{v\}$. We use ω for arbitrary (ie possibly nondeterministic) strategies and δ for deterministic strategies.

A strategy modeling the behaviour of the program's whole environment is a collection of individual channel strategies indexed by the security lattice. We say two strategies are equivalent with respect to a given security level if the channel strategies at and below that level are identical.

Definition 4. *A strategy* ω *is an L-indexed family such that each* ω_a *is an a-strategy.*

Let Strat denote the set of all strategies. We write $\omega =_a \omega'$ to mean $\omega_b = \omega_b'$ for all $b \sqsubseteq a$.

The interaction between a program and its environment is modelled by playing a strategy against a state of an IOLTS to produce a trace of input and output events. Let s be a state of an IOLTS. Playing strategy ω against state s may produce trace t, written $\omega \models s \xrightarrow{t}$, if t is a *possible* trace for s and, for every input event $a?v$ in t, v is a value which may be chosen by ω_a when applied to the sequence of events leading up to the input event. Formally:

Definition 5. $\omega \models s \xrightarrow{t}$ *iff* $s \xrightarrow{t}$ *and* $v \in \omega_a(t')$ *for all* $t'.a?v \leq t$, *where* $\leq$ *is the prefix ordering on traces.*

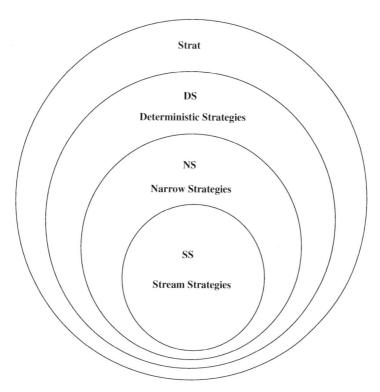

Fig. 2. An inclusion hierarchy of strategies

We define three interesting sub-classes of strategy:

DS. The deterministic strategies.

NS. The "narrow" strategies. This is the class of strategies considered in [14] (the term "narrow" is ours; in [14] they are simply called strategies). These are deterministic strategies such that the user's choice is influenced only by events on that particular channel, not by events on channels at lower security levels. The formal definition is as follows:

Definition 6 (Narrow Strategy). *A strategy ω is* narrow *iff it is deterministic and, for all a, if $t =_{\{a\}} t'$ then $\omega_a(t) = \omega_a(t')$.*

SS. The "stream" strategies. A stream strategy is just a family of streams (one for each channel) presented as a strategy. Concretely, each time a stream strategy is asked for an input on a channel it simply returns the next item in the stream for that channel. Each channel strategy in such a strategy returns a value which depends only on the number of inputs which have been requested on that channel so far, since this number is precisely the position in the stream which has been reached. For a channel a we say that traces t, t' are a-*stream-pointer equivalent*, written $t \bowtie_a t'$, iff t and t' contain the same number of a-input events. A stream strategy is thus a family of channel strategies each of which respects stream-pointer equivalence:

Definition 7 (Stream Strategy). *A strategy ω is a stream strategy iff it is deterministic and, for all a, if $t \bowtie_a t'$ then $\omega_a(t) = \omega_a(t')$*

Figure 2 illustrates how these sub-classes form an inclusion hierarchy. It is straightforward to verify that the inclusions shown do indeed hold and are, in fact, strict: $SS \subset NS \subset DS \subset Strat$.

4.2   Non-Interference

Our definition of non-interference [8] is framed in terms of strategies and traces. It is a generalisation of Definition 1 from [14]. The definition says that a state s of an IOLTS is non-interfering for a given set of strategies if, for each user, any two strategies drawn from the set which look the same, also produce sets of traces which look the same, when played against s.

Definition 8. *Let W be a set of strategies. A state s of an IOLTS is* non-interfering *for W (or W-NI for short) iff*

$$\forall \omega_1, \omega_2 \in W . (\omega_1 =_a \omega_2 \wedge \omega_1 \models s \overset{t_1}{\rightarrow}) \Rightarrow (\exists t_2 . t_2 =_a t_1 \wedge \omega_2 \models s \overset{t_2}{\rightarrow})$$

We say that s is simply non-interfering *(or NI for short) if it is non-interfering for the set of all strategies.*

We now explore the relationship between the NI properties corresponding to the sub-classes of strategy shown in Figure 2. We start with the obvious fact that inclusion of sub-classes of strategy implies reverse-inclusion of the corresponding NI properties:

Lemma 1. *Let $W_1, W_2 \subseteq Strat$. If $W_1 \subseteq W_2$ then W_2-NI $\Rightarrow W_1$-NI.*

We thus immediately have a sequence of inclusions of NI properties which mirrors the inclusions shown in Figure 2:

Proposition 1. *NI $\Rightarrow$ DS-NI $\Rightarrow$ NS-NI $\Rightarrow$ SS-NI.*

In Section 4.3, we establish that DS-NI and NI are actually equivalent. We conjecture that NS-NI is also equivalent to NI but verifying this is left for future work.

Note that SS-NI is essentially "property 1" from Section 3.1. By considering the sets of possible traces for the various programs in Section 3.1 it can be established, for example, that Program 1a is NI, whereas Program 1b is SS-NI but not NI. It is clear, therefore, that SS-NI is, in general, a strictly weaker property than NI. Nonetheless, we are able to show (Section 4.4) that for *deterministic* IOLTS, SS-NI and NI are equivalent.

4.3 Non-Interference for Deterministic Strategies

The following theorem says that, to establish non-interference, it is only necessary to consider deterministic strategies.

Theorem 1. *DS-NI $\iff$ NI.*

By Proposition 1, to prove the theorem it is sufficient to show that if s is DS-NI then s is NI. We prove the contrapositive.

Let s be a state of an IOLTS and suppose that s does *not* have the NI property. Thus there must be two (possibly nondeterministic) strategies W, W′, level B and trace T such that $W =_B W'$ and:

1. $W \not\models s \overset{T}{\twoheadrightarrow}$
2. For all t', if $W' \models s \overset{t'}{\twoheadrightarrow}$ then $t' \neq_B T$.

The key proof idea is to construct two B-equivalent deterministic strategies which, when played against s, result in the same NI-violating behaviours as W, W′.

First, we derive a deterministic strategy $\theta(W)$ from W, as follows. Let $\chi : (\wp(\mathbb{V}) - \emptyset) \to \mathbb{V}$ be some function such that $\chi(X) \in X$. Then:

$$\theta(W)_a(u) = \begin{cases} v & \text{if } \exists u' =_a u.\ u'a?v \leq T \\ \chi(W_a(u)) & otherwise \end{cases}$$

It is necessary to show that $\theta(W)$ is well-defined. In particular, we must show:

a) if $u' =_a u$ and $u'' =_a u$ and $u'a?v \leq T$ and $u''a?v' \leq T$, then $v = v'$;
b) if $u =_a u'$ then $\theta(W)_a(u) = \theta(W)_a(u')$.

First we need the following technical lemma:

Lemma 2. *Let $t_1a?v \leq t_2\ell$ be such that $t_1 \bowtie_a t_2$. Then $t_2 = t_1$ and $\ell = a?v$.*

Proof. Let n_i be the number of a-input events in t_i. Since $t_1 \bowtie_a t_2$, we have $n_1 = n_2$. Now suppose towards a contradiction that $t_1a?v \neq t_2\ell$, hence $t_1a?v \leq t_2$. But then we would have $n_1 + 1 \leq n_2$, which contradicts $n_1 = n_2$. □

Now we can established well-definedness of $\theta(W)$.

Proposition 2. *$\theta(W)$ is a well defined deterministic strategy.*

Proof

a) By assumption of $u' =_a u$ and $u'' =_a u$ we have $u' =_a u''$. Clearly $u' =_a u''$ implies that u', u'' have the same number of a-input events. Furthermore, by assumption that $u'a?v$ and $u''a?v'$ are both prefixes of T, one must be a prefix of the other. Thus, by Lemma 2, $a?v = a?v'$, hence $v = v'$.
b) Suppose $u =_a u'$. If the first case in the definition of $\theta(W)_a$ applies to u then, by essentially the same argument as in a), it must also apply to u' and give the same result. If the second case applies, then, since W_a is an a-strategy, $W_a(u) = W_a(u')$, hence $\chi(W_a(u)) = \chi(W_a(u'))$. □

Next we derive a deterministic strategy $\lambda(w')$ from w'. In this case we must ensure that $\lambda(w')_a = \theta(w)_a$ for all $a \sqsubseteq B$, since we want $\theta(w) =_B \lambda(w')$. We define:

$$\lambda(w')_a(u) = \begin{cases} \theta(w)_a(u) & \text{if } a \sqsubseteq B \\ \chi(w'_a(u)) & otherwise \end{cases}$$

The proof that $\lambda(w')$ is a well-defined deterministic strategy is essentially as for $\theta(w)$ and is omitted. It is immediate from the definition of $\lambda(w')$ that $\theta(w) =_B \lambda(w')$.

It remains to show that this pair of strategies constitute a counterexample to DS-NI and, for this, it suffices to show that:

1. $\theta(w)$ produces T when played against s.
2. The set of traces produced by $\lambda(w')$ is a subset of those produced by w'.

For the first of these, it is given that $s \xrightarrow{T}$, so we need only show that $\theta(w)_a(u) = v$ whenever $ua?v \le T$, and this is clear from the definition of $\theta(w)_a$, since $u =_a u$. For the second, say that strategy ω' *refines* strategy ω iff $\omega'_a(u) \subseteq \omega_a(u)$, for all a, u. It is then immediate from Definition 5 that the refining strategy produces a subset of the traces of the original when played against the same state. Formally:

Lemma 3. *If ω' refines ω and $\omega' \models s \xrightarrow{u} then \omega \models s \xrightarrow{u}$.*

It is straightforward to verify that $\theta(w)$ refines w and hence that $\lambda(w')$ refines w'. This completes the proof that DS-NI $\Rightarrow$ NI.

4.4   Non-Interference for Deterministic IOLTS

Here we establish our main result. That, *for deterministic IOLTS*, to establish NI it is only necessary to consider stream strategies. Thus, for deterministic systems, when reasoning about information flow it can suffice to work with a simple stream-based semantic model of the environment and a corresponding stream-based definition of NI, rather than strategies.

Theorem 2. *A state s of a deterministic IOLTS is NI iff it is SS-NI.*

Corollary 1. *For deterministic IOLTS: NI, DS-NI, NS-NI and SS-NI are all equivalent.*

Given Proposition 1 and Theorem 1, to prove Theorem 2 it suffices to show that, for any state s of a deterministic IOLTS, if s is SS-NI then s is DS-NI. Again, we prove the contrapositive.

Let s be a state of a deterministic IOLTS and suppose that s does *not* have the DS-NI property. Thus there must be two deterministic strategies D, D', level B and trace T such that D $=_B$ D' and:

1. D $\models s \xrightarrow{T}$
2. For all t', if D' $\models s \xrightarrow{t'}$ then $t' \ne_B$ T.

The proof mimics the one above for DS-NI $\Rightarrow$ NI, but this time we derive stream strategies from deterministic strategies. We derive the stream strategy $\phi(D)$ from D as follows:

$$\phi(D)_a(u) = \begin{cases} v & \text{if } \exists u' \bowtie_a u.\ D \models s \xrightarrow{u'a?v} \\ K & \text{otherwise} \end{cases}$$

where K is some (arbitrary) constant in $\mathbb{V}$.

We must show that $\phi(D)$ is a well-defined stream strategy. In particular, we must show:

a) If $u' \bowtie_a u$ and $u'' \bowtie_a u$ and $D \models s \xrightarrow{u'a?v}$ and $D \models s \xrightarrow{u''a?v'}$, then $v = v'$.
b) If $u \bowtie_a u'$ then $\phi(D)_a(u) = \phi(D)_a(u')$.

Part b) follows immediately from the definition of $\phi(D)$ once we have shown a).

To show a) we make use of a lemma which states an expected consequence of determinism: if we play a deterministic strategy against any state of a deterministic IOLTS, there will be no branching in the set of traces produced.

Lemma 4. *Let s be a state of a deterministic IOLTS and let δ be a deterministic strategy. If $\delta \models s \xrightarrow{t_1}$ and $\delta \models s \xrightarrow{t_2}$ then either $t_1 \leq t_2$ or $t_2 \leq t_1$.*

Proof. Suppose, without loss of generality, that $\text{length}(t_1) \leq \text{length}(t_2)$. Proceed by induction on $\text{length}(t_1)$ to show that $t_1 \leq t_2$.

If $\text{length}(t_1) = 0$ then $t_1 = \epsilon \leq t_2$.

If $\text{length}(t_1) > 0$ then t_1 has the form $t_1' \ell_1$ and $s \xrightarrow{t_1'} s_1' \xrightarrow{\ell_1} s_1''$. Then $\text{length}(t_1') < \text{length}(t_2)$ and by IH $t_1' \leq t_2$, hence $t_1' < t_2$. Thus, for some ℓ_2, $t_1' \ell_2 \leq t_2$ and $s \xrightarrow{t_1'} s_2' \xrightarrow{\ell_2} s_2''$. Part 2 of the definition of deterministic IOLTS (Definition 1) entails (by a simple induction on the length of t_1') that $s_2' = s_1'$. It thus remains to show that $\ell_1 = \ell_2$. Suppose towards a contradiction that $\ell_1 \neq \ell_2$. By part 1 of Definition 1 we must have $\ell_1 = a?v_1$ and $\ell_2 = a?v_2$. Then, since $\delta \models s \xrightarrow{t_1'a?v_1}$ and $\delta \models s \xrightarrow{t_1'a?v_2}$, we have $v_1 \in \delta_a(t_1')$ and $v_2 \in \delta_a(t_1')$. But then, since δ is deterministic, $v_1 = v_2$, a contradiction. $\square$

Well-definedness of $\phi(D)$ then follows:

Proposition 3. $\phi(D)$ *is a well-defined stream strategy.*

Proof. It remains to show that condition a) holds. That is, if $u' \bowtie_a u$ and $u'' \bowtie_a u$ and $D \models s \xrightarrow{u'a?v}$ and $D \models s \xrightarrow{u''a?v'}$ then $v = v'$. Now s is a state of deterministic IOLTS and D is deterministic, so, by Lemma 4, either $u'a?v \leq u''a?v'$ or $u''a?v' \leq u'a?v$. From $u' \bowtie_a u$ and $u'' \bowtie_a u$ we also have $u' \bowtie_a u''$. Hence by Lemma 2, $v = v'$. $\square$

Next we derive a stream strategy $\psi(D')$ from D'. For $a \sqsubseteq B$ we define $\psi(D')_a = \phi(D)_a$ and for $a \not\sqsubseteq B$ we derive $\psi(D')$ from D' exactly as we derived $\phi(D)$ from D:

$$\psi(D')_a = \begin{cases} \phi(D)_a & \text{if } a \sqsubseteq B \\ \phi(D')_a & \text{if } a \not\sqsubseteq B \end{cases}$$

The proof that $\psi(D')$ is a well-defined stream strategy is essentially as for $\phi(D)$ and is omitted. It is immediate from the definition of $\psi(D')$ that $\phi(D) =_B \psi(D')$.

For the final step in the proof that SS-NI $\Rightarrow$ DS-NI we introduce the notion of a-prefix:

Definition 9. *Trace u is an a-prefix of u', written $u \preceq_a u'$, iff $u =_a u''$ for some $u'' \leq u'$.*

We state without proof some obvious properties of $\preceq_a$:

- If $a_1 \sqsubseteq a_2$ then $\preceq_{a_2} \subseteq \preceq_{a_1}$.
- If $u \leq u' \preceq_a u''$ then $u \preceq_a u''$.
- If $u =_a u'$ then $u \preceq_a u'$.

We will use these freely in the remainder of the proof.

The proof is now essentially completed by the following lemma, which says that, when played against S, $\phi(\text{D})$ and D produce exactly the same sets of traces (including, in particular, T), whereas every trace produced by $\psi(\text{D}')$ is either also produced by D' or is not a B-prefix of T.

Lemma 5

1. $\phi(\text{D}) \models \text{S} \xrightarrow{u} \textit{iff } \text{D} \models \text{S} \xrightarrow{u}$.
2. $\textit{If } \psi(\text{D}') \models \text{S} \xrightarrow{u} \textit{and } u \preceq_\text{B} \text{T } \textit{then } \text{D}' \models \text{S} \xrightarrow{u}$.

Proof. The lemma holds vacuously if u is not a trace of S, so we need only show that it holds for all u such that $\text{S} \xrightarrow{u}$. Let $\#_\text{I}(u)$ denote the number of input events in u. We proceed by induction on $\#_\text{I}(u)$. Take the two parts in turn:

1. For $\#_\text{I}(u) = 0$ we have both $\phi(\text{D}) \models \text{S} \xrightarrow{u}$ and $\text{D} \models \text{S} \xrightarrow{u}$ by assumption that $\text{S} \xrightarrow{u}$. In the inductive case, $\#_\text{I}(u) = n+1$, hence $u'a?v \leq u$ for some u' with $\#_\text{I}(u') = n$. By IH $\phi(\text{D}) \models \text{S} \xrightarrow{u'}$ iff $\text{D} \models \text{S} \xrightarrow{u'}$. Note that, since $a?v$ is the last input event in u, we have:

   (i) $\text{D} \models \text{S} \xrightarrow{u}$ iff $(\text{D} \models \text{S} \xrightarrow{u'}) \wedge (\text{D}_a(u') = v)$

   (ii) $\phi(\text{D}) \models \text{S} \xrightarrow{u}$ iff $(\phi(\text{D}) \models \text{S} \xrightarrow{u'}) \wedge (\phi(\text{D})_a(u') = v)$

   Thus it suffices to show that, if $\text{D} \models \text{S} \xrightarrow{u'}$ then $\text{D}_a(u') = \phi(\text{D})_a(u')$. Let $\text{D}_a(u') = w$. Then, since $\text{S} \xrightarrow{u'a?v}$ and the IOLTS is input-neutral, we have $\text{S} \xrightarrow{u'a?w}$. Hence, since $u' \bowtie_a u'$, by definition of $\phi(\text{D})_a$ we have $\phi(\text{D})_a(u') = w$.

2. Assume $\psi(\text{D}') \models \text{S} \xrightarrow{u}$ and $u \preceq_\text{B} \text{T}$. The base case is as for part 1. In the inductive case, again we have $\#_\text{I}(u) = n+1$, hence $u'a?v \leq u$ for some u' with $\#_\text{I}(u') = n$. By assumption of $u \preceq_\text{B} \text{T}$ we have $u' \preceq_\text{B} \text{T}$, hence by IH $\text{D}' \models \text{S} \xrightarrow{u'}$. Thus it suffices to show $\text{D}'_a(u') = v$. We proceed by cases according to whether $a \sqsubseteq \text{B}$.

   If $a \not\sqsubseteq \text{B}$, let $w = \text{D}'_a(u')$. Then, since $\text{S} \xrightarrow{u'a?v}$ and the IOLTS is input-neutral, we have $\text{S} \xrightarrow{u'a?w}$. Thus, by definition of $\psi(\text{D}')$, $\psi(\text{D}')_a(u') = w$. But, by assumption of $\psi(\text{D}') \models \text{S} \xrightarrow{u}$, we have $\psi(\text{D}')_a(u') = v$, hence $w = v$.

   If $a \sqsubseteq \text{B}$ then, from $u \preceq_\text{B} \text{T}$, we have $u'a?v \preceq_a \text{T}$. Thus $u''a?v \leq \text{T}$ and $u'' =_a u'$, for some u''. Thus $\text{D}_a(u'') = \text{D}_a(u') = v$. But, since $\text{D} =_\text{B} \text{D}'$ and $a \sqsubseteq \text{B}$, we have $\text{D}'_a = \text{D}_a$, hence $\text{D}'_a(u') = v$. $\square$

Proposition 4. $\phi(\text{D}), \psi(\text{D}')$ *are a counterexample to SS-NI.*

Proof. By part 1 of Lemma 5, $\phi(\text{D}) \models \text{S} \xrightarrow{\text{T}}$. Now suppose $\psi(\text{D}') \models \text{S} \xrightarrow{t'}$ and $t' =_\text{B} \text{T}$. But then $t' \preceq_\text{B} \text{T}$ and hence, by part 2 of Lemma 5, $\text{D}' \models \text{S} \xrightarrow{t'}$, contradicting the original assumption that D, D' are a counterexample to NI. $\qquad\square$

This concludes the proof of Theorem 2.

5   Conclusions

We have defined a notion of Input-Output Labelled Transition System (IOLTS) suitable for modelling interactive programming languages. Following previous work by Wittbold and Johnson [16] and O'Neill, Clarkson and Chong [14] we have defined a notion of non-interference (NI) for IOLTS, modelling the users' input behaviours as strategies. Our main result has been to show that, for deterministic IOLTS, a simpler definition of NI, based on a stream model of user input, is equivalent.

5.1   Non-Interference and Nondeterminism

The definition of NI we use in this paper is (essentially) the one used for deterministic programs in [14]. However, although the definition can also be applied to nondeterministic programs (as our use of it illustrates) it is interesting to note that the authors of [14] actually modify the definition when they add non-determinism to the language. (Unfortunately, in modifying it, they render it unable to distinguish between the insecure Program 1b and its secure variant Program 1a). The modification is motivated by the desire to avoid so-called *refinement attacks*, in which refining a secure program (removing some nondeterminism) renders it insecure. We chose not to follow this route since it identifies two uses of nondeterminism which we prefer to differentiate: the use of nondeterminism to allow under-specification, and the use of nondeterminism as a programming construct, essentially as a source of deliberate "noise" intended to disrupt information flows. It is this latter use which is relevant in the covert channel examples described above.

But there is a possible weakness in the security delivered by our version of NI for nondeterministic programs. Consider the following example:

```
input x from H
if (1 | x) then
      output 0 to L
else
      while (true) do skip
```

(Recall that | here is nondeterministic choice.) This program is NI by our definition. Whether it should be regarded as secure depends on our assumptions about the observability of non-termination in the presence of nondeterminism. If we wish to make the definition of NI sensitive to the possibility of non-termination in this example, we might use a more sophisticated definition based, for example, on a form of bisimulation rather than trace-equivalence. This approach would suggest transposing the problem into a process algebraic setting, as explored in [7] (see Section 5.2 for further discussion on this point). Alternatively, we might consider *weakening* the definition of NI to make it, more generally, termination insensitive. In the latter case it would be interesting to try to adapt the work of [5] to establish computational bounds on the rate at which information could be leaked.

5.2   Future Work

Our longer term goal is to be able to reason about the security properties of programs in interaction with their environments in a compositional way. Ideally we do not want to treat these two actors differently. One stumbling block we face in achieving this is that a very common environment for a program is another program or even a set of programs. What is the relationship between programs and strategies?

A strategy is defined in Wittbold and Johnson [16] as a map from the history of inputs and outputs on a given channel to the next input on that channel. There is no computational content in that definition and, in general, a strategy could be non-computable (and clearly not representable by a program). On the other hand, not every program has a semantics which can be characterised as providing an appropriate input to another program whenever it is required. In fact the setting in which Wittbold and Johnson introduce strategies is a purely synchronous one in which inputs are always supplied to the program. So, in particular, a program written in the interactive core imperative language defined in this paper will not in general define a strategy for another program written in the same language, or even define a strategy at all. Consider for example a program which only updates its internal state and never engages with input or output at all.

If we assume the programs are interacting in an asynchronous fashion, a program which expects input on a given channel may never get it from the other programs in its environment. Even supposing a program is structured correctly so that it acts as a strategy for another program (and presumably vice versa) termination problems may mean that it never produces an expected output. For example:

```
P1:
input x from H;
input z from L;
output (z XOR x) on H;

P2:
output y on H;
while(x < 0)   x--;
output x on L;
input w from H;
```

Program P2 will provide input for Program P1 on L only some of the time. It could be described as a partial strategy. Any reasoning about environments formed from programs would have to take partiality into account.

There are two directions in which we could take this work.

We could continue to model environments as strategies and ask what kinds of systems could be strategies for each other and ask what kinds of constraints on the systems would that require. We have discussed some of the issues above but an interesting enquiry along these lines is the possibility of modelling the interaction using game semantics [1,2,9].

On the other hand, why constrain the model of the environment to be a strategy? Our use of IOLTS suggests some more general formal process model might be a suitable setting for extending our results, building on the foundational work of [7]. A potential issue to be addressed in this case would be that *sequentiality* seems to be an essential characteristic of the deterministic programs on which we have focused. It may be that security properties such as NDC and BNDC as defined in [7] are so strong as to effectively rule out many sequential systems of interest.

Orthogonal to these two lines of enquiry is the question of probabilistic models of the the behaviour of the environment. With respect to strategies, for example, Jürjens has shown [13] that Gray's security property Probabilistic Noninterference (PNI) [12] is a generalisation of Wittbold and Johnson's nondeducibility on strategies [16] while Aldini, Bravetti and Gorrieri have analysed probabilistic noninterference using a probabilistic process algebra [3,4].

Acknowledgments

This work was supported by EPSRC research grant EP/C545605/1 & EP/C009746/1 (Quantitative Information Flow). Thanks to Aslan Askarov, Catuscia Palamidessi, Andrei Sabelfeld and David Sands for their encouragement and comments on early versions of this work. We also thank the anonymous reviewers for their very helpful criticisms and suggestions for improvement.

References

1. Abramksy, S., McCusker, G.: Game semantics. In: Berger, U., Schwichtenberg, H. (eds.) Logic and Computation: Proc. 1997 Marktoberdorf Summer School. NATO Science Series. Springer, Heidelberg (1998)
2. Abramsky, S., Jagadeesan, R., Malacaria, P.: Full abstraction for pcf. Information and Computation, 409–470 (December 2000)
3. Aldini, A.: Probabilistic information flow in a process algebra. In: Larsen, K.G., Nielsen, M. (eds.) CONCUR 2001. LNCS, vol. 2154, pp. 152–168. Springer, Heidelberg (2001)
4. Aldini, A., Bravetti, M., Gorrieri, R.: A process-algebraic approach for the analysis of probabilistic noninterference. J. Comput. Secur. 12(2), 191–245 (2004)
5. Askarov, A., Hunt, S., Sabelfeld, A., Sands, D.: Termination-insensitive noninterference leaks more than just a bit. In: Jajodia, S., Lopez, J. (eds.) ESORICS 2008. LNCS, vol. 5283. Springer, Heidelberg (2008)
6. Denning, D.E.: A lattice model of secure information flow. Comm. of the ACM 19(5), 236–243 (1976)
7. Focardi, R., Gorrieri, R.: A classification of security properties for process algebras. J. Computer Security 3(1), 5–33 (1995)
8. Goguen, J.A., Meseguer, J.: Security policies and security models. In: Symposium on Security and Privacy, April 1982, pp. 11–20 (1982)

9. Harmer, R., Mccusker, G.: A fully abstract game semantics for finite nondeterminism. In: Proceedings of the Fourteenth Annual Symposium on Logic in Computer Science, LICS 1999, pp. 422–430. IEEE Computer Society Press, Los Alamitos (1999)

10. Honda, K., Yoshida, N., Carbone, M.: Multiparty asynchronous session types. In: Principles Of Programming Languages (January 2008)

11. Hunt, S., Sands, D.: Just forget it – the semantics and enforcement of information erasure. In: Drossopoulou, S. (ed.) ESOP 2008. LNCS, vol. 4960, pp. 239–253. Springer, Heidelberg (2008)

12. Gray III, J.W.: Toward a mathematical foundation for information flow security. In: Proc. of the 1991 Symposium on Security and Privacy, pp. 21–35. IEEE, Los Alamitos (1991)

13. Jürjens, J.: Secure information flow for concurrent processes. In: Palamidessi, C. (ed.) CONCUR 2000. LNCS, vol. 1877, pp. 395–409. Springer, Heidelberg (2000)

14. O'Neill, K.R., Clarkson, M.R., Chong, S.: Information-flow security for interactive programs. In: CSFW, pp. 190–201. IEEE Computer Society, Los Alamitos (2006)

15. Shannon, C.E.: Channels with side information at the transmitter. IBM journal of Research and Development 2(4), 289–293 (1958)

16. Wittbold, J.T., Johnson, D.M.: Information flow in nondeterministic systems. In: IEEE Symposium on Security and Privacy, pp. 144–161 (1990)

Information-Theoretic Modeling and Analysis of Interrupt-Related Covert Channels

Heiko Mantel and Henning Sudbrock[*]

Department of Computer Science, TU Darmstadt,
Hochschulstraße 10, 64289 Darmstadt, Germany
{mantel,sudbrock}@cs.tu-darmstadt.de

Abstract. We present a formal model for analyzing the bandwidth of covert channels. The focus is on channels that exploit interrupt-driven communication, which have been shown to pose a serious threat in practical experiments. Our work builds on our earlier model [1], which we used to compare the effectiveness of different countermeasures against such channels. The main novel contribution of this article is an approach to exploiting detailed knowledge about a given channel in order to make the bandwidth analysis more precise.

1 Introduction

Confidentiality and integrity on the application level heavily depend on mechanisms to restrict communication in underlying system layers. Even if one closes all communication channels between two applications, the danger of covert communication remains, i.e., that there are channels that are not intended as communication channels [2]. The problem of identifying covert channels and analyzing their bandwidth has received much attention by the research community (see, e.g., [3,4,5,6,7]), but covert channel analysis and mitigation is far from being solved.

Covert channels can be established based on various system-level resources that are virtualized or otherwise shared between multiple processes. For instance, the physical memory can be exploited to establish a covert channel as follows: a sender sends a signal by heavily allocating memory, and a receiver decides whether a signal was sent or not, depending on the paging rate that he observes when allocating memory. In this article, we focus on *interrupt-related covert channels*, i.e., covert channels that are established based on the CPU time used for handling interrupts. Unlike many other covert channels, interrupt-related channels cannot be mitigated by assigning a constant quota of resource usage to each process. Therefore, it is of particular interest to obtain reliable upper bounds on the bandwidth of such channels. More generally, if one cannot mitigate some covert channels then one should at least be able to assess their dangers.

In this article, we investigate the information-theoretic modeling of interrupt-related covert channels. The main novel contribution is an approach to exploiting detailed knowledge about a given channel in order to make the bandwidth analysis more precise. This contribution is twofold: On the one hand, we demonstrate how to refine a model

---

[*] The authors gratefully acknowledge support by the German Research Foundation (DFG). The authors furthermore thank the anonymous reviewers for their helpful comments.

P. Degano, J. Guttman, and F. Martinelli (Eds.): FAST 2008, LNCS 5491, pp. 67–81, 2009.

based on detailed knowledge about a given channel, and we show at two concrete examples that such refinements can result in significantly more precise upper bounds on the bandwidth. On the other hand, we show that even in the case when the knowledge needed for a refinement is incomplete, the available knowledge can still be exploited to improve the bandwidth analysis in a significant way.

In earlier work, we investigated several mechanisms to reduce the bandwidth of interrupt-related covert channels [1]. The model employed in this article constitutes an improvement over the earlier model as it faithfully reflects the capabilities of senders and receivers and is therefore suitable for obtaining reliable upper bounds on the bandwidth of interrupt-related covert channels.

To our knowledge, there is no prior work on refining models of covert channels by exploiting knowledge about probability distributions to improve the bandwidth analysis. Our work is the first to exploit incomplete knowledge about probability distributions in the bandwidth analysis of covert channels, in general. We have also implemented an exploit of interrupt-related channels that works in practice. Using a simple ad hoc encoding the exploit allows to transmit a four-digit PIN (i.e., approximately 13 bits of information) in about 30 seconds. However, the focus of the current article is not on such practical exploitations but rather on sound techniques for analyzing the bandwidth.

2   Modeling Interrupt-Related Covert Channels

In this section, we present the information-theoretic model for analyzing the bandwidth of covert channels. Before presenting the model, we recall how interrupt-related channels operate and select a class of such channels as a running example.

2.1   Interrupt-Related Covert Channels

The transmission of information over an *interrupt-related covert channel* is based on operations that result in asynchronous interrupt requests. The *receiving process* continuously probes a clock during its execution in order to notice when it has been preempted by an interrupt request. For instance, the observation that it was preempted at least once during a given time-slot could be interpreted as the value 1 and that it was not preempted as the value 0. To send a 0 over this channel, the *sending process* only needs to refrain from executing operations that result in interrupt requests during the receiving process' time-slot and, to send a 1, it performs such operations. Such an interrupt-related channel cannot be mitigated by assigning a constant quota of resource usage to each process [1], a technique that can be used to mitigate many other types of covert channels.

Interrupt-related covert channels can be established based on many different operations and various hardware devices. To make things concrete, we focus throughout this article on channels that are based on the transmission of packets via a network interface card (NIC). We call such an interrupt-related channel an *NIC-channel*.

More concretely, we consider an NIC that requests interrupts on two occasions: after a packet has been transmitted to the network and after a packet has been received from the network. An interrupt request causes the CPU to suspend its current activity in order to execute an interrupt handler. This behavior can be exploited to establish a covert channel as follows: The sending process requests the transmission of a packet

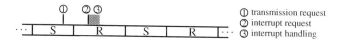

Fig. 1. Covert transmission of a single bit via an NIC-channel

via the NIC. After the NIC has transmitted the packet, it acknowledges the transmission by an interrupt request. The handling of this interrupt will occur during the receiving process' time-slot if the transmission request is issued at the proper time by the sending process. We illustrate the transmission of a single bit in a simple example scenario where the sending process and the receiving process are scheduled alternately, and no other processes are active. In Figure 1, each box in the time-line represents a time-slot of the process indicated by the label inside the box, i.e., by S and R for the sending process and the receiving process, respectively. Above the time-line, the occurrence of a transmission request and the occurrence of an interrupt request are indicated by the two vertical bars labeled with 1 and 2, respectively. The time interval used for handling the interrupt is indicated by the gray rectangle labeled with 3.

2.2 The Information-Theoretic Model

We model each NIC-channel as a discrete, memoryless channel C, i.e., as a triple (I_C, O_C, P_C). Further information about discrete, memoryless channels can be found in, e.g., [8]. The *input alphabet* I_C models the set of values that can be sent on C, and the *output alphabet* O_C models the set of values that can be received from C. The *channel matrix* $P_C = (p(o|i))_{i \in I_C, o \in O_C}$ defines the probability $p(o|i)$ that a given output o is received given that the input equals i. We first model the transmission from a given time-slot of the sender to a given time-slot of the receiver before we generalize the setting to multiple time-slots. In the model, we measure time abstractly in discrete *time units*, which could, e.g., be microseconds or clock cycles, and assume that all time-slots of the sending process and the receiving process have a fixed length of l time units.

The Input Alphabet. An input to the channel corresponds to the points in time at which the sending process requests the transmission of a network packet. Formally, an input is an ordered list $[t_1, \ldots, t_k]$, where each element t_i represents a transmission request at time t_i in the sending process' time-slot. We measure time relative to the starting point of the given time-slot and require $t_i \leq l$ for all elements of the list. The input alphabet is

$$I_C = \{[t_1, \ldots, t_k] \mid \forall i \in \{1, \ldots, k-1\}. 1 \leq t_i < t_{i+1} \leq l\}.$$

As an example, the input symbol $i = [2, 7, 8]$ is illustrated by the diagram on the left hand side of Figure 2. The three vertical bars on top of the sending process' time-slot represent the transmission requests after 2, 7, and 8 time units, respectively. An alternative, but equivalent representation of inputs are bit strings of length l.

The Output Alphabet. An output symbol contains information about interrupt handling in the receiving process' time-slot. For each interrupt request that is handled during that time-slot, the output symbol contains a pair (s, d), where s represents the time at which

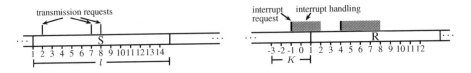

Fig. 2. Input symbol $[2, 7, 8]$ (left diagram) and output symbol $[(-1, 3), (4, 4)]$ (right diagram)

the interrupt request occurs, and d represents the duration of handling this request. This modeling is conservative as output symbols contain the information when interrupts occur and how long their handling takes, while the receiver only sees during which time intervals it was not running on the CPU. We use this approach as it allows us to model the correspondence between input and output symbols independently of how the system deals with interrupts that are requested during the handling of another interrupt request.

We formalize an output symbol as an ordered list $[(s_1, d_1), \ldots, (s_k, d_k)]$:

$$O_C = \{ [(s_1, d_1), \ldots, (s_k, d_k)] \mid$$
$$\forall i \in \{1, \ldots, k-1\} . (-K < s_i \leq s_{i+1} \leq l \wedge (s_i = s_{i+1} \Rightarrow d_i \leq d_{i+1}))\},$$

where K is the maximal amount of time that interrupt handling may take. Note that the lists in the output alphabet are ordered in the sense that either $s_i < s_{i+1}$ or $s_i = s_{i+1} \wedge d_i \leq d_{i+1}$ holds for $i \in \{1, \ldots, k-1\}$. If $s_i = s_j$ holds for $i \neq j$ then this represents that the two interrupt requests occur at the same time. Note that we demand $-K < s_i$ instead of $0 < s_i$ and $s_{i+1} \leq l$ instead of $s_{i+1} + d_{i+1} \leq l$. This ensures an adequate treatment of interrupt requests that occur at the boundaries of the receiving process' time-slot. That is, our output symbols include interrupt requests that occur before the receiving process' time-slot but that are handled at least partially during this time-slot as well as interrupts whose handling exceeds the receiving process' time-slot.

As an example, the output symbol $[(-1, 3), (4, 4)]$ is represented by the diagram on the right-hand side of Figure 2. In the diagram, the vertical bars represent the occurrence of interrupt requests, and the gray boxes represent the time used for interrupt handling.

The Channel Matrix. While the input alphabet and the output alphabet can be defined for NIC-channels in general, the channel matrix must be defined dependent on the particular instance of an NIC-channel. We illustrate this for a simple example channel.

Example 1. Assume a scenario where the sending process and the receiving process are scheduled alternately in a Round-Robin fashion and no other processes are active. The length of each time-slot shall be 100 milliseconds, the latency of the NIC shall be 10 milliseconds (i.e. an interrupt request occurs exactly 10 milliseconds after a given transmission request), and handling a single interrupt shall take exactly 1 millisecond.

We choose milliseconds as granularity of time in the model, i.e. one time unit in the model corresponds to one millisecond in reality. At each time unit, the sending process either requests a transmission or not. Given an input symbol $[t_1, \ldots, t_j, t_{j+1}, \ldots, t_{j+k}]$ with $t_j \leq l - 10$ and $t_{j+1} > l - 10$, the transmission requests at $t_1, \ldots, t_j$ do not result in interrupt requests in the receiver's time-slot and, hence, can be ignored in an input symbol. Given an input $[t_1, \ldots, t_k]$ with $t_1 > l - 10$ and $k \leq 10$, the receiver observes the output $[(t_1 - l + 10, 1), \ldots, (t_k - l + 10, 1)]$, which means that 2^{10} different output symbols can be generated. The channel matrix can then be defined as follows:

$$P_C[i, o] = p(o|i) = \begin{cases} 1 & \text{, if } i = [t_1, \ldots, t_j, t_{j+1}, \ldots, t_{j+k}], t_j \leq l - 10 < t_{j+1}, \\ & k \leq 10, \text{ and } o = [(t_{j+1} - l + 10, 1), \ldots, (t_{j+k} - l + 10, 1)] \\ 0 & \text{, otherwise.} \end{cases}$$

The channel in the prior example features a functional dependency between input and output. That is, for a given input $i \in I_C$, the corresponding output $o(i) \in O_C$ and a given list element (s_j, d_j) in the output $o(i)$, there is exactly one corresponding list element t_k in the input i. This is reflected in the model by the fact that no other values than 0 and 1 occur as entries in the channel matrix.[1]

Bandwidth Analysis. The capacity $CAP(C)$ of a discrete, memoryless channel C is defined as an upper bound on the amount of information (in number of bits) that can be transmitted over C on average with an arbitrarily small error probability. For the formal definition of capacity and of other basic concepts of information theory see, e.g., [8].

Example 2. In the scenario from Example 1, 2^{10} different output symbols can be generated. Each of these symbols can be generated by sending an input symbol $[t_1, \ldots, t_k]$ with $t_1 > l - 10$ and $k \leq 10$. Hence, we obtain a capacity of 10 bits per scheduler round for our simple example channel.

For a contemporary NIC and scheduler, it is plausible that a given time-slot of the receiving process is only influenced by transmissions in the immediately preceding time-slot of the sending process. This observation allows us to generalize the model to multiple scheduler rounds.

Example 3. In Example 1, a scheduling round consists of a time-slot of each of the two processes. Hence, 5 scheduler rounds occur every second. Since the capacity is 10 bits per scheduler round (see Example 2), we obtain a capacity of 50 bits per second.

In Examples 1–3, the latency of the NIC as well as the handling time of an interrupt request are constant. Random effects influencing these time values can be taken into account by an appropriate definition of the channel matrix.

Example 4. Reconsider the scenario from Examples 1–3, but with a non-constant latency of the NIC. We assume that the latency of the NIC is between 8 and 12 milliseconds, where the probability that the latency equals t milliseconds is denoted as $p(\text{latency} = t)$. For the probability distribution depicted in the following graph, we obtain a capacity of 2.3 bits per scheduler round, or equivalently 11.5 bits per second.[2]

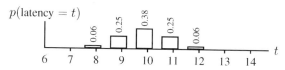

---

[1] Examples of channels where the dependency between input and output is not functional are given in Example 4 as well as in Section 3.2.

[2] Due to space restrictions, the formalization of the probabilities $P_C[i, o]$ used in the analysis is provided in an appendix to this article which is available on the second author's website (http://www.mais.informatik.tu-darmstadt.de/FAST08-app.html).

If the number of processes and the behavior of the interrupt mechanism remain constant over time, like in Examples 3 and 4, then the capacity per second can be calculated by the formula $CAP(C) * \frac{1}{L*(n+2)}$ where n is the number of active processes besides sender and receiver and L is the duration of a single time-slot in seconds. In a more dynamic setting where, e.g., the number of processes or the dependency between input and output changes over time, one would need to perform a more complicated calculation, possibly having to adapt the channel matrix between individual scheduler rounds.

Remark 1. In [1], we defined an information-theoretic model in order to analyze the effectiveness of various countermeasures against interrupt-related channels. In this model, we would obtain a capacity of approximately 3.5 bits per scheduler round for the scenario from Examples 1–3 (see Example 5 in [1]). This significant difference in the capacity is due to a somewhat ad hoc simplification in the model that results in an inaccurate treatment of the receiving process' capabilities. In our earlier model, the receiver could observe less than he can observe in reality and, therefore, the bandwidth analysis resulted in a capacity that is too low. More concretely, we assumed that the receiving process could only perceive the accumulated delay caused by all interrupts that occur in a given time-slot. Unlike our earlier model, the model proposed in this article (including all refinements presented in the subsequent sections) provides a suitable basis for determining reliable upper bounds on the bandwidth as it reflects the capabilities of senders and receivers in an adequate way.

3   Exploiting Additional Knowledge in a Bandwidth Analysis

Additional knowledge about a particular NIC-channel can be exploited in the bandwidth analysis. In this section, we demonstrate how our information-theoretic model can be refined based on such knowledge. We illustrate how to refine the model with two examples: the first exploits knowledge about the peculiarities of the NIC and the second exploits information about the run-time environment of the sender and receiver. In each case, the objective of refining the model is to increase the precision of the bandwidth analysis. The fact that the model from Section 2 is conservative already guarantees that the calculated bandwidths constitute reliable upper bounds. As we demonstrate by concrete examples, refinements of the model can lead to significant increases in precision.

3.1   Exploiting Peculiarities of the Network Interface Card

In Section 2, we made the rather conservative assumption that the sender can request a transmission at each time unit during its time-slot. Let us now consider an NIC that requires that two subsequent transmission requests are at least T_{tr} time units apart. Consequently, the sender can only generate input symbols from the following subset:

$$I'_C = \{[t_1, \ldots, t_k] \mid \forall i \in \{1, \ldots, k-1\}. \; 1 \le t_i < t_{i+1} \le l \wedge t_{i+1} - t_i \ge T_{tr}\} \subseteq I_C.$$

The number of ordered lists over a set $\{1, \ldots, j\}$ where two adjacent elements in a list have at least a distance of T_{tr} time units can be computed recursively as follows:

$$N(j) = j + 1 \qquad\qquad\qquad , \text{if } j \le T_{tr}$$
$$N(j) = N(j - T_{tr}) + N(j - 1) , \text{if } j > T_{tr}$$

The first equation above reflects the fact that there cannot be two elements in $\{1, \ldots, j\}$ with a distance of at least T_{tr} if $j \leq T_{tr}$ holds. In this case, the empty list $[\,]$ and the singleton lists $[1], \ldots, [j]$ are the only ordered lists that satisfy the given constraints. The second equation reflects the fact that the set of ordered lists can be partitioned into the following two subsets: the lists in which j occurs as the last element (hence, there are $N(j - T_{tr})$ possibilities for the prefix of a list without this last element) and the lists in which j does not occur (hence, there are $N(j - 1)$ possibilities for such lists).

Example 5. We consider the same scenario as in Examples 1–3 (i.e. $l = 100$ and $K = 1$), but with the additional knowledge that two subsequent transmission requests must be at least two time units apart (i.e. $T_{tr} = 2$). Like before, an input symbol $[t_1, \ldots, t_i, t_{i+1} \ldots, t_{i+k}]$ with $t_j \leq l - 10$, $t_{j+1} > l - 10$, and $k \leq 10$ results in the output symbol $[(t_{i+1} - l + 10, 1), \ldots, (t_{i+k} - l + 10, 1)]$. Note that the set of output symbols that can actually occur is only a proper subset of the one in Example 1. The cardinality of this subset equals $N(10)$ (for $T_{tr} = 2$) because only transmission requests in the last 10 milliseconds of the sender's time-slot are relevant and because two transmission requests must be at least 2 milliseconds apart. That is, we obtain a bandwidth of $\log_2(N(10)) = \log_2(144) \approx 7.2$ bits per scheduler round.

The above example demonstrates that our refinement of the model leads to an upper bound on the bandwidth that is significantly lower (reduction by more than 25%) than in the model from Section 2. This justifies the slightly more complex model that results from taking restrictions on the sender side into account. Note that the difference in the bandwidth becomes even greater if larger values of T_{tr} are used. The capacities for $T_{tr} \in \{1, \ldots, 9\}$ are depicted in in the following graph. For instance, for $T_{tr} = 6$, we obtain a capacity of approximately 4.4 bits per scheduler round.

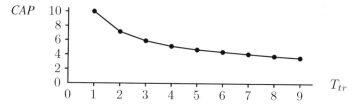

Remark 2. Refinements of the model, like the one just presented, must be constructed with care. In particular, one must be careful to not endanger the conservativity of the model. Otherwise, one could obtain bandwidths that are no reliable upper bounds.

We illustrate this by an example. To this end, we consider the same scenario as in Example 5, but define the set of input symbols that can be generated less carefully than before. To simplify the bandwidth analysis, we assume that transmission requests occur only at odd time units. This ensures that two subsequent transmission requests are at least two time units apart. Under this assumption, only elements from the following subset of I_C can be generated:

$$I_C'' = \{[t_1, \ldots, t_k] \mid \forall i \in \{1, \ldots, k-1\}. 1 \leq t_i < t_{i+1} \leq l \wedge t_i, t_{i+1} \text{ are odd}\}.$$

Under this assumption, the set of output symbols that can be generated is

$$O_C'' = \{[(t_1, 1), \ldots, (t_k, 1)] \mid \forall i \in \{1, \ldots, k-1\}. 1 \leq t_i < t_{i+1} \leq 10 \wedge t_i, t_{i+1} \text{odd}\}.$$

This set contains 2^5 different elements. Hence, we obtain a capacity of 5 bits per scheduler round. Note how much easier it is to determine the bandwidth here in comparison to Example 5, where we had to employ recursive equations. However, the calculated capacity does not constitute a reliable upper bound on the bandwidth of the channel because there are output symbols (e.g., $[(2, 1), (4, 1)]$) that can be generated under the given assumptions in reality, but that do not occur in O''_C. The deviation from the correct result is significant (5 bits instead of 7.2 bits in Example 5) and, hence, not acceptable.

This illustrates how careful one must be when exploiting additional knowledge about a channel in the bandwidth analysis. In particular, one should avoid ad hoc refinements that simplify the analysis technically because, otherwise, one might obtain significantly inaccurate results that do not constitute upper bounds on the bandwidth.

3.2   Exploiting Knowledge about Noise

So far, we only considered those interrupt requests in a time-slot of the receiver that are caused by transmission requests of the sender. In reality, however, other sources of interrupts could introduce noise into the communication and, thereby, lower the bandwidth of the covert channel. For instance, any hardware device that uses interrupt-driven communication could add to the noise. This includes the NIC, which also generates interrupt requests to signal other events than the successful transmission of a packet to the network. To simplify the presentation in the following, we focus on noise due to interrupts that the NIC requests to signal that a packet has arrived from the network.

Since the occurrences of additional interrupt requests depend on the behavior of the environment of the system, for instance on other clients attached to the network, the receiving process, in general, does not know in advance when interrupt requests caused by arriving network packets are handled during its time-slot. To model the occurrences of these interrupt requests, we use a random variable Env, which takes values in the set

$$\{[(r_1, d_1), \ldots, (r_k, d_k)] \mid \forall i \in \{1, \ldots, k-1\}. - K < r_i < r_{i+1} \leq l\},$$

where the list $[(r_1, d_1), \ldots, (r_k, d_k)]$ represents occurrences of interrupt requests caused by arriving network packets at the times $r_1, \ldots, r_k$ with respect to the receiving process' time-slot, and the interrupt request at time r_i is handled in d_i time units.

The probabilistic dependency of a channel's output on the input is captured by the probability matrix P_C in our model of the channel. If no noise disturbs the transmission over the channel, the dependency between input symbols and output symbols is functional, like in Examples 1–3. In the presence of noise, we usually loose this functional dependency. For instance, the input symbol $[91]$ could result in the output $[(1, 1)]$, which is the only possible output in the scenario without noise from Examples 1–3, but it could also result, e.g., in the output $[(1, 1), (3, 1)]$ where the second list element represents an interrupt request that signals the arrival of a network packet at time 3.

We introduce some notation for the definition of probability matrices. We write $o_1 \sqsubseteq o_2$ to express that the list o_2 contains all occurrences of elements in the list o_1. We use $o_2 \ominus o_1$ to denote the list that results by removing one occurrence of an element from the list o_2 for each occurrence of this element in o_1, given that the element occurs in o_2 (e.g., $[(1, 1), (1, 1), (3, 1)] \ominus [(1, 1)] = [(1, 1), (3, 1)]$). For a given input $i \in I_C$

and output $o \in O_C$, one can determine the list of all elements in o that are caused by transmission requests in i. We use $o(i) \in O_C$ to denote this sublist of o.

If an output symbol $o \in O_C$ occurs for a given input $i \in I_C$, then $o(i)$ denotes the sublist of o that contains all interrupts requests that are generated by transmission requests in i. Hence, all interrupt requests in $o \ominus o(i)$ must be caused by noise, i.e., by the arrival of packets from the network. Therefore, we define

$$P_C[i, o] = p(o|i) = \begin{cases} 0 & \text{, if } o(i) \not\subseteq o, \\ p(Env = o \ominus o(i)) & \text{, if } o(i) \subseteq o. \end{cases}$$

Note that $o(i) \not\subseteq o$ implies that o was not generated by i. Hence, $P_C[i, o] = 0$ must hold.

Example 6. We consider the scenario from Examples 1–3, but admit noise due to interrupt requests caused by the arrival of packets from the network. We assume that 3 network packets arrive, on average, during a 10 millisecond interval, and that each of the corresponding interrupt requests is handled within 1 millisecond. Additionally, we assume that the probability that the environment causes an interrupt request at a given time unit is independent of the same probability for another time unit, i.e.,

$$p(Env = [(r_1, 1), \dots, (r_k, 1)]) = 0.3^k * (1 - 0.3)^{l-k}.$$

For this scenario, we obtain a capacity of approximately 5.6 bits per scheduler round.[3]

Example 6 illustrates that using a more complex model, in which interrupt requests caused by the arrival of network packets are taken into account, can result in a significantly more precise upper bound on the bandwidth. Compared to Example 1, where we obtained an upper bound of 10 bits per scheduler round, the upper bound on the bandwidth is decreased by 4.4 bits per scheduler round, i.e., by 44%.

Remark 3. One must be careful when choosing a probability distribution for the random variable Env because an inappropriate choice may result in significant errors in the calculation. To illustrate this, we reconsider Example 6, but assume that it is likely that directly after the arrival of a packet from the network, further packets arrive. In such a scenario, the occurrence of an interrupt that signals the arrival of a packet increases the likelihood that further interrupts occur immediately afterwards. Therefore, we cannot assume anymore that the probability that noise occurs at one time unit is independent from the occurrence of noise at other points in time (which we assumed in Example 6).

Assume, for instance, that packets were always arriving in batches of size 2. Then one obtains a capacity of approximately 8.7 bits per scheduler round instead of 5.6 bits. That is, the effect of noise on the bandwidth is significantly reduced. However, note also that even if the effect of noise is limited in this way, we still obtain some increase in the precision of the calculated bandwidth (8.7 bits instead of 10 bits).

---

[3] An analytical computation of the capacity in this scenario is too difficult. For an approximation, we compute capacities here, and in the remainder of the article, using an algorithm due to Arimoto and Blahut [9,10] that allows the computation of arbitrarily precise approximations of the capacity of discrete, memoryless channels. The computations are performed using the authors' straightforward Java implementation of the algorithm.

4   Effects on the Analysis of a Countermeasure

In Section 3, we demonstrated that improving the information-theoretic model can have quite significant effects on the results of a bandwidth analysis. Interestingly, modifications to the model not only have an effect on the capacity of the channel, but can also influence the evaluation of the effectiveness of countermeasures against interrupt-related channels. In the current section, we investigate this second effect at the example of *interrupt-rate limiting*. We base our investigation on an earlier evaluation and comparison which covered interrupt-rate limiting and five other countermeasures [1].

Interrupt-rate limiting mitigates NIC-channels by interrupting the CPU less frequently. The technique is used in network interface cards, where interrupt requests are delayed until a certain number v of packets has arrived, rather than requesting an interrupt for each packet (see, e.g., [11]). The evaluation of interrupt-rate limiting as a countermeasure against covert channels in [1] led to two conclusions:

– The countermeasure is capable to reduce the bandwidth arbitrarily close towards 0.
– For high values of v, the capacity is decreasing only slowly.

Both of these observations remain valid for the improved information-theoretic model that we proposed in Section 2. Nevertheless, the modifications to the model can still have an observable effect on the effectiveness of the countermeasure, at least in some cases. We illustrate this more concretely in the remainder of this section.

Effects of Modeling the Receiver Adequately. To elaborate the effects of changing the output alphabet on the effectiveness of interrupt-rate limiting, let us revisit the scenario from Examples 1–3. The analysis shows that, at least for this scenario, the change of the output alphabet has a significant effect on the effectiveness of interrupt-rate limiting.

For the analysis, we integrate interrupt-rate limiting into the model by defining an appropriate channel matrix. The definition of the probabilities $P_C[i, o]$ is fairly straightforward. The only subtlety results from the need to take into account that an unknown number of network packets is pending at the NIC at the beginning of the receiving process' time-slot. Like in [1], we assume that the number of pending interrupts is uniformly distributed on the set $\{0, \ldots, v - 1\}$.

The analysis results for the model using the refined output alphabet from Section 2 as well as for the earlier model from [1] are displayed in Figure 3. The solid dots ($\bullet$) represent the resulting capacities for the refined output alphabet from Section 2, and the circles ($\circ$) those for the earlier model. When increasing the parameter v for small values, the reduction of the capacity is significantly stronger for the model from Section 2. For instance, increasing the value of v from 1 to 2 reduces the capacity by 39% in the refined model, but only by 27% in the earlier model. For larger values of v (i.e. for $v \geq 10$), interrupt-rate limiting reduces the capacity in both models nearly to the same level.

Effects of Exploiting Noise and Peculiarities of the NIC in the Model. Unlike the refinement of the output alphabet from Section 2, the two refinements from Section 3 do not have an observable effect on the effectiveness of interrupt-rate limiting. In both scenarios, we could not identify any significant differences in the reduction of the capacity when applying interrupt-rate limiting.

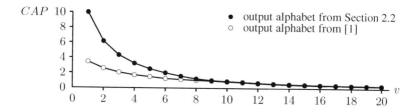

Fig. 3. Effect of the refined output alphabet on the analysis of interrupt-rate limiting

5   Incomplete Knowledge of Probabilistic Behavior

In Section 3, we demonstrated how additional knowledge about a particular covert channel can be exploited to increase the precision of the bandwidth analysis. When exploiting the bandwidth reduction due to noise in Section 3.2, we assumed the probability distribution to be known for the additional interrupts that disturb the covert communication. However, one can easily imagine cases where only incomplete information about the probability distributions is available. For instance, one might only know the number of packets that arrive from the network on average, but not what the exact probability distribution is. In such a scenario, one should refrain from simply choosing one arbitrary probability distribution from the set of possible distributions. Such an ad-hoc choice could lead to significant errors in the resulting capacity, as the difference between the capacities obtained in Example 6 and in Remark 2 prove (5.6 bits versus 8.7 bits per scheduler round). This raises the question whether there is any possibility to obtain reliable upper bounds on the bandwidth when exploiting incomplete knowledge about probability distributions for noise in order to increase the precision of the capacity analysis. In this section, we give an affirmative answer to this question and show how incomplete knowledge about probability distributions can be exploited.

The following example illustrates how reliable upper bounds can be achieved by performing the analysis in multiple instances of the refined model from Section 3.2. For the used approach it is essential that the refinement from Section 3.2 is parametric in the probability distribution of the noise represented by the random variable Env.

Example 7. We consider a scenario, where an interrupt request occurs exactly t time units after a given transmission request. Handling an interrupt request shall take exactly one time unit. Furthermore, on average, x interrupt requests are caused by arriving network packets during the first t time units of the receiving process' time-slot.

Without considering the additional information about arriving network packets, we obtain an upper bound on the capacity of t bits per scheduler round.

To obtain a more precise upper bound by using the additional knowledge, we denote with $\#_{Env}$ the number of interrupt requests caused by arriving network packets during the first t time units of the receiving process' time-slot, and with $\mu(\#_{Env})$ the mean value of $\#_{Env}$. In the scenario under consideration $\mu(\#_{Env})$ equals x. For different probability distributions of the random variable Env (see Section 3.2), $\mu(\#_{Env})$ takes different values. We denote with D the set of all possible probability distributions of the random variable Env for which $\mu(\#_{Env}) = x$. With the given information that, on average, x interrupt requests are caused by arriving network packets during the first t time units of the receiving process' time-slot, the distribution of the random variable Env could be any probability distribution in the set D.

Using the refined model from Section 3.2, we can compute an upper bound on the bandwidth for each $d \in D$. Note that when D is too large it becomes infeasible to calculate the upper bounds for all $d \in D$ in this fashion. We denote the upper bound obtained under the assumption that Env is distributed according to d with UB(d). Then the maximal value of UB(d), for $d \in D$, is an upper bound on the bandwidth of the channel, as this is the highest upper bound for those probability distributions of Env for which $\mu(\#_{Env}) = x$.

Assume that $t = 2$ and $x = 0.8$. In this case, the set D is small enough such that the individual computation of UB(d) for all $d \in D$ is feasible. To compute these values, we implemented the analysis for the refined model from Section 3.2 for arbitrary distributions of Env. In the implementation the probabilities $p(Env = [(r_1, 1), \dots, (r_k, 1)])$ are represented with a precision of four digits. To compute the upper bound, we needed to compute the capacity for approximately 160.000 instances of the model. The resulting upper bound (which equals the maximum of all computed capacities) equals approximately 1.7 bits per scheduler round.

The preceding example demonstrates that the consideration of additional knowledge that is not sufficient to instantiate the refined model from Section 3.2 still allows one to obtain more precise upper bounds. Compared to an analysis where the additional knowledge is not taken into account, the obtained upper bound is reduced by 15%.

The following example illustrates that exploiting further information can result in further improvements of the upper bound.

Example 8. We consider the scenario from Example 7, but assume in addition that the variance of the random variable $\#_{Env}$ equals 0.4. Using this additional information, we denote with D' the set containing all probability distributions of Env where the mean value of $\#_{Env}$ equals 0.8 and the variance of $\#_{Env}$ equals 0.4. By determining the maximal value of UB(d) for $d \in D'$, we obtain an upper bound on the bandwidth equal to approximately 1.3 bits per scheduler round.

Remark 4. When we consider the scenario from Example 7, the size of the set D for which UB(d) needs to be computed during the analysis grows exponentially when t is increased. This is because interrupt requests during the first t time units in the receiving process' time-slot can be caused by the sending process, therefore interrupt requests caused by arriving network packets that occur up to t time units after the start of the receiving process' time-slot influence the channel's capacity, and, hence, the analysis. In consequence, if the value of t is too large the brute-force approach used in Examples 7 and 8 is no longer feasible. Luckily, there are more efficient algorithms from the domain of global optimization [12] that can be used to compute the maximal value of UB(d) for $d \in D$. More precisely, we showed that the problem to find the maximal value of UB(d) for $d \in D$ in the above scenarios is a convex maximization problem over a linearly constrained set [13]. For this class of problems algorithms that are more efficient than the brute-force approach employed in Examples 7 and 8 have been developed [14].

6   Related Work

Covert channels have been firstly identified in [2]. They have been researched extensively throughout the last 35 years, where the main research areas were covert channel
identification, covert channel analysis, and covert channel mitigation.

The focus of the current article is on covert channel modeling and analysis, not on their
identification and their mitigation. A guide to covert channel identification is provided
in [3], covering various approaches including syntactic information flow analysis (e.g.,
[15,16]) and the shared resource matrix method [17,18]. More recent approaches use
security type systems for the identification of information leaks (e.g., [19,20]). Various
methods for the mitigation of covert timing channels have been proposed [21,22,23,24],
including mechanisms targeted specifically at interrupt-related channels [1].

Concerning the analysis of covert channels, the focus of most previous research has
been on deriving the bandwidth based on information theory. In [25,26] the connection
between notions of noninterference and the capacity of a channel is investigated. Various other articles (e.g., [27,28,29,30,31]) investigate how the capacity of certain abstract
classes of channels can be computed. In [28,32] effects of noise on the transmission time
of a symbol over a covert channel are studied. This differs from our treatment of noise
in Section 3.2, where noise affects the output symbol itself. Gray focuses on a particular
class of covert channels in [33,22], where the probabilistic behavior considered in the
analysis originates from two mechanisms for mitigating the channel. This is also the
case in the analysis of the NRL pump, another mitigation mechanism that targets covert
channels exploiting acknowledgments in conventional communication [23,34,24].

In [35], games between an attacker exploiting a covert channel and a jammer disturb-
ing the communication are investigated. Different jamming strategies result in a family
of channel models. In this setting, the jammer completely determines the probability
distributions. This differs from our treatment in Section 5, where we also consider families of probability distributions but assume that each distribution is possible given the
available knowledge. In [36] and [37], models of the NRL pump that are parametric in
the probability distributions are used to assess how parameter variations influence the
capacity of covert channels. However, these models are not used to find upper bounds
on the channel capacity when the concrete parameter values are unknown. We are not
aware of any prior work that derives upper bounds on the bandwidth in a probabilistic
model, where the information about the probability distributions is incomplete.

Most approaches, as also the current article, use information theory for the analysis
of covert channels. However, there are also a few other approaches. For instance, [38]
uses Markov models to compute the bandwidth of a covert channel. An approach that
does not consider a probabilistic setting is based on counting the number of different
sender behaviors that can be distinguished by the receiver [5].

7   Conclusion

In this article, we showed how additional knowledge about particular instances of covert
channels can be exploited to improve the precision of the bandwidth analysis. We
demonstrated with two concrete examples that such improvements can have a rather
significant effect on the calculated capacity. In addition, we showed that and how even

incomplete knowledge about probability distributions can be exploited in the bandwidth analysis in a sound way.

The employed information-theoretic model is similar to the model used in [1]. Our new model constitutes a technical improvement over our earlier model, and allows to compute reliable upper bounds on the bandwidth of interrupt-related channels.

In parallel to our theoretical investigations, we experimented with practical exploitations of interrupt-related covert channels and NIC-channels in particular. This effort is on-going, but the results obtained so far already strongly confirm that interrupt-related covert channels pose a threat that should be taken serious. Using the exploit, the transmission of a 13-bit PIN (i.e. the order of magnitude used in authentication mechanisms for banking machines) takes approximately 30 seconds. In contrast to our theoretical analysis which results in upper bounds on the bandwidth, the practical evaluation allows us to obtain lower bounds on the bandwidth of interrupt-related covert channels.

References

1. Mantel, H., Sudbrock, H.: Comparing Countermeasures against Interrupt-Related Covert Channels in an Information-Theoretic Framework. In: Proc. of the IEEE Computer Security Foundations Symposium, pp. 326–340 (2007)
2. Lampson, B.W.: A Note on the Confinement Problem. Communications of the ACM 16(10), 613–615 (1973)
3. Gligor, V.: A Guide to Understanding Covert Channel Analysis of Trusted Systems. CSC-TG-030, Rainbow Series (Light Pink Book) (1993)
4. Shieh, S.P.: Estimating and Measuring Covert Channel Bandwidth in Multilevel Secure Operating Systems. Journal of Inform. Science & Engineering 15, 91–106 (1999)
5. Lowe, G.: Quantifying Information Flow. In: Proc. of the IEEE Computer Security Foundations Workshop, pp. 18–31 (2002)
6. Beauquier, D., Lanotte, R.: Hiding Information in Multi Level Security Systems. In: Dimitrakos, T., Martinelli, F., Ryan, P.Y.A., Schneider, S. (eds.) FAST 2006. LNCS, vol. 4691, pp. 250–269. Springer, Heidelberg (2007)
7. Son, J., Alves-Foss, J.: Covert Timing Channel Analysis of Rate Monotonic Real-Time Scheduling Algorithm in MLS Systems. In: Proc. of the IEEE Information Assurance Workshop, pp. 361–368 (2006)
8. Cover, T.M., Thomas, J.A.: Elements of Information Theory, 2nd edn. John Wiley & Sons, Inc., Chichester (2006)
9. Arimoto, S.: An Algorithm for Computing the Capacity of Arbitrary Discrete Memoryless Channels. IEEE Trans. on Information Theory 18(1), 14–20 (1972)
10. Blahut, R.: Computation of Channel Capacity and Rate-Distortion Functions. IEEE Trans. on Information Theory 18(4), 460–473 (1972)
11. Intel Corporation: Interrupt Moderation Using Intel Gigabit Ethernet Controllers, Application Note (AP-450), Revision 1.1 (2003)
12. Horst, R., Tuy, H.: Global Optimization. Deterministic Approaches. Springer, Heidelberg (1996)
13. Horst, R.: On the Global Minimization of Concave Functions. OR Spectrum 6(4), 195–205 (1984)
14. Benson, H.P.: Deterministic Algorithms for Constrained Concave Minimization: A Unified Critical Survey. Naval Research Logistics 43(6), 765–795 (1996)
15. Denning, D.E.: A Lattice Model of Secure Information Flow. Communications of the ACM 19(5), 236–243 (1976)

16. Denning, D.E., Denning, P.J.: Certification of Programs for Secure Information Flow. Communications of the ACM 20(7), 504–513 (1977)
17. Kemmerer, R.A.: Shared Resource Matrix Methodology: An Approach to Identifying Storage and Timing Channels. ACM Trans. on Comp. Sys. 1(3), 256–277 (1983)
18. Kemmerer, R.A.: A Practical Approach to Identifying Storage and Timing Channels: Twenty Years Later. In: Proc. of the Annual Computer Security Applications Conference, pp. 109–118 (2002)
19. Volpano, D., Smith, G., Irvine, C.: A Sound Type System for Secure Flow Analysis. Journal of Computer Security 4(3), 1–21 (1996)
20. Sabelfeld, A., Myers, A.C.: Language-based Information-Flow Security. IEEE Journal on Selected Areas in Communication 21(1), 5–19 (2003)
21. Hu, W.-M.: Reducing Timing Channels with Fuzzy Time. In: Proc. of the IEEE Symposium on Research in Security and Privacy, pp. 8–20 (1991)
22. Gray III, J.W.: On Introducing Noise into the Bus-Contention Channel. In: Proc. of the IEEE Symposium on Research in Security and Privacy, pp. 90–98 (1993)
23. Kang, M.H., Moskowitz, I.S.: A Pump for Rapid, Reliable, Secure Communication. In: Proc. of the ACM Conference on Computer and Communications Security, pp. 119–129 (1993)
24. Kang, M.H., Moskowitz, I.S., Chincheck, S.: The Pump: A Decade of Covert Fun. In: Proc. of the Annual Computer Security Applications Conference, pp. 352–360 (2005)
25. Millen, J.K.: Covert Channel Capacity. In: Proc. of the IEEE Symposium on Security and Privacy, pp. 60–66 (1987)
26. Moskowitz, I.S.: Quotient States and Probabilistic Channels. In: Proc. of the IEEE Computer Security Foundations Workshop, pp. 74–83 (1990)
27. Millen, J.K.: Finite-State Noiseless Covert Channels. In: Proc. of the IEEE Computer Security Foundations Workshop, pp. 81–86 (1989)
28. Moskowitz, I.S.: Variable Noise Effects Upon a Simple Timing Channel. In: Proc. of the IEEE Symposium on Security and Privacy, pp. 362–372 (1991)
29. Moskowitz, I.S., Miller, A.R.: Simple Timing Channels. In: Proc. of the IEEE Symposium on Research in Security and Privacy, pp. 56–64 (1994)
30. Moskowitz, I.S., Greenwald, S.J., Kang, M.H.: An Analysis of the Timed Z-channel. In: Proc. of the IEEE Symposium on Security and Privacy, pp. 2–11 (1996)
31. Martin, K., Moskowitz, I.S.: Noisy Timing Channels with Binary Inputs and Outputs. In: Camenisch, J.L., Collberg, C.S., Johnson, N.F., Sallee, P. (eds.) IH 2006. LNCS, vol. 4437, pp. 124–144. Springer, Heidelberg (2007)
32. Moskowitz, I.S., Miller, A.R.: The Channel Capacity of a Certain Noisy Timing Channel. IEEE Trans. on Information Theory 38(4), 1339–1344 (1992)
33. Gray III, J.W.: On Analyzing the Bus-Contention Channel under Fuzzy Time. In: Proc. of the IEEE Computer Security Foundations Workshop, pp. 3–9 (1993)
34. Kang, M.H., Moskowitz, I.S., Lee, D.C.: A Network Pump. IEEE Trans. on Software Engineering 22(5), 329–338 (1996)
35. Giles, J., Hajek, B.: An Information-theoretic and Game-theoretic Study of Timing Channels. IEEE Trans. on Information Theory 48(9), 2455–2477 (2002)
36. Lanotte, R., Maggiolo-Schettini, A., Tini, S., Troina, A., Tronci, E.: Automatic Analysis of the NRL Pump. Electr. Notes Theor. Comput. Sci. 99, 245–266 (2004)
37. Aldini, A., Bernardo, M.: An Integrated View of Security Analysis and Performance Evaluation: Trading QoS with Covert Channel Bandwidth. In: Heisel, M., Liggesmeyer, P., Wittmann, S. (eds.) SAFECOMP 2004. LNCS, vol. 3219, pp. 283–296. Springer, Heidelberg (2004)
38. Tsai, C.R., Gligor, V.D.: A Bandwidth Computation Model for Covert Storage Channels and its Applications. In: Proc. of the IEEE Symposium on Security and Privacy, pp. 108–121 (1988)

Causality and Accountability

Dominic Duggan and Ye Wu

Department of Computer Science, Stevens Institute of Technology
Hoboken, New Jersey 07030, USA
Fax: +1 (201) 216-8249
{dduggan,ywu1}@cs.stevens.edu

Abstract. Noninterference is a standard correctness condition for information flow control, but achieving it may sometimes be too expensive to be practical, particularly for distributed applications. A framework is introduced for specifying what forms of information flow control should be secured. Accountable noninterference requires that there be no information leaks via accountable information flows. An example application is in delineating sequential and distributed information flows, allowing different enforcement mechanisms for each. As such, the framework allows the specification of mechanism, dual to policy, in information flow control.

1 Introduction

Decentralized information flow control is emerging as an organizing principle for decentralized secure software systems, and recent work is extending this to secure distributed systems [35]. Following Goguen and Meseguer [15], information flow control policies are formulated in terms of *noninterference*:

> Given two groups of users G and G', we say G does not interfere with G' if for any sequence of commands w, what users in G' can observe after executing w is the same as what users in G can observe after executing $PG(w)$, which is w with command initiated by users in G removed.

Noninterference is a strong condition, that implicitly prevents covert channels based on indirect control effects. Language-based security [30] has focused to a large extent on information flow control, applying techniques from programming languages to perform static analysis of software to verify information flow control properties such as noninterference. In distributed systems, noninterference is often characterized in terms of process equivalence.

In reality noninterference may too strong a condition for many applications. For example, in many situations the information flow control policy changes over time. There may also be circumstances under which information is allowed to be declassified. There are also practical barriers to the assurance of noninterference. In language-based security, noninterference focuses on preventing covert channels via control flow (assignment to a low variable based on examining the content of a high variable, for example). This ignores covert channels that are available through the runtime (e.g. the garbage collector or thread timing), disk I/O, aspects of the user interface etc. Noninterference for

P. Degano, J. Guttman, and F. Martinelli (Eds.): FAST 2008, LNCS 5491, pp. 82–96, 2009.

distributed processes is particularly difficult, since it must prevent traffic analysis by low-level attackers, a very strong condition for internet communications. Noninterference results for system designs are therefore often cited as "baseline" results, making strong assumptions (e.g. sequentiality) about the computing environment, with no connection made to the actual practical environments in which one would try to apply such systems.

We propose an alternative approach to considering the correctness of information flow control. In this approach, we focus on *causality* rather than process equivalence. Causality can be expressed in many ways. For example, Lamport's happened-before relation $\leadsto$ [24] assumes sequential processes running concurrently, and with events e and messages m uniquely identified:

1. If event e_2 happens after event e_1 at process P, then $e_1 \leadsto e_2$.
2. If event e_1 is the sending of message m and e_2 is the receipt of m, then $e_1 \leadsto e_2$.
3. If $e_1 \leadsto e_2$ and $e_2 \leadsto e_3$, then $e_1 \leadsto e_3$.

Stated in terms of causality, noninterference says that a low event cannot depend causally on a high event: $e_1 \not\leadsto e_2$ if e_1 is high and e_2 is low.

In this article, we propose a new framework in which different notions of causality can be used to relax the basic notion of noninterference, reflecting the characteristics of the operating environment and what is reasonably achievable. This not only brings the formal model closer to the operating environment, it also allows us to consider new mechanisms for information control and release based on the explication of these characteristics. By relaxing the stringency of the information flow control requirements, while not relaxing the actual security policy, this framework introduces reasoning about mechanism as well as policy in specifying desired levels of confidentiality.

Our approach considers two relations: a baseline causal relation, and a relaxed subset of causality that we term *accountability*. The accountability relation identifies the subset of the causal relationship between events for which confidentiality should be enforced. *Accountable noninterference* then specifies that there should be no *accountable* causal relation from high events to low events.

We define these concepts in the next section. We give several examples of these notions, in the context of distributed message-passing systems, in Sect. 3. We identify a "perfect" system that identifies causality and accountability, a much more limited system that is more clearly implementable, based on focusing on sequential causality, and a hybrid system that combines both notions of distributed and sequential causality. We give a specification of this hybrid system in Sect. 4. Sect. 5 considers related work, while Sect. 6 provides our conclusions.

2   Accountability and Accountable Noninterference

In this section, we define the notions of accountability and accountable noninterference, and provide examples in the rest of the article. We are principally interested in causal relationships between individual, observable events in distributed systems. This is in a framework where observable events within a subsystem may be masked from outside observation in the environment surrounding that subsystem (e.g. a firewall that blocks outside messages to or from a particular port or machine). The topology of the system may be dynamic [26]. We assume that there is an operational description of a system using a labeled transition system, with transitions of the form

$$K_1 \xrightarrow[\Delta]{a} K_2$$

where each transition between processes K_1 and K_2 is labelled by the observable action a that is offered to the environment, and a transition context Δ for that action being offered. Typically this context will have some way of uniquely identifying the event corresponding to the observable action. That event will typically have a security level, and be causally dependent on other events, as determined by the context Δ. A traditional labeled transition system for concurrent and distributed systems focuses only on the observable action.

The labeled transition system will also have internal events, with such internal transitions denoted by $K_1 \longrightarrow K_2$. We do not try to track causality for internal events directly, rather we focus on causal relationships between the observable events. We denote zero or more internal transitions by $K_1 \Longrightarrow K_2$. Then $K_1 \overset{a}{\underset{\Delta}{\Longrightarrow}} K_2$ denotes $K_1 \Longrightarrow K_1' \xrightarrow[\Delta]{a} K_2' \Longrightarrow K_2$ for some K_1' and K_2', i.e., zero or more internal transitions before and after an observable event.

Causality and accountability are specified as two dependency relations between events, identified by transition contexts Δ, where the semantics of the system is provided in the manner described above:

1. *Causality* $\Delta_1 \rightsquigarrow \Delta_2$ has the following property: if $K_1 \overset{a_1}{\underset{\Delta_1}{\Longrightarrow}} K_2$ and $K_2 \overset{a_2}{\underset{\Delta_2}{\Longrightarrow}} K_3$, and $\Delta_1 \not\rightsquigarrow \Delta_2$, then there is some K_2' such that $K_1 \overset{a_2}{\underset{\Delta_2}{\Longrightarrow}} K_2'$ and $K_2' \overset{a_1}{\underset{\Delta_1}{\Longrightarrow}} K_3$. In other words, we can permute the observation or execution of concurrent events.
2. *Accountability* $\Delta_1 \dashrightarrow \Delta_2$ is a subset of the causality relation: $\dashrightarrow \subseteq \rightsquigarrow$. It is the information flow for which a system developer is responsible, in which some information flows are ignored for the purposes of correctness.

Accountable noninterference requires that there be no accountable information flow from high level processes to low level processes. This means that $\Delta_1 \not\dashrightarrow \Delta_2$ for any high level event Δ_1 and low level event Δ_2.

We consider some examples of these definitions in the next section.

3   Examples

We now consider some examples of accountability and accountable noninterference. We work in the context of process calculi and labeled transition systems [19,25], in particular using Milner's CCS and pi-calculus [25,26]. CCS and the pi-calculus are formalisms for reasoning about distributed message-passing systems. For example, the syntax of CCS is given by:

$$P, Q ::= \alpha.P \mid (P \mid Q) \mid (P + Q) \mid (va)P \mid 0$$

where $\alpha.P$ denotes the process that offers action α and then becomes process P, $(P \mid Q)$ denotes parallel composition, $(P + Q)$ denotes a nondeterministic selection between behaviors P and Q, $(va)P$ denotes the local hiding of the channel name a within the subsystem P, and 0 denotes the empty process. Such systems are described operationally using labeled transitions of the form $P \xrightarrow{\alpha} Q$ for processes P and Q and observable action α. The latter may be a message send event on a channel ($\bar{a}$) or a message receive event (a), where a is the name of a communication channel. Such a transition denotes the transition from process P to process Q on the action (message send or receive event) α. Process equivalence is defined in terms of observable behavior (behaviors offered to the observing environment), for example, testing or bisimulation equivalence.

We can then provide several instantiations of the above scheme.

3.1 Global Causality

Our first system identifies causality and accountability: $\rightsquigarrow = \dashrightarrow$. Accountable noninterference requires that no low-level event be causally dependent on a high-level event. Therefore the occurrence of any low-level event can be permuted with the occurence of a high-level event, so that all low-level events precede high-level events. Therefore, the traces that result from removing high-level events are causally consistent: they are low-level events only, with no high-level events preceding them. Thus we obtain the original characterization of noninterference due to Goguen and Meseguer [15].

Such formalisms assume an interleaving semantics for concurrency: one reasons about the behavior of such systems in terms of the interleaving of their observable actions. There are several ways to incorporate causality into such a model. One prominent approach [22,3,11] is to label each observed action with a *cause*, represented by a unique event identifier k, and a *causal history* or set of causees A, in the operational semantics: $P \xrightarrow[A,k]{\alpha} Q$. The syntax of processes is extended to record causes:

$$P, Q ::= \dots \quad \mid \quad A :: P \quad \mid \quad k :: P$$

These are intended as placeholders for recording causation. The infix operator :: is essentially a *causal dependence* operator. The expression $A :: P$ denotes a process P with a causal history (set of causes) A that precedes execution of that process. This causal history may be extended by the context within which P executes. The expression $k :: P$ denotes a process P with a causal dependency on an event uniquely identified by the event identifier k. Event identifiers are generated by the atomic operations of the language, *viz*, message sending and receipt. For example, the operational semantics includes the transition $a.P \xrightarrow[\{\},k]{a} P$ that represents the communication (message receipt) on the channel a, with this particular communication event uniquely identified by the cause k. The dependence of further execution of the continuation process P on this cause is represented by the configuration $k :: P$.

A process $a.P$ transitions by offering the action a to the observer environment and transitioning to $k :: P$, for some new unique event identifier k. Any actions within P have their causal dependence on this occurrence of the a action recorded by the prefix containing k. A rule for synchronization between processes, when a message is sent and received, entails the swapping of the causally preceding events for the message send and receive:

$$\frac{P_1 \xrightarrow[A_1,k_1]{a} P_1' \quad P_2 \xrightarrow[A_2,k_2]{\bar{a}} P_2'}{(P_1 \mid P_2) \longrightarrow (\{A_2/k_1\}P_1' \mid \{A_1/k_2\}P_2')}$$

Here the expression $\{A/k\}P$ denotes the substitution of the event identifier k by the causal history A in the process P. We omit the details for lack of space. For example, in the following starting configuration, the message receive event has causal predecessors k_1 and k_2, and the message send event has causal predecessor k_3. These causal predecessors are exchanged when the processes synchronize:

$$(\{k_1,k_2\} :: a.P_1 \xrightarrow[\{k_1,k_2\},k]{a} \{k_1,k_2\} :: k :: P_1$$

$$\{k_3\} :: \bar{a}.P_2 \xrightarrow[\{k_3\},k']{\bar{a}} \{k_3\} :: k' :: P_2$$

$$\overline{(\{k_1,k_2\} :: a.P_1 \mid \{k_3\} :: \bar{a}.P_2) \longrightarrow (\{k_1,k_2,k_3\} :: P_1 \mid \{k_1,k_2,k_3\} :: P_2)}$$

where we have merged the sets of causal predecessors in the continuations of the two synchronizing threads. For example, the left continuation is actually $\{k_1,k)2\} :: \{k_3\} :: P_1$ while the right continuation is actually $\{k_3\} :: \{k_1,k_2\} :: P_2$. As a result of swapping causal histories, the two continuation processes share the same causal histories.

3.2 Local Causality

Our second system reflects a philosophical point of view, that focuses on sequential information flow control. Our motivation for considering control-flow-based information flow control is the following. Generally we are interested in lightweight data flow control in programs, statically (at compile time) making sure that secret data does not leak by an assignment from a high-security variable to a low-security variable. However focusing solely on data flow control is severely limited, for the following reason: it misses flows of data that go through transformations on the data, and in particular in data marshalling. For example, if a program variable has type int^H where the annotation H on the type restricts this variable to be high security, passing it through the Java serializer will produce a datum of type $\text{byte}[]$, an array of bytes without the security annotation on its type. The following piece of code demonstrates how a marshaller could bypass restrictions based on data flow control:

```
booleanH x; fileL f;
if (x) write(f,"true"); else write(f,"false");
```

We wish to strengthen the security guarantees by propagating data flow controls through sequential transformations of the data such as marshalling *but no further*.

Simply preventing the assignment of a high variable to a low variable is insufficient. Our second system chooses this as a reasonable juncture at which to draw the line for information flow control ("Security is always a question of economics," [6]). We track dependencies through sequential program execution, and in particular through transformations on the data being protected. However we do not attempt to track dependencies on data that is transmitted over the network, because we cannot prevent attacks such as traffic analysis and denial of service. In this case, we have $\dashrightarrow \subseteq \rightsquigarrow$, with at least the possibility that the inclusion is strict. The latter will be true if there are communication events of the sort that we do not attempt to track through the semantics. This prevents an information leak such as in the example above, but does not prevent the following information leak:

```
boolean^H x; file^L f; channel a, b;
( if (x) send(a); else send (b);
  | select a ⇒ write(f,"true"); [] b ⇒ write(f,"false"); )
```

where | denotes parallel composition, and the select statement performs nondeterministic selection between the two input channels a and b. In this example, a "high" process examines a high variable x and then sends empty messages on either communication channel a or b, depending on the value of the high variable. A low process then multiplexes between these two channels, and writes either "true" or "false" to a low security file depending on which channel it receives communication on. This example is exactly analogous to the example with the conditional above, where information leaks indirectly due to a control flow dependency; but in this case, the control flow is based on external communication. In the scenario where we only track local causality for accountability purposes, the dependency of the file write operations on the examination of the value of x is not tracked, and therefore accountable noninterference still holds. This is a form of declassification, but there is no explicit decision to release information at this point. Rather, the decision has been made, for pragmatic reasons, that we will allow information to leak in certain situations where it is infeasible or impossible to protect the data.

Describing this system is relatively straightforward. External transitions have the form $P_1 \xrightarrow[k]{a} P_2$, and we extend the syntax of processes with causal prefixes:

$$P ::= \ldots \quad | \quad k :: P$$

However synchronization no longer swaps causal sets for the synchronizing threads. Instead the semantics focuses solely on building up the sequential causal prefix for each process, ignoring dependencies from other processes.

3.3   Combining Local and Global Communication

Our third system combines the first two systems. In this system, we assume that there are parts of the communication infrastructure that can be tightly controlled (thread scheduler in a user-space thread package, kernel in an operating system, router in an enterprise network), so that it is possible to provide strong guarantees of information flow control, as in the first system. However this system also communicates with processes outside the enterprise network, on the internet, where it is infeasible to expect this tight level of control. The syntax of processes now includes both local and global causes, as well as some notion of locality to distinguish between local and global communication:

$$P ::= \ldots \quad | \quad A :: P \quad | \quad k :: P \quad | \quad \ell[P]$$

where $\ell[P]$ denotes a process P executing at a location ℓ. This system combines aspects of both of the preceding systems. Local sequential dependencies are the only basis for accountability. On the other hand, global dependencies, which include both sequential dependencies and those dependencies introduced by synchronization), are the basis for causality.

In this scenario, it may also be useful to allow data to be "released" for communication outside the trusted enterprise network. This release now becomes a matter of policy, while the leak of information above in the untrusted space is a matter of mechanism (in the sense that release happens because of the weakness of the enforcement mechanisms).

4   Formal Semantics

In this section we formalize the model of information flow control and accountability that was introduced at the conclusion of the previous section. This system includes both public and internal communications. The basic language is the polyadic pi-calculus, an extension of CCS that allows message payloads. The only kind of data in this system are message channels themselves, or rather the names of message channels. Such channel names may be sent as message payloads, for example, a client sending a server a private reply channel (a proxy object for accepting the reply, in the RMI setting). We choose a variant of this system where the language is asynchronous [31], to allow interesting information flows from "low" to "high." We assume we have the following syntactic categories:

$$
\begin{array}{llll}
\text{Channel Names} & a,b,c & \text{Causes} & k \\
\text{Channel Variables} & x,y,z & \text{Cause Sets} & A,B,C
\end{array}
$$

Then define the syntax of the language as follows:

$$
\begin{aligned}
v \in \text{Value} &::= a \mid x \\
P \in \text{Process} &::= \mathbf{0} \mid \overline{v_0}\langle \vec{v} \rangle \mid a(\vec{x}).P \mid \text{if } v_1 = v_2 \text{ then } P_1 \text{ else } P_2 \mid \\
& \quad (P_1 \mid P_2) \mid (va:LT)P \mid\ !P \\
K \in \text{Causal Net} &::= P \mid k::K \mid (A,B)::K \mid \ell[K] \mid (K_1 \mid K_2) \mid (va:LT)K
\end{aligned}
$$

A process consists (as with CCS) of the empty process, the message sending and message receiving operations, parallel composition and generation of a new channel name. In addition, the process language contains an operation for checking two channel names for equality. A couple of other differences from CCS are that (a) messages contain payloads (tuples of channel names) and (b) message sending is asynchronous. The latter allow more interesting information flows than the sychronous version of the system, allowing a low level process to send a message to a high level process without introducing a causal dependency from high back to low (due to the implicit acknowledgement in synchronous communication).

The syntax of causal nets provides the context in which processes evolve and exchange messages. Processes execute at a location $\ell[K]$; a local communication is between two processes at the same location ℓ, all other communications are global. There are also causal prefixes [22,3] $k::K$ and $(A,B)::K$. The former of these are generated as processes offer communication to the environment, recording the causal context of that observable action. The latter of these are introduced during synchronization, when a process that receives a message has its local cause replaced by the global causes for the message that it has just received. To understand why local causes are replaced rather than extended, consider the example at the end of Sect. 3.1. Fundamentally causes, or event identifiers, only exist as placeholders for establishing dependencies between subsystems of an overall system, and are only relevant within the context of that system. Outside of that system, external observers only see the behavior of the system as a whole, and so this semantics does not attempt to propagate this causal information beyond the system boundaries once it is clear what the complete causal history of an event is.

$$\overline{a}\langle \overrightarrow{b} \rangle \xrightarrow[\{\},\{\},\{\},k]{\overline{a}\langle \overrightarrow{b} \rangle} \mathbf{0} \qquad \text{(RED SEND)}$$

$$a(\overrightarrow{x}).P \xrightarrow[\{\},\{\},\{\},k]{a(\overrightarrow{b})} k :: \{\overrightarrow{b}/\overrightarrow{x}\}P \qquad \text{(RED RECV)}$$

$$\frac{P\,|\,!P \xrightarrow[A,B,C,k]{\alpha} K}{!P \xrightarrow[A,B,C,k]{\alpha} K} \qquad \text{(RED REPL)}$$

$$\frac{K \xrightarrow[A,B,C,k]{\alpha} K'}{k_0 :: K \xrightarrow[A\cup\{k_0\},B\cup\{k_0\},C\cup\{k_0\},k]{\alpha} k_0 :: K'} \qquad \text{(RED LOC CAUSE)}$$

$$\frac{K \xrightarrow[A,B,C,k]{\alpha} K'}{(A_0,B_0) :: K \xrightarrow[A\cup A_0,B\cup B_0,C,k]{\alpha} (A_0,B_0) :: K'} \qquad \text{(RED GLOB CAUSE)}$$

$$\frac{K \xrightarrow[A,B,C,k]{\alpha} K' \quad c_0 \notin names(\alpha)}{(vc_0 : LT)K \xrightarrow[A,B,C,k]{\alpha} (vc_0 : LT)K'} \qquad \text{(RED NEW)}$$

$$\frac{K \xrightarrow[A,B,C,k]{(v\overrightarrow{c}:\overrightarrow{LT})a(\overrightarrow{b})} K' \quad c_0 \neq a, c_0 \in \{\overrightarrow{b}\} - \{\overrightarrow{c}\}}{(vc_0 : LT)K \xrightarrow[A,B,C,k]{(v\overrightarrow{c},c_0:\overrightarrow{LT})a(\overrightarrow{b})} K'} \qquad \text{(RED NEW EXT)}$$

$$\frac{K_1 \xrightarrow[A,B,C,k]{\alpha} K_1' \quad boundNames(\alpha) \cap freeNames(K_2) - \{\}}{(K_1 \mid K_2) \xrightarrow[A,B,C,k]{\alpha} (K_1' \mid K_2)} \qquad \text{(RED PAR)}$$

$$\frac{K_1 \equiv K_1' \quad K_1' \xrightarrow[A,B,C,k]{\alpha} K_2' \quad K_2' \equiv K_2}{K_1 \xrightarrow[A,B,C,k]{\alpha} K_2} \qquad \text{(RED STRUCT)}$$

Fig. 1. Dynamic Semantics: External

$$K_1 \xrightarrow[A_1,B_1,C_1,k_1]{(v\vec{c}:\vec{LT})\overline{a}\langle \vec{b}\rangle} K_1' \quad K_2 \xrightarrow[A_2,B_2,C_2,k_2]{a(\vec{b})} K_2' \quad \{\vec{c}\}\cap \mathit{freeNames}(K_2) = \{\}$$
$$\overline{(\ell[K_1] \mid \ell[K_2]) \longrightarrow (v\vec{c}:\vec{LT})(\ell[K_1'] \mid \ell\{(A_1,B_1)/k_2\}K_2')} \qquad \text{(RED LOC SYNC)}$$

$$K_1 \xrightarrow[A_1,B_1,C_1,k_1]{(v\vec{c}:\vec{LT})\overline{a}\langle \vec{b}\rangle} K_1' \quad K_2 \xrightarrow[A_2,B_2,C_2,k_2]{a(\vec{b})} K_2' \quad \ell_1 \neq \ell_2 \quad \{\vec{c}\}\cap \mathit{freeNames}(K_2) = \{\}$$
$$\overline{(\ell_1[K_1] \mid \ell_2[K_2]) \longrightarrow (v\vec{c}:\vec{LT})(\ell_1[K_1'] \mid \ell_2[\{(A_1,\{\})/k_2\}K_2'])} \qquad \text{(RED GLOB SYNC)}$$

$$(\text{if } a = a \text{ then } P_1 \text{ else } P_2) \longrightarrow P_1 \qquad \text{(RED INT IFTRUE)}$$

$$\frac{a \neq b}{(\text{if } a = b \text{ then } P_1 \text{ else } P_2) \longrightarrow P_1} \qquad \text{(RED INT IFFALSE)}$$

$$\frac{P \mid !P \longrightarrow K}{!P \longrightarrow K} \qquad \text{(RED INT REPL)}$$

$$\mathbf{C}[\,] ::= [\,] \mid k_0 :: \mathbf{C}[\,] \mid (A_0,B_0) :: \mathbf{C}[\,] \mid \ell[\mathbf{C}[\,]] \mid (vc : LT)\mathbf{C}[\,] \mid (\mathbf{C}[\,] \mid K)$$
$$\frac{K \longrightarrow K'}{\mathbf{C}[K] \longrightarrow \mathbf{C}[K']}$$
$$\qquad \text{(RED INT CONG)}$$

$$\frac{K_1 \equiv K_1' \quad K_1' \longrightarrow K_2' \quad K_2' \equiv K_2}{K_1 \longrightarrow K_2} \qquad \text{(RED INT STRUCT)}$$

Fig. 2. Dynamic Semantics: Internal

Whereas in the system described in the previous section, these global causes are represented by a single set, in this system the local cause is replaced by a pair of cause sets (A,B). The former set A tracks all causal dependencies for the message that was received, and is the basis for defining the causality relation $\rightsquigarrow$. On the other hand, the latter set B is the basis for defining the accountability relation $--\rightarrow$ when accountability propagates across local communication but not across global communication.

In general the externally observable transitions of the system have the form

$$K \xrightarrow[A,B,C,k]{\alpha} K'$$

where α carries information about the action (message send or receive), A tracks global dependencies in order to propagate accountability through all communications, B tracks local dependencies in order to only propagate accountability through local communications, and C tracks sequential dependencies in a thread of execution. k is the event identifier for the observable action α.

For the labelled transition system for the semantics, define an action labelling an observable transition by:

$$\alpha \in \text{Action} ::= (v\vec{c} : \vec{LT})\overline{a}\langle \vec{b}\rangle \mid a(\vec{b})$$

The first of these corresponds to a message that has been sent (offered to the environment). The message has payload $\overrightarrow{b}$ and exports locally bound channel names $\overrightarrow{c}$ to the environment where it is received. The second of these corresponds to a message that has been received, with expected payload $\overrightarrow{b}$, using an "early" style of semantics for synchronization.

We assume some defined metafunctions:

$names(\alpha)$	Set of names (free and bound) in an action
$boundNames(\alpha), boundNames(K)$	Set of names bound in an action or process
$freeNames(\alpha), freeNames(K)$	Set of names free in an action or process
$\{a/x\}P$	Substitution of a variable with a name

The latter of these functions are defined by cases on the structure of processes, in the usual manner. We omit the details for lack of space. The rules for externally observable transitions are provided in Fig. 1. The (RED SEND) rule consumes a message in transit, offering the contents of that message to the environment; this rule is a manifestation of the asynchronous message-passing semantics that we assume for the system. The (RED RECV) rule instantiates the continuation P with an expected message payload of $\overrightarrow{b}$. This message receive should eventually synchronize with a message send with the same payload, at which time the sequential cause k will be instantiated with the global and local causes for the sent message.

The (RED LOC CAUSE) and (RED GLOB CAUSE) rules build up the components of the transition context as a labelled transition propagates through causal annotations. The first of these adds a sequential cause to all of the causal sets in the transition context, since such a cause is included in all causal histories of the offered behavior. The latter of these, the (RED GLOB CAUSE) rule, adds causes from global and local communication to the cause sets A and B, respectively. No causes are added to C by this rule because it only records local dependencies. The dependencies recorded in A and B correspond to those arising from receiving messages from other processes. The remaining rules in Fig. 1 are standard for propagating messages sent through a context that includes other processes and local channel name bindings.

Fig. 2 provides the internal transitions rules, and of these the most important are the first two, for synchronization. Both rules correspond to a message being received. Since we assume asynchronous communication, there is no implicit acknowledgement to impose a causal dependency on the message sender. The first rule corresponds to a local communication, where both sender and receiver are at location ℓ. The receiver's continuation has its sequential cause k_2 instantiated with the pair of (global, local) cause sets (A_1, B_1) from the sender. Since in this asynchronous system there is no continuation for the sender, its corresponding cause k_1 is ignored.

The second rule, Rule (RED GLOB SYNC), corresponds to synchronization between two processes at different locations ℓ_1 and ℓ_2. In this case, recording the cause set for the sender, at the receiver, would introduce an undesired causal dependency from the receiver to a sender at another network. Since the motivation for this system is to only track causal dependencies between local communications, the local cause set is instantiated as $\{\}$. On the other hand, the global cause set is properly instantiated with A_1. This will be used later to define the causality relation, that tracks all cause relations.

The rules in Fig. 2 rely on structural equivalence rules to push location identifiers down past name binding and parallel composition. We omit the straightforward details for lack of space.

It remains to relate this to our earlier definitions of accountability. At a first approximation, we can define:

$$\Delta = (A, B, C, k) \text{ for a transition } K \xrightarrow[A,B,C,k]{\alpha} K'$$

$$(A, B, C, k) \dashrightarrow_1 (A', B', C', k') \iff k \in A'$$
$$(A, B, C, k) \dashrightarrow_2 (A', B', C', k') \iff k \in C'$$
$$(A, B, C, k) \dashrightarrow_3 (A', B', C', k') \iff k \in B'$$

where these accountability relations correspond to the three examples in the previous section.

However these definitions only record subject dependencies, and not the object dependencies arising from the use of channels in one transition that are generated in another transition. Consider for example $(va : LT)(a().0 \mid \overline{b}\langle a \rangle)$, where any transition on a requires the transition on $\overline{b}$ first. Define:

$$exported(\alpha) = \begin{cases} \{\overrightarrow{b}\} \text{ if } \alpha = (v\overrightarrow{c} : \overrightarrow{LT})\overline{a}\langle \overrightarrow{b} \rangle \\ \{\overrightarrow{b}\} \text{ if } \alpha = a(\overrightarrow{b}) \end{cases}$$

Then for causality we must define:

$$\Delta = ((A, B, C, k), \alpha) \text{ for a transition } K \xrightarrow[A,B,C,k]{\alpha} K'$$
$$((A, B, C, k), \alpha) \rightsquigarrow ((A', B', C', k'), \alpha')$$
$$\iff k \in A' \text{ or } exported(\alpha) \cap freeNames(\alpha') \neq \{\}$$

reflecting that the event labelled by k' used a free name that was generated by the event labelled by k. This modification must be included into the definition of $\dashrightarrow_1$, which is equated with causality. It should be omitted from $\dashrightarrow_2$, which focuses only on sequential subject dependencies. There are some design choices in incorporating object dependencies into the definition of $\dashrightarrow_3$. The most reasonable alternative is to only consider object dependencies between local communications, but recording this requires adding a bit more machinery (recording the location where a communication happened in the labelled transition system). We omit the straightforward details for now, and assume that object dependencies are omitted from the definition of $\dashrightarrow_3$.

Proposition 1. *The relation $\rightsquigarrow$ defined above satisfies the definition of a causality relation: if $K_1 \xrightarrow[\Delta_1]{a_1} K_2$ and $K_2 \xrightarrow[\Delta_2]{a_2} K_3$, and $\Delta_1 \not\rightsquigarrow \Delta_2$, then there is some K_2' such that $K_1 \xrightarrow[\Delta_2]{a_2} K_2'$ and $K_2' \xrightarrow[\Delta_1]{a_1} K_3$.*

5   Related Work

Askarov and Sabelfeld [2] have proposed "gradual release" as an alternative to noninterference in information flow control systems with declassification. According to this policy, a computation is regarded as a sequential trace with designated declassification events, and the system is required to assure noninterference between high and low events between two consecutive declassification events: Gradual release assumes sequential execution, and in a concurrent framework some notion of causality is essential to properly relate high and low

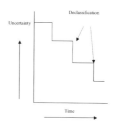

events and declassification events. For example, if h is high, l is low and d is a declassification, then $h.d.l$ would be a safe program but $(h.l \mid d)$ would not, even though both may produce the trace $(h.d.l)$, an undiscovered information leak.

Focardi and Gorrieri [12,13] introduced nondeterministic noninterference (NNI) and variants (SNNI, BNNI, etc) as a generalization of noninterference for concurrent and therefore nondeterministically interacting processes. They also introduce the notion of BNDC equivalence: a process P is BNDC if what a low level user sees of the system is not modified by composing that system with any high level process.

Busi and Gorrieri [5] consider noninterference for Petri net semantics, a popular operational model for true concurrency semantics. They show that the notion of BNDC for Petri nets is completely characterized by causality (high inputs enabling low outputs) and conflict (between high and low inputs for a transition). Busi and Gorrieri demonstrate that not all causalities and conflicts between high and low give rise to interference (for example, where a transition with high input is already enabled by the initial marking). These examples are related to work in interleaving models where some synchronization (for mutual exclusion) is allowed between high and low processes that access shared variables [14,23].

Crafa and Rossi [9], building on the BNDC notion of correctness, investigate the notion of "controlled information release" in a typed π-calculus extended with an explicit declassification expression. They allow a low action succeeding a high action, provided there is an intervening declassification operation. The declassification operation is only available to "high" (trusted) processes, and "low" processes are not able to view the declassification itself. This may require the addition of nondeterminism in some cases to mask the fact of declassification. Sewell and Vitek introduce the box-π process calculus to express wrappers encapsulating trusted/untrusted components intended for security policies enforcement [32]. They present a causal type system that statically captures legitimate flows between components, although it is not clear what the security guarantees of the system are.

Intransitive noninterference [28,33] has been applied to information flow control to require intervening processing before information is declassified. An example is adding a Password level to the standard lattice of Low and High, and allowing flows from High to Low through Password (requiring a dynamic password check), but not directly from High to Low. Intransitive noninterference should be viewed as orthogonal to accountable noninterference. Whereas the former involves the specification of a static declassification hierarchy, the latter is based on the operational behavior of processes.

Also declassification is not fundamentally part of accountable noninterference; security policies do not change while data is communicated over less secure channels.

A great deal of work on information flow control has been done in the concurrency community. Hennessy and Riely [17,18] develop a security π-calculus for which they study noninterference properties with respect to *may* and *must* testing. Honda and Yoshida [20] design a sophisticated system with linear and affine types for π-calculus to investigate noninterference expressed in terms of bisimulation. Boudol and Castellani [4] present a simple imperative language extended with parallelism to explore noninterference in a probabilistic setting. Ryan and Schneider characterize the absence of information flow in *CSP* [29] based on the notion of process equivalence. Bossi, Piazza and Rossi [1] generalize an unwinding framework for the definition of a security property that entails a noninterference principle described in a simple concurrent language. Similar approach related to this line of work can also be found in [8]. Most of these works are focused on strong noninterference properties usually characterized by a partial equivalence relation in a typed process language.

6   Conclusions

We have introduced a new approach to reasoning about correctness of information flow control, based on causal dependencies between events in a distributed systems, and a notion of *accountability* that provides a specification of allowable information flows based on abstracting from some of the flows that are tracked by causality. *Accountable noninterference* requires that developers not introduce causal flows that leak information, according to the notion of causality represented by accountability.

Some of the motivation provided for this approach is a recognition that noninterference is extremely difficult to achieve in many practical situations. The framework introduced here provides an opportunity to begin to reason about *mechanism* as well as *policy*. An example would be preventing the leaking of sensitive information outside a secure private network, even if the leaking is from one "high" principal to another. Under this scenario, data would be labelled both with a security level, say High and Low, reflecting a security policy, and also with a "sensitivity" level, say Local and Public, reflecting whether such information can be transmitted (presumably encrypted) over public networks, which exposes the possibility of hidden channels. In the latter case, the policy would not change, but the sensitivity level would reflect how securely the data should be handled. Many other possibilities suggest themselves. For example, if "high" information is to be allowed to flow over a public network, should it still be encrypted for security? There appear to be interesting avenues to pursue in this direction [28,7].

Although we have not considered explicit declassification, it appears straightforward to add declassification operations into this framework, generalizing the work of Askarov and Sabelfeld [2] from the sequential case. The example briefly described above suggests multiple forms of declassification: declassification of data from High to Low, and revelation of data from Local to Public.

Our framework is operational in nature, building on approaches developed for process calculi for reasoning about concurrent and distributed programming languages. For now, our notion of causality assumes single synchronization events, in a similar manner for example to notions of causality for developing and reasoning about distributed algorithms [24]. Other formulations, such as Communicating Sequential Processes (CSP), Petri nets and multiset rewriting logic [19,27,10], consider synchronizaion on several events, and it would be interesting to extend the framework based on these notions of multiway synchronization, particularly the latter two which are concerned with true concurrency semantics, with potential applications to workflow and multiparty interaction. It may also be interesting to consider a less operational and more logical framework for reasoning about causality, for example, using the notion of counterfactuals [21]. The theory of causality based on counterfactuals is focused on reasoning from causes to effects, motivated by applications in empirical reasoning, while our concern is rather for causal history and the absence of undesirable causal influences. Nevertheless causal explanations are an application of the theory of counterfactuals, so this is certainly an interesting avenue to explore further.

There is also a growing body of work in privacy, focusing not on preventing data from being released, but assuming the data will be released and focusing instead on tracking usage of the data and holding parties responsible [34]. There appear to be promising avenues to pursue here in delineating a connection between our notion of accountability and notions in the privacy field.

References

1. Piazza, C., Bossi, A., Rossi, S.: Compositional information flow security for concurrent programs. Journal of Computer Security 15(3), 373–416 (2007)
2. Askarov, A., Sabelfeld, A.: Gradual release: Unifying delassification, encryption and key release policies. In: IEEE Symposium on Security and Privacy (2007)
3. Boreale, M., Sangiorgi, D.: A fully abstract semantics for causality in the pi-calculus. Acta Informatica 35(5), 353–400 (1998)
4. Boudol, G., Castellani, I.: Noninterference for concurrent programs and thread systems. Theor. Comput. Sci. 281(1-2), 109–130 (2002)
5. Busi, N., Gorrieri, R.: Positive non-interference in elementary and trace nets. In: Cortadella, J., Reisig, W. (eds.) ICATPN 2004. LNCS, vol. 3099, pp. 1–16. Springer, Heidelberg (2004)
6. Cheswick, W., Bellovin, S., Rubin, A.: Firewalls and Internet Security. Addison-Wesley, Reading (2003)
7. Chothia, T., Duggan, D., Wu, Y.: Trusting the network. In: Foundations of Computer Security, Chicago, IL (2005)
8. Crafa, S., Rossi, S.: A theory of noninterference for the pi-calculus. In: De Nicola, R., Sangiorgi, D. (eds.) TGC 2005. LNCS, vol. 3705, pp. 2–18. Springer, Heidelberg (2005)
9. Crafa, S., Rossi, S.: Controlling information release in the pi-calculus. Information and Computation 285(8), 1235–1273 (2007)
10. de Oliveira Braga, C.: Rewriting Logic as a Semantic Framework for Modular Structural Operational Semantics. PhD thesis, Pontifícia Universidade Catolica do Rio de Janeiro (2001)
11. Degano, P., Priami, C.: Non-interleaving semantics for mobile processes. Theoretical Computer Science 216(1–2), 237–270 (1999)
12. Focardi, R., Gorrieri, R.: A taxonomy of security properties for process algebras. Journal of Computer Security 3(1), 5–34 (1995)
13. Focardi, R., Gorrieri, R.: Classification of security properties. In: Focardi, R., Gorrieri, R. (eds.) FOSAD 2000. LNCS, vol. 2171, pp. 331–396. Springer, Heidelberg (2001)

14. Focardi, R., Rossi, S.: Information flow security in dynamic contexts. In: Computer Security Foundations Workshop, pp. 307–319. IEEE Press, Los Alamitos (2002)
15. Goguen, J., Meseguer, J.: Security policies and security models. In: IEEE Symposium on Security and Privacy (1982)
16. Goguen, J., Meseguer, J.: Unwinding and inference control. In: IEEE Symposium on Security and Privacy (1984)
17. Hennessy, M.: The security picalculus and non-interference. Journal of Logic and Algebraic Programming 63, 3–34 (2004)
18. Hennessy, M., Riely, J.: Information flow vs resource access in the asynchronous pi-calculus. ACM Transactions on Programming Languages and Systems 24(5), 566–591 (2002)
19. Hoare, C.A.R.: Communicating Sequential Processes. Prentice-Hall, Englewood Cliffs (1985)
20. Honda, K., Yoshida, N.: A uniform type structure for secure information flow. In: POPL 2002: Proceedings of the 29th ACM SIGPLAN-SIGACT symposium on Principles of programming languages, pp. 81–92. ACM, New York (2002)
21. Pearl, J.: Causality: Models, Reasoning and Inference. Cambridge University Press, Cambridge (2000)
22. Kiehn, A.: Comparing locality and causality based equivalences. Acta Informatica (1994)
23. Kobayashi, N.: Type-based information flow analysis for the pi-calculus. Acta Informatica (2003)
24. Lamport, L.: Time, clocks and the ordering of events in a distributed system. Communications of the ACM 21(7), 558–565 (1978)
25. Milner, R.: Communication and Concurrency. Prentice-Hall, Englewood Cliffs (1989)
26. Milner, R.: The polyadic π-calculus: A tutorial. In: Bauer, F.L., Brauer, W., Schwichtenberg, H. (eds.) Logic and Algebra of Specification. Computer and Systems Sciences, vol. 94, pp. 203–246. Springer, Heidelberg (1993)
27. Reisig, W.: Petri Nets: An Introduction. EATCS Monographs on Theoretical Computer Science, vol. 4. Springer, Heidelberg (1988)
28. Rushby, J.M.: Noninterference, transitivity and channel-control security policies. Technical report, SRI (1992)
29. Ryan, P.Y.A., Schneider, S.A.: Process algebra and non-interference. In: CSFW 1999: Proceedings of the 12th IEEE workshop on Computer Security Foundations, Washington, DC, USA, p. 214. IEEE Computer Society, Los Alamitos (1999)
30. Sabelfeld, A., Myers, A.: Language-based information-flow security. IEEE Journal on Selected Areas in Communications (2002)
31. Sangiorgi, D.: Asynchronous process calculi: The first-order and higher-order paradigms. Theoretical Computer Science (253) (2001)
32. Sewell, P., Vitek, J.: Secure composition of untrusted code: Wrappers and causality types. In: CSFW 2000: Proceedings of the 13th IEEE workshop on Computer Security Foundations, Washington, DC, USA, p. 269. IEEE Computer Society, Los Alamitos (2000)
33. van der Meyden, R.: What, indeed, is intransitive noninterference? In: Biskup, J., López, J. (eds.) ESORICS 2007. LNCS, vol. 4734, pp. 235–250. Springer, Heidelberg (2007)
34. Weitzner, D., Abelson, H., Berners-Lee, T., Feigenbaum, J., Hendler, J., Sussman, G.J.: Information accountability. Communications of the ACM 51(6), 82–87 (2008)
35. Zeldovich, N., Boyd-Wickizer, S., Mazieres, D.: Securing distributed systems with information flow control. In: Network Systems Design and Implementation (2008)

Dynamics, Robustness and Fragility of Trust

Dusko Pavlovic*

Kestrel Institute and Oxford University
dusko@{kestrel.edu,comlab.ox.ac.uk}

Abstract. Trust is often conveyed through delegation, or through recommendation. This makes the trust authorities, who process and publish trust recommendations, into an attractive target for attacks and spoofing. In some recent empiric studies, this was shown to lead to a remarkable phenomenon of *adverse selection*: a greater percentage of unreliable or malicious web merchants were found among those with certain types of trust certificates, then among those without. While such findings can be attributed to a lack of diligence in trust authorities, or even to conflicts of interest, our analysis of trust dynamics suggests that public trust networks would probably remain vulnerable even if trust authorities were perfectly diligent. The reason is that the process of trust building, if trust is not breached too often, naturally leads to power-law distributions: the rich get richer, the trusted attract more trust. The evolutionary processes with such distributions, ubiquitous in nature, are known to be robust with respect to random failures, but vulnerable to adaptive attacks. We recommend some ways to decrease the vulnerability of trust building, and suggest some ideas for exploration.

1 Introduction

Background. In analyzing security protocols, we often reason under the assumption that a protocol participant, say Alice, is honest. This assumption simply means that Alice acts just as prescribed by the protocol, and does not engage in any other available runs. Such an assumption is sometimes justified, and sometimes not. When this assumption about Alice is made by another protocol participant, say Bob, then we say that Bob *trusts* Alice. The notion of protocol, according to which Alice is trusted to behave, is understood in the broadest sense of the word, as a general constraint on participants' behavior. E.g., a conversation protocol may consist of the requirement that the participants speak the truth, and Bob may trust Alice in that sense. While Alice's statements may be true or false, Bob's trust may go through many shades of gray, and through some nuances of other colors. Trust is dynamic, and can be many-valued. But note that it does not depend on any rules outside the specified protocol: e.g., a bank robbery protocol may involve a requirement that the robbers do not shoot at each other, so Bob may trust Alice in that sense. In any case, we write $B \xrightarrow{\Phi}_r A$, where Bob is the trustor, Alice is the trustee, Φ is the entrusted protocol (constraint, property), and r is a trust rating, which quantifies the level of trust.

---

* Supported by ONR and EPSRC.

P. Degano, J. Guttman, and F. Martinelli (Eds.): FAST 2008, LNCS 5491, pp. 97–113, 2009.
© Springer-Verlag Berlin Heidelberg 2009

In practice, this general notion of trust is usually restricted to some special cases:

– in web commerce, the seller and the buyer are trusted to act according to the established exchange protocols; more generally, trust plays an essential role in web services and service-oriented architectures at large;
– in access control, various types of principals (people, machines, services, channels) may entrust each other with various actions, or they may delegate authorities for such actions to each other [2,17];
– in public key cryptography, it is useful to view keys as principals[1], and to view the key hierarchies as trust relationships [3,19,24,30],
– various peer-to-peer and business-to-business transactions are based on trust, and the corresponding networks require various types of trust infrastructure [9,14,15,23].

When social relations need to be analyzed, the modeling techniques often proceed from two different points of view: local and global. E.g. in economics, when the questions of risk and utility are analyzed from a local point of view, they subsume under microeconomics; when they are analyzed from a global point of view, they fall under *macro*economics. Analyses of trust fall into two roughly analogous categories.

Local analyses of the trust relationship $B \xrightarrow[v]{\Phi} A$ are largely concerned with the logics of Φ, i.e. with the reasoning whereby the trustor B conveys or justifies entrusting the trustee A with Φ. As explained above, the trust statements internalize principals' beliefs and interactions, and vary through different forms of uncertainty, which lead to nonstandard logical features and formalisms. The examples of this kind of approach include [5,10,11,17,20,21]. E.g., when trust is analyzed in strand spaces [10], a trust relationship $B \xrightarrow[v]{\Phi} A$ is viewed on the level of a single send-receive interaction, where A is the sender and B the receiver. This interaction is annotated by a statement Φ, which the receiver B requires, and the sender A guarantees. By sending the message, A asserts Φ; when he receives the message, B assumes Φ. The statement that B trusts A thus means that B relies on A for Φ.

On the other hand, the *global* analyses of trust usually look at the *trust networks* spanned by the trust relationships $B \xrightarrow[v]{\Phi} A$ between the members $A, B \dots$ of some set of principals. While the local analyses focus on the logics of the entrusted properties Φ, the global analyses focus on the network structure and traffic dynamics leading to trust, and arising from it. The examples include [4,9,19,24,30]. In some cases [9], the entrusted properties are left implicit, because all trust relationships of interest concern the same Φ (e.g., $\Phi(A) = $"$A$ is a reliable merchant" or "A's keys are not compromised"). In other cases, the analyzed trust concerns boil down to two [3,19], or four [24] types of trust relationship, which are simply annotated by different types of arrows. Although the logics of trust have also been investigated in the context of trust networks [12,13], many basic questions about trust dynamics remain widely open even when there is only one entrusted property.

---

[1] Statically, two principals knowing the same keys are indistinguishable by cryptographic means. Dynamically, they may be distinguishable, e.g., by the fact that at some previous moment only one of them knew a particular key. Nevertheless, it is often useful and convenient to treat the keys as first-class citizens of cryptographic protocols, and to distinguish the principals only when necessary.

Summary of the Paper. We analyze dynamics of trust networks. It is driven by the users, who are trying to decide which web merchants to buy from, or in the Public Key Infrastructure model, which keys to use. The security problem for the user is that a trust authority, which she consults for trust recommendations, may be corrupt, just like any merchant, or any key. In order to decide which merchants to trust, the user must decide which recommenders to trust. And in order to decide which recommenders to trust, she must try some of the recommended merchants. The problem of the chicken and the egg arises. In order to protect herself, the user must not accept the trust recommendations passively, but needs to build up her private trust vectors, perhaps using some public recommendations on the way. While the public recommendations cover a broader range of trust objects and interactions, private trust vectors are less likely to be corrupt.

In section 2, we present an abstract model of public trust networks. In section 3, we analyze dynamics of the private trust building and updating. In section 4 we spell out the conclusions. In section 5, we discuss the applications, and propose some ideas how to combine private trust vectors with public recommendations, towards more reliable trust decisions.

Trust networks, as presented in section 2, consist of two components, echoing the distinction between the direct and indirect trust. This distinction is a common feature of most of the trust network models encountered in the literature [3,19,24,30]. Enriched with additional features, our model can be instantiated to these richer models. However, in order to present a picture simple enough for our analyses, we also show how to absorb, in a matrix form of a trust network, the chains of indirect trust, which is conveyed from one recommender to another, together with the direct trust, which is conveyed from the recommenders to the shops.

In section 3, we show that, under reasonable assumptions, the process of trust building asymptotically converges to a power-law distribution of trust vectors. This means that trust distributions have heavy tails of highly rated *trust hubs*. One consequence is that trust distributions are thus resilient to random perturbations. Another consequence is that they are vulnerable to adaptive attacks on their trust hubs. The proviso is that the cheaters do not wait too long with their deceit. In our trust model, this proviso is represented by the assumption that, the more trust a principal accumulates by acting honestly, the less likely it becomes that he will turn out to be dishonest.

The conclusions are spelled out in section 4. Our analysis of trust dynamics applies both to users' private trust vectors, and to recommenders' public recommendations. Since the latter are open to attacks, and turn out to obey the vulnerable power law distributions, they should not be directly used for trust decisions, but combined with the private trust values. This suggestion is supported by the empiric evidence that the public trust vectors are often actually subverted[8]. In section 5, we sketch some methods to combine public and private trust vectors, that need to be explored and evaluated in future research.

2   Modeling Trust Networks

In many communication networks, it is impossible, or unfeasible to fully authenticate and authorize all interactions. *Trust networks* provide a supplementary service of partial authentication or authorization. In many cases, authentication is bootstrapped by incrementally strengthening trust.

We begin by an informal description of the conceptual components of a trust network, and later provide the formal definitions. To determine thoughts, we first present the special case of a web shopping scenario. A shopper visits a virtual network of web merchants. If she has no prior experience with it, she can seek advice from some recommenders. Denote the set of merchants by J and the set of recommenders by U. The recommenders record and process the merchant ratings, submitted by the users after their interactions with the merchants. From these ratings, the recommenders derive their recommendations, and publish them as trust certificates. A trust certificate c is represented by an expression in the form $u \xrightarrow[r]{c} i$, where $u \in U$ is a recommender, $i \in J$ a merchant, and r is the trust rating in a previously agreed rating scale R. A *recommendation network* $\mathbb{A}$ is spanned by such certificates.

In addition to the merchant recommendation certificates $u \xrightarrow[r]{c} i$, a recommender u may issue the *endorsement certificates* $u \xrightarrow[r]{e} v$, where v is another recommender. The endorsement certificates span an *endorsement network* $\mathbb{E}$. The endorsement chains, represented by the paths through the endorsement network, allow analyzing the subtle problems of transitivity of trust.

We call *trust network* a pair $\mathbb{T} = \langle \mathbb{A}, \mathbb{E} \rangle$, where $\mathbb{A}$ is a recommendation network, and $\mathbb{E}$ is an endorsement network over the same set U of recommenders. Trust networks can be presented in many slightly different ways, but they all model the public infrastructure of trust.

Besides the shopping scenarios, trust networks also model the Public Key Infrastructures (PKI). In this interpretation, the trust authorities $u \in U$ are not recommenders, but simply keys. The endorsements $u \xrightarrow[r]{e} v$ between them are now the *delegation certificates*. The objects of trust $i \in J$ do not represent the web merchants any more, but the bindings between some principals' identities and their keys. A recommendation $u \xrightarrow[r]{c} i$ is now a *binding certificate* for i, signed by u. More details about this interpretation, and about other presentations of trust networks, can be found in [3,19,24,30].

We proceed with the formal definitions.

2.1 Recommendation Networks

A *recommendation (certificate)* network is an edge-labelled bipartite graph

$$\mathbb{A} = (R \xleftarrow{b} B \xrightarrow{\langle \partial, \varrho \rangle} U \times J)$$

where

- J is a set of *objects*,
- U is a set of *trust authorities*, or *recommenders*,
- B is a set of *certificates*, or *recommendations*, and
- R is a set of *values*, usually an ordered rig, where the *trust ratings* are evaluated.

A recommendation (certificate) $u \xrightarrow[r]{c} i$ is thus represented by an edge $c \in \mathsf{B}$ of the graph, with the source node $\partial(c) = u$ and the target node $\varrho(c) = i$. The value $r = b(c)$ is the trust rating assigned to i by u's recommendation c. The same recommender u may issue several recommendations $c_1, c_2 \ldots$ for the same object i, with the same or different trust ratings; he may also revoke some of them. The use of these multiple recommendations may be regulated by various policies, summing up or averaging the ratings, validating only the last one, and so on. For simplicity, in the present paper we assume that each trust authority takes care for this, and publishes at each point in time at most one recommendation for each object, which sums up (or averages) all its valid recommendations for that object. This allows us to conveniently reduce recommendation networks to matrices $A = (A_{ui})_{U \times J}$, where

$$A_{ui} = \sum_{u \xrightarrow{c} i} b(c)$$

The summation is taken in the *rig* structure of R. A *rig* $\mathsf{R} = (\mathsf{R}, +, \cdot, 0, 1)$ is a "ring without the negatives". This means that $(\mathsf{R}, +, 0)$ and $(\mathsf{R}, \cdot, 1)$ are commutative monoids[2] satisfying $a(b + c) = ab + ac$ and $0a = 0$. The typical examples include natural numbers $\mathbb{N}$, non-negative reals $\mathbb{R}_+$, but also distributive lattices, which in general cannot be embedded in a ring. For concreteness, we shall work mostly with $\mathsf{R} = \mathbb{N}$ or $\mathsf{R} = \mathbb{R}_+$, i.e. assume that the trust ratings are nonnegative real numbers. It should be noted, however, that in some concrete applications more general rigs are needed, e.g. of polynomials or affine functions over $\mathbb{R}_+$.

On the other hand, if the idea that our trust ratings have no upper bound seems strange, the reader can translate all our constructions to the interval $\mathsf{R} = [0, 1]$, with the rating function $\beta : \mathsf{B} \longrightarrow [0, 1]$ set to

$$\beta(c) = 1 - 2^{-b(c)}$$

The inverse transform is $b(c) = -\log_2 (1 - \beta(c))$. Being able to switch between these two equivalent views is useful because each simplifies different aspects of rating: the ratings over $\mathbb{R}_+$ are simpler when there are several parallel recommendations, which we want to add up, whereas the ratings over $[0, 1]$ are simpler when there is a chain of recommendations, and we want to multiply them.

Remarks. While $\mathbb{R}_+$ and $[0, 1]$ are just special cases of R, one could also raise the opposite objection, that they are needlessly general, since most real systems accept and generate their ratings over some very simple lattice (such as $\star < \star\star < \star\star\star$). But data analysis is never performed within that lattice. E.g., if the ratings are derived from users' feedback, then they usually need to be balanced, before they are entered in the same data set, because some users tend to rate more generously than others. In some other cases, the ratings need to be normalized into a given interval. So the rig operations are usually necessary. On the other hand, in relational data analysis, R is the boolean algebra $\{0, 1\}$, and the full ring structure is not given. So rigs are a reasonable compromise for general explorations.

---

[2] Rigs are sometimes called *semirings*. But it seems more reasonable to call semiring an algebra $\mathsf{R} = (\mathsf{R}, +, \cdot)$ where $(\mathsf{R}, +)$ and $(\mathsf{R}, \cdot)$ are semigroups, satisfying $a(b + c) = ab + ac$.

2.2   Endorsement Networks

We model an *endorsement* network as an edge-labelled graph

$$\mathbb{E} = (\mathsf{R} \xleftarrow{\;d\;} \mathsf{D} \xrightarrow{\langle \partial, \varrho \rangle} \mathsf{U} \times \mathsf{U})$$

where an endorsement (certificate) $u \xrightarrow{e} v$ is represented as element $e \in \mathsf{D}$ with $\partial(e) = u$ and $\varrho(e) = v$. The trust rating $r = d(c)$ this time quantifies u's endorsement of v. Like before, we reduce this network to a matrix $E = (E_{uv})_{\mathsf{U} \times \mathsf{U}}$, where

$$E_{uv} = \sum_{u \xrightarrow{e} v} d(e)$$

Abstractly, an endorsement network is similar to some of the popular network models, used for analyzing protein interactions, the Web, social groups, etc. (Cf. [18,27], and the references therein.) Its dynamics can always be analyzed in terms of promotion, discussed in [28]. In that paper, path completions were introduced to allow analyzing the multi-hop network interactions within a simple matrix framework. Here, they will allow us to analyze chains of trust in a similar framework.

2.3   Path Completions of Endorsement Networks

To some extent, trust is transitive: if u trusts w, and w trusts v, then u can accept some reliance on v. But not too much. Depending on the level of risk, and the presence of alternatives, u might prefer to avoid indirect trust. And in any case, it would be unwise for her to rely upon someone removed from her by 20 trustees of trustees of trustees... Can we capture such subtleties without complicating the model?

A *chain* or *path* $u \xrightarrow{e} v$ in an endorsement network E is a sequence of links $u \xrightarrow{e_1} w_1 \xrightarrow{e_2} w_2 \rightarrow \cdots \xrightarrow{e_n} v$. Given an endorsement network E, we would like to define another such network $E^{\#}$ over the same set of recommenders, but with the chains of the endorsement certificates as the new endorsement certificates. The naive idea is to simply take all finite chains of network links as the new network links; i.e., the paths through the old network become the links of the new network. The new network is then closed under composition: each path from u to v, as a composite of some links through other nodes, corresponds to a link from u to v. This amounts to generating the free category over the network graph.

Unfortunately, besides the trust dissipation, described above, this kind of closure destroys a lot essential information in all networks, just like the transitive closure of a relation does. E.g., in a social network, a friend of a friend is often not even an acquaintance. Taking the transitive closure of the friendship relation obliterates that fact. Moreover, the popular "small world" phenomenon suggests that almost *every two people* can be related through no more than six friends of friends of friends... So already adding all paths of length six to a social network, with a symmetric friendship relation, is likely to generate a complete graph. In fact, the average probability that two of node's neighbors in an undirected graph are also linked with each other is an important factor, called *clustering coefficient* [32]. On the other hand, in some networks, e.g. of protein interactions, a link $u \to v$ which shortcuts the links $u \to w \to v$ often denotes a direct *feed-forward* connection, rather than a composition of the two links, and leads to essentially different dynamics. For all these reasons, only some "short" paths can be added to a network. This is assured by penalizing the compositions.

As mentioned above, the ratings within $R = [0, 1]$ are more convenient for analyzing the chains of trust, so we use it in the next couple of definitions.

Definition 1. *For a given endorsement network* $\mathbb{E} = ([0, 1] \xleftarrow{\delta} D \underset{\varrho}{\overset{\partial}{\rightrightarrows}} U)$, *a trust threshold* $\eta \in [0, 1]$, *and a composition penalty* $\epsilon \in [0, 1]$, *we define the* path completion *to be the network*

$$\mathbb{E}^{\#} = ([0, 1] \xleftarrow{\delta} D^{\#} \underset{\varrho}{\overset{\partial}{\rightrightarrows}} U) \text{ where}$$

$$D^{\#} = \{e \in D^{+} \mid \delta(e) \geq \eta\} \text{ and}$$

$$\delta(u_0 \xrightarrow{e_1} u_1 \xrightarrow{e_2} u_2 \to \cdots \xrightarrow{e_n} u_n) = \epsilon^{n-1} \prod_{k=1}^{n} \delta(e_k)$$

with D^{+} *denoting the set of all nonempty paths in* $\mathbb{E}$, *i.e.* $n \geq 1$.

Remark. A path-complete network $\mathbb{E}^{\#}$ is closed under the compositions of high-trust endorsements, but not under the compositions which fall below the trust threshold. It is not hard to see that the path completion is an idempotent operation, i.e. $\mathbb{E}^{\#\#} = \mathbb{E}^{\#}$, but that it may fail to be a proper closure operation, because the endorsements $e \in \mathbb{E}$ such that $\delta(e) < \eta$ are not in $\mathbb{E}^{\#}$, so that generally $\mathbb{E} \not\subseteq \mathbb{E}^{\#}$.

2.4   Completions of Trust Networks

At the final step of completing a trust network, we bring the information captured in it into a more manageable form by folding the completion of the endorsement part into a new recommendation network. The trust matrix, extracted from this recommendation network in the same way as before, now captures not only the direct recommendations, but also a relevant part of indirect trust.

Definition 2. *Suppose that we are given a trust network* $\mathbb{T} = \langle \mathbb{A}, \mathbb{E} \rangle$ *with*

$$\mathbb{A} = ([0, 1] \xleftarrow{\beta} B \xrightarrow{\langle \partial, \varrho \rangle} U \times J)$$

$$\mathbb{E} = ([0, 1] \xleftarrow{\delta} D \xrightarrow{\langle \partial, \varrho \rangle} U \times U)$$

and moreover a trust threshold $\eta \in [0, 1]$, *and a composition penalty* $\epsilon \in [0, 1]$. *The* endorsement completion *of* $\mathbb{T}$ *is the recommendation network*

$$\mathbb{A}^{\#} = ([0, 1] \xleftarrow{\beta} B^{\#} \xrightarrow{\langle \partial, \varrho \rangle} U \times J) \text{ where}$$

$$B_{ui}^{\#} = \{\langle e, c \rangle \in \sum_{v \in U} D_{uv}^{*} \times B_{vi} \mid \beta(e, c) \geq \eta\} \text{ and}$$

$$\beta(u \xrightarrow{e} v \xrightarrow{c} i) = \delta(e) \cdot \beta(c)$$

where D^*_{uv} *denotes the set of all paths in from u to v in* $\mathbb{E}$, *including the empty path ø if* $u = v$, *in which case* $\delta(ø) = 1$.

Assumption. *In the rest of the paper, we work with recommendation networks* $\mathbb{A} = \mathbb{A}^{\#}$, *assumed to be endorsement complete.*

In the next section we analyze how individual users build their own trust vectors. The repercussions of this analysis to public trust networks are discussed in section 5.

3   PrivateTrust

For intuition, we introduce the mathematical model of the process of trust building and updating in terms of an imaginary shopper trying out some web merchants. The model is, however, completely general, and we explain later that a recommender also builds his trust vector by an analogous process.

3.1   Private Trust Vectors and Their Updating

The shopper records her trust in a *trust vector* $\tau \in R^J$. As the time $t = 0, 1, 2, \ldots$ ticks, the shopper interacts with the shops, and subsequently updates τ according to her shopping experiences. This evolution makes the trust vector into a stochastic process $\tau : \mathbb{N} \longrightarrow \mathcal{D}(R^J)$, which expresses the likely distribution of shopper's trust at time t as the random variable $\tau(t) \in \mathcal{D}(R^J)$. The stationary distribution of the stochastic process τ is the likely distribution of trust, which we would like to analyze.

On the side of the recommenders, the shopper may also maintain a trust vector $\sigma \in R^U$. The idea that a trusted recommender recommends reliable merchants is expressed through the invariant $\tau_i = \sum_{u \in U} \sigma_u A_{ui}$, which should be maintained as τ is updated. This makes $\sigma : \mathbb{N} \longrightarrow \mathcal{D}(R^U)$ into another stochastic process.

Initially, at $t = 0$, the shopper may assign all merchants the same trust rating $\tau_i(0) = 1$; or she may assign each recommender the same trust rating $\sigma_u(1) = 1$, and derive $\tau_i(0) = \sum_{u \in U} A_{ui}$.

The stochastic process $X : \mathbb{N} \longrightarrow \mathcal{D}J$ represents shopper's shopping history. Each random variable $X(t) \in \mathcal{D}J$ selects the merchant with whom the shopper interacts at time t. We assume that $X(0)$ is distributed uniformly at random, whereas the probability that the next shop $X(t + 1)$ will be $i \in J$ is either proportional to the trust $\tau_i(t)$, or it is a fixed value $\alpha \in [0, 1]$, if i has had a minimal trust rating, and selecting it means replacing it by a new, untested shop. Formally,

$$\text{Prob}\big(X(t + 1) = i\big) = \begin{cases} \alpha & \text{if } \tau_i(t) \text{ was minimal (so } i \text{ is now new)} \\ C(t)\tau_i(t) & \text{otherwise} \end{cases} \tag{1}$$

where $C(t) = \frac{1-\alpha}{\sum_{i \in J} \tau_i(t)}$ is the normalization factor. The minimality of $\tau_i(t)$ means that for all $j \in J$ holds $\tau_i(t) \leq \tau_j(t)$. The α-case corresponds to shopper's habit to, every once in a while replace an untrusted shop, with a minimal rating, with a new, untested shop.

After the transaction with the merchant $X(t + 1)$, the shopper updates her trust vector $\tau(t)$ to $\tau(t + 1)$, depending on whether the merchant acted honestly or not:

$$\tau_i(t + 1) = \begin{cases} \tau_i(t) & \text{if } i \neq X(t + 1) \\ 0 & \text{if } i = X(t + 1) \text{ is dishonest} \\ 1 & \text{if } i = X(t + 1) \text{ is honest, and new (i.e., } \tau_i(t) \text{ was minimal)} \\ 1 + \tau_i(t) & \text{if } i = X(t + 1) \text{ is honest, not new (i.e.,} \tau_i(t) \text{ not minimal)} \end{cases}$$

The interpretation of the third case is that the label $i = X(t + 1)$ is reassigned from some untrusted merchant, which had a minimal trust rating $\tau_i(t)$, to a new merchant, whose initial trust rating is set to 1 if the initial transaction with was satisfactory. In the fourth case, the merchant $i = X(t + 1)$ was tried out before, and has accumulated a trust rating $\tau_{X(t+1)}$, which is now increased to $\tau_{X(t+1)}(t + 1) = 1 + \tau_{X(t+1)}(t)$ because of a satisfactory transaction.

3.2 Private Trust Distribution

If the trust ratings evolve according to the process just described, how will they, in the long run, partition the set J of merchants? How many merchants will there be with a trust rating of 1, how many with a trust rating of 2, and so on? More precisely, we want to estimate the likely number of elements in each of the sets $W_\ell(t) = \{i \in J \mid \tau_i(t) = \ell\}$, for $\ell \in R$, as the time t ticks ahead. So we set up a system of equations, describing the evolution of

$$w_\ell(t) = |\{i \in J \mid \tau_i(t) = \ell\}|$$

where $|Y|$ denotes the number of elements of the set Y. Note that the disjoint union is $\cup_{\ell \in R} W_\ell(t) = J$, and therefore $\sum_{\ell \in R} w_\ell(t) = J$, where we write $J = |J|$.

The initial values $w_\ell(0)$ are determined by shopper's choice of $\tau(0)$. If she sets $\tau_i(0) = 1$ for all $i \in J$, then $w_1(0) = J$.

How does w_1 change at the time t? We claim that

$$\begin{aligned} w_1(t + 1) - w_1(t) = \quad & J \cdot \text{Prob}(X(t + 1) = i \mid \tau_i \text{ minimal}) \cdot \gamma_\perp \\ & - w_1(t) \cdot \text{Prob}(X(t + 1) = i \mid \tau_i(t) = 1) \\ = \quad & J\alpha\gamma_\perp - w_1(t) \cdot C(t) \end{aligned}$$

To justify this, note that the difference between $W_1(t + 1)$ and $W_1(t)$ comes about for one of the two reasons:

- either $i \in J$ is added to $W_1(t)$, because $\tau_i(t)$ was minimal, and $X(t + 1) = i$ was selected, with the probability α to be replaced with a new shop from J; and then that new shop, now called i, provided an honest transaction, the probability of which is $\gamma_\perp$; so i is now assigned the trust rating $\tau_i(t + 1) = 1$;
- or $i \in J$ is deleted from $W_1(t)$, because $\tau_i(t)$ was 1, and $X(t + 1) = i$ was selected from $W_1(t)$, with the probability $C(t) \cdot \tau_i(t)$; after the transaction, i's trust rating was updated either to $\tau_i(t + 1) = 2$ or to $\tau_i(t + 1) = 0$, depending on whether he acted honestly or dishonestly; but i was deleted from $W_1(t)$ in any case.

However, when the ratings $\ell > 1$ are updated, it will not be irrelevant whether i acts honestly or dishonestly. To describe dynamics of this process, we denote by $\gamma_\ell \in [0, 1]$ the probability that a shop with a rating ℓ is honest. With the described process of trust updating, accumulating a high trust rating ℓ takes time. In order to get a high trust rating, a dishonest shop has to act honestly for a long time. It is therefore reasonable to assume that the probability $1 - \gamma_\ell$ that an ℓ-rated shop is dishonest decreases to 0 as ℓ increases; i.e. that $\lim_{\ell \to \infty} \gamma_\ell = 1$.

Rating dynamics is now

$$w_\ell(t + 1) - w_\ell(t) = w_{\ell-1}(t) \cdot \text{Prob}(X(t + 1) = i \mid \tau_i(t) = \ell - 1) \cdot \gamma_{\ell-1}$$
$$-w_\ell(t) \cdot \text{Prob}(X(t + 1) = i \mid \tau_i(t) = \ell)$$
$$= w_{\ell-1}(t) \cdot C(t) \cdot (\ell - 1) \cdot \gamma_{\ell-1} - w_\ell(t) \cdot C(t) \cdot \ell$$

The difference between $W_\ell(t + 1)$ and $W_\ell(t)$ again comes from two sources:

- either $i \in J$ is added to $W_\ell(t)$, because $\tau_i(t)$ was $\ell - 1$ and $X(t + 1) = i$ was selected from $W_{\ell-1}(t)$ with the probability $C(t) \cdot (\ell - 1)$; and then this i turned out to be honest, with the probability $\gamma_{\ell-1}$, so that $\tau_i(t + 1)$ got updated to $1 + \tau_i(t) = \ell$;
- or $i \in J$ is deleted from $W_\ell(t)$, because $\tau_i(t)$ was ℓ, and $X(t + 1) = i$ was selected from $W_\ell(t)$, with probability $C(t) \cdot \ell$; if i acted honestly, his trust rating got updated to $\ell + 1$; if he acted dishonestly, it got updated to 0; in any case, he got removed from $W_\ell(t)$.

Conceptually, the above derivations follow Simon's master equation method [31]. To simplify the solution, we use a more contemporary approach of [6,33]. First of all, we do not seek the solutions for the sizes $w_\ell(t)$ of the sets $W_\ell(t)$, but rather for the densities $v_\ell(t) = \frac{w_\ell(t)}{J}$. Since $\sum_{\ell \in \mathbb{R}} v_\ell(t) = 1$, for every t, the functions $v_{(-)}(t) : \mathbb{R} \longrightarrow [0, 1]$ are probability distributions with a finite support. Together, they thus form a stochastic process $v : \mathbb{N} \longrightarrow \mathcal{D}\mathbb{R}$, described by the difference equations

$$\Delta v_1(t) = \alpha \gamma_\perp - C(t) v_1(t)$$
$$\Delta v_\ell(t) = \gamma_{\ell-1}(\ell - 1) C(t) v_{\ell-1}(t) - \ell C(t) v_\ell(t)$$

As shown in the Appendix, the steady state of this process turns out to be

$$v_1 = \frac{\alpha \gamma_\perp}{c + 1} \qquad v_n = \frac{\alpha \gamma_\perp G_{n-1}}{c} B\left(n, 1 + \frac{1}{c}\right)$$

where $G_n = \prod_{\ell=1}^{n} \gamma_\ell$, the constant c satisfies $\frac{c}{t} \approx C(t) = \frac{1-\alpha}{\sum_{i \in J} \tau_i(t)}$, and B is Dirichlet's Beta function. But Stirling's formula implies that $B(x, y) \approx x^{-y}$ holds as $x \to \infty$. We have thus proven that, with a sufficiently fine trust rating scale, and with the probability of honesty γ_ℓ increasing with the trust rating ℓ fast enough, the trust ratings obey the power law [25,26].

In summary, we have proven the following:

Theorem. *A trustor maintains trust ratings for a set of J trustees. The ratings take their values from a sufficiently large set, so that they can strictly increase whenever justified. They are updated according to the following procedure:*

- *Initially, the tustor assigns some fixed ratings (e.g., equal) to all trustees.*
- *Then the trustor repeatedly tests the trustees:*
  - *with a probability α, she tests an untested trustee, adds it to the set J, and deletes from it a trustee with the minimal rating;*
  - *otherwise, the turstor tests a previously tested trustee, with a probability proportional to its trust rating.*
- *After each step, the trustor updates the trust rating ℓ of the tested trustee as follows*
  - *with a probability γ_ℓ, she increases it (because of a satisfactory outcome of the test);*
  - *otherwise, she sets it to zero.*

If the probability γ_ℓ of a satisfactory transaction with an ℓ-rated trustee increases fast enough enough enough to satisfy $\frac{1}{e^{s_\ell}} \leq \gamma_\ell \leq 1$ for some convergent series $\sum_{\ell=1}^{\infty} s_\ell < \infty$, so that $G = \prod_{\ell=1}^{\infty} \gamma_\ell > 0$, then in the long run, the number w_n of trustees with the trust rating n obeys the power law

$$w_n \approx \frac{\alpha\gamma_\perp GJ}{c} \, n^{-\left(1+\frac{1}{c}\right)}$$

where c is a renormalising constant $c \approx \frac{1-\alpha}{1+\alpha\gamma_\perp}$, and $\gamma_\perp$ is the probability that an untested trustee will satisfy the test.

Remarks. As explained in section 2.1, the assumption that the trust can always increase does not mean that the trust ratings have to be unbounded: they can also increase asymptotically. This assumption is only needed to assure that the process of trust building will not become irrelevant after some threshold is reached. In reality, of course, only finitely many interactions with finitely many shops can be taken into account, but there is a real sense in which the trust process can always be refined, and trust increased.

The assumption that $G = \prod_{\ell=1}^{\infty} \gamma_\ell > 0$ means that the probability $1 - \gamma_\ell$, that a shop with a trust rating ℓ is not trustworthy, quickly decreases as ℓ increases. This assumption is not satisfied if many untrustworthy shops act honestly for a long time, waiting to accumulate trust, and then strike. If there are incentives for that, the heavy tail of the power component of w_n is trimmed by the exponential component $G_n = \prod_{\ell=1}^{n} \gamma_\ell$, and the distribution of trust is exponential.

But this leads to a negative feedback: as they decrease the range of trust distribution, the dishonest trust hubs actually decrease the vulnerability of the network. The more persistent attackers there are, the higher the cost of an attack.

Other Interpretations. Although our model was described and motivated as shopper's trust process, it seems likely that the stochastic process governing recommender's trust vector would be of the same type. The main difference is, of course, that the recommender does not select and test the merchant himself, but builds his trust vector from the merchant ratings that he obtains as the feedback from the shoppers. However, a shopper who comes back to submit the feedback is probably the same one who previously came to obtain recommender's recommendation. And it is furthermore just as likely that the shopper has selected the merchant following that recommendation. So the selection of the merchant whose trust rating will be updated at a time $t + 1$ was guided by recommender's trust vector at time t, just as it was the case with shopper's trust dynamics.

3.3 Robustness and Vulnerability of Private Trust

The upshot of the Theorem just proved is that there is a great variety of trust ratings: the distribution has a heavy tail. Money attracts money, and trust attracts more trust. As you extend the circle of merchants and the rating scale, you will find merchants with higher and higher trust rating. This applies to user's private trust vectors τ and σ, as well as to recommender's public trust vectors, displayed as the rows of the recommendation matrix $A = (A_{ui})_{U \times J}$. Moreover, although we did not describe dynamics of an endorsement network here, it seems certain that it also leads to a distribution of recommenders' influence, obeying the power law. The reason is that the endorsement dynamics is quite similar to promotion dynamics, described in [28], which is a version of one of the processes studied in Simon's seminal paper about the power law [31].

The structure and the properties of the distributions that obey the power law have been extensively analyzed [25,26,27]. As mentioned in the Introduction, because of the presence of highly rated hubs, such distributions tend to be robust under random perturbations, but vulnerable to adaptive attacks on their hubs[3]. Leaving the mathematical details aside, the security consequence is that *the power law distributions work for the attacker*: he only needs to attack a small number of nodes of high ranking, in order to gain control over a large part of the system. This phenomenon has been previously demonstrated on toy models of trust networks, involving the bottleneck nodes [19]. Although the recommender networks, currently deployed on the Web, still do not form a large network, the same phenomenon — that the main trust hubs become increasingly unreliable — has also been observed in practice: e.g., [8] describes some extreme examples.

4   Conclusions

The obvious security lessons, arising from our analyses, and supported by the empiric observations are thus:

- Trust decisions should not be derived from public trust recommendations alone. They should be based on private trust vectors, that the user should maintain herself.
- Public trust recommendations should be used to supplement and refine private trust.

5   Towards Applications: Combining Private Trust and Public Recommendations

Hoping that the gentle reader will not be too disturbed by the fact that the paper continues beyond its conclusions[4], in this final section we sketch some ways to implement

---

[3] One way to make this statement precise is to build a random graph with the given trust distribution as the degree distribution. The methods of [1] can serve for this purpose. The edges of the obtained graph can be interpreted as the interactions recorded in nodes' trust ratings. The trust hubs would then be the graph hubs in the usual sense: highly connected nodes. The robustness would manifest itself as a high phase transition: the graph remains connected even when many randomly selected edges are eliminated; and the fragility would mean that the graph falls apart very easily if some of the hubs are removed.

[4] A reviewer of a version of this paper where the above conclusions were not separated in their own section, objected that the paper ended abruptly, without any conclusions.

these conclusions. We propose for further exploration two methods for a user of a trust network to combine her private trust vectors with some public recommendations, in order to obtain more informative trust guidance. Although we attempt to provide intuitive explanations, understanding the technical details of these condensed ideas may require some familiarity with LSI and with the vector model.

5.1 Trust Communities

It is often emphasized that trust is relative to a community, or more generally to a module [28] within a network: e.g., a criminal may be trusted within the community of criminals, but not within a community of security researchers, and vice versa. The members of the same community can be recognized by similar trust vectors, or recommendations.

In this section, we briefly summarize how a recommendation matrix can be used to recognize communities in the space of recommenders on one hand, and in the space of merchants on the other. The merchants which deserve to be trusted for the same type of services are likely to be highly recommended by the same recommenders. This groups them into communities. The user can refine his trust by computing how much he trusts each community, and how is his trust distributed within each of them. While the public trust recommendations may be unreliable, and better not followed directly, they provide reliable and valuable information about the trust communities. By relativizing the private trust over the trust communities, the user can obtain significantly more precise guidance, distinguishing between the various forms of trust in the various communities, even in the model where the entrusted properties are kept implicit.

By suitably renormalizing the data, the similarity between the trust vectors φ and $\psi \in R^J$ can be viewed as the angle between the induced recommender vectors

$$s(\varphi, \psi) = \langle A\varphi \mid A\psi \rangle$$

where $\langle x|y \rangle = \sum_{v \in U} x_v \cdot y_v$ is the inner product in the space R^U. The angle is often used as the similarity measure in information retrieval and data mining [22]. It should be noted that it leads to subtle statistical problems, if applied to diverse samples [29]. The trust communities, as the subspaces of similar vectors within R^J, can be detected by spectral methods, using the data mining technique of Latent Semantic Indexing (LSI) [7,16,29]. The idea is to look for the vectors ξ where $s(\xi, \xi)$ attains the extremal values. Since the transpose A^T satisfies $\langle A\varphi \mid A\psi \rangle = \langle \varphi \mid A^T A\psi \rangle$, the similarity can be also be expressed as $s(\varphi, \psi) = \langle \varphi \mid A^T A\psi \rangle$. The extremal values of $s(\xi, \xi) = \langle \xi \mid A^T A\xi \rangle$ can thus be found as the eigenvalues $\{\lambda_1 > \lambda_2 > \cdots > \lambda_m\}$ of $A^T A$. The communities are the corresponding eigenspaces, described by the projectors $\{P_1, \ldots, P_m\}$.

There are at least two ways to refine private trust τ using the trust communities $\{P_1, \ldots, P_m\}$.

Community Specific Private Trust. Instead of using his trust vector $\tau \in R^J$ to select the trusted objects, the user can compute the *community specific* trust vectors

$$\tau^k = P_k \tau$$

obtained by projecting τ into each of the eigenspaces P_k, $k = 1, \ldots, m$, i.e. by relativizing it to the dominant merchant communities. In this way, even if the trust relations

$A \rightarrow B$ are not explicitly annotated by the entrusted properties Φ, the user can refine his trust decisions by recognizing the "latent" entrusted properties, uncovered as the dominant trust communities $\{P_1, \ldots, P_m\}$.

Personalized Recommendation Matrix. Intuitively, the spectrum $\{\lambda_1 > \lambda_2 > \cdots > \lambda_m\}$ expresses a notion of cohesion, i.e. the strength of the mutual trust within each of the communities $\{P_1, P_2, \ldots, P_m\}$. On the other hand, the degree to which a user with a trust vector τ trusts a community P_k can be measured by the similarity $s(\tau, \tau^k) = \langle \tau \mid P_k \tau \rangle$.

The Singular Value Decomposition (SVD) theorem tells that the spectral decomposition $A^T A = \sum_{k=1}^{m} \lambda_k P_k$ induces $A = \sum_{k=1}^{m} \sqrt{\lambda_k} \Pi_k$, for the suitable operators Π_k. The personalized recommendation matrix, remixed according to the community trust θ induced by user's trust vector τ is then $A_\tau = \sum_{k=1}^{m} \sqrt{\langle \tau \mid P_k \tau \rangle} \Pi_k$. Using this private matrix is equivalent to using the community specific trust vectors, within each of the trust communities; but it also allows evaluating trust for combinations of communities.

References

1. Aiello, W., Chung, F., Lu, L.: A random graph model for massive graphs. In: STOC 2000: Proceedings of the thirty-second annual ACM symposium on Theory of computing, pp. 171–180. ACM, New York (2000)
2. Benantar, M.: Access Control Systems: Security, Identity Management and Trust Models. Springer, Heidelberg (2006)
3. Beth, T., Borcherding, M., Klein, B.: Valuation of trust in open networks. In: Gollmann, D. (ed.) ESORICS 1994. LNCS, vol. 875, pp. 3–18. Springer, Heidelberg (1994)
4. Blaze, M., Feibenbaum, J., Lacy, J.: Decentralized trust management. In: Proceedings of Symposium on Security and Privacy, p. 164 (1996)
5. Carbone, M., Nielsen, M., Sassone, V.: A formal model for trust in dynamic networks. In: Cerone, A., Lindsay, P. (eds.) Proceedings of the First International Conference on Software Engineering and Formal Methods (2003)
6. Darling, R., Norris, J.R.: Differential equation approximations for Markov chains. Probability Surveys 5, 37–79 (2008)
7. Deerwester, S.C., Dumais, S.T., Landauer, T.K., Furnas, G.W., Harshman, R.A.: Indexing by latent semantic analysis. Journal of the American Society of Information Science 41(6), 391–407 (1990)
8. Edelman, B.: Adverse selection in online trust certifications. working paper, http://www.benedelman.org/publications/advsel-trust-draft.pdf
9. Guha, R., Kumar, R., Raghavan, P., Tomkins, A.: Propagation of trust and distrust. In: WWW 2004: Proceedings of the 13th international conference on World Wide Web, pp. 403–412. ACM, New York (2004)
10. Guttman, J.D., Thayer, F.J., Carlson, J.A., Herzog, J.C., Ramsdell, J.D., Sniffen, B.T.: Trust management in strand spaces: A rely-guarantee method. In: Schmidt, D. (ed.) ESOP 2004. LNCS, vol. 2986, pp. 325–339. Springer, Heidelberg (2004)
11. Jøsang, A.: A subjective metric of authentication. In: Quisquater, J.-J., Deswarte, Y., Meadows, C., Gollmann, D. (eds.) ESORICS 1998. LNCS, vol. 1485, pp. 329–344. Springer, Heidelberg (1998)
12. Jøsang, A.: An algebra for assessing trust in certification chains. In: NDSS. The Internet Society (1999)

13. Jøsang, A., Gray, E., Kinateder, M.: Simplification and analysis of transitive trust networks. Web Intelli. and Agent Sys. 4(2), 139–161 (2006)
14. Kamvar, S.D., Schlosser, M.T., Garcia-Molina, H.: The Eigentrust algorithm for reputation management in P2P networks. In: WWW 2003: Proceedings of the 12th international conference on World Wide Web, pp. 640–651. ACM Press, New York (2003)
15. Karabulut, Y., Kerschbaum, F., Massacci, F., Robinson, P., Yautsiukhin, A.: Security and trust in it business outsourcing: a manifesto. Electr. Notes Theor. Comput. Sci. 179, 47–58 (2007)
16. Kleinberg, J.M.: Authoritative sources in a hyperlinked environment. Journal of the ACM 46(5), 604–632 (1999)
17. Lampson, B., Abadi, M., Burrows, M., Wobber, E.: Authentication in distributed systems: theory and practice. SIGOPS Oper. Syst. Rev. 25(5), 165–182 (1991)
18. Langville, A.N., Meyer, C.D.: Google's PageRank and Beyond: The Science of Search Engine Rankings. Princeton University Press, Princeton (2006)
19. Levien, R., Aiken, A.: Attack-resistant trust metrics for public key certification. In: SSYM 1998: Proceedings of the 7th conference on USENIX Security Symposium, Berkeley, CA, USA, p. 18. USENIX Association (1998)
20. Li, N., Mitchell, J.C., Winsborough, W.H.: Design of a role-based trust-management framework. In: SP 2002: Proceedings of the 2002 IEEE Symposium on Security and Privacy, Washington, DC, USA, p. 114. IEEE Computer Society, Los Alamitos (2002)
21. Li, N., Mitchell, J.C., Winsborough, W.H.: Beyond proof-of-compliance: security analysis in trust management. J. ACM 52(3), 474–514 (2005)
22. Manning, C.D., Raghavan, P., Schtze, H.: Introduction to Information Retrieval. Cambridge University Press, Cambridge (2008)
23. Marti, S., Garcia-Molina, H.: Taxonomy of trust: categorizing P2P reputation systems. Comput. Netw. 50(4), 472–484 (2006)
24. Maurer, U.: Modelling a public-key infrastructure. In: Martella, G., Kurth, H., Montolivo, E., Bertino, E. (eds.) ESORICS 1996. LNCS, vol. 1146. Springer, Heidelberg (1996)
25. Mitzenmacher, M.: A brief history of generative models for power law and lognormal distribution. Internet Math. 1, 226–251 (2004)
26. Newman, M.: Power laws, Pareto distributions and Zipf's law. Contemporary Physics 46, 323 (2005)
27. Newman, M., Barabasi, A.-L., Watts, D.J. (eds.): The Structure and Dynamics of Networks. Princeton Studies in Complexity. Princeton University Press, Princeton (2006)
28. Pavlovic, D.: Network as a computer: Ranking paths to find flows. In: Hirsch, E.A., Razborov, A.A., Semenov, A., Slissenko, A. (eds.) Computer Science – Theory and Applications. LNCS, vol. 5010, pp. 384–397. Springer, Heidelberg (2008)
29. Pavlovic, D.: On quantum statistics in data analysis. In: Bruza, P. (ed.) Quantum Interaction 2008. AAAI, Menlo Park (2008)
30. Reiter, M.K., Stubblebine, S.G.: Authentication metric analysis and design. ACM Trans. Inf. Syst. Secur. 2(2), 138–158 (1999)
31. Simon, H.A.: On a class of skew distribution functions. Biometrika 42, 425–440 (1955)
32. Watts, D.J., Strogatz, S.H.: Collective dynamics of 'small-world' networks. Nature 393(6684), 440–442 (1998)
33. Wormald, N.C.: Differential equations for random processes and random graphs. The Annals of Applied Probability 5(4), 1217–1235 (1995)

Appendix: The Steady State of the Trust Process

The trust process $v : \mathbb{N} \longrightarrow \mathcal{D}\mathbb{R}$ is described by the difference equations

$$\Delta v_1(t) = \alpha\gamma_\perp - C(t)v_1(t)$$
$$\Delta v_\ell(t) = \gamma_{\ell-1}(\ell - 1)C(t)v_{\ell-1}(t) - C(t)\ell v_\ell(t)$$

Recall, first of all, from section 3.1 that $C(t) = \frac{1-\alpha}{S(t)}$, where $S(t) = \sum_{i \in J} \tau_i(t)$. The dynamics of τ, described at the end of section 3.1, implies that

$$S(t + 1) = \sum_{i \neq X(t+1)} \tau_i(t) + \gamma_{X(t+1)}\left(1 + \tau_{X(t+1)}(t)\right) + \alpha\gamma_\perp$$

where $\gamma_\perp$ is the probability that a shopper is satisfied after an interaction with a new shop. It follows that

$$\Delta S(t) = \gamma_{X(t+1)} - (1 - \gamma_{X(t+1)})\tau_{X(t+1)}(t) + \alpha\gamma_\perp \approx 1 + \alpha\gamma_\perp$$

is approximately constant and thus $S(t) \approx (1 + \alpha\gamma_\perp)t$. Hence $C(t) \approx \frac{c}{t}$, where $c = \frac{1-\alpha}{1+\alpha\gamma_\perp}$.

With this simplification, and with the martingale assumption of [33] satisfied, the solutions of the above system of difference equations can be approximated by the solutions of the corresponding differential system

$$\frac{dv_1}{dt} = \alpha\gamma_\perp - \frac{c}{t}v_1$$
$$\frac{dv_\ell}{dt} = \frac{\gamma_{\ell-1}c(\ell - 1)v_{\ell-1} - c\ell v_\ell}{t}$$

where the discrete time variable t has been made continuous. The steady state of the stochastic process $v : \mathbb{R} \longrightarrow \mathcal{D}\mathbb{R}$ can now be found in the form $v_\ell(t) = t \cdot v_\ell$, by expanding the recurrence

$$v_1 = \alpha\gamma_\perp - cv_1$$
$$v_\ell = \gamma_{\ell-1}c(\ell - 1)v_{\ell-1} - c\ell v_\ell$$

into

$$v_1 = \frac{\alpha\gamma_\perp}{c + 1}$$
$$v_\ell = \frac{(\ell - 1)\gamma_{\ell-1}c}{\ell c + 1}v_{\ell-1}$$

which further gives

$$v_2 = \frac{\alpha\gamma_\perp}{c+1} \cdot \frac{\gamma_1 c}{2c+1}$$

$$v_3 = \frac{\alpha\gamma_\perp}{c+1} \cdot \frac{\gamma_1 c}{2c+1} \cdot \frac{2\gamma_2 c}{3c+1}$$

$$\cdots$$

$$v_n = \alpha\gamma_\perp \left(\prod_{\ell=1}^{n-1} \gamma_\ell\right) c^{n-1} \cdot \frac{(n-1)!}{\prod_{k=1}^{n}(kc+1)}$$

$$= \frac{\alpha\gamma_\perp G_{n-1}}{c} \cdot \frac{(n-1)!}{\prod_{k=1}^{n}\left(k+\frac{1}{c}\right)}$$

$$= \frac{\alpha\gamma_\perp G_{n-1}}{c} \cdot \frac{\Gamma(n)\Gamma\left(1+\frac{1}{c}\right)}{\Gamma\left(n+1+\frac{1}{c}\right)}$$

$$= \frac{\alpha\gamma_\perp G_{n-1}}{c} \cdot B\left(n, 1+\frac{1}{c}\right)$$

Trust within the Context of Organizations: A Formal Approach

Emiliano Lorini[1], Rino Falcone[2], and Cristiano Castelfranchi[2]

[1] Institut de Recherche en Informatique de Toulouse (IRIT), France
[2] Institute of Cognitive Sciences and Technologies-CNR, Italy
Emiliano.Lorini@irit.fr,
rino.falcone@istc.cnr.it,
cristiano.castelfranchi@istc.cnr.it

Abstract. We present in this paper a logical model of trust within organizations. Three forms of trust are investigated: trust in an agent (i.e. interpersonal trust), trust in a role, trust in an agent *qua* player of a role. The relationships between the three forms of trust are investigated. A part of the paper is devoted to the analysis of trust of an authority (e.g. an employer) in a subordinate (e.g. an employee).

1 Introduction

When looking at human organizations, social scientists have been mostly interested in individuating the antecedents of collective behavior and collective action between interacting individuals and roles. A central concern of the field has been identifying the determinants of intraorganizational cooperation, coordination and delegation [20,2]. Among the different determinants, trust has been recognized as one of the most important [7,16].

In this paper, we will study trust and organizations from the perspective of computer scientists working in the field of multi-agent systems (MAS). Indeed, to provide a formal analysis of trust within the context of organizations is of definite importance for the theory and development of multi-agent systems. In the recent years, in the MAS field there has been a growing interest in the theory of organization. Several formal approaches to the characterization of organizational concepts have been proposed [22,10] as well as general methodologies for MAS [23,13] which are based on organizational concepts as their cornerstones and which provide the guidelines for the specification and the design of MAS environments. In these formal approaches and existing methodologies, a multi-agent system is conceived as an organization consisting of various interacting roles which can be played by different agents. Although the concept of organization has been extensively studied in the agent domain, there is still no comprehensive formal account of the issue of trust in agent organizations. For instance, the distinction between the concept of *trust in an agent* and the concept of *trust in a role* is not clearly and deeply analyzed. Indeed, most of formal models of trust proposed in the agent domain have a limited perspective and only focus on trust in information sources in the specific context of information exchange between agents (e.g. [17,14,8]). The aim of the present paper is to extend our conceptual and formal model of social trust [18,9] to

P. Degano, J. Guttman, and F. Martinelli (Eds.): FAST 2008, LNCS 5491, pp. 114–128, 2009.

the analysis of trust within organizations. This is in order to fill an existing gap in the literature about formal models of agents and multi-agent systems.

In particular, we will present in this paper a logical model of trust within the context of organizations. We model organizations as social entities in which agents play roles. Individual agents are described in terms of their mental attitudes (beliefs, goals, intentions). In an organization there are different roles to which certain powers are assigned. When an agent plays a certain role, he inherits the powers assigned to the role. We study trust at three different levels of generality. We start with the more general concept of an agent i's trust in another agent j abstracting away from the concept of role (*interpersonal trust*). We conceive interpersonal trust as an agent's disposition which is reducible to his beliefs and goals. In particular, we define trust in terms of a goal of the truster and the truster's belief that the trustee has the right properties (powers, abilities, dispositions) to ensure that his goal will be achieved. Then, we introduce the concept of role in order to investigate what it means that *an agent i trusts a certain role x* and *an agent i trusts another agent j qua player of a certain role x*. We focus on the relationships between the three different forms of trust (interpersonal trust, trust in a role and trust in an agent *qua* player of a role).

The paper is organized as follows. We start in Section 2 with a presentation of a modal logic which enables reasoning about actions and mental attitudes of agents (beliefs, goals and intentions), and about the roles that the agents play within the context of the organization. This logic will be used during the paper for formalizing the relevant concepts of our model of trust. The second part of the paper (Section 3) is devoted to present the three general concepts of trust that are relevant for a theory of organizations and for modeling and designing artificial organizations of agents: interpersonal trust (Section 3.1), trust in a role and and trust in an agent *qua* player of a role (Section 3.2). In Section 3.3, the three concepts are applied to the specific case of trust of an authority (e.g. an employer) in a subordinate (e.g. an employee). We conclude with a discussion of some directions for future works.

2 A Modal Logic of Mental Attitudes, Actions and Roles

We present in this section the multimodal logic $\mathcal{L}$ that we use to formalize the relevant concepts of our model of trust. $\mathcal{L}$ combines the expressiveness of dynamic logic [11] with the expressiveness of a logic of agents' mental attitudes [6]. Moreover, it enables reasoning about the relationships between different roles in the organization.

2.1 Syntax and Semantics

The syntactic primitives of the logic $\mathcal{L}$ are the following:

- a nonempty finite set of agents $AGT = \{i, j, \ldots\}$;
- a nonempty finite set of atomic actions $AT = \{a, b, \ldots\}$;
- a set of atomic formulas $ATM = \{p, q, \ldots\}$;
- a finite set of social roles $ROLE = \{x, y, \ldots\}$.

We add two additional formal constructions in order to specify the relationships between agents and roles and among different roles.

- a function $\mathscr{F}_{play} : ROLE \longrightarrow 2^{AGT} \setminus \emptyset$ which maps every role to a non-empty set of agents;
- a function $\mathscr{F}_{control} : ROLE \times ROLE \longrightarrow 2^{AT}$ which maps every couple of roles to a set of atomic actions.

Given a role $x \in ROLE$ and a non-empty set of agents $C \in 2^{AGT}$, $\mathscr{F}_{play}(x) = C$ means that C is the set of agents in the organization that play role x. Given two roles $x, y \in ROLE$ and a set of atomic actions $X \in 2^{AT}$, $\mathscr{F}_{control}(x, y) = X$ means that role x controls the atomic actions X of role y. More generally, the latter construction is used to specify a concept of right: $a \in \mathscr{F}_{control}(x, y)$ means that every agent playing role x has the *right* to require (resp. to authorize) an agent playing role y to do action a. We call the tuple $RS = \langle \mathscr{F}_{play}, \mathscr{F}_{control} \rangle$ a *role structure*.

We also introduce organizational actions of the form $req_j(a)$ and $auth_j(a)$ denoting respectively the action of requiring (or demanding) j to do the atomic action a and the action of authorizing (or allowing) j to do the atomic action a. Here we do not consider the negative counterparts of these organizational actions, that is, the action of forbidding j to do the atomic action a and the action of authorizing (or allowing) j not to do the atomic action a.

We define a set ACT of complex actions as the smallest superset of AT such that:

- if $a \in AT$ and $j \in AGT$ then $req_j(a) \in ACT$ and $auth_j(a) \in ACT$.

Since the sets AGT and AT are supposed to be finite, the set ACT is finite as well. We note $\alpha, \beta, \dots$ the elements in ACT.

The language $\mathcal{L}_{lang}$ of the logic $\mathcal{L}$ is defined as the smallest superset of ATM such that:

- if $\varphi, \psi \in \mathcal{L}_{lang}, \alpha \in ACT, i \in AGT, x, y \in ROLE$ and $a \in AT$ then $\neg\varphi, \varphi \vee \psi, After_{i:\alpha}\varphi, Does_{i:\alpha}\varphi, Bel_i\varphi, Goal_i\varphi, Obg\varphi, Control(x, y, a), Play(i, x) \in \mathcal{L}_{lang}$.

The classical boolean connectives $\wedge, \rightarrow, \leftrightarrow, \top$ and $\bot$ are defined from $\vee$ and $\neg$ in the usual manner.

The operators of our logic have the following intuitive meaning. $Bel_i\varphi$: the agent i believes that φ; $After_{i:\alpha}\varphi$: after agent i does α, it is the case that φ ($After_{i:\alpha}\bot$ is read: agent i cannot do action α); $Does_{i:\alpha}\varphi$: agent i is going to do α and φ will be true afterward ($Does_{i:\alpha}\top$ is read: agent i is going to do α); $Goal_i\varphi$: the agent i wants that φ holds; $Control(x, y, a)$: role x controls role y with respect to the action a; $Play(i, x)$: agent i plays role x; $Obg\varphi$: it is obligatory that φ. During the analysis of trust presented in Section 3, formula $After_{i:\alpha}\varphi$ will be often read: agent i has the power to ensure φ by doing α. Three abbreviations are given: $Can_i(\alpha) \overset{def}{=} \neg After_{i:\alpha}\bot$; $Int_i(\alpha) \overset{def}{=} Goal_i Does_{i:\alpha}\top$; $Perm\varphi \overset{def}{=} \neg Obg\neg\varphi$. $Can_i(\alpha)$ stands for: agent i can do action α (i.e. i has the capacity to do α). $Int_i(\alpha)$ stands for: agent i intends to do α. Finally, $Perm\varphi$ stands for: φ is permitted.

Models of the logic $\mathcal{L}$ are tuples $M = \langle W, RS, \mathscr{A}, \mathscr{D}, \mathscr{B}, \mathscr{G}, \mathscr{C}, \mathscr{V} \rangle$ defined as follows.

- W is a non empty set of possible worlds or states.
- RS is a role structure.

- $\mathscr{A} : AGT \times ACT \longrightarrow W \times W$ maps every agent i and action α to a relation $\mathscr{A}_{i:\alpha}$ between possible worlds in W. Given a world $w \in W$, if $(w, w') \in \mathscr{A}_{i:\alpha}$ then w' is a world which can be reached from w through the occurrence of agent i's action α.
- $\mathscr{D} : AGT \times ACT \longrightarrow W \times W$ maps every agent i and action α to a relation $\mathscr{D}_{i:\alpha}$ between possible worlds in W. Given a world $w \in W$, if $(w, w') \in \mathscr{D}_{i:\alpha}$ then w' is the *next* world of w which will be reached from w through the occurrence of agent i's action α.
- $\mathscr{B} : AGT \longrightarrow W \times W$ maps every agent i to a serial, transitive and euclidean relation $\mathscr{B}_i$ between possible worlds in W. Given a world $w \in W$, if $(w, w') \in \mathscr{B}_i$ then w' is a world which is compatible with agent i's beliefs at w.
- $\mathscr{G} : AGT \longrightarrow W \times W$ maps every agent i to a serial relation $\mathscr{G}_i$ between possible worlds in W. Given a world $w \in W$, if $(w, w') \in \mathscr{G}_i$ then w' is a world which is compatible with agent i's goals at w.
- $\mathscr{O}$ is a serial relation between possible worlds in W. Given a world $w \in W$, if $(w, w') \in \mathscr{O}$ then w' is a world which is ideal at world w.
- $\mathscr{V} : W \longrightarrow 2^{ATM}$ is a truth assignment which associates each world w with the set $\mathscr{V}(w)$ of atomic propositions true in w.

We distinguish the two types of relations R and D since we want to express both: the fact that at a given world w an agent performs an action α which will result in a next state w, the fact that if at w the agent did something different he would have produced a different outcome.

Given a model M, a world w and a formula φ, we write $M, w \models \varphi$ to mean that φ is true at world w in M, under the basic semantics. The rules defining the truth conditions of formulas are just standard for atomic formulas, negation and disjunction. The following are the remaining truth conditions for $After_{i:\alpha}\varphi$, $Does_{i:\alpha}\varphi$, $Bel_i\varphi$, $Goal_i\varphi$, $Obg\varphi$, $Control(x, y, a)$ and $Play(i, x)$.

- $M, w \models After_{i:\alpha}\varphi$ iff $M, w' \models \varphi$ for all w' such that $(w, w') \in \mathscr{A}_{i:\alpha}$
- $M, w \models Does_{i:\alpha}\varphi$ iff $\exists w'$ such that $(w, w') \in \mathscr{D}_{i:\alpha}$ and $M, w' \models \varphi$
- $M, w \models Bel_i\varphi$ iff $M, w' \models \varphi$ for all w' such that $(w, w') \in \mathscr{B}_i$
- $M, w \models Goal_i\varphi$ iff $M, w' \models \varphi$ for all w' such that $(w, w') \in \mathscr{G}_i$
- $M, w \models Obg\varphi$ iff $M, w' \models \varphi$ for all w' such that $(w, w') \in \mathscr{O}$
- $M, w \models Control(x, y, a)$ iff $a \in \mathscr{F}_{control}(x, y)$
- $M, w \models Play(i, x)$ iff $i \in \mathscr{F}_{play}(x)$

The following section is devoted to illustrate the additional semantic constraints over $\mathcal{L}$ models and the corresponding axiomatization of the logic $\mathcal{L}$.

2.2 Axiomatization

The axiomatizations of the logic $\mathcal{L}$ include all tautologies of propositional calculus and the standard rule of inference *modus ponens*.[1] Operators for actions of type $After_{i:\alpha}$ and $Does_{i:\alpha}$ are normal modal operators satisfying the axioms and rules of inference of system K.[2] Operators of type Bel_i and $Goal_i$ are just standard normal modal operators.

---

[1] If $\vdash \varphi$ and $\vdash \varphi \rightarrow \psi$ then $\vdash \psi$.

[2] This includes necessitation rule and Axiom K: $\dfrac{\vdash\varphi}{\vdash After_{i:\alpha}\varphi}$; $\dfrac{\vdash\varphi}{\vdash\neg Does_{i:\alpha}\neg\varphi}$; $(After_{i:\alpha}\varphi \wedge After_{i:\alpha}(\varphi \rightarrow \psi)) \rightarrow After_{i:\alpha}\psi$; $(Does_{i:\alpha}\varphi \wedge \neg Does_{i:\alpha}\neg\psi) \rightarrow Does_{i:\alpha}(\varphi \wedge \psi)$.

The former are modal operators for belief in Hintikka style [12] satisfying the axioms and rules of inference of system KD45. [3] The latter are modal operators for goal in Cohen & Levesque's style [6] satisfying the axioms and rules of inference of system KD.[4] Thus, we make assumptions about positive and negative introspection for beliefs and we suppose that an agent have no inconsistent beliefs or conflicting goals. Operators for obligations of type Obg are supposed to be KD normal modal operators as in SDL (standard deontic logic) [1].[5] Thus, we do not admit contradictory obligations.

We add the following constraint over every relation $\mathscr{D}_{i:\alpha}$ and every relation $\mathscr{D}_{j:\beta}$ of all $\mathcal{L}$ models. For every $i, j \in AGT$, $\alpha, \beta \in ACT$ and $w \in W$:

S1   if $(w, w') \in \mathscr{D}_{i:\alpha}$ and $(w, w'') \in \mathscr{D}_{j:\beta}$ then $w' = w''$

Constraint $S1$ says that if w' is the *next* world of w which is reachable from w through the occurrence of agent i's action α and w'' is also the *next* world of w which is reachable from w through the occurrence of agent j's action β, then w' and w'' denote the same world. Indeed, we suppose that every world can only have one *next* world. The semantic constraint $S1$ corresponds to the following axiom.

Alt$_{Act}$ $Does_{i:\alpha}\varphi \rightarrow \neg Does_{j:\beta}\neg\varphi$

Axiom **Alt**$_{Act}$ says that: if i is going to do α and φ will be true afterward, then it cannot be the case that j is going to do β and $\neg\varphi$ will be true afterward.

We also suppose that the world is never static in our framework, that is, we suppose that for every world w there exists some agent i and action α such that i is going to perform α at w. Formally, for every $w \in W$ we have that:

S2 $\exists i \in AGT, \exists \alpha \in ACT, \exists w' \in W$ such that $(w, w') \in \mathscr{D}_{i:\alpha}$

The semantic constraint $S2$ corresponds to the following axiom of our logic.

Active $\bigvee_{i \in AGT, \alpha \in ACT} Does_{i:\alpha}\top$

Axiom **Active** ensures that for every world w there is a *next* world of w which is reachable from w by the occurrence of some action of some agent. This is the reason why the operator X for *next* of LTL (linear temporal logic) can be defined as follows:

$$X\varphi \stackrel{\text{def}}{=} \bigvee_{i \in AGT, \alpha \in ACT} Does_{i:\alpha}\varphi$$

Note that X satisfies the standard property $X\varphi \leftrightarrow \neg X\neg\varphi$ (i.e. φ will be true in the next state iff $\neg\varphi$ will not be true in the next state).

The following relationship is supposed between every relation $\mathscr{D}_{i:\alpha}$ and the corresponding relation $\mathscr{A}_{i:\alpha}$ of all $\mathcal{L}$ models. For every $i \in AGT, \alpha \in ACT$ and $w \in W$:

S3   if $(w, w') \in \mathscr{D}_{i:\alpha}$ then $(w, w') \in \mathscr{A}_{i:\alpha}$

---

[3] This includes rule of necessitation, Axiom K for every operator Bel_i plus the following three axioms (so-called Axioms D, 4, 5): $\neg Bel_i\bot$; $Bel_i\varphi \rightarrow Bel_i Bel_i\varphi$; $\neg Bel_i\varphi \rightarrow Bel_i\neg Bel_i\varphi$.
[4] This includes rule of necessitation, Axiom K for every operator $Goal_i$ plus the following Axiom D: $\neg Goal_i\bot$.
[5] This includes rule of necessitation, Axiom K for Obg plus the following Axiom D: $\neg Obg\bot$.

The constraint $S3$ says that if w' is the *next* world of w which is reachable from w through the occurrence of agent i's action α, then w' is a world which is *possibly* reachable from w through the occurrence of agent i's action α. The semantic constraint $S3$ corresponds to the following axiom $\mathbf{Inc}_{Act,PAct}$.

$$\mathbf{Inc}_{Act,PAct} \quad Does_{i:\alpha}\varphi \rightarrow \neg After_{i:\alpha}\neg\varphi$$

According to $\mathbf{Inc}_{Act,PAct}$, if i is going to do α and φ will be true afterward, then it is not the case that $\neg\varphi$ will be true after i does α. The following axioms relates intentions with actions.

IntAct1 $(Int_i(\alpha) \wedge Can_i(\alpha)) \rightarrow Does_{i:\alpha}\top$
IntAct2 $Does_{i:\alpha}\top \rightarrow Int_i(\alpha)$

According to **IntAct1**, if i has the intention to do action α and has the capacity to do α, then i is going to do α. According to **IntAct2**, an agent is going to do action α only if he has the intention to do α. In this sense we suppose that an agent's *doing* is by definition intentional. Similar axioms have been studied in [19] in which a logical model of the relationships between intention and action performance is proposed. **IntAct1** and **IntAct2** correspond to the following semantic constraints over $\mathcal{L}$ models. For every $i \in AGT, \alpha \in ACT$ and $w \in W$:

S4   if $\forall(w,w') \in \mathscr{G}_i, \exists w''$ such that $(w',w'') \in \mathscr{D}_{i:\alpha}$ and $\exists v$ such that $(w,v) \in \mathscr{A}_{i:\alpha}$
        then $\exists v'$ such that $(w,v') \in \mathscr{D}_{i:\alpha}$
S5   if $\exists v'$ such that $(w,v') \in \mathscr{D}_{i:\alpha}$ then $\forall(w,w') \in \mathscr{G}_i, \exists w''$ such that $(w',w'') \in \mathscr{D}_{i:\alpha}$

We also suppose that goals and beliefs must be compatible, that is, if an agent has the goal that φ then, he cannot believe that $\neg\varphi$. Indeed, the notion of goal we characterize here is a notion of an agent's *chosen goal*, i.e. a goal that an agent decides to pursue. As some authors have stressed (*e.g.*[4]), a rational agent cannot decide to pursue a certain state of affairs φ, if he believes that $\neg\varphi$. Thus, for any $i \in AGT$ and $w \in W$ the following semantic constraint over $\mathcal{L}$ models is supposed:

S6 $\exists w'$ such that $(w,w') \in \mathscr{B}_i$ and $(w,w') \in \mathscr{G}_i$

The constraint $S7$ corresponds to the following axiom **WR** (*weak realism*) of our logic.

WR $Goal_i\varphi \rightarrow \neg Bel_i\neg\varphi$

In this work we assume positive and negative introspection over (chosen) goals, that is:

PIntrGoal $Goal_i\varphi \rightarrow Bel_i\,Goal_i\varphi$
NIntrGoal $\neg Goal_i\varphi \rightarrow Bel_i\neg Goal_i\varphi$

Axioms **PIntrGoal** and **NIntrGoal** correspond to the following semantic constraints over $\mathcal{L}$ models. For any $i \in AGT$ and $w \in W$:

S7   if $(w,w') \in \mathscr{B}_i$ then $\forall v$, if $(w,v) \in \mathscr{G}_i$ then $(w',v) \in \mathscr{G}_i$
S8   if $(w,w') \in \mathscr{B}_i$ then $\forall v$, if $(w',v) \in \mathscr{G}_i$ then $(w,v) \in \mathscr{G}_i$

We accept the following axiom relating obligations and beliefs:

BelObg $Obg\varphi \rightarrow Bel_i Obg\varphi$

This axiom is based on the assumption that every agent has complete information of what is obligatory. It is justified by the fact that if it is expected that an agent does every action which is obligatory, he must have a complete information about what is obligatory. Axiom **BelObg** corresponds to the following semantic constraint over $\mathcal{L}$ models: For any $i \in AGT$ and $w \in W$:

S9   if $(w, w') \in \mathcal{B}_i$ then $\forall v$, if $(w', v) \in \mathcal{O}$ then $(w, v) \in \mathcal{O}$

Note that by Axiom **BelObg**, the definition of the permission operator $Perm$ and Axiom D for Bel_i, the following formula can be derived as a consequence: $Bel_i Perm\varphi \rightarrow Perm\varphi$. This means that in our logical framework every agent has sound information of what is permitted.

We also have specific properties for the actions of requiring and authorizing. We suppose that, given two agents i and j playing respectively roles x and y in the organization, if role x controls role y with respect to the action a then: after i requires (resp. authorizes) j to do a, j has the obligation to do a (resp. has the permission to do a). Formally:

Control $(Play(i, x) \wedge Play(j, y) \wedge Control(x, y, a)) \rightarrow$
$(After_{i:req_j(a)} ObgDoes_{j:a}\top \wedge After_{i:auth_j(a)} PermDoes_{j:a}\top)$

Axiom **Control** corresponds to the following two semantic constraints over $\mathcal{L}$ models. For any $i, j \in AGT$, $x, y \in ROLE$, $a \in AT$ and $w \in W$ if $i \in \mathcal{F}_{play}(x)$, $j \in \mathcal{F}_{play}(y)$ and $a \in \mathcal{F}_{control}(x, y)$ then:

S10   if $(w, w') \in \mathcal{A}_{i:req_j(a)} \circ \mathcal{O}$ then $\exists w''$ such that $(w', w'') \in \mathcal{D}_{j:a}$
S11   if $(w, w') \in \mathcal{A}_{i:auth_j(a)}$ then $\exists w''$ such that $(w', w'') \in \mathcal{O} \circ \mathcal{D}_{j:a}$

where $\circ$ is the standard composition operator between two binary relations.

We call $\mathcal{L}$ the logic axiomatized by the axioms and rules of inference presented above. We write $\vdash \varphi$ if formula φ is a theorem of $\mathcal{L}$ (i.e. φ is the derivable from the axioms and rules of inference of the logic $\mathcal{L}$). We write $\models \varphi$ if φ is *valid* in all $\mathcal{L}$ models, i.e. $M, w \models \varphi$ for every $\mathcal{L}$ model M and world w in M. Finally, we say that φ is *satisfiable* if there exists a $\mathcal{L}$ model M and world w in M such that $M, w \models \varphi$. We can prove that the logic $\mathcal{L}$ is *sound* and *complete* with respect to the class of $\mathcal{L}$ models. Namely:

Theorem 1. $\vdash \varphi$ *if and only if* $\models \varphi$.

Proof. It is a routine task to check that the axioms of the logic $\mathcal{L}$ correspond one-to-one to their semantic counterparts on the frames. It is routine, too, to check that all of our axioms are in the Sahlqvist class. This means that the axioms are all expressible as first-order conditions on frames and that they are complete with respect to the defined frames classes, cf. [3, Th. 2.42]. ☐

3 Trust within the Context of Organizations

Trust relationships within the context of an organization can be analyzed at three general levels of abstraction:

- an agent's trust in another agent;
- an agent's trust in a role;
- an agent's trust in another agent *qua* player of a certain role.

The former kind of trust, also called interpersonal (or inter-agent) trust, is the trust that a certain agent i places in a different agent j. This kind of trust is based on i's ascription of specific properties to j including powers, abilities and dispositions. We call these j's *individual properties*.

On the contrary, an agent i's trust in a role x, with respect to the accomplishment of a given task φ, is based on i's attribution to role x of certain standard values and properties that are relevant for the achievement of the task φ. We call these *role properties*. For example, if i says that he trusts policemen with respect to the task of monitoring dangerous situations, i's trust in policemen is based on i's attribution to policemen of certain role properties that are relevant with respect to the task of monitoring dangerous situations (e.g. being armed, having the power to arrest suspected people, etc.).

Finally, an agent i's trust in another agent j *qua* player of a role x with respect to a certain task φ, is the trust that i places in j due to the fact that j plays role x and, according to i's beliefs, role x has certain (role) properties that are relevant for the accomplishment of task φ. In this situation, i's trust in j *qua* player of role x is based on the fact that i transfers the properties of role x (that are relevant for the accomplishment of task φ) to agent j playing role x. Differently from trust in a role, agent i's trust in agent j *qua* player of role x is also based on i's attribution to agent j of certain individual properties that are not necessarily properties of the role x. For example, i's trust in j *qua* policeman with respect to the task of monitoring dangerous situations has two facets. On the one side, it is based on the fact that j plays the role of policeman and, *qua* policeman, j inherits the role properties of policemen (e.g. being armed, having the power to arrest suspected people). On the other side, it is based on i's attribution of individual properties to j (e.g. being absent-minded and lazy). The individual properties of j might conflict with the properties that j inherits from the role of policeman leading i to negatively evaluate j with respect to the task of monitoring dangerous situations.

3.1 Interpersonal Trust

As we have stressed in our previous works [9], interpersonal trust should be conceived as a complex configuration of mental states in which there is both a motivational component and an epistemic component. More precisely, we assume that an agent i's trust in agent j necessarily involves a goal of the truster: if agent i trusts agent j then, necessarily, i trusts j with respect to some of his goals. The core of trust is a belief of the truster about some properties of the trustee, that is, if agent i trusts agent j then necessarily i trusts j because i has some goal and believes that j has the right properties to ensure that such a goal will be achieved.

In our perspective, interpersonal trust is based on the truster's *evaluation* of specific properties of the trustee (e.g. abilities, competencies, dispositions, etc) and of the environment in which the trustee is going to act, which are relevant for the achievement of a goal of the truster. From this perspective, trust is nothing more than the truster's belief about some relevant properties of the trustee with respect to a given goal. [6]

The following is the precise concept of interpersonal trust as an *evaluation* that interests us in the present work.

Definition 1. *Agent i's trust in agent j's action. Agent i trusts agent j to do α with regard to the achievement of φ if and only if i has the achievement goal that φ and i believes that:*

- *j, by doing α, will ensure φ AND*
- *j has the capacity to do α AND*
- *j intends to do α.*

The formal translation of Definition 1 is:

$$Trust(i, j, \alpha, \varphi) \stackrel{\text{def}}{=} AGoal_i\varphi \wedge Bel_i(After_{j:\alpha}\varphi \wedge Can_j(\alpha) \wedge Int_j(\alpha))$$

where $Trust(i, j, \alpha, \varphi)$ stands for "i trusts j to do α with regard to the achievement of φ", and formula $AGoal_i\varphi$, expressing agent i's achievement goal that φ, is defined as follows:

$$AGoal_i\varphi \stackrel{\text{def}}{=} Goal_iX\varphi \wedge \neg Bel_i\varphi$$

Our concept of achievement goal is similar to the concept studied in [6]. We say that an agent i has the achievement goal that φ if and only if, i wants φ to be true in the next state and does not believe that φ is true now. According to definition 1, i's trust in j with respect to the achievement of φ through action α is based on i's attribution of three main properties to j: the power to ensure φ by doing α ($After_{j:\alpha}\varphi$), the capacity to do action α ($Can_j(\alpha)$), the intention to do α ($Int_j(\alpha)$).

It is worth noting that in our logic the conditions $Can_j(\alpha)$ and $Int_j(\alpha)$ together are equivalent to $Does_{j:\alpha}\top$ (by axioms **Inc**$_{Act,PAct}$, **IntAct1** and **IntAct2**), so the definition of trust in the trustee's action can be simplified as follows:

$$Trust(i, j, \alpha, \varphi) \stackrel{\text{def}}{=} AGoal_i\varphi \wedge Bel_i(After_{j:\alpha}\varphi \wedge Does_{j:\alpha}\top)$$

Example 1. The two agents i and j are making a commercial transaction. After having paid j, i trusts j to deliver him a certain product with regard to his goal of having the product:

$$Trust(i, j, deliver, HasProduct(i)).$$

This means that i has the achievement goal of having the product:

$$AGoal_i HasProduct(i).$$

Moreover, according to i's beliefs, j, by delivering him the product, will ensure that he will have the product, and j is going to deliver the product:

$$Bel_i(After_{j:deliver}HasProduct(i) \wedge Does_{j:deliver}\top).$$

---

[6] In this paper we do not consider a related notion of *decision to trust*, that is, the truster's decision to bet and wager on the trustee and to rely on him for the accomplishment of a given task. For a distinction between trust as an *evaluation* and trust as a *decision*, see [9,21].

The following theorems highlight some interesting properties of the previous notion of interpersonal trust.

Theorem 2. *Let $i, j \in AGT$ and $\alpha \in ACT$. Then:*

1. $\vdash Trust(i, j, \alpha, \varphi) \rightarrow Bel_i X \varphi$
2. $\vdash Trust(i, j, \alpha, \varphi) \leftrightarrow Bel_i Trust(i, j, \alpha, \varphi)$
3. $\vdash (Trust(i, j, \alpha, \varphi) \wedge Trust(i, j, \alpha, \psi)) \rightarrow Trust(i, j, \alpha, \varphi \wedge \psi)$
4. $\vdash \neg Trust(i, j, \alpha, \top)$

Proof. We prove Theorems 2.1 and 2.4 as examples. We prove Theorem 2.1 first. $Trust(i, j, \alpha, \varphi)$ implies $Bel_i(After_{j:\alpha}\varphi \wedge Does_{j:\alpha}\top)$ (by def. of $Trust(i, j, \alpha, \varphi)$). $After_{j:\alpha}\varphi \wedge Does_{j:\alpha}\top$ implies $Does_{j:\alpha}\varphi$ (by Axiom **Inc**$_{Act,PAct}$ and standard principles of the normal operator $Does_{j:\alpha}$). $Does_{j:\alpha}\varphi$ implies $X\varphi$ (by definition of $X\varphi$). We conclude that $Bel_i(After_{j:\alpha}\varphi \wedge Does_{j:\alpha}\top)$ implies $Bel_i X\varphi$ (by Axiom K for Bel_i).

To prove Theorem 2.4, it is sufficient to prove that $Trust(i, j, \alpha, \top)$ implies $\bot$. $Trust(i, j, \alpha, \top)$ implies $\neg Bel_i \top$ (by def. of $Trust(i, j, \alpha, \top)$ and $AGoal_i \top$). The latter implies $\bot$ (by standard principles of the normal operator Bel_i). $\square$

According to Theorem 2.1, if i trusts j to do α with regard to φ then i has a positive expectation that φ will be true in the next state. Theorem 2.2 highlights the fact that trust is under the focus of the truster's awareness: i trusts j to do α with regard to φ if and only if, i is aware of this. Finally, Theorem 2.3 shows that trust aggregates under conjunction: if i trusts j to do α with regard to φ and i trusts j to do α with regard to ψ then, i trusts j to do α with regard to $\varphi \wedge \psi$. As Theorem 2.4 shows, in our logical model there is no trust about tautologies. This is for us an intuitive property of trust.

Trust in an Agent's Inaction. It is worth noting that an exhaustive ontology of trust must distinguish the concept *trust in an agent's action* as defined above (definition 1) from the concept of *trust in an agent's inaction*. The former concept is focused on the domain of gains whereas the latter is focused on the domain of losses. That is, in the former case the truster believes that the trustee is in condition to *further* the achievement of a pleasant state of affairs, and he will *do* that; in the latter case the truster believes that the trustee is in condition to *endanger* the maintenance of a pleasant state of affairs, but he will *refrain* from doing that. The concept of trust in an agent's inaction can be defined as follows.

Definition 2. *Agent i's **trust in agent** j's **inaction.** Agent i trusts j not to do α with regard to the maintenance of φ if and only if i has the maintenance goal that φ and i believes that:*

1. *j, by doing α, will ensure that $\neg\varphi$ AND*
2. *j has the capacity to do α AND*
3. *j does not intend to do α.*

The formal definition of trust in the trustee's inaction is given by the following abbreviation.

$$Trust(i, j, \neg\alpha, \varphi) \overset{\text{def}}{=} MGoal_i X\varphi \wedge Bel_i(After_{j:\alpha}\neg\varphi \wedge Can_j(\alpha) \wedge \neg Int_j(\alpha))$$

where $Trust(i, j, \neg\alpha, \varphi)$ stands for "i trusts j not to do α with regard to the maintenance of φ", and formula $MGoal_i\varphi$, expressing agent i's maintenance goal that φ, is defined as follows:

$$MGoal_i\varphi \stackrel{\text{def}}{=} Goal_iX\varphi \wedge Bel_i\varphi$$

Our concept of maintenance goal is similar to Cohen & Levesque's concept [6]: an agent i has the maintenance goal that φ if and only if, i wants φ to be true in the next state and believes that φ is true now. That is, an agent i has a maintenance goal that φ if and only if, agent i already has φ and has the goal to continue to have φ in the next state. More generally, a maintenance goal is the goal of preserving a certain state of affairs.

Example 2. Agent j is the webmaster of a public access website. Agent i is a regular reader of this website and he trusts j not to restrict the access to the website with regard to his goal of having free access to the website:

$$Trust(i, j, \neg restrict, freeAccess(i)).$$

This means that, i has the maintenance goal of having free access to the website:

$$MGoal_i freeAccess(i).$$

Moreover, according to i's beliefs, j has the capacity to restrict the access to the website and, by restricting the access to the website, j will ensure that i will not have free access to the website, but j does not intend to restrict the access:

$$Bel_i(After_{j:restrict}\neg freeAccess(i) \wedge Can_j(restrict) \wedge \neg Int_j(restrict)).$$

In this situation, i's trust in j is based on i's belief that j is in condition to restrict the access to the website, but j does not have the intention to do this.

Note that, differently from agent i's trust in agent j's action, agent i's trust in agent j's inaction with respect to the goal that φ does not entail i's positive expectation that φ will be true. Indeed, $Trust(i, j, \neg\alpha, \varphi) \wedge \neg Bel_iX\varphi$ is satisfiable in our logic. The intuitive reason is that $\neg\varphi$ may be the effect of another action than $j : \alpha$.

In the following Section 3.2 we will provide an analysis of trust in a role and trust in an agent *qua* player of a role.

3.2   Trust in a Role and Trust in an Agent *qua* Role Player

It is typical of organizations that an agent playing a certain role delegates the accomplishment of a task to another agent playing a different role. For example, an agent playing the role of director of the organization might require another agent playing the role of secretary the task of organizing a business meeting. Trust in roles plays a prominent role in organizational performance: it mediates the social interaction between agents and affects delegation mechanisms within the context of the organization [16,5].

As emphasized at the beginning of Section 3, an agent i's trust in a role x, with respect to the accomplishment of a given task φ, is based on i's attribution to role x of certain standard values and properties that are relevant for the achievement of the task φ (*role properties*). We here focus on a particular role property, that is, the (role) property of having the power to accomplish the task. In particular, we define an agent i's trust in a role x with respect to certain task as i's belief that playing role x is a sufficient condition for an agent to have the power to accomplish the task. The precise definition of trust in a role is the following one.

Definition 3. *Agent i's trust in role x. Agent i trusts role x with regard to the achievement of φ through action α if and only if i has the achievement goal that φ and believes that:*

- *every agent playing role x, by doing α, will ensure that φ.*

The formal translation of Definition 3 is:

$$Trust(i, x, \alpha, \varphi) \stackrel{def}{=} AGoal_i\varphi \wedge Bel_i(\bigwedge_{j \in \mathscr{F}_{play}(x)} After_{j:\alpha}\varphi)$$

where $\mathscr{F}_{play}(x)$ is the set of agents which play role x in the organization. The formula $Trust(i, x, \alpha, \varphi)$ is meant to stand for "agent i trusts role x with regard to the achievement of φ through action α". The following example clarifies the meaning of the concept of trust in a role.

Example 3. Suppose that agent i is the editor in chief of a scientific journal. Agent i trusts the members of his editorial board to review an article submitted to the journal with respect to his goal of having a good evaluation of the article. Formally:

$$Trust(i, boardMember, review, goodEvaluation).$$

This means that i has the achievement goal of having a good evaluation of the article and believes that every member of the board can provide a good evaluation of the article by reviewing it:

$$AGoal_i goodEvaluation \wedge$$
$$Bel_i(\bigwedge_{j \in \mathscr{F}_{play}(boardMember)} After_{j:review} goodEvaluation).$$

One might object that the previous definition of trust in a role x is quite strong since it requires that every agent playing role x has the power to ensure φ by doing α. One might define weaker forms of trust in a role. For instance, one might suppose that agent i trusts role x with regard to the achievement of φ through action α if and only if i has the achievement goal that φ and believes that the majority of agents playing role x can ensure φ by doing α. This alternative definition of trust in a role based on the concept of majority can be formally expressed as follows.

$$Trust(i, x, \alpha, \varphi) \stackrel{def}{=}$$

$$AGoal_i\varphi \wedge Bel_i(\bigvee_{C \subseteq \mathscr{F}_{play}(x), |C| > |\mathscr{F}_{play}(x) \setminus C|} (\bigwedge_{j \in C} After_{j:\alpha}\varphi))$$

The last kind of trust that we consider is an agent's trust in another agent *qua* player of a certain role. In our perspective, i trusts j *qua* player of role x with respect to a certain task if and only if, i trusts j *because* i thinks that j plays role x. As emphasized at the beginning of Section 3, agent i's trust in agent j *qua* player of role x has two facets. On the one side, it is based on the fact that i transfers some properties of role x (that are relevant for the accomplishment of the task) to agent j playing that role. On the other side, it is based on i's attribution of certain individual properties to j.

Definition 4. *Agent i's trust in agent j qua player of role x.* Agent i trusts agent j qua player of role x with regard to the achievement of φ through action α if and only if:

- agent i trusts role x with regard to the achievement of φ through action α (see definition 3) AND
- i believes that
  - j plays role x AND
  - j has the capacity to do α AND
  - j intends to do α.

According to definition 4, i's trust in j *qua* player of role x with respect to the achievement of φ through action α is based on i's trust in role x and i's attribution of two individual properties to j: the capacity to do α and the intention to do α. The definition can be formally translated as follows:

$$Trust(i, j, x, \alpha, \varphi) \stackrel{\text{def}}{=} Trust(i, x, \alpha, \varphi) \wedge Bel_i(Play(j, x) \wedge Can_j(\alpha) \wedge Int_j(\alpha))$$

where $Trust(i, j, x, \alpha, \varphi)$ stands for "agent i trusts agent j *qua* player of role x with regard to the achievement of φ through action α".

As for interpersonal trust, since in our logic the conditions $Can_j(\alpha)$ and $Int_j(\alpha)$ together are equivalent to $Does_{j:\alpha}\top$, the definition of trust in an agent *qua* player of a role can be simplified as follows:

$$Trust(i, j, x, \alpha, \varphi) \stackrel{\text{def}}{=} Trust(i, x, \alpha, \varphi) \wedge Bel_i(Play(j, x) \wedge Does_{j:\alpha}\top)$$

Before concluding this section, we consider some formal relationships between the three concepts of trust presented above. For instance:

- is it possible that agent j plays role x and agent i trust role x with respect to the achievement of φ, without i trusting j *qua* player of role x?
- is it possible that agent i trusts agent j *qua* player of role x with respect to the achievement of φ without i trusting j?

The answer to the first question is positive. Indeed, an agent i's trust in an agent j *qua* player of a role x with respect to the achievement of φ through action α is not only based on i's trust in role x but also on i's attribution of individual properties to j (i.e. j's capacity and j's intention to do action α). Thus, it might be the case that i trusts role x, under the condition that j plays role x and, i does not trust j *qua* player of role x. This is the reason why in our logic $\mathcal{L}$ the formula $\neg Trust(i, j, x, \alpha, \varphi) \wedge Trust(i, x, \alpha, \varphi) \wedge Play(j, x)$ is satisfiable. On the contrary, the answer to the second question is negative. Indeed, it is not possible that i trusts j *qua* player of role x with respect to the achievement of φ through α and, at the same time, agent i does not trust agent j with respect to the achievement of φ through α: $Trust(i, j, x, \alpha, \varphi) \rightarrow Trust(i, j, \alpha, \varphi)$ is a theorem of the logic $\mathcal{L}$. Note also that, in our logical model, interpersonal trust does not necessarily entail trust in an agent *qua* player of a certain role, that is, i might trust j with respect to φ without trusting j *qua* player of a role with respect to φ. This is the reason why the formula $Trust(i, j, \alpha, \varphi) \wedge Play(j, x) \wedge \neg Trust(i, j, x, \alpha, \varphi)$ is satisfiable in the logic $\mathcal{L}$. This is due to the fact that i's trust in j is not generalized to all agents playing the same role as j.

In the following Section 3.3, the definitions of trust in a role and trust in an agent *qua* player of a role are applied to the specific case of an authority's trust in a subordinate.

3.3   Trust of an Authority in an Subordinate

Trust of an authority in a subordinate (e.g. the trust of a leader in a follower, of an employer in an employee, of a trainer in a player, etc.) is based on the authority's belief that the subordinate will effectively try to complete a certain delegated task, that is, an authority's trust in a subordinate is based on the authority's belief that the subordinate will conform to the obligations that the authority has created by means of certain requests.

In some of our previous papers [18] we have formally characterized the concept of *obedience* as a general attitude of the subordinate concerning norm compliance. Let us reconsider it in the context of the present analysis. We say that a certain agent i is obedient if and only if, he intends to do a certain action α as a consequence of his fulfillment of the obligation to do this action. Formally:

$$Obed_i(\alpha) \stackrel{def}{=} Bel_i ObgDoes_{i:\alpha}\top \rightarrow Int_i(\alpha)$$

where $Obed_i(\alpha)$ stands for: i *is obedient to do the action* α.

The following Theorem 3 shows how the authority's belief that the subordinate is obedient intervenes to support the authority's trust in the subordinate.

Theorem 3. *Let* $i, j \in AGT$, $x, y \in ROLE$ *and* $a \in AT$ *then:*
$\vdash (Play(i,x) \wedge Play(j,y) \wedge Control(x,y,a) \wedge$
$After_{i:req_j(a)}(Trust(i,y,\alpha,\varphi) \wedge Bel_i(Obed_j(a) \wedge Can_j(a)))) \rightarrow$
$After_{i:req_j(a)}Trust(i,j,y,a,\varphi)$

Theorems 3 has the following meaning. Suppose that agents i and j play respectively roles x and y in the organization and role x controls role y with respect to the action a. In this sense, i has authority over j with respect to the action a. Then, if after i requires j to do a, i will trust role y with respect to the achievement of φ through a and i will believe j to be capable to do a and to be obedient to do a then, after i requires j to do a, i will trust j *qua* player of role y with respect to the achievement of φ through a.

4   Conclusion

We have presented in a modal logical framework a model of trust within organizations. We have defined three different forms of trust: interpersonal trust (i.e. trust in an agent), trust in a role and trust in an agent *qua* player of a role. The formal relationships between the three concepts have been investigated. In the last part of the paper we have considered the special case of an authority's trust in a subordinate (e.g. an employer's trust in a employee). Future works will be devoted to extend our analysis to a notion of *graded trust* based on a notion of *uncertain belief*. Indeed, in the present work we have only considered a notion of *binary trust* (i.e. either i trusts j or i does not trust j). Such a kind of extension will enable us to integrate the cognitive and qualitative analysis of trust presented in this paper with a quantitative analysis and, to compare our approach with existing probabilistic approaches to trust (e.g. [15]).

References

1. Åqvist, L.: Deontic logic. In: Gabbay, D.M., Geunther, F. (eds.) Handbook of Philosophical Logic. Kluwer Academic Publishers, Dordrecht (2002)
2. Arrow, K.: The Limits of Organization. Norton, New York (1974)
3. Blackburn, P., de Rijke, M., Venema, Y.: Modal Logic. Cambridge University Press, Cambridge (2001)
4. Bratman, M.: Intentions, plans, and practical reason. Harvard University Press (1987)
5. Castelfranchi, C.: Grounding organizations in the minds of agents. In: Dignum, V. (ed.) Multi-agent systems: semantics and dynamics of organizational models. IGI Global (forthcoming)
6. Cohen, P.R., Levesque, H.J.: Intention is choice with commitment. Artificial Intelligence 42, 213–261 (1990)
7. Coleman, J.: Foundations of Social Theory. Harvard University Press, Cambridge (1990)
8. Demolombe, R.: To trust information sources: a proposal for a modal logical framework. In: Castelfranchi, C.A., Tan, Y.H. (eds.) Trust and Deception in Virtual Societies, pp. 111–124. Kluwer, Dordrecht (2001)
9. Falcone, R., Castelfranchi, C.: Social trust: A cognitive approach. In: Castelfranchi, C., Tan, Y.H. (eds.) Trust and Deception in Virtual Societies, pp. 55–90. Kluwer, Dordrecht (2001)
10. Grossi, D., Royakkers, L., Dignum, F.: Organizational structure and responsibility: an analysis in a dynamic logic of organized collective agency. Artificial Intelligence and Law 15, 223–249 (2007)
11. Harel, D., Kozen, D., Tiuryn, J.: Dynamic Logic. MIT Press, Cambridge (2000)
12. Hintikka, J.: Knowledge and Belief. Cornell University Press, New York (1962)
13. Hübner, J.F., Sichman, J.S., Boissier, O.: Developing organised multi-agent systems using the MOISE+ model: programming issues at the system and agent levels. International Journal of Agent-Oriented Software Engineering 1(3/4), 370–395 (2007)
14. Jones, A.J.I.: On the concept of trust. Decision Support Systems 33(3), 225–232 (2002)
15. Jøsang, A.: A logic for uncertain probabilities. International Journal of Uncertainty, Fuzziness and Knowledge-Based Systems 9(3), 279–311 (2001)
16. Kramer, R.M.: Trust and distrust in organizations: emerging perspectives, enduring questions. Annual Review of Psychology 50, 569–598 (1999)
17. Liau, C.J.: Belief, information acquisition, and trust in multi-agent systems: a modal logic formulation. Artificial Intelligence 149, 31–60 (2003)
18. Lorini, E., Demolombe, R.: Trust and norms in the context of computer security: A logical formalization. In: van der Meyden, R., van der Torre, L. (eds.) DEON 2008. LNCS, vol. 5076, pp. 50–64. Springer, Heidelberg (2008)
19. Lorini, E., Herzig, A.: A logic of intention and attempt. Synthese 163(1), 45–77
20. March, J.G., Simon, H.: Organizations. John Wiley & Sons, Chichester (1958)
21. Marsh, S.: Formalising Trust as a Computational Concept. PhD thesis, University of Stirling, Scotland (1994)
22. Santos, F., Carmo, J., Jones, A.: Action concepts for describing organised interaction. In: Sprague, R.A. (ed.) Thirtieth Annual Hawai International Conference on System Sciences, pp. 373–382. IEEE Computer Society Press, Los Alamitos (1997)
23. Wooldridge, M., Jennings, N.R., Kinny, D.: The Gaia methodology for agent-oriented analysis and design. Autonomous Agents and Multi-Agent Systems 3(3), 285–312 (2000)

Know What You Trust[*]
Analyzing and Designing Trust Policies with Scoll

Fred Spiessens, Jerry den Hartog, and Sandro Etalle

Eindhoven Institute for the Protection of Systems and Information
University of Technology Eindhoven
Eindhoven, The Netherlands
a.o.d.spiessens@tue.nl, j.d.hartog@tue.nl, s.etalle@tue.nl

Abstract. In Decentralized Trust Management (DTM) authorization decisions are made by multiple principals who can also delegate decisions to each other. Therefore, a policy change of one principal will often affect who gets authorized by another principal. In such a system of influenceable authorization a number of principals may want to coordinate their policies to achieve long time guarantees on a set of safety goals.

The problem we tackle in this paper is to find minimal restrictions to the policies of a set of principals that achieve their safety goals. This will enable building useful DTM systems that are safe by design, simply by relying on the policy restrictions of the collaborating principals. To this end we will model DTM safety problems in Scoll [1], an approach that proved useful to model confinement in object capability systems [2].

1 Introduction

Structural (role based) decentralized trust management (DTM) systems address the problem of access and delegation control in a distributed setting where authorization emanates from multiple sources. The rights of the agents/users in/of a system are not determined by a single authority but is the effect of policies set by different parties.

Principals cannot only define roles and authorize other principals as members of these roles. They can also delegate the authorization of their roles to other principals. Several powerful role based delegation models and trust management languages have been proposed for this purpose in the literature, each with their own balance between simplicity and expressive power. In this paper we will use RT_0, the simplest in the RT [3,4] family of trust management languages, but our approach can easily be applied to more expressive members of that family.

The Running Example. The following simple example will be used and elaborated throughout this paper. The chair of the Open Conference defines a reviewer role and a submitter role for the conference. The chair designates Alice as a first

---

[*] This work has been supported in part by European Commission FP7 TAS3 project, nr. 216287 and the BSIK project Poseidon.

P. Degano, J. Guttman, and F. Martinelli (Eds.): FAST 2008, LNCS 5491, pp. 129–142, 2009.

reviewer. He then delegates all authorization responsibilities for both conference roles to the members of the reviewer role. This means that the policy of every conference reviewer can now influence the conference's role assignment. The safety concern the conference chair wants to be guaranteed is a simple mutual exclusion between the submitter and the reviewer role: no submitter should ever become also a reviewer.

The Problem. If the reviewers cooperate with each other to manage both conference roles, it is relatively easy for them to detect a breach of the mutual exclusion requirement: they would only have to check the members of both roles and raise alarm when both roles have a common member. However, it is not trivial for the reviewers to design their policies in such a way that the safety breach becomes guaranteed impossible.

For instance, it does not suffice for the reviewers to simply refrain from authorizing anyone directly to be a member of both roles. They must also watch their delegation statements, as these may have indirect effects that may not be obvious to predict. Disallowing the reviewers to assign anybody to the submitter role could be sufficient to guarantee the safety concern, but that solution would be too restrictive for the purpose of the conference.

The problem we want to solve concerning the running example is: in what way(s) can we restrict the policies of the reviewers no more than necessary to make sure that the conference roles are mutually exclusive regardless of the policies of the non-reviewers, while still allowing the submitter role to be filled.

The general form of the problem is as follows. In a DTM system in which every principal has a policy, and policies are finite sets of monotonic authorizations and delegations, let the following be given:

- let P_k be the set of principals of which we know the exact policies
- let P_u be the set of principals of which we do not know the policies or have no reliable way to restrict them, with $(P_u \cap P_k = \emptyset)$,
- let P_c be the set of cooperating principals: the ones of which we can restrict the policies, with $(P_c \cap P_u = \emptyset)$
- a number of safety concerns: what authorizations should not be allowed
- a number of availability concerns: what authorizations should be allowed

The problem is to find all restrictions R_i for the principals in P_c such that:

1. As long as the principals in P_c do not include any of the elements in R_i into their policy, it is impossible for the principals of P_u to break the safety requirements.
2. As long as the principals in P_c do not restrict their policies any further than described above, it is possible for the principals of P_u to reach the availability requirements .

We call R_i a solution to our problem. In practice, we will only calculate the minimal sets R_i for which both properties hold, and call them "optimal" solutions.

Property 1 indicates that every solution represents a set of sufficient restrictions for the cooperating principals that will guarantee safety, regardless of how the non-cooperative principals extend their policies. Property 2 merely indicates that no solution restricts the policies so strong that, even with maximally permissive policies of the principals in P_u, the reachability properties would not be guaranteed. Solutions are "optimal" if the restrictions are not only sufficient but also necessary for safety.

The approach we apply here will conservatively (over-)approximate all policies of the P_u principals to calculate upper bounds to the policies of the P_c principals. Our safety results are valid, even if the policies of the other principals are also conservatively approximated. However, this is not the case for availability requirements. That would require us to approximate the unknown policies from below and calculate lower bounds for the policies of the cooperating principals, which we regard as interesting future work.

A solvable problem will typically have multiple solutions, because a restriction in one principal's policy may render another restriction unnecessary.

The Proposed Solution. We propose to express and analyze safety problems in DTM systems using *Scoll* (Safe Collaboration Language), a formal model designed for general safety analysis.

First, we show that, thanks to its DataLog based structure and its explicit support for behavior-based effect analysis, Scoll provides a natural way to model such problems.

Secondly, we demonstrate how *Scollar* (Scoll's analysis tool) can calculate the minimal restrictions in the behavior of a set of entities that are necessary to avoid a given set of unwanted effects, without leading to overly restrictive solutions that prevent another given set of wanted effects. Our entities will be the principals and the role names of a DTM system. Our behaviors will correspond to the RT_0 policies of the principals.

Scoll and Scollar are explained in dept in "Patterns of Safe Collaboration" [1].

The remainder of this paper is organized as follows. We discuss related work in section 2. In Section 3 we give a quick account on the RT_0 language and express the running example in it. We then give an overview of Scoll in Section 4 while translating our example into Scoll. In Section 5 we calculate and interpret the solutions to the running example. We conclude in section 6.

2   Related Work

In decentralized trust management [3,4,5,6] decisions are made based on statements made by multiple principals. The decision who can be trusted, e.g. to access a resource, is not made by a single principal but takes into account information from multiple principals, i.e. the decision is in part *delegated* to these other principals.

Securely sharing statements made by principals can be achieved by certificates frameworks such as X.509 which provides certified but uninterpreted statements and systems such as SPKI/SDSI [7] which link statements to authorization. The PolicyMaker [5] and KeyNote [6] systems separate trust and security concerns, allowing the specification of trust relationships in the form of assertions by the different principals.

In the RT [3,4] family of trust management languages principals express their trust policies in the form of relationships between the principal's roles and those of other principals. The use of simple rules and a sequence of increasingly more expressive and complex optional language features allows us to express simple policies easily while also supporting more complex trust relations.

Delegation is very powerful and typically coarse-grained in trust management systems such as RT. Usually one cannot be certain that whoever you are delegating to will know, understand and adhere to your expectations about how they should use these delegated powers. Therefore you cannot be sure that the delegation works in the way you intended. RT in itself does not provide the means to express these intentions, nor to reason about what the policies should be, given your intentions of bounding the eventual authorization.

This problem does not go away if we treat delegation as a permission in itself and allow policies to restrict delegation rights as proposed by [8,9]. Even if such policies are more refined, the original problem remains: what should these refined policies be, given your intentions to bound the eventual authorization. Moreover, approaches using delegation-as-permission typically require a more elaborate and complex enforcement mechanism.

In [10] a different approach is followed; instead of restricting the delegation, a number of constraints on its consequences are stated explicitly. Cooperative, trusted parties are then expected to help *monitor* these constraints. The approach then calculates a minimal subset of roles whose policy changes must be monitored to guarantee the early detection of constraint violations. Control over the (consequences of the) delegation should then be kept within this group of trusted parties.

In contrast to this monitoring approach, we propose to define a set of cooperating principals and calculate alternative minimal sets of (RT_0) policy rules that should be disallowed for these principals, to *avoid* violating the safety constraints.

Certain security analysis problems about safety and reachability were solved in [11]. That work also focusses on calculating bounds for the algorithmical complexity of such problems.

In this paper we restrict ourselves to safety problems. We only take availability constraints into account to make sure that our proposed restrictions do not make the required availability impossible. The Scoll approach is meant for safety analysis and thus calculates minimal sets of policy restrictions. Our approach can therefor not provide real insights about availability, even though that would be very useful in the context of DTM. It is interesting future work to extend Scollar to also calculate minimal DTM policies for this purpose.

3   Policies and Safety Concerns in RT_0

In this section we first introduce the basics of the trust management language RT_0, see e.g. [12] for details. Next we introduce the notion of incomplete RT_0 policies and show how our running example can be expressed. Finally we introduce safety concerns for such policies.

Table 1. The 4 types of RT_0 policy expressions

example	type	meaning
A.r ← B	membership	principal A adds principal B to role A.r
A.r ← B.r1	simple inclusion	A considers every member of B.r1 to be a member of A.r
A.r ← A.r1.r2	linking inclusion	A considers everybody in the r2 role of anybody in A.r1 to be a member of A.r
A.r ← B.r1 ∩ C.r2	intersection	A considers every member of B.r1 who is also a member of C.r2 to be a member of A.r

In RT_0 *principals* are uniquely identified individuals or processes, denoted by names starting with an uppercase. A principal can define *roles*, which are denoted by the principal's name, followed by the *role name*, separated by a dot. Role names start with a lowercase. For instance "A.role1" denotes the role named "role1" as defined by principal A.

A *credential* is an expression of one of the four types listed and clarified in table 1. A *policy* system is a set of credentials. The policy $A_{\mathcal{P}}$ of a (group of) principal(s) A is the subset of S defining roles of A.

RT_0 Semantics: Given a system of RT_0 policies, the set of principals that are defined by the system to be members of the role A.r is denoted as $[\![A.r]\!]$ (see [12] for a formal definition). We will use this notation when expressing safety requirements about an RT_0 system.

When checking safety requirements we will need to distinguish fixed or controllable parts of the policy and parts of which we cannot be sure. To this end we add a classification to the principals. We refer to the resulting system as an incomplete RT_0 system to emphasise that to address safety concerns we will need to consider extensions of the system.

Definition 1 (Incomplete RT_0 system). *An* Incomplete RT_0 system is a RT_0 policy system *together with a labeling which assigns to each participant one of the following three labels:*

- *label* k *for the principals whose policies are static and completely known.*
- *label* c *for the principals whose policy changes we can control and bound if necessary.*
- *label* u *for the principals whose policies are not completely known or can change beyond our control*

We use P_l to denote all principals with label l. An extension *of the system is obtained by adding credentials for P_c or P_u (but not P_k).*

Table 2 shows our running example as an incomplete RT_0 system with three principals: Conference, Alice, and Bob.

Conference's label indicates that her policy is fixed and stable as described in the first three rules of table 2. In rule 1 Conference adds Alice to Conference.reviewer. In rules 2 and 3 Conference delegates the authorization decisions about both her roles to members of her reviewer role.

Table 2. An incomplete RT_0 policy system

Principal	label	rule	nr.
Conference	k	Conference.reviewer ← Alice	1
		Conference.reviewer ← Conference.reviewer.reviewer	2
		Conference.submitter ← Conference.reviewer. submitter	3
Alice	c	Alice.submitter ← Bob	4
		Alice. reviewer ← Alice. reviewer. reviewer	5
Bob	u		

Alice's label indicates that her policy changes can be controlled. In rule 4 she adds Bob to Alice.submitter. Rule 5 states that Alice allows her reviewers to make authorization decision about Alice.reviewer, just as Conference did in rule 2. Bob will become a member of Conference.submitter via the combined effects of rules 1, 3 and 4.

Bob's label indicates that we have no definite knowledge about Bob's policy and/or we cannot restrict his policy changes.

Safety and Availability Concerns: When defining roles we have will have certain restrictions on who is allowed to be in what role. These restrictions can be expressed by constraints on the roles, see e.g. [10]. Here we consider two types of constraints. The first are *Safety* constraints which are expressions of the form $[\![A_1^1.r_1^1]\!] \cap \ldots \cap [\![A_n^1.r_n^1]\!] \cup \ldots \cup [\![A_1^m.r_1^m]\!] \cap \ldots \cap [\![A_k^m.r_k^m]\!] \subseteq \emptyset$.

The safety requirement in our running example is: mutual exclusion between Conference's reviewer and submitter roles. That can be expressed as:
$[\![Conference.reviewer]\!] \cap [\![Conference.submitter]\!] \subseteq \emptyset$

The second type of constraints are availability requirements which are expressions of the form $[\![A_1^1.r_1^1]\!] \cap \ldots \cap [\![A_n^1.r_n^1]\!] \cup \ldots \cup [\![A_1^m.r_1^m]\!] \cap \ldots \cap [\![A_k^m.r_k^m]\!] \supset \emptyset$.

That at least one principal should be in Conference.submitter can be expressed as: $[\![Conference.submitter]\!] \supset \emptyset$.

Definition 2. *Given an incomplete policy system $\mathcal{P}$, a set of safety and a set of availability constraints we say that a set of credentials R for roles of principals in P_c (called a restriction) is a* solution *if*

- *any extension of $\mathcal{P}$ not containing credentials in R satisfies the safety constraints.*
- *there exists an extension of $\mathcal{P}$ not containing credentials in R which satisfies all the availability constraints.*

We say a solution is optimal *if any strict subset of R is not a solution.*

In the next section we will see how we specify incomplete RT_0 systems and safety and availability concerns in Scoll. After that we will show how to find optimal solutions.

4   Modeling DTM Safety Problems in Scoll

In this section we will give an intuition about Scoll's syntax and semantics while we show how the running example can be modeled.

Scoll is based on DataLog [13] and was designed to automate reasoning about the potential effects that can be caused by the (inter-)actions of entities in a system, and to calculate what limitations (to the system and/or the entities) are necessary and sufficient to avoid all unwanted effects (safety) without preventing any wanted effects (availability). For a detailed account on Scoll we refer to [1].

Scoll programs involve a static and finite set of *subjects*. Every subject conservatively models a (possibly dynamic and infinite) set of actual entities. To model our running example we have chosen to represent all the potential reviewers with a single subject Alice, and all potential submitters with a single subject Bob. Aggregating entities this way is a valid approach when analyzing safety, but it may represent an over approximation. This means that the policy restrictions we will calculate are guaranteed to be sufficient but may be refined in situations where not all reviewers are supposed to have the same policy. While Scoll provides support for iterative and selective refinement, we will not use this feature here as we don't need it to clarify our contributions.

Core Syntax Features: In Scoll all predicate labels and subject constants start with a lowercase letter. Variables range over all subjects, and start with a uppercase letter. Predicate labels can contain dot characters to increase readability. Behavior types are denoted in all capitals.

Figure 1 shows how we expressed the running example in Scoll. We can distinguish six parts in the Scoll program, indicated by keywords in bold. Each part will now be discussed in detail.

4.1   Part 1: **declare**

The first part declares the labels and arities of the predicates over the subjects in the program (see Figure 1). Scoll differentiates between three kinds of predicates:

> **state** predicates modeling the security state,
> **behavior** predicates modeling the intentions subjects can have, and
> **knowledge** predicates modeling the internal state of subjects: what a subject can "know" or "learn" about the system and about the other subjects.

The *state predicates* for our running example are clarified in table 3. They will be used in the system part (Section 4.2) and in the goal part (Section 4.6).

The canActAs predicate expresses role membership and is scenario independent. For each safety or availability constraint we add a predicate capturing violation of the constraint, such as shareMember/3 for the mutual exclusion constraint. If the constraint concerns a single role as in $[\![Conference.submitter]\!] \supset \emptyset$ we can omit the extra predicate as we can already express role membership.

Table 3. State predicates

predicate	example	meaning
canActAs/3	canActAs(a,b,r1)	$A \in [\![B.r1]\!]$
shareMember/3	shareMember(a,r1,r2)	$[\![A.r1]\!] \cap [\![A.r2]\!] \neq \emptyset$

declare
    state: canActAs/3 shareMember/3
    behavior: member/3 incl/4 link/4 intersect/6
    knowledge:
system
    /* Simple Member */
    A:member(R1,B) => canActAs(B,A,R1);
    /* Simple Inclusion */
    A:incl(R1,B,R2) canActAs(C,B,R2) => canActAs(C,A,R1);
    /* Linking Inclusion */
    A:link(R,R1,R2) canActAs(B,A,R1) canActAs(C,B,R2) => canActAs(C,A,R);
    /* Intersection */
    A:intersect(R,B1,R1,B2,R2) canActAs(C,B1,R1) canActAs(C,B2,R2)
    => canActAs(C,A,R);
    /* Mutex */
    canActAs(A,B,R1) canActAs(A,B,R2) => shareMember(B,R1,R2);
behavior
    NONE {}
    UNKNOWN {   => member(_,_) incl(_,_,_) link(_,_,_) intersect(_,_,_,_,_);}
    CONFERENCE { isAlice(X) isReviewerRole(R)=> member(X,R);
                isReviewerRole(R) => link(R1,R,R1);}
subject
    ? alice: NONE
    bob: UNKNOWN
    conference: CONFERENCE
    reviewer: NONE
    submitter: NONE
config
    conference:isAlice(alice) conference:isReviewerRole(reviewer)
goal
    ! shareMember(conference,reviewer,submitter)
    canActAs(bob,conference,submitter)
    canActAs(alice,conference,reviewer)

Fig. 1. Running example : an RT_0 based trust problem in Scoll

Behavior predicates express the behavior of the subject in the first argument of the predicate. Similarly, knowledge predicates express knowledge available to the subject in the first argument. To emphasize this, behavior and knowledge predicates will be denoted with their first argument in front of the predicate label, separated by a colon. For example we use conference:member(reviewer,alice) rather than member(conference, reviewer, alice) to make it clear that this is a predicate on conference's behavior.

The behavior predicates of Figure 1 are clarified in table 4. They correspond exactly to the RT_0 policy expressions of section 3. Instead of representing credentials (e.g. as in [12]), here they represent the authorization intentions of an issuer of credentials: his RT_0 policy.

Notice that we did not provide a behavior predicate to express the actual use of a role by a subject. Scoll is very suitable for modeling usage behavior as well, but we will not explore that in this paper.

Table 4. Behavior predicates

predicate	example	meaning in RT_0
member/3	a:member(r,b)	$A.r \leftarrow B$
incl/4	a:incl(r,b,r1)	$A.r \leftarrow B.r1$
link/4	a:link(r,r1,r2)	$A.r \leftarrow A.r1.r2$
int/6	a:int(r,b,r1,c,r2)	$A.r \leftarrow B.r1 \cap C.r2$

Knowledge predicates model what entities can learn from their own successful behavior. This knowledge can be used in behavior rules (Section 4.3). We will only use static, subject specific knowledge that can be declared in the config part (Section 4.5).

4.2   Part 2: system

This part contains the *system rules*: DataLog rules that conservatively and monotonically model *all* the mechanisms by which subject behavior can result in changes to the security state as represented by the state predicates.

All Scoll rules use a notation that is closer to logics than to logic programming: the conditions are to the left and the conclusions to the right of a logical implication sign "=>". To encourage correct conservative approximations, Scoll allows only variables in system rules. Knowledge of identity will be modeled explicitly with static, subject specific predicates in Section 4.5.

System rules typically include behavior predicates in their conditions to express that a subject's cooperation is a necessary condition to the state change. We refer to [2] for an explanation on how this approach can model discretionary access control. In our example the four types of RT_0 credentials each appear as a behavior condition in a system rule.

The first four system rules in Figure 1 should now be self explanatory. For every behavior predicate there is a rule that states the conditions in which a subject's behavior affects the security state. These four rules have similar effects: canActAs() facts are added to the security state.

To these scenario independent rules we add a rule capturing the meaning of each of the predicates used for the constraints: the last system rule derives a state predicate that will be used later to detect a breach of mutual exclusion:
canActAs(A,B,R1) canActAs(A,B,R2) => shareMember(B,R1,R2);

Remark: In the actual Scoll model of this problem we added some type restrictions to the conditions in the system rules, using unary state predicates that are not shown here. Their only effect is in speeding up the calculation and avoiding variable bindings that do not make sense. We did not show them here, to avoid cluttering up the example.

4.3   Part 3: behavior

Behavior rules are DataLog rules that express in what conditions a subject is ready to show what behavior. The first argument is dropped in every predicate of a behavior rule: it *implicitly* refers to the subject who's behavior is described.

Two standard behaviors are NONE and UNKNOWN which respectively model principals which will issue no credentials at all or freely issue any of the possible credentials. The latter is how we model unknown entities conservatively: as subjects that always show every possible behavior towards all other subjects. Notice the use of anonymous variables indicated with underbar "_".

In addition we have scenario specific behaviors. For each principal with a k label we define a corresponding behavior; i.e. a behavior which issues the credentials in their (fixed) policy. The CONFERENCE behavior type has two rules:

isAlice(X) isReviewerRole(R) => member(X,R); This is the way in which rule 1 of table 2 is expressed in Scoll. Basically we are saying that someone with this behavior makes Alice a member of their reviewer role. However, as no constants are allowed in Scoll behaviors, we introduce local knowledge predicates isAlice/2 and isReviewerRole/2 describing these values and initialize them in them in the **config** part (Section 4.5).

isReviewerRole(R) => link(R1,R,R1); Here we have used a shorthand. Rather than defining two rules, one for reviewer and one for submitter roles we link any role $R1$ thus capturing both rules 2 and 3 of table 2 in a single Scoll rule.

4.4   Part 4: subject

Every subject is listed in this part, and assigned a behavior type from the previous part. The behavior type should reflect the trust we have in the entity to not engage in any behavior other than specified in the rules of the behavior type.

? alice:NONE   The question mark before alice indicates that we want to find out how we far we can safely extend alice's behavior, starting from the NONE behavior type. All principals with a c label should be marked like this.

bob:UNKNOWN   To safely approximate bob's behavior we assume the worst.

conference:CONFERENCE   Subject conference has behavior CONFERENCE

reviewer:NONE   Subject reviewer is a role name and has no behavior

submitter:NONE   Subject submitter is a role name and has no behavior

4.5   Part 5: config

This part defines the initial configuration: a list of all state facts in the initial security state and all knowledge facts in the initial subject states. In Figure 1 this part initializes the private knowledge of subject conference.

4.6   Part 6: goal

The final part of a Scoll program is the "goal" part. It lists the facts that should *not* become true (safety requirements) preceded by an exclamation mark, and the facts that should become true (availability requirements) without an exclamation mark.

In the example we want one fact to *not* become true:

shareMember(conference, reviewer, submitter).

This goal corresponds to the mutual exclusion constraint: nobody should have both the reviewer role and the submitter role for this conference. Conservative modeling should guarantee that the safety properties satisfied in the Scoll model also hold in the actual system.

The availability goals are added to avoid solutions that restrict Alice's policy so much that there is no way for Bob to be in Conference.submitter, or for Alice to be in Conference.reviewer.

5   Scollar Finds Solutions for DTM Safety Problems

The Scoll program in Figure 1 expresses a mutual exclusion problem combined with basic availability requirements. Achieving mutual exclusions is generally a difficult problem in trust management systems. For example, in the RT family of languages a special construction (manifold roles [3]) is needed. In [10] mutual exclusion is monitored and detected early, rather than prevented, by introducing constraints and keeping control within a group of trusted, cooperating agents.

We turned our mutual exclusion constraint into a detectable state-predicate (Section 4.2), of which a particular fact should be avoided (Section 4.6).

As explained in [14], Scollar uses constraint programming to calculate the minimal sets of behavior restrictions that guarantee the safety requirements without preventing the availability requirements. By listing the ways in which Alice's policies can be restricted no more than necessary to achieve our safety goals, without preventing our availability goals, Scoll will tell us what the boundaries to Alice's allowed policies are.

When presented with the problem of Figure 1, Scollar finds two solutions (Figure 2) that minimize the restrictions on Alice's policy. To keep the table within reasonable size for a good overview, we removed the 6-ary predicate intersection() from the calculations.

	solution number	1	2
1	alice:member(reviewer,alice)		0
2	reviewer,bob)	0	0
3	submitter,alice)	0	0
4	alice:incl(reviewer,alice,submitter)	0	0
5	reviewer,bob,reviewer)	0	0
6	reviewer,bob,submitter)	0	0
7	submitter,alice,reviewer)	0	
8	submitter,bob,reviewer)	0	0
9	submitter,bob,submitter)	0	0
10	alice:link(reviewer, reviewer,submitter)	0	
11	reviewer,submitter,reviewer)	0	0
12	reviewer, submitter, submitter)	0	0
13	submitter, reviewer, reviewer)	0	
14	submitter,submitter,reviewer)	0	0
15	submitter, submitter,submitter)	0	0

Fig. 2. Overview of the 2 possible alternatives for restricting Alice's RT_0 policy (excluding the intersection statements)

The table in Figure 2 contains a row for every behavior fact (policy , see table 1) of Alice that is to be avoided in at least one of the two solutions. If the expression is to be avoided in a solution, it is indicated as a zero in the column representing this solution.

Let us first check the lines that contain 0 for both solutions. In no circumstances should Alice add the corresponding RT_0 credentials to her policy.

- line 2: Alice.reviewer ← Bob
  Alice should never make Bob a member of Alice.reviewer because, since the conference's roles are delegated to Alice, that would immediately violate the mutual exclusion constraint.
- line 3: Alice.reviewer ← Alice,
  Alice should never make herself member of her submitter role (line 3) because, since the conference's roles are delegated to Alice, that would immediately violate the mutual exclusion constraint.
- line 4: Alice.reviewer ← Alice.submitter
  Alice should never include here submitter role in her reviewer role.
- lines 5 and 6:
  Alice.reviewer ← Bob.reviewer,
  Alice.reviewer ← Bob.submitter
  Alice should never include any of Bob's roles in her reviewer role.
- lines 8 and 9:
  Alice.submitter ← Bob.reviewer,
  Alice.submitter ← Bob.submitter
  Alice should never include any of Bob's roles in her submitter role either.
- lines 11,12,14 and 15:
  Alice.reviewer ← Alice.submitter.reviewer,
  Alice.reviewer ← Alice.submitter.submitter,
  Alice.submitter ← Alice.submitter.reviewer,
  Alice.submitter ← Alice.submitter.submitter,
  Alice should never link any of her roles via her submitter role.

Solution 1 allows Alice to include herself to her own reviewer role (line 1), at the cost of further restricting the delegation via that role (lines 7, 10, and 13). Solution 2 represents the only alternative.

For improved understanding of the results, Scoll allows the user to check out the individual solutions in detail. The user then gets a complete overview showing the state, knowledge and behavior facts that would become true for every entity.

The solutions that are found in Scoll correspond to the optimal solutions (Definition 2).

Theorem 1 (Correctness and completeness). *Given an incomplete policy system with a set of safety and availability constraints and the Scoll program modeling the system and constraints as described in Section 4 we have that:*

- *Any restriction set calculated by Scollar is an optimal solution.*
- *Any optimal solution is found by Scollar.*

6   Conclusions and Future Work

We have shown that trust management research, particularly in DTM, can benefit from general techniques for safety analysis, in particular from analysis techniques that can model entity behavior.

We have shown how authorization and delegation policies can be modeled as subject behavior in the Scoll language, and how such models can be used to calculate how the cooperating principals can limit their policies to bound their direct and indirect consequences in the presence of unknown policies.

We have applied the Scollar tool to calculate the ways to restrict a principal's policy no more than necessary to avoid unwanted authorizations effects.

We have shown that Scollar can also take availability requirements into account when calculating the necessary restrictions. Even if these availability requirements are not guaranteed in a system of which the Scoll program is a conservative model, they are useful to detect and avoid solutions that would only model systems that cannot possibly comply to the availability requirements.

The advantages of Scoll and Scollar thus become available in the domains of Trust Management as well as Security research:

- The state predicates, behavior predicates and knowledge predicates can be chosen to model the effects and influences relevant for TM systems.
- The system rules can be chosen in accordance with the protection system that controls the modeled systems.
- The behavior types can be modeled in accordance with the relevant assumptions, trust, and knowledge about the entities or principals in the system.
- The detail of modeling can be adjusted to the requirements, and adapted for different parties in the same model. Scoll supports mechanisms for refinement of state, knowledge, and behavior.

Future Work: Since DTM requirements include proving availability as well as safety, we intend to adapt Scollar in the near future so that it supports availability and safety equally well.

We could consider modeling use-behavior as well in Scoll, should we want to bound the role *activations* of the cooperating principals, or guarantee dynamic mutual exclusion constraints.

The problem modeled in this paper is relatively simple and calculates a-priori properties and trust requirements for the cooperating principals. Future work may also focus on applying the proposed method to analyze trust management and usage control policies in a runtime system, during (updates in) actual delegation, authorization, and use. Future applications may for instance provide for dynamic adaptation of authorization, delegation, and use policies in accordance to knowledge gained from a-posteriori auditing or reputation systems.

The TAS3 project develops trusted architectures for shared services in domains such as healthcare and employability. This architecture implements trust policies which can depend both on structural and behavioral rules.

The Poseidon project, which conducts research on secure interoperation in ad hoc coalitions of heterogeneous parties in the maritime domain, could consider applying the approach and improving its scalability to match their demands for safety and trust analysis.

Scoll is available as open source at `http://www.scoll.evoluware.eu`, in the hope of attracting researchers and developers to help boost the scalability of the tool to the level necessary for more demanding research.

References

1. Spiessens, F.: Patterns of Safe Collaboration. PhD thesis, Université catholique de Louvain, Louvain-la-Neuve, Belgium (February 2007)
2. Spiessens, F., Van Roy, P.: A Practical Formal Model for Safety Analysis in Capability-Based Systems. In: De Nicola, R., Sangiorgi, D. (eds.) TGC 2005. LNCS, vol. 3705, pp. 248–278. Springer, Heidelberg (2005)
3. Li, N., Mitchell, J., Winsborough, W.: Design of a Role-based Trust-management Framework. In: Proc. IEEE Symposium on Security and Privacy, pp. 114–130. IEEE Computer Society Press, Los Alamitos (2002)
4. Artz, D., Gil, Y.: A survey of trust in computer science and the semantic web. Journal of Web Semantics (2007)
5. Blaze, M., Feigenbaum, J., Lacy, J.: Decentralized trust management. In: Press, I.C.S. (ed.) Proc. 1996 IEEE Symposium on Security and Privacy, pp. 164–173 (1996)
6. Blaze, M., Feigenbaum, J., Ioannidis, J., Keromytis, A.: The KeyNote trust-management system, version 2. IETF RFC 2704 (1999)
7. Ellison, C., Frantz, B., Lampson, B., Rivest, R., Thomas, B., Ylonen, T.: SPKI Certificate Theory. IETF RFC 2693 (September 1999)
8. Kagal, L., Cost, S., Finin, T., Peng, Y.: A framework for distributed trust management. In: Proc. of IJCAI 2001 Workshop on Autonomy, Delegation and Control (2001)
9. Kagal, L., Cost, S., Finin, T., Peng, Y.: A framework for distributed trust management. In: Proceedings of IJCAI 2001 Workshop on Autonomy, Delegation and Control (2001), `http://citeseer.nj.nec.com/kagal01framework.html`
10. Etalle, S., Winsborough, W.H.: Integrity constraints in trust management (extended abstract). In: Ahn, G.J. (ed.) 10th ACM Symp. on Access Control Models and Technologies (SACMAT), p. 10. ACM Press, New York (2005)
11. Li, N., Mitchell, J.C., Winsborough, W.H.: Beyond proof-of-compliance: security analysis in trust management. J. ACM 52(3), 474–514 (2005)
12. Czenko, M.R., Etalle, S., Li, D., Winsborough, W.H.: An introduction to the role based trust management framework RT. Technical Report TR-CTIT-07-34, University of Twente, Enschede (June 2007)
13. Gallaire, H., Minker, J. (eds.): Logic and Data Bases. Perseus Publishing (1978)
14. Spiessens, F., Jaradin, Y., Van Roy, P.: Using Constraints To Analyze And Generate Safe Capability Patterns. Research Report INFO-2005-11, Département d'Ingénierie Informatique, Université catholique de Louvain, Louvain-la-Neuve Belgium, CPSec 2005 (2005), `http://www.info.ucl.ac.be/~fsp/rr2005-11.pdf`

Privacy-Friendly Electronic Traffic Pricing via Commits

Wiebren de Jonge[1] and Bart Jacobs[2]

[1] TIP Systems BV, and
Vrije Universiteit Amsterdam
`wiebren@cs.vu.nl`
[2] Inst. for Computing and Information Sciences
Radboud Universiteit Nijmegen
`bart@cs.ru.nl`

Abstract. This paper introduces a novel approach or architecture for fraud-resistant and privacy-friendly Electronic Traffic Pricing (ETP). One salient contribution is that it can satisfy the seemingly incompatible requirements of a privacy-friendly and so-called "thin" solution.

The proposed approach relies on regularly sending to the traffic Pricing Authority (PA) only hashes of travelled trajectories and hashes of the corresponding fees due. This makes it possible to achieve that users keep almost all data on the trajectories they travel and on the amounts they should pay completely hidden from the PA, without having to rely for their privacy protection on a so-called Trusted Third Party (TTP). Only a very small percentage of all these privacy-sensitive data requires that the pre-image trajectories and pre-image fees are revealed to the PA for spot-checking purposes (to detect cheating).

The calculations of the amounts due for trajectories travelled can be done—at desire—inside or outside the vehicle. Thus, seamless integration of "thin" and "thick" in one ETP system with one and the same spot-checking approach is made possible and easy. The calculations can be performed in a privacy-friendly way, since they do not require any vehicle or On-Board Equipment (OBE) identification.

The proposal can, for example, be used as a declaration-based approach much in line with current tax declaration traditions in which the individual citizen is personally responsible. However, the proposal allows for much individual variation (including delegation) and many additional (commercial) services. For example, it is also possible to reduce user responsibility and/or user involvement to an absolute minimum.

1 Introduction

After years of discussion the Dutch government has decided to introduce distance-related Electronic Traffic Pricing (ETP) for all vehicles on all roads by means of modern satellite technology, such as GPS or Galileo. Particularly the inclusion of personal vehicles, requiring an appropriate level of privacy protection, and the choice for time, location and vehicle category dependent kilometre tariffs make this approach ambitious and new in the world (see also [3]). For each individual vehicle detailed time and location information must be collected and processed without endangering privacy. The correct amounts due can be calculated with the help of a digital tariff and/or road map. Now

P. Degano, J. Guttman, and F. Martinelli (Eds.): FAST 2008, LNCS 5491, pp. 143–161, 2009.
© Springer-Verlag Berlin Heidelberg 2009

and then—for example, once per three months—the total amount due for the period (the "fee") in question must be revealed to the Pricing Authority (PA) and then collected. Clearly, the shorter these fee reporting periods, the greater the impact on privacy.

In the Netherlands, this new ETP should replace—in about five years time—the current (flat) road tax and the existing special purchase tax for personal vehicles and motorcycles. The main aims of introducing ETP are:

- fairness: the fee one has to pay will depend on one's actual vehicle use;
- congestion reduction: traffic supply can be influenced via flexible pricing policies;
- environmental impact reduction: kilometre tariffs will partly depend on (environmental) vehicle characteristics.

The techniques for such a form of ETP, like GPS and GSM, are all available. The challenge is to integrate them in such a way that the system will be reliable, privacy-friendly, cost-effective, transparent and easy to use, and will allow easy enforcement and dispute resolution. It may be expected that some of the intended users of the system—drivers / holders / owners of vehicles that are registered in the Netherlands—are hostile users and may try to obstruct or abuse the system. At the same time, the system should be trusted, by the various stakeholders involved.

This paper is not about general requirements for ETP, but focuses on privacy and security aspects. So far this topic has received relatively little attention in the computer security community. Our aim is to design a system that is both secure and privacy-friendly, in which privacy is not treated as a *post hoc* add-on, but as an essential property that needs to be built deeply into the architecture of the system. We adopt Mitch Kapor's slogan "architecture is politics" (see *e.g.* also [6]) and wish to design ICT-systems in such a manner that individual autonomy and control over one's own user data is offered and can be ensured, contributing to public trust in the system. After all, centralised informational control supports centralised societal control. This is a highly relevant issue, also in ETP.

This paper presents only the main lines of a novel solution and is organised as follows. Sections 2 and 3 give an informal introduction to the issues in this area via two possible solutions, as opposite extremes. Sections 4 and 6 describe the main ideas of the proposed solution and protocol essentials. Section 5 discusses cryptographic techniques used. Sections 7 and 8 discuss some advantages and possible use scenarios. Finally, Section 9 discusses the proposed solution from a broader perspective.

The main idea of this article is due to the first author (WdJ), see also [4]. The current elaboration and presentation is the result of joint work.

2   Context

For ETP, vehicles will contain so-called On-Board Equipment (OBE). What this OBE should do precisely depends on the architecture chosen, but we assume that it can at least:

- determine its own location, *e.g.* via a Global Navigation Satellite System (GNSS), such as GPS or (in the future) Galileo;
- communicate with the outside world, *e.g.* via GSM or WiFi on specific locations;
- store information locally and perform elementary computations.

One must take into account many aspects, of which we mention only a few here. First, no physical protection measure can prevent a user from sending false signals to the GNSS receiver in a vehicle or from blocking the true signals originating from the navigation satellites. Second, the OBE should not only do the right things, but also be prevented from doing any wrong things, like surreptitiously leaking location data, *e.g.* via a hidden/covert channel. Third, frequent data transmission from the vehicle may endanger privacy.

Although the OBE must satisfy certain minimal requirements, it can vary much in type and in additional functionality offered (see Sections 7.1 and 8). We call the OBE:

- "fat" or "thick" when it performs itself the calculation of the fees due[1] for registered road use;
- "thin" if this calculation is performed outside the vehicle (by another device or organisation).

Thin OBE must be trusted by the parties involved to register correctly. Fat OBE must additionally calculate correctly. Both are sensitive operations.

In our model we also assume that there is a (traffic) Pricing Authority (PA) that collects relevant information in its back office and takes care of the collection of fees. This PA may be subdivided, but is, for our purposes, best regarded as a single unit. We assume that the (national, road tax) authorities are responsible for the PA.

We also assume that there will be an open standard for the representation of "Traffic data Parts" or "Trajectory Parts" (TP). In this text a TP is an elementary data structure with location data aggregated to a path of a certain duration (in our examples: 1 minute), comprising a number of positions (*e.g.* 61; one per second, including an endpoint) together with a time stamp marking the time of the first position.

Road use fees will be calculated on the basis of the relevant TPs. The process to collect payments and the precise (internal) organisation of TPs are not relevant for this paper.

3 Two Extremes

In order to further set the scene we shall sketch in this section two possible architectures for ETP. We shall call them "centralised" and "decentralised". This aspect of (de)centralisation refers to the place where the actual location data of vehicles will be stored: in the back office of the PA or in individual vehicles. In general, central storage implies that individuals loose control over their location data. For example, at a certain moment these data could be made available for marketing and surveillance/datamining

---

[1] Actually, it might be better to use the more general term 'usage' instead of the more specific 'fee due', since usage can also be expressed in other ways, for instance as readings of one or more counters that each represent the cumulative number of kilometres travelled in a certain category. For example, one might use three categories: 1) 'outside rush hours' or 'low price', 2) 'during rush hour in a moderately congested area' or 'normal price', and 3) 'during rush hour in a highly congested area' or 'high price'. For simplicity and without loss of generality, we will focus on the case of fee calculation and not explicitly treat the very similar case of usage calculation.

(*e.g.* for criminal investigations). Hence, in the end the choice between central or decentralised storage is a political one, involving societal issues of power and control. Here we focus on the technical aspects.

In the centralised architecture the OBE is thin and all intelligence resides with the PA. The OBE frequently sends, say at least once every day, its collected location data to the PA. At the end of each period, say each quarter year, the PA calculates the total fee due.

This architecture is simple, but also rather naive. It will be unacceptable to many that the PA gets detailed travel information about every vehicle and that the central database with location data is vulnerable. This database will be an attractive target for individuals or organisations with unfriendly intentions, like terrorists or blackmailers. The system administrators who control this database may not always behave according to the rules, voluntarily or unvoluntarily. In short, the main weak point concerns privacy and security.

In this approach one needs to have confidence that the thin OBE registers and transfers all actual road use correctly. The PA may enforce this by "spot-checks" based on observations (*e.g.* photographs of vehicles and their licence plates) made at random locations and times. These observations can be compared with the transferred registrations. A fine can be imposed in case of discrepancy. Notice that these spot-checks can in principle take place without drivers or vehicle equipment noticing. This has advantages, because it prevents drivers/vehicles from notifying and warning each other about where to expect spot-checks.

In the decentralised architecture that we sketch next, we assume that the OBE is fat and thus contains enough intelligence to calculate the fee itself. The main problems with this architecture have to do with the OBE and its complexity. For example:

- The OBE must contain the tariff and/or road map data to perform the calculations. Since these crucial data change over time, there must also be a way to update them both securely and timely. The combination of security and timeliness here is a critical factor involving serious problems.
- The OBE must now also be trusted to make the right calculations. Hence it requires more security measures. For example, the OBE uses a separate communication channel for enforcement of correct road use registration and fee calculation, see below.
- The OBE, and particularly its software, becomes complex. This makes the OBE fragile and requires an option to securely update its firmware.

Clearly, the OBE will be more costly due to extra hardware and software required for the additional functionality and for the additional security measures.

In the decentralised approach the road-side checks involve interrogation of OBE in order to be able to check that the last few registrations and associated fee calculations have been performed correctly. For this request-response communication one usually uses Dedicated Short Range Communication (DSRC). Due to the two-way communication, spot-checking locations can easily be noticed by vehicle equipment, and then automatically passed on as warnings to other vehicles. This has a substantially negative effect on spot-checking effectiveness and thus costs. On the positive side, possible discrepancies—such as between the actual (spot-checked) vehicle location and the vehicle locations registered in the most recent (requested) entries of the OBE—may be observed directly on the spot, and may result in immediate reaction of the authorities at the spot-checking location.

As extremes, we are thus faced with a simple centralised solution that is highly privacy-unfriendly and vulnerable to data abuse, and with a complicated and fragile decentralised solution that offers good privacy protection, at least potentially (if well-designed and well-implemented). Our novel approach makes it possible to integrate 'fat' and 'thin' and also to combine the best of these two approaches. It can offer good privacy protection, even when realised with thin OBE, and it makes it possible to keep many advantages of the thin approach, even when choosing for fat OBE. In particular, decentralised and 'thin' do not conflict anymore. Hence, the strong relations suggested (by others and in our text above) between centralised and 'thin' and between decentralised and 'fat' are no longer valid.

4   Underlying Ideas

The solution of this paper depends on a number of basic ideas and observations.

- The basic traffic data registration (*i.e.* the TPs) can be protected against fraud by using 'non-revealing' commits and remote spot-checking (*i.e.* remote from the vehicle). Indeed, commits can be performed without revealing any (privacy-sensitive) data contents. For example, by sending to the PA only the results of hashing the data with a secure hash function. Such non-revealing commits can also be used for committing to fees calculated. Thus, it is not necessary to reveal any privacy-sensitive data at first.
- Based on a remote (*e.g.* road-side) observation of a vehicle, the vehicle's OBE (or the user's PC or a party enlisted by the user; see Section 7.1) must later reveal the actual data concerning a short period around the time of observation. Note that these actual data (*i.e.* the TPs) are the pre-images of the hash values that have been transferred to the PA earlier. In other words, cheating can be detected. All in all, the only privacy-sensitive traffic and fee data that must be revealed to the PA are those involved in a spot-check. In fact, the privacy-sensitive data to be revealed for a vehicle can be limited to a very small percentage (*e.g.* $< 1\%$ or even $\ll 1\%$) of all fee and traffic data. Note that one can still apply to the spot-checking process many usual (or, say, 'more traditional') privacy protection measures in order to protect even this very small percentage as much as possible.
- The identity of a vehicle or of OBE involved is not required for calculating the fee due for a trajectory part (TP). Hence, traffic fee calculation can be done anonymously.
- Traffic fee calculations can be done anywhere (inside or outside the vehicle) and even by parties not trusted by the PA. For example, calculations can be performed by the vehicle user's PC or by one or more parties enlisted by the vehicle user. That parties not trusted by the PA can be used for the fee calculations stems from the fact that the fee is derived information. If the basic traffic data, *i.e.* the TPs, are protected against fraud, then it is easy to check later whether calculations have been performed correctly.

- Non-revealing fee commits can be organised in such a way that the PA only needs "local" spot-checks to convince itself of the correctness of the total fee reported. Spot-checks to verify the correctness of "subfees" calculated for individual TPs and spot-checks to verify that subfees committed are also included in the total sum reported.

5 Background about Hashes

A (secure) hash is a function that turns a digital message of arbitrary length into a garbled message of fixed length (usually 160 or 256 bits). This output value is called the hash (value) of that message. Other names are 'digital fingerprint' or 'message digest'. Hashing is a basic operation in cryptology and computer security and is described in any textbook (see *e.g.* [7,5]). A (secure) hash function, usually written as h, has two basic properties:

- it is not feasible, given only an output value $v = h(m)$, to find the "pre-image" m;
- it is not feasible, given a message m, to find a different m' with $h(m') = h(m)$.

However, if a value v is given (first) it is easy to check that it is the hash value of a (later) given message m, simply by calculating $h(m)$ and checking if $v = h(m)$. A hash value $v = h(m)$ is thus a bit-pattern that is closely related to its pre-image m, but keeps (the contents of) m excellently concealed. There are standard implementations for such a function h, such as SHA-256. But here we shall abstract from such concrete functions and shall simply write h for an arbitrary secure hash function.

5.1 Use of Hashes for Commitment

Hashes (*i.e.* results $h(m)$ of hash function applications) can thus be used for early commitment to a piece of information without revealing its contents. In our context, this can be explained in more detail as follows. Suppose the OBE of a vehicle sends to the PA at time t_1 the hash value $v = h(m)$ of a certain piece of information m (*e.g.* a trajectory part TP or the subfee due for a TP) that is confidential in the sense that the OBE (or the vehicle's user) does not wish to reveal it to the PA, at least not without the need to do so. Furthermore, suppose that at some later time t_2 this OBE must reveal the piece of information m (*i.e.* the pre-image of v) to the PA for spot-checking purposes and does so by sending to the PA bit-pattern x pretending that x is exactly the same as the bit-pattern m committed earlier at time t_1. Then the PA can easily verify whether this is really true (*i.e.* that the PA is not cheated) by computing $h(x)$ and checking whether indeed $h(x) = v$. Thus, when spot-checked by the PA (say at time t_2) the OBE or vehicle user cannot cheat the PA by sending a message (*e.g.* trajectory or fee) different from the one committed earlier. In other words, as soon as the PA has received the hash $v = h(m)$, the message m (and thus its information contents) becomes 'frozen' and 'irreversible' (more or less: unchangeable/immutable).

5.2 Omission of Cryptographic Details

Finally, we warn the reader that in our presentation many details are omitted, including many cryptographic details. For example, if party A must supply hashes of confidential bit-patterns to B with a very short maximum length (in our context *e.g.* the fee due for a TP), then A should first concatenate a fresh random number to each original bit-pattern[2] in order not to endanger its secrecy. The incorporation of a random number in the pre-image prevents the receiver B from being able to construct a 'deciphering' table by brute force, that is, by computing the hash of all possible pre-images.

6   Approach and Protocol Essentials

This section will elaborate some technical details in order to explain the essence of the proposed approach. We shall concentrate on the main lines, which are actually quite simple. Several variations are possible, some of which will also be discussed. We shall at first assume minimal OBE as described in Section 2, which can only determine its own location, communicate with the traffic Pricing Authority (PA), and store Trajectory Parts (TPs).

6.1   Road Use Reporting and Verification

In the approach proposed, commit messages must be sent to the PA regularly. Here we assume that the OBE of each vehicle (say, with identifier veh-id) daily sends a commit:

$$\text{OBE} \longrightarrow \text{PA} : \langle \text{veh-id}, \text{day}, \text{hash}_{\text{day}} \rangle \tag{1}$$

where the "hash of the day" is a two-level nested hash defined as the hash of $24 \times 60 = 1440$ concatenated hashes of one minute length trajectory parts, *i.e.*:

$$\text{hash}_{\text{day}} = h\big(h(\text{TP}_{\text{day},1}) \,\|\, \cdots \,\|\, h(\text{TP}_{\text{day},1440}) \big) \tag{2}$$

Notice that (1) is a very short message, typically in the order of 40 bytes, that completely freezes a vehicle's movements and whereabouts (*i.e.* parking and/or travelling) of a particular day (indicated by the variable day) without revealing anything about the actual vehicle locations (the contents of the TPs of that day). The OBE stores all these trajectory parts $\text{TP}_{\text{day},i}$ forming the pre-images of the hash function h. It does so for all the reports it sends, until it can safely drop them (see Section 6.4).

It is important to understand that the PA can use observations for spot-checking the underlying book-keeping. Suppose that the PA has legal proof that a specific vehicle has been at location ℓ between 8:42 and 8:43 AM on February 13th (*i.e.* in minute 523 of day 44). Within some reasonable period after that day the PA can demand that both the pre-image (say, x) of the (outer hash of) hash_{44} and $\text{TP}_{44,523}$ (say, y) must be sent in. After receiving x and y, the PA verifies:

– whether x really corresponds to (*i.e.* is really the pre-image of) the fingerprint hash_{44} earlier received as commit (2);
– whether y indeed corresponds to (*i.e.* is really the pre-image of) the 523rd fingerprint present in x—using that hashes have a fixed length;

---

[2] Another detail omitted is that A has to keep the relationship between the original short bit-pattern and the random number, because otherwise A cannot reveal the correct pre-image later on.

- whether the trajectory data in y is in correspondence with the observation, that is, whether location ℓ is covered by trajectory part $y = \mathsf{TP}_{44,523}$.

If all three verifications are successful, then the book-keeping regarding the whereabouts in said minute, as frozen at the time of commit, is in accordance with the observed reality. If one of the three verifications fails, this indicates a possible fraud attempt. Of course, more investigation may be needed to exclude certain exceptional causes, such as an equipment failure that has been reported earlier (and in accordance with the rules). We will not digress on such issues further.

Reasons for Using the Nested, Two-Level Hash. In the next few paragraphs we digress on the two-level fingerprint $\mathsf{hash}_{\mathsf{day}}$ as described in (2). Instead of this nested hash, one could simply transfer the fingerprint of the concatenation of all TPs of the day in question:

$$h\big(\mathsf{TP}_{\mathsf{day},1} \parallel \cdots \parallel \mathsf{TP}_{\mathsf{day},1440}\big) \tag{3}$$

However, then a spot-check based on car-location-time evidence would require revealing all TPs of the day in question. Obviously, this would make privacy protection considerably worse. So, our main reason for using nested hashes is the considerably better privacy protection that can be achieved without changing to a higher frequency of sending commit messages to the PA.

A second reason is that the spot-checking as described—the spot-checking based on two-level hashes (2)—requires less data to be communicated. For, the pre-image x of hash $\mathsf{hash}_{\mathsf{day}}$ consists of 1440 hashes while the pre-image would consist of 1440 TPs in case of a single-level hash (3) of all TPs of the day in question. Assuming hashes of 32 bytes (256 bits), the 1440 hashes take up 45 KByte. Assuming the 61 positions in a trajectory part require an average of four bytes each, the 1440 TPs would require about 340 Kbyte.

A third reason is that one might use the hash of each TP to improve fraud resistance or to reduce the intensity of the spot-checking required, particularly by storing these inner hashes $h(\mathsf{TP}_{\mathsf{day},i})$ given in (2) more or less safely into an Authority's Trusted Element (ATE), inside the OBE. If such is done, we say that the inner hashes are used for "internal commits", while the outer hash given in (2) is said to be used for "external commit". Of course, the degree of safety offered by internal commits depends on the quality of the ATE's physical protection and will never be 100%.

Actually, the above three reasons explain why the first-level (bottom-level or inner) hashes are present, but do not explain yet why also the outer hash is used in (2). For, one also could drop this outer hash and simply transfer the concatenation of the hashes of all TPs of the day in question. However, the concatenation of 1440 hashes takes up 1440 times the number of bytes of one hash. Thus, the outer hashes are only present in order to reduce the size of the commit messages. Indeed, this comes at the price of having to (request for and) transfer during each spot-check an extra pre-image consisting of the concatenation of the (in our example: 1440) hashes. But spot-checks are performed for only a small percentage of all commit messages, so the net savings are considerable. In short, the outer hashes are there for efficiency reasons, that is, for reducing the communication costs.

6.2   Fee Calculation

The subfee due for each individual TP (trajectory part) can be calculated by publicly available software that uses a publicly available tariff and road map. This software may be run on the user's own PC or on computers of many independent Calculation Service Providers (CSPs), that is, organisations offering such calculations as a service. CSPs only have to run the calculation software and are supposed to prevent that this software—which may have been produced and distributed on behalf of the PA—leaks in some way any information to the PA or to others in the outside world. CSPs do not have to be trusted by the PA. Of course this software may also be run inside fat OBE.

The crucial point regarding privacy protection is that fee calculation need not involve any identity. Actually, one can organise things such that even the vehicle's category does not have to be revealed to the CSP.

Sending a TP to a CSP and then receiving back the subfee due can be done via a number of anonymity guaranteeing servers. (See *e.g.* Chaum's mixes [1]). If one fully trusts one particular CSP—one's own PC may act as such—all subfee calculations can be performed by that particular CSP. However, one can also organise that for each TP the CSP to be used will be chosen randomly from a set of independent (less trusted or even non-trusted) CSPs. Here we assume that 'dossier linking' (*i.e.* conspiracy) between a CSP and the PA via the hash of each TP will be hindered by a little trick/variation: for committing a particular TP one sends to the PA the hash of that TP concatenated with a random number. All in all, privacy can be protected as long as a sufficient percentage of the chosen CSPs do not cheat. More countermeasures exist, but are outside the scope of this article.

6.3   Fee Reporting and Verification

In order to enable the PA to collect payment, for each vehicle the total traffic fee due must be reported regularly, but—for privacy reasons—not too often. Here we assume that the OBE quarterly sends a fee report:

$$\text{OBE} \longrightarrow \text{PA} : \langle \text{veh-id}, \text{quarter}, \text{fee}_{\text{quarter}} \rangle \tag{4}$$

The PA must be able to check for each vehicle that a) subfees of individual TPs (*i.e.* $\text{fee}_{d,i}$) have been calculated correctly, and b) all these subfees add up to the reported total fee (*i.e.* $\text{fee}_{\text{quarter}} = \sum_{d \leq N \,\&\, i \leq 1440} \text{fee}_{d,i}$ where N denotes the number of days in the quarter). These checks must be carried out in a privacy-friendly way, revealing as few subfees (and subtotals) as possible. After all, subfees (and subtotals) show a little bit about an individual's behaviour, for instance whether or not the vehicle has been used or not. There are several possible ways to organise such fee reporting and verification. For illustrative purposes, we will first sketch an interactive way with a game-theoretic flavour. Then we will sketch our main solution using non-revealing commits via hashes. Finally, we will suggest possible use of homomorphic encryption for the hashing.

Interactive Verification. The PA may communicate as follows with an owner of a particular vehicle (or with a software agent acting on this owner's behalf).

- The PA says: "well, so your quarter amount is $\mathsf{fee_{quarter}}$". Tell me the three amounts of the months that are in this quarter. Of course, the owner should produce amounts that add up to $\mathsf{fee_{quarter}}$.
- The PA then picks one particular month from this quarter and proceeds to ask the amounts for the weeks in that month. Again they should add up correctly.
- Now the PA picks one particular week from the chosen month and asks the amounts for the days in that week. Again they should add up correctly.
- The PA continues to ask the amounts of the four quarters of a day, picks one, asks for the six hour amounts of that quarter day, picks one hour, asks for the four quarter (of an hour) amounts of that hour, picks one quarter, and asks for the three five-minute amounts of that quarter, and finally picks one five-minute period and asks for the minute amounts of that period. Of course the questions of the PA are organised in such a way that the pre-chosen day-minute pair (day, i) is in this five-minute period.
- Now the PA asks for $\mathsf{TP}_{\mathsf{day},i}$ and for the pre-image of the "hash of the day" as described in (2). The PA performs the checks from Section 6.1 to verify that $\mathsf{TP}_{\mathsf{day},i}$ is indeed the version committed earlier, computes the fee due for $\mathsf{TP}_{\mathsf{day},i}$ and checks whether this amount is indeed equal to the minute amount reported in the previous step.

By breaking up the path to the pre-chosen day-minute pair in many small substeps the PA learns relatively little about the fees of all other trajectory parts. In this verification method it is essential that the questions are posed and answered interactively, because otherwise the vehicle owner could successfully cheat and adjust amounts outside the path chosen by the PA (which are not checked) so that (sub)totals still add up correctly.

Non-Interactive Verification Via Hashes. Suppose that during the quarter (see also Section 7.6) the PA also receives for each day d a "fee hash of the day":

$$\mathsf{fee\text{-}hash}_d = h\big(h(\mathsf{fee}_{d,1}) \parallel \cdots \parallel h(\mathsf{fee}_{d,1440}) \big) \tag{5}$$

Then checking the correctness of an individual subfee $\mathsf{fee}_{d,i}$ is easy and very similar to the spot-checking described in Section 6.1. In this case the PA also asks for both $\mathsf{fee}_{d,i}$ and the pre-image of $\mathsf{fee\text{-}hash}_d$. The spot-check now includes verifying whether the latter is indeed the pre-image of $\mathsf{fee\text{-}hash}_d$, verifying whether $\mathsf{fee}_{d,i}$ is indeed the pre-image of the i-th hash in the concatenated string of 1440 hashes, computing itself the fee due for $\mathsf{TP}_{d,i}$ and verifying that this amount is indeed equal to $\mathsf{fee}_{d,i}$.

However, this is not sufficient yet. For one could cheat by committing correct subfees and reporting a false sum as total fee. Our solution is to change the list of all $h(\mathsf{fee}_{d,i})$ of a quarter into an "enriched" list representing (in post-order tree walk) the tree of hashes given in Figure 1, which 'freezes' all calculation steps involved. Note that a) the interactive verification that we described above, implicitly also involves a tree structure, and b) our 'freezing' allows the interactivity to be removed. Now the PA can spot-check the summation by selecting and checking a number of "triangles" consisting of an internal node and its children. Hereto one must reveal to the PA the pre-images of the hashes in these triangles of the form:

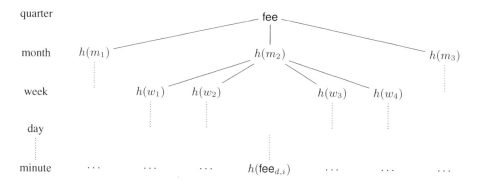

Fig. 1. Tree representation of hashes of subtotals of subfees, in which for instance the quarterly fee is the sum $m_1 + m_2 + m_3$ of the month amounts, and the (second) month amount m_2 is the sum $w_1 + w_2 + w_3 + w_4$ of the week amounts, *etc*

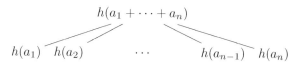

All in all, the PA can convince itself in a privacy-friendly manner of the correctness of the fee report. The sketched approach for committing (sub)fees via a tree of hashes requires a certain amount of elementary bookkeeping and communication that can be automated easily. It is not difficult to arrange that, for example, the OBE automatically does all the work required (without user involvement, if such is desired).

Possible Use of Homomorphic Hashing. Our third approach to fee reporting does not need a tree of hashes, but is computationally more involved. We will only sketch it very rudimentarily. Let G be a suitable finite group with modular multiplication and generator $g \in G$. The discrete log problem refers to the infeasibility of calculating $n \in \mathbb{N}$ when $g^n \in G$ is given. Hence, we can use the function $x \mapsto g^x$ as a homomorphic hash, since $g^x \cdot g^y = g^{x+y}$. The homomorphism property is often useful, for instance in counting protected votes via multiplication in e-voting, see *e.g.* [2]. In a similar way one may use homomorphic hashing in the current setting. Subfees $\mathsf{fee}_{d,i}$ of trajectory parts $\mathsf{TP}_{d,i}$ can be sent to the PA as $g^{\mathsf{fee}_{d,i}}$. The PA can then multiply these hashed values and check that $\prod_{d \leq N \,\&\, i \leq 1440} g^{\mathsf{fee}_{d,i}} = g^{\mathsf{fee}_{\mathsf{quarter}}}$.

There are a number of subtle points that need to be addressed, among which the following. The amounts $\mathsf{fee}_{d,i}$ are typically small numbers that should be "blinded" to prevent that $\mathsf{fee}_{d,i}$ can be obtainded from $g^{\mathsf{fee}_{d,i}}$ by trying a limited number of values. Blinding can occur by multiplying $g^{\mathsf{fee}_{d,i}}$ with $g_0^{R_{d,i}}$, where $R_{d,i}$ is a random value (or actually a well-chosen hash value that also acts as binder) and $g_0 \in G$ is coprime with g. Use of g_0 (instead of g) hinders interfering with the fee by "shifting" between the exponents in the product. The sum R of the random values must be submitted together with $\mathsf{fee}_{\mathsf{quarter}}$ so that the PA can check the equation $\prod_{d \leq N \,\&\, i \leq 1440} g^{\mathsf{fee}_{d,i}} g_0^{R_{d,i}} = g^{\mathsf{fee}_{\mathsf{quarter}}} g_0^{R}$.

6.4 Confirmations

At various stages a user or his/her OBE needs to receive (digitally) signed information from the PA. For example:

- confirmations of receipt of the trajectory commit messages (2) and of the fee reports that have been submitted to the PA;
- requests for disclosure of certain TPs or (sub)fees;
- clearance messages stating that all book-keeping (such as pre-images/TPs) can be dropped up to a certain day.

Confirmation messages typically involve return messages by the PA comprising a time-stamped and digitally signed copy of the data submitted to and received by the PA. If such a confirmation message does not arrive within a certain time frame, the OBE may notify the user. Clearly, OBEs need to be able to check digital signatures of the PA. This requires that they contain a certificate for the public key of the PA. This public key may also be used to encrypt messages to the PA. However, as already has been mentioned in Section 5.2, such cryptographic details are outside the scope of the current paper.

7 Some Properties

This section will explicitly discuss some of the properties of the proposed approach using non-revealing commits. One main point is that this approach makes privacy-friendly (decentralised) and fraud-resistant solutions possible, even when using thin OBE. Another main point is that existing fat solutions can be improved substantially by adding the use of non-revealing commits, thus making a number of advantages of 'thin' (*e.g.* related to spot-checking, costs, monitoring ability and system continuity) also available for 'fat'. For example, fat solutions can be made less vulnerable to compromise of the OBE's physical protection (*i.e.* to tampering). Below we treat several aspects in more detail.

7.1 Wide Range of Realisation Options

The proposed approach allows much implementation freedom. The only two tasks that certainly must be performed in the vehicle are determining the relevant traffic data (*e.g.* trajectory data) and temporarily registering these data piece by piece (*e.g.* per minute) locally. All other work—except the optional 'internal commits' (see Section 6.1)—can be performed, at desire, inside or outside the vehicle.

Clearly, for doing all work (including subfee calculations) inside the vehicle fat OBE is required. In case of minimal work inside the vehicle, the (thin) OBE must transfer the relevant traffic data to equipment outside the vehicle taking care of all other work. This latter equipment may be the user's own PC or the processing equipment of a party chosen by the user. However, thin OBE may also do all work with only the exception of subfee calculations outside the vehicle. The thin OBE then takes care of committing to the traffic data, distributing automatically and anonymously fee calculations to selected Calculation Service Providers, collecting the results, committing to these results, reporting the quarterly fee to the PA and reacting to messages from the PA, such as verification requests. Note that all this processing can be fully automated and can be performed by OBE, if desired.

In short, users have a wide range of OBE options to choose from. Their choice may depend on additional services offered and on how much control they wish to have themselves. That is, on whether they wish to trust one or more other parties and, if so, how much.

7.2 'Thin' and 'Fat' Can Be Integrated Gracefully

The proposed approach makes ETP systems possible in which some vehicles use thin and others fat OBE and in which the same spot-checking approach is used for all vehicles.

7.3 Simple and Effective Spot-Checks

Spot-checks in our approach can be based on random observations, just as in case of 'conventional thin' (*i.e.* the centralised approach from Section 3). During an observation no real-time communication with the vehicle is required, which greatly reduces the complexity (and costs) of spot-checking. Furthermore, unnoticed spot-checking is made possible, at least during daylight. Without further explanation we mention that unnoticed spot-checks can be much more effective than detectable ones and thus can be used to (further) reduce the spot-checking costs (or to achieve better fraud resistance at the same costs).

The simple and effective observation-based spot-checks can be used to monitor the actual fraud resistance level (see below) and also to replace either all or only part of spot-checks based on real-time interrogation of the OBE (*e.g.* via DSRC). If one chooses for exclusively making use of observation-based spot-checks, one saves the costs for the hardware and software required for the real-time communication channel and gives up the ability to stop a vehicle on the spot immediately after an unsatisfactory interrogation.

An advantage of the proposed approach is that these simple, effective and cost-efficient observation-based spot-checks can also be used for fat OBE.

7.4 Spot-Checking and Physical Protection Can Work 'In Parallel'

In our approach (as well as in 'conventional thin') spot-checks can produce effect even if the OBE is not protected at all against manipulation of trajectory data. Indeed, manipulating the contents of a trajectory data part (TP) does not make much sense as long as that TP is committed (in case of 'conventional thin': transferred to the PA) before the forger could find out at which locations and times the probability of his vehicle having been observed is sufficiently low to make the risk of being caught acceptable. Thus, if the PA manages to keep the times and locations of a considerable part of all random observations secret until the TPs have been committed (in case of 'conventional thin': have been transferred), then fraudulent TPs may be uncovered by spot-checks. In other words, the effectiveness of observation-based spot-checks depends on the amount of increased knowledge that potential forgers can timely acquire on the likelihood of having been observed, but not on the physical protection of OBE (against trajectory data manipulation).

The property just described is very important. It implies that the protection achieved by spot-checking (say, the logical protection) and the physical protection can work 'in parallel' and thus provide for two independent layers of protection. In other words, the total level of fraud resistance is equal to the sum of the fraud resistance achieved by physical protection and of the fraud resistance achieved by spot-checking. This has the advantage that one can get rid of the risks that adhere to full reliance on physical protection measures.

Note that in the decentralised fat approach from Section 3 the logical and physical protection are 'serial', since the (effectiveness of) spot-checking by real-time interrogation of the OBE depends on the physical protection of the OBE.

The 'parallelism' property of the proposed approach (and of 'conventional thin') leads to important advantages. In the following we will treat three such advantages (related to costs, system continuity and monitoring ability). Note that the proposed approach makes these advantages now also available for fat OBE.

Cost Optimal Balance between Spot-Checks and Physical Protection. In general, a really high level of physical protection is expensive and in the long run (often) not sufficient to prevent successful manipulation. One problem is that perfect physical protection does not exist. Another problem is that almost perfect physical protection—fully in accordance with the law of diminishing returns—probably results in high or even prohibitive costs. In our context a third problem is that—as far as we know—no physical protection measure can prevent one from sending false signals to the GNSS receiver in a vehicle and/or altogether blocking the true signals originating from the navigation satellites.

If spot-checking and physical protection of OBE work in parallel, then the desired level of fraud resistance can be achieved by a combination of both. This offers as advantage that one can head for a cost optimal balance between spot-checking and physical protection measures. If the marginal costs for additional physical protection measures (required for achieving the last few percent of the required level of fraud resistance) are higher than the marginal costs for the additional spot-checking (required for achieving that same last few percent), then one can choose for increasing the intensity of spot-checking and for not applying additional physical protection measures. And if not, then one can increase the physical protection instead of increasing the spot-checking intensity.

The proposed approach makes this balancing now also possible for 'fat'.

System Continuity Is Less Vulnerable. Some level of (hardware and software) protection will be used in OBE implementations. For instance, to make manipulation of trajectory data sufficiently difficult. But when that protection gets broken at some stage in the future, this event does not undermine the essence of the system and disrupt it fundamentally, at a large scale. After all, one can temporarily increase the intensity of spot-checking to keep the level of fraud resistance (roughly) intact. As soon as the problems with the physical protection have been solved (which may take quite some time), one can decrease the intensity of spot-checking to an appropriate level.

In short, the system continuity is less vulnerable, since there is less (vulnerable) dependence on physical protection measures. This now also works for 'fat'.

Ability to Monitor the Actual Fraud Resistance Level. Since the observation-based spot-checking that we have described, works independent of the OBE's physical protection, it can be used to monitor the fraud resistance level actually achieved, that is, the real percentage of violators.

Suppose that the PA allows multiple traffic pricing Service Providers (SPs) that each make use of a different type of equipment. Suppose also that each SP guarantees to the PA a certain level of fraud resistance (*e.g.* by physical protection only, or *e.g.* by a combination of physical protection for the OBE and of interrogation-based spot-checking by or on behalf of the SP). Then the PA can use the observation-based spot-checking to monitor in the field whether the SPs really succeed in keeping fraud below the level agreed upon.

The proposed approach makes such monitoring now also possible for 'fat'.

7.5 Privacy and Data Protection

Sending messages need not be done continually while driving and can be limited to, say, once a day. Thus, one can allow users to influence the moments and places of transmission. This is beneficial for privacy protection, because, for instance, a GSM provider might determine the vehicle's location at the time of transmission.

Furthermore, privacy-sensitive travel and fee data can be stored decentralised, under control of participants, instead of in some massive central database of the PA, where they might be misused in various ways, for instance as result of function creep.

Apart from the total fee due and from the location and fee data involved in spot-checks, no privacy-sensitive data needs to be revealed to the PA or a TTP. This amount of data seems to be optimal (for privacy). Note that spot-checks are always necessary, at least if one does not wish to fully rely on physical protection measures.

Assuming that a certain fixed level of fraud resistance must be achieved, one can reduce the spot-checking—and thus increase the privacy protection—in proportion as one increases the physical protection applied to the OBE.

All this is true both for the decentralised fat approach from Section 3 and for our approach, even when the latter makes use of thin OBE. As a consequence, our 'thin' (which is decentralised) offers important advantages over 'conventional thin' (*i.e.* centralised 'thin').

In order to prevent the PA from spot-checking individual vehicles too much, a limit (*i.e.* maximum) can be set to the number of spot-checks allowed per vehicle per period. Furthermore, the PA can also be kept from asking detailed whereabouts (*i.e.* TPs) of particular vehicles without having a corresponding observation, by obligating the PA to specify in requests for TPs both the time of observation and the location of the observed vehicle. Based on the time and location specified, it is easy (*e.g.* for the OBE) to automatically detect possible abuse attempts by the PA.

7.6 Communication and Critical Time Paths

In case of 'conventional thin', the OBE commits to traffic data parts by transferring them to the PA. As suggested in Section 7.4, this transferring preferably[3] should be performed before users can find out at which locations and times the probability of their vehicle having been observed is sufficiently low to make the risk of being caught

---

[3] Otherwise, the logical protection (*i.e.* the additional independent layer of protection) will be weak and one must rely (almost) fully on the OBE's physical protection, which we do not advocate.

acceptable. Similarly, in our approach the committing to trajectory parts is (to a certain extent) 'time critical'.

If a request for details (*i.e.* for a TP) is only allowed if the PA has observed the vehicle at the corresponding time and location (see Section 7.5), then calculating the fee due for a traffic data part and committing to the result has also 'time critical' aspects[4].

All communication and other work afterward is not 'time critical'. Indeed, the communication required for spot-checking is not sensitive for, say, a substantial break down of the communication system, such as a breakdown of several days. Note that much or most of the communication can be done at specific moments or places, when a cheap connection (*e.g.* WiFi) is available, for instance at home or at a fueling station offering such connectivity. All this may be used to reduce the communication costs. We do not wish to discussion the communication costs of different approaches further, because these costs are rather unclear at this stage. For example, they depend much on the type of communication channel(s) used. Furthermore, this issue is not crucial for the purpose of our presentation.

7.7   Individual Responsibility

With our approach it is possible (but not necessary) to give users individual autonomy by allowing them to take maximal responsibility. This is to a certain extent comparable to the current responsibility of individual citizens for the submittal and correctness of the contents of tax forms for income and revenue. Indeed, there are some developments that tax authorities support citizens by providing partly pre-filled forms, but in the end the responsibility still lies with the citizen. The role of the state is to (statistically/randomly) check these tax reports, to collect the associated fees and to punish those individuals (or organisations) that do not fulfil their duties.

A system in which the state takes the full responsibility—that is, determines all by itself (without user involvement) the amount of taxes due—is completely different. Citizens then are turned into passive subjects whose behaviour is being monitored almost constantly in order to obtain the relevant data for calculating fees. Such a system may seem more convenient for users, but is definitely also more threatening than the traditional declaration-based one. It constitutes a fundamental change in the balance of power and responsibilities.

In the end it is of course a political decision in which direction our societies are moving. Our approach at least provides a technical basis to uphold individual autonomy a bit longer.

8   Use Scenarios: Granny, Gadget and Geek

This section will elaborate, to some extent, three different use scenarios of the proposed ETP approach, which we shall (respectfully) label 'granny', 'gadget' and 'geek'.

---

[4] If ample time is available, one might succeed in acquiring almost complete knowledge on where and when observation teams have been active and then committing to a zero fee for all TPs where the risk of having been observed is negligible. Note that: a) the PA may provide for a sufficient number of unnoticed observations as countermeasure, b) external commits may be seen as less 'time critical' if internal commits (see Section 6.1) are used, and c) internal commits rely on physical protection (just as fat OBE does).

'Granny' is well-aware of painful periods in history and is not happy with the idea that others (in particular, the state) know her car movements, but she definitely does not want much ado. She uses computers, in a limited way, but does not (wish to) understand the internal workings. She simply buys a black box that handles everything for her. Our 'granny' chooses for thin OBE that computes and sends the trajectory hashes itself, distributes fee calculations to selected Calculation Service Providers, sends hashes of the results (see Section 6.3) to the PA and also automatically handles the verification requests from the PA. After each quarter the device informs her via a display (or an SMS or e-mail) how much she has to pay for that quarter. On her request, the device will show her other aggregations of fee calculations. For example, the fee due for a particular trip, day or week.

The 'gadget' person does not care very much about his privacy. He is willing to exchange it for extra services. He chooses some organisation that he trusts and that sells fancy car navigation systems (including for instance a car assistance or breakdown service) with embedded traffic pricing functionality. He buys such a device and signs a service contract so that the company will take care of all road fee submissions and checks on his behalf. The device sends his location information (trajectory parts) to the company, which handles the hash and fee submissions and the answers to spot-checks. The company to which he has delegated his road pricing duties thus knows his whereabouts, but offers additional services in return, like safety surveillance and tailored real-time congestion information with personalised suggestions for alternative routes.

Our 'geek' does not trust anyone. She wants a minimal system in her car that only stores trajectory parts and communicates their daily hashes to the PA. She frequently transfers her trajectory parts (pre-images) to her PC, *e.g.* via WiFi or perhaps even via a dump on a USB memory stick or on her Bluetooth cell-phone. She uses open source software to do all the work required. Her software calculates the (sub)fees on the basis of publicly available map information, sends their hashes (see Section 6.3) as well as the fee due for each quarter to the PA via the web, and handles all spot-checking requests from the PA. With every spot-check request concerning a trajectory part, the software on her PC first checks whether the time and location as specified by the PA are correct (see Section 7.5). If not, she asks for the photograph to find out whether this may have been an understandable error of the PA or an abuse attempt. She uses the additional functionality of her software package to keep a personal record of all her travels and can visualise them in Google maps (via Tor). She also keeps them to show to her boss, if needed, to substantiate her occasional reclaims for business trips. Note that a reasonable possibility is that the open source software package and the required map information are produced and published on behalf of the PA, say via a web site.

All these three fictitious individuals fulfil, in quite different ways, the duties associated with a system for ETP as proposed here. It shows that there is ample room for individual variation and for contributions and additional services by commercial organisations.

9   Final Remarks

The main idea in this paper is simple and general. It may be described as follows. Consumers use certain 'goods'. Examples are use of transport infrastructure (such as a whole road network as described in previous sections, or toll roads, or parking lots, or a public transportation system) or consumption of, say, electricity. Each consumer's usage is measured by equipment in the consumer's environment, which is 'potentially hostile' for the goods provider. Correct functioning of and reporting by the equipment may be the responsibility of the consumer, of a party chosen by the consumer (*e.g.* an independent equipment provider), of the goods provider (*e.g.* in certain cases that it also provides for the equipment or parts thereof) or of any combination of these. Our approach is useful and suitable for all these cases of individual or shared responsibility. For the following, let us assume the user is (mainly) responsible. Then the consumer (or actually equipment on his behalf) commits himself to the measurements by transferring hashes (fingerprints) of the measured values to the goods provider (or a pricing authority), while keeping secret the measured values. The measured values (*i.e.* the pre-images of the hashes) are used for the calculation of fees due (for short periods). These calculations can be done separately and in a privacy-friendly way and hashes of their results must also be transferred to the goods provider. Only the total fee due for a longer period (*i.e.* the sum of the fees due for many short periods) is reported to the goods provider in 'readable' form. The goods provider can guarantee fraud resistance by spot-checking in a way similar to what has been described in previous sections.

Underlying such an architecture is a certain view on the organisation of our society in which individuals remain responsible for what they do and their behaviour is not constantly monitored and checked. To make this view more concrete, consider a toll gate, for instance at the entrance of a bridge or of a congestion fee area. The traditional way to organise such a fee is to identify (for instance via license plate recognition or via some DSRC-tag) each vehicle passing by and to charge a fee on the basis of such observations. This is in a sense the most obvious solution. It is rather privacy-unfriendly however, because all passages of individual vehicles are—at least temporarily—registered in some database (of the authority in question) that is open to various forms of secondary use. A different solution, in line with the approach presented in this paper, is the following. The gate constantly broadcasts messages of the form "you are passing this-and-this gate at this-and-this time and this-and-this tariff table must be applied", which are recorded by the OBE of vehicles that pass by. The OBE of these vehicles regularly transfer hashes of these records to a central authority and also hashes of the fees due for such passages. Vehicles may be photographed now and then in order to randomly check the correctness of the total fee reported for a longer period. Thus, only a small subset of all passages is recorded (temporarily) by the authority.

Which approach do you prefer? In the end this is a societal issue. This paper provides a technical framework for more privacy-friendly (but also more fraud-resistant) solutions than are currently being employed.

Acknowledgments

Thanks are due to Eric Verheul, Michel Oey, Gert Maneschijn, Gerke Paulusma, Gerhard de Koning Gans, Erik Poll, Jaap-Henk Hoepman, Marko van Eekelen and Engelbert Hubbers for helpful discussions and suggestions.

References

1. Chaum, D.: Untraceable electronic mail, return addresses, and digital pseudonyms. Communications of the ACM 24(2), 84–88 (1981)
2. Cramer, R., Gennaro, R., Schoenmakers, B.: A secure and optimally efficient multi-authority election scheme. In: Fumy, W. (ed.) EUROCRYPT 1997. LNCS, vol. 1233, pp. 103–118. Springer, Heidelberg (1997)
3. Eisses, S., de Jonge, W., Habers, V.: Privacy and distance-based charging for all vehicles on all roads. In: Proceedings of the 13th ITS World Congress (2006),
   www.rapp.ch/documents/papers/Privacy_and_RUC_ITSLondon-doc.pdf
4. de Jonge, W.: Kilometerheffing op basis van elektronische aangifte. Informatie, 22–27 (2003),
   www.cs.vu.nl/~wiebren/TIP/ArtikelInformatie.pdf
5. Kaufman, C., Perlman, R., Speciner, M.: Network Security. Private Communication in a Public World. Prentice Hall, Englewood Cliffs (2002)
6. Lessig, L.: The Future of Ideas. Vintage (2001)
7. Schneier, B.: Applied cryptography, 2nd edn. John Wiley & Sons, Chichester (1996)

A Formal Privacy Management Framework

Daniel Le Métayer

Inria Grenoble Rhône-Alpes, 655 venue de l'Europe, Montbonnot, France
Daniel.Le-Metayer@inrialpes.fr

Abstract. Privacy is a complex issue which cannot be handled by exclusively technical means. The work described in this paper results from a multidisciplinary project involving lawyers and computer scientists with the double goal to (1) reconsider the fundamental values motivating privacy protection and (2) study the conditions for a better protection of these values by a combination of legal and technical means. One of these conditions is to provide to the individuals effective ways to convey their consent to the disclosure of their personal data. This paper focuses on the formal framework proposed in the project to deliver this consent through software agents.

1 Context and Motivations

In the same way as the growing use of photography at the end of the 19th century prompted Warren and Brandeis seminal paper [31], the changes imposed nowadays by information and communication technologies require a deep reflection on the fundamental values underlying privacy and the best way to achieve their protection [15,27]. Furthermore a multidisciplinary approach is necessary to tackle this challenge because privacy can neither be apprehended nor guaranteed by exclusively legal or technical means. As a step in this direction, the collaborative projects PRIAM[1] and LISE[2] gather lawyers and computer scientists with the dual goal of putting forward effective (legal and technical) instruments to protect privacy and to establish liabilities in IT systems.

One of the greatest challenges posed by pervasive computing or ambient intelligence to privacy is the fact that communications and computations can occur without the user's notice ("invisibility principle"). Indeed, most legal instruments for privacy protection explicitly refer to the unambiguous consent of the person as one of the conditions for the collection of his/her personal data. But requiring that the user provides his consent before each single data communication would not only be ineffective in terms of privacy protection (or even counterproductive, as it already is on the Internet, because the harassed user would end up accepting all requests and relinquishing his privacy altogether), it would also defeat the very purpose of these systems. Possible ways to reconcile the principle of unambiguous consent and the essential features of ubiquitous computing have thus been central to the legal and technical studies conducted in the PRIAM project.

In this paper we start from the requirements and recommendations resulting from the legal study and focus on the technical aspects, more precisely on the definition of

---

[1] Privacy Issues in Ambient Intelligence.
[2] Liability Issues in Software Engineering.

P. Degano, J. Guttman, and F. Martinelli (Eds.): FAST 2008, LNCS 5491, pp. 162–176, 2009.

a formal framework for privacy management. The overall approach, which involves a natural language setting as well as informal and formal descriptions, is sketched in Section 2. The formal framework itself is defined in Sections 3, 4 and 5 which introduce respectively the language of events, compliance and global correctness. Section 6 is a review of related work and Section 7 draws some conclusions.

2   Approach

The fact that a person ("data subject" following the terminology of [28]) must provide his informed consent before his personal data may be collected (unless otherwise authorized by law) is the cornerstone of most data protection regulations [29]. For example, Article 7 of the EU Directive 95/46/EC [28] states that

> Personal data may be processed only if: (a) the data subject has unambiguously given his consent; or (b) processing is necessary for the performance of a contract to which the data subject is a party or in order to take steps at the request of the data subject prior to entering into a contract; or (c) processing is necessary for compliance with a legal obligation to which the controller is subject; or (d) processing is necessary in order to protect the vital interests of the data subject, ...

In addition, this consent must be *informed* in the sense that the entity collecting the data ("controller" following the terminology of [28])[3] must provide sufficient information to the data subject, including "the purposes of the processing for which the data are intended".

In situations such as pervasive computing where an action from the user before each disclosure of data is not practically feasible, the natural question for the computer scientist is then: why not using the technology itself to cure the problems caused by the technology? In other words, if privacy rights are jeopardized by the highest level of automation provided by pervasive computing, why not also increasing the level of automation on the side of the defense of these rights ? This idea leads to the notion of *Privacy Agent*, a dedicated software which would play the role of "representative" or "proxy" of the user and manage his personal data on his behalf [20,21]. Not surprisingly, this possibility triggers a whole bunch of new questions from the legal side: to what extent should a consent delivered via a software agent be considered as legally valid? Are current regulations flexible enough to accept such kind of delegation to an automated system? If it is the case, what technical and legal constraints should be imposed on a software agent to be used as a valid representative of a subject? What would be the consequences of any error (bug, misunderstanding, etc.) in the process? The conclusions of our legal analysis of these issues are presented in [22]. The most important recommendations as far as the present paper is concerned are the following:

1. The technical framework should ensure, as much as possible, that the meaning and impact of the consent are defined without any ambiguity and properly understood by all the actors involved.

---

[3] More precisely, [28] defines the controller as the legal entity which determines the purposes and means of the processing of personal data.

2. The actors involved are not only the data subject and the controller, but also the software agent providers and the Data Authority[4]. In particular, since software agents are not granted any legal personality (even though this issue is debated among lawyers [12,10]), it is the software agent provider who should be liable for the correct implementation of the privacy policy of the data subject.
3. All actors should be held accountable for their actions and precise procedures should be put in place to ensure that liabilities can be established after the facts. Such procedures should be usable in a formal procedure in case of litigation[5].

In order to implement the above recommendations, the legal and technical framework put forward in the PRIAM project involves the following ingredients:

1. A restricted natural language (SIMPL: SIMple Privacy Language) used by data subjects and data controllers to express respectively their privacy requirements and commitments.
2. Specifications of a subject software agent and a controller software agent ("Subject Agent", or "SA", and "Controller Agent" or "CA" in the sequel). These specifications are mostly expressed in a formal framework, based on a trace semantics, complemented with informal requirements.
3. Link between SIMPL policies and software agent specifications.
4. Link between software agent specifications and their implementations.
5. Legal contracts between the Subject Agent provider (respectively the Controller Agent provider) and the data subject (respectively the controller) referring to the above items.

The PRIAM framework thus involves different languages (SIMPL, trace language, implementation language) which, we believe, is essential due to the variety of actors involved. The position taken in PRIAM is that, in order to reduce potential sources of ambiguities:

– The most appropriate language should be used for each purpose.
– Each of these languages should be kept minimal.
– The correspondences between these languages should be defined precisely.

These conditions are necessary to ensure that each actor has the proper understanding and that these understandings are consistent. For example, the aforementioned links should ensure that there is no gap between the wishes of a data subject (expressed through the SIMPL language) and the actual behaviour of his Subject Agent. In any circumstances, if a disagreement arises concerning the treatment of personal data by a controller (or the software agent acting on his behalf), then the proposed framework should make it possible to discover the origin of the problem and to identify the liable actor.

In this paper, we focus on the formal part of the specification and provide some hints on the other aspects.

---

[4] In addition, other certification authorities may also be involved, e.g. to authentify or to certify software agents.

[5] As set forth in Article 23 of [28] the controller is liable for damages suffered by the data owner as a result of unlawful processing of personal data.

3   Events Language

Before entering into the presentation of the events language used to define the semantics of software agents, it is necessary to start with a quick introduction to the SIMPL language. Let us call "disclosure policy" and "collection policy" the privacy policies defined by data subjects and controllers respectively. The following is an example disclosure policy statement in SIMPL:

> I consent to disclose data of category Cultural to a third party only if the aforementioned third party has provided the following pieces of information pursuant to this disclosure of data:
> - His identity and such identity belongs to Book Store.
> - His verification level and such verification level is at least 2.
> - His privacy policy with respect to the aforementioned category of data and such policy includes the following commitments :
>   - Use only this data for the following purpose(s): Order Processing.
>   - Delete this data within a delay of 1 month.
>   - Transfer this data always accompanied with the present privacy and only to third parties allowed to receive this data according the present privacy policy after commitment of such third party to respect this privacy policy provided I am previously informed of such disclosure and the identity of the third party.
>   - Ensure that any valid request from my side to access such data will be satisfied within a delay of 3 days.
>   - Ensure that any valid request from my side to delete such data will be satisfied within a delay of 3 days.
>   - Ensure that any valid request from my side to modify such data will be satisfied within a delay of 3 days.

Similarly, the controller can express privacy commitments of the form:

> The management of data of category Book Order shall meet, if requested by their Sticky Policy, the following requirements:
> - Use of the data shall be only for the following purpose(s): Order Processing.
> - The data shall be deleted within a delay of 3 months after its collection.
> - The data may be transferred or disclosed (i) always accompanied with its Sticky Policy; (ii) only in contexts allowed by this Sticky Policy; (iii) only to third parties allowed to receive the data according this Sticky Policy after commitment of such third party to comply with this Sticky Policy.
> - Any Valid Request from the owner of the data to access the data will be satisfied within the delay of 1 week.

SIMPL has a slightly legal flavour because it is the language used to express policies as they are signed by individuals (subjects and controllers) but users can define their policies through a friendly interface which relieves them from the burden of writing the sentences by themselves. The above examples illustrate only some of the possibilities of the SIMPL language. A more complete account of the language is conveyed through the presentation of the semantics domains below.

Following the minimality principle stated in the previous section, we define the semantics of privacy agents (Subject Agents and Controller Agents) in terms of traces of events. In the following subsections, we introduce some of the most significant events for, successively, Subject Agents and Controller Agents.

3.1   Subject Agent Events

Subject Agents can communicate with Controller Agents and with the subject himself. By convention, events $E(Id_1, Id_2, \ldots)$ represent communications from Id_1 to Id_2:

- *DisclosureRequest*$(Id_1, Id_2, Category, Verification, Commitment)$ is a communication from a CA to a SA : the CA asks for the disclosure of information of category *Category* of subject Id_2. Id_1 is the name of the controller, *Verification* his verification level and *Commitment* his commitments for the treatment of the requested data. The verification level can be seen as a trust level granted to the controller by a certification authority, which may come with a certificate from this authority. For this information to make sense for the subject, a standard (or widely accepted) ranking must be available[6]. The subject can also require that the certificate originates from specific authorities.
- *DataDisclosure*$(Id_1, Id_2, Category, Value, StickyPolicy)$ is the disclosure of data as a reply to the previous request. *Value* is the requested value and *StickyPolicy* its associated privacy policy. In our framework, a personal data should never be separated from its privacy policy. Id_1 is the name of the subject and Id_2 the name of the controller.
- *SDefineDisclosure*$(DisclosurePolicy, Id)$ is a communication from a subject to his SA : the subject defines a new disclosure policy and identity[7].

3.2   Controller Agent Events

In addition to the communications with Subject Agents introduced in the previous subsection, Controller Agents can interact with their controller (defining a new collection policy), with third parties (requesting the transfer of personal data collected by the controller) and with applications requesting access to the data. Applications represent accesses to the data which are local to the controller's site or device. The following are examples of Controller Agent events:

- *DefineCollection*$(CollectionPolicy)$ is a communication from the controller to the CA : the controller defines a new collection policy[8].

---

[6] The ranking used in the PRIAM project includes level 1 (minimum level) which corresponds to controllers having committed to comply with automated auditor requests, level 2 which includes the same commitment for physical audits and level 3 which includes the certification of the Controller Agent.

[7] This feature allows the subject to use different identities (or pseudonyms) at different points of time.

[8] Note that, in contrast with subjects, controllers cannot change their identity. This limitation makes it easier to implement the accountability requirement set forth in Section 2.

- $TransferRequest(Id_1, Id_2, Id_3, Category, Verification, Commitment)$ is a communication from the CA of name Id_1 to the CA of name Id_2. The controller Id_1 requests the transfer of data of category $Category$ pertaining to the subject of name Id_3. $Verification$ is the verification level of Id_1 and $Commitment$ his commitments.
- $TransferData(Id_1, Id_2, Id_3, Category, Value, StickyPolicy)$ is the reply to the previous request. $Value$ is the value of data $Category$ of the subject of name Id_3 and $StickyPolicy$ its sticky policy.

4   Compliance

The semantics of a software agent is defined in terms of compliant agent traces. An agent trace is a pair (E, S) with E a finite list of event values $E_1, \ldots, E_n$ and S a finite list of state values $S_1, \ldots, S_n$.

States are functions from variables to their domains. Any Subject Agent state includes at least the following variables:

- $MyData$: function of type $Categories \rightarrow Values$ representing the personal data of the subject.
- $MyDPolicy$: disclosure policy of the subject (belonging to $DisclosurePolicies$, as defined below).
- $MyIdentity$: identity of the subject.
- $MyTime$: local time of the subject.

It can also include context variables such as $MyLoc$ (localization). Note that time is simply treated as a state variable here: the faithful implementation of a clock is typically a commitment which is left in the informal part of the specification.

Controller Agent states include at least the following variables:

- $MyImport$: personal data with their collection date and sticky policy. Its type is $(Identities \otimes Categories) \rightarrow (Times \otimes Values \otimes StickyPolicies)$.
- $MyCPolicy$: collection policy of the controller (belonging to $CollectionPolicies$, as defined below).
- $MyIdentity$: identity of the controller.
- $MyTime$: local time of the controller.
- $MyLevel$: verification level of the controller.

Similarly to Subject Agent states, Controller Agent states can also include context variables.

Events are tuples of values tagged by their event type. Events can either be internal or external. External events are events of the types introduced in the previous subsection. Internal events include other actions which can have an impact on the state of the agent. For the sake of simplicity (and without loss of generality), we consider only one type of internal event here: $internal$.

The parameters of external events take values in the following domains:

$DisclosurePolicy : DisclosurePolicies$
$CollectionPolicy : CollectionPolicies$
$Id, Id_1, Id_2, Id_3 : Identities$

Category : *Categories*
Value : *Values*
Application : *Applications*
Purpose : *Purposes*
Commitment : *Commitments*
Verification : *Verifications*
StickyPolicy : *StickyPolicies*

The main domains are defined as follows[9]:

$DisclosurePolicies = Categories \rightarrow StickyPolicies$
$CollectionPolicies = Categories \rightarrow Commitments$
$StickyPolicies = \{(X_1, X_2, X_3, X_4) \|$
$\qquad X_1 \in IdentityPolicies,$
$\qquad X_2 \in VerificationPolicies,$
$\qquad X_3 \in Commitments,$
$\qquad X_4 \in Contexts\}$
$IdentityPolicies = \{(X, Y) \| X = \nabla \text{ or } X \subseteq Nat, Y = \nabla \text{ or } Y \subseteq Authorities\}$
$VerificationPolicies = \{(X, Y) \| X \in \{\nabla, 1, 2, 3\}, Y = \nabla \text{ or } Y \subseteq Authorities\}$
$Commitments = \{(X_1, X_2, X_3, X_4, X_5, X_6) \|$
$\qquad X_1 \subseteq Purposes,$
$\qquad X_2 \in Delays,$
$\qquad X_3 \in \{\perp, \nabla, information, authorization\},$
$\qquad X_4, X_5, X_6 \in Delays\}$
$Delays = Nat_\nabla$
$Identities = Nat \otimes Certificates$
$Contexts = (Vars \rightarrow Bool)_\nabla$
$Certificates = (Nat \otimes Authorities)_\nabla$

We use the notation S_∇ to denote the set $S \cup \{\nabla\}$. The value ∇ represents the absence of constraint or commitment: for example if the deletion delay is equal to ∇ (X_2 in the definition of *Commitments*) for a given category in a disclosure policy, it means that no commitment is required from the controllers with respect to the deletion of data of that category; if the value of X in the definition of *IdentityPolicies* is ∇, it means that no constraint is imposed on the identity of the controllers which are allowed to receive the data. A disclosure policy associates a sticky policy with each category of data. Sticky policies involve three constraints on the controllers (X_1, X_2 and X_3) and one constraint on the context (X_4). The first component of identity policies is the set of identities of controllers allowed to receive the data and the second component is the set of recognized certification authorities to certify this identity. The components of *Commitments* represent respectively: the set of authorized purposes (X_1); the deletion delay (X_2); the commitment with respect to transfer of the data to a third party (X_3 where $\perp$ means no transfer right); and delays for complying with requests from the data subject (respectively X_4 for access requests, X_5 for deletion requests and X_6 for modification requests). Certificates contain the actual value of the certificate and the certification authority.

---

[9] The other domains are pre-defined sets of basic values: for example, $Applications = Nat$.

For the purpose of this paper, we use Definition 1 as the compliance property for Subject Agent traces, which is sufficient to convey the essence of the approach. The complete definitions of compliance include additional requirements to ensure, for example, that agents forward messages towards (and from) subjects and controllers.

Definition 1. *A Subject Agent trace* (E, S) *is said to be compliant if the following conditions hold:*

$\forall\, i,\, E_i = DataDisclosure(Id_1, Id_2, Ca, Va, Po) \Rightarrow$
$\qquad \exists\, j < i,\, \exists\, Ve_2,\, \exists\, Co_2,\, E_j = DisclosureRequest(Id_2, Id_1, Ca, Ve_2, Co_2)$ *and*
$\qquad \forall k\ j < k < i,\, E_k \neq DataDisclosure(Id_1, Id_2, Ca, *, *)$ *and*
$\qquad S_i(MyIdentity) = Id_1$ *and* $S_i(MyData)(Ca) = Va$ *and*
$\qquad Po = S_i(MyDPolicy)(Ca) = (Id, Ve, Co_2, Cx)$ *and*
$\qquad Id_2 \triangleright Id$ *and* $Ve_2 \triangleright Ve$ *and* $S_i \triangleright Cx$
$\forall\, i, E_i = DefineDisclosure(Dp, Id) \Rightarrow$
$\qquad S_i = S_{i-1}[MyDPolicy \mapsto Dp;\ MyIdentity \mapsto Id]$
$\forall\, i,\, E_i = Internal \Rightarrow$
$\qquad S_i(MyDPolicy) = S_{i-1}(MyDPolicy)$ *and*
$\qquad S_i(MyIdentity) = S_{i-1}(MyIdentity)$
$\forall\, i,\, E_i = External$ *and* $E_i \neq DefineDisclosure \Rightarrow S_i = S_{i-1}$

Definition 2. *The "satisfies" relation $\triangleright$ is defined as follows for, respectively, identities, verification levels and states:*

Let $Id = (Id_1, Cer_1)$, $Id' = (Id'_1, Au'_1)$, *then* $Id \triangleright Id'$ *if and only if*
$\qquad (Id'_1 = \nabla$ *or* $Id_1 \in Id'_1)$ *and* $(Au'_1 = \nabla$ *or* $(Cer_1 = (*, Au_1)$ *and* $Au_1 \in Au'_1))$
Let $Ve = (Ve_1, Cer_1)$, $Ve' = (Ve'_1, Au'_1)$, *then* $Ve \triangleright Ve'$ *if and only if*
$\qquad (Ve'_1 = \nabla$ *or* $Ve_1 \geq Ve'_1)$ *and* $(Au'_1 = \nabla$ *or* $(Cer_1 = (*, Au_1)$ *and* $Au_1 \in Au'_1))$
$S \triangleright Cx$ *if and only if* $Cx = \nabla$ *or* $(\forall y \in Domain(Cx),\, S(y) \Rightarrow Cx(y))$

The most important rule for the compliance of Subject Agents is the rule defining the conditions for data disclosure. First a request for disclosure must have been received previously by the Subject Agent (and must not have been answered before). In addition, this request must come from an authorized controller for this category of data $(Id_2 \triangleright Id)$, his verification level must be sufficient $(Ve_2 \triangleright Ve)$ and the current state must satisfy the context requirement in the disclosure policy for this category of data $(S_i \triangleright Cx)$. Last but not least, the controller must commit to the sticky policy for this category of data $(S_i(MyPolicy)(Ca) = (Id, Ve, Co_2, Cx)$ with Co_2 equal to the commitment in the *DisclosureRequest* event). Another important rule is the rule stating that the disclosure policy and identity must not be modified by internal events[10].

The compliance property for Controller Agents, which is not presented here for the sake of conciseness, characterizes honest behaviours of Controller Agents: for example, when requesting a data disclosure, the Controller Agent must provide its true identity, verification level and privacy policy for the category of data requested; the Controller Agent must ensure that collected data are not kept longer than permitted; it cannot modify sticky policies, etc.

---

[10] Note that internal events can change other parts of the state : typically, they can modify the current context (e.g. time or location) and the personal data of the subject.

The compliance properties apply to software agents individually. Not surprisingly, the semantics of a complete system (set of software agents) is defined as the sets of the traces of the software agents composing the system[11]. The only additional requirement for a set of traces to be compliant is consistency, which amounts to ensure the matching of communication events: any communication event $E(Id_1, Id_2, *, *, \ldots)$ must match with the corresponding (identical) event in exactly one other trace in the set.

5   Global Correctness

The compliance conditions stated in the previous section impose constraints on the behaviour of software agents. What remains to be shown however is that these constraints are sufficient to ensure that personal data are appropriately protected by the system. Property 1 and Property 2 state two desirable properties of the system:

- Property 1 expresses the fact that if a value of a subject is in the data space of a controller, then this value is associated with a sticky policy Po and the subject has defined at some stage a privacy policy allowing a controller with this identity to receive this data with this sticky policy.
- Property 2 states that if the value of a subject is contained in the data space of a controller and the subject has never defined a privacy policy allowing any controller to forward this data, then the subject must have disclosed this data to this controller directly.

Property 1. If Σ is a compliant set of traces of a system of software agents then

$$\forall (E, S) \in \Sigma,$$
$$\exists i, \exists Id_2, \exists Ca, \exists Po, \ S_i(MyImport)(Id_2, Ca) = (*, *, Po)$$
$$\Rightarrow$$
$$\exists (E', S') \in \Sigma, \exists j,$$
$$S'_j(MyIdentity) = Id_2 \text{ and}$$
$$Po = S'_j(MyDPolicy)(Ca) = (Id, *, *, *) \text{ and}$$
$$S_i(MyIdentity) \triangleright Id$$

Property 2. If Σ is a compliant set of traces of a system of software agents then

$$\forall (E, S) \in \Sigma,$$
$$\exists i, \exists Id_2, \exists Ca, \ S_i(MyImport)(Id_2, Ca) \neq \bot \text{ and}$$
$$(\forall (E', S') \in \Sigma, \forall j,$$
$$S'_j(MyIdentity) = Id_2 \text{ and}$$
$$S'_j(MyDPolicy)(Ca) = (*, *, Co, *)$$
$$\Rightarrow Co = (*, *, \bot, *, *, *))$$
$$\Rightarrow$$
$$\exists (E', S') \in \Sigma, \exists k, \ S'_k(MyIdentity) = Id_2 \text{ and}$$
$$E_k = DataDisclosure(Id_2, S_i(MyIdentity), Ca, *, *)$$

The complete definition of global correctness includes other properties which can be defined in a similar way such as the compliance with deletion delays and purpose restrictions. A significant benefit of the approach is that the compliance of the set of

---

[11] We assume a finite and fixed set of software agents in this paper.

software agent traces is sufficient to establish global correctness. For example, Property 1 can be proven by recurrence on the length of the software agent traces and decomposition into two subcases corresponding respectively to (1) the collection of the data through direct disclosure from the subject and (2) the collection of the data through transfer by another controller[12]. The conclusion follows from the compliance of the Subject Agent in the first case and from the recurrence hypothesis and compliance of the sending Controller Agent in the second case. The second property can be proven in a similar way.

6   Related Work

Privacy policies have triggered a fair amount of interest during the last decade. The approach followed in [24] consists in extending the access control matrix model to deal with privacy rules. The extended model has been used to express the HIPAA [14] consent rules in a formal setting and to check properties of different versions of the HIPAA. The main extensions to the access control matrix model concern the introduction of specific operations for notification and logging. The motivations for this project are thus significantly different from our own goals: as a consequence [24] does not deal with sticky policies, agent compliance or future obligations (obligations used in [24] are conditions on the current context). The same access control matrix approach has been applied to the expression of privacy policies for location-based services [13] based on a Personal Digital Rights Management (PDRM) architecture. [25] has introduced a very generic framework encompassing several families of policies including usage control policies. These controls can be used to enforce some kinds of obligations at different points of time (which differ according to the families) but typical privacy obligations such as deletion or compliance with modification requests do not seem to be amenable to this model.

The Obligation Specification Language (OSL) put forward in [16] is mostly exemplified through DRM policies but can also be used to express privacy policies. It includes usage requirements such as duration, number of times, purpose, notification, etc. OSL is a rich language for obligations including different modalities (such as "must" and "may") and temporal operators. The semantics of OSL is defined in terms of traces expressed in the Z notation. The work presented here shares with [16] the trace semantics approach but differs in terms of scope and focus: we start with a simple language dedicated to privacy (deriving from natural language statements) and provide a framework for the definition of compliant agents acting as representative of the individuals. In contrast, the objective of [16] was to propose "a language for expressing requirements from many application areas of usage control" and thus dos not include any specific provision for privacy management.

Other contributions aim at providing a formal semantics to existing languages or frameworks, such as EPAL (Enterprise Privacy Authorization Language [1]) in [3] and

---

[12] The occurrence of a *DataDisclosure* or a *TransferData* event are the only possibilities to extend the *MyImport* data space of a compliant controller.

[2] or the P3P (Platform for Privacy Preferences [30]) in [23][13]. The semantics of EPAL presented in [3] is a decision procedure for the evaluation of access requests. The semantics is then used to define a notion of refinement of policies (satisfaction of a policy by another one) and the composition of policies. The approach followed in [23] and [32] is similar in spirit but uses a relational framework to define P3P privacy policies and APPEL (A P3P Preference Exchange Language) preferences. Similarly [2] proposes an embedding of EPAL into Prolog to benefit from the unification mechanisms for solving privacy queries. The formalism proposed in [19] is a first order predicate calculus built upon an XML framework. This formalism is used to support regulatory information management and compliance assistance. The main challenge tackled by these projects is the complexity and subtleties of languages which were not designed originally with a formal semantics and contain various sources of ambiguities. As a consequence, these efforts focus on the decision procedure to answer access requests and do not consider, as presented here, compliance properties of individual software agents or global correctness properties. Again, the approach followed here is more focused and top-down (defining a minimal setting to satisfy the legal and technical needs in order to secure the delegation of user's consent to software agents).

The semantics models proposed in [6] are based on RNLS (Restricted Natural Language Statements), a syntax for describing goals in terms of actors, actions and objects. Privacy related statements expressed in a natural language have first to be restated (manually) into RNLS. [6] suggests different kinds of quantitative and qualitative analyses which can then be performed on RNLS statements (for example to assess the level of privacy protection or to answer specific queries about the access to personal data) and [5] presents a method for generating natural language policy statements. Examples of analyses of privacy regulations derived from the HIPAA rules are presented in [7]. [26] also proposes a "semi-structured English syntax" which is used as an intermediate step to translate the Canadian FIPPA (Freedom of Information and Protection of Privacy Act) into EPAL. We share with this trend of work the use of natural language descriptions of privacy policies. However our main target is the definition of privacy policies (by subjects as well as controllers) and their correct implementation (as opposed to the analysis or translation of regulations in [6], [7] and [26]). We also share with the Sparcle project ([8] and [17]) the objective of assisting users to edit privacy policies expressed in a natural language but the user interface issues have been left outside the scope of this paper.

The interest of "a-posteriori" policy enforcement has been strongly advocated in [9] and [11], for example to cope with emergency actions that need to be taken in unexpected circumstances or to address the lack of control of the subjects in a distributed environment. The APPEL (A-Posteriori PoLicy Enforcement) core presented in [11] combines an audit logic with trust management techniques. As in our framework, it makes it possible to define sticky data policies; in addition, it includes provisions for constraining the join of documents and defining policy refinement rules. Trust

---

[13] The work reported in [18] is also related to this paper because it shows how to transform privacy practices expressed in E-P3P into privacy promises expressed in P3P. In contrast with our approach this transformation is bottom-up rather than top-down and it does not rely on a formal semantics.

and accountability are central in [11] and the formal setting is based on audit logs. Even though we have focused on the communications between subjects and controllers agents here (rather than the interactions with the auditor's agent), we also endorse the accountability principle and the introduction of automatic audits in the framework. The audit logic presented in [9] provides a general framework for defining agent accountability based on a proof system and proof obligations of the agents (when they are audited). The main difference between our approach and [9] and [11] is again a matter of focus: considering our goal to specify agents implementing the requirements of data subjects and controllers, we deal with specific obligations such as commitments on actions to be performed in the future (e.g., data deletion), purpose control, rights of the subject to be implemented by the controller (access, modification, deletion, etc.). In addition we consider subject as well as controller policies.

7   Conclusions

The work presented in this paper is part of a broader multidisciplinary project which follows a top-down approach, starting from the legal analysis and defining technical and legal requirements for the development of an effective solution to privacy issues in ambient intelligence environments. Due to space considerations, we have focused on one specific aspect in this paper, namely the specification of privacy agents and only the concepts necessary to convey the essence of the approach have been introduced. The complete framework includes, for example, provisions to define hierarchies of categories and purposes (with cumulative policy constraints), to deliver data with sticky policies stronger than the required policy (using implication rather than equality for compliance checking), to define the commitments of the controller in terms of audit (audit request and audit answer events), etc. Also the actual sets of events, compliance properties and global correctness properties are richer than the versions presented here.

As far as the legal framework is concerned, the roles of the different actors have been defined precisely and contract models have been proposed to formalize the commitments of the software agent providers with respect to the subjects and to the controllers. These commitments establish a double link between statements in SIMPL and software agent implementations: the first link is defined through the formal semantics introduced in this paper and a refinement relation between abstract execution traces and actual logs; the second link is expressed in terms of informal constraints. Typical constraints which have to be expressed informally concern the faithful implementation of the clock (variable *MyTime* in the software agent states) and the delivery of personal data to applications consistent with the purpose stated in their sticky policy. As far as the formal path is concerned, the locality property put forward in Section 5 is significant both from the technical point of view and from the legal point of view: technically speaking, it makes it possible to reason at the level of individual software agents; legally speaking, it means that liabilities can be associated with software agent providers based on individual commitments.

We believe that the two most important features of the framework presented here are minimality and generality : we have focused on the needs arising from the legal analysis for the specific issue of privacy protection and used the minimal technical setting to reach our goal. Minimality is a pre-requisite in this context both at the level of the natural language used to communicate with the users (to minimize the risks of misunderstanding by a subject or controller) and with respect to the formalization (to minimize the risk of misunderstanding or rejection of the elements of proof by juridical experts in case of litigation). Another significant design choice made in the project is the separation of issues which also corresponds to the legal position to isolate privacy from economical issues: according to this view, personal data are not considered as assets for bargaining but values to be protected independently of any other consideration[14]. As a result, Subject Agents can be seen as a "Privacy Monitors" in charge of controlling all disclosures of data, but strictly limited to this role.

Another consequence of this choice of separation of issues is that security is seen as orthogonal to privacy here: in other words, we have defined privacy as a functional model which should be complemented by appropriate security measures[15]. Note that the framework presented here is flexible enough to refer to security issues though: for example authentication rules or trust policies can be linked to the framework through the management of appropriate sets of identities, certification authorities and protocols can be integrated as conditions before the disclosure of data.

Acknowledgements. This work has been partially funded by the INRIA ARC (Action de Recherche Coopérative) PRIAM (Privacy Issues in Ambient Intelligence) and ANR (Agence Nationale de la Recherche) under the grant ANR-07-SESU-007 (project LISE: Liability Issues in Software Engineering).

References

1. Ashley, P., Hada, S., Karjoth, G., Powers, C., Schunter, M.: Enterprise privacy authorization language (EPAL). Technical Report 3485, IBM (2003)
2. Backes, M., Durmuth, M., Karjoth, G.: Unification in privacy policy evaluation - translating EPAL into Prolog. In: Fifth IEEE Int. Workshop on Policies for Distributed Systems and Networks (POLICY 2004) (2004)
3. Backes, M., Pfitzmann, B., Schunter, M.: A toolkit for managing enterprise privacy policies. In: Snekkenes, E., Gollmann, D. (eds.) ESORICS 2003. LNCS, vol. 2808, pp. 162–180. Springer, Heidelberg (2003)
4. Bibas, S.A.: A contractual approach to data privacy. Harvard Journal of Law and Public Policy, 17 (1994)
5. Breaux, T.D., Anton, A.I.: Analysing goal semantics for rights, permissions, and obligations. In: Sixth IEEE Int. Conference on Requirements Engineering (RE 2005) (2005)
6. Breaux, T.D., Anton, A.I.: Deriving semantics models from privacy principles. In: Sixth IEEE Int. Workshop on Policies for Distributed Systems and Networks (POLICY 2005) (2005)
7. Breaux, T.D., Anton, A.I.: Mining rule semantics to understand legislative compliance. In: ACM Workshop on Privacy in the Electronic Society (WPES 2005) (2005)

---

[14] This view, which is widely adopted in Europe, is not accepted by all lawyers though, especially in the US [4].

[15] Indeed, the European Directive [28] explicitly sets forth the liability of the controller to ensure the security of the personal data but does not provide further details on this topic.

8. Brodie, C.A., Karat, C.-M., Karat, J.: An empirical study of natural language parsing of privacy policy rules using the Sparcle policy workbench. In: Symposium On Usable Privacy and Security (SOUPS) (2006)

9. Cederquist, J.G., Corin, R., Dekker, M., Etalle, S., den Hartog, J.: An audit logic for accountability. In: Sixth IEEE Int. Workshop on Policies for Distributed Systems and Networks (POLICY 2005) (2005)

10. Dehiyat, E.: Intelligent agents and intentionality: should we begin to think outside the box? Computer Law and Security Report 22(1), 472–482 (2006)

11. Etalle, S., Winsborough, W.: A posteriori compliance control. In: ACM Symposium on Access Control Models And Technologies (SACMAT 2007) (2007)

12. Finocchiaro, G.: Electronic contracts and software agents. Computer Law and Security Report 19(1), 20–24 (2003)

13. Gunter, C., May, M.J., Stubblebine, S.: A formal privacy system and its application to location based services. In: Martin, D., Serjantov, A. (eds.) PET 2004. LNCS, vol. 3424, pp. 256–282. Springer, Heidelberg (2005)

14. Health Resources and Services Administration. Health Insurance Portability and Accountability Act. Public Law, 104–191 (1996)

15. Hildebrandt, M.: Profiling: from data to knowledge. DuD: Datenschutz und Datensicherheit 30(9), 548–552 (2006)

16. Hilty, M., Pretschner, A., Basin, D., Schaefer, C., Walter, T.: A policy language for distributed usage control. In: Biskup, J., López, J. (eds.) ESORICS 2007. LNCS, vol. 4734, pp. 531–546. Springer, Heidelberg (2007)

17. Karat, J., Karat, C.-M., Brodie, C.A., Feng, J.: Privacy in information technology: designing to enable privacy policy management in organizations. Int. Journal on Human-Computer Studies 63 (2005)

18. Karjoth, G., Schunter, M., Van Herreweghen, E.: Translating privacy practices into privacy promises - How to promise what you can keep. In: Fourth IEEE Int. Workshop on Policies for Distributed Systems and Networks (POLICY 2003) (2003)

19. Kerrigan, S., Law, K.H.: Logic-based regulation compliance-assistance. In: ICAIL 2003 (2003)

20. Langheinrich, M.: A privacy awareness system for ubiquitous computing environments. In: Borriello, G., Holmquist, L.E. (eds.) UbiComp 2002. LNCS, vol. 2498, pp. 237–245. Springer, Heidelberg (2002)

21. Langheinrich, M.: Personal privacy in ubiquitous computing. Tools and system support. Dissertation Document ETH 16100 (2005)

22. Le Métayer, D., Monteleone, S.: Computer assisted consent for personal data processing. In: 3D LSPI Conference on Legal, Security and Privacy Issues in IT (2008)

23. Li, N., Yu, T., Anton, A.: A semantics-based approach to privacy languages. Technical Report 2003-28, CERIAS (2003)

24. May, M.J., Gunter, C., Lee, I.: Privacy APIs: Access control techniques to analyze and verify legal privacy policies. In: Computer Security Foundations Workshop (CSFW) (2006)

25. Park, J., Sandhu, R.: The $UCON_{ABC}$ usage control model. ACM Transactions on Information and System Security (2004)

26. Powers, C., Adler, S., Wishart, B.: EPAL translation of the freedom of information and protection of privacy act. Technical Report Version 1.1, Tivoli Software, IBM (2004)

27. Rouvroy, A.: Privacy, data protection, and the unprecedented challenges of ambient intelligence. Social Science Research Network (2007)

28. The European Parliament and the Council of the European Union. UE directive 95/46/EC on the protection of individuals with regard to the processing of personal data and on the free movement of such data. Official Journal of the European Communities (1995)
29. Veldhuisen, A., Kohras, M., et al.: Analysis of privacy principles: Making privacy operational. Technical Report Version 2.0, International Security Trust and Privacy Alliance (May 2007)
30. W3C. Platform for privacy preferences (P3P). W3C recommendation. Technical report, W3C (2002), http://www.w3.org
31. Warren, S., Brandeis, L.: The right to privacy. Harvard Law Review, 193–220 (1890)
32. Yu, T., Li, N., Anton, A.I.: A formal semantics for P3P. In: ACM Workshop on Secure Web Services (2004)

Parameterised Anonymity

Jan Friso Groote and Simona Orzan

Department of Computer Science, Eindhoven University of Technology,
P.O. Box 513, NL-5600MB, Eindhoven, The Netherlands

Abstract. We introduce the notion of parameterised anonymity, to formalize the anonymity property of protocols with an arbitrary number of participants. This definition is an extension of the well known CSP anonymity formalization of Schneider and Sidiropoulos [18]. Using recently developed invariant techniques for solving parameterised boolean equation systems, we then show that the Dining Cryptographers protocol guarantees parameterised anonymity with respect to outside observers. We also argue that although the question whether a protocol guarantees parameterised anonymity is in general undecidable, there are practical subclasses where anonymity can be decided for any group of processes.

1 Introduction

Anonymity refers to the ability of a user to own some data or take some actions without being tracked down as the owner of that data or the originator of those actions. This property is essential in group protocols that might involve sensitive personal data, like electronic auctions, voting, anonymous broadcasts, file-sharing etc. Due to its relevance and subtle nature, anonymity has been given many definitions and has been the subject of theoretical studies and formal analysis work [1,8,9,17,10]. Protocols where anonymity is one of the aims are typically meant for large groups of users. However, formal verification of anonymity only treat (small) examples of individual protocols [13,18,19] and claims about the correctness of anonymity protocols *for any group size* are generally not made.

In this paper, we propose a parameterised possibilistic definition of anonymity based on a notion of secret choices of participants. The main inspiration is the CSP definition in [18], where anonymity is formalized as the impossibility of an observer to distinguish a protocol behaviour where a participant i acts according to a choice c from a protocol behaviour where i has taken a different choice d.

We then give a formal correctness proof for Chaum's Dining Cryptographers protocol [2], arguably the most well-known example of a protocol where anonymity is the main requirement. Starting with [18], where DC has been proved correct for 3 cryptographers, various verification approaches, both process theoretical and logical, have been applied to it, e.g. [18,1,13] — but only *for concrete instances*, the maximum instance being as large as 15 cryptographers [4]. No formal proof exists so far for an arbitrary number of parties, although a mathematical argument has already been given by Chaum in the original paper. We use a recently developed theory where standard verification problems like

P. Degano, J. Guttman, and F. Martinelli (Eds.): FAST 2008, LNCS 5491, pp. 177–191, 2009.

model checking and equivalence checking are encoded as *parameterised boolean equation systems (PBES)* [7]. PBESs are usually solved by symbolic approximation and by discovering equation patterns and invariants [7,16]. In solving the PBES corresponding to the DC protocol, we make essential use of invariants.

We also formulate the *parameterised anonymity problem* for $n \geq N$ processes (NPA) as the problem of deciding whether, for every instance of a group protocol description, a different instance can be found whose observable behaviour is indistinguishable from that of the first one. We show that this is undecidable in general, but practically usable subsets exists where anonymity can be decided.

We are aware of only one other previous anonymity proof for an arbitrary number of parties. There [10], the pi-calculus has been used for modeling and the correctness argument is based on the congruence of observational equivalence w.r.t. the parallel composition operator. This approach works essentially due to the absence of communication in the model. The matters get much more complex when communication is involved, as illustrated also in the current paper. A basic referendum protocol has been briefly analysed using PBESs in [16].

Decidability of the traditional security properties *secrecy* and *authentication* has been well understood in various models - atomic or complex keys, Dolev-Yao intruder with (un)bounded message size, (dis)allow equality tests etc. [11]. Recently, the need to answer decidability questions for other security properties like *anonymity, privacy, fairness* etc. was recognized [5] and gained interest. For the case of two-party protocols, effectiveness, fairness and balance of contract-signing is decidable [12], as well as a property related to anonymity, called *opacity* [15].

2   Preliminaries

A short introduction to mCRL2. mCRL2 is a process algebraic specification language with data types [6]. Processes are built from atomic multi-actions (e.g. $a|b|c$ is a multi-action where actions a, b and c happen simultaneously). Behaviour is combined by sequential composition ($\cdot$), non-deterministic choice ($+$) and parallel compositions ($\|$). There are two special processes: the deadlock δ and the internal action τ. Actions of parallel processes lead to multi-actions if they happen simultaneously. The *communication operator* Γ_C is used to let such actions communicate, under the restriction that they carry the same data arguments. E.g., if $\Gamma_{\{a|b \to c\}}$ is applied to a multi-action $a|b$, it becomes c. The *allow operator* $\nabla_V(p)$ allows only the multi-actions from V occurring in p to happen. The renaming operator $\rho_R(p)$ where R is a function from actions to actions renames the actions in p according to R. The *hiding* operator τ_I turns all occurrences of actions from the set I into the internal action τ.

There are a number of ways to tie processes up with data types. First, both processes and atomic actions can be parameterised with data elements, as in $P(x, 3)$ or $\text{send}(x)$. Then, $\sum_{x \in D} P(x)$ denotes alternative (possibly infinite) choice over data domain D, i.e. for any value $x_0 \in D$, the process can behave as $P(x_0)$. Finally, if b is a boolean term and p and q are processes, then the conditional construct $b \to p \diamond q$ is the process 'if b then p else q'.

PBES. A parameterised boolean equation is a fixed-point equation having as left-hand side a predicate variable with data parameters and as right-hand side a defining *predicate formula*, which is a boolean expression with quantifiers and predicate variables. Formally, a predicate formula is defined by the grammar $\phi ::= b \mid \phi_1 \wedge \phi_2 \mid \phi_1 \vee \phi_2 \mid \forall d{:}D.\ \phi \mid \exists d{:}D.\ \phi \mid X(e)$, where b is a data term of Boolean sort $\mathbb{B}$. X (taken from some domain of variables $\mathcal{P}$) is a (sorted) predicate variable of sort D_X and e is a vector of data terms of the sort D_X. The data variables occurring in a predicate formula are taken from a set $\mathcal{D}$.

Parameterised boolean equation systems (PBES) [7] provide a fundamental framework for solving verification problems. They can encode model checking questions [7], checking of various process equivalences [3], static analysis problems etc. The PBES solution is then the solution to the encoded problem. The basic PBES solving techniques are successive symbolic approximation of the system's equations and instantiation of the data parameters.

PBES invariants. In general, due to their complexity, it is not possible to solve PBESs automatically, but heuristics and interactive approaches are necessary. *Invariants* are predicates over data only (thus, no predicate variables involved), expressing a fixed relation between data variables. An invariant of a predicate variable X provides in fact an overapproximation of X's solution. In a recent extended study [16], many useful results and examples on the characterisation and use of invariants are discussed. For the current paper, we restrict those to the specific case of a PBES with one maximal fixed-point (ν) equation. An invariant for a parameterised boolean equation is defined formally as follows:

Definition 1. *Let $(\sigma X(d{:}D_X) = \phi)$ be an equation and let f be a simple predicate formula. Then f is an invariant of X iff $f \wedge \phi \leftrightarrow (f \wedge \phi)[(f(e) \wedge X(e))/X(e)]$, where $\leftrightarrow$ denotes boolean bi-implication and $[(f(e) \wedge X(e))/X(e)]$ denotes the substitution of all occurrences of X's instantiations $X(e)$ (for all possible data parameters e) with $f(e) \wedge X(e)$.*

A sufficient characterisation of an invariant for an equation is that it transfers its truth from the data parameters on the left-hand side to the data parameters on the right-hand side. Proposition 1 is a variation of this general principle.

Proposition 1 (from [16]). *Let $(\sigma X(d{:}D_X) = \phi)$ be an equation, with $\sigma \in \{\mu, \nu\}$ and ϕ of the form $\phi(d) = \chi \wedge \bigwedge_{\star \in I}(\psi_\star \Rightarrow X(g_k(d)))$, for I some index set, $\Rightarrow$ denoting the usual logical shortcut, χ, $\psi_\star$ simple predicate formulae and $g_\star(d)$ data terms. Moreover, let $f \in \mathcal{P}$ be a simple predicate such that, for all $\star \in I$, $f(d) \wedge \chi \wedge \psi_\star \Rightarrow f(g_\star(d))$. Then f is an invariant for the given equation.*

Definition 2. *Let $\mathcal{E} \equiv (\sigma X(d{:}D_X) = \phi)$ be an equation and f an invariant for it. $\mathcal{E}$ strengthened with f is the equation $\mathcal{E}' \equiv (\sigma X(d{:}D_X) = f \wedge \phi)$.*

Equations strengthened with well-chosen invariants are (much) easier to solve than the original equations. The main theorem in [7,16] identifies the conditions that ensure preservation of PBES solutions under strengthening with invariants. Instantiated for one equation $\mathcal{E}$, this theorem states that the solution of $\mathcal{E}$ coincides with the solution of $\mathcal{E}$ strengthened with an invariant f, on data domains satisfying f. This provides the technical base for the invariant-driven approach to equation solving. More specifically, once a good invariant is found, that characterizes the reachable data space without restricting it to uninteresting subsets, the strengthened version of an equation can be solved instead of the original one. In some specific cases, when an equation fits certain patterns, invariants can immediately lead to its solution. Such a pattern is described below.

Proposition 2 (from [16]). *Let $\mathcal{E} \equiv (\nu X(d{:}D_X) = \phi)$ be an equation. Let f be an invariant for $\mathcal{E}$ and assume ϕ has the form ($Q_l \in \{\forall, \exists\}$ for any l):*

$$f \wedge \bigwedge_{\star \in I} Q_1 \, e_\star^1{:}E_\star^1 \dots Q_{m_\star} \, e_\star^{m_\star}{:}E_\star^{m_\star}. \ (\psi_\star \Rightarrow X(g_\star(d, e_\star^1, \dots, e_\star^{m_\star})))$$

where, for any $\star \in I$, $\psi_\star$ is a simple predicate formula and $g_\star$ is a data term that depends only on the values of d and $e_i^1, \dots, e_i^{m_i}$. Then X has the solution f.

The Dining Cryptographers protocol. This protocol is a metaphor for anonymous broadcast and the story goes as follows: n cryptographers have dinner together. At the end, they learn that the bill has been payed anonymously by one of them, or by the NSA (National Security Agency). They wish to find out whether the payer was NSA or not, but if the payer was one of the cryptographers, nobody should learn her identity. To achieve this, they use the following protocol: each neighbouring pair of cryptographers generates a shared bit, by flipping a coin; then each cryptographer computes the exclusive or (XOR, denoted $\oplus$) of the two random bits she shares with her neighbors. Then, if she hasn't paid, she publicly announces the result. If she was herself the payer, she announces the flipped result. Every cryptographer collects all the announcements and XORs them. The result indicates whether the payer was an insider or not - true ($\top$) means cryptographer, false ($\bot$) means NSA.

3   A Parameterised Formalization of Anonymity

We give a formal scalable notion of anonymity, using mCRL2 and taking inspiration in existing process theoretic definitions like the one using CSP in [18]. We take the general view that anonymity for a participant means hiding parts of his behaviour or data from possible observers. We consider a *passive intruder*, who observes protocol runs but doesn't have the power to change its course. Group protocols like the ones we're interested in can usually be written as a parallel composition of n parties and an environment process:

$$\texttt{Protocol}(x) \stackrel{def}{=} \tau_I \rho_R \nabla_V \Gamma_C(P(0, x_0) \| P(1, x_1) \| \cdots \| P(n{-}1, x_{n-1}) \| Q(n)) \quad (1)$$

where $x = (x_0, x_1, \dots, x_{n-1})$ is a vector of secret choices. The parameters x_i come from a known, usually small, domain D. The processes $P(i, x_i)$ represent the behaviour of participant i and the process $Q(n)$ is some environmental process. The operator Γ_C prescribes the communications among the processes. The set C contains clauses of the form $a|b{\rightarrow}c$ expressing that actions a and b must communicate to c provided the parameters of a and b are equal. The allow operator ∇_V with V a set of multi-actions each of the form $a_1|\cdots|a_n$, shows which multi-actions are visible. All multi-actions that are not in V are blocked. The renaming operator ρ_R is used to give certain actions a different name. Finally, the operator τ_I renames actions in the set I to τ, effectively hiding them.

A typical example of a protocol where anonymity is desired, is a voting protocol, where x_i represents i's vote. The essence of anonymity is that the intruder should not be able to conclude from his observations x_i must be i's secret choice. More precisely, the intruder should not be able to observe any difference in the behaviours of the protocol with different values for x_i.

Definition 3 (anonymity). *Let* Protocol *be the formal specification of a protocol, D the domain of secret choices, $Restriction : D^* \rightarrow \{\top, \bot\}$ a predicate on arrays of D elements, $\sim$ a process equivalence modeling the intruder's observing power. We say that* Protocol *is anonymous for participant i out of n iff*

$$\forall x \in D^n \text{ with } Restriction(x)$$
$$\exists v \in D^n \text{ s.t. } Restriction(v), \ v_i \neq x_i \text{ and } \texttt{Protocol}(x) \sim \texttt{Protocol}(v).$$

The predicate *Restriction* is optional and captures possible conditions imposed by the protocol on the parameter array, describing the situations when the protocol is expected to guarantee anonymity. For instance, in the Dining Cryptographers (DC) protocol, $D = \{\top, \bot\}$ and x satisfies the condition that $x_i = \top$ for exactly one i (if nobody pays, anonymity is not guaranteed). In voting protocols, anonymity is expected only in non-unanimous votes, so the restriction there is that the parameter array should list at least two different values (votes).

The equivalence $\sim$ is a behavioural congruence (w.r.t. the operators that are used in the specification and which the intruder can use for his observations) and should be sufficiently strong, in order to ensure a sound analysis. In general, strong, branching or weak bisimulation are suitable. For standard process operators, failure and trace equivalence are also congruences.

4   A Symbolic Parameterised Correctness Proof for the Dining Cryptographers Protocol

In this section, we give a formal proof that the DC protocol guarantees anonymity w.r.t. an external intruder to any participant i ($i : 0 \leq i < n$), for any number of parties $n > 1$. We consider strong bisimulation equivalence (denoted $\underline{\leftrightarrow}$) as the equivalence expressing the intruder's observing power. Mostly, in the literature, trace equivalence is considered for this purpose. However, strong bisimulation is a sound choice, since whenever we prove a protocol correct according to it, it will also be correct in the trace model.

Formal model. We formalize DC as a parallel composition of n processes, each modelling the behaviour of a cryptographer. The secret choice as discussed in

Section 3 is the decision to pay or not (the paying bit), represented by the Boolean values $x_i \in \{\top, \bot\}$. The characterizing condition $Restriction(x)$ is that x should contain exactly one value $\top$, since anonymity should hold when there is exactly one payer. A cryptographer process executes a series of actions corresponding to the three main steps of the protocol. The decision whether to pay or not is modelled by the execution of a $\mathbf{pay}(i, x_i)$ action. Flipping of the ith coin is modelled as follows: process $Crypt(i, x_i)$ executes a $\mathbf{flip}$ action and then shares the result with the right hand neighbour in the ring, by executing $\mathbf{tell}$ while its right hand neighbour gets to know the result of this coin flipping by executing the action $\mathbf{recv}$. The synchronisation of these two actions results into the communication action $\mathbf{com}$. The mCRL2 specification looks like this:

$$DC(x{:}ChoiceVector) = \quad \rho_{\{\forall i,d.\mathbf{flip}(i,d)\to\mathbf{flip}(i),\forall i,d.\mathbf{com}(i,d)\to\mathbf{com}(i)\}}$$
$$\nabla_{\{\mathbf{flip},\mathbf{tell},\mathbf{com},\mathbf{syncbcast},\mathbf{nsa}\}} \quad \Gamma_{\{\mathbf{tell}|\mathbf{recv}\to\mathbf{com}\}}$$
$$(Crypt(0,x_0)\|Crypt(1,x_1)\|\cdots\|Crypt(n-1,x_{n-1}))$$

$$Crypt(i{:}\mathbb{N}, x_i{:}\mathbb{B}) \quad = \sum_{coinL:\mathbb{B}}(\,\mathbf{flip}(i, coinL)\cdot$$
$$(\mathbf{tell}((i+1) \bmod n, coinL)\|\sum_{coinR:\mathbb{B}}\mathbf{recv}(i, coinR))\cdot$$
$$CryptAnnounce(n, 0, i, x_i \oplus coinR \oplus coinL)$$

The $CryptAnnounce(n, m, i, v)$ process models the third step: broadcasting the result of i's local computation (v) and computing the XOR of all broadcasted values. Since the broadcast implementation is not an actual part of the protocol and for lack of space, we do not show this subprocess here. Its visible actions are the synchronous broadcast $\mathbf{syncbcast}$ and the protocol's conclusion $\mathbf{nsa}$. These actions have been added to the linearized version of the model. The renaming rules occurring as argument of ρ specify how much of the cryptographer's actions is visible for the intruder.

Proof idea. The proof, presented in the rest of the section, proceeds as follows:

- *linearisation*: First, the parallel composition is eliminated from the model above, by replacing it with choice and sequential composition. This is a standard operation for virtually all automatic and manual verifications in mCRL2 and can be done completely automatically. The result in our case is the linear process $LDC(S, x, v, m, n)$, shown in Fig. 1. We denote LDC_i the instance of this specification for the case when i is the payer. Then proving parameterised anonymity becomes the problem of proving that for some fixed target participant i, there is another participant j such that $LDC_i \leftrightarrow LDC_j$. In particular, we will prove that $LDC_i \leftrightarrow LDC_{(i+1) \bmod n}$.
- *building a PBES*: We encode the above equivalence question as a PBES, using the translation established in [3].
- *solving the PBES*: We identify relevant invariants, and use them to prove that the solution for the PBES is $\top$ (true).
- *interpreting the solution*: This positive solution translates back to a positive answer for the equivalence $LDC_i \leftrightarrow LDC_{(i+1) \bmod n}$, which justifies parameterised anonymity for DC, as will be concluded in Theorem 1.

Linearisation. Eliminating the parallel composition operator from the DC process is a tool supported exercise, dictated by the mCRL2 linearisation rules [6].

$$\mathsf{LDC}(S, x, v, m, n) =$$

(a) $\displaystyle \sum_{j\in\{0,\dots,n-1\}} \sum_{b\in\{0,1\}} S_j \approx 0 \to \mathbf{flip}(j)\cdot\mathsf{LDC}(S[j \leftarrow 1], x[j \leftarrow \oplus b], v[j \leftarrow b], m, n)$

(b) $\displaystyle +\sum_{j\in\{0,\dots,n-1\}} S_j \approx 1 \wedge S_{j+1} \approx 1 \to \mathbf{com}(j+1)\cdot\mathsf{LDC}(S[j \leftarrow 2, j+1 \leftarrow 3], x[j+1 \leftarrow \oplus v_j], v, m, n)$

(c) $\displaystyle +\sum_{j\in\{0,\dots,n-1\}} S_j \approx 1 \wedge S_{j+1} \approx 2 \to \mathbf{com}(j+1)\cdot$

$\qquad\qquad \mathsf{LDC}(S[j \leftarrow 2, j+1 \leftarrow 4], x[j+1 \leftarrow \oplus v_j], v[j+1 \leftarrow x_{j+1} \oplus v_j], m, n)$

(d) $\displaystyle +\sum_{j\in\{0,\dots,n-1\}} S_j \approx 3 \wedge S_{j+1} \approx 1 \to \mathbf{com}(j+1)\cdot$

$\qquad\qquad \mathsf{LDC}(S[j \leftarrow 4, j+1 \leftarrow 3], x[j+1 \leftarrow \oplus v_j], v[j \leftarrow x_j], m, n)$

(e) $\displaystyle +\sum_{j\in\{0,\dots,n-1\}} S_j \approx 3 \wedge S_{j+1} \approx 2 \to \mathbf{com}(j+1)\cdot$

$\qquad\qquad \mathsf{LDC}(S[j \leftarrow 4, j+1 \leftarrow 4], x[j+1 \leftarrow \oplus v_j], v[j \leftarrow x_j, j+1 \leftarrow x_{j+1} \oplus v_j], m, n)$

(f) $\displaystyle +\sum_{j\in\{0,\dots,n-1\}} m_j \approx \perp \wedge \forall k. S_k \approx 4 \to \mathbf{syncbcast}(j, x_j)\cdot\mathsf{LDC}(S, x, v[(\forall k)k \leftarrow \oplus x_j], m[j \leftarrow \top], n)$

(g) $\displaystyle +\sum_{j\in\{0,\dots,n-1\}} S_j \approx 4 \wedge \forall k. m_k \approx \top \to \mathbf{nsa}(j, !v_j)\cdot\mathsf{LDC}(S[j \leftarrow 5], x, v, m, n)$

Fig. 1. The linearized specification of the Dining Cryptographers protocol. The following shortcuts have been used: $\forall j$, $\forall k$ denote $\forall j \in \{0, \dots, n-1\}$, $\forall k \in \{0, \dots, n-1\}$; $j+1$ denotes $(j+1) \bmod n$. Let LDC_i denote the protocol instance where cryptographer i is the payer: $\mathsf{LDC}_i \equiv \mathsf{LDC}\,(\overline{S}, \overline{x^i}, \overline{v}, \overline{m}, n)$.

The linear process resulted, LDC, is shown in Figure 1. Its parameters are the number of cryptographers n and a few data arrays of length n, basically obtained by concatenating the local parameters of the n *Crypt* processes. For every index j, S_j (from $\mathbb{N}$) represents the current local state of process *Crypt*(j, x_j). x_j, v_j and m_j are booleans representing j's paying bit, j's currently computed all-XOR value and a mark whether j broadcasted, respectively. Initially, the array S is 0 everywhere, while v and m are $\perp$ everywhere. We denote these default initial values by $\overline{S}$, $\overline{v}$, $\overline{m}$. Suppose i is the payer. Then the initial choice vector x is $\perp$ everywhere except for the ith position which is $\top$ (we denote this array $\overline{x^i}$).

For an array A, we write $A[k \leftarrow expr]$ to denote A after that element A_k has been assigned the expression $expr$. In particular, if the assignment involves an operation op on the old value of A_k, we write $A[k \leftarrow op\ expr]$. For instance, $A[k \leftarrow \top]$ denotes A updated with the assignment $A_k := \top$ and $A[k \leftarrow \oplus\top]$ denotes A updated with the assignment $A_k := A_k \oplus \top$. To keep the description readable, we also write everywhere $j + 1$ instead of $(j + 1) \bmod n$.

The PBES. The strong bisimilarity question $\mathsf{LDC}_i \leftrightarroweq \mathsf{LDC}_{i+1}$ is encoded, by applying the translation rules from [3] and several logical rewritings, to the equation $\mathcal{E}$ shown in Fig. 2. The data parameters of variable **E** represent in fact two states $\langle S, x, v, m, n \rangle$ and $\langle S', x', v', m', n' \rangle$ of the two linear specifications LDC_i

$\nu\mathbf{E}(S, x, v, m, n, S', x', v', m', n') =$

(a) $\quad \forall j. \forall b \in \{0, 1\}. \ (S_j \approx 0 \ \Leftrightarrow \ S'_j = 0 \ \wedge \ \underline{S_j \approx 0} \Rightarrow$

$\quad\quad \mathbf{E}(S[j \leftarrow 1], x[j \leftarrow \oplus b], v[j \leftarrow b], S'[j \leftarrow 1], x'[j \leftarrow \oplus(b \oplus (j = i))], v'[j \leftarrow (b \oplus (j = i))])$

(b) $\quad \wedge \forall j. \ ((S_j \approx 1 \wedge S_{j+1} \approx 1 \ \Leftrightarrow \ S'_j \approx 1 \wedge S'_{j+1} \approx 1) \ \wedge \ \underline{(S_j \approx 1 \wedge S_{j+1} \approx 1)} \Rightarrow$

$\quad\quad \mathbf{E}(S[j \leftarrow 2, j+1 \leftarrow 3], x[j+1 \leftarrow \oplus v_j], S'[j \leftarrow 2, j+1 \leftarrow 3], x'[j+1 \leftarrow \oplus v'_j]))$

(c) $\quad \wedge \forall j. \ ((S_j \approx 1 \wedge S_{j+1} \approx 2 \ \Leftrightarrow \ S'_j \approx 1 \wedge S'_{j+1} \approx 2) \ \wedge \ \underline{(S_j \approx 1 \wedge S_{j+1} \approx 2)} \Rightarrow$

$\quad\quad \mathbf{E}(S[j \leftarrow 2, j+1 \leftarrow 4], x[j+1 \leftarrow \oplus v_j], v[j+1 \leftarrow x_{j+1} \oplus v_j],$

$\quad\quad\quad\quad S'[j \leftarrow 2, j+1 \leftarrow 4], x'[j+1 \leftarrow \oplus v'_j], v'[j+1 \leftarrow x'_{j+1} \oplus v'_j]))$

(d) $\quad \wedge \forall j. \ ((S_j \approx 3 \wedge S_{j+1} \approx 1 \ \Leftrightarrow \ S'_j \approx 3 \wedge S'_{j+1} \approx 1) \wedge \underline{(S_j \approx 3 \wedge S_{j+1} \approx 1)} \Rightarrow$

$\quad\quad \mathbf{E}(S[j \leftarrow 4, j+1 \leftarrow 3], x[j+1 \leftarrow \oplus v_j], v[j \leftarrow x_j],$

$\quad\quad\quad\quad S'[j \leftarrow 4, j+1 \leftarrow 3], x'[j+1 \leftarrow \oplus v'_j], v'[j \leftarrow x'_{j'}]))$

(e) $\quad \wedge \forall j. \ ((S_j \approx 3 \wedge S_{j+1} \approx 2 \ \Leftrightarrow \ S'_j \approx 3 \wedge S'_{j+1} \approx 2) \ \wedge \ \underline{(S_j \approx 3 \wedge S_{j+1} \approx 2)} \Rightarrow$

$\quad\quad \mathbf{E}(S[j \leftarrow 4, j+1 \leftarrow 4], x[j+1 \leftarrow \oplus v_j], v[j \leftarrow x_j, j+1 \leftarrow x_{j+1} \oplus v_j],$

$\quad\quad\quad\quad S'[j \leftarrow 4, j+1 \leftarrow 4], x'[j+1 \leftarrow \oplus v'_j], v'[j \leftarrow x'_j, j+1 \leftarrow x'_{j+1} \oplus v'_j]) \ )$

(f) $\quad \wedge \forall j. \ ((m_j \approx \perp \wedge (\forall k. S_k \approx 4) \ \Leftrightarrow \ m'_j \approx \perp \wedge (\forall k. S'_k \approx 4))$

$\quad\quad \wedge \ \underline{(m_j \approx \perp \wedge (\forall k. S_k \approx 4))} \Rightarrow x_j \approx x'_j$ $\hspace{3cm} (\alpha(j))$

$\quad\quad \wedge \ \underline{(m_j \approx \perp \wedge (\forall k. S_k \approx 4))} \Rightarrow$

$\quad\quad\quad\quad \mathbf{E}(v[(\forall k)k \leftarrow \oplus x_j], m[j \leftarrow \top], v'[(\forall k)k \leftarrow \oplus x'_j], m'[j \leftarrow \top]))$

(g) $\quad \wedge \forall j. \ ((S_j \approx 4 \wedge (\forall k. m_k \approx \top) \ \Leftrightarrow \ S'_j \approx 4 \wedge (\forall k. m'_k \approx \top))$

$\quad\quad \wedge \ \underline{(S_j \approx 4 \wedge (\forall k. m_k \approx \top))} \Rightarrow v_j \approx v'_j$ $\hspace{2.8cm} (\beta(j))$

$\quad\quad \wedge \ \underline{(S_j \approx 4 \wedge (\forall k. m_k \approx \top))} \Rightarrow \mathbf{E}(S[j \leftarrow 5], S'[j \leftarrow 5]))$

Fig. 2. The PBES encoding the equivalence question $\mathsf{LDC}_i \leftrightarrows \mathsf{LDC}_{i+1}$. The same shortcuts as in Fig. 1 are used. Moreover, only the modified data parameters variables are shown in the parameter lists of $\mathbf{E}$ occurrences. For readability, the guards are underlined and the guard equivalences are italicized. $\approx$ is used as equality symbol for the data parameters and is assumed defined for (arrays of) $\mathbb{B}$ and $\mathbb{N}$.

and LDC_{i+1}. Intuitively, this equation enumerates all conditions that need to be satisfied for the two states to be strongly bisimilar. The first subterm originally contained an extra existential quantification $\exists b':\mathbb{B}$, and the update for v' was $v'[j \leftarrow b']$. This quantification has been replaced by a concrete instantiation for b', namely $b \oplus (j = i)$ maintaining bisimulation.

Solving the PBES. We start by noticing that the right-hand side of our equation fits the form of Proposition 1 and that the predicate $\iota_1(d) : (S \approx S' \wedge m \approx m' \wedge n \approx n')$ satisfies the condition in Proposition 1, so it is an invariant. All predicate variables occurring in this section have the same sort as $\mathbf{E}$. However, we will sometimes write only a sub-list of the parameters, in order to outline the exact parameters on which a predicate depends. d is the whole list.

Proposition 1 also immediately holds for the expression $\kappa(d) : (\forall j.S_j \approx 0 \Rightarrow (x_j \approx (i=j)))$, which formalizes the intuition that participant i is the payer in the run specified by LDC_i. Strengthening $\mathcal{E}$ with $(\iota_1 \wedge \kappa)$ leads to a first significant simplification: the seven predicates expressing guard equivalences (shown in italics in the figure) rewrite to $\top$, because they follow from ι_1. The resulting equation $\mathcal{E}'$ has a form that still fits Proposition 1:

$$\nu \mathbf{E}(d) = (\kappa \wedge \iota_1 \wedge \forall j.\alpha(j) \wedge \forall j.\beta(j)) \wedge \bigwedge_{\star \in \{a \ldots g\}} \forall j.\phi_\star(d,j) \Rightarrow \mathbf{E}(g_\star(d,j)). \quad (2)$$

The main difficulty of a parametric proof is to find the right invariants that significantly reduce the complexity of the equation, without excluding the relevant solutions. In our case, invariants that are not satisfied by the initial parameters $\langle \overline{S}, \overline{x^i}, \overline{v}, \overline{m}, n, \overline{S}, \overline{x^{i+1}}, \overline{v}, \overline{m}, n \rangle$ are not useful, because then the solution of the strengthened equation will not necessarily satisfy the original equation. Since ι_1 holds, we now need a powerful invariant relation between the rest of the parameters, (x, v, x', v'). In fact, we are intuitively aiming to properly map the states of the "actual" protocol behaviour, as modeled by the (S, x, v, m, n) parameters, to the states of the "alternative protocol" behaviour, captured by the (S', x', v', m', n') parameters. Let $\mathtt{mx}(S_k, x_k, k)$ denote the following formula:

$$((S_k \approx 0) \wedge (k = i+1) \vee (S_k \in \{1,2\} \wedge (x_k \oplus (k = i+1))) \vee (S_k \in \{3,4\} \wedge (x_k))),$$

which can be read as the short routine "if $S_k \approx 0$, then return $k = i + 1$; else if $S_k \in \{1,2\}$ then return $(x_k \oplus (k = i+1))$; else if $S_k \in \{3,4\}$ then return x_k; else return $\bot$". Moreover, let $\mathtt{mV}(S_k, v_k, k)$ denote the following formula:

$$(S_k \in \{1,2,3\} \wedge (v_k \oplus (i = k))) \vee (S_k \in \{4,5\} \wedge (v_k)).$$

Intuitively, $\mathtt{mx}$ and $\mathtt{mV}$ are our proposed x-mapping and v-mapping, linking parameters (S, x) to x' and, respectively, (S, v) to v' (k is an index). The central piece of the correctness proof is showing that these connections are invariant. We do this in the following lemma.

Lemma 1. *The predicates $\iota_2(S, x, x') : \forall k. x'_k = \mathtt{mx}(S_k, x_k, k)$ and $\iota_3(S, v, v') : \forall k. v'_k = \mathtt{mV}(S_k, v_k, k)$ are invariants for the equation $\mathcal{E}'$.*

Proof. We will prove, for each subterm $\forall j.\phi_\star(d,j) \Rightarrow \mathbf{E}(g_\star(d,j))$ of the right-hand side of (2), that $(\iota_2(d) \wedge \iota_3(d) \wedge \phi_\star(d,j)) \Rightarrow \iota_2(g_\star(d,j)) \wedge \iota_3(g_\star(d,j))$ holds. From this we will then conclude using Proposition 1 that ι_2 and ι_3 are invariants.

The proof is more or less mechanical. For each subterm $a \ldots g$, assuming that the left-hand side of the implication holds, we rewrite the two terms in the right-hand side to $\top$. Note that a part of the left-hand side is common to all 7 subterms:

$$(\iota_2(d) \wedge \iota_3(d)) : \quad \forall k. x'_k = \mathtt{mx}(S_k, x_k, k) \wedge \forall k. v'_k = \mathtt{mV}(S_k, v_k, k) \quad (3)$$

Let us use $\langle S[], x[], v[], S'[], x'[], v'[] \rangle$ as a shortcut for the updates suffered by d at the currently analyzed subterm. The proof obligation is, for all subterms,

$$(\iota_2(d[])) \wedge \iota_3(d[]) : \forall k. x'[]_k = \mathtt{mx}(S[]_k, x[]_k, k) \wedge \forall k. v'[]_k = \mathtt{mV}(S[]_k, v[]_k, k). \quad (4)$$

(a) For this subterm, $\phi(d,j) \equiv (S_j \approx 0)$ and $d[] \equiv \langle S[j \leftarrow 1], x[j \leftarrow \oplus b], v[j \leftarrow b], S'[j \leftarrow 1], x'[j \leftarrow \oplus(b \oplus (j = i))], v'[j \leftarrow (b \oplus (j = i))]\rangle$. For $k \neq j$, $d[]_k = d_k$. In particular, this means that $x'[]_k = x'_k$ and $\mathtt{mx}(S[]_k, x[]_k, k) = \mathtt{mx}(S_k, x_k, k)$, and similarly for v' and $\mathtt{mV}$. Therefore we only need to prove

$$(A) \quad x'[]_j = \mathtt{mx}(S[]_j, x[]_j, j) \qquad\qquad (B) \quad v'[]_j = \mathtt{mV}(S[]_j, v[]_j, j).$$

By projecting $d[]$ on j, these equalities rewrite to

$$(A) \quad x'_j \oplus b \oplus (j = i) = \mathtt{mx}(1, x_j \oplus b, j) \qquad\qquad (B) \quad b \oplus (j = i) = \mathtt{mV}(1, b, j).$$

We can now unfold the definitions of $\mathtt{mx}, \mathtt{mV}$ and obtain:

$$(A) \quad x'_j \oplus b \oplus (j = i) = (x_j \oplus b) \oplus (j = i + 1)$$
$$(B) \quad b \oplus (j = i) = b \oplus (j = i)$$

(B) is trivially true. $\iota_2(d)$ holds, so we can rewrite x'_j, taking into account that $S_j \approx 0$, and obtain $(A)(j = i+1) \oplus b \oplus (j = i) = (x_j \oplus b) \oplus (j = i+1)$, which further rewrites to $x_j = (i = j)$. Note that $\kappa(d)$ can be used as a premise, in conjunction with any ϕ_*, since it stands as an independent term in the expression (2). Since in the current situation $S_j = 0$, κ ensures $x_j = (i = j)$.

(b) For this subterm, $\phi(d,j)) \equiv (S_j \approx 1 \wedge S_{j+1} \approx 1$ and $d[] \equiv \langle S[j \leftarrow 2, j+1 \leftarrow 3], x[j+1 \leftarrow \oplus v_j], S'[j \leftarrow 2, j+1 \leftarrow 3], x'[j+1 \leftarrow \oplus v'_j]\rangle$. For $k \notin \{j, j+1\}$, $d[]_k = d_k$. This means that $x'[]_k = x'_k$ and $\mathtt{mx}(S[]_k, x[]_k, k) = \mathtt{mx}(S_k, x_k, k)$, and similarly for v' and $\mathtt{mV}$. Therefore we only need to prove

$$(A1) \quad x'[]_j = \mathtt{mx}(S[]_j, x[]_j, j) \qquad\qquad (A2) \quad x'[]_{j+1} = \mathtt{mx}(S[]_{j+1}, x[]_{j+1}, j+1)$$
$$(B1) \quad v'[]_j = \mathtt{mV}(S[]_j, v[]_j, j) \qquad\qquad (B2) \quad v'[]_{j+1} = \mathtt{mV}(S[]_{j+1}, v[]_{j+1}, j+1).$$

By projecting $d[]$ on j and $j+1$, these rewrite to

$$(A1) \quad x'_j = \mathtt{mx}(2, x_j, j) \qquad\qquad (A2) \quad x'_{j+1} \oplus v'_j = \mathtt{mx}(3, x_{j+1} \oplus v_j, j+1)$$
$$(B1) \quad v'_j = \mathtt{mV}(2, v_j, j) \qquad\qquad (B2) \quad v'_{j+1} = \mathtt{mV}(3, v_{j+1}, j+1).$$

Further, we unfold the definitions of $\mathtt{mx}, \mathtt{mV}$ and obtain:

$$(A1) \quad x'_j = x_j \oplus (j = i+1) \qquad\qquad (A2) \quad x'_{j+1} \oplus v'_j = x_{j+1} \oplus v_j$$
$$(B1) \quad v'_j = v_j \oplus (j = i) \qquad\qquad (B2) \quad v'_{j+1} = v_{j+1} \oplus (j+1 = i)$$

Instantiation of $\iota_2(d)$ and $\iota_3(d)$ for j and $j+1$, while taking into account that $S_j \approx 1 \wedge S_{j+1} \approx 1$, leads to the truth of formulae (A1),(B1),(B2). (A2) transforms to $(x_{j+1} \oplus (j+1 = i+1)) \oplus (v_j \oplus (i = j)) = x_{j+1} \oplus v_j$, which obviously holds since $(j+1 = i+1) = (j = i)$, $x \oplus x = \bot$ and $x \oplus \bot = x$.

(c) For this subterm, $\phi(d,j) \equiv (S_j \approx 1 \wedge S_{j+1} \approx 2)$ and $d[] \equiv \langle S[j \leftarrow 2, j+1 \leftarrow 4], x[j+1 \leftarrow \oplus v_j], v[j+1 \leftarrow x_{j+1} \oplus v_j], S'[j \leftarrow 2, j+1 \leftarrow 4], x'[j+1 \leftarrow \oplus v'_j], v'[j+1 \leftarrow x'_{j+1} \oplus v'_j]\rangle$. An argument identical to the one at **(b)** justifies that we only need to prove

$$(A1) \quad x'[]_j = \mathtt{mx}(S[]_j, x[]_j, j) \qquad\qquad (A2) \quad x'[]_{j+1} = \mathtt{mx}(S[]_{j+1}, x[]_{j+1}, j+1)$$
$$(B1) \quad v'[]_j = \mathtt{mV}(S[]_j, v[]_j, j) \qquad\qquad (B2) \quad v'[]_{j+1} = \mathtt{mV}(S[]_{j+1}, v[]_{j+1}, j+1).$$

By projecting $d[]$ on j and $j+1$, and then applying the definitions of $\mathtt{mx},\mathtt{mV}$:

$(A1)\ x'_j = x_j \oplus (j = i+1)$ $(A2)\ x'_{j+1} \oplus v'_j = x_{j+1} \oplus v_j$
$(B1)\ v'_j = v_j \oplus (j = i)$ $(B2)\ x'_{j+1} \oplus v'_j = x_{j+1} \oplus v_j$

Since $S_j = 1 \wedge S_{j+1} = 2$, the instantiation of $\iota_2(d)$ and $\iota_3(d)$ for j gives exactly (A1) and (B1). By instantiating $\iota_2(d)$ for $j+1$ and $\iota_3(d)$ for j, $(A2)$ becomes $x_{j+1} \oplus (j + 1 = i + 1) \oplus v_j \oplus (j = i) = x_{j+1} \oplus v_j$, which evaluates to $\top$.

(d) For this subterm, $\phi(d,j) \equiv (S_j \approx 3 \wedge S_{j+1} \approx 1)$ and $d[] \equiv \langle S[j \leftarrow 4, j+1 \leftarrow 3], x[j+1 \leftarrow \oplus v_j], v[j \leftarrow x_j], S'[j \leftarrow 4, j+1 \leftarrow 3], x'[j+1 \leftarrow \oplus v'_j], v'[j \leftarrow x'_j]\rangle$. As with the previous subterms, we only need to prove

$(A1)\ x'[]_j = \mathtt{mx}(S[]_j, x[]_j, j)$ $(A2)\ x'[]_{j+1} = \mathtt{mx}(S[]_{j+1}, x[]_{j+1}, j+1)$
$(B1)\ v'[]_j = \mathtt{mV}(S[]_j, v[]_j, j)$ $(B2)\ v'[]_{j+1} = \mathtt{mV}(S[]_{j+1}, v[]_{j+1}, j+1)$.

By projecting $d[]$ on j and $j+1$, and then applying the definitions of $\mathtt{mx},\mathtt{mV}$:

$(A1)\ x'_j = x_j$ $(A2)\ x'_{j+1} \oplus v'_j = x_{j+1} \oplus v_j$
$(B1)\ x'_j = x_j$ $(B2)\ v'_{j+1} = v_{j+1} \oplus (i = j+1)$.

Since $S_j = 3 \wedge S_{j+1} = 1$, the instantiation of $\iota_2(d)$ for j is exactly formula (A1), and the instantiation of $\iota_3(d)$ for $j+1$ is exactly formula (B2). By instantiating $\iota_2(d)$ for $j+1$ and $\iota_3(d)$ for j, $(A2)$ becomes $(x_{j+1} \oplus (j+1 = i+1) \oplus v_j \oplus (i = j)) = x_{j+1} \oplus v_j$, which is true, due to $x \oplus x = \bot$ and $x \oplus 0 = x$.

(e) For this subterm, $\phi(d,j) \equiv (S_j \approx 3 \wedge S_{j+1} \approx 2)$ and $d[] \equiv \langle S[j \leftarrow 4, j+1 \leftarrow 4], x[j+1 \leftarrow \oplus v_j], v[j \leftarrow x_j, j+1 \leftarrow x_{j+1} \oplus v_j], S'[j \leftarrow 4, j+1 \leftarrow 4], x'[j+1 \leftarrow \oplus v'_j], v'[j \leftarrow x'_j, j+1 \leftarrow x'_{j+1} \oplus v'_j]\rangle$.

The same argument as above ensures that we only need to prove

$(A1)\ x'[]_j = \mathtt{mx}(S[]_j, x[]_j, j)$ $(A2)\ x'[]_{j+1} = \mathtt{mx}(S[]_{j+1}, x[]_{j+1}, j+1)$
$(B1)\ v'[]_j = \mathtt{mV}(S[]_j, v[]_j, j)$ $(B2)\ v'[]_{j+1} = \mathtt{mV}(S[]_{j+1}, v[]_{j+1}, j+1)$.

By projecting $d[]$ on j and $j+1$, then applying the definitions of $\mathtt{mx},\mathtt{mV}$:

$(A1)\ x'_j = x_j$ $(A2)\ x'_{j+1} \oplus v'_j = x_{j+1} \oplus v_j$
$(B1)\ x'_j = x_j$ $(B2)\ x'_{j+1} \oplus v'_j = x_{j+1} \oplus v_j$.

Since $S_j = 3 \wedge S_{j+1} = 2$, the instantiation of $\iota_2(d)$ for j is (A1). By instantiating $\iota_2(d)$ for $j+1$ and $\iota_3(d)$ for j, $(A2, B2)$ becomes $(x_{j+1} \oplus (j+1 = i+1) \oplus v_j \oplus (j = i)) = x_{j+1} \oplus v_j$, which is $\top$, due to $x \oplus x = \bot$ and $x \oplus 0 = x$.

(f) Here, $\phi(d,j) \equiv (m_j \approx \bot \wedge (\forall k.S_k \approx 4))$ and $d[] \equiv \langle v[(\forall k)k \leftarrow \oplus x_j], m[j \leftarrow \top], v'[(\forall k)k \leftarrow \oplus x'_j], m'[j \leftarrow \top]\rangle$. We project $d[]$ on a random k. So, we now have to prove $x'_k = \mathtt{mx}(S_k, x_k, k)$ and $v'_k \oplus x'_j = \mathtt{mV}(S_k, v_k \oplus x_j, k)$. The first formula is true (from $\iota_2(d)$). We rewrite the second one using the definition of $\mathtt{mV}$ and $(\iota_2(d) \wedge \iota_3(d))$. The result is $v_k \oplus x_j = v_k \oplus x_j$, trivially true.

(g) For this subterm, $\phi(d,j) \equiv (S_j \approx 4 \wedge (\forall k.m_k \approx \top))$ and $d[] \equiv \langle S[j \leftarrow 5], S'[j \leftarrow 5]\rangle$. We project $d[]$ on a random k. So, we now have to prove: $x'_k = \mathtt{mx}(5, x_k, k)$ and $v'_k = \mathtt{mV}(5, v_k, k)$. They are both true, due to $\iota_2(d) \wedge \iota_3(d)$ and the fact that $\mathtt{mx}(4, x, y) = \mathtt{mx}(5, x, y)$ and $\mathtt{mV}(4, x, y) = \mathtt{mV}(5, x, y)$. $\qquad\square$

Now we can strengthen $\mathcal{E}'$ with the invariants proved at Lemma 1:

$$\nu\mathbf{E}(d) = \iota_2(d) \wedge \iota_3(d)$$
$$\wedge\kappa(d) \wedge \iota_1(d) \wedge \forall j.\alpha(j) \wedge \forall j.\beta(j) \wedge \bigwedge_{\star\in\{a...g\}} \forall j.\phi_\star(j) \Rightarrow \mathbf{E}(g_\star(d,j)).$$

Note that $\forall j.\alpha(j) \wedge \forall j.\beta(j)$ follows from $\iota_2(S, x, x')$ and $\iota_3(S, v, v')$. Then the equation is equivalent to $\nu\mathbf{E}(d) = \iota_2(d)\wedge\iota_3(d)\wedge\kappa(d)\wedge\iota_1(d)\wedge\bigwedge_{\star\in\{a...g\}} \forall j.\phi_\star(j) \Rightarrow \mathbf{E}(g_\star(d,j))$, which fits the form in the assumption of Proposition 2. Therefore, the solution is $\iota_1(d)\wedge\iota_2(d)\wedge\iota_3(d)$. Since all the used invariants $\iota_1, \iota_2, \iota_3, \kappa$ are satisfied by our instance of interest $d \equiv \langle \overline{S}, \overline{x^i}, \overline{v}, \overline{m}, n, \overline{S}, \overline{x^{i+1}}, \overline{v}, \overline{m}, n\rangle$, it follows that the solution of the original equation $\mathcal{E}$ for this instance is $\top$. We can then conclude that the solution to the encoded equivalence problem $\mathsf{LDC}_i \leftrightarrows \mathsf{LDC}_{i+1}$ is true and thus, the parameterised anonymity property holds for the DC protocol:

Theorem 1. *For any $i \geq 0$ and any $n > max(i,1)$, the protocol DC is anonymous for i out of n w.r.t. an external intruder.*

As a final remark, we note that the proof can be adapted to accommodate internal observers, i.e. for the more interesting case when a cryptographer j is the intruder. Then the mCRL2 model specifying j's view on the protocol behaviour would allow visibility of the secret bit x_j, thus the set R from ρ_R would *not* contain any renamings for actions of the form $\mathbf{flip}(j,d)$, $\mathbf{com}(j,d)$ and $\mathbf{com}(j-1,d)$ (for any d). For checking the condition $\exists v \dots$ from Def. 3, which in the DC case is $\exists \overline{x^k} \dots$, we need to make the distinction $j \neq i+1$ or $j = i+1$. In the first case, the proof proceeds exactly as above, since the weakening of the renaming set does not influence the validity (proof) of the used invariants. In the second case, we need to choose another k, for instance $(i-1) \bmod n$ and prove, in a very similar way, that $\mathsf{LDC}_i \leftrightarrows \mathsf{LDC}_{(i-1) \bmod n}$. Note that in both cases, i,j,k should be different, therefore the assumption $n > 2$ would be needed.

5   (Un)decidability

We now study the general question: given a multiparty protocol, can it be decided whether it guarantees anonymity to its participants, whatever their number?

(**NPA**) Given a domain D, a constant $N\geq 1$ and a parameterised protocol $\mathtt{Protocol}(x)$, decide whether $\mathtt{Protocol}(x)$ is anonymous for 0 with at least N processes present. In other words, decide whether for all $n\geq N$:

$\forall x\in D^n$ with $Restriction(x)$
$\quad\quad \exists v\in D^n$ s.t. $Restriction(v)$, $v_0\neq x_0$ and $\mathtt{Protocol}(x)\sim\mathtt{Protocol}(v)$.

Note that using index 0 in this definition is not a loss of generality. In most protocols, the behaviours of honest parties are isomorphic and renaming schemes can reduce the anonymity question about a participant index $i \geq 0$ to NPA.

The following theorem says that for all reasonable weak equivalences (those satisfying $a\cdot\tau\cdot x = a\cdot x$), preserving the alphabet of a process, when sequential programs can be expressed in the specification formalism, there is in general no hope to decide anonymity.

Theorem 2. *Let $\sim$ denote any behavioural congruence refining weak trace equivalence satisfying $a \cdot \tau \cdot x = a \cdot x$. Then NPA is undecidable for any number $N \geq 1$ of processes.*

Proof. We encode the question of deciding program termination as an instance of NPA. Let M be a program translated to mCRL2 (mCRL2 is sufficiently expressive for this) without visible behaviour — i.e., all its actions are τ steps. Let us construct a protocol as follows where **stop** is a visible action and $D = \{0, 1\}$:

$$
\begin{aligned}
P(i, x_i) &= i {\not\approx} 0 \rightarrow \delta \ + \ i {\approx} 0 \rightarrow (x_i {\approx} 1 \rightarrow \tau \cdot M \cdot \textbf{stop} + x_i {\approx} 0 \rightarrow \tau \cdot \textbf{stop}) \\
Q(n) &= \delta \\
\texttt{Protocol}(x) &= P(0, x_0) \| P(1, x_1) \| \cdots \| P(n{-}1, x_{n-1}) \| Q(n)
\end{aligned}
$$

By applying the parallel composition laws, this protocol process linearizes to:

$$
\texttt{Protocol}(x) = x_0 {\approx} 1 \rightarrow \tau \cdot M \cdot \textbf{stop} \cdot \delta \ + \ x_0 {\approx} 0 \rightarrow \tau \cdot \textbf{stop} \cdot \delta. \tag{5}
$$

Suppose NPA is decidable. Then we get an answer to whether this protocol is anonymous or not. NPA can be formulated as $\forall n \geq 1 \ \forall x \in \{0,1\}^n \ \exists v \in \{0,1\}^n \ v_0 \neq x_0 \wedge \texttt{Protocol}(x) \sim \texttt{Protocol}(v)$. So, according to (5), $\tau \cdot M \cdot \textbf{stop} \cdot \delta \sim \tau \cdot \textbf{stop} \cdot \delta$. Using the requirements on $\sim$, this can only be the case iff M terminates. As termination of M is undecidable, NPA is also undecidable. □

Undecidability holds even for protocols without loops:

Theorem 3. *If $\sim$ denotes strong-, weak- or branching bisimilarity then NPA is undecidable, even if the protocol specification language does not contain loops (but contains the choice operator $\sum$ essentially quantifying over infinite domains).*

Proof. We reduce the problem of deciding strong bisimulation between two mCRL2 processes to NPA. Let M_1 and M_2 be two arbitrary mCRL2 processes. In a similar fashion as above, we construct a protocol that, after the linearisation of the parallel composition, looks as: $\texttt{Protocol}(x) = x_0 {\not\approx} 0 \rightarrow M_1 \cdot \delta \ + \ x_0 {\approx} 0 \rightarrow M_2 \cdot \delta$. A positive answer to NPA means that $M_1 \cdot \delta \not\sim M_2 \cdot \delta$ and a negative answer means that $M_1 \cdot \delta \sim M_2 \cdot \delta$. According to [14], strong, branching and weak bisimulation are all undecidable for processes with infinite choice, hence NPA is undecidable as well. □

So, unsurprisingly, parameterised anonymity is in general undecidable. However, in many cases it can still be decided by inspecting a finite collection of processes only. Let us call the communication function Γ_C *behaviour preserving* for an equivalence relation $\sim$ and processes p and q iff $\Gamma_C(p) \sim \Gamma_C(q)$ implies $p \sim q$. This is for instance the case if C is functional (i.e. $C(\alpha) = C(\alpha')$ implies $\alpha = \alpha'$) and no communication action $C(\alpha)$ occurs in p or in q.

Theorem 4. *Consider a protocol as defined (1). Assume D is finite, the set of hidden actions I is empty, renaming is effectively the identity, the set of allowed actions V does not block any actions and the communication function is behaviour preserving for $\sim$ and parallel combinations of $P(i, x_i)$ and $Q(n)$. Moreover, $\sim$ respects commutativity of the parallel operator. For any $N \geq 1$, NPA is decidable iff it can be decided that, for any $n \geq N$ and $x_1, \ldots, x_{N-1}, y_1, \ldots, y_{N-1} \in D$,*

$$P(0, x_0)\| \cdots \|P(N-1, x_{N-1})\|Q(n) \sim P(0, y_0)\| \cdots \|P(N-1, y_{N-1})\|Q(n). \quad (6)$$

Proof. The first step is to determine whether for every x with $Restriction(x)$ a v can be found such that $Restriction(v)$ and $v_0 \neq x_0$ satisfy (6). As x and v can only attain a finite number of values, this can be done by explicit enumeration.

Suppose this fails for some x. So, for any v either $Restriction(v)$, $v_0 \neq x_0$ or (6) would not hold. In the last case, Protocol(x)$\not\approx$Protocol(v) as Γ_C is behaviour preserving. Thus NPA does not hold for $n = N$. As NPA should hold for every $n \geq N$ processes, we can conclude that NPA is invalid.

Now assume that the procedure above yields a v for every x. We find that as (6) holds, and as $\sim$ is a behavioural congruence for which $\|$ is commutative:

$$P(0, x_0)\| \cdots \|P(N-1, x_{N-1})\|P(N, x_N)\| \cdots \|P(n-1, x_{n-1})\|Q(n) \sim$$
$$P(0, v_0)\| \cdots \|P(N-1, v_{N-1})\|P(N, x_N)\| \cdots \|P(n-1, x_{n-1})\|Q(n)$$

By applying the communication operator Γ_C and the ∇_V, ρ_R and τ_I operators (which effectively do nothing), all the conditions of NPA are made valid.   □

Verification of (6) might be tricky, as n is an arbitrary number. Unless the behaviour of Q is very essentially dependent on n, which it rarely is, this will not pose a problem for the verification tools of mCRL2 as they are essentially symbolic manipulators. Note furthermore that this decision procedure often does not apply because the communication operator is not behaviour preserving or the allow, renaming or hiding operators are not trivial. But as only one side of the decision procedure requires these properties, it can still be useful to determine anonymity by just investigating a finite number of processes. The procedure as sketched here is exponential in N as all vectors x must be investigated. Fortunately, in practical cases we already want to achieve anonymity for small groups of processes, so N is a fairly small number.

6   Conclusion

We gave a formal correctness proof for the Dining Cryptographers protocol with an arbitrary number of parties, using the modeling language mCRL2 and its supporting PBES theory. The model in our proof considers an external passive intruder, but a very similar proof would work for single internal intruders. Due to the fact that data plays an explicit central role in PBES equations, compact symbolic representations are possible, of, e.g., systems consisting of a number of components with similar behaviour. Finding the right invariants requires, as in other frameworks, use of intuition and protocol understanding. However, proving that the proposed predicates are invariants is a mechanical exercise, as well as the application of those invariants to simplifying and eventually solving the target PBES. This makes the PBES framework a comfortable and powerful formalism for such complex correctness proofs. We also showed that the parameterised anonymity problem is undecidable. However, under some restrictions, decidability is possible based on the investigation of a small subgroup of processes.

References

1. Bhargava, M., Palamidessi, C.: Probabilistic anonymity. In: Abadi, M., de Alfaro, L. (eds.) CONCUR 2005. LNCS, vol. 3653, pp. 171–185. Springer, Heidelberg (2005)
2. Chaum, D.: The dining cryptographers problem: unconditional sender and receiver untraceability. Journal of Cryptology 1, 65–75 (1988)
3. Chen, T., Ploeger, B., van de Pol, J., Willemse, T.A.C.: Equivalence checking for infinite systems using parameterized boolean equation systems. In: Caires, L., Vasconcelos, V.T. (eds.) CONCUR 2007. LNCS, vol. 4703, pp. 120–135. Springer, Heidelberg (2007)
4. Chothia, T., Orzan, S.M., Pang, J., Torabi Dashti, M.: A framework for automatically checking anonymity with μCRL. In: Montanari, U., Sannella, D., Bruni, R. (eds.) TGC 2006. LNCS, vol. 4661, pp. 301–318. Springer, Heidelberg (2007)
5. Comon, H., Shmatikov, V.: Is it possible to decide whether a cryptographic protocol is secure or not? J. Telecomm. and Inf. Tech. 4, 3–13 (2002)
6. Groote, J.F., Mathijssen, A.H.J., Reniers, M.A., Usenko, Y.S., van Weerdenburg, M.J.: The formal specification language mCRL2. In: MMOSS, Dagstuhl Seminar Proceedings 06351 (2007)
7. Groote, J.F., Willemse, T.A.C.: Parameterised boolean equation systems. Theor. Comput. Sci. 343(3), 332–369 (2005)
8. Halpern, J.Y., O'Neill, K.R.: Anonymity and information hiding in multiagent systems. Journal of Computer Security, 483–514 (2005)
9. Hughes, D., Shmatikov, V.: Information hiding, anonymity and privacy: A modular approach. Journal of Computer Security 12(1), 3–36 (2004)
10. Kremer, S., Ryan, M.D.: Analysis of an electronic voting protocol in the applied pi-calculus. In: Sagiv, M. (ed.) ESOP 2005. LNCS, vol. 3444, pp. 186–200. Springer, Heidelberg (2005)
11. Küsters, R., Wilke, T.: Automata-based analysis of recursive cryptographic protocols. In: Diekert, V., Habib, M. (eds.) STACS 2004. LNCS, vol. 2996, pp. 382–393. Springer, Heidelberg (2004)
12. Kähler, D., Küsters, R., Wilke, T.: Deciding properties of contract-signing protocols. In: Diekert, V., Durand, B. (eds.) STACS 2005. LNCS, vol. 3404, pp. 158–169. Springer, Heidelberg (2005)
13. Lomuscio, A., Raimondi, F.: MCMAS: A model-checker for multi-agent systems. In: Hermanns, H., Palsberg, J. (eds.) TACAS 2006. LNCS, vol. 3920, pp. 450–454. Springer, Heidelberg (2006)
14. Luttik, B.: On the expressiveness of choice quantification. Ann. Pure Appl. Logic 121(1), 39–87 (2003)
15. Mazaré, L.: Decidability of opacity with non-atomic keys. In: Proc. FAST 2004, pp. 71–84 (2004)
16. Orzan, S.M., Willemse, T.A.C.: Invariants for parameterised boolean equation systems. In: van Breugel, F., Chechik, M. (eds.) CONCUR 2008. LNCS, vol. 5201, pp. 187–202. Springer, Heidelberg (to appear, 2008)
17. Pfitzmann, A., Hansen, M.: Anonymity, unobservability, and pseudonymity: A proposal for terminology, draft v0.23 (August 2005)
18. Schneider, S., Sidiropoulos, A.: CSP and anonymity. In: Martella, G., Kurth, H., Montolivo, E., Bertino, E. (eds.) ESORICS 1996. LNCS, vol. 1146. Springer, Heidelberg (1996)
19. Shmatikov, V.: Probabilistic model checking of an anonymity system. Journal of Computer Security 12(3/4), 355–377 (2004)

Automatic Methods
for Analyzing Non-repudiation Protocols
with an Active Intruder

Francis Klay[1] and Laurent Vigneron[2,*]

[1] France Telecom R&D, Lannion, France
francis.klay@orange-ftgroup.com
[2] LORIA - Nancy Université, Vandoeuvre-lès-Nancy, France
laurent.vigneron@loria.fr

Abstract. Non-repudiation protocols have an important role in many areas where secured transactions with proofs of participation are necessary. Formal methods are clever and without error, therefore using them for verifying such protocols is crucial. In this purpose, we show how to partially represent non-repudiation as a combination of authentications on the Fair Zhou-Gollmann protocol. After discussing the limitations of this method, we define a new one, based on the handling of the knowledge of protocol participants. This second method is general and of natural use, as it consists in adding simple annotations in the protocol specification. It is very easy to implement in tools able to handle participants knowledge. We have implemented it in the AVISPA Tool and analyzed the Fair Zhou-Gollmann protocol and the optimistic Cederquist-Corin-Dashti protocol, discovering attacks in each. This extension of the AVISPA Tool for handling non-repudiation opens a highway to the specification of many other properties, without any more change in the tool itself.

Keywords: Cryptographic protocols, non-repudiation, fairness, authentication, automatic analysis, AVISPA Tool.

1 Introduction

Authentication and secrecy properties of security protocols have been intensively studied for years [23], but the interest of other properties such as non-repudiation and fairness has been raised only in the 1990s with the explosion of Internet services and electronic transactions.[1]

Non-repudiation protocols are designed for verifying that, when two parties exchange information over a network, neither one nor the other can deny having participated to this communication. Such a protocol must therefore generate

---

[*] This work is supported by the ANR AVOTÉ, http://www.lsv.ens-cachan.fr/anr-avote/

[1] See [1] for a detailed list of publications related to the analysis of non-repudiation protocols.

P. Degano, J. Guttman, and F. Martinelli (Eds.): FAST 2008, LNCS 5491, pp. 192–209, 2009.

evidences of participation to be used in case of a dispute. The basic tools for non-repudiation services have been digital signatures and public key cryptography. Indeed, a signed message is an evidence of participation and identity of the other party [14].

The majority of the non-repudiation property analysis efforts in the literature are manually driven though. One of the first efforts to apply formal methods to the verification of non-repudiation protocols has been presented by Zhou et al. in [31], where they have used SVO logic. In [25] Schneider uses process algebra CSP to prove the correctness of a non-repudiation protocol, the well-known Fair Zhou-Gollmann protocol. With the same goal, Bella et al. have used the theorem prover Isabelle [4]. Schneider has defined a rank function for encoding that in an execution trace, an event happens before another event. The verification is done by analyzing traces in the stable failures models of CSP. Among the automatic analysis attempts, we can cite Shmatikov and Mitchell [26] with Murφ, a finite state model-checker, to analyze a fair exchange and two contract signing protocols, Kremer and Raskin [15] with a game-based model, Armando et al. [3] using LTL for encoding resilient channels in particular, the work of Gürgens and Rudolph [9] based on the asynchronous product automata (APA) and the simple homomorphism verification tool (SHVT) [19], raising flaws in three variants of the Fair Zhou-Gollmann protocol and in two other optimistic fair non-repudiation protocols [13,29]. Wei and Heather [27] have used FDR, with an approach similar to Schneider, for a variant of the Fair Zhou-Gollmann protocol with timestamps.

The common point between all those works is that they use rich logics, with a classical bad consequence for model checkers, the difficulty to consider large protocols. For avoiding this problem, Wei and Heather [28] have used PVS [22], but some of the proofs still had to be done by hand.

Fairness is a property that is more difficult to achieve: no party should be able to reach a point where he has the evidence or the message he requires, without the other party also having his required evidence. Fairness is not always required for non-repudiation protocols, but it is usually desirable.

A variety of protocols has been proposed in the literature to solve the problem of fair message exchange with non-repudiation. The first solutions were based on a gradual exchange of the expected information [14]. However this simultaneous secret exchange is troublesome for actual implementations because fairness is based on the assumption of equal computational power for both parties, which is very unlikely in a real world scenario. A possible solution to this problem is the use of a trusted third party (TTP), and in fact it has been shown that this is impossible to achieve fair exchange without a TTP [18,20]. The TTP can be used as a delivery agent to provide simultaneous share of evidences. The Fair Zhou-Gollmann protocol [30] is a well known example using a TTP as a delivery agent; a significant amount of work has been done over this protocol and its derivations [4,10,21,25,31]. However, instead of passing the complete message through the TTP and thus creating a possible bottleneck, recent evolution of protocols resulted in efficient, *optimistic* versions, in which the TTP is only involved in case something goes wrong. Resolve and abort sub-protocols must guarantee that every party can complete the protocol in a fair manner and without waiting for actions of the other party.

One of these recent protocols is the optimistic Cederquist-Corin-Dashti (CCD) non-repudiation protocol [6]. The CCD protocol has the advantage of not using session labels, unlike many others in the literature [14,17,30,25]. A session label typically consists of a hash of all message components. Gürgens et al. [10] have shown a number of vulnerabilities associated to the use of session labels and, to our knowledge, the CCD protocol is the only optimistic non-repudiation protocol that avoids altogether the use of session labels.

This paper presents a method for automatically verifying non-repudiation protocols in presence of an active intruder. Our method has been implemented in the AVISPA Tool [2][2] and we illustrate it with examples. This tool, intensively used for defining Internet security protocols and automatically analyzing their authentication and secrecy properties, did not provide any help for considering non-repudiation properties.

We first consider non-repudiation analysis as a combination of authentication problems, applied to the Fair Zhou-Gollmann protocol. We show the limitations of this representation and the difficulties for proving non-repudiation properties using only authentications. Then, we define a method based on the analysis of agents knowledge, permitting to handle non-repudiation and fairness properties in a uniform framework. Our approach allows one to specify the logical properties in a natural way: they correspond to state invariants that are convincing properties for the user. This method is easy to integrate in lazy verification systems, such as the AVISPA Tool, and can also be integrated in any system able to handle agents (or intruder) knowledge. This should permit, contrarily to more complex logics like LTL, to set up abstractions more easily for considering unbounded cases. This should also permit to get a more efficient verification for bounded cases. We illustrate this fact with the analysis of the optimistic Cederquist-Corin-Dashti protocol.

In this paper, the defined techniques are based on the formal semantics presented in [7,8] for the AVISPA Tool.

2   Non-repudiation Properties

Non-repudiation (NR) is a general property that is usually not clearly defined. It is described by protocols designers as a set of required services, depending on the protocol and the required security level. In particular, non-repudiation properties may differ whether a trusted third party (TTP) is used or not in the protocol.

In the following, we recall the classical model independent definitions of non-repudiation services required by most of the existing security applications (for e-commerce for example). All these services are defined for a message sent by an originator agent to a recipient agent, possibly via a delivery agent, a TTP.

---

[2] http://www.avispa-project.org

Definition 1. *The service of **non-repudiation of origin**, denoted $NRO_B(A)$, provides the recipient B with a set of evidences which ensures that the originator A has sent the message. The evidence of origin is generated by the originator and held by the recipient. This property protects the recipient against a dishonest originator.*

Definition 2. *The service of **non-repudiation of receipt**, denoted $NRR_A(B)$, provides the originator A a set of evidences which ensures that the recipient B has received the message. The evidence of receipt is generated by the recipient and held by the originator. This property protects the originator against a dishonest recipient.*

Definition 3. *The service of **non-repudiation of submission**, denoted $NRS_A(B)$, provides the originator A a set of evidences which ensures that he has submitted the message for delivery to B. This service only applies when the protocol uses a TTP. Evidence of submission is generated by the delivery agent, and will be held by the originator. This property protects the originator against a dishonest recipient.*

Definition 4. *The service of **non-repudiation of delivery**, denoted $NRD_A(B)$, provides the originator A a set of evidences which ensures that the recipient B has received the message. This service only applies when the protocol uses a TTP. Evidence of delivery is generated by the delivery agent, and will be held by the originator. This property protects the originator against a dishonest recipient.*

Definition 5. *A service of **fairness** (also called strong fairness) for a non-repudiation protocol provides evidences that, at the end of the protocol execution, either the originator has the evidence of receipt of the message and the recipient has the evidence of origin of the corresponding message, or none of them has any valuable information. This property protects the originator and the recipient.*

Definition 6. *A service of **timeliness** for a non-repudiation protocol guarantees that, whatever happens during the protocol run, all participants can reach a state that preserves fairness, in a finite time.*

Note that in general, sets of evidences such as $\mathcal{NRO}$, $\mathcal{NRR}$, $\mathcal{NRS}$ and $\mathcal{NRD}$ are composed with messages signed by an agent.

After this informal use of the notion of evidence, let us consider for the sequel of this paper the following definition.

Definition 7. *An **evidence** for an agent A and a non-repudiation property P is a message, a part of a message, or a combination of both, received by A that is necessary for guaranteeing property P.*

We will also consider the following definition of a valid service.

Definition 8. *A non-repudiation service is **valid** if is satisfies the corresponding property.*

Remark: In this paper, we consider the evidences given by the protocol designer as valid: without intervention of an intruder, those evidences are sufficient to guarantee the non-repudiation service; and in case of a dispute, a judge analyzing them will always be able to protect honest agents. Thus, we suppose that evidences are correctly chosen, so that a judge can use them for building proofs protecting honest agents.

3 Non-repudiation as Authentication

It is well known that non-repudiation is a form of authentication [23]. In this section we use the Fair Zhou-Gollmann protocol to demonstrate that properties like NRO, NRR,... can be at least partially represented by authentication properties. However we show some strong limitations of this approach, motivating the introduction of a new approach in the next section.

3.1 Running Example: The FairZG Protocol

In this section we describe the Fair Zhou-Gollmann protocol (FairZG) [31], a fair non-repudiation protocol that uses a TTP. We have chosen this protocol as a case study to demonstrate our analysis approach because of the existence of significant related work [4,10,21,25]. The protocol is presented below in Alice&Bob notation, where fNRO, fNRR, fSUB and fCON are labels used to identify the purpose of messages.

1. $A \to B$:   fNRO.B.L.C.NRO
2. $B \to A$:   fNRR.A.L.NRR
3. $A \to TTP$: fSUB.B.L.K.SubK
4. $B \leftrightarrow TTP$: fCON.A.B.L.K.ConK
5. $A \leftrightarrow TTP$: fCON.A.B.L.K.ConK

where A (for Alice) is the originator of the message M, B (for Bob) is the recipient of the message M, TTP is the trusted third party, M is the message to be sent from Alice to Bob, C is a commitment (the message M encrypted by a key K), L is a unique session identifier (also called label), K is a symmetric key defined by Alice, NRO is a message used for non-repudiation of origin (the message fNRO.B.L.C signed by Alice), NRR is a message used for non-repudiation of receipt (the message fNRR.A.L.C signed by Bob), SubK is a proof of submission of K (the message fSUB.B.L.K signed by Alice), ConK is a confirmation of K (the message fCON.A.B.L.K signed by the TTP).

Non-repudiation properties of origin and receipt are defined by the protocol designers by the following sets of terms:

$$\mathcal{NRO}_B(A) = \{\mathsf{NRO}, \mathsf{ConK}\}$$
$$\mathcal{NRR}_A(B) = \{\mathsf{NRR}, \mathsf{ConK}\}$$

The main idea of this FairZG protocol is to split the delivery of a message into two parts. First a commitment C, containing the message M encrypted by a key K, is exchanged between Alice and Bob (message fNRO). Once Alice has an evidence of commitment from Bob (message fNRR), the key K is sent to a trusted third party (message fSUB). Once the TTP has received the key, both Alice and Bob can retrieve the evidence ConK and the key K from the TTP (messages fCON). This last step is represented by a double direction arrow in the Alice&Bob notation because it is implementation specific and may be composed by several message exchanges between the agents and the TTP. In this scenario we assume that the network will not be down forever and both Alice and Bob have access to the TTP's shared repository where it stores the evidences and the key. This means that the agents will be able to retrieve the key and evidences from the TTP even in case of network failures.

3.2   Non-repudiation of Origin as Authentication

In our example, the FairZG protocol, non-repudiation of origin should provide the guarantee that if Bob owns $\mathcal{NRO}$ then Alice has sent M to Bob. Proposition 1 shows how this can be partially ensured with a set of authentications.

Definition 9. auth(X,Y,D) *is the non injective authentication, and means agent* X *authenticates agent* Y *on data* D.

The semantics of such a predicate is standard and can be found in [16]. The next two lemmas present standard properties of authentication.

Lemma 1 (Subterm property). *Given agents A and B, and message M, if* auth(A,B,M), *then for each subterm s of M, accessible by composition/decomposition of M by both agents,* auth(A,B,s) *is true.*

Lemma 2 (Transitivity of authentication). *Given agents A, B and C, and message M, if* auth(A,B,M) *and* auth(B,C,M), *then* auth(A,C,M).

Proposition 1. *Given the FairZG protocol, if* auth(B,A,NRO), auth(B,TTP, ConK) *and* auth(TTP,A,SubK) *are valid, then the non-repudiation service of origin* $NRO_B(A)$ *is valid.*

Proof. For the two evidences of $\mathcal{NRO}_B(A) - \{$NRO, ConK$\}$, we have:

- NRO = Sig$_A$(fNRO.B.L.$\{$M$\}_K$): since auth(B,A,NRO) is valid, there is an agreement between B and A on Sig$_A$(fNRO.B.L.C). From the subterm property, this also means an agreement on $\{$M$\}_K$, thus A has sent the $\{$M$\}_K$ that B holds.
- ConK = Sig$_{TTP}$(fCON.A.B.L.K): as above auth(B,TTP,ConK) implies an agreement on K between B and TTP. Furthermore SubK=Sig$_A$(fSUB, B, L, K), thus auth(TTP,A,SubK) implies an agreement on K between TTP and A. By transitivity we have an agreement on K between B and A which means that A has sent K to TTP, that same K that B got from TTP.

As A has sent $\{M\}_K$ and K, it means that he has generated M and run the protocol in order to transmit it to B.

Non-injective authentication is only required for auth(B,TTP,ConK) because B can ask many times ConK. However since all authentications imply an agreement on the unique session identifier L, this protects from authentication across different sessions.   □

3.3 Non-repudiation of Receipt as Authentication

In our example, the FairZG protocol, non-repudiation of receipt should provide the guarantee that if Alice owns $\mathcal{NRR}$ then Bob has received M from Alice. Proposition 2 shows how this can be partially done with a set of authentications.

Proposition 2. *Given the FairZG protocol, if* auth(A,B,NRR), auth(A,TTP, ConK) *and* auth(B,TTP,ConK) *are valid, then the non-repudiation service of receipt* $NRR_A(B)$ *is valid.*

Proof. For the two evidences of $\mathcal{NRR}_A(B) = \{NRR, ConK\}$, we have:

- NRR = $Sig_B(fNRR.A.L.\{M\}_K)$: a reasoning as for NRO in Proposition 1 ensures that B has received $\{M\}_K$.
- ConK = $Sig_{TTP}(fCON.A.B.L.K)$: auth(A,TTP,ConK) implies an agreement on K between A and TTP. Furthermore auth(B,TTP,ConK) implies an agreement on K between B and TTP. This means that there is an agreement on K between A and B, thus when A holds ConK, B has received or will be able to receive K.

The proof end is similar to the one of Proposition 1.   □

3.4 Limitations and Difficulties

We have just illustrated on the FairZG protocol how to represent some non-repudiation properties using authentication. This shows that non-repudiation can be handled by most existing protocol analyzers, as most of them can handle authentication.

However, this only permits to partially handle non-repudiation:

1. The main problem is to apply Propositions 1 and 2 in automatic tools, since the authentication property is usually encoded by an annotation pair (for example "witness"/"request" in AVISPA). In such a situation we cannot handle dishonest agents since for example with the $NRO_B(A)$ service, a dishonest Bob could forge a fake evidences set without executing the "request" annotation. In such a case there is no authentication failure but the service is not valid.

     More generally dishonest agents can always act so that authentications in which they are involved fail or not, by generating wrong authentication "requests", or wrong "witnesses". This is the reason why tools like AVISPA do not handle authentications involving the intruder. This is also why with our representation of non-repudiation, the AVISPA tool does not find any error in the FairZG protocol, while this is possible to prove that the protocol is not fair when agent A is dishonest [9] (see Section 4.4 for details of this attack).

In order to avoid this kind of problems we need to prove that Bob could only own $\mathcal{NRO}$ if Alice has actually sent the correct protocol messages. This may be done as for example in [25], [27] or [10] but this is not trivial.

2. Another problem with the handling of non-repudiation as authentications is that it is difficult to apply to optimistic non-repudiation protocols that include sub-protocols like *abort* and *resolve* as presented in the next section. One of the main difficulties is that such protocols are non-deterministic.

As a conclusion, proving non-repudiation with the help of authentications does not seem to be the best way; this is why in the next section we propose another simple and complete approach for handling non-repudiation.

4   Non-repudiation Based on Agent Knowledge

In this section, we present a new method for considering non-repudiation services and fairness in a uniform framework: we introduce a logic permitting to describe states invariants. This logic is a very classical one, except that we define two new predicates, deduce and aknows that permit to consider agents knowledge in the description of goals. The aknows predicate is also used as a protocol annotation, with the following semantics: *agent X knows (or can deduce) term t.*

All our work is based on the standard formal semantics described in [7,8] for the AVISPA Tool.

4.1   Description of Non-repudiation Properties

The main role of a non-repudiation protocol is to give evidences of non-repudiation to the parties involved in the protocol. To analyze this kind of protocol, one must verify which participants have their non-repudiation evidences at the end of the protocol execution. For example, if the originator has all its evidences for non-repudiation of receipt, then the service of non-repudiation of receipt is guaranteed. If the recipient has all its evidences for non-repudiation of origin, then the service of non-repudiation of origin is guaranteed. If both parties (or none of them) have their evidences, fairness is guaranteed. In other words, to analyze non-repudiation, we need to verify if a set of terms is known by an agent at the end of the protocol execution.

And for considering a large class of non-repudiation protocols, we shall not restrict evidences to a set of terms, but we have to consider them as a combination of terms using standard logical connectors (conjunction, disjunction, negation).

For considering non-repudiation and fairness properties involving honest and dishonest agents, we have defined a new predicate that permits to access the knowledge of protocol participants. This predicate, named aknows (for *agent knows*), is used in protocols specifications for annotating transitions and for defining properties.

Definition 10 ($\mathcal{NR}_{-X}(Y)$). *Let $\mathcal{A}$ be a set of agents playing a finite number of sessions of a protocol, $\mathcal{T}$ a set of terms sent in the messages of this protocol and $\mathcal{E}$ the subset of terms in $\mathcal{T}$ that are part of the evidences of non-repudiation in the protocol. For agents $X, Y \in \mathcal{A}$, $\mathcal{NR}_{-X}(Y)$ is a logical combination of terms $t \in \mathcal{E}$ that constitute the evidence for a service of non-repudiation NR_- for agent X wrt. agent Y.*

Definition 11 (aknows). *Let $\mathcal{A}$ be a set of agents playing a finite number of sessions of a protocol, $\mathcal{P}$ the set of processes (ie. instances of protocol roles) involved in those sessions, and $\mathcal{T}$ a set of terms. The protocol annotation $\mathsf{aknows}(X, p, t)$ is a predicate with $X \in \mathcal{A}$, $p \in \mathcal{P}$ and $t \in \mathcal{T}$, asserting that agent X, playing a role of the protocol as process p, knows (or can deduce) the term t.*

The semantics of predicate $\mathsf{aknows}(X, p, t)$ is that the term t can be composed by agent X, according to its current knowledge in process p of the protocol, whether this agent is honest or not. This composability test can be easily done by any tool that is able to manage agents knowledge or intruder knowledge.

By abuse of notation, we may write $\mathsf{aknows}(X, p, L)$, for a logical formula L combining evidences ($\mathcal{NR}_{-X}(Y)$ for example), considering that the predicate aknows is an homomorphism:

$$\mathsf{aknows}(X, p, L_1 \wedge L_2) = \mathsf{aknows}(X, p, L_1) \wedge \mathsf{aknows}(X, p, L_2)$$
$$\mathsf{aknows}(X, p, L_1 \vee L_2) = \mathsf{aknows}(X, p, L_1) \vee \mathsf{aknows}(X, p, L_2)$$
$$\mathsf{aknows}(X, p, \neg L) = \neg \mathsf{aknows}(X, p, L)$$

Definition 12 (deduce). *Let $\mathcal{A}$ be a set of agents playing a finite number of sessions of a protocol and $\mathcal{T}$ a set of terms. We define $\mathsf{deduce}(X, t)$, with $X \in \mathcal{A}$ and $t \in \mathcal{T}$, as the predicate which means that X can deduce t from its knowledge.*

We will use the same abuse of notation for deduce as for aknows.

The aknows predicate is used in protocol transitions for indicating that an agent knows an important information; it corresponds to a fact; it has the same meaning when used in the description of a property, but also indicates that protocol transitions have really been run.

The deduce predicate is used in properties description for indicating a deducible knowledge.

As a consequence, we can assume that each aknows annotation in protocols transitions corresponds to a valid deduce predicate on the same information; this assumption permits to avoid bad annotations.

Definition 13 (well-formedness). *The evidence $\mathcal{NR}_{-X}(Y)$ is well-formed if it contains information that uniquely identifies X, Y, M. This set, held by X, is used for proving to a judge that Y has run the protocol in a coherent way wrt. X's run.*

Note that in this context, the interesting case to study is when X is dishonest and has forged the set of evidences, while Y did not run the protocol (eg. has not sent M for a service of non-repudiation of origin).

We now give the results obtained by this representation.

Proposition 3. *Given a non-repudiation service of B against A about a message M with the well-formed evidence $\mathcal{NR}_{-B}(A)$ for processes p_B and p_A of B and A respectively. If the following formulae are true at the end of process p_B of B, then the non-repudiation service is valid.*

$$\texttt{aknows}(B, p_B, \mathcal{NR}_{-B}(A)) \Rightarrow \texttt{aknows}(A, p_A, M)$$
$$\texttt{deduce}(B, \mathcal{NR}_{-B}(A)) \quad\ \Rightarrow \texttt{aknows}(B, p_B, \mathcal{NR}_{-B}(A))$$

Proof. A sketch of proof is as follows: by the second implication if B is able to deduce $\mathcal{NR}_{-B}(A)$ then $\texttt{aknows}(B, p_B, \mathcal{NR}_{-B}(A))$ is included in its knowledge, since by well-formedness of $\mathcal{NR}_{-B}(A)$, $\mathcal{NR}_{-B}(A)$ and $\texttt{aknows}(B, p_B, \mathcal{NR}_{-B}(A))$ are related to the same process p_B.

And again by well-formedness of $\mathcal{NR}_{-B}(A)$, it includes all the information uniquely identifying M, thus the first implication implies an agreement on M between B and A. Finally as $\texttt{aknows}(A, p_A, M)$ is an annotation, this means that A has followed the protocol, thus he has done what he must do with M. □

Remark: Verifying formulae given in the above Proposition is not a problem, because a priori any theorem prover (able to consider secrecy) can compute whatever can be deduced by an agent at a given step of the protocol, especially concerning the $\texttt{deduce}$ predicate [12].

Corollary 1. *Given a non-repudiation service of origin for B against A about message M, involving processes p_B and p_A of B and A respectively. If$\mathcal{NRO}_B(A))$ is well-formed and the following formulae are true at the end of process p_B, then the service is valid.*

$$\texttt{aknows}(B, p_B, \mathcal{NRO}_B(A)) \Rightarrow \texttt{aknows}(A, p_A, M)$$
$$\texttt{deduce}(B, \mathcal{NRO}_B(A)) \quad\ \Rightarrow \texttt{aknows}(B, p_B, \mathcal{NRO}_B(A))$$

Corollary 2. *Given a non-repudiation service of receipt for A against B about message M, involving processes p_A and p_B of A and B respectively. If$\mathcal{NRR}_A(B))$ is well-formed and the following formulae are true at the end of process p_A, then the service is valid.*

$$\texttt{aknows}(A, p_A, \mathcal{NRR}_A(B)) \Rightarrow \texttt{aknows}(B, p_B, M)$$
$$\texttt{deduce}(A, \mathcal{NRR}_A(B)) \quad\ \Rightarrow \texttt{aknows}(A, p_A, \mathcal{NRR}_A(B))$$

4.2 Description of Fairness

In the literature, authors often give different definitions of fairness for non-repudiation protocols. In some definitions none of the parties should have more evidences than the others at any given point in time. Others have a more flexible definition in which none of them should have more evidences than the others at the end of the protocol run. In many works it is also not very clear if only successful protocol runs are taken into account, or partial protocol runs are valid as well.

In this paper we consider the flexible definition of fairness, taking into account complete protocol runs. By complete protocol runs we mean a run where, even though the protocol could not have reached its last transition for all agents, there is no executable transition left, i.e. all possible protocol steps have been executed, but this does not mean that all agents are in a final state.

We define this standard notion of fairness as a function of non-repudiation of origin and of non-repudiation of receipt. If both properties, NRO and NRR, are ensured or both are not valid for a given message M, then we have fairness.

Proposition 4. *Given a protocol whose purpose is to send a message from Alice to Bob, we have the following equivalence concerning the standard definition of fairness for processes p_A and p_B of Alice and Bob respectively. If the non-repudiation is valid for the NRO and NRR services then:*

$$Fairness \equiv (\texttt{aknows}(Bob, p_B, \mathcal{NRO}_{Bob}(Alice)) \textit{ iff } \texttt{aknows}(Alice, p_A, \mathcal{NRR}_{Alice}(Bob)))$$

This result can be generalized to fairness wrt. a set of non-repudiation services as follows.

Theorem 1. *Given a protocol involving a finite number of agents, given a finite set of valid non-repudiation services NR, the protocol is fair wrt. NR iff*

$$\forall \mathcal{NRS}_{1X_1}(Y_1), \mathcal{NRS}_{2X_2}(Y_2) \in \mathcal{NR},$$
$$\texttt{aknows}(X_1, p_1, \mathcal{NRS}_{1X_1}(Y_1)) \textit{ iff } \texttt{aknows}(X_2, p_2, \mathcal{NRS}_{2X_2}(Y_2))$$

4.3 Running Example: CCD

For illustrating the analysis method described above, we use in this section a recent protocol, the Cederquist-Corin-Dashti (CCD) optimistic non-repudiation protocol [6]. The CCD protocol has been created for permitting an agent A to send a message M to an agent B in a fair manner. This means that agent A should get an evidence of receipt of M by B (EOR) if and only if B has really received M and the evidence of origin from A (EOO). EOR permits A to prove that B has received M, while EOO permits B to prove that M has been sent by A. The protocol is divided into three sub-protocols: the main protocol, an *abort* sub-protocol and a *resolve* sub-protocol.

The Main Protocol. It describes the sending of M by A to B and the exchange of evidences in the case where both agents can complete the entire protocol. If this direct communication cannot be completed, in order to finish properly the protocol, the agents execute the *abort* or the *resolve* sub-protocol with a trusted third party (TTP).

The main protocol is therefore composed of the following messages exchanges, described in the Alice&Bob notation:

1. $A \rightarrow B : \{M\}_K.EOO_M$ where $EOO_M = \{B.TTP.H(\{M\}_K).\{K.A\}_{Kttp}\}_{inv(Ka)}$
2. $B \rightarrow A : EOR_M$ where $EOR_M = \{EOO_M\}_{inv(Kb)}$
3. $A \rightarrow B : K$
4. $B \rightarrow A : EOR_K$ where $EOR_K = \{A.H(\{M\}_K).K\}_{inv(Kb)}$

where K is a symmetric key freshly generated by A, H is a one-way hash function, Kg is the public key of agent g and $inv(Kg)$ is the private key of agent g (used for signing messages). Note that we assume that all public keys are known by all agents (including dishonest agents).

In the first message, A sends the message M encrypted by K and the evidence of origin for B (message signed by A, so decryptable by B). In this evidence, B checks his identity, learns the name of the TTP, checks that the hash code is the result of hashing the first part of the message, but he cannot decrypt the last part of the evidence; this last part may be useful if any of the other sub-protocols is used.

B answers by sending the evidence of receipt for A, A checking that EOR_M is EOO_M signed by B.

In the third message, A sends the key K, permitting B to discover the plaintext message M.

Finally, B sends to A another evidence of receipt, permitting A to check that the symmetric key has been received by B.

The *Abort* Sub-Protocol. The *abort* sub-protocol is executed by agent A if he does not receive the message EOR_M at step 2 of the main protocol. The purpose of this sub-protocol is to cancel the messages exchange.

1. $A \rightarrow TTP$: $\{\texttt{abort}.H(\{M\}_K).B.\{K.A\}_{Kttp}\}_{inv(Ka)}$

2. $TTP \rightarrow A$: $\begin{cases} E_{TTP} & \text{where } E_{TTP} = \{A.B.K.H(\{M\}_K)\}_{inv(Kttp)} \\ & \text{if } \texttt{resolved}(A.B.K.H(\{M\}_K)) \\ AB_{TTP} & \text{where } AB_{TTP} = \{A.B.H(\{M\}_K).\{K.A\}_{Kttp}\}_{inv(Kttp)} \\ & \text{otherwise} \end{cases}$

In this sub-protocol, A sends to the TTP an abort request, containing the $\texttt{abort}$ label and some information about the protocol session to be aborted.

According to what the TTP knows about this protocol session, he has two possible answers: if this is the first problem received by the TTP for this protocol session, the TTP sends a confirmation of abortion, AB_{TTP}, and stores in its database that this protocol session has been aborted; but if the TTP has already received a request for resolving this protocol session, he sends to A the information for completing his evidence of receipt by B, E_{TTP}.

The *Resolve* Sub-Protocol. The role of this second sub-protocol is to permit agents A and B to finish the protocol in a fair manner, if the main protocol cannot be run until its end by some of the parties. For example, if B does not get K or if A does not get EOR_K, they can invoke the *resolve* sub-protocol.

1. $G \rightarrow TTP$: EOR_M

2. $TTP \rightarrow G$: $\begin{cases} AB_{TTP} & \text{if } \texttt{aborted}(A.B.K.H(\{M\}_K)) \\ E_{TTP} & \text{otherwise} \end{cases}$

where G stands for A or B.

A resolve request is done by sending EOR_M to the TTP. If the protocol session has already been aborted, the TTP answers by the abortion confirmation, AB_{TTP}. If this is not the case, the TTP sends E_{TTP} so that the user could complete its evidence of receipt (if G is A) or of origin (if G is B). Then the TTP stores in its database that this protocol session has been resolved.

Agents' Evidences. For this protocol, according to [6], the logical expressions of evidences are:

$$\mathcal{NRO}_B(A) = \{M\}_K \wedge EOO_M \wedge K$$
$$\mathcal{NRR}_A(B) = \{M\}_K \wedge EOR_M \wedge (EOR_K \vee E_{TTP})$$

Note that there are two possibilities of evidences for non-repudiation of receipt, according to the way the protocol is run.

According to our method, we simply have to annotate protocol steps with aknows predicates, and then write the logical formula to be verified.

Non-Repudiation of Origin. The following table shows where those annotations take place in the three CCD sub-protocols, for considering non-repudiation of origin.

$\mathcal{NRO}_B(A)$	Protocol - step
aknows$(B, p_B, \{M\}_K)$	Main - 1.
aknows(B, p_B, EOO_M)	Main - 1.
aknows(B, p_B, K)	Main - 3.
aknows(B, p_B, K)	Resolve - 2.

Note that the key K can be obtained either by the third message of the main protocol, or by the second message of the resolve sub-protocol. One annotation has to be put in each of those protocol steps.

By Corollary 1, **non-repudiation of origin** for the CCD protocol is represented by the following invariant formulae:

aknows$(B, p_B, \{M\}_K \wedge EOO_M \wedge K) \Rightarrow$ aknows(A, p_A, M)
deduce$(B, \{M\}_K \wedge EOO_M \wedge K) \Rightarrow$ aknows$(B, p_B, \{M\}_K \wedge EOO_M \wedge K)$

Non-Repudiation of Receipt. The following table shows where those annotations take place in the three CCD sub-protocols, for considering non-repudiation of receipt.

$\mathcal{NRR}_A(B)$	Protocol - step
aknows$(A, p_A, \{M\}_K)$	Main - 1.
aknows(A, p_A, EOR_M)	Main - 2.
aknows(A, p_A, EOR_K)	Main - 4.
aknows(A, p_A, E_{TTP})	Abort - 2.
aknows(A, p_A, E_{TTP})	Resolve - 2.

For this property, E_{TTP} can be obtained from the second message of the abort sub-protocol or of the resolve sub-protocol.

According to Corollary 2, **non-repudiation of receipt** for the CCD protocol is represented by the following invariant formulae:

$$\text{aknows}(A, p_A, \{M\}_K \wedge EOR_M \wedge (EOR_K \vee E_{TTP})) \Rightarrow \text{aknows}(B, p_B, M)$$
$$\text{deduce}(A, p_A, \{M\}_K \wedge EOR_M \wedge (EOR_K \vee E_{TTP})) \Rightarrow$$
$$\text{aknows}(A, p_A, \{M\}_K \wedge EOR_M \wedge (EOR_K \vee E_{TTP}))$$

Fairness. For analyzing **fairness**, this protocol requires timeliness, that is each participant should reach a final state before testing fairness. Fairness for the CCD protocol is described by the following logical formula, a very simple application of Theorem 1:

$$\text{aknows}(A, p_A, \mathcal{NRR}_A(B)) \Leftrightarrow \text{aknows}(B, p_B, \mathcal{NRO}_B(A))$$

Basically the property states that if A knows the EOR evidence ($\{M\}_K$, EOR_M, and EOR_K or E_{TTP}), then B knows the EOO evidence. And symmetrically for B, if B knows the EOO evidence ($\{M\}_K$, EOO_M and K), then A knows the EOR evidence.

Experiments. The CCD protocol has been specified in the AVISPA Tool, with the description of the fairness property given above. The detailed formulae used in the AVISPA Tool, with an LTL syntax, are:

$$\Box \left(\left(\begin{array}{l} \text{aknows}(A, p_A, \{M\}_K) \wedge \\ \text{aknows}(A, p_A, EOR_M) \wedge \\ (\text{aknows}(A, p_A, EOR_K) \vee \text{aknows}(A, p_A, E_{TTP})) \end{array} \right) \Rightarrow \left(\begin{array}{l} \text{aknows}(B, p_B, \{M\}_K) \wedge \\ \text{aknows}(B, p_B, EOO_M) \wedge \\ \text{aknows}(B, p_B, K) \end{array} \right) \right)$$

$$\Box \left(\left(\begin{array}{l} \text{aknows}(B, p_B, \{M\}_K) \wedge \\ \text{aknows}(B, p_B, EOO_M) \wedge \\ \text{aknows}(B, p_B, K) \end{array} \right) \Rightarrow \left(\begin{array}{l} \text{aknows}(A, p_A, \{M\}_K) \wedge \\ \text{aknows}(A, p_A, EOR_M) \wedge \\ (\text{aknows}(A, p_A, EOR_K) \vee \text{aknows}(A, p_A, E_{TTP})) \end{array} \right) \right)$$

Several scenarios have been run, and two of them have raised an attack, showing that the CCD protocol does not provide the fairness property for which it has been designed.

The **first attack** has been found for a scenario with only one protocol session where A, an honest agent, plays the protocol with a dishonest agent B (named i, for *intruder*). As soon as i has received the first message from A, he builds EOR_M and sends it to the TTP as resolve request. Later, when A, not receiving EOR_M, decides to abort the protocol, this is too late: the protocol has already been resolved, the intruder can get M and build the proof that A has sent M, and A cannot build the evidence of receipt, as he will never get EOR_M.

The trace of this attack is the following:

1. $A \rightarrow i :$ $\{M\}_K.EOO_M$
2. $i \rightarrow TTP :$ RESOLVE
3. $TTP \rightarrow i :$ E_{TTP}
*** timeout for A ***
4. $A \rightarrow TTP :$ ABORT
5. $TTP \rightarrow A :$ E_{TTP}

The **second attack** is a variant where both A and B are honest agents. The only difference is that B sends EOR_M to A, but this message is intercepted by the intruder and never delivered to A. At this point, the protocol is blocked, both agents waiting for a message. So, each agent will ask the help of the TTP for concluding the protocol: A will invoke the *abort* sub-protocol and B will invoke the *resolve* sub-protocol. And if the resolve request reaches the TTP before the abort request [3], B will get all his necessary evidences from the TTP, while A, having asked for an abort, will not be able to get all his evidences even with the help of the TTP.

The originality of this attack is that, at the end:

- A will guess (according to the answer received to his abort request) that the protocol has been resolved by B, so he will assume that B knows M and can build the proof that A has sent it; but A cannot prove this;
- B has resolved the protocol and has received from the TTP the information for getting M and building the proof that A has sent M; but he does not know that A does not have his proof;
- the TTP cannot know that A has not received EOR_M; so he knows that B can build its evidences, but he cannot know if A can or not.

So, those attacks show that the CCD protocol is not fair, even if both agents A and B are honest. The attack is due to a malicious intruder or a network problem, and the TTP is of no help for detecting the problem.

Correcting the protocol is not difficult, for example by sending EOR_M together with E_{TTP} in the *abort* sub-protocol, when the protocol is already resolved. The numerous scenarios that have been tried for this new version have not raised any attack. This experiment on the CCD protocol is detailed in [24].

4.4   Back to the FairZG Protocol

We have illustrated in Section 3 the representation of non-repudiation properties by authentications with the FairZG protocol, raising some limitations and difficulties for an automatic analysis. We have also analyzed this protocol with our second method, based on agents knowledge.

This protocol is known for having an attack when agent A is dishonest [9]. Indeed in [31], it is not specified whether or not the TTP should store ConK forever. And from the TTP point of view, a transaction is closed once both A and B have retrieved ConK, so he could delete all the information about this transaction.

When the TTP acts in that way, Gürgens and Rudolph have described an attack: a first session is run until its end between A and B; then, A starts a second session with B, using the same K and L as in the first session, but with a different message M_2; if B does not remark the similarity of the sessions, he will answer to A; but once A has got NRR, he can stop the session, not sending

---

[3] Note that this is possible even if channels are protected or pervasive, as agents use different channels; this is also possible if B has a shorter timeout than A; this notion of timeout is essential in the implementation of protocols, as demonstrated by Carbonell et al. in [5].

the third message of the protocol; at that point, A owns NRR from the second session and ConK from the first session, and this constitutes the evidences of receipt of M$_2$ by B; on his side, B will never be able to get ConK from the TTP and will never know how to decrypt M$_2$.

So, this attack is due to the hypothesis that the TTP does not keep information on closed sessions. We have modeled this hypothesis by using two parallel processes for the TTP, one for each session. And we have found the same attack.

5 Conclusion

Non-repudiation protocols have an important role in many areas where secure transactions with proofs of participation are necessary. The evidences of origin and receipt of a message are two examples of elements that the parties should own at the end of a communication. We have given two very different examples of such protocols. The FairZG protocol is an intensively studied protocol in which the role of the trusted third party is essential. The CCD protocol is a more recent non-repudiation protocol that avoids the use of session labels and distinguishes itself by the use of an optimistic approach, the trusted third party being used only in case of a problem in the execution of the main protocol.

The fairness of a non-repudiation protocol is a property difficult to analyze and there are very few tools that can handle the automatic analysis of this property.

The contribution of this work is twofold. First, we have illustrated with the FairZG protocol how difficult it is to consider full non-repudiation properties using only a combination of authentications.

Second, we have defined a new method that permits to handle in a very easy way non-repudiation properties and fairness in a uniform framework. This method is based on the handling of agents knowledge and can be used to automatically analyze non-repudiation protocols as well as contract signing protocols [26]. We have implemented it in the AVISPA Tool and have successfully applied it to the CCD and FairZG protocols, proving that they are not fair. We have also tested other specifications of the CCD protocol, for example with secure communication channels between agents and the TTP, no attack has been found; but using such channels is not considered as acceptable, because it generates an overload of the TTP activity.

Our method, based on the writing of simple state invariants, is of easy use, and can be implemented in any tool handling agents (or intruder) knowledge. It should be very helpful for setting abstractions for handling unbounded scenarios, and it should be very efficient for bounded verifications, as it has been the case in our implementation. We hope that this work will open a highway to the specification of many other properties, without any more change in the specification languages and the analysis engines.

Our work has been done for analyzing non-repudiation protocols. A complementary approach has been defined by Guttman in [11], where he describes a protocol design process, based on authentication tests, permitting to guarantee some security properties, including some non-repudiation properties. Note that in the example presented by Guttman, fairness is not considered.

References

1. http://www.lsv.ens-cachan.fr/~kremer/FXbib/references.php
2. Armando, A., Basin, D.A., Boichut, Y., Chevalier, Y., Compagna, L., Cuéllar, J., Drielsma, P.H., Héam, P.-C., Kouchnarenko, O., Mantovani, J., Mödersheim, S., von Oheimb, D., Rusinowitch, M., Santiago, J., Turuani, M., Viganò, L., Vigneron, L.: The AVISPA Tool for the Automated Validation of Internet Security Protocols and Applications. In: Etessami, K., Rajamani, S.K. (eds.) CAV 2005. LNCS, vol. 3576, pp. 281–285. Springer, Heidelberg (2005)
3. Armando, A., Carbone, R., Compagna, L.: LTL Model Checking for Security Protocols. In: 20th IEEE Computer Security Foundations Symp., CSF, pp. 385–396. IEEE Computer Society, Los Alamitos (2007)
4. Bella, G., Paulson, L.C.: Mechanical Proofs about a Non-repudiation Protocol. In: Boulton, R.J., Jackson, P.B. (eds.) TPHOLs 2001. LNCS, vol. 2152, pp. 91–104. Springer, Heidelberg (2001)
5. Carbonell, M., Sierra, J.M., Onieva, J.A., Lopez, J., Zhou, J.: Estimation of TTP Features in Non-repudiation Service. In: Gervasi, O., Gavrilova, M.L. (eds.) ICCSA 2007, Part II. LNCS, vol. 4706, pp. 549–558. Springer, Heidelberg (2007)
6. Cederquist, J., Corin, R., Dashti, M.T.: On the Quest for Impartiality: Design and Analysis of a Fair Non-repudiation Protocol. In: Qing, S., Mao, W., López, J., Wang, G. (eds.) ICICS 2005. LNCS, vol. 3783, pp. 27–39. Springer, Heidelberg (2005)
7. Chevalier, Y., Compagna, L., Cuellar, J., Hankes Drielsma, P., Mantovani, J., Mödersheim, S., Vigneron, L.: A High Level Protocol Specification Language for Industrial Security-Sensitive Protocols. In: Proc. of Work. on Specification and Automated Processing of Security Requirements, SAPS, Linz, Austria, vol. 180. Oesterreichische Computer Gesellschaft (Austrian Computer Society) (September 2004)
8. Compagna, L.: SAT-based Model-Checking of Security Protocols. PhD thesis, Università degli Studi di Genova and the University of Edinburgh (2005)
9. Gürgens, S., Rudolph, C.: Security Analysis of Efficient (Un-)fair Non-repudiation Protocols. Formal Aspects of Computing 17(3), 260–276 (2005)
10. Gürgens, S., Rudolph, C., Vogt, H.: On the Security of Fair Non-repudiation Protocols. Int. Journal of Information Security 4, 253–262 (2005)
11. Guttman, J.D.: Authentication tests and disjoint encryption: A design method for security protocols. Journal of Computer Security 12(3-4), 409–433 (2004)
12. Jacquemard, F., Rusinowitch, M., Vigneron, L.: Compiling and Verifying Security Protocols. In: Parigot, M., Voronkov, A. (eds.) LPAR 2000. LNCS, vol. 1955, pp. 131–160. Springer, Heidelberg (2000)
13. Kremer, S., Markowitch, O.: Optimistic Non-repudiable Information Exchange. In: Biemond, J. (ed.) 21st Symp. on Information Theory in the Benelux, Wassenaar, NL, pp. 139–146. Werkgemeenschap Informatieen Communicatietheorie, Enschede (2000)
14. Kremer, S., Markowitch, O., Zhou, J.: An Intensive Survey of Fair Non-repudiation Protocols. Computer Communications 25(17), 1606–1621 (2002)
15. Kremer, S., Raskin, J.-F.: A Game-Based Verification of Non-repudiation and Fair Exchange Protocols. In: Larsen, K.G., Nielsen, M. (eds.) CONCUR 2001. LNCS, vol. 2154, pp. 551–565. Springer, Heidelberg (2001)
16. Lowe, G.: A Hierarchy of Authentication Specification. In: 10th Computer Security Foundations Work., CSFW, Rockport, Massachusetts, USA, pp. 31–44. IEEE Computer Society, Los Alamitos (1997)

17. Markowitch, O., Kremer, S.: An Optimistic Non-repudiation Protocol with Transparent Trusted Third Party. In: Davida, G.I., Frankel, Y. (eds.) ISC 2001. LNCS, vol. 2200, pp. 363–378. Springer, Heidelberg (2001)

18. Markowitch, O., Roggeman, Y.: Probabilistic Non-Repudiation without Trusted Third Party. In: 2nd Work. on Security in Communication Networks, Amalfi, Italy (1999)

19. Ochsenschläger, P., Repp, J., Rieke, R., Nitsche, U.: The SH-Verification Tool - Abstraction-Based Verification of Co-operating Systems. Formal Aspects of Computing 10(4), 381–404 (1998)

20. Pagnia, H., Gärtner, F.C.: On the Impossibility of Fair Exchange without a Trusted Third Party. Technical Report TUD-BS-1999-02, Darmstadt University of Technology, Darmstadt, Germany (1999)

21. Pancho-Festin, S., Gollmann, D.: On the Formal Analyses of the Zhou-Gollmann Non-repudiation Protocol. In: Dimitrakos, T., Martinelli, F., Ryan, P.Y.A., Schneider, S. (eds.) FAST 2005. LNCS, vol. 3866, pp. 5–15. Springer, Heidelberg (2006)

22. Roscoe, A.W., Hoare, C.A.R., Bird, R.: The Theory and Practice of Concurrency. Prentice Hall PTR, Englewood Cliffs (1997)

23. Ryan, P., Goldsmith, M., Lowe, G., Roscoe, B., Schneider, S.: Modelling and Analysis of Security Protocols. Addison Wesley, Reading (2000)

24. Santiago, J., Vigneron, L.: Optimistic Non-repudiation Protocol Analysis. In: Sauveron, D., Markantonakis, K., Bilas, A., Quisquater, J.-J. (eds.) WISTP 2007. LNCS, vol. 4462, pp. 90–101. Springer, Heidelberg (2007)

25. Schneider, S.: Formal Analysis of a Non-Repudiation Protocol. In: Proc. of The 11th Computer Security Foundations Work, pp. 54–65. IEEE Computer Society Press, Los Alamitos (1998)

26. Shmatikov, V., Mitchell, J.C.: Analysis of abuse-free contract signing. In: Frankel, Y. (ed.) FC 2000. LNCS, vol. 1962, pp. 174–191. Springer, Heidelberg (2001)

27. Wei, K., Heather, J.: Towards verification of timed non-repudiation protocols. In: Dimitrakos, T., Martinelli, F., Ryan, P.Y.A., Schneider, S. (eds.) FAST 2005. LNCS, vol. 3866, pp. 244–257. Springer, Heidelberg (2006)

28. Wei, K., Heather, J.: A theorem-proving approach to verification of fair non-repudiation protocols. In: Dimitrakos, T., Martinelli, F., Ryan, P.Y.A., Schneider, S. (eds.) FAST 2006. LNCS, vol. 4691, pp. 202–219. Springer, Heidelberg (2007)

29. Zhou, J., Deng, R.H., Bao, F.: Evolution of fair non-repudiation with TTP. In: Pieprzyk, J.P., Safavi-Naini, R., Seberry, J. (eds.) ACISP 1999. LNCS, vol. 1587, pp. 258–269. Springer, Heidelberg (1999)

30. Zhou, J., Gollmann, D.: A Fair Non-repudiation Protocol. In: IEEE Symp. on Security and Privacy, Oakland, CA, USA, pp. 55–61. IEEE Computer Society, Los Alamitos (1996)

31. Zhou, J., Gollmann, D.: Towards verification of non-repudiation protocols. In: Proc. of Int. Refinement Work. and Formal Methods Pacific, Canberra, Australia, pp. 370–380 (September 1998)

Petri Net Security Checker: Structural Non-interference at Work

Simone Frau[1,*], Roberto Gorrieri[2], and Carlo Ferigato[3]

[1] Information Security, ETH Zurich, 8092 Zurich, Switzerland
`simone.frau@inf.ethz.ch`
[2] Dipartimento di Scienze dell'Informazione, Università di Bologna,
Mura A. Zamboni, 7, 40127 Bologna, Italy
`gorrieri@cs.unibo.it`
[3] Joint Research Centre - European Commission,
Via E. Fermi, 1, 21027 Ispra (VA), Italy
`carlo.ferigato@jrc.it`

Abstract. Structural non-interference is a semi-static technique defined over Petri nets to check the absence of illegal information flows. This paper presents the main algorithmic features of this new technique and its implementation in a software tool, called the Petri Net Security Checker.

1 Introduction

Non-interference has been defined in the literature as an extensional property based on some observational semantics: the high part of a system does not interfere with the low part if whatever is done at the high level produces *no visible effect* on the low part of the system. The original notion of non-interference in [10] was defined, using trace semantics, for system programs that are deterministic. Generalized notions of non-interference were then designed to include (nondeterministic) labeled transition systems and finer notions of observational semantics such as bisimulation (see, e.g., [14,6,13,15,8]). The security properties in this class are based on the dynamics of systems; they are defined by means of one (or more) equivalence check(s); hence, non-interference checking is as difficult as equivalence checking, a well-studied hard problem in concurrency theory.

One relevant property in this class is the bisimulation-based property *BNDC* (Bisimulation Non-Deducibility on Composition) proposed by Focardi and Gorrieri some years ago [6,8] on a CCS-like [12] process algebra. *BNDC* basically states that a system R is secure if it is bisimilar to R in parallel with any high level process Π w.r.t. the low actions the two systems can perform.

Intuitively, the many definitions of non-interference that have been proposed try to capture the essence of information flow as an extensional property. On

---

[*] Frau's work was mainly conducted at the Joint Research Centre of the European Commission, Ispra.

P. Degano, J. Guttman, and F. Martinelli (Eds.): FAST 2008, LNCS 5491, pp. 210–225, 2009.

the contrary, one may think that there are clear physical reasons for the occurrence of an information flow, that can be better understood if one exploits a computational model where causality of actions and conflict among actions can be modelled directly. Indeed, this is not the case of labeled transitions systems, a typical example of an *interleaving* model, where parallelism is not primitive.

For this reason, in [1,2,3] Busi and Gorrieri have shown that these extensional non–interference properties can be naturally defined also on Petri Nets, in particular on Elementary Nets [5], a well-known model of computation where causality and conflict are primitive concepts. More interestingly, they address the problem of defining statically non-interference for Elementary Nets, by looking at the structure of the net systems under investigation:

- in order to better understand the relationship between a flow of information and the causality (or conflict) relation between the activities originating such a flow, hence grounding more firmly the intuition about what is an interference, and
- in order to find more efficiently checkable non-interference properties that are sufficient (sometimes also necessary) conditions for those that have already received some support in the literature, such as *BNDC*.

Structural non-interference is defined on the basis of the absence of particular places in the net. We identify two special classes of places: *causal places*, i.e., places for which there are an incoming high transition and an outgoing low transition; and, *conflict places*, i.e. places for which there are both low and high outgoing transitions. Intuitively, causal places represent potential source of interference because the occurrence of the high transition is a prerequisite for the execution of the low transition. Similarly, conflict places represent potential source of interference because if the low event is not executable, then we can derive that a certain high transition has occurred. The absence of causal and conflict places is clearly a static property that can be easily checked by a simple inspection of the (finite) net structure; interestingly enough, this is a sufficient condition to ensure *BNDC*.

In order to characterize more precisely *BNDC*, the notion of causal place and conflict place is slightly refined, yielding the so-called *active* causal place and *active* conflict place. These new definitions are based also on a limited exploration of the state-space of the net (i.e. of its marking graph), hence, the absence of such places is not a purely structural property, rather a hybrid property. When active causal and active conflict places are absent, we get a property, called *Positive Place–Based Non–Interference* (*PBNI+* for short), which turns out to be equivalent to *BNDC* (proof in [3]). This result is rather surprising because the two properties are defined in a very different way.

1.1   Contribution of This Paper

In this paper, we investigate the algorithmic properties of *PBNI+*. First we show that, given an elementary net with p places, n transitions and f arcs, the complexity of checking for the absence of potential causal/conflict places is $O(f + p)$. Then, once singled out potential causal/conflict places, the check that such a potential place is active takes $O(pn2^{3p})$ in the worst case, because it is necessary to build the whole marking graph (that is exponential in the size of the net). Therefore, depending on the shape of the net, the complexity of *PBNI+* varies in the range between $O(f + p)$ and $O(pn2^{3p})$.

It is interesting to observe that *BNDC* was proved to be decidable in [11] over labeled transitions systems with an algorithm that is *exponential* in the number of the states. Even if the two models are different and so a comparison may be unfair, we point out that our procedure for deciding *BNDC* is *cubic* in the number of states of the marking graph of the net, which in turn is exponential in the number of the places of the net.

These algorithms have been implemented in a software tool, called the Petri Net Security Checker (PNSC for short), which provides functionalities for creating, editing and executing Petri nets, as well as automatically detecting places that are potential/active and causal/conflict.

The paper is organised as follows. In Section 2 we recall the basic definitions about Elementary Net systems, the dynamic non-interference property *BNDC* and the structural property *PBNI+*. In Section 3 we discuss the complexity of checking *PBNI+*. In Section 4 we describe the details of the PNSC tool, its functionalities and its implementation, besides showing its application to a small case study. Finally, some conclusive remarks are drawn in Section 5.

2   Background

2.1   Elementary Net Systems

Here we introduce basic definitions about the class of Petri Nets we use. Some familiarity with Petri net terminology is assumed. More details in [5,2].

Definition 1. *A transition system is a triple $TS = (St, E, \rightarrow)$ where*

- *St is the set of states*
- *E is the set of events*
- *$\rightarrow\, \subseteq St \times E \times St$ is the transition relation.*

In the following we use $s \xrightarrow{e} s'$ to denote $(s, e, s') \in\, \rightarrow$. Given a transition $s \xrightarrow{e} s'$, s is called the source, *s' the* target *and e the* label *of the transition. A* rooted transition system *is a pair (TS, s_0) where $TS = (St, E, \rightarrow)$ is a transition system and $s_0 \in St$ is the* initial state.

Definition 2. *An* elementary net *is a tuple $N = (S, T, F)$, where*

- *S and T are the (finite) sets of* places *and* transitions, *such that $S \cap T = \emptyset$*
- *$F \subseteq (S \times T) \cup (T \times S)$ is the flow relation, usually represented as a set of directed arcs connecting places and transitions.*

A subset of S is called a *marking*. Given a marking m and a place s, if $s \in m$ then we say that the place s contains a token, otherwise we say that s is empty.

Let $x \in S \cup T$. The *preset* of x is the set $^\bullet x = \{y \mid F(y, x)\}$. The *postset* of x is the set $x^\bullet = \{y \mid F(x, y)\}$. The preset and postset functions are generalized in the obvious way to set of elements: if $X \subseteq S \cup T$ then $^\bullet X = \bigcup_{x \in X} {}^\bullet x$ and $X^\bullet = \bigcup_{x \in X} x^\bullet$. A transition t is enabled at marking m if $^\bullet t \subseteq m$ and $t^\bullet \cap m = \emptyset$. The firing (execution) of a transition t enabled at m produces the marking $m' = (m \setminus {}^\bullet t) \cup t^\bullet$. This is usually written as $m[t\rangle m'$. With the notation $m[t\rangle$ we mean that there exists m' such that $m[t\rangle m'$.

An *elementary net system* is a pair (N, m_0), where N is an elementary net and m_0 is a marking of N, called *initial marking*. With abuse of notation, we use (S, T, F, m_0) to denote the net system $((S, T, F), m_0)$.

The set of *markings reachable from* m, denoted by $[m\rangle$, is defined as the least set of markings such that

- $m \in [m\rangle$
- if $m' \in [m\rangle$ and there exists a transition t such that $m'[t\rangle m''$ then $m'' \in [m\rangle$.

The set of *firing sequences* is defined inductively as follows:

- m_0 is a firing sequence;
- if $m_0[t_1\rangle m_1 \ldots [t_n\rangle m_n$ is a firing sequence and $m_n[t_{n+1}\rangle m_{n+1}$ then also $m_0[t_1\rangle m_1 \ldots [t_n\rangle m_n[t_{n+1}\rangle m_{n+1}$ is a firing sequence.

Given a firing sequence $m_0[t_1\rangle m_1 \ldots [t_n\rangle m_n$, we call $t_1 \ldots t_n$ a *transition sequence*. We use σ to range over transition sequences.

The *marking graph* of a net system N is the transition system

$$MG(N) = ([m_0\rangle, T, \{(m, t, m') \mid m \in [m_0\rangle \wedge t \in T \wedge m[t\rangle m'\})$$

A net is *transition simple* if the following condition holds for all $x, y \in T$: if $^\bullet x = {}^\bullet y$ and $x^\bullet = y^\bullet$ then $x = y$. A marking m contains a *contact* if there exists a transition $t \in T$ such that $^\bullet t \subseteq m$ and $not(m[t\rangle)$. A net system is *contact–free* if no marking in $[m_0\rangle$ contains a contact. A net system is *reduced* if each transition can occur at least one time: for all $t \in T$ there exists $m \in [m_0\rangle$ such that $m[t\rangle$. In the following we consider contact-free elementary net systems that are transition simple and reduced.

2.2 A Dynamic Non-interference Property: *BNDC*

Our aim is to analyse systems that can perform two kinds of actions: high level actions, representing the interaction of the system with high level users, and low level actions, representing the interaction with low level users. We want to verify if the interplay between the high user and the high part of the system can affect the view of the system as observed by a low user. We assume that the low user knows the structure of the system, and we check if, in spite of this, he is not able to infer the behavior of the high user by observing the low view of the execution of the system. Hence, we consider nets whose set of transitions is partitioned into two subsets: the set H of high level transitions and the set L of low level transitions. To emphasize this partition we use the following notation. Let L and H be two disjoint sets: with (S, L, H, F, m_0) we denote the net system $(S, L \cup H, F, m_0)$.

Among the many non-interference properties defined by Focardi and Gorrieri in [6,7,8], here we consider *BNDC* (Bisimulation Non-Deducibility on Composition). To properly define it over Petri nets, we need some auxiliary definitions: the operations of parallel composition (in TCSP-like style [4]) and restriction (in CCS-like style [12]), as well as a notion of low-view bisimulation.

Definition 3. *Let $N_1 = (S_1, L_1, H_1, F_1, m_{0,1})$ and $N_2 = (S_2, L_2, H_2, F_2, m_{0,2})$ be two net systems such that $S_1 \cap S_2 = \emptyset$ and $(L_1 \cup L_2) \cap (H_1 \cup H_2) = \emptyset$. The parallel composition of N_1 and N_2 is the net system*

$$N_1 \mid N_2 = (S_1 \cup S_2, L_1 \cup L_2, H_1 \cup H_2, F_1 \cup F_2, m_{0,1} \cup m_{0,2})$$

Note that synchronization occurs over those (low or high) transitions that are shared by the two nets, i.e., a transition t that occurs both in N_1 and N_2 has preset (postset), in $N_1 \mid N_2$, given by the union of the disjoint presets (postsets) in N_1 and N_2, respectively.

Definition 4. *Let $N = (S, L, H, F, m_0)$ be a net system and let U be a set of transitions. The restriction on U is defined as $N \backslash U = (S, L', H', F', m_0)$, where:*

$$L' = L \setminus U$$
$$H' = H \setminus U$$
$$F' = F \setminus (S \times U \cup U \times S)$$

The non-interference property we are going to introduce is based on some notion of *low* observability of a system, i.e., what can be observed of a system from the point of view of low users. The low view of a transition sequence is nothing but the subsequence where high level transitions are discarded.

Definition 5. *Let $N = (S, L, H, F, m_0)$ be an elementary net system. The* low view *of a transition sequence σ of N is defined as follows:*

$$\Lambda_N(\varepsilon) = \varepsilon$$
$$\Lambda_N(\sigma t) = \begin{cases} \Lambda_N(\sigma)t & \text{if } t \in L \\ \Lambda_N(\sigma) & \text{otherwise} \end{cases}$$

Then, a variant of bisimulation [12] can be defined in such a way that only the low behaviour is considered.

Definition 6. *Let $N_1 = (S_1, L_1, H_1, F_1, m_{0,1})$ and $N_2 = (S_2, L_2, H_2, F_2, m_{0,2})$ be two net systems. A low–view bisimulation from N_1 to N_2 is a relation R on $\mathcal{P}(S_1) \times \mathcal{P}(S_2)$ such that if $(m_1, m_2) \in R$ then for all $t \in \bigcup_{i=1,2} L_i \cup H_i$:*

- *if $m_1[t\rangle m_1'$ then there exist σ, m_2' such that $m_2[\sigma\rangle m_2'$, $\Lambda_{N_1}(t) = \Lambda_{N_2}(\sigma)$ and $(m_1', m_2') \in R$*
- *if $m_2[t\rangle m_2'$ then there exist σ, m_1' such that $m_1[\sigma\rangle m_1'$, $\Lambda_{N_2}(t) = \Lambda_{N_1}(\sigma)$ and $(m_1', m_2') \in R$*

If $N_1 = N_2$ we say that R is a low–view bisimulation on N_1.

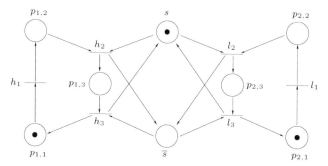

Fig. 1. The net system for a mutually exclusive access to a shared resource

We say that N_1 is low–view bisimilar to N_2, denoted by $N_1 \approx^{\Lambda}_{bis} N_2$, if there exists a low–view bisimulation R from N_1 to N_2 such that $(m_{0,1}, m_{0,2}) \in R$.

Now we are ready to define *BNDC*.

Definition 7. *Let $N = (S, L, H, F, m_0)$ be a net system. N is BNDC iff for all high-level nets $K = (S_K, \emptyset, H_K, F_K, m_{0,K})$: $N \backslash H \approx^{\Lambda}_{bis} (N \mid K) \backslash (H \setminus H_K)$.*

The left-hand term $N \backslash H$ represents the system N when isolated from high-level users (hence, the low view of N in isolation), while the right-hand term expresses the low view of N interacting with the (common transitions of the) high environment K (note that the activities resulting from such interactions are invisible by the definition of low view equivalence). *BNDC* is a very intuitive property: whatever high level system K is interacting with N, the low effect is unobservable. However, it is difficult to check this property because of the universal quantification over high systems.

Example 1. As a simple case study and running example, consider the net in Figure 1, which represents a mutually exclusive access to a shared resource (represented by the token in s) by a high-user (left part of the net) and a low-user (right part of the net). Even if it might appear, at first sight, that the system is secure (and indeed, it is *BSNNI* (Bisimulation Strong Nondeterministic Non-Interference) [8]), actually it is not secure because a low level user can detect if a high-level user has deadlocked the system. Indeed, if the high-level user represented in the net K in Figure 2 wants to interact with the user in Figure 1, then a deadlock is reached after performing the sequence $h_1 h_2$ and the low level user can detect this because (s)he is not able to interact with the net. As a matter of fact, *BNDC* is not satisfied, as K makes invalid the equivalence check in the definition of *BNDC*.

2.3   Structural Non-interference

Consider a net system $N = (S, L, H, F, m_0)$. Consider a low level transition l of the net: if l can fire, then we know that the places in the preset of l are marked before the firing of l; moreover, we know that such places become unmarked

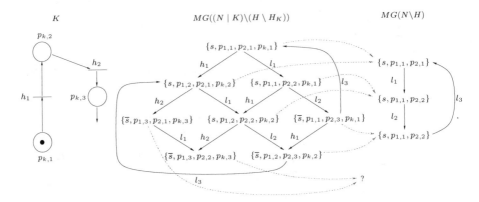

Fig. 2. The shared resource net system is not $BNDC$

after the firing of l. If there exists a high level transition h that produces a token in a place s in the preset of l (see the system N_1 in Figure 3), then the low level user can infer that h has occurred if he can perform the low level transition l. We note that there exists a causal dependency between the transitions h and l, because the firing of h produces a token that is consumed by l. In this case we will say s is a potential causal place.

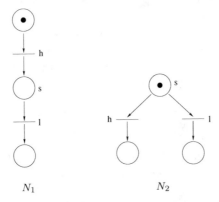

Fig. 3. Examples of net systems containing causal and conflict places

Consider now the situation illustrated in the system N_2 of Figure 3: in this case, place s is in the preset of both l and h, i.e., l and h are competing for the use of the resource represented by the token in s. Aware of the existence of such a place, a low user knows that the high-level action h has been performed, if he is not able to perform the low-level action l. Place s represents a conflict between transitions l and h, because the firing of h prevents l from firing. In this case we will call s a potential conflict place.

In order to avoid the definition of a security notion that is too strong, and that rules out systems that do not reveal information on the high-level actions that have been performed, we need to refine the concepts illustrated above. In particular the potential causal place is an active causal place if there is an execution where the token produced by the high level transition is eventually consumed by the low level transition. Similarly, a potential conflict place is active if the token that could be consumed immediately by a high level transition can be later on also consumed by a low level transition. The formal definitions follow.

Definition 8. *Let* $N = (S, L, H, F, m_0)$ *be an elementary net system. Let* s *be a place of* N *such that* $s^\bullet \cap L \neq \emptyset$ *(i.e., a token in* s *can be consumed by a low transition).*

The place $s \in S$ *is a* potentially causal place *if* $^\bullet s \cap H \neq \emptyset$ *(i.e., a token in* s *can be produced by a high transition). A potentially causal place* s *is an* active causal place *if the following condition holds: there exist* $l \in s^\bullet \cap L$, $h \in {}^\bullet s \cap H$, $m \in [m_0\rangle$ *and a transition sequence* σ *such that* $m[h\sigma l\rangle$ *and* $s \notin t^\bullet$ *for all* $t \in \sigma$.

The place $s \in S$ *is a* potentially conflict place *if* $s^\bullet \cap H \neq \emptyset$ *(i.e., the token in* s *can be consumed also by a high transition). A potentially conflict place is an* active conflict place *if the following condition holds: there exist* $l \in s^\bullet \cap L$, $h \in s^\bullet \cap H$, $m \in [m_0\rangle$ *and a transition sequence* σ *such that* $m[h\rangle$, $m[\sigma l\rangle$ *and* $s \notin t^\bullet$ *for all* $t \in \sigma$.

Definition 9. *Let* $N = (S, L, H, F, m_0)$ *be an elementary net system. We say that* N *is PBNI+ (positive Place Based Non-Interference) if, for all* $s \in S$, s *is neither an active causal place nor an active conflict place.*

The following non-trivial result, proved in [3], states that the behavioural non-interference property *BNDC* is equivalent to the semi-static, structural property *PBNI+*.

Theorem 1. *Let* $N = (S, L, H, F, m_0)$ *be an elementary net system. Then* N *is PBNI+ iff* N *is BNDC.*

An obvious consequence is that if N has no *potentially causal* and *potentially conflict* places, then N is *BNDC*. Hence, a simple strategy to check if N is *BNDC* is to first identify potential causal/conflict places, a procedure that we show in the next section to be of complexity $O(f + p)$ in the size of the net (p is the number of places and f of arcs). If no place of these sorts is found, then N is *PBNI+*, hence *BNDC*. Otherwise, any such a candidate place should be better studied to check if it is actually an *active* causal/conflict place, a procedure that requires a limited exploration of the marking graph.

Observe that the net in Figure 1 of our running example is not *PBNI+* because place s is an active conflict (and also active causal) place.

3   *PBNI+* **Verification Algorithms**

Verification of *PBNI+* requires two separate steps: first, detection of potential causal places and potential conflict ones; then, checking if such places are active (causal/conflict) places.

We assume to use certain data structures. Precisely, a *Net* will be a structure containing an ordered list of *places*, an ordered list of *transitions* and a list of places (subset of the above mentioned *places* list) representing the *initial marking*. We also assume places in the *initial marking* list maintain the same order they have in the *places* list, so that all operations on sets of places (such as union, intersection and difference) can be done in $O(p)$.

Each place (each transition) has associated its own *preset* and *postset*, that are represented by lists of the opposite elements (transitions or places, respectively). As for the *initial marking* list in a *Net*, we will assume the nodes in the *preset* and *postset* lists appear in the same order they do in the lists they are taken from, so to be able to perform all operations on sets in linear time w.r.t. the number of nodes ($O(p)$ or $O(n)$, respectively). For convenience, we will assume a *Net* also contains a list of *arcs* (as specified by the flow relation F, $|F| = f$), thus that we can occasionally cycle on it in $O(f)$ time rather than $O(np)$ (inherent upper bound for f).

3.1   Potential Places Detection

Detecting potential places is a purely structural procedure, easy and computationally light-weight. Let us consider detection of potential causal places in a net N with p places and f arcs, and each place has three dedicated boolean variables for keeping track of the examined arcs: $highPre$, $lowPost$ and $highPost$. This consists of the following steps (each one annotated with an estimate of its worst-case computational cost):

- for each arc a in the net N: – $O(f)$ times
    - if a's source is a transition t – $O(1)$
        - if t is high then set $highPre$ of a's target as $true$ – $O(1)$
    - else
        - if t is low then set $lowPost$ of a's source as $true$ – $O(1)$
- for each place p in the net N: – $O(p)$ times
    - if p's $highPre$ and $lowPost$ are true, then add p to the set of computed potential causal places – $O(1)$

Detection of potential conflict places differs slightly, in that it will only set $highPost$ instead of $highPre$.

As all inner instructions cost $O(1)$, the final procedure cost will be the sum of the two cycles, namely $O(f + p)$.

3.2   Active Places Detection

Differently from the above, detection of active places is a complex (hence, also heavier) procedure because it has to analyze – though partially – the dynamic behaviour of the net.

First of all, we need a procedure to build the marking graph, i.e., the state space of the net.[1] We represent such a graph as a list of structures. Each of these structures is composed of a marking m, (where each marking is a set of places represented in the same fashion as the *initial marking* in Net), and of a list of pairs (t, m'), where t is an enabled transition and m' is the marking reached by firing t, i.e., $m[t\rangle m'$.

Under these modelling assumptions, the algorithm is composed of the following instructions (each annotated with an estimate of its worst-case, computational cost):

- create the marking list *list* with the initial marking as its only element – $O(1)$
- for each marking m in *list*: – $O(2^p)$ times
  - for each transition t: – $O(n)$ times
    - if t is enabled at m: – $O(p)$
      - compute the marking m' reachable from m by firing t – $O(p)$
      - if m' is not already in *list*, add $(m', emptylist)$ to *list* – $O(2^p)$
      - add to the list associated to m the new pair (t, m') – $O(1)$

The procedure acts mostly as a breadth-first visit: we add first the initial marking, and start a cycle exploring the graph. For each marking in the list, we compute the marking every enabled transition leads to and add the corresponding pair (enabled transition, reached marking) to the currently examined marking. When we meet a new marking, we add it to the queue and this will be examined later as the cycle proceeds.

Since the heaviest operation in the innermost cycle is checking whether the marking graph already contains a marking ($O(2^p)$), the procedure's cost is bound to the product of this by the weight of the nested cycles over the places and transitions of the net. Therefore the procedure's final cost will be $O(n 2^{2p})^2$.

Notice also that this procedure can take any marking as initial marking, which means that it can compute every possible subgraph rooted in the given marking. Furthermore, also a procedure for creating a marking graph restricted on a set of transitions can be easily obtained from the above. It is easy to see this trivially involves including only one more check and does not change computational costs.

We can now introduce a procedure that searches for active causal places over the net. Intuitively, we do the following steps:

- find potentially causal places – $O(f + p)$
- for each place s among these: – $O(p)$ times

---

[1] Notice that, since each marking is a set of places, the marking graph can contain up to 2^p states. Hence, the state space we are dealing with is inherently exponential in the number p of places.

[2] A further optimization could be using a search tree instead of a list for representing the *marking graph*, once an appropriate order on the places is introduced such that induces an order on the markings as well. That would reduce look up time from $O(2^p)$ to $O(p)$, and the whole procedure would cost $O(np2^p)$.

- scan the markings in the marking graph, and single out only those which are reached through high transitions in $\bullet s$. – $O(2^{2p})$
- for each marking m among these: – $O(2^p)$ times
  - create a new marking graph rooted in m and restricted on all transitions containing s in their postset – $O(n2^{2p})$
  - search among its markings for one enabling any low transition in $s^\bullet$. If any is found, add s to the list of active causal places returned – $O(2^p)$

The active places so found perfectly comply with Definition 8. Indeed, for each potential causal place we single out all markings reached through a high transition h in $\bullet s$, that is $m[h\rangle m'$. Then, for each of these, we create a marking graph rooted in m and restricted on all transitions belonging to $\bullet s$. In such a marking graph every marking is reached through a sequence of transitions that do not produce new tokens in s ($s \notin t^\bullet$ for all $t \in \sigma$), therefore if we find one that enables a low transition $l \in s^\bullet$, we have $m'[\sigma l\rangle$, and hence $m[h\sigma l\rangle$.

The procedure is as heavy as computing the restricted marking graph ($O(n2^{2p})$) for each marking ($O(2^p)$) and each place in the net ($O(p)$), therefore it has a final cost of $O(pn2^{3p})$ (or $O(p^2 n2^{2p})$ if the optimization in footnote 2 is implemented).

Finally, a procedure verifying *PBNI+* would just call the previous one and the one to detect active conflict places (which, intuitively enough, has same computational costs). Needless to say, procedure's final cost, in the worst case, is $O(pn2^{3p})$ as well. Note that, since the number of states is $O(2^p)$, the procedure for verifying *PBNI+* (hence *BNDC*) is actually *cubic* in the number of states.

Note, moreover, that in practice, the cost of checking *PBNI+* is much lower: (*i*) it might be the case that there are no potential causal/conflict places and so in this case the complexity is $O(f + p)$; (*ii*) the number of potential places is usually small w.r.t. to p; and, in particular, (*iii*) the number of reachable markings of the marking graph is generally much lower than 2^p.

4 Petri Net Security Checker

The tool, named *Petri Net Security Checker* (*PNSC* for short) [9], was written in Java [16], using the Eclipse development platform [17].

Figure 4 shows the tool's interface, which provides the user, in a single working environment, with different functionalities, that can be grouped into three main categories: editing, execution and net properties checking.

4.1 Editing

First of all, *PNSC* allows the user to create, save and open Petri nets. For these operations the tool uses the *Petri Net Markup Language* format [18], the standard format for Petri nets interchange, thus ensuring compatibility with external programs for further analysis of the nets (e.g. PIPE2 [19]).

By means of an intuitive toolbar, the user can draw the net. This includes basic operations as drawing places and (both high and low) transitions, draw

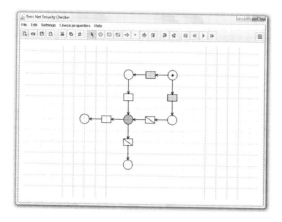

Fig. 4. Petri Net Security Checker main window

arcs between them and set the initial marking of the net. Furthermore, it is possible to select portions of the net to carry out further operations as deleting, cutting, copying and pasting.

Being designed for incremental editing of nets in conjunction with checking their security, we developed different view modes to make comparison easier. In fact, nets can be cloned and placed side by side to be edited and compared concurrently, as shown in Figure 5.

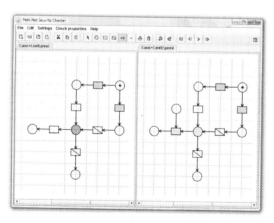

Fig. 5. Comparison mode

In addition, the tool keeps track of all editing steps, so that each one can be undone/redone.

4.2   Execution

It is also possible to graphically simulate net executions (commonly referred to as *token game animation*).

The user can either fire one of the currently enabled transitions (highlighted in green as in Figure 4 and in Figure 5) by double clicking on it, or he can start a timed random execution, which consists of firing, at regular time intervals, a random transition among the enabled ones. In this case also, the tool keeps track of all firing steps, so that it is possible to step back (and, afterwards, forward) to previous (respectively, following) markings.

4.3   Properties Check

Finally, the most distinctive functionalities of $PNSC$ pertain to the verification of the net's properties.

First, it is possible to check whether a net is simple, reduced and contact free[3]. Whenever one of these does not hold, all nodes that do not comply with it ·are highlighted in grey (as in Figure 6).

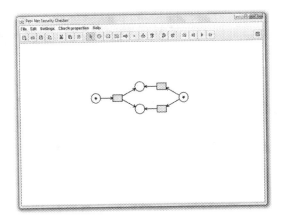

Fig. 6. A not contact-free net

The main functionality of our tool though is finding both potential and active causal/conflict places in the net, using the algorithms described in Section 3. When these checks are activated, potential causal/conflict places will be highlighted in orange, while active causal/conflict ones will be highlighted in red, as shown in Figure 7, which depicts the net already discussed in Figure 1.

Furthermore, for each potential/active place found it is possible to pinpoint and highlight the transitions and markings involved in the causality or conflict situation from the rest of the net, as in Figure 8, allowing a better inspection of the problem.

---

[3] These checks are of minor complexity, namely $O(np^2)$, $O(n2^p)$ and $O(pn2^p)$, respectively.

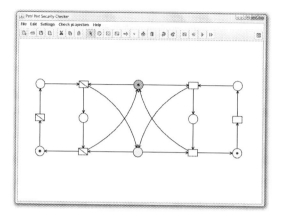

Fig. 7. Potential causal/conflict places will be highlighted in orange, active ones in red

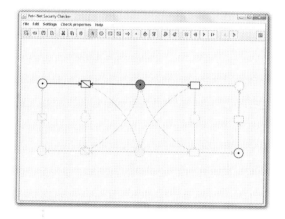

Fig. 8. Focus on the active conflict situation

5   Conclusion

In this paper we presented the tool *Petri Net Security Checker* for building Petri nets with transitions of two different confidentiality levels and check a structural security property on them, namely *PBNI+*.

The tool can actually check also some behavioural security properties, such as *SBNDC* and *BSNNI* [2]. Interestingly enough, *PBNI+* is proved to be equivalent to the behavioural property *BNDC* which is not obviously decidable; hence, the algorithms we presented in Section 3 offer a decidability proof for *BNDC* over Elementary Net Systems. The only paper we know offering a decidability result for *BNDC* is [11] where an exponential (in the number of states) procedure is presented for labeled transition systems. Our result is actually for a rather different model (unlabeled elementary net systems) and so it might be unfair to make a comparison; nonetheless, our decision procedure is cubic in the number of states of the marking graph (in turn exponential in the number of places).

We considered, for theoretical reasons in the implementation of our tool, only *Elementary Net Systems*, where places can contain at most one token. A natural generalization of this approach is to consider Place/Transition systems, where each place can contain more than one token. Such a class of nets is particularly interesting because the marking graph associated to a finite P/T net system may be infinite. In [3] Busi and Gorrieri claim that *PBNI+* can be easily defined also on this richer class of nets and checked in a finite amount of time, and keep on being the same as *BNDC* and *SBNDC* also for P/T net systems. This is particularly interesting because bisimulation is not decidable over P/T nets, hence *BNDC* as well as *SBNDC* are not checkable at all! This extension would also possibly provide the first result of decidability of a behavioural information flow security property, like *BNDC*, on a class of infinite state systems. It is likely that an extension of *PBNI+* to cover P/T nets also could be easily followed by a corresponding extension of the tool.

Acknowledgements

The authors would like to thank the anonymous referees for helpful comments.

References

1. Busi, N., Gorrieri, R.: A Survey on Non-Interference with Petri Nets. In: Desel, J., Reisig, W., Rozenberg, G. (eds.) Lectures on Concurrency and Petri Nets. LNCS, vol. 3098, pp. 328–344. Springer, Heidelberg (2004)
2. Busi, N., Gorrieri, R.: Positive Non-Interference in Elementary and Trace Nets. In: Cortadella, J., Reisig, W. (eds.) ICATPN 2004. LNCS, vol. 3099, pp. 1–16. Springer, Heidelberg (2004)
3. Busi, N., Gorrieri, R.: Structural Non-Interference in Elementary and Trace Nets. In: Mathematical Structures in Computer Science (2008) (accepted for publication) (2008/4/3), http://www.cs.unibo.it/~gorrieri/Papers/bg08.ps
4. Brooks, S.D., Hoare, C.A.R., Roscoe, A.W.: A Theory of Communicating Sequential Processes. Journal of the ACM 31(3), 560–599 (1984)
5. Engelfriet, J., Rozenberg, G.: Elementary Net Systems. In: Reisig, W., Rozenberg, G. (eds.) APN 1998. LNCS, vol. 1491, pp. 12–121. Springer, Heidelberg (1998)
6. Focardi, R., Gorrieri, R.: A Classification of Security Properties. Journal of Computer Security 3(1), 5–33 (1995)
7. Focardi, R., Gorrieri, R.: The Compositional Security Checker: A Tool for the Verification of Information Flow Security Properties. IEEE Transactions on Software Engineering 23(9), 550–571 (1997)
8. Focardi, R., Gorrieri, R.: Classification of Security Properties (Part I: Information Flow). In: Focardi, R., Gorrieri, R. (eds.) FOSAD 2000. LNCS, vol. 2171, pp. 331–396. Springer, Heidelberg (2001)
9. Frau, S.: Uno strumento sotware per l'analisi di proprietà di sicurezza su reti di Petri. Master thesis (in Italian), University of Bologna (March 2008)

10. Goguen, J.A., Meseguer, J.: Security Policy and Security Models. In: Proc. of Symposium on Security and Privacy, pp. 11–20. IEEE CS Press, Los Alamitos (1982)
11. Martinelli, F.: Partial Model Checking and Theorem Proving for Ensuring Security Properties. In: Proc. of Computer Security Foundations Workshop, pp. 44–52. IEEE CS Press, Los Alamitos (1998)
12. Milner, R.: Communication and Concurrency. Prentice-Hall, Englewood Cliffs (1989)
13. Roscoe, A.W.: CSP and Determinism in Security Modelling. In: Proc. of IEEE Symposium on Security and Privacy, pp. 114–127. IEEE CS Press, Los Alamitos (1995)
14. Ryan, P.Y.A.: Mathematical models of computer security. In: Focardi, R., Gorrieri, R. (eds.) FOSAD 2000. LNCS, vol. 2171, pp. 1–62. Springer, Heidelberg (2001)
15. Ryan, P.Y.A., Schneider, S.: Process Algebra and Noninterference. In: Proc. of 12th Computer Security Foundations Workshop, pp. 214–227. IEEE CS Press, Los Alamitos (1999)
16. Java Technology. Sun Microsystems (2008/4/3), http://java.sun.com/
17. Eclipse.org. Eclipse Foundation (2008/4/3), http://www.eclipse.org/
18. http://www2.informatik.hu-berlin.de/top/pnml/download/about/PNML_LNCS.pdf (2008/4/3)
19. Platform Independent Petri Net Editor (2008/4/3), http://pipe2.sourceforge.net/

Verifying Multi-party Authentication Using Rank Functions and PVS*

Rob Verhoeven and Francien Dechesne

Department of Mathematics and Computer Science,
Technische Universiteit Eindhoven, The Netherlands
{r.h.a.verhoeven,f.dechesne}@tue.nl

Abstract. In this paper we present a fully formal correctness proof of a multi-party version of the Needham-Schroeder-Lowe public key authentication protocol. As the protocol allows for an arbitrary number of participants, the model consisting of all possible protocol executions exceeds any bounds imposed by model checking methods. By modelling the protocol in the CSP-framework and using the Rank Theorem we obtain an abstraction level that allows to give a correctness proof in PVS for the protocol with respect to authentication, for the protocol running in parallel in multiple instantiations, possibly with different numbers of agents for each instance.

This specific result shows how, more generally, the formalisation in CSP and application of the theorem prover PVS make full formal verification of multi-party security protocols possible.

1 Introduction

Mathematical modelling of security protocols and their requirements allows to reason about their correctness, under clearly stated assumptions. With formal verification methods subtle flaws of security protocols have been discovered and made expressible (a notable example being [1]).

A well-developed formal verification method is the use of model checkers. Although the capacity of model checking tools has increased significantly by the development of both hardware and theory, they require the protocol model to remain within certain practical bounds. For protocols designed for an *arbitrary* number of participants, the trace model can easily grow beyond these bounds. Therefore, multi-party protocol verification requires a higher abstraction level.

In this paper, we demonstrate how the (interactive) theorem prover PVS (Prototype Verification System) [2] can be successfully used for the verification of a multi-party authentication protocol. We analyse the generalisation, introduced in [3], of the Needham-Schroeder-Lowe public key protocol (NSL). It has been checked for a strong authentication requirement (*injective synchronisation* [4])

* Research funded by the Dutch Organisation for Scientific Research (NWO), project number 612.000.528: *Verification and Epistemics of Multi-Party Protocol Security*.

P. Degano, J. Guttman, and F. Martinelli (Eds.): FAST 2008, LNCS 5491, pp. 226–241, 2009.

with the model checker Scyther [5] for some small numbers of participants [6]. While [6] also gives a general proof on paper in terms of the operational semantics underlying Scyther, leaving some steps to intuition, we here present a first complete machine-checked correctness proof. For the proof, we used the framework in Communicating Sequential Processes (CSP) for security protocols and the rank function approach to prove authentication properties [7,8,9,10], and their implementation [11] in PVS. As a contribution to this framework, we updated the implementation for a current version of PVS (from version 3.2 to 4.2) and made the updated implementation available for use at [12]. Furthermore, we believe the proof presented here is the first fully formalised correctness proof for a multi-party authentication protocol, and the first *complete* correctness proof in the PVS-implementation to be available.

Related work. The rank function approach has succesfully been applied before to two-party protocols (NSL in [7], Woo-Lam in [13]). Another multi-party protocol, the Diffie-Hellman group protocol A-GDH.2, was analysed using the rank function approach in [14]. However, as [15] proved this protocol to be essentially flawed, [14] only finds a rank function (and thereby a correctness proof) for a restricted version of the protocol, assuming a weak intruder. From the failure to find a valid rank function for the original protocol, an attack was derived.

The theorem prover PVS has also been used before in the context of verification of multi-party protocols, viz. in [16] for an intrusion tolerant group communication protocol. However, there the relevant *authentication* requirements are only checked for some concrete instances using a model checker (Murphi). In the seminal paper [17] on using the theorem prover Isabelle for the verification of security protocols, a recursively defined multi-party authentication protocol is verified in an instantiation for 3 agents (*loc.cit.* Ch.6).

The use of signalling events to specify different authentication properties in CSP is discussed in [18]. The notion of authentication we prove in this paper amounts to injective agreement, which is weaker [4] than the property proven in [6]: injective *synchronisation*. It is an open question whether our result can be improved to injective synchronisation within the rank function approach.

Heather and Schneider have developed theory to systematically find a rank function for a protocol with its corresponding authentication requirements [8]. However, their automated implementation of this theory only works for two-party protocols (possibly involving a server) and although the theory is certainly capable of dealing with multi-party protocols, it requires too much effort to apply manually in our opinion.

Structure of the paper. In the next section, we introduce the multi-party generalisation of NSL we have verified. In Sect. 3 we describe the components of the CSP-framework that constitute the protocol model and its requirements, in order to show in Sect. 4 how these were filled in to build the PVS-proof.

For considerations of space, we assume familiarity with standard security protocol notions (nonces, public key cryptography, protocol roles) and CSP (cf. [19] for an extensive account), and we omit PVS-code: the code is available at [12].

2   A Multi-party Authentication Protocol

In this paper we analyse a generalisation of the well-known Needham-Schroeder-Lowe public key protocol (NSL)[1]. This generalisation aims to authenticate all participants of a protocol run to each other. Authentication informally means that after termination of a protocol run, all users involved are sure of each other's identity. This generalisation is a variation of the generalisation given by Cremers and Mauw [6]. We will refer to the original generalisation as the Generalised NSL public key protocol (GNSL) and the generalisation used here as GNSL'.[1]

As an example, an instantiation of the protocol for four users can be seen in Fig. 1, given as a Message Sequence Chart (MSC).[2] The formal protocol definition, in the style of [6], is shown in Fig. 2.

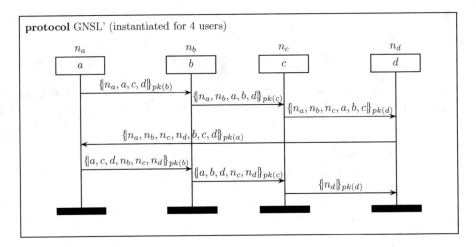

Fig. 1. The adaptation of the GNSL protocol studied in this paper (GNSL'), instantiated with four users

We see that in the first chain of messages that is sent around (the MsgA's) every user adds his nonce to the nonces he has received and forwards them along with information on the protocol run's participants. In the second chain of messages (the MsgB's) each user gets his nonce back and forwards the other nonces along. Since each user sends his nonce to the next user in line, encrypted with that user's public key, each user personally authenticates his successor, but delegates authentication of all other users to each of their predecessors.

Because of this delegation, the authentication property only has to hold when the users involved (in the property) are honest [6]. Honesty of a user means that

---

[1] The original generalisation does not include user identities in the second chain of messages. User identities are still omitted here in the last protocol message so that the protocol remains a generalisation of NSL. For the underlying reasons of considering the protocol version with user identities, please refer to [20].

[2] MSC made with [21].

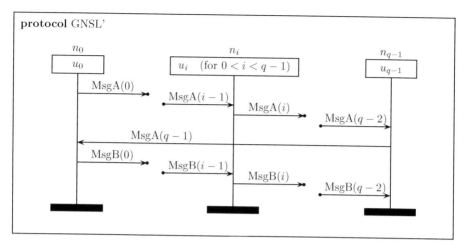

where $\mathrm{MsgA}(i) = \{\![[n_0 \ldots n_i], \mathrm{AL}(next(i))]\!\}_{pk(next(i))}$ $0 \le i < q$

$\mathrm{MsgB}(i) = \begin{cases} \{\![\mathrm{AL}(next(i)), [n_{i+1} \ldots n_{q-1}]]\!\}_{pk(next(i))} & 0 \le i < q-2 \\ \{\![[n_{q-1}]]\!\}_{pk(next(q-2))} & i = q-2 \end{cases}$

$next(i) = u_{(i+1) \bmod q}$

$\mathrm{AL}(x) = [u_0, u_1, \ldots, u_{q-1}] \backslash \{x\}$

Fig. 2. The definition of GNSL' for a run with q users ($2 \le q$). Slightly adapted from the definition of GNSL in [6].

he acts according to the protocol, will ignore any messages offered to him that do not fit into the protocol and is not controlled by the enemy, in the sense that the enemy does not possess his secret key. The network over which the protocol is communicating may be in control of an enemy (and arbitrarily many dishonest users). Note that such a requirement still allows for scenarios such as the famous attack on the Needham-Schroeder public key protocol (as in that case the property is 'authentication of a user a to b', who are both honest, even though the attack involves dishonest users) [1].

Note that the order of nonces and identities in the second chain of messages is reversed when compared to the order in the first chain of messages. This is to introduce a structural difference between both chains, so a message from the second chain will not be misinterpreted as a message from the first chain, and vice versa, assuming messages can be typechecked. Being able to typecheck messages is a reasonable assumption, as in practice, protocol messages can simply be tagged with typechecking information [22].

3   Technical Background

In this section, we present the technical background that is necessary for the treatise of our analysis of GNSL'. To verify its authentication properties, we have made use of Schneider's Rank Theorem [10] which applies to a CSP model of a network controlled by a Dolev-Yao enemy [23]. Firstly we will introduce this network, followed by the Rank Theorem and a short discussion on authentication.

3.1   Network Model

Here we present a standard Dolev-Yao network model, i.e. a network that is controlled by a virtually omnipotent enemy that can block, reroute, duplicate, fake and eavesdrop on messages. We use the CSP model for this network as presented in [8], as it is this model to which the Rank Theorem applies. This model has four parameters, namely

- a message datatype,
- a message generation relation,
- the enemy's initial knowledge, and
- the user processes.

The first parameter prescribes the types of the messages that are communicated over the network.

The two subsequent parameters of the network model belong to the process *Enemy*, modelling the Dolev-Yao intruder. These parameters are a set of messages *Init*, representing the enemy's initial knowledge, and a message generation relation $\vdash$ that prescribes which new messages can be derived from existing ones. $S \vdash m$ denotes that message m can be formed with knowledge of all messages in set S. This relation is used to model the enemy's ability to fake messages. With $\Box$ as the CSP operator for choice, the entire *Enemy* process is:

$$Enemy(S) = \bigsqcup_{\substack{i,j \in \mathcal{U} \\ \wedge\, m \in Message}} trans.i.j.m \rightarrow Enemy(S \cup \{m\})$$
$$\Box$$
$$\bigsqcup_{\substack{i,j \in \mathcal{U}\, \wedge \\ m \in Message\, |\, S \vdash m}} rec.i.j.m \rightarrow Enemy(S) \ .$$

The last parameter is a set $\mathcal{U}$, which contains the identities of all those who will use the network. For every identity $u \in \mathcal{U}$, there is a CSP process U (denoted in the upper case of the corresponding lower case user identity) describing the behaviour of user u. Each process U communicates by transmitting messages over channel *trans.u* and receiving messages over channel *rec.u*. The ability for users to perform multiple, concurrent runs of a protocol is modelled by partitioning nonces among users and then further partitioning them among every protocol role [8], parametrising the user processes on these nonces and interleaving these processes over an infinite set of nonces for each role and user. Then, there are infinitely many processes (one for each nonce). Due to the nature of the partitioning, this models each user being able to perform infinitely many concurrent runs and being able to act according to any protocol role. Furthermore, by distinctness of the sets of nonces for each user and role, the perfect cryptography assumption that each nonce is truly random is incorporated in the model.

Inspired by the naming conventions of Heather and Schneider [8], upper case $U^r(n)$ will provide the process of user u (lower case) fulfilling role r (from a set of protocol roles $\mathcal{R}$) in a protocol run using nonce n. User u's nonce n will come from the set $\mathcal{N}_u^r$, an infinite subset of all nonces $\mathcal{N}$. With $|||$ denoting CSP interleaving, a full user process (for any $u \in \mathcal{U}$) is then defined as:

$$U = \underset{r \in \mathcal{R}}{|||} \left(\underset{n \in \mathcal{N}_u^r}{|||} U^r(n) \right) .$$

As an example, consider a possible process definition for the initiator role of NSL (in the right part of Fig. 4):

$$U^{initiator}(n) = \underset{\substack{j \in \mathcal{U} \wedge \\ n_j \in \mathcal{N}}}{\square} \quad \begin{aligned} &trans.i.j.\{\!|n, i|\!\}_{pk(j)} \rightarrow \\ &rec.i.j.\{\!|n, n_j, j|\!\}_{pk(i)} \rightarrow \\ &trans.i.j.\{\!|n_j|\!\}_{pk(j)} \rightarrow \\ &commit(i, j, n) \rightarrow Stop . \end{aligned}$$

In order to model a network with a Dolev-Yao enemy, all communication passes through the enemy. This is accomplished by putting all user processes in parallel with the process modelling the enemy (*Enemy*) and having them synchronise on the *trans* and *rec* events. The CSP description of the network is given in (1). A visualisation of the network is shown in Fig. 3.

$$Network = \left(\underset{u \in \mathcal{U}}{|||} U \right) |[\{trans, rec\}]| \; Enemy(Init) . \tag{1}$$

3.2 Authentication

To illustrate the notion of 'authentication', we show NSL on the left in Fig. 4. Its goal as a security protocol is to authenticate user a to user b (and vice

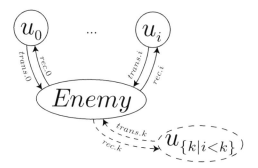

Fig. 3. A graphical representation of a network, where all communication is controlled by the enemy. u_0 to u_i represent honest users whereas $u_{\{k|i<k\}}$ represent users controlled by the enemy.

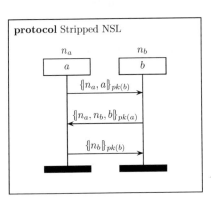

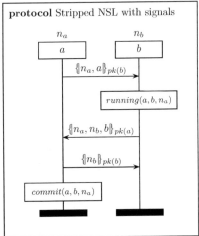

Fig. 4. The (stripped) Needham-Schroeder-Lowe public key protocol (NSL)

versa). To formalise such a goal, we add signalling events *running* and *commit* to the protocol (see the right part of Fig. 4), representing respectively a user's involvement in and completion of a particular protocol run. Authentication can then be formalised by demanding that, on any network running the protocol, no *commit*-event may have occurred without a corresponding *running*-event having occurred [9]. So we define a predicate **precedes** for sets of events R and T, acting on a process trace t:

$$R \text{ precedes } T \equiv t \upharpoonright T \neq \langle\rangle \Rightarrow t \upharpoonright R \neq \langle\rangle \; ,$$

then we want for all possible traces of the *Network* process, instantiated with NSL, that

$$\langle \forall i, j, n : i, j \in User \; \wedge \; n \in Nonce : \\ running(i, j, n) \text{ precedes } commit(i, j, n)\rangle \; .$$

Note that the informal term 'authentication' has many formalised interpretations [24,18,4]. The formalisation given here corresponds to non-injective agreement [10].

3.3 Rank Theorem

Schneider's Rank Theorem was first introduced in [7]. Here we use a slightly updated form of the theorem from [10,8], which we shall only briefly elaborate upon. For more information on the Rank Theorem, please refer to either of [10,8,11].

Theorem 1. *With the aforementioned Enemy process, initial knowledge Init, set of users U (with corresponding processes) and for sets of events R and T, if I is a predicate on messages (including signalling events) such that:*

R1: $\langle \forall m : m \in Init : I(m) \rangle$
R2: *For all sets of messages* S, $(\langle \forall m : m \in S : I(m) \rangle \wedge S \vdash m') \Rightarrow I(m')$
R3: $\langle \forall m : m \in T : \neg I(m) \rangle$
R4: $\langle \forall u : u \in \mathcal{U} : U \ \|[\ R\ ]\|\ Stop$ **sat maintains** $I \rangle$
then $\left(\||_{u \in \mathcal{U}} U \right) \ \|[\ \{trans, rec\}\ ]\|\ Enemy(Init)$ **sat** R **precedes** T .

The intuition is that the predicate (or 'rank function') I will hold for all 'safe' messages (messages the enemy may gain knowledge of). In addition, the predicate will fail for all 'unsafe' messages (messages that the enemy must not obtain).

The first condition, R1, can be interpreted as requiring that the enemy's initial knowledge is safe. R2 expresses that no unsafe messages can be derived from a set of safe messages and R3 demands that the messages in T are considered unsafe. Condition R4 is a bit more complicated, as it contains the predicate **sat maintains** I. The definition of a process P satisfying a specification S is:

$$P \text{ sat } S \equiv \langle \forall t : t \in traces(P) : S(t) \rangle \ ,$$

S is therefore a predicate on traces. The **maintains** I predicate is specific for this setting and states that all transmission events in a trace must satisfy I, unless there has been a reception event not satisfying I beforehand. As a whole, R4 expresses that no user process, when blocked on the events in set R (meaning it will halt when trying to perform an event from R), may produce an unsafe message if it has not received one earlier.

The rank theorem turns proving a trace predicate of the form 'R **precedes** T' into finding a predicate that satisfies conditions R1–R4. As we have chosen to formalise authentication as such a predicate, our task is reduced to providing the parameters for the network model and finding such a predicate.

3.4 PVS

The network model and Rank Theorem have been implemented in PVS by Evans [11]. We have obtained this implementation from him through personal correspondence and have updated it to the current version of PVS (4.2). Along with the complete code belonging to this paper (in the same PVS version) it is available online [12].

4 Verification

In this section we discuss the verification of the GNSL' protocol, within the network model of Sect. 3.1. The authentication property to prove is that each participant in a protocol run with q participants (where $2 \leq q$) is authenticated to each other participant, even if the protocol is running in a hostile environment and when arbitrarily many instantiations of the protocol (with any amount of users) are running in parallel. Code of the PVS theory corresponding to the analysis is available online [12].

For application of the rank theorem, we instantiated the network model by providing the message datatype, message generation relation, the enemy's initial knowledge and the user process. Each of these will be provided in the upcoming subsections. After that, we present a rank function that satisfies the conditions of the Rank Theorem.

4.1   Messages

This protocol uses standard concepts found in most security protocols (user identities, nonces, keys, concatenation, encryption). Furthermore, messages in GNSL' contain sequences of nonces and user identities of arbitrary length, which can be elegantly modelled using lists, rather than by using concatenation as this does not distinguish between types. We therefore introduced a list-type explicitly for nonces and one explicitly for user identities. This led to the following message datatype:

$$
\begin{aligned}
Key \quad &= SK \mid PK \\
Message &= \mathcal{U} \mid \mathcal{N} \mid [\mathcal{U}, \ldots, \mathcal{U}] \mid [\mathcal{N}, \ldots, \mathcal{N}] \\
&\quad \mid Message.Message \mid Key(Message) \ .
\end{aligned}
$$

4.2   Message Generation Relation

The message generation relation ($\vdash$) describes how the enemy may construct a new message m from the set S of messages he has in his possession. The enemy can do this through encryption[3], by concatenation of messages or by extracting a part from such a concatenation:

$$
\begin{aligned}
m \in S &\Rightarrow S \vdash m \\
S \vdash m_1.m_2 &\Leftrightarrow S \vdash m_1 \wedge S \vdash m_2 \\
S \vdash k \wedge S \vdash m &\Rightarrow S \vdash \{m\}_k \ .
\end{aligned}
$$

The enemy must also be able to deal with the information contained in lists. He must be able to extract this information from lists and make new lists containing known information, so with $+\!\!+$ denoting list concatenation:

$$
\begin{aligned}
S \vdash m &\Leftrightarrow S \vdash [m] \\
S \vdash l_1 \wedge S \vdash l_2 &\Leftrightarrow S \vdash l_1 +\!\!+ l_2
\end{aligned}
$$

4.3   Proof Goal

We have verified a single instantiation of GNSL', namely an instantiation for p users (where p is left unspecified, except that $p \geq 2$), running concurrently with other instantiations of any size. Because p is further left unspecified, all proofs on this p-instantiation are valid for all instantiations of GNSL' involving two or more users.

We observed, looking at Fig. 2, that there are three distinct types of users in any instantiation of GNSL':

---

[3] In PVS, decryption is treated as encryption with an inverse key.

u_0: the 'first' user in the chain, the 'initiator'

u_{p-1}: the 'last' user in the chain

u_i $_{(0<i<p-1)}$: a 'middle' user, any user between the first and last user (if $p = 2$, there is none)

After this observation, we split up the proof into pairs, as shown in Fig. 5, where each arrow represents a proof of one of the aforementioned categories of users being authenticated to another category. In this paper, we treat only the proof of the last user being authenticated to the first user (*). The other proofs are similar in nature and all have been completed in PVS.

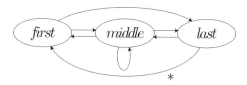

Fig. 5.

Signalling events were added to the user processes, as discussed in Sect. 3.2. CSP processes for each of the three categories of users, including these signals, are given in Fig. 6. These processes are combined in the next section to form a process describing the entire protocol.

Per the protocol definition in [6], its authentication requirements need only be satisfied if they contain exclusively honest users [6], therefore the set $\mathcal{U}$ will contain a subset of distinct, honest users $hu_0, \ldots, hu_{p-1}$. The analysis involves an authentication requirement with these users (in ascending order). Since these users are arbitrarily chosen and their processes identical, the proof holds for any authentication involving p honest users [8].

Protocol roles are defined as a numbered tuple (q, i) where q is the size of the protocol instantiation and i $(0 \leq i < q)$ enumerates the q distinct roles in that instantiation. The concrete proof goal, for the protocol extended with the signalling events, is:

$$\langle \forall n : n \in \mathcal{N}_{hu_0}^{(p,0)} : running_{p-1}([hu_0, \ldots, hu_{p-1}], n) \; \texttt{precedes}$$
$$commit_0([hu_0, \ldots, hu_{p-1}], n) \rangle \; . \tag{2}$$

We have proven this goal by proving it for one particular nonce [8], which we refer to as nonce n_0.

4.4   Enemy's Initial Knowledge

The enemy's initial knowledge must reflect that users $hu_0, \ldots, hu_{p-1}$ are honest. That means he is not in possession of any of their secret keys. The nonce n_0 is also assumed to be secret and therefore unavailable to the enemy. Apart from these restrictions, the enemy knows all identities, nonces and keys:

$$Init = \mathcal{U} \cup \mathcal{N} \setminus \{n_0\} \cup Key \setminus \{sk(hu_0) \ldots sk(hu_{p-1})\} \; .$$

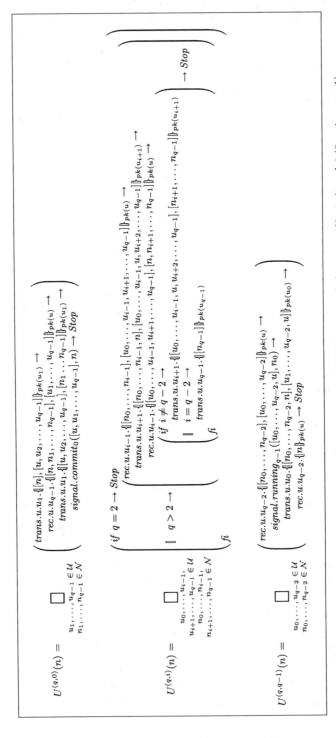

Fig. 6. CSP processes that, combined, model the GNSL' protocol, for any q ($2 \leq q$) and i ($0 < i < q - 1$)

4.5   User Processes

The last parameter to the network model is the process modelling users running the protocol. By simply combining the processes shown in Fig. 6 through interleaving, we obtain the process in (3). Because we interleave over the set of nonces that is constructed as discussed in Sect. 3.1, we are indeed modelling arbitrarily many users running the protocol in different sized instantiations concurrently.

$$\underset{u \in \mathcal{U}}{|||} \left(\underset{q \in \{x|2 \leq x\}}{|||} \left(\underset{i \in \{x|0 \leq x < q\}}{|||} \left(\underset{n \in \mathcal{N}_u^{(q,i)}}{|||} U^{(q,i)}(n) \right) \right) \right) . \tag{3}$$

By using the reasoning followed by Heather and Schneider in [8] we have altered the definition of process $U^{(q,0)}(n)$ given in Fig. 6. We have split off the case when nonce n_0 is used and shown that in that particular case, we can fix the users in the process to be $hu_1 \ldots hu_{p-1}$. The renewed definition is:

$$
\begin{aligned}
U^{(q,0)}(n) = \ & \textit{if } n \neq n_0 \rightarrow \text{'original process' of Fig. 6} \tag{4} \\
& \llbracket \quad n = n_0 \rightarrow \text{as } U^{(p,0)}(n) \text{ according to the definition of Fig. 6,} \\
& \qquad \qquad \text{but with } [u_1, \ldots, u_{p-1}] = [hu_1, \ldots, hu_{p-1}] \\
& \textit{fi}
\end{aligned}
$$

Note that $n = n_0$ also implies that $u_0 = hu_0$ and the performed protocol role is $(p, 0)$, due to the fact that $n_0 \in \mathcal{N}_{hu_0}^{(p,0)}$.

4.6   Finding a Rank Function

Since a rank function assigns boolean values to messages (and signalling events), we say of a message that it has either a 'false' or a 'true' rank. We have found a rank function ρ that satisfies conditions R1–R4 of the Rank Theorem by the reasoning presented in this section.

To satisfy R3, an explicit clause in ρ assigns a false rank to a *commit* signal if it corresponds to $commit_0([hu_0, \ldots, hu_{p-1}], n_0)$. To satisfy R4, the message received by process $HU_0(n_0)$, that outputs this false ranking *commit* signal, must be of a false rank. To satisfy R2, one of its atomic parts must rank false as well. Luckily, nonce n_0 is deemed secret, meaning it is not in the enemy's initial knowledge, and is therefore given a false rank without the risk of compromising R1. Everything else is given a true rank. For list, concatenation and encryption structures, the rank function acts as expected on their arguments:

$$\rho(commit_x([u_v, \ldots, u_w], n)) \equiv x \neq 0$$
$$\vee \ [u_v, \ldots, u_w] \neq [hu_0, \ldots, hu_{p-1}]$$
$$\vee \ n \neq n_0 \tag{5}$$
$$\rho(n) \equiv n \neq n_0 \tag{6}$$
$$\rho([n_v, \ldots, n_w]) \equiv n_0 \notin [n_v, \ldots, n_w] \tag{7}$$
$$\rho(m_0.m_1) \equiv \rho(m_0) \wedge \rho(m_1) \tag{8}$$
$$\rho(\{\!|m|\!\}_k) \equiv \rho(m) . \tag{9}$$

However, there is a problem with the way ρ is defined on encryption structures in (9). Although this definition ensures that the message process $HU_0(n_0)$ receives (containing n_0) evaluates to a false rank, it also gives a false rank to all other messages containing n_0. As such messages are passed around in the protocol run in which users $hu_0, \ldots, hu_{p-1}$ communicate with each other and hu_0 uses nonce n_0, requirement R4 is not met. Therefore these messages, up to the point where process HU_{p-1} is blocked on the *running*-event, need to be explicitly given a true rank (see Fig. 7). HU_{p-1} respects R4 because it is blocked on the running-event before outputting the false ranking message to hu_0.

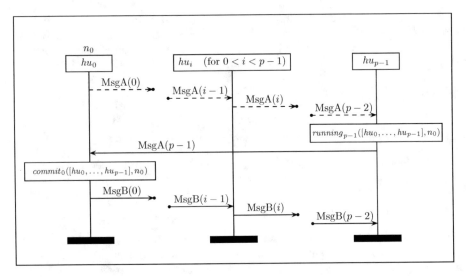

Fig. 7. The GNSL' protocol run with nonce n_0 between $hu_0, \ldots, hu_{p-1}$. The dotted arrows are the messages which are explicitly given a true rank.

Defining ρ on encrypted messages in such a way necessitates the need for a false rank to all secret keys of the honest users, as otherwise condition R2 can be violated by 'decrypting' one of said messages to produce n_0. The rank function of (5)–(8) was completed by adding the following clauses:

$$\rho(\{\!|m|\!\}_k) \equiv \rho(m)$$
$$\vee \ \langle \exists i : 0 < i < p : k = sk(hu_i)$$
$$\wedge \ \langle \exists l : l = [n_x, \ldots, n_{x+i}] :$$
$$m = (n_0 +\!\!+ l).[hu_0, \ldots, hu_{i-1}, hu_{i+1}, \ldots, hu_{p-1}]\rangle\rangle \tag{10}$$

$$\rho(sk(u)) \equiv u \notin \{hu_0, \ldots, hu_{p-1}\} \ . \tag{11}$$

Note that the fact that we are prying into the structure of an encrypted message enforces the typechecking assumption made in Sect. 2.

4.7 Proof

We verified the fact that ρ found in Sect. 4.6 does indeed satisfy the requirements of a rank function by transferring our CSP model into Evans' formalisation of CSP in PVS [11]. Requirements R1 and R3 can be proved by simply expanding definitions and R2 is proved by structural induction on messages. Requirement R4 is proved per protocol role and for each protocol role per event, where it is proved that a transmission event has true rank when assuming that previous reception events had true rank. It is the most labour-intensive requirement to check, as many cases are to be distinguished (e.g. a received message's assumed true rank may in fact be false, producing a contradiction, or it might indeed be true, but for several different reasons, based on the rank function). Using a theorem prover is useful here, as it enforces the consideration of each possible case, where it is easy to oversee a case when proving by hand. It can also take care of bookkeeping, in particular the repeated expansion of definitions.

The amount of interaction required for proving the general multi-party case turned out to be significantly more than for the standard two-party NSL-protocol, or for a finite (e.g. 4-user) instantiation of GNSL', mainly caused by proof obligations following from the message-list datatype. Our use of lists necessitated the development of a separate PVS theory containing lemmata for lists, specific to this context.

5 Conclusion and Future Work

We have shown for a specific multi-party authentication protocol, how formalisation in CSP and application of PVS make its full formal verification possible. The existing framework turned out to be adaptable to accommodate the arbitrary numbers of participants in the interleaving instantiations of the protocol. The new element in the PVS-implementation of the protocol specification, was the addition of a message-*list* datatype. We have updated the existing PVS-implementation for the rank function approach to protocol verification, and made it readily available for further use at [12]. As a general result, this paper demonstrates that the formalisation in CSP and its implementation in PVS can be used for full formal verification of multi-party security protocols.

We expect that proving security properties of other non-recursive multi-party security protocols involving the same cryptographic primitives (nonces and public-key cryptography) can be tackled in an almost identical way as the way presented in this paper and that much of the PVS code will be reusable in other analyses.

5.1 Injective Agreement

In this paper, we have proven the authentication property of *non-injective agreement* for the GNSL'-protocol, by proving the property in (2). Yet we can show that we have in fact proven the stronger property of injective agreement. For injective agreement, we require that each protocol run of an authenticator corresponds to a unique run of the authenticee, i.e. the mapping of authenticator runs to authenticee runs is injective [24]. In a protocol that establishes injective agreement, an enemy replaying messages of an old protocol run will not cause an honest user to believe he has successfully concluded a new protocol run.

When using signalling events, proving injective agreement requires that the number of *commit*-events never exceed the number of corresponding *running*-events in any trace [18]. In the case of our proof goal in (2), it is easy to see that the *commit*-event can occur at most once. This is because only honest users can generate signalling events [9] and the *commit*-event in question contains hu_0's secret nonce, so only hu_0 can generate it. Since hu_0 is assumed to use a nonce only once, the *commit*-event can only occur once and since we have already proven that it is always preceded by at least one corresponding *running*-event, we have reached injective agreement.

Recently [25], the operational semantics in terms of which the even stronger property of injective synchronisation is proven for the protocol in [6], has been implemented in the theorem prover Isabelle/HOL. Once possible, it would be highly interesting to formalise the proof of [6] in Isabelle/HOL, and compare both the proof and the formalisation process with the work presented in this paper.

References

1. Lowe, G.: Breaking and Fixing the Needham-Schroeder Public-Key Protocol Using FDR. In: Margaria, T., Steffen, B. (eds.) TACAS 1996. LNCS, vol. 1055, pp. 147–166. Springer, Heidelberg (1996)
2. Owre, S., Rushby, J.M., Shankar, N.: Prototype Verification System, http://www.csl.sri.com/
3. Cremers, C., Mauw, S.: A Family of Multi-Party Authentication Protocols. In: First Benelux Workshop on Information and System Security (WISSec) (2006)
4. Cremers, C.J.F., Mauw, S., de Vink, E.P.: Injective Synchronisation: an Extension of the Authentication Hierarchy. Theor. Comput. Sci. 367(1-2), 139–161 (2006)
5. Cremers, C.: Scyther tool, http://people.inf.ethz.ch/cremersc/scyther/
6. Cremers, C.: Scyther – Semantics and Verification of Security Protocols. PhD thesis, Technische Universiteit Eindhoven (November 2006)
7. Schneider, S.: Verifying Authentication Protocols with CSP. In: CSFW 10, pp. 3–17. IEEE Computer Society Press, Los Alamitos (1997)
8. Heather, J., Schneider, S.: A Decision Procedure for the Existence of a Rank Function. Journal of Computer Security 13(2), 317–344 (2005)
9. Ryan, P., Schneider, S.: Modelling and Analysis of Security Protocols. Addison-Wesley, Reading (2001)
10. Schneider, S., Delicata, R.: Verifying Security Protocols: An Application of CSP. In: Abdallah, A.E., Jones, C.B., Sanders, J.W. (eds.) Communicating Sequential Processes. LNCS, vol. 3525, pp. 243–263. Springer, Heidelberg (2005)
11. Evans, N., Schneider, S.: Verifying Security Protocols with PVS: Widening the Rank Function Approach. Journal of Logic and Algebraic Programming 64(2), 253–284 (2005)

12. Verhoeven, R.: PVS-code for this paper, http://www.win.tue.nl/~fdechesn/
13. Shaikh, S., Bush, V.: Analysing the Woo-Lam Protocol Using CSP and Rank Functions. Journal of Research and Practice in Information Technology 38(1), 19–29 (2006)
14. Delicata, R., Schneider, S.A.: A Formal Model of Diffie-Hellman Using CSP and Rank Functions. Technical Report CSD-TR-03-05, Department of Computer Science, Royal Holloway, University of London (2003)
15. Pereira, O., Quisquater, J.J.: Generic Insecurity of Cliques-Type Authenticated Group Key Agreement Protocols. In: CSFW 17, pp. 16–19. IEEE Computer Society Press, Los Alamitos (2004)
16. Layouni, M., Hooman, J., Tahar, S.: On the correctness of an intrusion-tolerant group communication protocol. In: Geist, D., Tronci, E. (eds.) CHARME 2003. LNCS, vol. 2860, pp. 231–246. Springer, Heidelberg (2003)
17. Paulson, L.C.: The Inductive Approach to Verifying Cryptographic Protocols. Journal of Computer Security 6(1-2), 85–128 (1998)
18. Shaikh, S.A., Bush, V.J., Schneider, S.A.: Specifying authentication using signal events in CSP. In: Feng, D., Lin, D., Yung, M. (eds.) CISC 2005. LNCS, vol. 3822, pp. 63–74. Springer, Heidelberg (2005)
19. Roscoe, A.W., Hoare, C.A.R., Bird, R.: The Theory and Practice of Concurrency. Prentice Hall, NJ (1997)
20. Verhoeven, R.: Proving Correctness of a Multi-Party Authentication Protocol with Rank Functions. Master's thesis, Technische Universiteit Eindhoven (2007)
21. Mauw, S., Bos, V.: Drawing Message Sequence Charts with LaTeX. TUGBoat 22(1-2), 87–92 (2001)
22. Heather, J., Lowe, G., Schneider, S.: How to prevent type flaw attacks on security protocols. In: CSFW 13, pp. 255–268. IEEE Computer Society Press, Los Alamitos (2000)
23. Dolev, D., Yao, A.: On the Security of Public Key Protocols. IEEE Transactions on Information Theory 29(2), 198–208 (1983)
24. Lowe, G.: A Hierarchy of Authentication Specifications. In: CSFW 10, pp. 31–44. IEEE Computer Society Press, Los Alamitos (1997)
25. Meier, S.: A Formalization of an Operational Semantics of Security Protocols. Diploma thesis, ETH Zurich (August 2007)

The Append-Only Web Bulletin Board

James Heather and David Lundin

University of Surrey, Guildford, Surrey, UK

Abstract. A large number of papers on verifiable electronic voting that have appeared in the literature in recent years have relied heavily on the availability of an *append-only web bulletin board*. Despite this widespread requirement, however, the notion of an append-only web bulletin board remains somewhat vague, and no method of constructing such a bulletin board has been proposed.

This paper fills the gap. We identify the required properties of an append-only web bulletin board, and introduce the concept of *certified publishing* of messages to the board. We show how such a board can be constructed in order to satisfy the properties we have identified.

Finally, we consider how to extend the scheme to make the web bulletin board robust and able to offer assurance to writers of the inclusion of their messages.

Although the work presented here has been inspired and motivated by the requirements of electronic voting systems, the web bulletin board is sufficiently general to allow use in other contexts.

1 Introduction

A number of verifiable electronic voting systems require specific data to be made publicly available after or during the election [1, 2, 3, 4, 5, 6, 7, 8, 10, 11, 12, 13, 14, 15, 17, 18]. Sometimes the means of publication is left undiscussed; where it is raised, it is often referred to as an *append-only web bulletin board*. The existence of such a publication vehicle is typically assumed, but the required properties of the web bulletin board are usually not given significant air time, and certainly no attempt has been made at a systematic treatment or at providing a mechanism for implementing an append-only web bulletin board. This is perhaps rather surprising considering the sheer number of papers that rely on the existence of something along these lines.

Our aim here is to identify the properties that the append-only web bulletin board needs to possess, and then to show how one can be built.

1.1 The Web Bulletin Board

The basic idea that emerges from reading through the many papers listed above is as follows. There are three types of agent involved in the system: the *web bulletin board*, *readers*, and *writers*. The web bulletin board needs to allow various parties—the writers—to publish information on the board, so that it can be read

P. Degano, J. Guttman, and F. Martinelli (Eds.): FAST 2008, LNCS 5491, pp. 242–256, 2009.

by any of the readers. The board is *append-only* in the sense that once something is published it should never be removed or altered, and when something new is published it should be placed at the end of the ordered sequence of messages listed on the board. If something is inserted out of sequence, removed, or altered, this needs to be detectable.

The board is not responsible for generating the content, of course; that is down to the parties that write to the board. When they write something, they provide a digital signature to enable others to verify the origin of the message. The board is, however, responsible for ensuring that signatures are correct, and for ensuring that the content of the board does not change after publication. In the context of a national election, there would presumably be laws governing these responsibilities, with severe sanctions for contravention.

It is, of course, very hard to build a system that can guarantee that information written to it cannot be lost. If the published information is stored in only one place, and that repository suffers catastrophic failure, it might not be possible to recover it, though it might be possible to prove that information has indeed gone missing. For this reason, the first part of this paper looks only at being able to *detect* corruption rather than being able to *prevent* it. This issue of fault tolerance and disaster recovery is one that we will return to in a later section.

The possibility of collusion between a writer of a message and the board itself should be borne in mind. We will ensure that nothing can be published to the board unless it is signed by both the writer and the board; but even if the two collude, we should still have protection against insertion, deletion or alteration of messages.

1.2 Motivation

The main motivating context, as we have suggested, is that of electronic voting.

Electronic voting. In a verifiable electronic voting system, there are usually various parties who collectively transform the encrypted votes into an election result. Verifiability of the system then rests on allowing these parties to publish certain information that enables anyone (voters, the political parties, the media, election observers, and so on) to check various claims; for example:

- all the encrypted votes [6,7,17] might be published, so that voters can check that their votes have been included in the process;
- all the decrypted votes might be published (without anyone knowing the link from encrypted vote to decrypted vote), so that anyone can check the tallying;
- those involved in the decryption might publish zero-knowledge proofs [19] or other information as evidence that they have done their jobs without underhand tactics [6,7].

Other applications. Although electronic voting provides the primary motivation, our scheme has other applications. For instance:

1. *Auctions.* In the auction context the bidder wishes to place a bid at a particular time, based on a current (opened or closed) bid and receive proof of receipt of the bid. The auctioneer wants protection against allegations of malfeasance, and thus needs to publish a proof that the sequence of bids has not been manipulated in any way.
2. *Auditable discussion boards.* It may be desirable to create a web-based discussion board or forum that provides an auditable history of the discussion.
3. *System logs.* In some contexts, it might be useful to have a verifiable online log of the activities of a distributed system. Typically, log files are written as plain text files, with full trust invested in the system writing the log; sometimes we may wish to weaken the level of trust required in the logger.
4. *Petitions.* One current fashion seems to be signing of online petitions. However, there is usually no security provided at all: no-one can verify that the signatures are not faked, and those who do sign cannot verify that the text of the petition is not subsequently changed. It would clearly increase trust in the final signed petition if we could find a way round these problems.

1.3   Roadmap

The contribution of this paper is split into Sections 2 and 3. In Section 2, we introduce the *certified publishing* concept, identify the properties required of the web bulletin board, and show that our system satisfies those properties. Section 3 then discusses how to extend this with more thorough robustness properties. Finally, we sum up and give conclusions in Section 4.

2   Certified Publishing

The web bulletin board must accept submissions only from accredited writers; similarly it must protect itself from accountability that arises from the published data by keeping proof of the origin of messages.

In this section, we start by listing the properties we require of our web bulletin board; then we introduce our scheme and show that it satisfies these properties.

2.1   Required Security Properties

We identify a number of security properties that an append-only web bulletin board should satisfy.

A web bulletin board is a sequence $\langle wbb_1, \ldots, wbb_n \rangle$, where each wbb_i contains a message, along with some metadata about the message. We will leave this metadata abstract for the moment, and give details in Section 2.2 of what metadata the web bulletin board publishes in our scheme.

Unalterable history

Definition 21. *A web bulletin board has* unalterable history *if, whenever a reader retrieves the contents of the board at time T_0 and again at time T_1, it is able to check that the board it read at T_0 is a prefix of the board at T_1, in the* *sense that the board at T_1 has the same content as previously, except for possibly having had messages appended. If this is not the case, the reader can detect that the board has become corrupted.*

Definition 22. *A web bulletin board has* certified publishing *if whenever a reader retrieves the contents of the board, either he can detect corruption of the board, or he will have proof, for each message on the board:*

1. *of who wrote the message;*
2. *that the writer intended the message to be published with the stated timestamp and at this point in the board's sequence of messages.*

These guarantees should hold even if the bulletin board and the writer collude.

Proof of timeliness of acceptance. The following guarantees enable agents to verify that messages were accepted for publication in a timely fashion.

Timeliness is difficult to tie down in a clean fashion, because networks are usually asynchronous, and we have to allow for latency. Although we would like to say, for instance, that if a reader checks the board at time T, he should not subsequently discover a new message published with an earlier date of writing than T, we must allow for the possibility that a writer has constructed a message with a timestamp of $T - \delta$ for some small δ, and the message is still in transit, and so has not yet appeared on the board. For this reason, we introduce some small, fixed security parameter ϵ that appears as a parameter to the following definitions. Increasing the value of ϵ reduces the number of times the board has to reject a message because its claimed publication date is too old by the time it arrives, but increases the extent to which the web bulletin board can deliberately delay decisions on whether to publish a particular message. We do not anticipate that this will cause problems: it should be possible to choose a value of the order of a few milliseconds and still have decent protection against latency. If a message is rejected because the delay exceeds ϵ, the message can always be sent again with a fresh timestamp.[1]

Definition 23. *The bulletin board has* timely publication *if, whenever a reader views the web bulletin board at a time T, and a message is subsequently published to the web bulletin board with a claimed publication date that is earlier than $T - \epsilon$, the reader can prove that the board has been corrupted.*

The above definition is not subsumed under Definition 21. Here, we are dealing with the *time* of publication; there, we were dealing with the *order*. Definition 23 says essentially that once someone has viewed the board, nothing more can be published to the board with a publication date of *before* the time of reading.

Definition 24. *Suppose that the web bulletin board currently contains λ messages. Suppose further that writer W attempts at time T to write message m as*

---

[1] In fact, we could get away with sending only a fresh timestamp and signature. This might save a lot of time if the message was very long.

message $\lambda + 1$, *and that* W' *attempts at time* T' *to write* m' *as message* $\lambda + 1$. *If in such cases the later of the two messages always wins—that is, if whenever (without loss of generality)* $T + \epsilon < T'$, *and the earlier message* m *is published to the board,* W' *can prove that the board has become corrupted—then we say that the board has* early rejection. *(If* $|T - T'| < \epsilon$ *then we get no guarantees.)*

This last point initially seems strange: one might expect the earlier message to win over the later message. But it makes very little difference which wins, as long as there is a clear and enforceable policy. The practical upshot of forcing the later message to take priority is that if the web bulletin board is to claim that the first message never arrived, it will have to make this decision before allowing any other writers to submit messages. This prevents the web bulletin board from collecting a pool of potential next messages from various writers, and delaying its decision over which to publish until it has received a favourable one.

2.2   The History

The implementation of the bulletin board in our scheme is as follows. The web bulletin board stores a sequence $\langle wbb_1, \ldots, wbb_n \rangle$, indexed starting from 1, where each $wbb_i = \langle m_i, T_i, W_i, H_i, WSign_i, BSign_i \rangle$, where m_i is a message, T_i is a timestamp, W_i is the name of a writer, and H_i is a hash, and $WSign_i$ and $BSign_i$ are signed terms. The intention is that T_i will store the writer W_i's timestamp at the time of writing message m_i, H_i is a hash that identifies the message as occurring at this point in the sequence, $WSign_i$ is the writer's commitment to the message, and $BSign_i$ is the board's commitment to accepting the message for publication.

Definition 25. *Such a sequence is called a* history.

Definition 26. *The web bulletin board is required to ensure that its history always satisfies the following invariant:*

1. $H_i = H(m_i.T_i.W_i.H_{i-1})$, *where* $H_0 = 0$;
2. $WSign_i = S_{W_i}(H_i)$;
3. $BSign_i = S_B(WSign_i.T_i')$, *with* T_i' *being the web bulletin board's timestamp at the time of signing;*
4. $T_i \le T_i' < T_i + \epsilon$.

A history that has these properties is called a consistent *history.*

Lemma 21. *If a history is consistent, then any prefix of the history is also consistent.*

Proof. The proof is a simple induction on the length of the history.

Definition 27. *We will use 'wbb_λ' to denote the last element of* $\langle wbb_1, \ldots, wbb_n \rangle$ *(that is, the most recent entry on the web bulletin board). The current* state hash *is the value of* H_λ. *This is the hash value that the next writer will need to use as the third component in constructing* $H_{\lambda+1}$.

2.3   Assumptions

There are various assumptions that are required in order to ensure that the web bulletin board achieves the security properties we desire.

In practice, the following assumption would normally be ensured by putting some adequate private key infrastructure (PKI) in place.

Assumption 21. *All agents know the public keys of all writers and of the web bulletin board itself, but each writer's secret key is known only to that writer, and the web bulletin board's secret key is known only to the web bulletin board.*

We need further to assume that the cryptography does its job adequately. Assumptions 21 and 22 together mean that a message signed with S_{W_i} must have originated with W_i, and a message signed with S_B must have originated with the web bulletin board. Assumption 21 is enough to ensure that anyone who sees a signed message can verify the signature.

Assumption 22. *Signed messages can be produced only by an agent who knows the signing key.*

The most important consequence of the following assumption is that the hash function we are using is treated as injective. This is obviously not strictly true of a hash function; however, a good collision-free hash function will effectively achieve this for us by ensuring that hashes do not accidentally collide, and that agents are unable to produce two distinct terms that hash to the same value.

Assumption 23. *The terms form a free algebra. Essentially, this means that concatenation of terms is associative, and that any two syntactically distinct terms have different values.*

2.4   Reading

All information written to the web bulletin board is considered public, and so anyone can act as a reader. The fact that this is usually termed a *web* bulletin board suggests that the transfer is to be done over HTTP, although that will not concern us here. It is also quite possible that, for efficiency reasons, readers might want to retrieve only part of the contents of the board rather than the whole of it, but again, we are not here concerned with questions of how to present the material to the reader. For the purposes of this paper, we shall assume that readers retrieve all of $\langle wbb_1, \ldots, wbb_n \rangle$ whenever required.

Whenever anything is read from the web bulletin board, it also returns a signed and dated copy of the current state hash:

$$\text{Message 1.} \quad B \to R \ : \ \langle wbb_1, \ldots, wbb_n \rangle . S_B(H_\lambda . T_B)$$

This makes it impossible for the web bulletin board subsequently to change what was on the board before this point. If the web bulletin board tries to do so, R can prove that the board has been corrupted by producing $S_B(H_\lambda, T_B)$. We will return later to this point.

2.5   Writing

Writing to the board involves three stages: getting the current state hash; sending the message to the board; getting a receipt. The protocol looks like this:

$$\begin{aligned}
\text{Message 1.} \quad & B \to W \;:\; S_B(H_\lambda, T_B) \\
\text{Message 2.} \quad & W \to B \;:\; m.T.W.H.S_W(H) \\
\text{Message 3.} \quad & B \to W \;:\; S_B(S_W(H).T')
\end{aligned}$$

where $H = H(m.T.W.H_\lambda)$.

In the first message, the board sends the current state hash H_λ to the writer, signed and dated. The writer rejects Message 1 if T_B is more than ϵ old.

In Message 2, the writer sends the message he wishes to publish, along with a newly generated hash, based on the message, the time of writing, the writer's name, and the current state hash; he also sends a signed version of this hash. The web bulletin board rejects Message 2 if $T - T_B > \epsilon$. On receipt of Message 2, the web bulletin board checks the signature, and thus obtains proof that the writer really did write the message at this point; it also checks the hash. The writer's signature commits to the message, to the timestamp, and to the current state hash; this guarantees that the writer intended the message to appear as the next message in the sequence after the one that resulted in this state hash.

Finally, the board sends back a signed and dated copy of the writer's signed hash. The writer will reject Message 3 if $T' - T > \epsilon$. The writer also checks the signature, and gets proof that the web bulletin board has accepted the message as appearing next in the sequence. If anything else appears in place of m, the writer can produce m and the web bulletin board's signature to show that the web bulletin board has deleted or altered the message.

Of course, when the writer sends Message 2, he has no guarantee of receiving a Message 3 at all, and thus no guarantee of getting proof that the message has been accepted.

At the end of the protocol, provided that the signature and the hash are both correct, and provided that T is fresh, the web bulletin board appends $\langle m.T.W.H.S_W(H).S_B(S_W(H).T') \rangle$ to the history. The new state hash now becomes H.

Proposition 22. *If the history was consistent before appending this new message, it will still be consistent afterwards.*

Proof. By inspection.

2.6 *Analysis of Security Properties

We now consider the security properties we set out in Definitions 21 to 24, and show that our implementation of the bulletin board satisfies those properties. We start with some preliminary results.

Lemma 23. *Any reader who reads the entire history of the web bulletin board has enough information to check that it is consistent.*

Proof. All signatures are immediately verifiable because by Assumption 21 all agents have all public keys. The only remaining question is whether the hashes can be verified; this amounts to asking whether the reader knows the information being hashed, in order to reconstruct the hash and check that the values are equal. But this is trivially true. All agents know H_0, because $H_0 = 0$. Then, for every other hash value $H_{k+1} = H(m_{k+1}.T_{k+1}.W_{k+1}.H_k)$, the first three components inside the hash appear in the clear in entry $k+1$ of the web bulletin board, and the last appears in entry k. Finally, anyone can check that $T_i' - T < \epsilon$ for all i.

We define equivalence of histories based on whether the messages they store, along with the times they were written and the names of the writers, are the same.

Definition 28. *Suppose that we have two web bulletin board histories $\langle wbb_1, \ldots, wbb_n \rangle$ and $\langle wbb_1^*, \ldots, wbb_{n^*}^* \rangle$.*

Suppose that the ith terms of the histories are $\langle m_i, T_i, W_i, H_i, WSign_i, BSign_i \rangle$ for the first history, and $\langle m_i^*, T_i^*, W_i^*, H_i^*, WSign_i^*, BSign_i^* \rangle$ for the second. We say that the two histories are equivalent *if and only if*

1. $n = n^*$;
2. *for all $1 \le i \le n$, we have $m_i = m_i^*$, $T_i = T_i^*$, $W_i = W_i^*$.*

Remark 1. *This notion of equivalence is an equivalence relation.*

Lemma 24. *Two histories have the same state hash if and only if the histories are equivalent.*

Proof. We first show that two histories with the same state hash are equivalent. To do this, we prove the contrapositive: that two inequivalent consistent web bulletin board histories have different state hashes.

Suppose that we have two consistent histories $\langle wbb_1, \ldots, wbb_n \rangle$ and $\langle wbb_1', \ldots, wbb_{n'}' \rangle$, where the ith term of the former is $\langle m_i, T_i, W_i, H_i, WSign_i, BSign_i \rangle$ and the ith term of the latter is $\langle m_i^*, T_i^*, W_i^*, H_i^*, WSign_i^*, BSign_i^* \rangle$. If they are inequivalent, then they differ on some m_i, T_i or W_i, or else the histories are of different length. Since the two histories are consistent, the state hashes for each are correctly constructed from these m_i, T_i and W_i terms; that is, with the first history, for each $1 \le i \le n$ we have

$$H_i = H(m_i.T_i.W_i.H_{i-1})$$

and similarly for the second web bulletin board.

A simple mathematical induction on n, together with Assumption 23, now establishes that $H_n \ne H_{n^*}^*$.

For the reverse direction, we must show that two equivalent histories have the same state hash. This is also a simple induction. If the histories are equivalent then they are of the same length; suppose our two histories are $\langle wbb_1, \ldots, wbb_n \rangle$ and $\langle wbb_1', \ldots, wbb_n' \rangle$. Now an induction on n establishes the result. If $n = 0$, then the state hash in each case is 0. Now suppose that the result holds for all histories of length k. When $n = k + 1$, the state hash for the first board is $H_{k+1} = H(m_{k+1}.T_{k+1}.W_{k+1}.H_k)$, and for the second it is $H'_{k+1} = H(m'_{k+1}.T'_{k+1}.W'_{k+1}.H'_k)$. But the equivalence of the histories tells us that

$$m_{k+1}.T_{k+1}.W_{k+1} = m'_{k+1}.T'_{k+1}.W'_{k+1}$$

and the inductive hypothesis tells us that $H_k = H'_k$; thus, $H_{k+1} = H'_{k+1}$, and the histories have the same state hash.

We are now in a position to consider the security properties we require of our web bulletin board.

Unalterable history. Retrieving the contents of the web bulletin board, as we have already seen, returns to the reader R the sequence $\langle wbb_1, \dots, wbb_n \rangle$. $S_B(H_\lambda, T_B)$.

By performing appropriate checks when reading the board, the reader can confirm that the board has not been corrupted. By remembering the signed state hash $S_B(H_\lambda, T_B)$, the reader will have enough information to be able to detect later if anything he has already read has changed.

Theorem 25. *The web bulletin board has unalterable history (Definition 21).*

Proof. Suppose a reader retrieves the contents of the board at time T_0. He will receive, along with the contents $\langle wbb0_{n_0} \rangle$ of the board, $S_B(H_{\lambda_0}, T_0)$. The reader then checks that H_{λ_0} is indeed the state hash of $\langle wbb0_{n_0} \rangle$; he also checks that $\langle wbb0_{n_0} \rangle$ is consistent. Having made these checks, he need store only $S_B(H_{\lambda_0}, T_0)$; he need not cache the entire board.

If he later retrieves the contents $\langle wbb1_{n_1} \rangle$ of the board at T_1, he will receive $S_B(H_{\lambda_1}, T_1)$. He performs the same checks on $\langle wbb1_{n_1} \rangle$ as he did when he retrieved the board the first time.

If all of these checks pass, then $\langle wbb1_{n_1} \rangle$ is consistent. If $n_1 < n_0$ then the later board is shorter than it was, and the reader will know that the board has been corrupted, because something must have been deleted for the board to have shortened. Otherwise, he now considers the sequence consisting of the first n_0 elements of $\langle wbb1_{n_1} \rangle$. This is a prefix of the later board, and so by Lemma 21 this is also consistent.

He now looks at this prefix and considers the last element $\langle m_{n_0}, T_{n_0}, W_{n_0}, H_{n_0}, WSign_{n_0}, BSign_{n_0} \rangle$. The state hash of the prefix is H_{n_0}. By Lemma 24, the state hash of this prefix is the same as that of $\langle wbb0_{n_0} \rangle$ if and only if the prefix is equivalent to $\langle wbb0_{n_0} \rangle$; so he checks that $H_{n_0} = H_{\lambda_0}$. If this is the case, then he knows that no message or message timestamp or message origin has been altered, and that nothing has been deleted or inserted before this point. If not, he will know that the board has been corrupted.

Note that this works even in the presence of collusion between the web bulletin board and the writers. Even if the writers produce old signatures (with old timestamps) for the web bulletin board to insert into the sequence, the change of history will mean that the state hash of the prefix will change, and the reader will be able to detect this.

Theorem 26. *The web bulletin board has certified publishing (Definition 22).*

Proof. When a reader retrieves the contents $\langle wbb_1, \ldots, wbb_n \rangle$ of the web bulletin board, he first checks that the history is consistent. If not, he is able to detect that the board has been corrupted. If it is consistent, then each element is of the form $\langle m_i, T_i, W_i, H_i, WSign_i, BSign_i \rangle$, where $WSign_i = S_{W_i}(H(m_i.T_i.W_i.H_{i-1}))$. This signature is enough to show that writer W_i created the message—by Assumption 21, only W_i has the signing key, and the only time a writer signs a message is when sending one to the board for publication. The writer chooses the timestamp when creating the signature, so the reader knows that the writer intended this to be the timestamp associated with the message.

That the writer intended the message to appear at this point in the sequence is clear from the fact that the writer was prepared to use H_{i-1} as the last component inside the hash to be signed: this value, H_{i-1}, was the state hash before m_i was added to the history.

Proof of timeliness of acceptance

Theorem 27. *The web bulletin board has timely publication (Definition 23).*

Proof. If a reader views the board at time T, he will obtain a value of the form $S_B(H_\lambda, T_B)$ from the web bulletin board, with $T < T_B < T + \epsilon$. But this commits the web bulletin board to the claim that at time T_B, the state hash was H_λ. This, by Lemma 24, corresponds to some particular history $\langle wbb_\lambda \rangle$.

Suppose that the board subsequently publishes a new message, not present in $\langle wbb_\lambda \rangle$, with a claimed publication date of T_0, where $T_0 + \epsilon < T$. This involves placing an entry into the history of the form $\langle m, T_0, W, H, WSign, BSign \rangle$, where $BSign = S_B(S_W(H(m.T_0.H').T_0'))$, with $T_0' < T_0 + \epsilon$. But now $T_0' < T_0 + \epsilon < T < T_B$.

But this commits the web bulletin board to the claim that at time T_0', the state hash corresponded to a history that includes this new entry. Since $T_0' < T_B$, the history at T_0' should have been a prefix of the history at T_B. But this means that the history at T_B should also have included the new entry, contrary to our previous assumption.

Theorem 28. *The web bulletin board has early rejection (Definition 24).*

Proof. Early rejection is an immediate consequence of timely publication and the fact that writing a message involves first reading the state hash from the board.

The first message of the writing protocol is

$$\text{Message 1.} \quad B \to W \ : \ S_B(H_\lambda, T_B)$$

which returns the state hash H_λ to the writer. If another writer now manages to publish a message using the same state hash but at a time earlier than $T_B - \epsilon$, the same argument as that used in Theorem 27 will enable the writer to show that the board has become corrupted.

2.7 Summary

In this section, we have developed a scheme for implementing the append-only web bulletin board, and shown that it satisfies the security properties we required of it.

This is already sufficiently powerful to meet the demands of most, if not all, of the systems that have assumed the existence of an append-only web bulletin board. It provides an implementation that guarantees that the bulletin board cannot manipulate the messages on the board and hope to escape detection.

The bulletin board as presented thus far, however, does not provide any liveness guarantees. There is nothing to stop the board from refusing to communicate with one or more agents. Although the board cannot manipulate the history of previously published messages, it can certainly prevent them from being published or read.

The main motivation for developing an append-only web bulletin board is that many electronic voting systems require such a board. Most of the voting systems that have been proposed are rather weak at present on their ability to recover from disaster, and are unable to cope if one of the core components of the system crashes or refuses to perform its function; consequently, if the board were to be used for one of these applications, it would not significantly weaken the liveness properties of the system as a whole.

However, it is clearly desirable to make the web bulletin board as robust as possible. It would be better if we could construct a distributed board in such a way that guarantees can be made about publication and retention of messages even in the event of one or more machines crashing or becoming compromised.

The aim of the next section is to make some progress towards constructing such a board.

3 Robust Publishing

Although the writer and the web bulletin board both seek to gain proof from the other of their correct function, the principal weakness of the scheme presented thus far in the paper is that the web bulletin board may suffer some catastrophic failure that prohibits it from fulfilling its duty to publish the data it has accepted from the writers, or the web bulletin board may stage a denial of service attack, by refusing to communicate with some or all of the readers or writers, with the same result.

3.1 Web Bulletin Board Peers

A natural way of improving the scheme is to create a distributed web bulletin board, consisting of some number of geographically disparate linked peers, each run by a separate organisation. We can then simply replicate the published data across all of them, and if one fails, the others can still function and fulfil the duty of the *collective*.

However, although there exist many practical methods for replicating databases across a set of servers, these do not offer the amount of trust that we seek. If, for example, a particular web bulletin board peer B_x successfully replicates the data it has accepted from the writers and issued certificates for to another peer B_y this does not necessarily give the writers any higher level of confidence in the correct publishing of the data, because they have not been issued a certificate by the web bulletin board *collective* but merely by a single peer. If B_x were to fail—perhaps by having its private key compromised!—and a writer, with a certificate proving the receipt by that peer of a message, were to complain, there would (still) be no way of recovering the messages that had not been replicated to other peers. The writer must be guaranteed, at the time of writing, that its message will survive because it has been replicated to a large enough number of web bulletin board peers.

The approach we adopt here is to require that as long as some threshold set k out of n bulletin board peers survive and function correctly, the integrity of the election should be guaranteed by the collective. In terms of the scheme presented in the previous section, this means that the certificate issued by the web bulletin board to the writer is issued by the web bulletin board peers as a collective. This is facilitated by a threshold cryptography scheme.

3.2   Threshold Cryptography Scheme

For this improved version of the web bulletin board, we will assume that some particular threshold cryptography scheme, such as ElGamal [9] or Paillier [16], has been agreed upon, and that each peer has been given a secret share of a threshold signing key. The scheme that we present here is not dependent on the particular cryptographic mechanism used.

We require two things from the threshold scheme: first, that it is a public key scheme, meaning that an encryption under a generally available public key can only be decrypted by the secret (threshold) private key; and secondly, that the private key can be split into n parts in such a way that a threshold subset of k key holders can co-operate to perform the decryption, but $k - 1$ key holders together still have no useful information about the threshold key.

3.3   Distributed History: Synchronized

The information stored by each peer is exactly the same information as was stored in Section 2. The bulletin board's signing key S_B is now the threshold key, split among the n peers; any k of these can together sign a message.

The rough idea for writing a message is that the writer should send his message to a peer of his choice; the peer will then form a threshold set of peers who can sign the receipt; and this signed receipt is then returned to the writer as proof of acceptance and publication of the message. All of the k peers involved in signing now add the message to their own history, and the message is also sent to the other $n - k$ peers for publication on their boards too. Each of those peers must accept the message as authentic, because it has already been signed by the threshold key.

This is nearly sufficient to give us what we want, but there are a couple of loose ends that want tying up.

Locking the peers. If the peers are to stay synchronized, it is important that we do not have two messages written concurrently. But we need a threshold set of peers to sign a message, and this gives us a neat way round the problem. We start by stipulating that a threshold set must contain more than half of the peers; that is, that $2k > n$. In this way, we can ensure that two threshold sets can never be constructed concurrently.

Peers should never allow themselves to be part of two signing sets at the same time. They may still respond to read requests when in the middle of a signing operation, but they may not respond to other writing requests.

(Coding this would need to be done carefully, of course, to prevent deadlock when two peers each try to construct a threshold set to get a message signed.)

Publish or be damned. When a message is signed by a threshold set, it must then be distributed to the other $n - k$ peers. One must ask what happens if a peer refuses to publish a message on its board.

By this point, the message has been accepted by a threshold set, and is therefore deemed to have been certified by the collective. A peer must not refuse to publish a certified message on its board. If it does so, this constitutes breaking its contract, and it should thereafter be dropped by the other peers.

3.4   Distributed History: Unsynchronized

Another possibility for maintaining a distributed web bulletin board is to drop the requirement that all peers should keep track of all of the messages. It is possible to construct the board in such a way that writing to one peer results in a signature from a threshold set, and a consequent guarantee that the message has been replicated to those peers, but not necessarily to all n peers. This involves changing the structure somewhat from that presented in Section 2. What we get is a web bulletin board that maintains a *local* append-only structure, in the sense that each peer keeps an ordered sequence of messages.

Following this approach has two interesting consequences. First, the writing of messages need no longer be done strictly sequentially: two or more messages can be written concurrently. In a very large-scale system, this could be a considerable advantage, because locking a threshold set of peers might be a time-consuming operation.

Secondly, in order to make sure one has read all of the messages, one now needs to consult $n - k + 1$ peers. (Each message is guaranteed to be written on k boards, so we need to check enough boards to leave only $k - 1$ boards unchecked.)

Whether one chooses the synchronized distributed web bulletin board or the unsynchronized distributed web bulletin board depends entirely on the nature of the application. If one requires a strict ordering of all messages to be maintained, one must use the synchronized board; this would apply to an auction, or audited discussion board. For an online petition, the ordering of the signatures is presumably not crucial, and the unsynchronized board would work well.

For many electronic voting systems, the ordering of messages is unimportant. Often what is required is simply a record of all encrypted votes, or some such. In this context, either option would work, but the unsynchronized board might be more efficient.

4   Conclusion

In this paper, we have provided a way of implementing the append-only web bulletin board whose existence has been assumed in so much of the electronic voting literature.

We introduced the notion of *certified publishing*, in which a writer and a bulletin board are protected from false allegations of misconduct. We then introduced our scheme, and demonstrated that it satisfies the properties that one requires of an append-only web bulletin board.

Finally, in Section 3, we discussed how to distribute the board among a number of peers to make it robust in the face of system failure or deliberate misconduct.

Future work will focus on the distributed web bulletin board and on its security properties. We aim to define the liveness properties we would expect of the two flavours of distributed board, and then prove that they satisfy those properties.

4.1   The Application to Electronic Voting

A robust web bulletin board and the issuing of encrypted receipts are vital components of verifiable electronic voting systems. When an encrypted receipt is submitted to the web bulletin board by a voting machine/scanner, the web bulletin board collective responds with a certificate indicating that the receipt has been received and published in the robust collective history. This certificate can be printed onto the voter's receipt, giving the individual further opportunities to audit the election. Furthermore, if the voter is able to verify, using the certificate, that the encrypted receipt has been correctly entered onto the web bulletin board, he need not check the receipt on the web bulletin board after the close of the election. This improves the security of the whole election: it means that the integrity of the election requires a smaller number of voters to check their receipts.

Acknowledgements

Warm thanks to Roger Peel and Zhe Xia for their comments on the scheme presented here.

References

1. Adida, B., Rivest, R.: Scratch & vote: self-contained paper-based cryptographic voting. In: Proceedings of the fifth ACM workshop on Privacy in electronic society, pp. 29–40 (2006)

2. Aditya, R., Lee, B., Boyd, C., Dawson, E.: An efficient mixnet-based voting scheme providing receipt-freeness. In: Katsikas, S.K., López, J., Pernul, G. (eds.) TrustBus 2004. LNCS, vol. 3184, pp. 152–161. Springer, Heidelberg (2004)
3. Araujo, R., Custodio, R.F., van de Graaf, J.: A verifiable voting protocol based on farnel. In: Proceedings of Workshop On Trustworthy Elections (WOTE 2007) (2007)
4. Baudron, O., Fouque, P.-A., Pointcheval, D., Stern, J., Poupard, G.: Practical multi-candidate election system. In: Proceedings of the twentieth ACM Symposium on Principles of Distributed Computing (PODC 2001), pp. 274–283 (2001)
5. Benaloh, J., Tuinstra, D.: Receipt-free secret-ballot elections (extended abstract). In: Proceedings of the twenty-sixth Symposium on Theory of Computing (STOC 1994), pp. 544–553 (1994)
6. Chaum, D.: Secret ballot receipts: true voter-verifiable elections. IEEE: Security and Privacy Magazine 2(1), 38–47 (2004)
7. Chaum, D., Ryan, P.Y.A., Schneider, S.: A practical voter-verifiable election scheme. In: di Vimercati, S.d.C., Syverson, P.F., Gollmann, D. (eds.) ESORICS 2005. LNCS, vol. 3679, pp. 118–139. Springer, Heidelberg (2005)
8. Cramer, R., Gennaro, R., Schoenmakers, B.: A secure and optimally efficient multi-authority election scheme. In: Fumy, W. (ed.) EUROCRYPT 1997. LNCS, vol. 1233, pp. 103–118. Springer, Heidelberg (1997)
9. ElGamal, T.: A public key cryptosystem and a signature scheme based on discrete logarithms. IEEE Transactions on IT 31(4), 467–472 (1985)
10. Fisher, K., Carback, R., Sherman, T.: Punchscan: Introduction and system definition of a high-integrity election system. In: Pre-proceedings, pp. 19–29. IAVoSS Workshop On Trustworthy Elections (2006)
11. Fujioka, A., Okamoto, T., Ohta, K.: A practical secret voting scheme for large scale elections. In: Zheng, Y., Seberry, J. (eds.) AUSCRYPT 1992. LNCS, vol. 718, pp. 244–251. Springer, Heidelberg (1993)
12. Juels, A., Catalano, D., Jakobsson, M.: Coercion-resistant electronic elections. In: Proceedings of the 2005 ACM Workshop on Privacy in the Electronic Society, pp. 61–70 (2005)
13. Lee, B., Boyd, C., Dawson, E., Kim, K., Yang, J., Yoo, S.: Providing receipt-freeness in mixnet-based voting protocols. In: Lim, J.-I., Lee, D.-H. (eds.) ICISC 2003. LNCS, vol. 2971, pp. 245–258. Springer, Heidelberg (2004)
14. Neff, C.A., Adler, J.: Verifiable e-voting: indisputable electronic elections at polling places. VoteHere Inc. (2003)
15. Ohkubo, M., Miura, F., Abe, M., Fujioka, A., Okamoto, T.: An improvement on a practical secret voting scheme. In: Zheng, Y., Mambo, M. (eds.) ISW 1999. LNCS, vol. 1729, pp. 225–234. Springer, Heidelberg (1999)
16. Paillier, P.: Public-key cryptosystems based on discrete logarithms residues. In: Stern, J. (ed.) EUROCRYPT 1999. LNCS, vol. 1592, pp. 223–238. Springer, Heidelberg (1999)
17. Punchscan, http://www.punchscan.org
18. Rivest, R.: The threeballot voting system (2006), http://crypto.csail.mit.edu/~rivest/Rivest-TheThreeBallotVotingSystem.pdf
19. Schneier, B.: Applied Cryptography: protocols, algorithms, and source code in C, 2nd edn. John Wiley, United States of America (1996)

Secure Broadcast Ambients

Elsa L. Gunter and Ayesha Yasmeen

Department of Computer Science, University of Illinois at Urbana-Champaign,
Urbana, IL, USA
egunter@cs.uiuc.edu, yasmeen@uiuc.edu

Abstract. Broadcast mechanism is prevalent in many forms of electronic networks. Modeling broadcast protocols succinctly and reasoning about how secure these protocols are is gaining importance as society increasingly comes to depend on a wide variety of electronic communications. In this work we present a modified ambient calculus where the nature of communication is broadcast within domains. We allow reconfigurable configurations of communication domains, access restrictions to domains and the capability of modeling cryptographic communication protocols in broadcast scenarios.

Keywords: Ambient calculi, process calculi, broadcast, bisimulations, congruence, security.

1   Introduction

In a world of increasing dependence on electronic communications between reconfigurable and mobile devices, there is a clear need for accurate formal systems to model these devices and their communications to facilitate guaranteeing such properties as functionality and security (especially privacy and integrity). Ambients [9], including boxed ambients [5,2], are formalisms that have been developed to model such mobile devices and their communication. Ambients have an associated topology that confines their movement and their communication options. This topology has traditionally been restricted to tree structures, and communication and movement have been restricted to adjacent ambients. The tree structure implies that an ambient can only be "in" one other ambient at a given time. This poses problems for modeling aspects of networks, such as routers. A router is most naturally modeled as being "in" multiple domains at once. Similarly, a laptop with an ethernet connection, a bluetooth connection and a dialup-modem connection, can be thought of as being "in" three different domains at once. The restriction of the topology to tree structures prevents modeling these devices that way. In this work, we loosen this constraint to allow the topology to be that of a dynamically reconfigurable directed acyclic graph, thus allowing one ambient to be in more than one other ambient at a given time, or possibly none at all.

In theoretical models of systems, and ambients in particular, communication is often modeled using point-to-point channels. Depending on the particular calculus, many processes may have access to a given channel, but each communication

P. Degano, J. Guttman, and F. Martinelli (Eds.): FAST 2008, LNCS 5491, pp. 257–271, 2009.
© Springer-Verlag Berlin Heidelberg 2009

will have a unique recipient. Within such frameworks, modeling broadcast and multicast communications must be done using multiple unicasts. Let us consider a π-calculus [15] implementation of a message being broadcasted over a channel. In order to ensure that this message can be received by every possible recipient, the message sending action has to be replicated.

Server $=!(\overline{c}\langle M\rangle.\mathsf{nil})$; Client$_i = c(x_i).P_i$; Network = Server | Client$_1$ | Client$_2$ | $\ldots$

This implementation of a broadcast communication using π-calculus is incorrect in the sense that it does not enforce receiving the message M simultaneously by every recipient. One recipient may receive it much later than another recipient. An adversary can choose to come in any time after the message has been sent to sniff the message. As a result, it allows for possible behaviors in the model that can not arise in practice.

Alternatives to this have been devised using broadcast communications. These include broadcast communication limited to a specified domain. However, in frameworks with broadcast within a domain, the domains are relatively static with only at most code moving among them. Because the code alone is mobile, it carries no identity with it, which limits the ability to concisely and accurately model the organization of the domains, and model the restriction of access to the domains by other domains. In our work, we have broadcast communication within ambients. Messages announced to the ambient are heard by the ambient and all ambients directly within it. Ambients may restrict access to themselves, and hence to the privilege of the communication within them, based on the identity of potential entrants, without requiring that their names be hidden.

Let us now consider a wifi network existing in a home. *The wireless network usually continually broadcasts its identity (SSID) to the rest of the world on its wavelength. Anyone capable of capturing wireless communication on that wavelength is capable of listening to this name. The wireless network gets to announce its name even when no one is listening for it. If the network does not secure itself, then typically anyone who knows its name, can enter it. Once a rogue computer enters this network, it can send and receive packets of its own and listen to all the communication occurring inside the network, as all packets are essentially broadcasted in a wireless network. In order to be able to prevent indiscriminate access to the home network, the network should not be allowing everyone to gain access to itself. The simplest method of access control is Machine Authentication Code (MAC) filtering, where a computer is allowed access to a network only if it has a network card with a pre-approved MAC. This can allow the home network to deny access to an unauthorized computer from the house next door. Also, the router of the wifi network connects the computers connected to the home wireless network with the outside world. This router is capable of directly communicating to the outside internet network and the home computers. Hence, virtually it is present in multiple communication domains simultaneously. Any computer such as a laptop belonging to a household member should be allowed access and also it should be allowed to leave the network whenever the user of the laptop simply shuts it off. Finally, each computer on the home network should be able to hide from all other computers whatever it is communicating with the rest of the world.*

This scenario leads to the necessity of a calculus which is able to model (i) distinct regions of computation; (ii) broadcast communication within the regions of communication, where all listeners get to listen to the communication simultaneously, irrespective of whether the speaker knows of the listeners' identities or not, and also irrespective to whether there is anyone actually listening for the communication or not; (iii) allowing indiscriminate access to a region; (iv) allowing access control via selective permission to enter a region; (v) allowing elegant representation of regions being inside multiple domains, for example, as said before, a laptop computer connected to the home wifi network, may also be connected to a workplace network via dialup connection; (vi) allowing the hierarchy of the regions to be a directed acyclic graph with the capability of modeling that a region can be a standalone region, that is, it may at some times be adjacent to no other region, (vii) allowing regions to leave other regions at their free will, without requiring any permission from the regions that it is trying to leave; (viii) allow regions to engage in cryptographic communication protocols to be able to secure their data. None of the existing process calculi, especially the ambient calculi and the broadcast calculi, are capable of modeling all these aspects of the home wireless network. We list what aspects the other existing related process calculi can encode in the related works section in Section 6. Our directed acyclic hierarchy of ambients and broadcast communication is however a novel combination.

2   Secure Broadcast Ambients

2.1   Syntax of Secure Broadcast Ambients

In order to define the syntax of Secure Broadcast Ambients we use the following categories of identifiers: ambient names: $n, m \in Amb$, message variables: $x \in MessVar$ and key variables: $k \in Keys$. The syntax of Secure Broadcast Ambients is presented in Table 1. *Messages*, *Processes* and *Systems* are the main syntactic categories. We only mention interesting aspects of the syntax. Apart from the variables, a message can be a pair of messages or an encrypted message. Each ambient contains a process. Processes are built from the usual constructs, such as replication. parallel combination, and prefixing with actions.

An ambient n can indicate its intention to move into another ambient by a in m prefix. However, this movement can only be successful if a corresponding permission is there to allow this move. The corresponding permission can be either $\overline{\text{in}}\, n$ allowing specifically n to enter, or $\overline{\text{in}}\, \_$ indicating permission for any ambient. As we shall see in Section 3, the only further restriction placed on entrance is that an ambient is not allowed to enter a descendant of itself. This interpretation of ambient movement leads to a directed acyclic graph structure for the hierarchy of ambients. In Secure Broadcast Ambients, an ambient can be in multiple ambients at the same time. An ambient may even fail to be in any ambient, for example, a laptop that has been turned off. An ambient n exits from the ambient m by the out m action without requiring any permission from any other ambient, and without affecting the relationship of n to any other ambient.

Table 1. Syntax of Broadcast Ambients

Messages:

$M, N ::= x$ message ident

      $| \quad m$ ambient name

      $| \quad (M, N)$ pairing

      $| \quad k$ key

      $| \quad \{M\}_k$ encrypted message

Format:

$F ::= m$ ambient name

     $| \quad \{x\}_k$ decryption

     $| \quad (x, y)$ pairs

Prefixes:

$\pi ::= \overline{in\ \mu}$ allow enter

    $| \quad in\ m$ enter

    $| \quad out\ m$ exit

    $| \quad (x)^m$ input

    $| \quad \nu k$ new key

    $| \quad \langle M \rangle^m$ output

Processes:

$P, Q ::= $ nil   nil process

      $| \quad P \mid Q$ composition

      $| \quad !P$ replication

      $| \quad \pi.P$ prefixing

      $| \quad$ cond M is N in P data comparison

      $| \quad$ case M of $F : P$ case analysis

Systems:

$S ::= $ nilsystem   empty system

    $| \quad m[P]$ ambient

    $| \quad (x)^m(S)$ broadcast receive

    $| \quad \nu k.(S)$ key restrict

    $| \quad \nu m :: \mathcal{L}.(S)$ ambient restrict

    $| \quad S_1 \| S_2$ parallel

Ambient Pattern:

$\mu ::= \ _-$ any ambient

    $| \quad m$ ambient name

The processes have sending and receiving prefixes for communication. We do not have channels to be used for inter-ambient communication. In our calculus the name of a parent ambient acts as the broadcast channel for both itself and its children. This way, any ambient can listen to any conversation that is going on between any of its parents and their children. Henceforth channels are synonymous with ambients.

A process can also perform matching, or case analysis on a message much in the manner of [1]. The case analysis patterns are given by the formats. In this work we only consider symmetric encryption and so the decryption key is the same as the encryption key for every encrypted message.

We introduce systems, which are collections of ambients. A system can be an empty system, an ambient, a system waiting to receive a message or multiple systems in parallel. Systems can create a new key or a new ambient name with a given parent list by restriction.

The free variables, free ambient names and free keys of messages, processes and systems will be denoted by the function fv(), fn() and fk() respectively and is defined the usual way. We use fi() for their union. Ambient and key restriction, message input and case analysis are the binding constructs.

We now encode the components in the wireless home network as described in the introduction using our syntax:

$$\text{Wifi}[\overline{!in\ \text{Laptop}}.\text{nil}] \| \text{Laptop}[in\ \text{Wifi}.(x)^{\text{Wifi}}.P] \|$$
$$\text{Router}[!((x)^{\text{Wifi}}.\langle x \rangle^{\text{ISP}}.\text{nil}) \mid !((x)^{\text{ISP}}.\langle x \rangle^{\text{Wifi}}.\text{nil})]$$

The router, Router captures all outgoing packets in the home network, Wifi, and forwards them to the ISP (its code is omitted here) and vice versa. Currently, the wireless home network allows only the laptop, Laptop to enter the network.

The laptop first tries to enter the network and then as an example code we make it listen on the network.

2.2 Structural Equivalence of Broadcast Ambients

Structural equivalence is defined for each of processes and systems. It is the smallest equivalence relation containing the rules in Table 2, closed under alpha equivalence (where ν, message receipt and case analysis are the binding constructs), and the associativity and commutativity of parallel composition of each of processes and systems, with nil and nilsystem as the respective identities. We omit some rules that are very similar to rules for ambients and process calculi in general. Rules for restriction, permutation and pattern matching are very similar to rules provided in [1]. Decryption is also performed by pattern matching in an abstract fashion as in [1]. We use bi() to indicate the identifier that is being bound in a restriction. We sometimes use u as an abbreviation for $\nu m :: \mathcal{L}$ or νk.

The rule (STRSYSPAR) indicates that one ambient can have multiple scattered pieces with the same name. However, there will be only one ambient with a particular name. The last four rules in Table 2 are the rules that enable broadcast communication. The rule (STRBRDCSTLISTEN) allows an ambient to lift the receive action on a particular broadcast channel of a process within it up to the level of the ambient system. The rule (STRCOMBLISTEN) can then be used to combine the listening systems. It is the principal rule that is used to model broadcast systems. This rule combines multiple ambients listening on the same channel so that later on only one transition is needed to send a message simultaneously to all the ambients listening on this ambient. In addition to being able to send a message to multiple parties simultaneously, in a broadcast scenario, the broadcaster can send out a message even if no one is listening on the broadcast channel being used. The rule (STRNOLISTEN) enables us to model this scenario.

3   Operational Semantics

The operational semantics of Secure Broadcast Ambients relies heavily on the topological layout of the ambients under consideration. We now introduce *configurations*, which keep track of the topology of the ambients in a system.

3.1 Configuration

We first introduce the concept of a parent list, Π, for the ambients. The parent list keeps track of the ancestors for each ambient. A parent list is a finite ordered list of pairs of ambients and ambient lists, written as $[m_0 :: \mathcal{L}_0, m_1 :: \mathcal{L}_1, \ldots, m_n :: \mathcal{L}_n]$ where each $\mathcal{L}_i$ is the list of parent ambients of ambient m_i and for each i and j such that $0 \leq i, j \leq n$ we have that $m_i \neq m_j$ and if $i \leq j \leq n$ then $m_i \notin \mathcal{L}_j$.

We allow our ambients to be decomposed into several parallel pieces as the structural equivalence rules suggest. Hence, we need to consolidate the hierarchy information for each ambient, so that all pieces have the same view of their

Table 2. Structural Equivalence

(STRREPPAR)	$!P \equiv P \mid !P$	(STRNIL SYS)	$m[\text{nil}] \equiv \text{nilsystem}$
(STRPROCSYS)	$P \equiv Q \Rightarrow m[P] \equiv m[Q]$	(STRSYSPAR)	$m[P_1 \mid P_2] \equiv m[P_1] \| m[P_2]$
(STRSYSKEY)	$m[\nu k.P] \equiv \nu k.m[P]$	(STRKEY)	$\nu u.\nu k.S \equiv \nu k.\nu u.S$
(STRPKEY)	$\nu k_1.\nu k_2.P \equiv \nu k_2.\nu k_1.P$	(STRRESNIL)	$\nu u.\text{nilsystem} \equiv \text{nilsystem}$

(STRRES PAR)	$\nu u.(S_1 \| S_2) \equiv S_1 \| \nu u.S_2,$ if $bi(u) \notin fi(S_1)$
(STRRES REC)	$\nu u.(x)^n.S \equiv (x)^n.\nu u.S$ if $n \neq bi(u)$
(STRRES RES)	$\nu n :: \mathcal{L}_1.\nu m :: \mathcal{L}_2.S \equiv \nu m :: \mathcal{L}_2.\nu n :: \mathcal{L}_1.S,$
	if n $\neq$ m and m $\notin \mathcal{L}_1$ and n $\notin \mathcal{L}_2$
(STRBRDCSTLISTEN)	$\nu m :: \mathcal{L}.\nu n_1 :: \mathcal{L}'_1 \ldots \nu n_k :: \mathcal{L}'_k.m[(x)^n.P] \equiv \nu m :: \mathcal{L}.\nu n_1 :: \mathcal{L}'_1 \ldots$
	$\nu n_k :: \mathcal{L}'_k.((x)^n(m[P])),$ if $m = n \vee (m \notin \{n_1, \ldots, n_k\} \wedge n \in \mathcal{L})$
(STRNOLISTEN)	$(x)^n(\text{nilsystem}) \equiv \text{nilsystem}$
(STRNEUTRAL)	$(x)^n.(S_1 \| S_2) \equiv S_1 \| ((x)^n.S_2)$ if $x \notin fv(S_1)$
(STRCOMBLISTEN)	$(x)^n.S_1 \| (y)^n.S_2 \equiv (z)^n.(S_1[z/x] \| S_2[z/y]),$ z fresh in S_1, S_2

ancestry, and so that no cycle can arise in the hierarchical graph of the ambients. Hence we introduce the idea of a configuration, Δ. Configurations represent the partial ordering of the ambients by the parent-child relation, and are a linearization of that order with parents always occurring to the left.

Definition 1. *A configuration is a parent list* $\Pi = [m_0 :: \mathcal{L}_0, m_1 :: \mathcal{L}_1, \ldots, m_n :: \mathcal{L}_n]$ *with the additional constraint that* $\forall i.0 \leq i \leq n.p \in \mathcal{L}_i \Rightarrow \exists j.0 \leq j < i.p = m_j$. *The set of all first components in a configuration* Δ *will be denoted by* $\mathbf{dom}(\Delta) = \{m \mid \exists \mathcal{L}.(m, \mathcal{L}) \in \Delta\}$. *We define a function* # *which concatenates an ambient-parent list pair to a configuration as* $[m_0 :: \mathcal{L}_0, m_1 :: \mathcal{L}_1, \ldots, m_n :: \mathcal{L}_n]\#(m :: \mathcal{L}) = [m_0 :: \mathcal{L}_0, m_1 :: \mathcal{L}_1; \ldots, m_n :: \mathcal{L}_n, m :: \mathcal{L}]$ *if* $m \notin \mathbf{dom}(\Delta)$ *and* $\mathcal{L} \subseteq \mathbf{dom}(\Delta)$, *and otherwise it is undefined. We define* $\Delta\#\Pi$ *as the iterative folding of* # *over* Π.

We shall refer to the pair of a configuration and a system, $\Delta \triangleright S$, as a *formation* where $\text{ambsinsys}(S) \subseteq \mathbf{dom}(\Delta)$. $\text{ambsinsys}(S)$ is a function that returns all ambients of the form $m[P]$ syntactically appearing in the system S (definition omitted in this work). The set of all formations will be denoted by $\mathcal{F}$. Notice that $\Delta\#(m :: \mathcal{L})$ is a configuration if it is defined. Also notice, $\Delta = [m_0 :: \mathcal{L}_0, m_1 :: \mathcal{L}_1, \ldots, m_n :: \mathcal{L}_n] = []\#m_0 :: \mathcal{L}_0\#m_1 :: \mathcal{L}_1\# \ldots \#m_n :: \mathcal{L}_n$. When looking an ambient up in a configuration, we will start at the right, moving to the left. Because the parents of any ambient are always to the left of this ambient in the configuration, we are ensured that a configuration always encodes a directed acyclic graph.

Definition 2. *We define a permutation relation* perm *as the reflexive, symmetric, transitive closure of the following rule: if* $m \notin \mathcal{L}_n$, $n \notin \mathcal{L}_m$, $m \neq n$ *then* $perm(\Delta \# m :: \mathcal{L}_m \# n :: \mathcal{L}_n \# \Pi, \Delta \# n :: \mathcal{L}_n \# m :: \mathcal{L}_m \# \Pi)$.

This permutation relation creates equivalence classes of configurations that have the same topological structure that is induced by the hierarchical relationship of the ambients in the domain of the configurations. Let us now extend the structural equivalence of systems, $\equiv$, to structural equivalence of formations, where

Table 3. Barbs

BARB IN:

$$\frac{m \in \mathrm{dom}(\Delta) \wedge m \notin \mathcal{L}_n}{\Delta \;\#\; n :: \mathcal{L}_n \;\#\; \Pi \triangleright \\ n[\mathsf{in}\; m\, .P] \downarrow \mathsf{in}(n,m)}$$

BARB CO-IN:

$$\frac{\mu = \_ \vee (\mathrm{match}(n,\mu) = \mathsf{false} \wedge \\ \mu \notin \mathrm{dom}(\Delta) \cup \mathcal{L}_n)}{\Delta \;\#\; n :: \mathcal{L}_n \;\#\; \Pi \triangleright n[\overline{\mathsf{in}\;\mu}\, .P] \downarrow \overline{\mathsf{in}}(n,\mu)}$$

BARB SEND:

$$\frac{m \in (\{n\} \cup \Delta(n))}{\Delta \triangleright n[\langle M \rangle^m .P] \downarrow \mathsf{send}\; m}$$

FORMATIONSTRUCTBARB:

$$\frac{\Delta_1 \triangleright S_1 \equiv \Delta_2 \triangleright S_2 \quad \Delta_2 \triangleright S_2 \downarrow \xi}{\Delta_1 \triangleright S_1 \downarrow \xi}$$

SYSPARBARB:

$$\frac{\Delta \triangleright S_1 \downarrow \xi}{\Delta \triangleright (S_1 \| S_2) \downarrow \xi}$$

NEWKEYBARB:

$$\frac{\Delta \triangleright S \downarrow \xi}{\Delta \triangleright \nu k.S \downarrow \xi}$$

NEWAMBBARB:

$$\frac{\Delta \;\#\; n :: \mathcal{L} \triangleright S \downarrow \xi \quad n \notin fn(\xi)}{\Delta \triangleright \nu(n :: \mathcal{L}).S \downarrow \xi}$$

two formations $\Delta_1 \triangleright S_1$ and $\Delta_2 \triangleright S_2$ are structurally equivalent if $\mathrm{perm}(\Delta_1, \Delta_2)$ and $S_1 \equiv S_2$.

3.2 Barbs

Our aim is to provide co-inductive relations that relate two formations that are externally indistinguishable. However, since we are considering secrecy of confidential information contained in systems, we want to reason about systems whose actions are indistinguishable even while sending and receiving different secrets. In that regard, we now define a predicate traditionally referred to as *barbs* that describes the actions a system can be observed to take. These actions will not indicate what messages (if any) are involved in the actions. We define the set of barbs exhibited by a system using the rules in Table 3, where we denote S exhibits a barb ξ in the configuration Δ by $\Delta \triangleright S \downarrow \xi$. We define the barbs by descending through the syntax of the systems. Systems are mainly composed of ambients in parallel. Each ambient contains a process and hence we consider all the visible actions such processes can take. The empty system does not exhibit any barb. For the process inside an ambient only movement and communication actions are observable; other process constructs like pattern matching are not observable. The barb send m indicates that an ambient wants to send some message over the channel m. However receiving a message is not a barb in our system. The reason is that in a broadcast system a broadcaster or sender of a message can send a message, but whether the message was actually heard by anyone is not observable. An ambient may even send a message in a channel to which no one is listening. Similarly, entering, but not exiting, an ambient is an observable action as exiting does not require any form of permission from the ambients involved. The barb in (n,m) indicates that the ambient n is trying to enter ambient m. Similarly, the barb $\overline{\mathsf{in}}(n,\mu)$ indicates that the ambient n is allowing some ambient to enter it. The *match* operator takes an ambient name

Table 4. Labeled Transition System

BROADCAST MESSAGE:

$$m_j \in \mathrm{dom}(\Delta), j = 0, \ldots, k \;\wedge\; n \in \bigcap_{j=0}^{k}(\{m_j\} \cup \Delta(m_j))$$

$$\overline{\Delta \rhd (m_0[\langle M \rangle^n.P] \| (x)^n(m_1[P_1] \| \ldots \| m_k[P_k]))} \xrightarrow{\text{send } m_0}$$
$$\Delta \rhd m_0[P] \| (m_1[P_1] \| \ldots \| m_k[P_k])[M/x]$$

ENTER:

$$\mathrm{match}(n,\mu) \;\wedge\; m \notin \mathcal{L}_n \;\wedge\; m \in \mathrm{dom}(\Delta)$$
$$\overline{\Delta \;\#\; n :: \mathcal{L}_n \;\#\; \Pi \rhd n[\mathrm{in}\; m.P] \| m[\overline{\mathrm{in}}\; \mu.Q]}$$
$$\xrightarrow{\mathrm{in}(n,m)} \Delta \;\#\; n :: \mathcal{L}_n \cup \{m\} \;\#\; \Pi \rhd n[P] \| m[Q]$$

EXIT:

$$m \in \mathcal{L}_n$$
$$\overline{\Delta \;\#\; n :: \mathcal{L}_n \;\#\; \Pi \rhd n[\mathrm{out}\; m.P]}$$
$$\xrightarrow{\tau} \Delta \;\#\; n :: \mathcal{L}_n \setminus \{m\} \;\#\; \Pi \rhd n[P]$$

FORMATIONEQUIV:

$$\Delta_1 \rhd S_1 \equiv \Delta_1' \rhd S_1'$$
$$\Delta_1' \rhd S_1' \xrightarrow{\xi} \Delta_2' \rhd S_2'$$
$$\Delta_2' \rhd S_2' \equiv \Delta_2 \rhd S_2$$
$$\overline{\Delta_1 \rhd S_1 \xrightarrow{\xi} \Delta_2 \rhd S_2}$$

AMBRESTRICT:

$$\Delta \;\#\; n :: \mathcal{L} \rhd S_1 \xrightarrow{\xi}$$
$$\Delta' \;\#\; n :: \mathcal{L}' \rhd S_2$$
$$\overline{\Delta \rhd \nu n :: \mathcal{L}.S_1 \xrightarrow{\xi}}$$
$$\Delta' \rhd \nu n :: \mathcal{L}'.S_2$$

PARALLEL:

$$\Delta \rhd S_1 \xrightarrow{\xi}$$
$$\Delta' \rhd S_1'$$
$$\overline{\Delta \rhd (S_1 \| S_2) \xrightarrow{\xi}}$$
$$\Delta' \rhd (S_1' \| S_2)$$

and a μ and determines whether the μ in the provided permission matches the name of the ambient which is trying to enter, as $\mathrm{match}(n,\mu) = (\mu = \_ \vee \mu = n)$.

3.3   Labeled Transition Semantics

Using formations, we introduce the labeled transition relation $\xrightarrow{\mathcal{L}} \subseteq \mathcal{F} \times \mathcal{L} \times \mathcal{F}$ for Secure Broadcast Ambients, where the transitions take one formation to another with the label $\mathcal{L}$ where $\mathcal{L}$ can either be a barb or the silent unobservable action τ. The transition semantics is given in Table 4. We now describe some interesting transition rules. In the BROADCAST MESSAGE rule, we have a number of recipients waiting to receive a message being sent to an ambient, n. When an ambient sends a message to n, the communication completes. However, the communication should only occur if the configuration implies that the sender is either n itself or a child of n and the recipients are all children of n or n itself. Hence, we impose some side conditions for this rule. The first condition ensures that all ambients mentioned are described by the configuration Δ. The second condition ensures that n is either the sender or the sender is a child of n. It also ensures that the recipients are either children of n or n itself. After the communication, the sender proceeds with the rest of its code and a message variable substitution occurs for the recipient system.   We now consider the ambient entry rule. As mentioned earlier an ambient needs specific permission to be able to enter another ambient. If there is a matching permission then an enter action is performed.   In the rule Enter, n wants to enter ambient m. Ambient m has a permission prefix which has to either allow any ambient access to enter m or specifically allow ambient n to enter m. We also impose restrictions so that an ambient cannot enter an ambient it is already in. The other condition for this rule is to ensure that adding m as a parent of n will not introduce a cycle in the ancestry of n. After gaining entry into the ambient m, the parent list of n is updated. For the exit action in rule EXIT, we check that the ambient requesting to exit from an ambient is actually a child of that ambient. The unlabeled transition system, $\rightarrow \subseteq \mathcal{F} \times \mathcal{F}$ is obtained by simply removing the labels from the labeled transitions.

3.4 Testing Equivalence

We now define the concept of *testing* a system in the manner of [1]. Intuitively it represents all tests an external system can make on any context in order to gather information about it. A formation $\Delta \triangleright T$ is a *context* for a formation $\Delta' \triangleright S$ if $\Delta' \circ \Delta \triangleright (S \| T)$ is a formation. $\circ$ is a function which composes two configurations and returns another configuration. Its formal definition is omitted here. First we define barb convergence in the manner of [1]. The predicate $\Delta \triangleright S \Downarrow \xi$ is true when S is a system which can exhibit the barb ξ after zero or more transitions under the configuration Δ. The rules for barb convergence are as follows:

$$
\begin{array}{cc}
\text{BARB:} & \text{REDUCT:} \\[4pt]
\dfrac{\Delta \triangleright S \downarrow \xi}{\Delta \triangleright S \Downarrow \xi} & \dfrac{\Delta \triangleright S \rightarrow \Delta' \triangleright S' \quad \Delta' \triangleright S' \Downarrow \xi}{\Delta \triangleright S \Downarrow \xi}
\end{array}
$$

Definition 3. *A test of $\Delta \triangleright S$ is a pair containing a formation $\Delta' \triangleright T$ and a barb ξ. $\Delta \triangleright S$ passes the test $(\Delta' \triangleright T, \xi)$ if and only if $(\Delta \circ \Delta') \triangleright (S \| T) \Downarrow \xi$.*

Definition 4. *A testing preorder, $\sqsubseteq$ for two formations $\Delta_1 \triangleright S_1$ and $\Delta_2 \triangleright S_2$ is defined as follows: $\Delta_1 \triangleright S_1 \sqsubseteq \Delta_2 \triangleright S_2$ if for any test $(\Delta \triangleright T, \xi)$, we have that if $\Delta_1 \triangleright S_1$ passes the test $(\Delta \triangleright T, \xi)$ then $\Delta_2 \triangleright S_2$ passes the test $(\Delta \triangleright T, \xi)$.*

Definition 5. *Two formations $\Delta_1 \triangleright S_1$ and $\Delta_2 \triangleright S_2$ are testing equivalent, denoted by $\Delta_1 \triangleright S_1 \simeq \Delta_2 \triangleright S_2$, if $\Delta_1 \triangleright S_1 \sqsubseteq \Delta_2 \triangleright S_2$ and $\Delta_2 \triangleright S_2 \sqsubseteq \Delta_1 \triangleright S_1$.*

3.5 Barbed Equivalence and Barbed Congruence

As mentioned in [1], testing equivalence, though elegant in concept, is hard to deal with. Hence we need another co-inductive relation that is easier to deal with to reason about systems being equivalent as to externally observable actions. Such a relation will be useful if it implies testing equivalence thereby removing the need to come up with all possible tests to determine testing equivalence. Let us define barbed simulation as a binary relation $\mathcal{R} \subseteq \mathcal{F} \times \mathcal{F}$ such that for two formations F_1 and F_2, $F_1 \mathcal{R} F_2$ implies that,

- if $F_1 \downarrow \xi$ then $F_2 \downarrow \xi$
- if $F_1 \rightarrow F_1'$ then there exists F_2' such that $F_2 \rightarrow F_2'$ where $F_1' \mathcal{R} F_2'$

A *barbed bisimulation* is a relation $\mathcal{R}$ such that both $\mathcal{R}$ and $\mathcal{R}^{-1}$ are barbed simulations. *Barbed equivalence*, written $\dot\sim$, is the greatest barbed bisimulation.

Definition 6. *Two formations $\Delta_1 \triangleright S_1$ and $\Delta_2 \triangleright S_2$ are barbed congruent, denoted by $\Delta_1 \triangleright S_1 \sim \Delta_2 \triangleright S_2$, if for any context $\Delta \triangleright T$, we have that $(\Delta_1 \circ \Delta) \triangleright (S_1 \| T) \sim (\Delta_2 \circ \Delta) \triangleright (S_2 \| T)$*

Proposition 1

- *Barbed congruence is reflexive, transitive and symmetric.*
- *Barbed congruence is a congruence on closed systems.*
- *Structural equivalence implies barbed congruence.*
- *Barbed congruence implies testing equivalence.*

4   Secrecy

Secrecy of confidential information is a big issue in computer networks. The confidential information can be login information for an online banking facility, medical information of a patient or grades of a student in a university online grade processing system. The importance of confidentiality of these type of information is tremendous. In this section we focus on whether, during the execution of a communication protocol, any message from a set of (secret) messages is ever disclosed to ambients who are not trusted or authorized to receive that message. We will use behavioral congruence to characterize processes with nondisclosure assurance.

In real life scenarios, it is typical to have that some of the agents under consideration are trusted. For example, in a WPA-enabled Wi-Fi network the RADIUS authentication server is considered to be trusted; in an online banking scenario, any authorized client and the server at the bank are considered trusted and the login information is assumed to be known to both these parties. Hence we wish to determine whether a system will ever reveal a set of confidential information to distrusted agents in any possible context. In order to do that we will introduce the concept of safe contexts. The behavioral congruence that we have introduced before considers all possible contexts. But in order to determine whether a system can keep some confidential information secret, we have to impose the restriction that the context does not already contain the secrets, because that would imply that the secret has already been revealed to the world and is no longer a secret. We will concentrate our focus on whether contexts that do not already know about secrets can possibly distinguish among systems using different secrets at different times. Our analysis is an adaptation of the work done by Abadi *et al.* in [1].

4.1   Safe Contexts and Secrecy in Safe Contexts

Let us now define a formation in which a set of keys are secret from ambients not in a given set of trusted ambients. A formation $(\Delta \triangleright T)$ is safe with respect to a set of ambients $\mathcal{A}$ and a set of secret keys $\mathcal{K}$ if ambients not in $\mathcal{A}$ only see confidential messages encrypted with the keys in $\mathcal{K}$ which are unknown to them. This allows us to specify restrictions that will be imposed upon the environments that will be composed with systems whose secrecy property we wish to check.

Definition 7. *Let $\mathcal{A}$ be a set of ambients, $\mathcal{K}$ be a set of keys, X be a set of variables and $\Delta \triangleright T$ be a formation. $\Delta \triangleright T$ is safe with respect to $\mathcal{A}$, X and $\mathcal{K}$ denoted by $\clubsuit_{\mathcal{A},X,\mathcal{K}}(\Delta \triangleright T)$ if $\Delta \triangleright T$ is a well formed formation, $\mathrm{fv}_{\bar{\mathcal{A}}}(T) \subseteq X$ and $\mathrm{fk}_{\bar{\mathcal{A}}}(T) \cap \mathcal{K} = \{\}$.*

Here by $\mathrm{fv}_{\bar{\mathcal{A}}}(T)$ and $\mathrm{fk}_{\bar{\mathcal{A}}}(T)$ we indicate the free variables and free keys appearing in the ambients not in the set $\mathcal{A}$ appearing in the form $m[P]$ in the system T. We now define substitutions for the free variables appearing in safe contexts where the substitution functions will only replace each free variable with messages encrypted with the keys that are secret from untrusted ambients. We call them *safe* substitutions.

Definition 8. *A substitution function $\sigma : X \longrightarrow M$ is a safe substitution with respect to a set of variables X and a set of keys $\mathcal{K}$ denoted by $\Upsilon_{X,\mathcal{K}}(\sigma)$ if $\mathrm{dom}(\sigma) = X$, σ is injective and for all $x \in X$, $\sigma(x)$ is of the form $\{M\}_k$ where $k \in \mathcal{K}$.*

The following lemma states that a safe formation is structurally equivalent to safe formations no matter what safe substitution is applied to it. Similarly a safe formation only transitions to safe formations irrespective of the safe substitution applied to it.

Lemma 1. *Let $\mathcal{A}$ be a set of ambients, X be a set of variables and $\mathcal{K}$ be a set of keys and $\Delta \triangleright T$ be a formation where $\clubsuit_{\mathcal{A},X,K}(\Delta \triangleright T)$. Let σ be a substitution such that $\Upsilon_{X,\mathcal{K}}(\sigma)$.*

- *If $\Delta \triangleright \sigma(T) \equiv \Delta' \triangleright T'$ then there exists a system S such that $\clubsuit_{\mathcal{A},X,\mathcal{K}}(\Delta' \triangleright S)$, $\mathrm{fv}(S) \subseteq \mathrm{fv}(T)$, $\mathrm{fk}(S) \subseteq \mathrm{fk}(T)$, and $T' = \sigma(S)$ such that whenever $\Upsilon_{X,\mathcal{K}}(\sigma')$, $\Delta \triangleright \sigma'(T) \equiv \Delta'' \triangleright \sigma'(S)$, where $\mathrm{perm}(\Delta', \Delta'')$.*
- *If $\Delta \triangleright \sigma(T) \xrightarrow{\xi} \Delta' \triangleright T'$ then there exists a system S such that $\clubsuit_{\mathcal{A},X,\mathcal{K}}(\Delta' \triangleright S)$, $\mathrm{fv}(S) \subseteq \mathrm{fv}(T)$, $\mathrm{fk}(S) \subseteq \mathrm{fk}(T)$, and $T' = \sigma(S)$ such that whenever $\Upsilon_{X,\mathcal{K}}(\sigma')$, $\Delta \triangleright \sigma'(T) \xrightarrow{\xi} \Delta'' \triangleright \sigma'(S)$, where $\mathrm{perm}(\Delta', \Delta'')$.*

Proof. By induction on the structure of T.

The next lemma states that the observable behaviors of a safe formation is indistinguishable under different safe substitutions.

Lemma 2. *Let $\mathcal{A}$ be a set of ambients, X be a set of variables and $\mathcal{K}$ be a set of keys. Let σ and σ' be two substitutions such that $\Upsilon_{X,\mathcal{K}}(\sigma)$ and $\Upsilon_{X,\mathcal{K}}(\sigma')$. Then $\{(\Delta \triangleright \sigma(T)), (\Delta \triangleright \sigma'(T)) | \clubsuit_{\mathcal{A},X,\mathcal{K}}(\Delta \triangleright T)\}$ is a barbed bisimulation.*

This lemma along with Proposition 1 allows us to reason about untrusted ambient systems without having to figure out all possible tests the untrusted ambients can perform on a system.

5   Example in **Secure Broadcast Ambients**

We first show how to impose configurations on systems by adding a configuration on top of part of our encoding for the home network. Assume Router is already in the Wifi ambient and Laptop and Wifi are not inside any ambient. A possible configuration can be [Laptop :: empty # Wifi :: empty # Router :: (Wifi; empty)]. Now the first action Laptop attempts is entering Wifi. However, the formation $F_0 =$ [Laptop :: empty # Wifi :: empty # Router :: (Wifi; empty)] ▷ Wifi[!$\overline{\text{in Laptop}}$.nil] ∥ Laptop[in Wifi .$(x)^{\text{Wifi}}.P$] will not allow this transition as ambient Laptop is trying to enter an ambient which appears later than itself in the configuration. In order to enable this transition, we permute the configuration to [Wifi :: empty#Laptop :: empty#Router :: (Wifi; empty)]. This configuration is going to allow the ambient Laptop to enter the ambient Wifi. Here is the transition:

$$F_0 = [\text{Laptop} :: \text{empty} \# \text{Wifi} :: \text{empty} \# \text{Router} :: (\text{Wifi}; \text{empty})] \triangleright$$
$$\text{Wifi}[!\overline{\text{in Laptop}}.nil] \| \text{Laptop}[\text{in Wifi} .(x)^{\text{Wifi}}.P]$$
$$\equiv F_1 = [\text{Wifi} :: \text{empty} \# \text{Laptop} :: \text{empty} \# \text{Router} :: (\text{Wifi}; \text{empty})] \triangleright$$
$$\text{Wifi}[!\overline{\text{in Laptop}}.nil] \| \text{Laptop}[\text{in Wifi} .(x)^{\text{Wifi}}.P] \rightarrow$$
$$F_2 = [\text{Wifi} :: \text{empty} \# \text{Laptop} :: (\text{Wifi}; \text{empty}) \# \text{Router} :: (\text{Wifi}; \text{empty})] \triangleright$$
$$\text{Wifi}[!\overline{\text{in Laptop}}.nil] \| \text{Laptop}[(x)^{\text{Wifi}}.P]$$

Now in the manner of [1], we show how to reason about ambient systems to determine whether they are distinguishable from the outside world as to what messages are being communicated in an encrypted form among them. If the components of the home network encrypt their messages then usually the router decrypts them and then forwards them to the worldwide internet network outside the home network. The corresponding code for the router and the Laptop can look like:

$$\Delta = [\text{Wifi} :: \text{empty} \# \text{Laptop} :: (\text{Wifi}; \text{empty}) \# \text{Router} :: (\text{Wifi}; \text{empty})]$$
$$S_1(M) = \text{Laptop}[\langle M \rangle^{\text{Wifi}}.nil]$$
$$S_2 = \text{Router}[(x)^{\text{Wifi}}. \text{ case } x \text{ of } \{y\}_{k_{\text{Wifi\_Laptop}}} : S(y)]$$
$$F(M) = \Delta \triangleright (\nu k_{\text{Wifi\_Laptop}}.(S_1(M) \| S_2))$$
$$S_{2\,spec}(M) = \text{Router}[(x)^{\text{Wifi}}. \text{ case } x \text{ of } \{y\}_{k_{\text{Wifi\_Laptop}}} : S(M)]$$
$$F_{spec}(M) = \Delta \triangleright (\nu k_{\text{Wifi\_Laptop}}.(S_1(M) \| S_{2\,spec}(M)))$$

Now what we would like to have is that for any closed term M, $F(M) \simeq F_{spec}(M)$, that is for any closed term, the external world will not be able to distinguish among whether a system sending a specific message was being considered or whether a system handling any message was being considered. In other words the outside world will not be able to distinguish among systems handling different set of messages, and will get same set of responses from all possible tests. However, as we have Proposition 1, we do not need to test the two systems with all possible tests, we only need to determine whether they are barb congruent or not:

$$\Delta \triangleright (\nu k_{\text{Wifi\_Laptop}}.(S_1(M) \| S_{2\,spec}(M))) \sim \Delta \triangleright (\nu k_{\text{Wifi\_Laptop}}.(S_1(M) \| S_2)$$

By the definition of $\sim$, we know that we need to show that for all contexts $\Delta' \triangleright T$,

$$\Delta \circ \Delta' \triangleright (\nu k_{\text{Wifi\_Laptop}}.(S_1(M) \| S_{2\,spec}(M))) \| T \overset{.}{\sim} \Delta \circ \Delta' \triangleright (\nu k_{\text{Wifi\_Laptop}}.((S_1(M) \| S_2) \| T)$$

Without loss of generality we can assume that $k_{\text{Wifi\_Laptop}} \notin \text{fk}(T)$. Then we will need to show that for all contexts,

$$\Delta \circ \Delta' \triangleright \nu k_{\text{Wifi\_Laptop}}.(S_1(M) \| S_{2\,spec}(M) \| T) \overset{.}{\sim} \Delta \circ \Delta' \triangleright \nu k_{\text{Wifi\_Laptop}}.(S_1(M) \| S_2 \| T)$$

Since barb equivalence is preserved by restriction (proof not given in this work), we only need to show that

$$\Delta \circ \Delta' \rhd (S_1(M) \| S_{2\,spec}(M) \| T) \,\dot{\sim}\, \Delta \circ \Delta' \rhd (S_1(M) \| S_2 \| T)$$

To prove that, we use a substitution function $\sigma = \{x \mapsto \{M\}_{k_{\mathsf{Wifi\_Laptop}}}\}$ where $\Upsilon_{\{x\},\{k_{\mathsf{Wifi\_Laptop}}\}}(\sigma)$. We then introduce a relation $\mathcal{S}$: $F_1 \mathcal{S} F_2$ if and only if $F_1 = \Delta \circ \Delta' \rhd (S_{2\,spec}(M) \| T_1\sigma)$ and $F_2 = \Delta \circ \Delta' \rhd (S_2(M) \| T_1\sigma)$ for some T_1 such that $\clubsuit_{\mathcal{A},X,\mathcal{K}}(\delta \circ \Delta' \rhd T_1)$ where $\mathcal{A} = \{\mathsf{Router}, \mathsf{Laptop}\}$, $X = \{x\}$ and $\mathcal{K} = k_{\mathsf{Wifi\_Laptop}}$. Here, $\delta \circ \Delta' \rhd T_1\sigma$ represents both $S_1(M)$ and contexts that they do not already know of the key being used between the Router and the Laptop, that is $k_{\mathsf{Wifi\_Laptop}}$ is not known by any ambient other than Router and Laptop in them. The rest of the proof consists of proving that $\mathcal{S} \cup \dot{\sim}$ is a barbed bisimulation.

6   Related Work

Mobile ambients have been extended in various ways since their introduction. In [3], *boxed ambients* removed the ability of ambients to open, and added the ability for parent and child ambients to communicate by communication channels. *Safe ambients* [12] and subsequently *NBA(New Boxed Ambients)*[4] allowed the ambient being entered or exited the power to grant (or by omission, deny) the requested entrance or egress. We removed the egress permission to be able to model situations where a mobile device is simply turned off.

Let us now consider the existing broadcast calculi like CBS [20] and $b\pi$[7]. They overcome the limitations of CCS and π-calculus respectively, by allowing one-to-many communication. However, these calculi were not designed to model regions of computation where the regions are capable of restricting access to themselves. Hennessy *et al.* gives a theory of bisimulation equivalence and equational theory and finitary proof system for both the strong and weak versions of the bisimulation equivalences for CBS in [10]. The calculus for Higher Order Broadcast System, HOBS is presented in [19], which is a higher order extension of CBS. Nanz *et al.* extend CBS to CBS# in [17], where they confine broadcast communication to local rooms and impose graphical restrictions on being able to listen in a particular region. However, their regions are not actively mobile. Moraru *et al.* suggests in [16] how the broadcast communication mechanism of CBS can be extended to the ambient calculus as given in [9]. Prasad suggests ways of modeling "globally asynchronous, locally synchronous" broadcast communication scenarios using Mobile Broadcasting Systems, MBS in [21]. Mezzetti *et al.* present Calculus of Wireless Systems (CWS) in [13], where they extend CBS to accommodate nonatomic communication action of wireless networks. Their focus is on modeling wireless communication protocols among usually immobile domains like sensor networks. They use locations and radius to define transmission regions instead of connectivity graphs like CBS#. Their regions, like CBS# are also immobile.

Among the process calculi where the method of communication is not broadcast, a related work is the work on distributed π-calculus [11] by Hennessy *et al.* where we have locations and code mobility among locations. The topology of locations is flat in their calculus and they have code movement but not location movement. Another related calculus is the m-calculus as given in [22] which is a higher-order extension of [8]. Their location topology is tree-structured, with the programmable access control to locations. Another related calculus is the seal calculus given in [6]. However, seals are different from ambients in the structure of their hierarchy and because seals are not subjectively mobile like ambients. *Discretionary ambients* by Nielson *et al.* [18] equip safe ambients with discretionary and mandatory access control.

A related work is that of bigraphs by Milner presented in [14]. Bigraphs are actually a pair of two graphs, a topograph, describing actual physical location and a link graph which describes communication links which does not care about the physical positions. Place graphs are forests of unordered trees whereas our topology is a collection of directed acyclic graphs. Link graphs allow channels between arbitrary pair of agents. They do not have to be adjacent in any way. They lack any mechanism of enforcing access restrictions.

7   Conclusion

We defined Secure Broadcast Ambients which is capable of modeling broadcast communication within a domain. Our calculus allows a directed acyclic graph topology of the location of our agents, hence our topology is more flexible than the usual tree structured one. Our domains or systems are also capable of restricting access to themselves. We then provide co-inductive relations to reason about whether an ambient system keeps a set of messages secret by using encryption. We provide a scenario which our calculus can model more succinctly than other calculi. We present the modeling of this scenario in our calculus to demonstrate the strengths and capabilities of our calculus.

Our calculus however only handles symmetric encryption at this point. Hence we are not capable of modeling communication protocols requiring asymmetric encryption. Developing a complete theory for handling asymmetric encryption is a future goal for us. Also, we intend to apply our calculus for modeling and reasoning about workflows specially workflows where confidentiality and integrity of the data involved is a very significant concern. We have modeled the Automated Identification and Data Capture (AIDC) workflow for hospital data management, being developed at UIUC, using our calculus. We are working towards proving security properties of such scenarios.

References

1. Abadi, M., Gordon, A.D.: A Calculus for Cryptographic Protocols: The Spi Calculus. Inf. Comput. 148(1), 1–70 (1999)
2. Bugliesi, M., Castagna, G., Crafa, S.: Reasoning about security in mobile ambients. In: Larsen, K.G., Nielsen, M. (eds.) CONCUR 2001. LNCS, vol. 2154, pp. 102–120. Springer, Heidelberg (2001)

3. Bugliesi, M., Castagna, G., Crafa, S.: Access Control for Mobile Agents: The Calculus of Boxed Ambients. ACM Transactions on Programming Languages and Systems 26(1), 57–124 (2004)

4. Bugliesi, M., Crafa, S., Merro, M., Sassone, V.: Communication and mobility control in boxed ambients. Inf. Comput. 202(1), 39–86 (2005)

5. Cardelli, L., Gordon, A.D.: Mobile Ambients. Theoretical Computer Science 240(1), 177–213 (2000); Le Métayer, D. (ed.) Special Issue on Coordination

6. Castagna, G., Vitek, J., Nardelli, F.Z.: The seal calculus. Inf. Comput. 201(1), 1–54 (2005)

7. Ene, C., Muntean, T.: A broadcast-based calculus for communicating systems. In: IPDPS, p. 149. IEEE Computer Society, Los Alamitos (2001)

8. Fournet, C., Gonthier, G.: The join calculus: A language for distributed mobile programming. In: Barthe, G., Dybjer, P., Pinto, L., Saraiva, J. (eds.) APPSEM 2000. LNCS, vol. 2395, pp. 268–332. Springer, Heidelberg (2002)

9. Gordon, A.D., Cardelli, L.: Equational properties of mobile ambients. Mathematical Structures in Computer Science 13(3), 371–408 (2003)

10. Hennessy, M., Rathke, J.: Bisimulations for a calculus of broadcasting systems. Theor. Comput. Sci. 200(1-2), 225–260 (1998)

11. Hennessy, M., Rathke, J., Yoshida, N.: safeDpi: a language for controlling mobile code. Acta Inf. 42(4-5), 227–290 (2005)

12. Levi, F., Sangiorgi, D.: Controlling Interference in Ambients. Transactions on Programming Languages and Systems 25(1), 1–69 (2003)

13. Mezzetti, N., Sangiorgi, D.: Towards a calculus for wireless systems. Electr. Notes Theor. Comput. Sci. 158, 331–353 (2006)

14. Milner, R.: Bigraphical reactive systems. In: Larsen, K.G., Nielsen, M. (eds.) CONCUR 2001. LNCS, vol. 2154, pp. 16–35. Springer, Heidelberg (2001)

15. Milner, R., Parrow, J., Walker, D.: A Calculus of Mobile Processes. Information and Computation 100, 1–40 (1992)

16. Moraru, V., Muntean, T., Gutuleac, E.: Towards a model for broadcasting secure mobile processes. In: ISPDC, pp. 168–172 (2006)

17. Nanz, S., Hankin, C.: A framework for security analysis of mobile wireless networks. Theor. Comput. Sci. 367(1-2), 203–227 (2006)

18. Nielson, H.R., Nielson, F., Buchholtz, M.: Security for mobility. In: Focardi, R., Gorrieri, R. (eds.) FOSAD 2001. LNCS, vol. 2946, pp. 207–265. Springer, Heidelberg (2004)

19. Ostrovsky, K., Prasad, K.V.S., Taha, W.: Towards a primitive higher order calculus of broadcasting systems. In: PPDP, pp. 2–13 (2002)

20. Prasad, K.V.S.: A calculus of broadcasting systems. Sci. Comput. Program. 25(2-3), 285–327 (1995)

21. Prasad, K.V.S.: A prospectus for mobile broadcasting systems. Electr. Notes Theor. Comput. Sci. 162, 295–300 (2006)

22. Schmitt, A., Stefani, J.-B.: The m-calculus: a higher-order distributed process calculus. In: POPL, pp. 50–61 (2003)

Extending Anticipation Games with Location, Penalty and Timeline

Elie Bursztein

LSV, ENS Cachan, CNRS, INRIA, France
eb@lsv.ens-cachan.fr

Abstract. Over the last few years, attack graphs have became a well recognized tool to analyze and model complex network attack. The most advanced evolution of attack graphs, called anticipation games, is based on game theory. However even if anticipation games allow to model time, collateral effects and player interactions with the network, there is still key aspects of the network security that cannot be modeled in this framework. Theses aspects are network cooperation to fight unknown attack, the cost of attack based on its duration and the introduction of new attack over the time. In this paper we address these needs, by introducing a three-fold extension to anticipation games. We prove that this extension does not change the complexity of the framework. We illustrate the usefulness of this extension by presenting how it can be used to find a defense strategy against 0 days that use an honey net. Finally, we have implemented this extension into a prototype, to show that it can be used to analyze large networks security.

1 Introduction

As networks of hosts continue to grow, evaluating their vulnerability to attacks becomes increasingly more important. When evaluating the security of a network, it is not enough to consider the presence or the absence of public vulnerabilities. Inevitably, a large network will contain undisclosed vulnerabilities that can be the target of undisclosed attacks called zero day exploits. To setup a defense strategy that mitigates this kind of attack, network cooperation defense needs to be considered. Using network topological information along with other information such as average deployment cost and time, an analyst can produce an **anticipation game**. The anticipation game framework [5,4] is the most advanced evolution of attach graphs. This framework is based on game theory [7] and TATL [8] (Timed Alternating-time Temporal Logic).

Modeling network cooperation strategy cannot be achieved in the current anticipation games framework, because some rules and strategies need to be restrained to specific set of services, whereas other need to be global to model network communication. For example, patching rules should not be applied to a honey-net network. This is why location restriction needs to be introduced in the framework. Moreover dealing with a zero day exploit requires taking into account the vulnerability cycle timeline. To do so one need to be able to express a timeline of events which is a succession of events that takes place one after the other.

We also extend anticipation games with penalties. Intuitively a penalty is a cost added for each unit of time a constraint holds. As additional benefit penalty allow to model

P. Degano, J. Guttman, and F. Martinelli (Eds.): FAST 2008, LNCS 5491, pp. 272–286, 2009.

another important relation between time and cost: cost diminishing. A cost diminishing occurs when the same action is executed multiple times. It also occurs when an on-going process is done for an extended period. *e.g* service monitoring.

Finally this extension allows us to model player's simultaneous actions and event branching. Event branching is used to model that at a certain point, several options are available to the player, such as using one kind of patch or an other.

The main contribution of this paper is an extension of the anticipation game framework that allows to model network cooperation, intrusion cost based on their duration, and the introduction of new event over the time. To the best of our knowledge, our extended framework is the first which is able to model and analyze those aspects of network security. We prove that anticipation games with locations and penalties are decidable and that the complexity of the model remains EXPTIME-complete. We also have implemented our framework into an freely available tool called NetQi [3] to evaluate the effectiveness of the approach. In the evaluation section we will show that it is possible to analyze complex multiple-sites scenarios even on large networks with thousand of services. To illustrate how our extension works, we provide a running example that discusses a network multiple-sites defense strategy that uses a honey-net as a defense against various types of exploits including zero day ones.

The reminder of this paper is organized as follows. In Sect. 2, we will survey related work and in Sect. 3 we recall what an anticipation game is. We also detail the game example that is used as a guideline for the rest of the paper. Sect. 4 presents the notion of locations. In Sect 5 the timeline of events is illustrated. Sect. 6 introduces the notion of penalty and cost diminishing. Sect 7 covers the multiple-sites defense strategies that were found by analyzing the running example with our prototype. In sect. 8 we evaluate the effectiveness of the approach. We conclude in Sect. 9

2   Related Work

Model checking for attack graphs was introduced by Ammann and Ritchey [17]. They are used to harden security [14]. Various methods have been proposed for finding attack paths, i.e., sequences of exploits, including logic-based approaches [15,19,9,18], and graph-based approaches [21,20,13]. Anticipation game are based on timed automata, timed games, and timed alternating-time temporal logic (TATL) [8], a timed extension to alternating-time Kripke structures and temporal logic (ATL) [1]. The TATL framework was specifically introduced in [7]. Game strategies have been used to predict players actions in numerous domains ranging from economy to war [2,16]. the notion of cost diminishing appears in [6]. The use of games for network security was introduced by Lye and Wing [11]. Game theory was used to analyze denial of service in [12]. The anticipation game framework was presented by Bursztein and Goubault-Larrecq [5] and network strategies for anticipation games were introduced in [4].

3   Anticipation Games

An anticipation game is a timed game [7], the key difference between standard timed games and anticipation games is the dual-layer structure used in anticipation games.

Its lower-layer called the **Network Layer** is used to represent network information. Its upper-layer called the **Attack Layer** is a regular TATL game structure used to model the network state evolution induced by players actions such as exploiting a vulnerability. An anticipation games can be thought as a graph of graphs where the lower graph is the network state and the above graph describes the transition between one network state to an other. The players of an anticipation games are called **administrator** and **intruder** and their actions are modeled by **timed rules**. Typical actions range from patching, to exploiting a vulnerability, to firewalling a service. They are called timed rules because a rule execution requires a certain amount of time to be executed. Each Attack Layer transition represents the execution of one rule. In an anticipation game a path is called a **play**. More formally a play is a path (a sequence of action and states) $\rho : s_0 r_0 s_1 r_1 \ldots$ where $\forall j : s_j \xrightarrow{r_j} s_{j+1}$, s_j and s_{j+1} are network states, and r_j is the rule used to make the transition. Using a network initial configuration and a set of rules, an anticipation game is used to answer questions such as : *what should I do to counter this type of attack ?*

In the anticipation games framework, a questions is specified in term of **strategies objectives** and its answer, the **strategy**, is the play that fulfill best these objectives. Strategies objectives are composed of two main parts: a set of constraints and a set of goals. Constraints are used to express conditions on the network state that a play must satisfy to be considered as a potential strategy. A typical defense strategy constraint is that no service is ever compromised during the play and that at the end of the play no service is vulnerable anymore. Goal are used to select among all the plays that satisfy the set of constraints the one that is the most relevant by analyzing the cost, reward and time outcome. A typical defense strategy goal is to minimize the cost of the strategy.

The cost reward and timing used in this paper are not meant to be realistic, they are only here for example purpose. While interesting, computing the real value of cost, reward and timing is out of the scope of this paper that aims at providing a mean to reason on them.

3.1   Network Layer

The Network Layer is composed of two parts. First the **Dependency Graph** which is the graph that represents the dependency relations that exist in the network. It is meant to be static and does not evolve over game execution. Secondly a finite **set of states** associated to each Dependency Graph vertex that describes the current network state. This set of states is meant to evolve over game execution. Formally, let $\mathcal{A}$ be a finite set of so-called *atomic propositions* $A_1, \ldots, A_n, \ldots$, denoting each base property. Each atomic proposition is true or false at each vertex. E.g., Vuln is true at each vertex that is vulnerable. Thus each atomic proposition is true or false for each of Dependency Graph vertices. *States* on Dependency Graph are then simply functions $\rho : \mathcal{A} \to \mathbb{P}(V)$ mapping each atomic proposition to the set of vertices that satisfies it. We describe ρ in a finite way, as a table of all pairs $(A, v) \in \mathcal{A} \times \mathbb{P}(V)$ such that $v \in \rho(A)$; hence there are finitely many states. The Dependency Graph used as an example and the corresponding set of states are represented in Figure 1.

This Dependency Graph is composed of six real vertices and a virtual one (vertex 1). The edges are the dependencies that exist between services. Concrete dependencies are

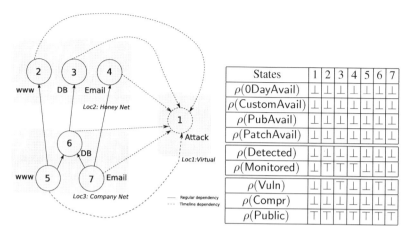

Fig. 1. Dependency Graph (left) and Initial set of states (right)

represented with a plain line and virtual dependencies used for the timeline of events with a dashed line. The role of the virtual vertex and its incoming dependencies is to model the timeline of events as detailed in Section 5. Concrete dependencies are used to model that a service is dependent on another. In our example the vertex *www (5)*, which is a web server, depends on the vertex *DB (6)*, which is a database, to retrieve user credential for authentication purpose. From a security perspective it means that if the vertex *DB (6)* is unavailable by **collateral effect** the vertex *www (5)* will be also unavailable. It also means that the trust relation that exists between those two vertices may be exploited by an attacker. These dependencies are used in game rules to model collateral effects and trust abuse. The three dependencies from the company's network services to their twins services located in the honey network are used for the multiple-sites defense purpose. The fake honey-net services are used to lure the attacker and catch him when he tries to attack them. Using an honey-net allow to catch unknown attack because the only traffic they get are attacks. Hence if the traffic is not a known attack, it is likely that its a new type of attack. That is why each company's services depend on its honey-net fake twin service to defeat a zero day attack.

The complete set of variables mapping used in the example can be divided into three parts. The first part is variables `0DayAvail`, `CustomAvail`, `PubAvail` and `PatchAvail` which are used to model the timeline of events. The second part is variables `Detected` and `Monitored` which are used for multiple-sites defense purpose. Finally the third part is used to describe the network's initial state. The variable `Vuln` is used to model that the company web and email services along with their fake twin services located on the honey-net are vulnerable to an unknown vulnerability. The variable `Compr` is used to say that no service is compromised. Finally the variable `Public` is used to indicate that every service is public (not firewalled).

3.2 Attack Layer

TATL [8] extends ATL [1] with the notion of timed game by adding time cost to transitions. From the network security perspective this is important because it models that player actions on a network require a certain amount of time to be executed. This prevents meaningless strategies such as being able to patch every network vulnerability in an instant. Hence an anticipation game can be viewed as a race between players where the fastest wins. This time race introduces a so called element of surprise [7]. For example the intruder can take the administrator by surprise if he can exploit a vulnerability faster than the administrator can patch it. This is coherent with real network security where you cannot foresee what attacker will come up next.

3.3   Rules of the Game

The actions of each player are described by a set of timed rules. Each rule is of the form:

$$\Gamma_x : \textbf{Pre } F \xrightarrow{\Delta,\, \text{p},\, \text{a},\, \text{c}} P$$

where F is the set of **preconditions** that need to be satisfied in order to use the rule. Δ is the amount of time needed to execute the rule, p is the player who uses the rule, a is the rule label (string), and c is the rule cost. P is the rule **post-condition**, that states rule effects. It is required for F preconditions to hold not just when the rule is selected, but also during the whole time it takes the rule to actually complete (Δ time units). Γ_x is the rule location. Anticipation games use two types of rules [4]. **Granting rule** use the $\Longrightarrow$ double arrow and **regular rules** use the $\longrightarrow$ single arrow. A granting rule allows the player to receive a reward based on the target Dependency Graph vertex value when the rule is successfully executed whereas regular rules do not grant any reward. Regular rules are used for temporary actions and for the timeline of events. For example the following rule is used to model trust abuse attack:

$$\Gamma : \textbf{Pre } \Diamond Compr \wedge \neg Compr \xrightarrow{2,\text{I},\text{Trust abuse},\, 200} Compr$$

It says that the intruder (I) can compromise a non compromised ($\neg Compr$) vertex by exploiting a trust relation if one of its successors is compromised ($\Diamond Compr$) in 2 units of time for a cost of \$200. The $\Diamond$ is a modal operator used to speak of Dependency Graph successors. The other operators used in rule preconditions and effects are standard modal operators. If the intruder chooses to use this rule, then to have a successful rule execution it is required that the preconditions are fulfilled when he chooses to apply the rule, and also after the 2 units of time required to complete it. This is mandatory because the network state might evolve due to administrator actions during these 2 units of time. For example the administrator might have restored the successor vertex. In this case, the intruder is taken by surprise, and the compromise rule fails.

4   Location

In the original anticipation games [5] a rule can be applied to any Dependency Graph vertex as long as its set of constraints meets the rule preconditions requirements. However in many cases such behavior is not suitable. In particular it is not possible to model network multiple-sites defense analysis without restricting the scope of rules. This impossibility is mainly due to the fact that different rules need to be applied to the different networks. Therefore we distinguish three type of rules: the **transitional** ones, the **local** ones, and the **global** ones. Transitional rules are used to model inter-site interaction. Local rules are used for site specific action. In our example the rule used to model trust abuse attacks needs to be restricted to company's network, and timeline of events rules to the virtual location. Finally global rules are meant to be used on any vertex. Similarly strategies objectives might be restricted to a given set of vertices. In our example finding a defense strategy that prevents service compromising should obviously not apply to honey-net fake services. In order to restrict rules and strategy objectives to a given set of vertices, we extend anticipation games with locations. A location is a non-empty set of services that belongs to the same site. More formally a location is a set of Dependency Graph vertices represented by an integer. Location integer is added to every Dependency Graph vertex as a label. Locations are specified in rules and strategy objectives to restrict their scopes.

4.1 Type of Rule

We use the set of an **operational rules** depicted in figure 2 in the example. We speak of operational set because it is used to model attack and defense actions. At the opposite the set of **timeline rules** depicted in section 5 is used to model timeline events. This operational set combines the three types of rules to model multiple site defense. The three type of rules are more formally defined as:

Definition 1 (Global rule). *A rule is global if no location restriction is specified.*

Definition 2 (Local rule). *A rule is local if the same location restriction is specified for the rule target vertex and the rule target successor vertex.*

Definition 3 (Transitional rule). *A rule is transitional if a different location restriction is specified for the rule target vertex and the rule target successor vertex.*

4.2 Global Rules

The first three rules are comparable, as they model the same action: an intruder (I) that exploits a remote service vulnerability to compromise a public service. The rule

1) Γ : **Pre** : $\lozenge 0DayAvail \wedge Vuln \wedge Public \wedge \neg Compr$
$\implies$ 3, I, 0 day exploit, 20000
Effect : $Compr$

2) Γ : **Pre** : $\lozenge CustomAvail \wedge Vuln \wedge Public \wedge \neg Compr$
$\implies$ 4, I, Custom exploit, 2000
Effect : $Compr$

3) Γ : **Pre** : $\lozenge PubAvail \wedge Vuln \wedge Public \wedge \neg Compr$
$\implies$ 7, I, Public exploit, 200
Effect : $Compr$

4) $\Gamma_{3:3}$: **Pre** : $\neg Compr \wedge \lozenge Compr$
$\implies$ 2, I, Trust Abuse, 200
Effect : $Compr$

5) $\Gamma_{1:1}$: **Pre** $Monitored \wedge Compr \wedge \neg Detected$
$\longrightarrow$ 1, A, Attack Detected, 2000
Effect $Detected$

6) $\Gamma_{2:2}$: **Pre** $\neg Vuln \wedge \neg Public$
$\longrightarrow$ 1, A, Unfirewall, 100
Effect $Public$

7) $\Gamma_{3:2}$: **Pre** $\lozenge Detected \wedge Vuln \wedge Public$
$\longrightarrow$ 0, A, Firewall, 100
Effect $\neg Public$

8) $\Gamma_{3:1}$: **Pre** $\lozenge PatchAvail \wedge Vuln$
$\longrightarrow$ 6, A, Patch, 500
Effect $\neg Vuln$

Fig. 2. Set of rules used to model a players action

preconditions ensure that the targeted service is vulnerable ($Vuln$ has to be true) and remotely accessible ($Public$ has to be true). The rule effects when the execution is successful is that the vertex becomes compromised ($Compr$ become true). Since these rules are meant to attack fake and real services they are global (Γ has no index). They differ because due to the events timeline, they are available at a different time. The 0Day exploit is released first, then the custom exploit and finally the public exploit. For instance $0DayAvail$ is set to true for the virtual vertex by a timeline rule after 48 hours. This constraint is used to prevent the intruder from using it earlier in the game. Accordingly the Custom exploit cannot be used before it is available because until then, the $CustomAvail$ is set to false for the virtual vertex. The cost of the three rules also differs researching a vulnerability is more costly than making a custom exploit which is more costly than simply using a public exploit. The conjunction of cost and timeline allows us to model the trade-off between the advantage awarded by an undisclosed vulnerability exploit and the investment required to find it.

4.3   Local Rules

Rules 4, 5, and 6 are local rules. Their Γ index is of the form $n : n$ where the first n is the vertex location and the second n is the successor location. Rule 4 says that if a service is not compromised ($\neg Compr$) and if one of its successor is compromised ($\Diamond Compr$) then it can be compromised by the intruder (I) in 2 hours for \$200. This rule must be local because otherwise erroneous actions are possible: as visible in diagram 1 a dependency exists between each company's service and its corresponding honey-net service. When the trust abuse rule is not restricted to a local scope these relations can be used for trust abuse. As a result a compromised honey-net service can be used to compromise a company's service by trust abuse, which is clearly an erroneous action. This is why this rule needs to be restricted to the company's network context to be executed only on services where real trust relation exists. Rule 5 is local to the honey-net network. It states that if a service is monitored ($Monitored$), compromised ($Compr$) and an alert has not been already raised ($\neg Detected$) then an alert is raised. The time required to trigger the rule also includes the alert propagation time in order to achieve simultaneous service firewalling execution as explained in Section 5. The $Monitored$ set is used as detailed in Section 6 to compute monitoring ongoing process cost. The rule 6 is local to the company's network because since the firewall rule applies only to the company's network this one should only apply to it as well. It states that if a service is not public ($\neg Public$) and not vulnerable ($\neg Vuln$) then it can be made public ($Public$).

4.4   Transitional Rules

Rules 7 and 8 are transitional rules. Their Γ index is of the form $n : m$ where n is the vertex location and m the successor location. They are used for multiple-sites interaction. In the example there are two kinds of such interactions. First the interaction between the honey-net (location 2) and the company's network (location 3). This interaction allows the company's network to defend itself against unknown attacks by firewalling a company's service when the corresponding honey-net service experience an attack. This interaction is described by the rule 7 which states that if an attack is detected on a remote location ($\Diamond Detected$) and the vertex is public (*Public*) and vulnerable (*Vuln*) then it can be firewalled by the administrator. The location restriction ensures that only company's network will be affected by the rule. It also ensures that the successor belongs to the honey-net. The other transitional rule is the patching rule. It is restricted to the company network location because honey-net services are not meant to be patched. Its successor has to be the virtual location because this is where the timeline of events evolves. The timeline information is needed to know when the patch is available. This rule can only be transitional: if it is global, it can be applied to honey-net and if it is local it does not work because the timeline of events evolution take place in the virtual location.

4.5 Strategy with Location

Definition 4 *(Strategy). A strategy is the tuple* S : (name, P, $\mathcal{O}$, $\mathcal{R}$, $\mathcal{C}$, $\mathcal{L}$) *where* name *is the strategy name,* P *its owner,* $\mathcal{O}$ *is the strategy objectives set,* $\mathcal{R}$ *is the objectives priority strict order,* $\mathcal{C}$ *is the set of constraints for the play and* $\mathcal{L}$ *is the set of constraint for the location.*

In our example the following defense strategy objectives are used:

$$S : (\text{Defense strategy}, Admin, MIN(Cost) \wedge MAX(OCost), OCost > Cost, \Box\neg Compr, \neg 2)$$

They are used to find the play for the administrator that primarily maximizes intruder cost ($MIN(OCost)$), and secondarily minimizes the administrator cost ($MIN(Cost)$), and ensures that no service in every location except the honey-net location ($\neg 2$) is ever compromised ($\Box\neg Compr$). Adding the opponent cost maximization objective aims at finding the **(weakly) dominant strategy**.

Definition 5 (weakly) dominant strategy. *A dominant strategy is the strategy that beats every opponent strategy (strict dominance) or at least maximizes the number of strategies beaten (weak dominance).*

The strategy returned for these objectives can be view as the play where the opponent plays his best game against the targeted player. Model-checking strategies constraints against Anticipation games with location is still decidable.

Lemma 1. *Model-checking strategies constraints against Anticipation games extended with locations is decidable.*

5   Using a Timeline of Events

Being able to model a timeline of events is mandatory because many network security scenarios need it. For instance the classical vulnerability cycle [10] follows a timeline of events: the patch for a given flaw is developed only after the vulnerability is either reported, or caught in the wild and reverse engineered. Similarly an attack can be detected by a misuse IDS `only after` its signature has been added to the database. Such a timeline of events can be modeled in anticipation games by using a combination of rules, states and dependencies. The key idea is to add a virtual vertex in the dependency graph that is used to model the timeline of events evolution thanks to a set of states. An additional set of dependencies from real services to this virtual vertex is added in order to be able to use timeline of events state in rule preconditions and effects (as in the Dependency Graph depicted in figure 1). Locations are used to ensure that the virtual vertex is the only one used in timeline of events evolution rules. Otherwise, every timeline rule will apply successively to every vertex leading to an erroneous strategy.

5.1 Discreet Timeline of Events Illustration

The multiple-site defense example uses a timeline of events inspired by the standard vulnerability cycle represented in diagram 3 which is modeled by the four sets and four rules presented in figure 3. Intuitively in this model states are used to model which points have been reached so far and rules are used to advance in the timeline. One distinct state is required for each event because states are Boolean values. Accordingly each state used for the timeline of events is set to false in initial conditions. The rule execution time represents the time interval between two consecutive events. For example the custom exploit is available 14 days after the vulnerability is discovered (global time), and 12 days after the zero day exploit (relative time). The availability of the custom exploit is modeled by the rule 2. This rule states that if the Custom exploit is not available ($\neg CustomAvail$) and the zero day is ($0DayAvail$) then after 288 units of time (12 days) the attacker will have access to custom exploit.

Using a relative time allows us to model branching. For example if the timeline presented above is not sufficient, because one wants to model multiple ways to disclose the vulnerability and make the custom exploit available, then it is possible to use multiple rules that have the same effect but different preconditions, time, and cost. For example to model that the disclosure is the result of an intrusion caught by the honey-net

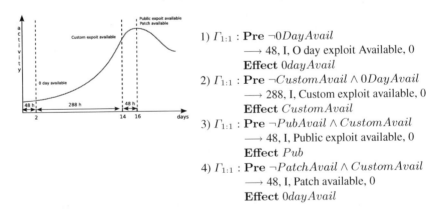

1) $\Gamma_{1:1}$: **Pre** $\neg 0DayAvail$
   $\longrightarrow$ 48, I, O day exploit Available, 0
   Effect $0dayAvail$

2) $\Gamma_{1:1}$: **Pre** $\neg CustomAvail \wedge 0DayAvail$
   $\longrightarrow$ 288, I, Custom exploit available, 0
   Effect $CustomAvail$

3) $\Gamma_{1:1}$: **Pre** $\neg PubAvail \wedge CustomAvail$
   $\longrightarrow$ 48, I, Public exploit available, 0
   Effect Pub

4) $\Gamma_{1:1}$: **Pre** $\neg PatchAvail \wedge CustomAvail$
   $\longrightarrow$ 48, I, Patch available, 0
   Effect $0dayAvail$

Fig. 3. Vulnerability timeline of events (left) and the set of rules used to model timeline evolution (right)

and reverse engineered the following rule can be used with the proper set of dependencies:

$$\Gamma_{1:2} : \textbf{Pre } Detected \xrightarrow{288, \text{A, Reverse Engineering}, 500} \textbf{Effect} Custom Avail$$

This transitional rule states that if a honey-net service is compromised then in 12 day the administrator staff is able to reverse engineer it for a cost of $500. Branching was not introduced in the example for the purpose of clarity.

Another type of timeline of events occurs when multiple actions take place at the same time. In the multiple-site defense this occurs when the attack on the honey-net is caught: every site has to use the firewall simultaneously. Otherwise the time required to firewall x sites is equal to $x \times t$ where t is the time required to firewall one site. To have a constant time regardless of the number of sites a state is used as a validation point. In the example this is the state $Detected$. The time required to firewall the site is modeled by the rule 5 of figure 2. Once this rule is executed the administrator is able to use simultaneously as many firewall rules as she wants. This is achieved by setting the firewall rule time to 0.

6 Linking Cost and Time

In the original anticipation games model with strategies [4], costs are bounded to rule executions: each time a player executes a rule, his cost increases. This is a natural way to model that player action has a cost. However this approach has an important limitation: it does not allow to model costs that are time dependent. Such cost exists for on-going processes which are prominent in network security. Two well known examples of such on-going processes are service DOSing (Denial Of Service)[12], and intrusion detection monitoring. The longer they last, the higher the cost is. To model this type of cost, anticipation games need to be extended with the notion of penalty. Intuitively a penalty is a cost that is added for every unit of time a constraint holds on a given dependency graph vertex. More formally a penalty is defined as follows:

Definition 6 (Penalty). *A penalty is the tuple $P : (\mathsf{P}, \mathsf{N}, \mathsf{C}, \mathsf{F})$ where P is the player targeted by the penalty, $\mathsf{N} \in \mathbb{N}^*$ is the Dependency Graph vertex where the constraint has to hold, C is the constraint that needs to be satisfied to trigger the penalty, and $\mathsf{F}(x)$ is the function $\mathsf{F}(x) : \mathbb{N}^* \to \mathbb{N}$ that takes as parameter the integer x which is the number of units of time elapsed since the penalty has been triggered and returns the corresponding cost for this unit of time. The total cost generated by the penalty is therefore the sum of all the costs returned by the penalty function.*

Here is how penalty can be used to model a DOS cost. Assume that the Dependency Graph vertex 5 is a HTTP service used to sell company products. Every hour, the amount of income generated by this service is $1000. Therefore for every unit of time the service is unavailable ($\neg Avail$) because of the DOS, the company loses $1000 of income. This can be modeled by adding the following penalty to the game:

$$P : (\text{Administrator}, 5, \neg Avail, f(x) \to 1000)$$

which states that for each unit of time where the vertex 5 (www service) is not available the administrator cost is increased by 1000. The use of such penalty allows the incident strategy cost minimization objective to take into account the relation between the loss of income and the time elapsed. In the running example we use the same kind of penalty to compute the cost associated with the action of firewalling a public service. The use of a function based on the number of units of time elapsed allows to use various cost models such as an exponential cost or a diminishing cost model as presented above.

Another important time/cost relation to consider is when the cost diminishes over the time [6]. This reduction occurs when the same action is performed multiple times, or when an on-going process is run for an extended period of time. Performing the same action again and again is a common practice in network security. For instance the action of patching similar services or the action of reusing the same exploit. In this context the cost of the first use is more expensive than later ones. In the patching case, the first use is more expensive because it requires to download and test the patch. In the exploit case, the first use requires the attacker to develop and test the code whereas subsequent exploitations only require it to be launched. This type of cost reduction is modeled in anticipation games by using two rules with different costs and a timeline of events to ensure that the cheaper rule is only used after the most expensive one has been used. To model a diminishing supervision cost with a lower bound the following kind of penalty can be used:

$$P : (\text{Administrator}, 5, \text{Monitored}, f(x) \rightarrow int(1000/x) + y)$$

Where x is the number of time units elapsed, $y \in \mathbb{N}$ is the lower bound cost and $int(x)$ the standard function that returns a rounded integer from a float. We use two kinds of penalties in the example. The first kind is induced by monitoring honey-net service, we assume that monitoring a honey-net service costs \$10 by hour. Accordingly we add three penalties to the analysis, one for each honey-net service. For example the following penalty is added for the vertex 2:

$$P : (\text{Administrator}, 2, \text{Monitored}, f(x) \rightarrow 10)$$

6.1   Decidability and Complexity of the Extended Model

Even if adding penalty allows to model a brand new range of cost, from the decidability perspective, extending the framework with penalty does not change the decidability.

Lemma 2. *Model-checking strategies constraints against Anticipation games extended with penalty is decidable.*

From Lemma 1 and Lemma 2 it follows:

Theorem 1. *Model-checking strategies constraints against Anticipation games extended with penalties and locations is decidable.*

Which is the central theoretical result. Additionally we prove that locations and penalties does not change the anticipation games complexity bound which is a key result for the practicality of the approach:

Theorem 2. *Model-checking strategies constraints over anticipation games extended with penalties and locations remain EXPTIME-Complete.*

7   Multiple Sites Strategies Illustration

We use the Dependency Graph, Set of states, and rules sets presented above to illustrate how multiples-sites defense analysis can be achieved in anticipation games thanks to strategies. To do so we consider the two following cases. In the first case the company's network does not rely on honey-net information to detect zero day attacks and therefore the honey-net is removed from the simulation. In the second case, the interaction between the honey-net and the company's network occurs. This is the exact configuration described earlier during the paper. For both cases, we run the analysis to find the administrator dominant strategy objective as introduced in 4:

$$S : (\text{Defense strategy}, Admin, MIN(Cost) \wedge MAX(OCost), OCost > Cost, \Box \neg Compr, \neg 2)$$

When the honey-net is not present the only type of attack that can be countered is the public exploit attack one. This is done by patching the vulnerable service as soon as the patch is available. This defense strategy is presented in figure 4. In this figure, rule names have been abbreviated. Column abbreviations are Ts for time, Pl for player, Ac action, Ta target vertex, S successor vertex, Pa payoff and C for cost. A denote the administrator player and I for the intruder.

The row one of the table on the left is read as follows: at time 0 the Intruder (I) selects (sel) the rule 0day avail on vertex 2, there is no successor involved ($\bot$). The intruder reward and cost are not yet intialized (−). Accordingly the line 2 states

Ts	Pl	Ac	Rule	Ta	S	Pa	C
0	I	sel	0day avail	2	$\bot$	-	-
48	I	**exec**	0day avail	2	$\bot$	0	0
48	I	sel	Custom avail	2	$\bot$	-	-
336	I	**exec**	Custom avail	2	$\bot$	0	0
337	I	sel	Public avail	2	$\bot$	-	-
337	A	sel	Patch avail	2	$\bot$	-	-
385	I	**exec**	Public avail	2	$\bot$	0	0
385	I	sel	Compr public	7	2	-	-
385	A	**exec**	Patch avail	2	$\bot$	0	2700
385	A	sel	Patch	7	2	-	-
391	A	**exec**	Patch	7	2	1	3500
392	I	fail	Compr public	7	2	0	200

Ts	Pl	Ac	Rule	Ta	S	Pa	C
0	I	sel	0day avail	2	$\bot$	-	-
48	I	**exec**	0day avail	2	$\bot$	0	0
48	I	sel	Compr 0 day	4	2	-	-
51	I	**exec**	Compr 0 day	4	2	1	20000
52	I	sel	Compr 0 day	7	2	-	-
52	A	sel	Attack catched	4	$\bot$	-	-
52	A	**exec**	Attack catched	4	$\bot$	0	2000
52	A	sel	Firewall	7	4	-	-
52	A	**exec**	Firewall	7	4	0	4800
54	I	fail	Compr 0 day	7	2	1	40000
54	I	sel	Custom avail	2	$\bot$	-	-
342	I	**exec**	Custom avail	2	$\bot$	1	40000
343	I	sel	Public avail	2	$\bot$	-	-
343	A	sel	Patch avail	2	$\bot$	-	-
390	I	**exec**	Public avail	2	$\bot$	1	40000
391	A	**exec**	Patch avail	2	$\bot$	0	4000
391	A	sel	Patch	7	2	-	-
397	A	**exec**	Patch	7	2	1	4500
397	A	sel	UnFirewall	7	$\bot$	-	-
398	A	**exec**	UnFirewall	7	$\bot$	1	4803

Fig. 4. Defense strategy without Honey-net (left) Defense strategy with honey-net (right)

that at time 48 the intruder (I) execute (exec) the rule 0day avail on vertex 2, his current cost is 0 and his current reward is 0. And so on.

The defense efficiency can be improved by taking preventive action when the vulnerability is disclosed. For instance by firewalling the vulnerable service. This is however not a suitable course of action in most case because this also prevent access from legitimate users. When the honey-net is used, the defense strategy can mitigate zero day attacks as long as the honey-net is targeted first by the intruder, as detailed in figure 4 (on the right). Even with the introduction of an honey-net, the intruder has a strictly dominant strategy that involves attacking company's network services first This is consistent with real world honey-net purpose that aims at mitigate 0 day attack by catching unknown threats without the guaranty catch them all.

8 Evaluation

To evaluate the effectiveness of anticipation games to analyze complex multiple-sites scenarios, we have implemented the full framework in a tool written in C for performance reasons. Evaluations were conducted on a Linux core 2 desktop using the tool built-in benchmark option. The game used in the evaluation is the one presented in this paper with more company networks and more services per network. Benchmark results are summarized in the table below. Time is in second. The prototype includes many optimizations to delay the execution time blowup. It follows that it is possible to find the optimal strategy for 50 services divided into 4 sites and 1 honey-net. When more services are added, the execution time blowup as predicted by the theoretical complexity bound. That is why for larger network, we have designed an heuristic that is able to find an approximate strategy by using a dynamic rules ordering algorithm. The strategy returned by this algorithm is sound, it satisfies the strategy constraint, but there is no guarantee that it is the best one. However on small examples, it appears to be so. This evaluation shows that anticipation games is suitable to analyze complex scenarios even on very large networks.

Analysis	Num of service	Num of network	Analysis time in sec
Exact	30	2	0.03
Exact	40	3	0.1
Exact	50	4	1020
Appro	2000	1	0.48
Appro	5000	4	0.82
Appro	10000	3	2.26

9 Conclusion

We have introduced an extension for anticipation games that allows to analyze network cooperation and cost over the time. We have also proved that this extension does not change anticipation games complexity. Finally we have shown with our prototype that anticipation games with this extension can be used in practice to model complex scenario even when each network have thousand services. As a future direction of work, we will focus on dependency graph static analysis to improve the scalability of the exact solution.

Acknowledgements

Thanks to Richard Lippmann for his advices on multi-sites defense and Marc Dacier for the discussion about the notion of cost diminishing.

References

1. Alur, R., Henzinger, T.A., Kupferman, O.: Alternating-time temporal logic. J. ACM 49(5), 672–713 (2002)
2. Myerson, R.B.: Game Theory: Analysis of Conflict. Harvard University Press (1997)
3. Bursztein, E.: NetQi: A model checker for anticipation game. In: Cha, S(S.), Choi, J.-Y., Kim, M., Lee, I., Viswanathan, M. (eds.) ATVA 2008. LNCS, vol. 5311. Springer, Heidelberg (2008)
4. Bursztein, E.: Using strategy objectives for network security analysis. In: 4th International Conferences on Information Security and Cryptology INSCRYPT. Springer, Heidelberg (2008)
5. Bursztein, E., Goubault-Larrecq, J.: A logical framework for evaluating network resilience against faults and attacks. In: Cervesato, I. (ed.) ASIAN 2007. LNCS, vol. 4846, pp. 212–227. Springer, Heidelberg (2007)
6. Dacier, M., Deswarte, Y., Kaaniche, M.: Models and tools for quantitative assessment of operational security. In: 12th International Information Security Conference, pp. 177–186 (May 1996)
7. de Alfaro, L., Faella, M., Henzinger, T., Majumdar, R., Stoelinga, M.: The element of surprise in timed games. In: Amadio, R., Lugiez, D. (eds.) CONCUR 2003. LNCS, vol. 2761, pp. 144–158. Springer, Heidelberg (2003)
8. Henzinger, T., Prabhu, V.: Timed alternating-time temporal logic. In: Asarin, E., Bouyer, P. (eds.) FORMATS 2006. LNCS, vol. 4202, pp. 1–18. Springer, Heidelberg (2006)
9. Jha, S., Sheyner, O., Wing, J.: Two formal analysis of attack graphs. In: CSFW 2002: Proceedings of the 15th IEEE Computer Security Foundations Workshop (CSFW 2002), Washington, DC, USA, pp. 49–63. IEEE Computer Society Press, Los Alamitos (2002)
10. Lippmann, R., Webster, S., Stetson, D.: The Effect of Identifying Vulnerabilities and Patching Software on the Utility of Network Intrusion Detection. In: Wespi, A., Vigna, G., Deri, L. (eds.) RAID 2002. LNCS, vol. 2516, pp. 307–326. Springer, Heidelberg (2002)
11. Lye, K.-w., Wing, J.M.: Game strategies in network security. Int. J. Inf. Sec. 4(1-2), 71–86 (2005)
12. Mahimkar, A., Shmatikov, V.: Game-based analysis of denial-of-service prevention protocols. In: 18th IEEE Computer Security Foundations Workshop (CSFW), Aix-en-Provence, France, pp. 287–301. IEEE Computer Society, Los Alamitos (2005)
13. Noel, S., Jajodia, S.: Managing attack graph complexity through visual hierarchical aggregation. In: VizSEC/DMSEC 2004: Proceedings of the 2004 ACM workshop on Visualization and data mining for computer security, pp. 109–118. ACM Press, New York (2004)
14. Noel, S., Jajodia, S., O'Berry, B., Jacobs, M.: Efficient Minimum-Cost Network Hardening Via Exploit Dependency Graphs. In: 19th Annual Computer Security Applications Conference, pp. 86–95 (December 2003)

15. Ramakrishan, C., Sekar, R.: Model-based analysis of configuration vulnerabilities. Journal of Computer Security 1, 198–209 (2002)
16. Rasmusen, E.: Games and Information. Blackwell publishing, Malden (2007)
17. Ritchey, R.W., Ammann, P.: Using model checking to analyze network vulnerabilities. In: SP 2000: Proceedings of the 2000 IEEE Symposium on Security and Privacy, Washington, DC, USA, pp. 156–165. IEEE Computer Society, Los Alamitos (2000)
18. Shahriari, H.R., Jalili, R.: Modeling and analyzing network vulnerabilities via a logic-based approach
19. Sheyner, O., Haines, J., Jha, S., Lippmann, R., Wing, J.M.: Automated generation and analysis of attack graphs. In: SP 2002: Proceedings of the 2002 IEEE Symposium on Security and Privacy, Washington, DC, USA, pp. 273–284. IEEE Computer Society, Los Alamitos (2002)
20. Swiler, L.P.: A graph-based network-vulnerability analysis system. In: New Security Paradigms Workshop, pp. 71–79. ACM Press, New York (1998)
21. Zerkle, D., Levitt, K.: Netkuang: a multi-host configuration vulnerability checker. In: SSYM 1996: Proceedings of the 6th conference on USENIX Security Symposium, Focusing on Applications of Cryptography, pp. 195–201. Usenix (1996)

Do You Really Mean What You Actually Enforced?[*]
Edit Automata Revisited

Nataliia Bielova and Fabio Massacci

DISI - University of Trento, Italy
surname@disi.unitn.it

Abstract. In the landmark paper on the theoretical side of Polymer, Ligatti and his co-authors have identified a new class of enforcement mechanisms based on the notion of edit automata, that can transform sequences and enforce more than simple safety properties.

We show that there is a gap between the edit automata that one can possibly write (e.g. by Ligatti himself in his running example) and the edit automata that are actually constructed according the theorems from Ligatti's IJIS paper and IC follow-up papers by Talhi et al. "Ligatti's automata" are just a particular kind of edit automata.

Thus, we re-open a question which seemed to have received a definitive answer: you have written your security enforcement mechanism (aka your edit automata); does it really enforce the security policy you wanted?

Keywords: Formal models for security, trust and reputation, Resource and Access Control, Validation/Analysis tools and techniques.

1 Introduction

The explosion of multi-player games, P2P applications, collaborative tools on Web 2.0, and corporate clients in service oriented architectures has changed the usage models of the average PC user: users demand to install more and more applications from a variety of sources. Unfortunately, the full usage of those applications is at odds with the current security model.

The first hurdle is certification. Certified application by trusted parties can run with full powers while untrusted ones essentially without any powers. However, certification just says that the code is trusted rather than trustworthy because the certificate has no semantics whatsoever. Will your apparently innocuous application collect your private information and upload it to the remote server [16]? Will your corporate client developed in out-sourcing dump your hard disk in a shady country? You have no way to know.

Model carrying code [18] or Security-by-Contract [4] which claim that code should come equipped with a security claims to be matched against the platform policies could be a solution. However this will only be a solution for certified code.

---

[*] Research partly supported by the Project EU-FP7-IP-MASTER.

P. Degano, J. Guttman, and F. Martinelli (Eds.): FAST 2008, LNCS 5491, pp. 287–301, 2009.

To deal with the untrusted code either .NET [12] or Java [7] can exploit the mechanism of permissions. Permissions are assigned to enable execution of potentially dangerous functionalities, such as starting various types of connections or accessing sensitive information. The drawback is that after assigning a permission the user has very limited control over its usage. An application with a permission to upload a video can then send hundreds of them invisibly for the user (see the Blogs on UK Channel 4's Video on Demand application). Conditional permissions that allow and forbid use of the functionality depending on such factors as the bandwidth or some previous actions of the application itself are currently out of reach. The consequence is that either applications are sandboxed (and thus can do almost nothing), or the user decided that they are trusted and then they can do almost everything.

To overcome these drawbacks a number of authors have proposed to enforce the compliance of the application to the user's policies by execution monitoring. This is the idea behind security automata [5,8,1,17], safety control of Java programs using temporal logic specs [10] and history based access control [11].

In order to provide enforcement of security policies at run time by monitoring untrusted programs we want to know what kind of policies are enforceable and what sorts of mechanisms can actually enforce them. In a landmark paper [2] Bauer, Ligatti and Walker seemed to provide a definitive answer by presenting a new hierarchy of enforcement mechanisms and classification of security policies that are enforceable by these mechanisms.

Traditional *security automata* were essentially action observers that stopped the execution as soon as an illegal sequence of actions was on the eve of being performed. The new classification of enforcement mechanisms proposed by Ligatti included *truncation, insertion, suppression* and *edit automata* which were considered as execution transformers rather than execution recognizers. The great novelty of these automata was their ability to transform the "bad" program executions in good ones.

These automata were then classified with respect to the properties they can enforce: precisely and effectively enforceable properties. It is stated in [2] that as precise enforcers, edit automata have the same power as truncation, suppression and insertion automata. As for effective enforcement, it is said that edit automata can insert and suppress actions by defining *suppression-rewrite* and *insertion-rewrite* functions and thus can actually enforce more expressive properties than simple safety properties. The proof of Thm. 8 in [2] provides us with a construction of an edit automaton that can effectively enforce any (enforceable) property.

Talhi et al. [19] have further refined the notion by considering bounded version of enforceable properties.

1.1   Contribution of the Paper

If everything is settled why we need to write this paper? Everything started when we tried to formally show "as an exercise" that the running example of edit automaton from [2] provably enforces the security policy described in that paper by applying the effective enforcement theorem from the very same paper. Much to our dismay, we failed.

As a result of this failure we decided to plunge into a deeper investigation and discovered that this was not for lack of will, patience or technique. Rather, the impossibility of reconciling the running example of a paper with the theorem on the very same paper is a consequence of a gap between the edit automata that one can possibly write (e.g. by Ligatti himself in his running example) and the edit automata that are actually constructed according Thm. 8 from [2] and Thm. 8 from [14] and the follow-up papers by Talhi et al. [19]. "Ligatti's automata" are just a particular kind of edit automata. Figure 3 later in the paper shows that we were trying to prove the equivalence of automata belonging to different classes, even though they are the "same" according to [2].

The contribution of this paper is therefore manyfold:

- We show the difference between the running example from [2] and the edit automata that are constructed according Thm. 8 in the very same paper.
- We introduce a more fine grained classification of edit automata introducing the notion of *Delayed Automata* and related security properties and relation between different notion of enforcement.
- We further explain the gap by showing that the particular automata that are actually constructed according Thm. 8 from [2] are a particular form of delayed automata that have an all-or-nothing behavior and that we named Ligatti's automata.

The remainder of the paper is structured as follows. At first we sketch the difference between the edit automaton from the running example and Thm. 8 from [2] (§2). Then we present the basic notions of policies, enforcement and automata in Section 3. We give a more fine grained classification of edit automata introducing the notion of *Delayed Automata* (§4). Section 5 explains relation between different notions of enforcement and types of edit automata. Finally we conclude with a discussion of future and related works (§6).

2   The Example Revised

Example 1 (Verbatim from [2]). To make our example more concrete, we will model a simple market system with two main actions, take(n) and pay(n), which represent acquisition of n apples and the corresponding payment. We let a range over all the actions that might occur in the system (such as take, pay, window-shop, browse, etc.) Our policy is that every time an agent takes n apples it must pay for those apples. Payments may come before acquisition or vice versa, and take(n); pay(n) is semantically equivalent to pay(n);take(n). The edit automaton enforces the atomicity of this transaction by emitting take(n);pay(n) only when the transaction completes. If payment is made first, the automaton allows clients to perform other actions such as browse before committing (the take-pay transaction appears atomically after all such intermediary actions). On the other hand, if apples are taken and not paid for immediately, we issue a warning and abort the transaction. Consistency is ensured by remembering the number of apples taken or the size of the prepayment in the state of the machine. Once acquisition and payment occur, the sale is final and there are no refunds (durability)."

In order to formally define the allowed and prohibited behavior described in the market policy we present: 1) a predicate $\widehat{P}$ over sequences of executions; 2) the expected output for every input sequence according the original example in Table 1.

Let us explain the expected output of some examples form Table 1, e.g. sequence 7:

- It contains take(1) action and browse action after it.
- Since there is no pay(1) action, the policy is violated. We expect the action take(1) be suppressed and output the warning action instead.
- The browse action does not violate the policy hence we output it.
- Next actions pay(2);take(2) do not violate the policy.
- Therefore the output is warning;browse;pay(2);take(2).

In the sequences 13-15 the text of original example leaves opened a number of interpretations. It is clear that good sequences must have a pair of take(n) and pay(n) as the text implies, but it is not clear whether we allow interleaving of pay(n) and pay(m). The text seems to imply that this is not possible so we mark them as violations.

We say that expected output is defined if either a take-pay transaction is completed (after the last pay(n) action there is a take(n) action) or the transaction is violated (after take(n) action there is an action different from pay(n)).

Table 1. Sequences of actions for market policy

No.	Sequence of actions σ	Expected output	$\widehat{P}(\sigma)$
1	take(1)	.	×
2	pay(1)	.	×
3	take(1);browse	warning; browse	×
4	pay(1);browse	browse	×
5	pay(1); take(1)	pay(1);take(1)	√
6	take(1);browse;pay(2)	warning;browse	×
7	take(1);browse;pay(2);take(2)	warning;browse;pay(2);take(2)	×
8	take(1);browse;pay(1)	warning;browse	×
9	take(1);browse;pay(1);take(2)	warning;browse	×
10	take(1);browse;pay(1);take(2);browse	warning;browse;warning;browse	×
11	take(1);browse;pay(1);take(2); browse;pay(2)	warning;browse; warning;browse	×
12	take(1); pay(2); take(2)	pay(2);take(2)	×
13	pay(1);browse;pay(2)	browse	×
14	pay(1);browse;pay(2);take(2)	browse;pay(2);take(2)	×
15	pay(1);browse;pay(2);take(2);browse	browse;pay(2);take(2);browse	×

But it is not clear how the sequence 14 should be transformed because we don't know if the `pay(1)` action should still be followed by the `take(1)` action or it should be simply suppressed.

The edit automaton that, as authors of [2] say, effectively enforces the market policy is shown in Fig. 1. But the definition of effective enforcement includes the notion of property $\widehat{P}$: the predicate over the sequences of actions and this predicate is not given explicitly in [2]. That is why following the example in English we are presenting the Table 1 as a market policy. Assuming that our presentation of the policy corresponds to the Example 1, the given edit automaton [2] should effectively enforce the policy in Table 1.

According to the Thm. 8 of [2], any property $\widehat{P}$ can be effectively enforced by some edit automaton. We will construct such automaton according to the proof of this theorem (for more details about construction see technical report [3]).

After construction we discovered that edit automaton that effectively enforces $\widehat{P}$ (Fig. 1) and the one constructed by the proof of Theorem 8 (some edit automaton that effectively enforces $\widehat{P}$) produce different output for the same input. Let us show in Table 2 some cases of input and output of both automata.

Analysing the Table 2 we find out that the transformed sequences of actions are not always the ones expected from the edit automaton. So the question arises:

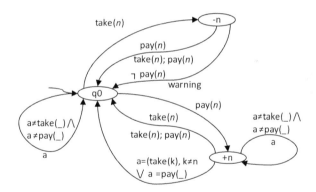

Fig. 1. An edit automaton that "effectively" enforces the market policy [2]

Table 2. Difference in output for edit automata

No.	Input	Output	
		EA from Fig. 1 [2]	Constructed EA by Thm.8 [2]
1	pay(1); take(1)	take(1);pay(1)	pay(1);take(1)
2	take(1); browse; pay(1); take(2); browse; pay(2)	warning;browse	·
3	take(1); pay(2); take(2)	warning	·
4	take(1); browse; pay(2); take(2)	warning;take(2); pay(2)	·
5	pay(1); browse; pay(2); take(2); browse	browse; warning	·

Why the output is predictable in some cases and unpredictable in the others? The answer to this question is:

1. Both edit automata produce the expected output when the input sequence is legal (sequence 1 in the example)
2. The edit automaton constructed following the proof of Thm. 8 [2] is a very particular kind of the edit automaton.

When the sequence is illegal the output of both edit automata is unexpected. In Fig. 2 we show the relation between input and output for edit automaton from Fig. 1 [2] and edit automata constructed by Thm.8 [2] with respect to the "good" and "bad" traces. In case of "bad" input sequences edit automaton constructed by Thm.8 [2] outputs only the longest valid prefix: so either it outputs some valid sequence (ex.1 in Tab.2) or suppresses all the sequence (ex.2-5 in Tab.2). While edit automaton from Fig. 1 [2] always outputs some "good" sequence of actions even if the longest valid prefix is an empty sequence (ex.2-5 in Tab.2).

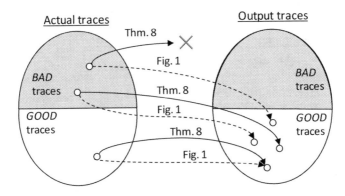

Fig. 2. Relation between input and output for edit automaton from Fig. 1 [2] and edit automaton constructed by Thm.8 [2]

In order to explain this difference we analyze different classifications of edit automata that explain the behavior of the edit automaton constructed following the proof of Thm. 8 and the edit automaton from Fig. 1 [2]. For example, all theorems referring to edit automata in [19] are about the particular kind of automaton that is constructed following the proof of Thm. 8 [2].

3 Basic Notions of Policies, Enforcement and Automata

Similarly to [2] we specify the system at a high level of abstraction, where the set Σ is the set of program actions; the set of all finite sequences over Σ is denoted by Σ^*, similarly the set of all infinite sequences is Σ^ω, and the set $\Sigma^* \cup \Sigma^\omega$ is a set of all finite and infinite executions. Execution σ is a finite sequence of actions $a_1, a_2, ..., a_n$. In scope of this paper we assume only finite executions leaving infinite sequences of actions to be considered in future work.

With · we denote an empty execution. The notation $\sigma[i]$ is used to denote the i-th action in the sequence (begin counting at 0). The notation $\sigma[..i]$ denotes the subsequence of σ involving the actions $\sigma[0]$ through $\sigma[i]$, and $\sigma[i+1..]$ denotes the subsequence of σ involving all other actions. We use the notation $\tau; \sigma$ to denote the concatenation of two sequences.

As showed in Section 2 the constructed edit automaton following the algorithm in [2] and edit automaton presented in [2] are different. We give the original definition of edit automata from [2]:

An *Edit Automaton E* is described by a 5-tuple of the form $\langle Q, q_0, \delta, \gamma, \omega \rangle$ with respect to some system with actions set Σ. Q specifies possible states, and q_0 is the initial state. The partial function $\delta : (\Sigma \times Q) \to Q$ specifies the transition function; the partial function $\omega : (\Sigma \times Q) \to \{-, +\}$ has the same domain as δ and indicates whether or not the action is to be suppressed (-) or emitted(+); the partial function γ is an insertion function, $\gamma : (\Sigma \times Q) \to \Sigma^* \times Q$. The partial functions δ and γ have disjoint domains.

$$(\sigma, q) \xrightarrow{\tau}_E (\sigma', q') \tag{1}$$

$$(\sigma, q) \xrightarrow{a}_E (\sigma', q') \text{ if } \sigma = a; \sigma' \wedge \delta(a, q) = q' \wedge \omega(a, q) = + \tag{2}$$

$$(\sigma, q) \xrightarrow{\cdot}_E (\sigma', q') \text{ if } \sigma = a; \sigma' \wedge \delta(a, q) = q' \wedge \omega(a, q) = - \tag{3}$$

$$(\sigma, q) \xrightarrow{\tau}_E (\sigma, q') \text{ if } \sigma = a; \sigma' \wedge \gamma(a, q) = \tau; q' \tag{4}$$

$$(\sigma, q) \xrightarrow{\cdot}_E (\cdot, q) \text{ otherwise} \tag{5}$$

Assuming that the function γ always inserts all necessary actions that have to appear before the a action, we can rewrite the case of insertion as statement (4) and then statement (2). We consider that after inserting some actions τ at the next step the automaton will accept the current action a (if inserting $\tau; a$ makes the output illegal then one can simply suppress a without inserting τ). Hence, the equation (4) can be represented as follows:

$$(\sigma, q) \xrightarrow{\tau; a}_E (\sigma', q') \text{ if } \sigma = a; \sigma' \wedge \gamma(a, q) = \tau; q' \tag{6}$$

In this way, the sequences σ and σ' are not relevant in the definition of transitions. Loosely speaking this was a Mealy-Moore transformation [9]. In order to give a formal definition in our notations, we will use the σ_S sequence to define the sequence that was read but is not in the output yet.

Definition 1 (Edit Automata (EA)). *An* Edit Automaton E *is a 5-tuple of the form* $\langle Q, q_0, \delta, \gamma_o, \gamma_k \rangle$ *with respect to some system with actions set Σ. Q specifies possible states, and $q_0 \in Q$ is the initial state. The partial function $\delta : (Q \times \Sigma) \to Q$ specifies the transition function; the partial function $\gamma_o : (\Sigma^* \times Q) \to \Sigma^*$ defines the output of the transition according to the current state and the sequence of actions that is read but not in the output yet; the partial function $\gamma_k : (\Sigma^* \times Q) \to \Sigma^*$ defined the sequence that will be kept after committing the transition. The dependence between the transition, output and* keep function is following: if $\delta(q,a)$ is defined then $\gamma_o(q,a,\sigma)$ and $\gamma_k(q,a,\sigma)$ must be defined for all σ.

$$(q, \sigma_S) \xrightarrow{\gamma_o(q,\sigma_S;a)} E(q', \gamma_k(q, \sigma_S; a)) \tag{7}$$

In order for the enforcement mechanism to be effective all functions δ, γ_k and γ_o should be decidable.

Proposition 1. *The Definition 1 of edit automaton has the same expressive power of the original definition [2].*

The proofs of all propositions and theorems are in the technical report [3].

4   A New Classification of Automata

Let us now give a deeper look at the automaton constructed according the proof of Thm. 8 [2]. In this construction at every state the automaton has emitted the sequence σ', and σ' is the *longest valid prefix* of the input sequence σ. Indeed, Table 2 shows that this statement holds for edit automaton constructed by Thm. 8 and it doesn't hold for the edit automaton from Fig. 1 [2]. Therefore, in order to understand what kind of edit automaton is in Fig. 1 we need to give a formal definition of this kind of automaton. This automaton outputs some valid prefix only when the sequence can become valid again in the future (e.g. for the sequence take(1);pay(1);take(2) after reading take(1);pay(1) the automaton will output these actions, and after reading the take(2) action it will still output the valid prefix take(1);pay(1)). And it outputs some corrected sequence (current valid prefix and some other sequence) if the sequence cannot become valid in the future(in example 2 of Table 2 after reading take(1);browse actions the automaton outputs another action warning).

This corresponds to the following intuition:

Remark 1. The automaton constructed according to the proof of Thm. 8 in [2] just delays the appearance of input actions until the input has built up a correct sequence again.

Formally, we propose a notion of wider class of such automata called *Delayed Automata*. They simply output some prefix of the input. These class will be the container of other less trivial cases when the property $\widehat{P}$ will be called into account.

Definition 2 (Delayed Automata). Delayed automaton A *is an edit automaton that is described by a 5-tuple of the form* $A = \langle Q, q_0, \delta, \gamma_o, \gamma_k \rangle$, *where the transition is defined as in equation (7) with the restriction that it always outputs some prefix of the input:*

$$\sigma_S; a = \gamma_o(q, \sigma_S; a); \gamma_k(q, \sigma_S; a) \tag{8}$$

In order to give a formal definition of the automata from Thm. 8 [2] for any property $\widehat{P}$ we present also a wider class of automata called *All-Or-Nothing Automata*. These automata always output a prefix of the input (hence it is a particular kind of the Delayed Automata). Moreover, at every step of the transition either it outputs all suspended inputs or suppresses the current action.

Definition 3 (All-Or-Nothing Automata). *All-Or-Nothing automaton A is an edit automaton described by a 5-tuple of the form $A = \langle Q, q_0, \delta, \ \gamma_o, \gamma_k \rangle$, where the transition relation is defined as in equation (7) with the following restrictions:*

- *This automaton outputs a prefix of the input: the statement (8) holds.*
- *At every step of the transition either it outputs the whole suspended sequence of actions or suppresses the current action:*

$$\gamma_o(q, \sigma_S; a) = \begin{cases} \sigma_S; a \\ . \end{cases} \tag{9}$$

The next step is the refinement of this class towards what we call *Ligatti Automata for $\widehat{P}$*. These automata always output a prefix of the input (hence it is a particular kind of the Delayed Automata) and they are particular kind of All-Or-Nothing automata. Moreover, they output the longest valid prefix. The definition of Ligatti Automaton for property $\widehat{P}$ given below was made according to the construction of edit automaton given in the proof of Thm. 8 [2].

Definition 4 (Ligatti Automata for property $\widehat{P}$). *Ligatti automaton E for property $\widehat{P}$ is an edit automaton described by a 5-tuple of the form $E = \langle Q, q_0, \delta, \gamma_o, \gamma_k \rangle$, where the set of states $Q = \Sigma^*$ (every state contains the already accepted sequence σ) and the transition relation is defined in a similar way as in equation (7):*

$$(\sigma, \sigma_S) \xrightarrow{\gamma_o(\sigma, \sigma_S; a)} E(\sigma; \gamma_o(\sigma, \sigma_S; a), \gamma_k(\sigma, \sigma_S; a)) \tag{10}$$

With the following restrictions:

- *The automaton outputs a prefix of the input (the statement (8) holds)*
- *Either it outputs the whole suspended sequence of actions or suppress the current action (the statement (9) holds).*
- *Output is a valid prefix of the input*

$$\widehat{P}(\sigma; \gamma_o(\sigma, \sigma_S; a)) \tag{11}$$

- *If the current sequence is valid then it outputs the whole sequence:*

$$\text{If } \widehat{P}(\sigma; \sigma_S; a) \text{ then } \gamma_o(\sigma, \sigma_S; a) = \sigma_S; a. \tag{12}$$

At every state a Ligatti automaton for property $\widehat{P}$ keeps the sequence σ that was read till the current moment in order to decide whether $\widehat{P}(\sigma; \sigma_S; a)$ holds. This explains why $Q = \Sigma^*$. In our definition a Ligatti Automaton for property $\widehat{P}$ is obviously a particular kind of Edit Automatfon. We will show that this statement holds in the original definition as well.

Proposition 2. *The Ligatti Automaton for property $\widehat{P}$ is an Edit Automaton according to Ligatti's own Definition.*

Let us now show the inverse of this claim: the edit automaton constructed following the proof of Thm. 8 [2] is a Ligatti Automaton for property $\widehat{P}$.

Proposition 3. *The Edit automaton constructed following the proof of Thm. 8 in [2] for property $\widehat{P}$ is a Ligatti Automaton for $\widehat{P}$.*

In a nutshell, the difference between edit automata and Ligatti automata for property $\widehat{P}$ is the following: edit automata suppress and insert arbitrary actions according to the given rewriting functions ω and γ while Ligatti automata for property $\widehat{P}$ can only insert those actions that were read before; suppressed actions either will be inserted when the input sequence becomes valid or all subsequent actions will be suppressed. Thus Ligatti automata for property $\widehat{P}$ outputs the longest valid prefix of the input sequence.

Since the automaton constructed following the proof of Thm. 8 [2] is a Ligatti automaton for property $\widehat{P}$ while the automaton given in [2] (Fig. 1) is an edit automaton, the difference between their behaviors is not clear.

Still, the automaton of Fig. 1 is not a completely arbitrary edit automaton and we propose a notion of *Delayed Automaton for property $\widehat{P}$*. If the sequence is valid it outputs a valid prefix of the input, otherwise it can output some valid sequence (i.e. fixing the input).

Definition 5 (Delayed Automata for property $\widehat{P}$). Delayed automaton A for $\widehat{P}$ is an edit automaton that is described by a 5-tuple of the form $A = \langle Q, q_0, \delta, \gamma_o, \gamma_k \rangle$, where the transition is defined in the same way as in equation (7) with the following restrictions:
   If $\widehat{P}(\sigma; \sigma_S; a)$ then

   - Output is a prefix of the input (the statement (8) holds) and
   - Output is a valid prefix of the input (the statement (11) holds).

Later in Fig. 3 we will pictorially describe the situation. However, in order to explain more relations present in that picture we need first to define the notion of enforcement in the next section.

5   A New Classification of Enforcement Properties

The principles of soundness and transparency were presented in [2] in order to be able to compare different enforcement mechanisms. Let us first see an intuitive description of these mechanisms. The notion of *soundness* requires all the observable output of enforcement mechanism to be valid. The notion of *transparency* means that an enforcement mechanism must preserve the semantics of executions that are already valid. The notion of *precise* enforcement by [2] obeys both of these properties. According to that definition, the automaton in question outputs program actions in lock-step with the target program's action stream if the action stream σ is valid. Suppose that at the current moment the automaton reads i-th action in the sequence, and the sequence $\sigma[..i+1]$ is not valid. Then the automaton will not output any other actions.

In order to formalize the behavior where the automaton suppresses some actions and later insert them when the sequence turns out to be legal, we present the notion of *Delayed precise enforcement*.

Definition 6 (Delayed Precise Enforcement). *An edit automaton A with starting state q_0 delayed precisely enforces a property $\widehat{P}$ on the system with action set Σ iff $\forall \sigma \in \Sigma^* \ \exists q' \ \exists \sigma' \in \Sigma^*$.*

1. $(\sigma, q_0) \xrightarrow{\sigma'} {}_A (\cdot, q')$, *and*
2. $\widehat{P}(\sigma')$, *and*
3. $\widehat{P}(\sigma) \Rightarrow \sigma = \sigma' \wedge \forall i \ \exists j. \ j \leq i \ \exists q_*. \ (\sigma, q_0) \xrightarrow{\sigma[..j]} {}_A (\sigma[i+1..], q_*).$

There is another notion of enforcement called "effective=enforcement" [14], which also obeys the properties of soundness and transparency.

Definition 7 (Effective=Enforcement). *An automaton A with starting state q_0 effectively= enforces a property $\widehat{P}$ on the system with action set Σ iff $\forall \sigma \in \Sigma^* \ \exists q' \ \exists \sigma' \in \Sigma^*$.*

1. $(\sigma, q_0) \xrightarrow{\sigma'} {}_A (\cdot, q')$, *and*
2. $\widehat{P}(\sigma')$, *and*
3. $\widehat{P}(\sigma) \Rightarrow \sigma = \sigma'$

Let us show the relation between delayed precise enforcement and effective=enforcement.

Theorem 1. *If edit automaton A delayed precisely enforces a property $\widehat{P}$ then it effectively= enforces property $\widehat{P}$.*

Let us come back to Example 1. As it is said in [2] the given edit automaton (Fig. 1) effectively=enforces the market policy. But since the market policy is given only in natural language and the predicate $\widehat{P}$ is not given, statement "An edit automata effectively enforces the market policy" is stretching the definition.

Let us show in Fig. 3 all edit automata and its' particular subclasses presented above. The following theorems show the relation between different types of edit automata.

Proposition 4. *If edit automaton A is a Delayed Automaton then it is not necessary that A is a Delayed Automaton for property $\widehat{P}$.*

Proposition 5. *If edit automaton A is a Delayed Automaton for property $\widehat{P}$ then it is not necessary that A is a Delayed Automaton.*

From the Thm. 4 and Thm. 5 we can conclude that classes of Delayed Automata and Delayed Automata for $\widehat{P}$ have some common subclass but none of them include the other.

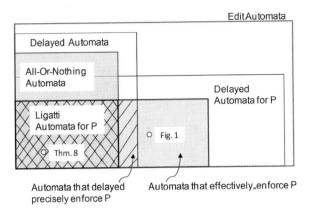

Fig. 3. The classes of Edit Automata

Theorem 2. *If edit automaton A effectively$_=$enforces property $\widehat{P}$ then A is a Delayed Automaton for property $\widehat{P}$ and it is not necessary that A is a Delayed Automaton.*

Proposition 6. *If edit automaton A is a Delayed Automaton for property $\widehat{P}$ then it is not necessary that A effectively$_=$enforces property $\widehat{P}$.*

From Thm. 2 and Proposition 6 we conclude that the class of edit automata that effectively$_=$enforces property $\widehat{P}$ is a particular class of Delayed Automata for $\widehat{P}$ and is not a proper subset of Delayed Automata.

Thm. 1 shows that edit automata that delayed precisely enforce property $\widehat{P}$ are a particular type of edit automata that effectively$_=$enforce $\widehat{P}$. The key point is that in the definition of delayed precise enforcement it is left open how illegal input is transformed.

Let us have a look at the 2d and 3d conditions of precise enforcement [2]:

$$\widehat{P}(\sigma')$$

$$\widehat{P}(\sigma) \Rightarrow \forall i \, \exists q''. \, (\sigma, q_0) \xrightarrow{\sigma[..i]}_A (\sigma[i+1..], q'')$$

These conditions mean that the automaton will produce an output *in a step-by-step* fashion with the monitored action stream and will output only a valid prefix. As soon as input sequence becomes illegal, the automaton will stop outputting. Therefore, in case of precise enforcement for illegal input, it will output some valid prefix $\sigma' = \sigma[..k]$ such that $\forall i. \, i \leq k. \, \widehat{P}(\sigma[..i]) \wedge \neg\widehat{P}(\sigma[..k+1])$. In case of delayed precise enforcement for illegal input the output will be some valid prefix $\sigma' = \sigma[..k]$ such that $\forall i. \, i \leq k. \, \widehat{P}(\sigma[..i])$.

Theorem 3. *Edit automaton A delayed precisely enforces a property $\widehat{P}$ if and only if A is a Delayed Automaton, A is a Delayed Automaton for $\widehat{P}$ and it effectively$_=$enforces property $\widehat{P}$.*

Proposition 7. *Delayed automaton A that delayed precisely enforces property $\widehat{P}$ is not necessarily a Ligatti Automaton for $\widehat{P}$.*

Proposition 8. *All-Or-Nothing automaton A is a Delayed Automaton but not necessarily a Delayed Automaton for property* $\widehat{P}$.

Theorem 4. *All-Or-Nothing automaton A delayed precisely enforces a property* $\widehat{P}$ *if and only if A is a Ligatti Automaton for property* $\widehat{P}$.

Now we will define type of edit automaton constructed following the proof of Theorem 8 in [2] for property $\widehat{P}$ and type of edit automaton presented by the authors in [2] (Fig. 1).

As the Proposition 3 states, edit automaton constructed following the proof of Theorem 8 in [2] for property $\widehat{P}$ is a Ligatti Automaton for $\widehat{P}$. The edit automaton given in Fig. 1 [2] is an edit automaton that effectively_enforces $\widehat{P}$: the 2d condition of effective_enforcement is fulfilled (automaton always outputs the valid sequence) and the 3d condition is valid because in case of valid input it always outputs all the sequence. The edit automaton given in Fig. 1 [2] is not a Delayed Automaton because it does not always output some prefix of the input (see examples 2-5 in Tab.2)

Therefore we can conclude that both automata from Theorem 8 [2] and from Fig. 1 [2] are edit automata that effectively_enforce property $\widehat{P}$. But when one wants to construct such an automaton and follows the proof of Theorem 8 [2], he obtains Ligatti Automaton for $\widehat{P}$ that delayed precisely enforces $\widehat{P}$.

6   Related Work and Conclusions

Schneider [17] was the first to introduce the notion of enforceable security policies. The follow-up work by Hamlen et al. [8] fixed a number of errors and characterized more precisely the notion of policies enforceable by execution monitors as a subset of safety properties. They also analyzed the properties that can be enforced by static analysis and program rewriting. This taxonomy leads to a more accurate characterization of enforceable security policies. Ligatti, Bauer, and Walker [2] have introduced edit automata; a more detailed framework for reasoning about execution monitoring mechanisms. As we already said, in Schneider's view execution monitors are just sequence recognizers while Ligatti et al. view execution monitors as sequence transformers. Having the power of modifying program actions at run time, edit automata are provably more powerful than security automata [13].

Fong [6] provided a fine-grained, information-based characterization of enforceable policies. In order to represent constraints on information available to execution monitors, he used abstraction functions over sequences of monitored programs and defined a lattice on the space of all congruence relations over action sequences aimed at comparing classes of EM-enforceable security policies. Still his policies are limited to safety properties over finite executions.

Martinelli and Matteucci [15] have shown how to synthesize program controllers that monitor behavior of the untrusted components of the system. Given the system and a security policy represented as a μ-calculus formula the user can choose the controller operator (truncation, suppression, insertion or edit automata). Then he can generate a program controller that will restrict the behavior of the system to those specified by the formula.

When a security policy is represented by a predicate $\widehat{P}$ over set of finite executions we can conclude that both automata from Thm. 8 [2] and from Fig. 1 [2] are edit automata that effectively$_=$enforce property $\widehat{P}$. If one wants to construct such an automaton and follows the proof of Thm. 8 [2], he obtains a Ligatti automaton for $\widehat{P}$ that delayed precisely enforces $\widehat{P}$. A problem that is present in the construction of Thm. 8 is that it assumes an oracle that can tell for each sequence σ whether $\widehat{P}(\sigma)$ holds or not.

A security policy in Thm. 8 [2] is a predicate $\widehat{P}$ on all possible finite sequences of executions, but in this case the edit automaton which effectively enforces this policy is only of theoretical interest: following the proof of Thm. 8 only infinite states automata can be constructed.

In summary, we have shown that the difference between the running example from [2] and the edit automata that are constructed according Thm. 8 in the very same paper is due to a deeper theoretical difference. In order to understand this difference we have introduced a more fine grained classification of edit automata introducing the notion of *Delayed Automata*. The particular automata that are actually constructed according Thm. 8 from [2] are a particular form of delayed automata that have an all-or-nothing behavior and that we named Ligatti's automata after their inventor.

Hence, the construction from Talhi et al. [19] only applies to Ligatti's automata. Given a Ligatti automaton they can extract the Büchi automaton that represent the policy effectively enforced by the Ligatti automaton. What happens if the automaton is not a Ligatti automaton? For example the automaton from Fig. 1? Proposition 6.24 [19] simply does not apply. It needs to be shown whether given a general edit automaton one can construct a Büchi automaton so that the latter represents the policy that is effectively enforced by the former. We leave this question open for future investigation.

What remains to be done? Our results shows that the edit automaton that you can actually write (e.g. by using Polymer) does not necessarily correspond to the theoretical construction that provably guarantees that your automaton enforce your policy. A first step would be to find a construction that given a security policy represented as a Büchi automaton gives the Ligatti automaton that effectively enforces it.

So we fully re-open the most intriguing question that the stream of papers on execution monitors seemed to have closed: *you have written your security enforcement mechanism (aka your edit automata); how do you know that it really enforces the security policy you specified?*

References

1. Bauer, L., Ligatti, J., Walker, D.: Composing security policies with polymer. In: Proceedings of the ACM SIGPLAN 2005 Conference on Programming Language Design and Implementation, pp. 305–314. ACM Press, New York (2005)

2. Bauer, L., Ligatti, J., Walker, D.: Edit automata: Enforcement mechanisms for run-time security policies. International Journal of Information Security 4(1-2), 2–16 (2005)

3. Bielova, N., Massacci, F.: Do you really mean what you actually enforced? Technical Report DISI-08-033, UNITN (2008)

4. Dragoni, N., Massacci, F., Naliuka, K., Siahaan, I.: Security-by-Contract: Toward a Semantics for Digital Signatures on Mobile Code. In: López, J., Samarati, P., Ferrer, J.L. (eds.) EuroPKI 2007. LNCS, vol. 4582, pp. 297–312. Springer, Heidelberg (2007)

5. Erlingsson, U.: The Inlined Reference Monitor Approach to Security Policy Enforcement. Technical report 2003-1916, Department of Computer Science, Cornell University (2003)

6. Fong, P.W.L.: Access control by tracking shallow execution history. In: Proceedings of the 2004 IEEE Symposium on Security and Privacy, pp. 43–55 (May 2004)

7. Gong, L., Ellison, G.: Inside Java(TM) 2 Platform Security: Architecture, API Design, and Implementation. Pearson Education, London (2003)

8. Hamlen, K.W., Morrisett, G., Schneider, F.B.: Computability classes for enforcement mechanisms. ACM Transactions on Programming Languages and Systems 28(1), 175–205 (2006)

9. Hartmanis, J.: Algebraic structure theory of sequential machines. Prentice-Hall, Englewood Cliffs (1966)

10. Havelund, K., Rosu, G.: Efficient monitoring of safety properties. International Journal on Software Tools for Technol. Transfer (2004)

11. Krukow, K., Nielsen, M., Sassone, V.: A framework for concrete reputation-systems with applications to history-based access control. In: Proceedings of the 12th ACM Conference on Communications and Computer Security (2005)

12. LaMacchia, B., Lange, S.: .NET Framework security. Addison-Wesley, Reading (2002)

13. Ligatti, J., Bauer, L., Walker, D.: Enforcing non-safety security policies with program monitors. In: di Vimercati, S.d.C., Syverson, P.F., Gollmann, D. (eds.) ESORICS 2005. LNCS, vol. 3679, pp. 355–373. Springer, Heidelberg (2005)

14. Ligatti, J.A.: Policy Enforcement via Program Monitoring. PhD thesis, Princeton University (June 2006)

15. Martinelli, F., Matteucci, I.: Through modeling to synthesis of security automata. In: Proceedings of the Second International Workshop on Security and Trust Management. Electr. Notes Theor. Comp. Sci., vol. 179, pp. 31–46 (2007)

16. Ray, B.: Symbian signing is no protection from spyware (May 2007), http://www.theregister.co.uk/2007/05/23/symbian_signed_spyware/

17. Schneider, F.B.: Enforceable security policies. ACM Transactions on Information and System Security 3(1), 30–50 (2000)

18. Sekar, R., Venkatakrishnan, V.N., Basu, S., Bhatkar, S., DuVarney, D.C.: Model-carrying code: a practical approach for safe execution of untrusted applications. In: Proceedings of the 19th ACM Symposium on Operating Systems Principles, pp. 15–28. ACM Press, New York (2003)

19. Talhi, C., Tawbi, N., Debbabi, M.: Execution monitoring enforcement under memory-limitation constraints. Information and Computation 206(2-4), 158–184 (2007)

Delegating Privileges over Finite Resources: A Quota Based Delegation Approach*

Isaac Agudo, Carmen Fernandez-Gago, and Javier Lopez

Department of Computer Science, University of Malaga, Malaga 29071 Spain
{isaac,mcgago,jlm}@lcc.uma.es

Abstract. When delegation in real world scenarios is considered, the delegator (the entity that posses the privileges) usually passes the privileges on to the delegatee (the entity that receives the privileges) in such a way that the former looses these privileges while the delegation is effective. If we think of a physical key that opens a door, the privilege being delegated by the owner of the key is opening the door. Once the owner of the key delegates this privilege to another entity, by handing over the key, he is not able to open the door any longer. This is due to the fact that the key is not copied and handed over but handed over to the delegatee.

When delegation takes place in the electronic world, the delegator usually retains also the privileges. Thus, both users have them simultaneously. This situation, which in most cases is not a problem, may be undesirable when dealing with certain kind of resources.

In particular, if we think of finite resources, those in which the number of users accessing simultaneously is finite, we can not allow that a user delegating his access privilege is also granted access when the delegation if effective.

In this paper we propose an approach where each user is delegated an access quota for a resource. If further delegating of the delegated quota occurs, this is subtracted from his quota. That is, when delegating, part of the quota remains with the delegator and another part goes to the delegatee. This allows a more fairly access to the resource. Moreover, we show that this approach can also be applied to any kind of resources by defining appropriate authorization policies.

1 Introduction

When delegation in real world scenarios is considered, the delegator (the entity owning the privileges) usually passes the privileges on to the delegatee (the entity that receives the privileges) in such a way that the former looses these privileges while the delegation is effective. If we think of a contact-less ID card used for

---

* This work has been partially funded by the European Commission through the research project SPIKE (FP7-ICT-2007-1-217098), and the Spanish Ministry of Science and Education through the research project ARES (CONSOLIDER CSD2007-00004).

P. Degano, J. Guttman, and F. Martinelli (Eds.): FAST 2008, LNCS 5491, pp. 302–315, 2009.
© Springer-Verlag Berlin Heidelberg 2009

opening a door, the privilege being delegated by the owner of the card is opening the door. Contact-less ID cards are meant to be tamper resistant and hence non feasible to be copied. Then, once the owner of the card delegates this privilege to another entity, by handing over the key, he is not able to open the door any longer. This is due to the fact that the key is not copied and handed over but just handed over to the delegatee.

When delegation takes place in the electronic world, the delegator usually retains the privileges. Thus, both users hold the privilege simultaneously . This situation, which in most cases is not a problem, may be undesirable when dealing with certain kind of resources. Current solutions for privilege management with support for delegation (see PolicyMaker [3], KeyNote [2], SPKI [4], PMI [7]) do not address this situation.

In particular, if we think of finite resources, those in which the number of users accessing simultaneously is finite, we can not allow that a user delegating his access privilege is also granted access when the delegation is effective.

In our approach each user is delegated an access quota for a resource and when further delegation occurs the delegated quota is subtracted from his given quota. Thus, when delegating, part of the quota remains with the delegator another part goes to the delegatee.

In this paper we propose a model useful for delegating rights or authorization in order to use a specific resource that can be split in several parts. Granting a part of a resource can be seen as granting a percentage of it. Thus, when issuing credentials together with the resource we should specify the percentage, or quota, of it that is being delegated. Our model uses Markov's chains, widely used as a statistics model [8, 13].

This quota percentage can be compared with a trust value in the sense that the higher it is, the more power the holder of the credential has. In fact, the approach presented in this work is similar, and related, to some existing approaches for trust management. One of these methods is PageRank [12] that represents a way of ranking the best search results based on a page's reputation. Flow models such as Advogato's reputation system [9] or Appleseed [14, 15] use of transitivity. In these type of systems the reputation of a participant increases as a function of incoming flow and decreases as a function of ongoing flow.

The paper is organized as follows. In Section 3 we describe two scenarios where our model could be applied. The model is presented in Section 4 and its complexity in Section 4.2. Section 6 outlines the future work and concludes the paper.

2   Related Work

As we mentioned in the introduction, current delegation schemes used in authorization systems do not fully take into consideration the scenario where the delegated privilege can not or must no be shared between the delegator and the delegatee. Some works have defined the privilege transfer scenario, but nothing has been mentioned about the quota based approach.

PolicyMaker [3] is a general and powerful solution that allows the use of any programming language to encode the nature of the authority being granted as well as the entities to which it is being granted. KeyNote [2] is a derivation of PolicyMaker, and has been supported by IETF.

Blaze, Feigenbaum and Lacy introduced in [3] the notion of Trust Management. In that original work they proposed the PolicyMaker scheme as a solution for trust management purposes. It addresses the authorization problem directly, without considering two different phases (one for authentication and another for access control).

Keynote [2] uses a specific assertion language that is flexible enough to handle the security policies of different applications. Assertions delegate the authorization to perform operations to other principals. KeyNote considers two types of assertions called policies and credentials.

In both approaches, once users obtain privileges they can delegate it to any other user while also being able to use it at the same time. This is why none of these solutions can be used in our scenarios.

SKPI [4] was proposed by the IETF working group. The SPKI certificate contains at least an Issuer and a Subject, and it can contain validity conditions, authorization and delegation information. The delegation information is used to specify the maximal length of a delegation path. When set to 0 delegation is not allowed. This approach does not deal neither with finite resources nor with privileges that can not be shared.

Privilege Management Infrastructure (PMI) is defined in X.509 ITU-T Recommendation [7] as the framework for the extended use of attribute certificates. The Recommendation establishes four PMI models, one of them is the Delegation model. Initially, the Source of Authority (SOA) assigns or delegates the privilege to Attribute Authorities (AA). These can delegate the privileges to other AAs or to end entities (EE). AAs and EEs can use their delegated privileges and present them to the Privilege Verifier (PV) that verifies the certification path to determine the validity of the privileges. The mechanism used to contain the delegation statements is the attribute certificate. The extensions field is used by the authorities to include the delegation policy.

Even though PMIs do not directly deal neither with finite resources nor with privileges that can not be shared, we can take advantage of the extension mechanism in order to be able to manage them.

3   Applicability Issues or Scenarios

The type of scenarios where the quota model scheme can be applied are those where an entity has all the access to a resource and it could hand over shares of the access to this resource to some other entities. In this section we will outline two cases.

3.1   Residential Network Scenario

Let us assume a residential environment where the residents could use limited resources such as file space in a shared hard disk or the internet connection bandwidth. Those resources are shared among users in the residential environment according to some parameters such as how much they contribute to the residential network (e.g. money or hardware) or another less objective parameters such as friendship or trust relationships.

How are new users introduced to the residential network? How are resources assigned to them? All these questions could be answered according to the initial network configuration.

We assume a simple scenario where there are only two users in the residential network and a new user wants to access its services, in particular, the shared space and the bandwidth. In case both initial users had the same relevance in the network, both of them will own a half of the space and a half of the bandwidth. Then, one of them, or both, will hand over some of his space and bandwidth to the new user.

The easiest way for the new user to use the resources is to make an arrangement with one of the initial users in order to share his part of the network. This arrangement may involve some payment from the new user. In case the initial user shares half of his resources with the new user, the new configuration will include 3 users with a share of 50%, 25% and 25%. This process can be repeated in order to include new users in the system.

The situation is even more interesting when a new user knows two current users and obtains from them a part of their shares. In this case the share of the new user will be the sum of the parts handed to him. Thus, a new user can accumulate more quota by dealing with existing users.

The structure of the network could then be encoded as a weighted trust graph. This makes easier to define a central authorization module that takes as input the graph of the network and controls access to the resources in the network.

3.2 Grid Organization

Another scenario where the quota delegation policy is applicable is the following. Let us assume a grid composed of different organizations sharing multimedia resources. Each organization has a participating quota that determines the influence in the authorization process in order to use the resources.

When making authorization decisions this hierarchy, and the participation indexes of quota, have to be taken into account. There are several ways of doing this.

Each entity may issue different certificates, and those will be weighted according to their participation index.

Each entity participating in the grid has a share of quota. This share of quota could be handed over to external users. Usually, each organization would keep some of this quota for its use and will 'sell' the surplus of resources. This process could take place in a cascade effect. That is, if an external organization has bought a participation in a particular resource, this organization could also sell a portion to another external organization.

As consecutive sales advance, the quota that the new organizations obtain decreases. That means that more external organizations to the grid will have less influence on managing rights to access the resources of the grid.

There should also be a policy of access for each resource established by the grid and a common agreement where the minimum quota needed for accessing such a resource is reflected. Depending on the nature of the resource, this quota will be higher or lower. For instance, if the resource is a cluster, a request for a minute slot of use requires a lower quota than for using it for longer. Also, if there are two or more users competing for the same resource the quota can be used in order to prioritize the access to the resource.

4   A Quota Approach for Delegation

In Section 3 we have presented a scenario where the entities participating in a grid delegate rights management to another organizations, from inside and outside the grid. In this section we will introduce a mathematical model that formalizes the situation of the scenarios described above. We will call this model the *Quota Delegation Model*.

Since organizations in lower levels have been delegated less quota as we descend one level in the chain, we are interested in the exact quota that any organization retains. The quota is a real number in the interval $[0, 1]$, representing a percentage of the total quota where 1 corresponds to 100%. A user expresses the quota delegated to other entities relatively to the actual quota they obtain. The actual quota that a user delegates to another one is computed by multiplying the relative quota (encoded in the delegation quota credential) and the actual quota of the delegator. The absolute quota of a user is computed by summing up all the absolute quotas delegated by all the users of the system. In this section we will provide with an iterative mechanism for computing the absolute quota of each user.

In order to compute the quota of a certain organization we will use the product of all the quota of the links in the chain from the root node to the node we want to compute, minus the quota that this entity delegates. In fact, for each entity we can distinguish the delegated quota, which is the quota that reaches this entity trough delegation paths, and the actual quota of this entity that is computed by subtracting the quota delegated to other entities from the delegated quota of this entity.

If there are several chains for delegating quota to organizations, the final quota will be the addition of all the quotas obtained from all the different chains.

Loops are not allowed in our quota delegation model and have to be solved outside of it. For instance, if entity X has delegated some of its quota to entity Y and later, Y wants to delegate some of its quota to X, then there are two possibilities:

- If the absolute quota that Y wants to delegate to X is greater than the absolute quota X delegates to Y, then the quota delegation credential from X to Y should be removed from the system and a new quota delegation credential from Y to X should be added, where the delegated quota corresponds to the difference between the absolute quota that Y wants to delegate to X and the absolute quota delegated from X to Y expressed relatively to the quota of Y.

– If the absolute quota that Y wants to delegate to X is lower than the absolute quota X delegates to Y, then the current quota delegation credential from X to Y should be removed from the system and a new quota delegation credential from X to Y should be added. Then the delegated quota corresponds to the difference between the absolute quota delegated from X to Y and the absolute quota that Y wants to delegate to X expressed relatively to the quota of X.

In both cases the resulting quota delegation graph has no loops.

We have initially used attribute certificate credentials [7,5] to implement our Quota Delegation Model. The privilege delegated is encoded as an attribute and the value of the attribute is set to the quota. All the credentials have to be passed to a central server which checks that the quota assignments that each user does for each privilege is fair, i.e. the quotas of each credential issued by the same user and regarding the same privilege sum less than 1, which represents 100% of the quota. This central server stores all the delegated quotas in a matrix form.

If we establish an equivalence between nodes or organizations and states, and between the quota that an entity X hands over to Z and the statistical concept of transition from one X to Z, our particular problem could be modelled as a discrete Markov's chain where the number of phases or stages corresponds to the length of the chain that we consider.

4.1   Computational Model

The initial organization or entity that first holds all the quota is called the *initiator* and it will be the initial state of the Markov's chain. The values of the quotas could be placed in a matrix such as the addition of the elements in each row is lower or equal than 1 ('almost' a stochastic matrix). The reason is that the addition of all quota could never be greater than 1 but it can be less, i.e., there could be states without any assigned quota. Therefore, in order to make this matrix a stochastic matrix we should add an additional state, namely, the state of the non-assigned quota. This new state will mean a new column and row for the matrix of the states where the values in the columns are calculated in such a way that the addition of the values in the row is 1. If we call this matrix A, the associated stochastic matrix A^* is as follows:

$$\left(\begin{array}{c|c} A & \begin{array}{c} 1 - \sum_{j=1}^{n} a_{1,j} \\ \vdots \\ 1 - \sum_{j=1}^{n} a_{n,j} \end{array} \\ \hline 0 \cdots 0 & 1 \end{array} \right)$$

The state of 'non-assigned' quota is a non-transition state as once it has been reached no other state can be reached afterwards.

This matrix can be expressed in its canonical form as

$$\left(\begin{array}{c|c} A & R \\ \hline 0 & I \end{array} \right)$$

where A is the matrix of quota delegation that contains all the transition states; R is the matrix that contains the non-assigned quota by entities and I is the identity matrix of length 1. As there are no loops in the quota delegation graph, the matrix A is upper triangular or at least we can make it upper triangular by reordering the nodes using a topological sort algorithm over the quota delegation graph. Therefore, the matrix of the chain, N, is calculated as follows:

$$N = (I - A)^{-1}$$

Next we will show that the element n_{ij} of N is the share of quota that entity i hands over to entity j.

An element $a_{ij}^{(k)}$ of matrix A^k represents the percentage of quota that node i hands over node j indirectly, if we only consider chains of length k. Also, $A^n = 0$ if n is greater or equal than the size of the matrix, as this is an upper triangular matrix. Therefore, we can define matrix $\widehat{A}$ as

$$\widehat{A} = \sum_{i=1}^{\infty} A^i = \sum_{i=1}^{n-1} A^i$$

The elements of $\widehat{A}$ can be calculated in the following way:

$$\hat{a}_{ij} = \sum_{s=1}^{n-1} a_{ij}^{(s)}$$

$$\widehat{A} = (\hat{a}_{ij})$$

The elements $\hat{a}_{ij}$ of $\widehat{A}$ are the addition of all the quota that node i hands over to node j for chains of any length.

Next we will show that $N = I + \widehat{A}$, i.e., $I + \widehat{A}$ is the inverse of $I - A$. In order to do this, we will show that the matrix is invertible from the right-hand side (it is analogous from the left-hand side).

$$(I - A)(I + \widehat{A}) = (I - A)(\sum_{s=0}^{n-1} A^s)$$

$$= \sum_{s=0}^{n-1} A^s - \sum_{s=1}^{n} A^s$$

$$= I + \sum_{s=1}^{n-1} A^s - \sum_{s=1}^{n-1} A^s - A^n$$

$$= I$$

This gives us two ways of obtaining the percentage of quota handed over by entity i to entity j. Either by calculating the element ij of matrix N or by calculating the element (i, j) of matrix $\widehat{A}$.

In both cases, we can use the first row of those columns to form the vector of quota delegation from the initiator.

Definition 1 (quota delegation vector). *The quota delegation vector is the vector v consisting of all the quota delegation values from the initiator to the rest of the entities. The first element is set to 1.*

In order to obtain the actual quota that remains in each entity, we have to subtract the quota it delegates from the quota it has been delegated. This can be easily done by multiplying the corresponding element of the quota delegation vector, v_i, by the element r_i of the column vector R.

By multiplying the column vector R by v, element by element, we obtain the quota distribution over the entities. The sum of all the elements of this vector is 1.

4.2 Efficiency Analysis

The quota delegation model presents a feature that, in some cases, could be an advantage and, in some others, a disadvantage depending on the nature of the system. This feature is that if all the available quota has been assigned and we would be interested in assigning quota to a new entity, this should be taken away from the previously assigned quota.

Taking quota away could affect the entities which already had them assigned and therefore, the quota should be re-distributed again. This re-distribution will affect more to entities closer to the entity that it is the root of the quota. Thus, if we establish an order where the entity origin of the quota is of order 1 and the other entities' order follows from the order how the quota is assigned, as higher the order is, less impact will have the new distribution on this entity.

Taking into account all the above considerations we can make some remarks concerning the complexity of the calculation of matrix $\widehat{A}$. First, the consecutive powers of matrix A have mainly zeros as their elements. Thus, for example, while A is an upper triangular matrix, the elements of the diagonal $a_{i\,i+1}^2$ of the matrix $A^2 = (a_{i\,j}^2)$ are all 0. Also, if the size of the matrix A is n then A^{n-1} has only one element which is not 0. This element is a_{1n}^n. Thus, in order to calculate the elements of the diagonal $\hat{a}_{i,i+k}$ of matrix $\widehat{A}$, we only need elements of the powers of A which are less or equal than k.

Next, we will see how many elemental operations we need in order to calculate those elements.

Let d_k be the diagonal k for $k \in \{1, \dots, n-1\}$ of any matrix $A = (A_{ij})$. This diagonal has $n - k$ elements which are

$$d_k(A) = \{a_{j\,j+k}\}_{j=1}^{n-k}$$

The number of operations needed in order to calculate $d_m(A^p)$ is $(m - p + 1)(n-m)$ multiplications and $(m-p)(n-m)$ additions (the detailed explanation is beyond the scope of this paper).

Therefore, the number of multiplications needed in order to calculate $\widehat{A}$ and the number of additions needed in order to calculate the powers of A are respectively

$$\frac{(n + 1)n(n - 1)(n - 2)}{24} \text{ and } \frac{n(n - 1)(n - 2)(n - 3)}{24} \tag{1}$$

In order to calculate $d_m(\widehat{A})$ we have to add the non-null diagonals $d_m(A^p)$, i.e., $m - 1$ diagonals. Since these diagonals have $n - m$ elements, the number of additions for adding the consecutive powers of A is

$$\frac{n(n-1)(n-2)}{6} \qquad (2)$$

From those results we can calculate the total number of additions that are required for calculating $\widehat{A}$ and the total number of operations. Those two numbers are respectively

$$\frac{n(n^3 - 2n^2 - n + 2)}{24} \quad \text{and} \quad \frac{n(n^3 - 2n^2 - n + 2)}{12}$$

As a remark we can say that this algorithm for calculating the distribution of quota for n entities is of the order $\mathcal{O}(n^4)$.

If we used the matrix N instead, we can determine the complexity of the method by analyzing the complexity of the calculation of the inverse of $I - A$.

This matrix is invertible and its inverse is $I + \widehat{A}$. It is also upper triangular. In this case, we could solve as n systems of simultaneous equations $(I - A)x^i = b_i$, where b_i are the consecutive columns of matrix I in order to calculate the inverse. This inverse will be the matrix, in columns, $(I - A)^{-1} = (x^{(1)} \| \ldots \| x^{(n)})$. We can deduce that the inverse matrix is also upper triangular by observing the sub-system of the $n - i$ equations of each system,

$$\begin{pmatrix} 0 & 1 & \cdots & -a_{i+1\,n} \\ \vdots & \vdots & & \vdots \\ 0 & 0 & \cdots & 1 \end{pmatrix} \begin{pmatrix} x^{(i)}_{i+1} \\ \vdots \\ x^{(i)}_n \end{pmatrix} = \begin{pmatrix} 0 \\ \vdots \\ 0 \end{pmatrix}$$

therefore, $x^{(i)}_j = 0$ for $j > i$. Thus, resolving the remaining i equations of the system they can be simplified as follows

$$\begin{pmatrix} 1 & -a_{12} & \cdots & -a_{1i} \\ 0 & 1 & \cdots & -a_{i+1\,i} \\ \vdots & \vdots & & \vdots \\ 0 & 0 & \cdots & 1 \end{pmatrix} \begin{pmatrix} x^{(i)}_1 \\ x^{(i)}_2 \\ \vdots \\ x^{(i)}_i \end{pmatrix} = \begin{pmatrix} 0 \\ 0 \\ \vdots \\ 1 \end{pmatrix}$$

This triangular system of i equations can be resolved by performing i^2 operations by using the substitution method. Thus, the final number of operations needed for calculating the inverse of $I - A$ will be

$$\sum_{i=1}^{n} i^2 = \frac{n(n+1)(2n+1)}{6}$$

This means that by using the matrix N we can reduce the complexity to $\mathcal{O}(n^3)$.

5   Quota Based Delegation and Authorization Policies

Our quota based delegation model is mainly focused on facilitating delegation of access to resources that can be measured and consequently divided among users according to the specified quota percentage. Examples of such a kind of resources are the Internet connection bandwidth (see Section 3.2), file storage space, CPU load in cluster environments, etc. In those cases there is not need for a specific authorization policy to be used against the certificates, as they encode both things. The rights are already included in the credential, therefore we do not need to contrast it with an authorization policy. However, not all the resources are easily split and furthermore, sometimes it is undesirable to include the resource in the credential. In those cases, we use a role or group membership attribute and split this attribute among the users in the system. The grid scenario is a clear example of this situation. In those cases, we do need an authorization policy, therefore actual privileges or rights can be derived from the quota membership to a particular attribute. In Figure 1 we illustrate how those two scenarios are characterized according to where more effort is needed, either in the definition of credentials or in the definition of the authorization policies.

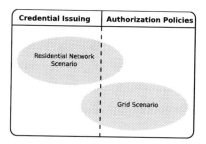

Fig. 1. Characterization of the two scenarios

Even though we have made a distinction here between these two examples, there might be cases where it is not that easy to make it. For the definition of the authorization policy we take as an input the quota or the percentage of the attribute that the user holds, and the higher it is, the more privileges it will be delegated.

The authorization problem can be also tackled by using negative statements, such as 'this user will never access this resource'. As each user is delegated a quota of the resource, an authorization credential can be given a weight associated to the quota of the issuer. Then, positive authorization credentials, i.e., those granting some privileges but not delegating them, can be counted as positive votes for authorization decisions and negative ones as negative votes. Those votes are proportional to the quota of the issuers of the credentials, in such a way that at the end, we can sum up all the positive votes and subtract from them all the negative ones. If the result is positive the authorization request will be granted. However, this is just a simple authorization policy. More complex solutions can be defined, such as requesting a lower bound for the delegated quota.

5.1   Example

Let us assume a grid of four organizations X, Z, V and W. Let us also assume that the X is the user who initially possesses 100% of the quota of a given resource, i.e. X is the owner of the resource and wants to contribute a share of it to the grid. X hands over a third of the quota to V and another third to W. V and W also delegate 3/4 of their quota to Z. We are interested in calculating the exact quota that each entity in the grid retains after all the quota delegations are effective.

In order for the matrix A to be upper triangular, we can establish the following order of the nodes: $X \rightarrow 1$, $V \rightarrow 2$, $W \rightarrow 3$ and $Z \rightarrow 4$.

Figure 2 shows the distribution of the quota. The Figure on the left-hand side describes how the quota originally is distributed among peers and, on the one on the right-hand side the distribution of quota is represented as a States Transition Diagram (STD) of the associated Markov's chain which includes the 'non-assigned' quota states.

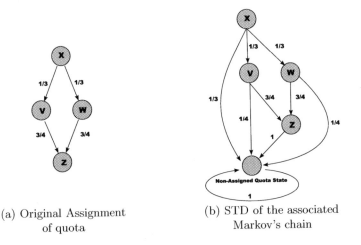

(a) Original Assignment   (b) STD of the associated
of quota   Markov's chain

Fig. 2. From quota assignment graph to Markov's chain STD

The matrix representing the quota assigned is as follows

$$A = \begin{pmatrix} 0 & \frac{1}{3} & \frac{1}{3} & 0 \\ 0 & 0 & 0 & \frac{3}{4} \\ 0 & 0 & 0 & \frac{3}{4} \\ 0 & 0 & 0 & 0 \end{pmatrix}$$

From this matrix we can obtain the stochastic matrix by including the non-assigned quota in the last row and column.

$$A^* = \begin{pmatrix} 0 & \frac{1}{3} & \frac{1}{3} & 0 & \frac{1}{3} \\ 0 & 0 & 0 & \frac{3}{4} & \frac{1}{4} \\ 0 & 0 & 0 & \frac{3}{4} & \frac{1}{4} \\ 0 & 0 & 0 & 0 & 1 \\ \hline 0 & 0 & 0 & 0 & 1 \end{pmatrix}$$

The fifth row and column correspond to the state of non-assigned quota.

In order to calculate the quota that X hands over Z we should calculate, in Markov's processes terminology, the probability of going from state X to Z. We will use matrix N for doing it.

$$N = (I - A)^{-1} = \begin{pmatrix} 1 & \frac{1}{3} & \frac{1}{3} & \frac{1}{2} \\ 0 & 1 & 0 & \frac{3}{4} \\ 0 & 0 & 1 & \frac{3}{4} \\ 0 & 0 & 0 & 1 \end{pmatrix}$$

In order to obtain the actual quota belonging to each user, we have to subtract the quota that has already been delegated. We can do this by multiplying the first row of this matrix by the column of the non-assigned quota, element by element.

$$(1, \frac{1}{3}, \frac{1}{3}, \frac{1}{2}) \times (\frac{1}{3}, \frac{1}{4}, \frac{1}{4}, 1) = (\frac{1}{3}, \frac{1}{12}, \frac{1}{12}, \frac{1}{2})$$

Therefore, the shares of assigned quota of all the participants are the corresponding elements of this vector. Note that the sum of the elements of this vector is one, therefore the quota property holds.

If we implement an authorization policy such as the simple one defined in the previous section in such a way that Z and W decide that access to a third party has to be granted, it does not matter what X and Y state, as the votes of Z and W count more than 50%. Thus, the decision will be to grant access.

6 Conclusions and Future Work

In this work we have presented a delegation mechanism for finite resources or environments where there could be a conflict of interest among the entities involved in the decision making process.

By specifying quotas in credentials we allow for fair delegation among the participants, as we can control that a resource is never overflowed by a massive access from participants. When using the quota delegation mechanism in conjunction with attributes, instead of with proper resources, fairness is not the main objective but solving disputes between participants about which other users are granted some privileges.

Currently we are exploring how this quota can be included in standard X.509 attribute certificates in a more coherent manner. We are using ideas from [10,1]. For doing this, we should first implement a mechanism such that a user is not allowed to issue credentials for more than 100% of his quota.

The trivial solution consists of storing all the credentials in a central server that performs consistence checking over delegated quota. However, we believe that distributed solutions, or at least semi-distributed solutions, can be achieved.

We are also focusing our efforts on exploring the field of encrypted databases [11, 6] in order to try to implement a quota service database where each user stores all the quota delegation credentials in an encrypted manner. Thus, this quota service database, that may also be distributed, could answer consistence queries, i.e. the delegated quota does not exceed the 100% of the own quota, without revelling information neither about the delegated entities nor the actual quota being delegated to them, to the privilege verifier.

The privilege verifier would therefore be able to compute at least a lower bound for the delegated quota, based on a subset of the actual delegation paths. In order to determine a lower bound of the delegated quota to a user, it should be feasible to verify with the Quota Service Database that the specified quotas in each of the credentials paths are part of fair assignment of quota. That is, the summation of all the quotas of credentials of a given issuer for the same privilege should never exceed 100%.

Furthermore, the Quota Service Database would allow us to use both, push and pull mechanisms for authorization. By using the quota service database, the privilege verifier can check that the credentials a user has sent to in order to attest his quota are all the existing one.

References

1. Agudo, I., Lopez, J., Montenegro, J.A.: A representation model of trust relationships with delegation extensions. In: Herrmann, P., Issarny, V., Shiu, S.C.K. (eds.) iTrust 2005. LNCS, vol. 3477, pp. 116–130. Springer, Heidelberg (2005)
2. Blaze, M., Feigenbaum, J., Keromytis, A.D.: KeyNote: Trust Management for Public-Key Infrastructures (position paper). In: Christianson, B., Crispo, B., Harbison, W.S., Roe, M. (eds.) Security Protocols 1998. LNCS, vol. 1550, pp. 59–63. Springer, Heidelberg (1999)
3. Blaze, M., Feigenbaum, J., Lacy, J.: Decentralized Trust Management. In: IEEE Symposium on Security and Privacy (1996)
4. Ellison, C.: SPKI Certificate Theory, Request for Comments 2693. IETF SPKI Working Group (September 1999)
5. Farrell, S., Housley, R.: An Internet Attribute Certificate Profile for Authorization. IETF PKIX Working Group, Request for Comments 3281 (April 2002)
6. Haber, S., Horne, W., Sander, T., Yao, D.: Privacy-preserving verification of aggregate queries on outsourced databases. Technical report, Trusted Systems Laboratory, HP Laboratories Palo Alto (2007)
7. ITU-T Recommendation X.509. ITU-T X.509, ISI/IEC 9594-8, Information technology - Open Systems Interconnection - The Directory: Public-key and attribute certificate frameworks (August 2005)
8. Kemeny, J.G.: Finite Markov Chains. New York (1976)
9. Leiven, R.: Attack Resistant Trust Metrics. PhD thesis, University of California, Berkeley (2003)

10. Montenegro, J., Moya, F.: A practical approach of X.509 attribute certificate framework as support to obtain privilege delegation. In: Katsikas, S.K., Gritzalis, S., López, J. (eds.) EuroPKI 2004. LNCS, vol. 3093, pp. 160–172. Springer, Heidelberg (2004)
11. Narasimha, M., Tsudik, G.: Authentication of outsourced databases using signature aggregation and chaining. In: Li Lee, M., Tan, K.-L., Wuwongse, V. (eds.) DASFAA 2006. LNCS, vol. 3882, pp. 420–436. Springer, Heidelberg (2006)
12. Page, L., Brin, S., Motwani, R., Winograd, T.: The PageRank Citation Ranking: Bringing Order to the Web. Technical report, Stanford Digital Library Technologies Project (1998)
13. Papoullis, A.: Brownian Movement and Markoff Processes. In: Papoullis, A. (ed.) Probability, Random Variables and Stochastic Processes, New York, pp. 515–553 (1984)
14. Ziegler, C.N., Lausen, G.: Spreading Activation Models for Trust Propagation. In: IEEE International Conference on e-Technology, e-Commerce, and e-Service (EEE 2004), Taipei (March 2004)
15. Ziegler, C.-N., Lausen, G.: Propagation Models for Trust and Distrust in Social Networks. Information Systems Frontiers 7(4-5), 337–358 (2005)

Access Control and Information Flow in Transactional Memory*

Ariel Cohen[1], Ron van der Meyden[2], and Lenore D. Zuck[3]

[1] New York University
arielc@cs.nyu.edu
[2] University of New South Wales
meyden@cse.unsw.edu.au
[3] University of Illinois at Chicago
lenore@cs.uic.edu

Abstract. The paper considers the addition of access control to a number of transactional memory implementations, and studies its impact on the information flow security of such systems. Even after the imposition of access control, the Unbounded Transactional Memory due to Ananian et al, and most instances of a general scheme for transactional conflict detection and arbitration due to Scott, are shown to be insecure. This result applies even for a very simple policy prohibiting information flow from a high to a low security domain. The source of the insecurity is identified as the ability of agents to cause aborts of other agents' transactions. A generic implementation is defined, parameterized by a "may-abort" relation that defines which agents may cause aborts of other agents' transactions. This implementation is shown to be secure with respect to an intransitive information flow policy consistent with the access control table and "may-abort" relation. Using this result, Transactional Memory Coherence and Consistency, an implementation due to Hammond et al, is shown to be secure with respect to intransitive information flow policies. Moreover, it is shown how to modify Scott's arbitration policies using the may-abort relation, yielding a class of secure implementations closely related to Scott's scheme.

1 Introduction

Multicore architectures have become ubiquitous in the design of microprocessor chips, and they require developers to produce concurrent programs in order to gain a full advantage of the multiple number of processors. Parallel programming, however, is very challenging. It requires programmers to carefully coordinate and synchronize objects that access shared data in order to ensure that programs do not produce inconsistent, incorrect or nondeterministic results. Locks, semaphores, mutexes, and similar constructs are difficult to compose, and their incorrect application may introduce undesirable effects such as deadlocks, priority inversion, and convoying.

---

* The research of the first and third co-authors was sponsored in part by ONR grant N00014-99-1-0131 and NSF Award CNS-0420477. The work of the second author was supported by ARC Discovery grant DP0451529.

P. Degano, J. Guttman, and F. Martinelli (Eds.): FAST 2008, LNCS 5491, pp. 316–330, 2009.

Transactional Memory (TM) avoids these pitfalls, and simplifies parallel programming by transferring the burden of concurrency management from the programmers to the system designers, thus enabling programmers to safely compose scalable applications. Consequently, transactional memory is considered to be a promising alternative method for coordinating objects and numerous new implementations have been proposed recently (see [11] for an excellent survey).

A *transaction* is a sequence of operations that are executed *atomically* – either all complete successfully (and the transaction commits), or none completes (and the transaction aborts). Moreover, committed transactions should be *serializable* – there should be a permutation of the operations of the committed transactions where the operations of each transaction are consecutive and in their original order. Transactional memory allows transactions to run concurrently as long as atomicity and serializability are preserved.

Shared memory systems are often decomposed into security domains, with access control mechanisms used to restrict actions, such as reading and writing memory locations not associated to these domains. This can be for reasons of structural decomposition as well as to enforce an information flow security policy. The latter has been a particular concern in military security applications. An *intransitive noninterference policy* can be viewed as a specification of the permitted causal influences in such architectures.

A great deal of research has focused on construction of multi-level secure systems, but, in practice, such systems continue to be plagued with known insecurities. An alternative that has been advocated is to build a multilevel secure system as a distributed system comprised of single-level systems [13,14]. Multicore processors offer the potential for such architectures for secure systems to be realised on a single chip. However, appropriate controls on features such as transactional memory will be required to realise this possibility. To our knowledge, the literature on transactional memory has not yet turned to consideration of how access control should be managed in such systems.

In this paper we develop a model of access control in transactional memories, in which transactional memory systems can be seen as extensions of Rushby's [15] access control model that add operations for opening, closing and aborting transactions. We then study the extent to which the theory of information flow in access control systems carries over to the extension. A standard memory system with an access control table can be associated with a "minimal" information flow policy (which is, in general, intransitive). It can be established that a system satisfies the associated minimal information flow policy. We study whether this is also the case for transactional memories, where we focus on different approaches to transactional memory implementation. Specifically, we consider Transactional Memory Coherence and Consistency (TCC) [8], Unbounded Transactional Memory (UTM) [2], and a general scheme for conflict detection and arbitration [16]. Some of these implementations turn out to be secure with respect to the policy associated to arbitrary access control tables, others turn out to be insecure even for the very simple information flow policy involving two agents **H** and **L** with information flow from **H** to **L** prohibited.

Finally, we identify the source of the insecurity to be the ability of one agent's activity to cause another agent's transaction to abort and propose a fix to the classical access control policy that avoids this type of insecurity. We define a generic transactional implementation that incorporates this idea. This result is then used to prove the security of TCC as well as a modification of Scott's arbitration rules so as to obtain secure variants for all instances of Scott's scheme.

A Simple Example. To demonstrate the ideas of this paper, consider *Unbounded Transactional Memory* (UTM) that eagerly updates the main memory with new values while maintaining copies of old values in a *transaction log*. A conflict between pending transactions occurs when one tries to read a block that was written by another, or write a block that was read or written by another. The arbitration policy is to abort the younger transaction, i.e., the one that started while the other was already pending.

Suppose a single memory block, x, and two security domains, **H** (high) and **L** (low), where **H** can only read x and **L** can both read and write x. As commonly assumed, the permitted information streams are from each domain into itself and from **L** to **H**. Let α be a trace of the system where **H** opens a transaction, then **L** opens a transaction, and then **H** reads x. Now, assume **L** attempts to write x. According to UTM, since this implies a conflict and **L**'s pending transaction is younger than **H**'s, **L**'s transaction would be aborted. From this, **L** would be able to infer that **H** has an older pending transaction that read x. Consequently, in this case, UTM allows information flow from **H** into **L**, contrary to policy.

The violation of the security policy occurred because of **L**'s ability to infer information about **H** from its *failure* to perform an action successfully, and not, as is usual the case in memory systems, from its ability to read a value written by **H**. This leads us to the observation that, to avoid such forbidden information flow, one should alter the arbitration policy as to avoid aborting transactions of lower security clients in lieu of actions performed by their higher security peers. As we show in the sequel, in this particular case it suffices to abort the older **H** if aborting the younger **L** would lead to security violation, and to follow the usual arbitration policy in all other cases.

Overview. The rest of the paper is organized as follows: Section 2 describes the formal model and recalls the definitions that we use from the theory of information flow security. Section 3 gives a general description of transactional memory system, enhances transactional memory systems with an access control table and proves several implementation of them to be insecure. Section 4 presents a generic secure protocol, and shows security of some transactional memory systems that implement the generic protocol. Section 5 shows how to fix the systems shown insecure in Section 3 so as to be secure. Section 6 reviews the data base literature related to our results. Finally, Section 7 provides some conclusions and discusses future work.

2   Model and Access Control

Several different abstract system models have been used in the literature on noninterference. In this paper, we use an *action-observed* model [15], where the observations are outputs received on performing an action. In later sections we refine this model in order to capture specific detail of interest in transactional memory systems.

Let $\mathcal{D}$ be a set of *security domains*, or *agents*, and let $\mathcal{O}$ be a set of *outputs*, or *observations*. An *action-observed* security system (AOSS) is a deterministic machine of the form $\langle S, s_0, A, \texttt{step}, \texttt{out}, \texttt{dom} \rangle$, where

1. S is a set of states (typically, the set of all assignments to some set of variables V),
2. $s_0 \in S$ is the *initial state*,
3. A is a set of actions,
4. $\mathrm{dom}: A \to \mathcal{D}$ associates each action to an element of the set of security domains $\mathcal{D}$,
5. $\mathrm{step}: S \times A \to S$ is a deterministic transition function, and
6. $\mathrm{out}: S \times A \to \mathcal{O}$ is a function such that $\mathrm{out}(s, a)$ is the output received by domain $\mathrm{dom}(a)$ when action a is performed in state s.

We write $s \cdot \alpha$ for the state reached by performing the sequence of actions $\alpha \in A^*$ from state s, defined inductively by $s \cdot \epsilon = s$ for ϵ the empty sequence, and $s \cdot \alpha a = \mathrm{step}(s \cdot \alpha, a)$ for $\alpha \in A^*$ and $a \in A$.

A *non-interference* policy captures when "actions of agent p_1 are permitted to interfere with agent p_2," or "information is permitted to flow from domain p_1 to domain p_2." See Section 6 for a brief survey on the history of non-interference. Formally, a *noninterference policy* is a binary relation $\rightarrowtail$ over $\mathcal{D}$, with $p \rightarrowtail q$ intuitively meaning that "actions of agent p are permitted to interfere with agent q." Since a domain should be allowed to interfere with, or have information about, itself, $\rightarrowtail$ is always assumed to be reflexive.

The simplest nontrivial noninterference policy (and the one most studied in the literature) is the one mentioned in Section 1, that comprised of two security domains **L** (low security) and **H** (high security), with information permitted to flow from **L** to **H** but not the other way around. Formally, this policy is captured by the (transitive) relation $\rightarrowtail = \{(\mathbf{L}, \mathbf{L}), (\mathbf{H}, \mathbf{H}), (\mathbf{L}, \mathbf{H})\}$.

As mentioned in Section 1, access control systems can naturally be associated to intransitive noninterference policies (we give the construction at the end of this section). Such policies can be given a number of different semantic interpretations. We use here the notion of *TA-Security* [12] (which avoids some unintuitive information flows allowed in [15]; see [12] for a discussion).

Formally, given sets L and I, let $H(L, I)$ be the smallest set H containing L and such that if $x, y \in H$ and $i \in I$ then $(x, y, i) \in H$. Intuitively, the elements of $H(L, I)$ are binary trees with L-labeled leaves and I-labeled interior nodes. Given a policy $\rightarrowtail$, define, for each agent $p \in D$, the function $\mathrm{ta}_p: A^* \to H(\{\epsilon\}, A)$ inductively by $\mathrm{ta}_p(\epsilon) = \epsilon$, and, for $\alpha \in A^*$ and $a \in A$:

$$\mathrm{ta}_p(\alpha a) = \begin{cases} (\mathrm{ta}_p(\alpha), \mathrm{ta}_{\mathrm{dom}(a)}(\alpha), a) & \mathrm{dom}(a) \rightarrowtail p \\ \mathrm{ta}_p(\alpha) & \text{otherwise} \end{cases}$$

Informally, the definition builds an operational model of the maximal permitted flow of information, where an action adds to the maximal permitted information of domains with which it is permitted to interfere – the fact that the action occurs, as well as all information available to its domain at the time it occurs.

An AOSS is TA-*secure with respect to* $\rightarrowtail$ if for all $\alpha, \alpha' \in A^*$, and $p \in \mathcal{D}$, if $\mathrm{ta}_p(\alpha) = \mathrm{ta}_p(\alpha')$ then $\mathrm{out}(s_0 \cdot \alpha, a) = \mathrm{out}(s_0 \cdot \alpha', a)$ for every $a \in A$ such that $\mathrm{dom}(a) = p$. That is, a system is secure if the output of an action returns no more information than the maximal information permitted to be known to its agent.

A simple example of an AOSS is a standard memory equipped with a read/write access control table. Let Loc be a set of memory locations, Val a set of values that these locations may store, and let $\mathcal{R}: \mathcal{D} \to \mathcal{P}(\text{Loc})$ and $\mathcal{W}: \mathcal{D} \to \mathcal{P}(\text{Loc})$ represent the locations that each agent is permitted to read and write, respectively. Consider a system in which the set of states is the set of all assignments $s: \text{Loc} \to Val$, and there are two types of actions: $\text{read}_p(x)$ (a read request by agent $p \in \mathcal{D}$ on location $x \in \text{Loc}$) $\text{write}_p(x, v)$ (a request by agent $p \in \mathcal{D}$ to write value v in location $x \in \text{Loc}$.) These actions have the expected semantics: $\text{read}_p(x)$ returns the value of x unless $x \notin \mathcal{R}(p)$, in which case it returns err. Similarly, $\text{write}_p(x, v)$ updates x by v (and returns ack) unless $x \notin \mathcal{W}(p)$ (in which case it returns err).

We remark that, given the access control structure $\mathcal{T} = (\mathcal{R}, \mathcal{W})$ on such a standard memory, we may define a policy $\rightarrowtail_{\mathcal{T}}$ by $p \rightarrowtail_{\mathcal{T}} q$ iff $p = q$ or $\mathcal{W}(p) \cap \mathcal{R}(q) \neq \emptyset$. (Generally, $\rightarrowtail_{\mathcal{T}}$ is not guaranteed to be transitive.) Intuitively, if $p \rightarrowtail_{\mathcal{T}} q$ then information flow from p to q cannot be prevented, since there is some location that p may write and q may read. Conversely, it can be shown [12] that this relation captures precisely the information flow policies enforced by the access control structure, in the sense that the memory system is TA-secure with respect to a policy $\rightarrowtail$ iff $\rightarrowtail_{\mathcal{T}} \subseteq \rightarrowtail$. In the sequel we examine the extent to which this result generalizes to transactional memories.

3   Transactional Memories

Transactional memory systems extend standard memory systems by allowing only for atomic and serializable sequences of operations. Transactional memories vary in their atomicity and serializability policies and in the implementation details by which they guarantee these policies. Consequently, they vary in the data structures they maintain (i.e., set of states) and the algorithms they employ (i.e., "step" function). See [4] for a treatment of issues, which we ignore here.

Assume a set of *clients* that direct transactional requests to a memory system that assigns a value from a set Val to every location x in a set Loc of locations. For every client p, let the set of actions a with $\text{dom}(a) = p$ (also referred to as *p-actions*) be:

- $\blacktriangleleft_p$ – An open transaction request.
- $\text{read}_p(x)$ – A request to read from address $x \in \text{Loc}$.
- $\text{write}_p(x, v)$ – A request to write the value $v \in Val$ to address $x \in \text{Loc}$.
- $\blacktriangleright_p$ – A close transaction request.
- $\blacktriangleright\!\!\!\!/_p$ – An abort transaction request.

Most current transactional memory implementations assume that each client can read from, and write to, every memory location. Here we take the view that clients are restricted in the locations they may access. Hence, we associate each client p with two subsets of Loc, $\mathcal{R}(p)$ and $\mathcal{W}(p)$, that indicate which locations p can read from and write to.

The memory provides a response to each action: ack acknowledges that a non-read has been carried out successfully, a value $v \in Val$ is returned in response to a successful read, err signals that the action is invalid, and $aborted$ signals that the transaction within which the action occurs must be aborted. An action is invalid when either it is a local violation of the transactional sequence, (for example, when a client issues a ➤̸ and its previous action is also an ➤̸), or when it attempts to access memory locations that are forbidden. Determining when a transaction is to be aborted depends, however, on the history of the transactional accesses and the transactional policies enforced.

A *conflict* occurs when concurrent transactions access the same location and at least one writes to it. When a conflict occurs, at least one of the participating transactions should be aborted. An implementation has an *eager conflict detection* if it detects conflicts as soon as they occur, and a *lazy conflict detection* if it delays the detection until one of the transactions requests to commit. *Arbitration* policies determine which transaction should abort.

Under *eager version management* the memory is updated with every acknowledged write action (which implies that aborts may require a roll-backs), and under *lazy version management* memory updates are delayed until the write-ing transaction commits (which entails no roll-backs). Note that eager version management may not be combined with lazy conflict detection.

In [16], Scott studied various notions of conflicts. Let $\prec$ denote the precedence relation on events of a given trace, $e \prec e'$ meaning that e occurred before e' (in the trace). Let T_p and T_q be concurrent (interleaved) transactions of agents p and q, respectively. The best known of Scott's conflicts are (1) *lazy invalidation* where T_p and T_q conflict if a write of one transaction may invalidate a read of the other, i.e., if for some memory address x, we have $\mathtt{read}_q(x), \mathtt{write}_p(x, \_) \prec \blacktriangleright_p \prec \blacktriangleright_q$ (Here the read and write can occur in either order); (2) *eager W-R* where T_p and T_q conflict if they have a lazy invalidation conflict, or if for some memory address x, we have $\mathtt{write}_p(x, \_) \prec \mathtt{read}_q(x) \prec \blacktriangleright_p$, and (3) *eager invalidation* where T_p and T_q conflict if they have an eager W-R conflict, or if for some memory address x, we have $\mathtt{read}_q(x) \prec \mathtt{write}_p(x, \_) \prec \blacktriangleright_q$. Scott also studies two arbitration policies. An *eagerly aggressive* policy aborts the transaction that opened first, and a *lazily aggressive* commits a transaction if only if it does not conflict with previously committed transactions.

Example 1. *Unbounded Transactional Memory* (UTM), proposed in [2], is a hardware transactional memory (HTM) that eagerly updates the main memory with new values while maintaining copies of old values in a transaction log. The description of UTM is outlined in Section 1.

To cast a transactional memory as a AOSS, we assume that the set $\mathcal{D}$ of security domains includes the set of clients, the set $\mathcal{O}$ of outputs includes $Val \cup \{err, ack, aborted\}$, and the set V of variables includes the set Loc of memory locations.

Given a sequence of actions $\alpha = a_1 \ldots a_n$ and a state s, we define the *trace* of α from s to be the sequence $trace(\alpha, s) = (a_1, o_1), (a_2, o_2), \ldots, (a_n, o_n)$, where $o_i = out(s \cdot (a_1 \ldots a_{i-1}), a_i)$ for $i = 1 \ldots n$. The trace indicates the sequence of outputs that are obtained for the sequence of actions α when initiated at s. We call a pair (a, o) an *event*. We say that $p \in \mathcal{D}$ has a *pending transaction* at α if for some $i \in [1..n]$, $(a_i, o_i) = (\blacktriangleleft_p, ack)$, and (a_j, o_j) is neither $(\blacktriangleright_p, ack)$ nor $(\blacktriangleright̸_p, ack)$ for all $j \in [i+1..n]$, i.e., p has a open transaction which has neither aborted nor committed at α. Similarly, p has a *pending aborted transaction* at α if it has a pending transaction and for the maximal $\ell \in [1..n]$ such that a_ℓ is a p-action, $o_\ell = aborted$.

Some properties of the output function out are relevant for our discussion. As described above, out returns err when an action violates a reasonable transaction sequence or attempts to access forbidden memory locations. More formally, for a sequence of actions α and a p-action a, $\text{out}(s_0 \cdot \alpha, a) = err$ iff one of the following holds:

1. a is $\blacktriangleleft_p$ and p has a pending transaction in α;
2. a is not $\blacktriangleleft_p$ and p has no pending transaction in α;
3. a is $\text{read}_p(x)$ and $x \notin \mathcal{R}(p)$;
4. a is $\text{write}_p(x)$ and $x \notin \mathcal{W}(p)$;

(Note that an err output depends solely on local history of agents; If one assumes agents attempt only syntactically "legal" actions, err can be removed.)

An *aborted* output depends on the implementation details. For simplicity's sake, we require that once an action generates an *aborted* output, all subsequent actions of the same transaction which do not attempt to abort it, also generate an *aborted* output. That is, to simplify the exposition, it is assumed that if p has an open aborted transaction in α and a is a p-action which is not $\blacktriangleright_p$, then $\text{out}(s_0 \cdot \alpha, a) = aborted$. The other cases for which out returns *aborted* are implementation dependent.

When the transactional memory receives an action, it first checks whether it is syntactically valid, returning err if it is not. It then checks whether an *aborted* output is due. For all other cases, it outputs ack, or some value $v \in Val$ if the action is a read action, which, again, depends on the transactional memory implementation. (For example, in UTM, the value is the last value written, while in other implementations it may be the last value written by a committed transaction). We assume that actions that return err because of an access violation do not update states. That is, that if $a = \text{read}_p(x)$ and $x \notin \mathcal{R}(p)$, or if $a = \text{write}_p(x)$ and $x \notin \mathcal{W}(p)$, then for every state s, $s \cdot a = s$.

Consider a transactional memory, and let $\mathcal{T} = (\mathcal{R}, \mathcal{W})$ be its access control table. As we did above, for a standard memory, we may define the policy $\rightarrowtail_{\mathcal{T}}$ on $\mathcal{D}$ to be the minimal policy consistent with $\mathcal{T}$. More precisely, we have $p \rightarrowtail_{\mathcal{T}} q$ iff $p = q$ or $\mathcal{W}(p) \cap \mathcal{R}(q) \neq \emptyset$. In the case of standard memories, this relation captures precisely the possible flows of information in the system. This proves no longer to be the case when we add the transactional memory structure. In fact, UTM from Example 1, as well as five out of the six combinations of [16]'s conflict and arbitration policies lead to insecure transactional memories, even after we impose access control:

Theorem 1. *The following transactional memory protocols are not* TA-*secure with respect to* $\rightarrowtail_{\mathcal{T}}$:

1. UTM *as defined in Example 1;*
2. *Protocols with eagerly aggressive arbitration and conflict detection which is lazy invalidation, eager W-R, or eager invalidation;*
3. *Protocols with lazily aggressive arbitration and conflict detection that is either eager W-R or eager invalidation.*

Consequently, the only combination of [16]'s conflict and arbitration policies that Theorem 1 does not cover is that of lazy invalidation conflict and a lazily aggressive arbitration. This is the focus of the next section.

4 A Secure Protocol

While standard memories equipped with an access control table $\mathcal{T}$ are TA-secure with respect to $\rightarrowtail_{\mathcal{T}}$ (and, consequently with any policy $\rightarrowtail$ that contains $\rightarrowtail_{\mathcal{T}}$), the results of Section 3 show that, once transactional features are added to a memory, this is no longer the case, since aborts provide a covert channel. All security breaches of Section 3 stem from allowing the output of a one client's action to depend on another's past events it *should* have no access to. Here we propose a remedy to this situation, by restricting the *out*put function so it depends only on the parts of the history that can safely impact the issuer of the action. Our key idea is to equip transactional memories not just with an access control table, but also with an additional control mechanism, that provides a way to constrain this covert channel. After describing the restriction, we present a *generic* protocol that uses the restriction, which we show to be secure. We also show that a well known protocol, TCC, is TA-secure by showing it to be an implementation of the generic protocol. Since TCC employs a lazy invalidation conflict detection and a lazily aggressive arbitration, it shows that the only combination of [16]'s conflicts and arbitrations that is not covered by Theorem 1 has a TA-secure implementation.

Let $\rightarrowtail_{ma}$ (*may abort*) be a reflexive binary relation on $\mathcal{D}$. Intuitively, if $p \not\rightarrowtail_{ma} q$, then in the event of a conflict between a transaction of p and a transaction of q, it is p's transaction that should be aborted, else we would have p activity causing an abort of an q transaction, which the relation prohibits.

The Generic Protocol. We introduce a protocol that uses the relation $\rightarrowtail_{ma}$ to impose the desired properties of out. The protocol is "full information" in the sense that it stores, for each client, all the information of actions of clients that may cause it to abort, in the order in which the actions occur. Security of this protocol implies that any implementation of it that allows for less information to be stored is also secure. We refer to this protocol as the *generic protocol*. It is general enough to allow for detection and arbitration of Scott-like transactional memory mechanisms. We show that this generic protocol is secure with respect to a minimal information flow policy derived from the access control and abort restrictions.

The generic protocol is presented as an AOSS. We follow the general model of Section 3, and include, for every client $p \in \mathcal{D}$, an event sequence $Cache_p$ consisting of sequences of events of the form (a, o) where $o \neq err$ and a is a q-event for some q such that $q \rightarrowtail_{ma} p$. Thus, the set V of the system's variables consists of:

- For each $x \in$ Loc a variable $mem[x]$ of type Val, representing the persistent memory. Initially, $mem[x] = v_0$ for all $x \in$ Loc, where $v_0 \in Val$ is some default initial value.
- For every $p \in \mathcal{D}$, a sequence $Cache_p$, initially empty. At each point in time, $Cache_p$ consists of actions (and their responses) of p as well as those of clients that may abort it.

To give operational meaning to the may-abort relation, we construct the implementation so that a client's transactions can be aborted based only on information locally available in the client's cache, and restrict the flow of information into the client's cache to comply with the relation $\rightarrowtail_{ma}$.

We furthermore paramaterize the implementation by means of a *cache policy* whereby each client manages its local cache. This policy, C, is represented by a pair of functions $C_p = (doomed_p, clean_p)$ for each $p \in \mathcal{D}$, where $doomed_p$ is a boolean function that takes $Cache_p$ and an p-action a and returns $true$ iff p's pending transaction should be aborted if a is performed. The function *clean* defines how each client updates its cache when aborting or committing a transaction. It takes $Cache_p$, and returns a subsequence of it that includes no p-events.

The function *doomed* is assumed to be monotonic: if $doomed_p(C, a) = true$, then so is $doomed_p(C; (a, aborted), b)$ for any p-action b other than $\blacktriangleright_p$. That is, appending further events after a transaction becomes doomed cannot change the fact that it is doomed.

Based on an access control table $\mathcal{T} = (\mathcal{R}, \mathcal{W})$ over the set of locations Loc, a may-abort relation $\rightarrowtail_{ma}$ and a cache policy C, we construct a transactional memory system $TM(\mathcal{T}, \rightarrowtail_{ma}, C)$. The states of the system are based on the variables described above. Fig. 1 describes the steps and output of the generic implementation. For readability, we included only the actions whose output is not err (recall that an err output is a result only of actions that the issuing clients can determine as erroneous). The first column is the action, say a. Then second column describes conditions under which a is taken. They are to be read as in a case-statement: the line corresponding to the first condition that holds is to be used. Thus, each can be interpreted as a predicate over states. The third column is $\mathrm{out}(s, a)$ – the output returned when action a is taken from state s that satisfies the associated predicate. The fourth column describes the update to the variables between the current state s and its successor $s' = \mathrm{step}(s, a)$. We use the following two abbreviations: For a set of clients $Q \subseteq \mathcal{D}$, let

$$\mathrm{Update}(Q) := \bigwedge_{q \in Q} Cache_q := Cache_q; (a, \mathrm{out}(s, a))$$

Thus, $\mathrm{Update}(Q)$ is the result of appending the action and its output to all clients in Q. For all clients $p \in \mathcal{D}$, $\mathrm{Apply}(Cache_p, mem)$ is executed by taking, for each $x \in \mathrm{Loc}$, the most recent occurrence of $(\mathrm{write}_p(x, v), ack)$ in $Cache_p$, and executing $mem[x] := v$. If no such event exists, that $mem[x]$ remains intact. We restrict the set of system states to those reachable from the initial state by means of a sequence of these actions.

The following theorem implies that the *only* way that information may flow between two clients in the generic implementation is by direct reading of written variables and by aborts of one of the client's transactions.

Theorem 2. *Given an access control table $\mathcal{T}$, a may-abort relation $\rightarrowtail_{ma}$, and a cache policy C, the system $TM(\mathcal{T}, \rightarrowtail_{ma}, C)$ is* TA-*secure with respect to the policy $\rightarrowtail_{\mathcal{T}} \cup \rightarrowtail_{ma}$.*

An immediate corollary of Theorem 2 is that $TM(\mathcal{T}, \rightarrowtail_{ma}, C)$ is TA-secure with respect to any policy $\rightarrowtail$ that contains both $\rightarrowtail_{\mathcal{T}}$ and $\rightarrowtail_{ma}$.

Theorem 2 can be similarly proved for protocols that record less information than the generic protocol above. For example, if p performs read or write actions on locations not observable by q, then such operations need not be recorded in q's cache. Other variants

action (a)	case (use first that applies)	output	updates
$\blacktriangleleft_p$		ack	$\texttt{Update}(\{q : p \rightarrowtail_{ma} q\})$
$\texttt{read}_p(x)$	$doomed_p(Cache_p, \texttt{read}_p(x))$	$aborted$	$\texttt{Update}(\{q : p \rightarrowtail_{ma} q\})$
	$Cache_p$ has $\texttt{write}_p(x,v)$ not proceeded by $\texttt{write}_p(x,-)$	v	$\texttt{Update}(\{q : p \rightarrowtail_{ma} q\})$
	$Cache_p$ contains $(\texttt{read}_p(x), v)$	v	$\texttt{Update}(\{q : p \rightarrowtail_{ma} q\})$
	otherwise	$mem[x]$	$\texttt{Update}(\{q : p \rightarrowtail_{ma} q\})$
$\texttt{write}_p(x,v)$	$doomed_p(Cache_p, \texttt{write}_p(x,v))$	$aborted$	$\texttt{Update}(\{q : p \rightarrowtail_{ma} q\})$
	otherwise	ack	$\texttt{Update}(\{q : p \rightarrowtail_{ma} q\})$
$\not\blacktriangleright_p$		ack	$\texttt{Update}(\{q : p \rightarrowtail_{ma} q\})$; $Cache_p := clean_p(Cache_p)$
$\blacktriangleright_p$	$doomed_p(Cache_p, \blacktriangleright_p)$	$aborted$	$\texttt{Update}(\{q : p \rightarrowtail_{ma} q\})$
	otherwise	ack	$\texttt{Apply}(Cache_p, mem)$; $Cache_p := clean_p(Cache_p)$

Fig. 1. Steps of generic implementation

(that still maintain the soundness of Theorem 2, with some modifications to its proof and system definitions) are protocols where the *clean* functions do not necessarily wipe out the most recent transaction of a client.

Consider now the case of Scott's scheme with a lazy invalidation and lazily aggressive arbitration: a conflict occurs when a transaction that writes to some memory location commits while there is another transaction that had read from this memory location, and it is arbitrated by aborting the reading transaction. Note that [16] is implicitly confined to lazy version management, which implies lazy conflict detection. We denote such a transactional memory system by M_{Lazy}. That is, given a set of locations Loc, M_{Lazy} is the transactional memory system over the locations Loc in which the states are just sequences of actions, the initial state is the empty sequence ϵ, and the step function is defined by concatenation: $\texttt{step}(\alpha, a) = \alpha a$. The observations in this system are uniquely defined once we specify that the system is a transactional memory system with lazy invalidation conflict, lazily aggressive arbitration, and lazy version management: $\texttt{out}(\alpha, a)$ is the unique output value implied by this specification when the sequence α is followed by action a. (We assume here that the output of any read in a transaction, but the first one, is handled by the local cache rather than by access to the main memory.)

An example of a M_{Lazy} system is the Transactional Coherence and Consistency (TCC) system of [8]. There, each client executes its transaction speculatively in its cache, and at commit, updates the memory and broadcasts all the write locations of the entire transaction to the other clients, notifying them about those locations that have been updated. When a client receives the broadcast, it aborts its current transaction if the broadcast indicates that some memory location read in the current transaction had been updated by the transaction of the broadcasting client.

Theorem 3. *For each access control table $\mathcal{T}$, the systems $M_{Lazy}(\mathcal{T})$ and TCC$(\mathcal{T})$ are TA-secure with respect to the policy $\rightarrowtail_{\mathcal{T}}$.*

Thus, the one case of Scott's schema where we did not show insecurity is in fact secure.

5   Securing the Insecure Implementations

The may-abort relation of Section 4 can also be used to enforce security on transactional memory systems that are not inherently secure, for example, the five schemata that are shown insecure in Theorem 1.

Recall the conflicts studied here (see Section 1). According to the definition of the relation $\rightarrowtail_T$ (Section 3), if $p \rightarrowtail_T q$ then there is a potential for a conflict between pending transactions of client p and client q. Since in the case of a conflict one of the transactions must be aborted, it is only reasonable to assume that $p \rightarrowtail_T q$ implies that at least one of $p \rightarrowtail_{ma} q$ or $q \rightarrowtail_{ma} p$ holds.

The arbitration policies determine, in a case of a conflict, which of the conflicting transactions should abort. As we saw, however, some such aborts may lead to security violations. We propose to remedy the situation by altering the arbitration rule, taking into account the $\rightarrowtail_{ma}$ relation. The policies are identical to Scott's when the client selected for abort may be aborted by the other according to the $\rightarrowtail_{ma}$ relation; it makes opposite decision in other cases.

Assume that pending transactions T_p and T_q conflict, and T_p attempts to close. The proposed arbitration policy is:

eagerly aggressive. Let $r \in \{p, q\}$ be the client whose transaction opened *first*, and let $\bar{r}$ be the other client. If $\bar{r} \rightarrowtail_{ma} r$, then abort T_r, and otherwise abort $T_{\bar{r}}$. That is, if the client whose transaction opened later may abort the one whose transaction opened earlier (and is about to close), then abort the latter's transaction. Otherwise, abort the transaction that opened later (which is consistent with traditional arbitration).

lazily aggressive. If $p \rightarrowtail_{ma} q$, then abort T_q. Otherwise, abort T_p.

We now show that, with these revised arbitration rules, all six combinations of conflict and arbitration policy lead to secure implementations. Given an access control table T, a Scott conflict rule CONF, and a modified arbitration rule ARB with respect to the may-abort policy $\rightarrowtail_{ma}$, let $M(T, \text{CONF}, \text{ARB}, \rightarrowtail_{ma})$ be the transactional memory system that applies the access control policy T and makes abort decisions by resolving conflicts generated by CONF according to arbitration rule ARB wrt $\rightarrowtail_{ma}$.

Theorem 4. *Suppose that T is an access control table and $\rightarrowtail_{ma}$ is a may-abort relation such that if $p \rightarrowtail_T q$ then $p \rightarrowtail_{ma} q$ or $q \rightarrowtail_{ma} p$.*
Then the system $M(T, \text{CONF}, \text{ARB}, \rightarrowtail_{ma})$ is TA-secure with respect to the policy $\rightarrowtail_T \cup \rightarrowtail_{ma}$.

6   Related Work

The notion of noninterference was proposed by Goguen and Meseguer [6] in order to provide an abstract characterization of information flow. The original theory was for *transitive* security policies (where, if information is permitted to flow from A to B and from B to C, it is permitted to flow from A to C). Intransitive noninterference policies, for which the semantics of [6] is insufficient, are gaining renewed significance in the context of the MILS (Multiple Independent Levels of Security and Safety) approach to high-assurance systems design [1,17]. This approach envisages the utilization of recent advances in, e.g., the efficiency of separation kernels, to increase the degree of componentization of systems, enabling secure systems to be built from a mix of small, trusted and more complex, untrusted components [14], with global security properties assured from the separation property and a verification effort focused on the trusted components. An intransitive noninterference policy can be viewed as a specification of the permitted causal influences in such an architecture. As we have noted, access control structures in shared memory systems are also associated with implicit noninterference policies, that are generally intransitive.

Haigh and Young [7], generalized the work of [6] to *intransitive* policies. Their theory was refined by Rushby [15], who also presented results showing that for a certain class of access control systems, if the read/write constraints in the system are compatible with an information flow policy then the system is in fact information flow secure with respect to that policy (which is, in general, intransitive). The definitions and theory of intransitive noninterference have recently been clarified by van der Meyden [12], whose definitions we follow here.

A significant body of literature exists on multilevel secure databases, in which the issue of transaction processing has been addressed. The area is surveyed in [3]. Covert channels that are similar to those identified in this paper are known for many of the traditional database transaction processing protocols. Closest to the transactional memory protocols we have considered are the multi-version (corresponding to lazy version management) optimistic schedulers (which, like transactional memory, do not delay requests, but execute them speculatively). Keefe et al [10] discuss a multi-version optimistic protocol with the following rule for aborts: "A transaction attempting to commit is aborted if its read set conflicts with the write set of another transaction that committed after it started." They show that this protocol, is secure for "class 2-SS" transactions, which are transactions that may write to variables of a higher security level, but involve only a single subject, i.e. agent. With respect to Scott's scheme, this amounts to lazy invalidation, but the arbitration rule differs from Scott's rules. Note that it causes unnecessary aborts when the reads all occur after the commitment of the closed transaction. Downing et al. [5] discuss another optimistic protocol that seems to be more closely related to $\text{TCC}(\mathcal{T})$.

There are some differences to our work, however. The database literature has concentrated on transaction scheduling on uniprocessor systems whereas the motivation for our study of transactional memory is multi-processor systems. The literature on multilevel database transactions assumes a partially ordered set of security levels, which corresponds to a transitive security policy. In this respect our work is more general in that we deal with intransitive policies, and note that these arise naturally from access control tables and the may-abort relation.

On the other hand, the database literature has considered several issues that we have not attempted to address. These include transactions involving multiple agents, and transactions for a single agent operating at multiple security levels - we have treated just transactions operating with respect to a single security classification. Distributed transaction processing issues such as atomic commitment protocols have also been studied from the perspective of information flow security. We have assumed here that each transaction executes on a single processor. It would also be interesting to consider such questions in the context of transactional memory.

7   Conclusion and Future Work

Mechanisms for shared use of resources in concurrent systems, such as locks and caches, are well-known to be potential sources of covert communication channels. Our results show that transactional memory, while it may help to reduce the requirement for mechanisms such as locks, may well open up new covert channels.

We first extended Rushby's access control model to transactional memory by adding operations for opening, closing and aborting transactions, and obtained a model of access control for transactional memories. We then studied the theory of information flow as applied to this model. Several well-known implementations were shown to be insecure. UTM was found to be insecure even for the very simple information flow policy involving two agents **H** and **L** with information flow from **H** to **L** prohibited. We also examined various combinations of conflict and arbitration functions that were introduced by Scott. Similarly to UTM, five out six combinations that were explored were found to be insecure for the very simple information flow policy that involves two agents.

The first straightforward conclusion from these results is that just extending implementations with an access control table is not sufficient for obtaining a secure system, and further methods and restrictions must be applied. It is worth pointing out that through our research we reviewed many implementations that do not even provide basic means for preventing restricting information flow between clients. Some implementations, e.g., DSTM [9], allow clients to directly abort transactions of other clients, or to modify their local data without any additional mechanism that prevents them from abusing it to signal (and thus pass information) the other clients. We therefore suggest that the issue of security should be considered at the early stages of design of transactional memory.

We have proposed the specific mechanism of adding a "may-abort" relation to the implementation. Based on this idea, we defined a generic implementation that is parameterized by an access control table and a may-abort relation as well as a cache management policy. We showed that all instances of this generic implementation are secure with respect to a policy derived from the access control table and may-abort policy. Using this result, we proved the security of the well known implementation TCC, which employs lazy version management and lazy conflict detection and executes transactions speculatively in the clients' caches. We were also able to propose a modification of Scott's arbitration policies that ensures security of all instances of Scott's scheme, by conditioning aborts to comply with the may-abort policy.

The most natural next step is to consider additional implementations from the perspective of our results. We note that UTM, since it employs eager version management, is not an instance of the generic implementation, which is based on lazy-version management. It would be of interest to also develop a generic secure implementation that covers variants of implementations based on earger version management. Another direction is to explore other sources that may potentially lead to insecurity in transactional memory, e.g., overflow in HTM.

The field of transactional memory is very open and relatively little formal work has been done. We have studied a particular formal model here, but others are conceivable. In particular, one could take a very different view as to what constitutes the interface of a transactional memory that should be studied from the point of view of information flow. For example, whereas we have considered aborts to be observable and left it open that an aborted transaction might be abandoned (rather than retried), one could consider a level of abstraction at which aborted transactions are automatically retried by the transactional memory system and the outcome of transactions is only visible at the interface once the transaction has successfully committed. Given our asynchronous semantics, the information flow violations that we have identified would probably not occur at this level of abstraction, though they would still be reflected as observable latencies on a timed model. Whatever one's opinion of such matters, our work demonstrates that information flow errors are an issue in transactional memories, and gives insight into how they might be resolved.

Finally, we note that the formal notions of security we have applied are based on an asynchronous model of computation, and do not take timing channels into account. With caches being a key implementation detail of transactional memory, temporally sensitive notions of information flow also need to be considered.

References

1. Alves-Foss, J., Harrison, W.S., Oman, P., Taylor, C.: The MILS architecture for high-assurance embedded systems. International Journal of Embedded Systems 2(3/4), 239–247 (2006)
2. Ananian, C.S., Asanovic, K., Kuszmaul, B.C., Leiserson, C.E., Lie, S.: Unbounded transactional memory. In: Proceedings of the Eleventh International Symposium on High-Performance Computer Architecture, pp. 316–327 (February 2005)
3. Atluri, V., Jajodia, S., George, B.: Multi-level secure transaction processing. Kluwer, Dordrecht (2000)
4. Cohen, A., O'Leary, J.W., Pnueli, A., Tuttle, M.R., Zuck, L.D.: Verifying correctness of transactional memories. In: Proceedings of FMCAD 2007 (November 2007)
5. Downing, A.R., Greenberg, T.F., Lunt, T.F.: Issues in distributed database security. In: Proceedings of Fifth Annual Computer Security Applications Conference, pp. 196–203 (December 1989)
6. Goguen, J.A., Meseguer, J.: Security policies and security models. In: Proc. IEEE Symp. on Security and Privacy, Oakland, pp. 11–20 (1982)
7. Haigh, J.T., Young, W.D.: Extending the noninterference version of MLS for SAT. IEEE Trans. on Software Engineering SE-13(2), 141–150 (1987)
8. Hammond, L., Wong, V., Chen, M., Carlstrom, B.D., Davis, J.D., Hertzberg, B., Prabhu, M.K., Wijaya, H., Kozyrakis, C., Olukotun, K.: Transactional memory coherence and consistency. In: Proceedings of the 31st Annual International Symposium on Computer Architecture, p. 102. IEEE Computer Society, Los Alamitos (2004)
9. Herlihy, M., Luchangco, V., Moir, M., Scherer III, W.N.: Software transactional memory for dynamic-sized data structures. In: PODC 2003: Proceedings of the twenty-second annual symposium on Principles of distributed computing, pp. 92–101. ACM Press, New York (2003)

10. Keefe, T.K., Tsai, W.T., Srivastava, J.: Database concurrency control in multilevel secure database management systems. IEEE Trans. Knowledge and Data Engineering 5(6), 1039–1055 (1993)
11. Larus, J.R., Rajwar, R.: Transactional Memory. Morgan & Claypool Publishers, San Francisco (2007)
12. van der Meyden, R.: What, indeed, is intransitive noninterference? In: Biskup, J., López, J. (eds.) ESORICS 2007. LNCS, vol. 4734, pp. 235–250. Springer, Heidelberg (2007)
13. Proctor, N.E., Neumann, P.G.: Architectural implications of covert channels. In: Proc. 15th National Computer Security Conference, pp. 28–43 (1992)
14. Rushby, J.M., Randell, R.: A distributed secure system. IEEE Computer 16(7), 55–67 (1983)
15. Rushby, J.: Noninterference, transitivity, and channel-control security policies. Technical report, SRI international (December 1992)
16. Scott, M.L.: Sequential specification of transactional memory semantics. In: Proc. TRANSACT the First ACM SIGPLAN Workshop on Languages, Compiler, and Hardware Suppport for Transactional Computing, Ottawa (2006)
17. Vanfleet, W.M., Beckworth, R.W., Calloni, B., Luke, J.A., Taylor, C., Uchenick, G.: MILS: architecture for high assurance embedded computing. Crosstalk: The Journal of Defence Engineering, 12–16 (August 2005)

Author Index